# KYRIOS CHRISTOS

# WILHELM BOUSSET

# KYRIOS CHRISTOS

translated by John E. Steely

A History of the Belief in Christ from
the Beginnings of Christianity to Irenaeus

Nashville • **ABINGDON PRESS** • New York

SET UP, PRINTED, AND BOUND BY THE
PARTHENON PRESS, AT NASHVILLE,
TENNESSEE, UNITED STATES OF AMERICA

# TRANSLATOR'S PREFACE

No argument needs to be offered to justify the translation of Wilhelm Bousset's *Kyrios Christos*. One can only wonder why it was not done long ago. The same intrinsic merit of the book which evoked such a continuing appreciation of it in its German dress, and which has called forth the fifth and sixth editions within the past five years, may be cited as explanation enough for the work of bringing it to the public that reads no German.

The work of translating has been made more enjoyable, if not easier, by the author's creative imagination and his sometimes lyrical grace. While this book builds painstakingly upon a foundation of detailed documentary evidence, the vigorous use of an informed imagination is evident on every page. The necessarily tedious style of much of the book gives way now and then to a poetic expression that is eminently suited to the task of summarizing a mood, an outlook, a yearning. It will be evident that these passages have been the most difficult part of the translator's work.

It is a pleasure to express thanks to the Christian Research Foundation, Inc., for the prize awarded this translation in the 1966-67 competition. Appreciation is due also to the Southeastern Baptist Theological Seminary alumni, whose Alumni Fund helped with the cost of typing the manuscript. Mrs. Norma Owens Hash worked faithfully and with great skill in the preparation of the typescript. Mr. James Anderson and other unnamed friends gave help for which I am deeply grateful. Above all, my thanks must go to my family, who encouraged and assisted me in innumerable ways toward the completion of this undertaking.

JOHN E. STEELY

*Wake Forest, North Carolina*
*June 1969*

# INTRODUCTORY WORD
# TO THE FIFTH EDITION

Among the works of New Testament scholarship the study of which I used to recommend in my lectures to students as indispensable, above all belonged Wilhelm Bousset's *Kyrios Christos*. I rejoice that this work is now to appear in a new edition, for it is still true that its study is indispensable; indeed one can say that this has today become all the more true. For this work introduces in incomparable fashion the questions which today are stirring New Testament scholarship, and in fact for the very reason that the work itself has brought about the present situation with the questions and discussions which concern it. In this work the demands raised by Bousset's predecessors and contemporaries of the so-called history-of-religions school (I mention only W. Wrede, H. Gunkel, J. Weiss, and W. Heitmüller) for the first time have been brought to fulfillment in a coherent and comprehensive presentation.

I need only at a few points to illustrate the significance which *the history-of-religions school* has had for the study and understanding of the New Testament.

1. The significance of *eschatology*—a topic which down to the present dominates the discussion to a large measure—was first fully recognized by the history-of-religions school. Johannes Weiss (in 1892 and 1900) showed how Jesus' preaching of the kingdom of God must be understood from the perspective of eschatology. In Bousset's *Kyrios Christos* the topic becomes directly relevant in the presentation of the primitive Palestinian community, but indirectly it remains current throughout the entire work, because according to Bousset in Hellenistic Christianity the cultically revered "Kyrios Christos" has appeared in the place of the eschatological figure of the "Son of Man." The problem of the relation of eschatology and cultus is thus raised.

2. This indicates a second point. *Hellenistic Christianity*, within which Paul and John first become understandable, *is to be distinguished from the primitive Palestinian community*. Bousset now has clearly seen that it is

7

necessary to develop a picture of pre-Pauline Hellenistic Christianity, and he prefaces the chapters on Paul and John with just such a presentation. One may say that this view in the meantime has become the common property of the historical study of the New Testament.

3. The theme of the distinction between Palestinian and Hellenistic Christianity includes the stimulating topics *"Jesus and Paul"* and *"The historical Jesus and the kerygmatic Christ,"* the second of which especially is being discussed today.

4. Also the themes of *the sacrament and the church,* which today play an essential role in theological discussion, have been made current by the history-of-religions school and especially by Bousset's *Kyrios Christos.*

5. Bousset sought to gain an understanding of the *peculiarity of Hellenistic Christianity* from the study of the involvement of Christian thought and concepts with the thought-world and conceptualizations of pagan Hellenism. While he stressed therein especially the significance of the mystery religions and the worship of the Kyrios, still he also kept in view Gnosticism, and the present-day discussion of the problem of a pre-Christian Gnosticism received an important impetus from his work.

6. Bousset intended, by portraying the development of belief in Christ down to the time of Irenaeus, *to remove the wall of separation between New Testament theology and the history of doctrine in the early church.* Only a reference to the *Theologisches Wörterbuch zum Neuen Testament* is needed for proof that this intention is justified. In connection with this also, the traditional interpretation of the canon is called in question, as Wrede had already done before Bousset. The consequence of Wrede's demand now becomes very evident in *Kyrios Christos.*

The correctness of Bousset's posing of the questions and the weight of all these themes and motifs become impressively clear to the student when he sees how they have developed in the works of the history-of-religions school. But in a quite special way, he can learn it from Bousset's *Kyrios Christos,* because in this comprehensive presentation he becomes acquainted with the inner connection of these themes.

It goes without saying that since Bousset, research has gone further, and that in particular much of a critical nature has been said about *Kyrios Christos.* If this criticism is directed especially against Bousset's thesis that Jesus was first characterized and addressed as "Lord," not in the primitive community but in Hellenistic Christianity, still it must be said that the correctness of Bousset's total view and of his representation of the cultic Kyrios worship in Hellenistic Christianity is in no way dependent upon the correctness of this thesis. Though it can be regretted above all that in his presentation, essential motifs of the New Testament, especially of Pauline theology, have not been brought into operation adequately, one still must remember that in *Kyrios Christos* Bousset did not intend to write a theology of the New Testament, but that he wrote a monograph, the theme of which to be sure can be characterized as the central theme of New Testament theology: "the history of belief in Christ from the beginnings of Christianity down to Irenaeus."

Finally, a word should be said about the intention of the history-of-religions school to represent *the religion* of primitive Christianity and to use the New Testament as a source for this. Today we can ask whether this intention can do justice to the New Testament, and whether we are not rather to turn back again to the old question about the *theology* of the New Testament. But here it must be recalled that that intention, to investigate the religion of primitive Christianity instead of the theology of the New Testament, is grounded in the opposition of the history-of-religions school to the view dominant up to that time (if we leave out of consideration the one exception of Schlatter), namely, in opposition to the view which inquired after the so-called doctrinal concepts. To this extent the history-of-religions school signified a decisive step toward a better understanding of the New Testament. For when inquiry was made as to religion, in so doing inquiry was being made basically as to the existential meaning of the theological expressions of the New Testament. This furthermore shows up, also, in the fact that instead of "religion," "piety" is preferred, and Christology is interpreted as Christ-oriented piety.

RUDOLF BULTMANN

*Marburg, 1964*

# FOREWORD TO
# THE FIRST EDITION

The present work has gradually grown, as from a seed, out of some work on the meaning of the term κύριος in the New Testament. It could almost seem doubtful now, after the conclusion of the whole work, whether the book's title *Kyrios Christos* is fitting and makes sense. And one could object to the selection of it the fact that in the work itself the proof is adduced that the primitive Palestinian community was not acquainted with this designation. Nevertheless after mature reflection I have decided to hold to this title. The theme "Kyrios Christos" still dominates the presentation of this book; anyone who surveys the whole work will readily recognize that. At the same time, with this title at its head a peculiarity of the present work should be identified. Kyrios Christos is Jesus of Nazareth in essence as the Lord of his community, venerated in the cultus. The present work in general attempts to take its point of departure from the practice of the cultus and of the community's worship and to understand the way things developed from this perspective. This is not an entirely new point of view; in recent times there has been an increase in the voices that vigorously call attention to the importance and necessity of this consideration. Still I think that for our area the present work has probably sought for the first time to actualize the programmatic demands here raised, in a coherent and comprehensive presentation.

I have, moreover, made an effort in this presentation to remove, as much as lay within my power, a dual restriction by which the study in these areas previously was limited.

In the first place this involved the removal of the wall of partition between New Testament theology and the history of doctrine in the early church. Long ago overcome in *theory*, at least to a large extent, it still dominates *practice* quite extensively, as a result of the division of labor which indeed is necessary. New Testament theologies conclude with the end of the New Testament, although most of the investigators probably are oppressed with the unsatisfying feeling that at the conclusion they are compelled to offer broken fragments, and rather arbitrarily broken ones at that. The histories of doctrine often give a quick backward glance at the New Testament age. But this appears then as the closed and, as it were, classical period; phenomena such as those of Paul and John are not actually set completely into the stream of the development of the history of doctrine.

Here at the same time the great and yet perverse basic thesis of Ritschl is still exerting its influence: that all the great phenomena of the New Testament are above all and in the first place to be understood on the ground of the Old Testament, and that they therefore stood at a specific distance from all the following formulations of Christianity. But even this view will not maintain itself. The great and decisive turning point in the development of Christianity is marked by its transition to Gentile-Christian territory in its very earliest beginnings. No other event approaches this in importance. The history of Christology presented here seeks to bring forward a proof of this, and Christology still represents the center of the whole development. In the presentation the distance between the Palestinian and the Jerusalem primitive communities, between Jerusalem and Antioch, will stand out sharply, and at the same time it will become clear, I hope, to what extent Paul belonged from the very first to the milieu of the Hellenistic primitive communities. Thus a contribution would then be made to the great problem of Paul and Jesus. The first two chapters of my book, which deal with the primitive church in Jerusalem, form only the introduction, as it were, the prelude to the following presentation, which leads on in a steady flow to the end of the second century.

It was naturally more difficult to decide upon the end point of the study. For of course the account must be broken off somewhere. I believe, however, that I have seen correctly here when I set Irenaeus at the end of my work. One may judge, I believe, that with Irenaeus a provisional conclusion is reached. It is actually the figure of this church father that stands in a totally dominating position at the end of the first volume of Harnack's *Dogmengeschichte*. Tertullian and Hippolytus stand on his shoulders, and for the development of specifically ecclesiastical theology Irenaeus means more than Clement and Origen, in spite of their great intellectual significance. In the realm of Christology the present treatment will, I hope, make it especially clear how it is precisely in Irenaeus that all the lines of the previous development clearly converge. With him, in fact, the conclusion is given; the formation of christological dogma is here approximately completed, so that all which yet comes after him can be regarded as further consequence and explication. And while in my opinion one can nowhere else in the second century conclude a coherent presentation without an awkward interruption, yet here it comes to a natural conclusion.

The second restriction for the study which I have further striven to remove in the present work is that of the separation of the religious history of primitive Christianity from the general development of the religious life surrounding Christianity in the time of its earliest childhood. Not that I would somehow raise the claim that here something new and unexpected has happened for the first time. In one area the demands here expressed have already met with success. For the gospel of Jesus and the tradition of the primitive community now practically all students are ready to acknowledge the fruitfulness of a consideration which takes into account the milieu of late Jewish patterns of thought in a determined and comprehensive way. For the later time Harnack with his *Dogmengeschichte* has effectively demolished the dividing wall between history of the Christian religion and the surrounding outside world, though he also turns his attention chiefly to the contacts of Christian theology with Greek philosophy. Already in the works of Anrich and Wobbermin on the Greek mysteries and in the work of Anz on the origin of Gnosticism this consideration was significantly expanded and extended from philosophy and theology to include the whole of piety.

Still there remains one area that is disputed, that of the Pauline-Johannine piety; indeed, one may say, that of the development of Christianity once it passed over into the Hellenistic milieu with the transition from Jerusalem to Antioch. Here the new demands present themselves; in spite of all the influences which are to be recognized for this Christianity from the side of Judaism and the Old Testament, yet in my opinion one will have to decide to set the total development within the cultural world of the Graeco-Roman empire in the larger history-of-religions connections which are here set forth. And it is to be expected that this sort of work will result in just as great or perhaps even greater fruitfulness, enrichment, and clarification of our knowledge than in its own time the utilization of the Palestinian milieu for the understanding of the gospel of Jesus and the evangelical tradition of the primitive community. Here in this area we stand at the beginning of a

13

new task with far-reaching and not yet completely foreseeable results and consequences.

But we would not be so far along with these beginnings if the work of the philologists had not come to our aid here in a previously unheard-of fashion. Only since classical philology, going beyond the boundaries of its earlier area of labor, has applied itself in ever increasing measure to the late antiquity of the age of the Diadochi and beyond; only since Droysen's great plan for a history of Hellenism, at the center of which the inception of Christianity would have to stand, has moved a long stride toward fulfillment, have things reached the point that now the theological work in this area can also begin and can face the gigantic task that is set particularly before it. Here it is the obligation of gratitude to mention a whole series of researchers who have blazed the trail. Without the great stimulation and advances, without the comprehensive labors of such men as Usener and Dieterich, Cumont and Wendland, Reitzenstein and Norden, E. Schwartz and Geffcken and so many others, the work as it is now posed for us would still be an impossibility, and the present work would not yet be written. But theological researchers also have for a long time placed themselves at the side of the philologists as fellow-workers toward the same goal; I refer in the first place to the stimuli which Pfleiderer, Eichhorn, and Gunkel have provided, to the penetrating studies of Heitmüller, as well as to the labors of Deissmann and J. Weiss, Lietzmann and others. It is a particular joy to see how the old master of our area of study, Heinrich Holtzmann, who has been taken from us by death, still showed in the second edition of his great work on New Testament theology an open mind and a clear eye for the new tasks which are here set forth. We younger ones have to continue the work with the same alertness for new questions and formulations of the problems which distinguished him, and with gratitude.

But on the other side the stoutest reservations likely will be voiced about this strong assimilation of the developmental process of Christology into the general history-of-religions context. And at the outset people will predictably confront us now with Cumont's large-scale and finely drawn statements in the foreword[1] to his work, *Die orientalischen Religionen im römischen Heidentum!* Against this we cannot emphatically enough draw attention to the fact that Cumont himself limits his judgment to the relation of Christianity to the developed form of the mystery religion in which it con-

---

[1] Incorporated into Gehrich's German translation (1910), pp. VI-XIII.

fronts us in the West in the course of the second century of the Christian era. On the other side he explicitly points out that with his statements the problem of how Christianity was related to Hellenistic Oriental syncretism was not to be settled. "Thus the investigation of the doctrines and usages common to Christianity and the Oriental mysteries almost always leads beyond the boundaries of the Roman empire and back into the Hellenistic Orient. *There* were the religious ideas shaped which were naturalized in Latin Europe under the Caesars; *there* is the key to still unsolved riddles to be sought."

Those students who *a limine* reject our entire approach by pointing to the fact that the heyday of the mystery religion in the Roman Empire falls only at the end of the second century A.D. may no longer appeal to these statements of Cumont. It is indeed true that in the upper strata of Roman (-Greek) society, religious syncretism and Oriental mysticism only begin about the time of Commodus' reign. In the literature of the educated this oppressive mysticism first comes gradually to a dominant position in the second half of the second century. I mention such names as Numenius of Apamaea, Aristides, Apuleius, Maximus of Tyre, and others. Theretofore Roman literature—I think of Seneca and Pliny, Epictetus and Marcus Aurelius—is dominated throughout by the spirit of the genuine Stoa, and even the still relatively moderate Oriental-mystical elements which with Poseidonius of Apamaea two centuries earlier flowed into the Stoa and into Greek philosophy here come into play less effectively.

But here an important distinction must be made. Rome and especially Greece, in spite of all the syncretistic currents, are not the Orient. What breaks forth into the open here in the second half of the second century has a long prehistory which has transpired especially in Syria (Asia Minor) and Egypt. But Christianity came out of the Orient, and the intellectual home base of the Gentile Christian church was first Syria (Antioch) and southern Asia Minor (Tarsus), and in the second place from the earliest times onward, Egypt. And further, in its beginnings, to which especially Paul, John, and Gnosticism belong, Christianity has nothing, nothing at all, to do with the truly philosophical literature of the educated circles and its historical development. What here first begins to climb up the ladder in the course of the second century can have been lively for a long time in a lower stratum.

And this was in fact the case. Recently it has become ever more widely recognized that the movement of Christian Gnosticism becomes under-

15

standable only under the presupposition that in it an intellectual current already present in the pre-Christian age and developed independent of Christianity (and of Judaism), and of a quite specific orientation, pushes its way into Christianity. In the second edition of his *Die hellenistisch-römische Kultur* Wendland properly removed his section on Gnosticism from the portrayal of Christianity and placed it before the latter. That this could be done without any serious alteration of the text, indeed that only now everything in the presentation appears in its proper place, best shows how everything is moving in the direction of this new recognition. A further bit of evidence for this view is offered by the observation that alongside the Gnosticism especially affected by Christianity and reshaped by Christian influences, we possess a purely Hellenistic Gnostic literature. Now—thanks to the most recent research in this area—it lies before us, clearly recognizable, in the Hermetic tractates, in the Oracula Chaldaica and other related manifestations; with Numenius of Apamaea it enters into philosophical literature, it extends with its influence deep into Neo-Platonic philosophy. For although Plotinus rejected this whole tendency and engaged in bitter struggle with it, his successors fell from the free intellectual heights of their master.

Now it is true that in the face of the striking parallels to New Testament piety which are offered by just this literature and particularly by the Hermetic tractates, some have the practice of taking refuge behind the problem of the proof of age. They reassure themselves with the fact that here was a literary circle whose age one could not with certainty and definiteness trace back beyond the third century A.D. Over against this, Reitzenstein is still correct in his attempt to trace this literature in its foundations and oldest component parts back into the first century. I hope to be able to carry the investigation even further on this point. Here we may only say that with the foundations of the Hermetic literature we find ourselves in the early age of Gnosticism. Here, indeed, for those who have relied entirely too much on the hitherto acknowledged *terminus ad quem* for this literature, every day can bring fresh surprises which will compel them to do some relearning. In this connection I refer only to the fact that recently a Latin author whose name often appears in connection with this mystical literature and whom most students were accustomed to dating in the Neo-Platonist age, Cornelius Labeo, has definitely assured his place, it appears to me, in the first century, through the evidence that he was used by Suetonius.[2]

---

[2] Cf. the splendid work of B. Boehm, *De Cornelii Labeonis aetate,* Diss. Koenigsberg, 1913.

Now it only needs the further demonstration that this Cornelius was essentially the opponent with whom Arnobius is contending in the second book of his *Adv. Nationes*—an assumption which already has often and with good reason been made—and then the syncretistic writing of the Oracula Chaldaica and in particular the central doctrine of the older Hermetic tractate (the staining of the soul by the wickedness of the planetary spheres) would be demonstrably put back into the first century, into the Pauline-Johannine era.

Indeed, when we go further back, the Jewish philosopher Philo also enters into this connection. One gradually begins to recognize that the total phenomenon of Philo is understandable neither when one takes his point of departure from Greek philosophy nor when one begins with the Old Testament and Judaism, nor finally when one conceives of Philo as a mixture of the two elements. In Philo a third element shows itself, and it is this that first gives to his figure the characteristic stamp, namely a strong touch of Hellenistic-Oriental mystical piety. Philo is neither a philosopher nor simply a representative of Jewish-Old Testament religiousness. In him is revealed as a *novum* a religious mysticism whose rise and origin are still a problem.

And again, if we proceed from here to Plutarch at the end of the first century A.D., we find in him an entire world of psychological, eschatological, and demonological views, and in addition, cosmological speculations and dualistic fundamental attitudes, which people often have previously sought to ascribe to older philosophical speculations of a Poseidonius or a Xenocrates. Here also is revealed a surplus element of half popular, half learned speculations, syncretistically and orientally conditioned fantasies, the sources of which have not yet been explored.

Thus the links come together to form a chain: Philo, the Hermetic literature, the sources of Plutarch's popular fantastic speculations, *Oracula Chaldaica,* the forerunners of Christian Gnosticism—and to this is assimilated a part of the literature which goes under the name of Neo-Pythagoreanism, and thus many fragments of religious literature which are preserved for us among the magical papyri—all this forms a strange world of its own with a special and unmistakable structure.

This literature, if one may call it literature, also stands in discernible continuity with that practical-cultic piety which we can hardly comprehend other than under the name of mystery piety and the concept of mystery religion. Bréhier in particular in his work on Philo has splendidly demonstrated how so many basic ideas and basic attitudes of Philonic piety find their explanation only on this basis. The collection of the Hermetic tractates, as it lies before us in Hermes Trismegistus as a selection from a much more extensive literature and in related fragments, is in this form quite certainly semi-philosophical literature. But it clearly points back, on its own part, to a religious literature of directly cultic purpose and to a practically observed piety as well as to circles in which these were dominant. Christian Gnosticism is a movement of explicitly practical character, a piety of mysterious initiations and sacraments.

This connection with practical religiousness, with cult and communal piety, gives to that entire body of literature its character and its stance. That characteristic blending of religion and a philosophical framing of ideas, of mysticism and thoughtful reflection, is explained in this way. The frame of mind of the small religiously motivated circles of the initiated, who are self-consciously in opposition to the world and the masses without, by means of all sorts of speculations wraps itself in a sharply dualistic outlook; the experience of ecstasy engenders a religious psychology of an amazingly supernaturalistic tendency; the cultus with its mysterious initiations is intellectualized into a world view which rests upon secret revelation, in which heightened intellectuality and nature-oriented supernaturalism lie amazingly intertwined.

In the face of the broad connections and of the question which consequently forces itself upon our attention, as to whether the development of Hellenistic Christianity and in particular the thought-world of Paul and John are not to be set into these contexts, one will no longer be able to answer from the outset with the insistence that the exact proof of age has not been established for many of the witnesses being considered. Here I cannot fully agree with Cumont (*Oriental Religions in Roman Paganism*, p. xviii) when he says: "All these facts constitute a series of very delicate problems of chronology and interrelation, and it would be rash to attempt to solve them *en bloc*. Probably there is a different answer in each particular case, and I am afraid that some cases must always remain unsolved." For what we have here are not questions of literary dependence in particular. No scholar will wish to assert that Paul had read this particular bit of Hermetica, or, more generally, that Christianity is dependent upon this or that particular mystery religion. Not even the question of whether Paul and John were acquainted with Philo will yield its solution. The main thing is rather the recognition of broad intellectual connections, the insight that perhaps with these above-mentioned phenomena the intellectual atmosphere, within which the growth of the Christian religion occurred and from which its development in considerable measure becomes understandable, has been transposed. On the other side, what is involved here is not a set of relatively irrelevant and merely interesting analogies and parallels, but rather the recognition that a form of piety which grew in its own soil quite early merged with the gospel of Jesus and with the latter entered into a new form which would remain beyond our understanding so long as we were unacquainted with the former. One should consider this question with the same freedom from prejudice with which one confronts the contacts of the Gospels and the Pauline literature with the Jewish literature. If, for example, we establish contacts between Paul and the Jewish literature of the end of the first century A.D. and from still later times, say on the theme of faith and works or on the theology of inherited sin and death (IV Ezra, the Syriac Book of Baruch); if we see that later fellow-rabbis of Paul also on their own part were acquainted with the experience of ecstatic ascent into Paradise, we will not make an issue of the difference in time, and hardly even assume a dependence of rabbinic thought upon Paul, but rather will readily trace the parallel phenomena back to the common ground on which they grow. This is what Cumont also does in his judicious and considered statements. In one particular case (the interpretation of religion in terms of military service) he demonstrates the impossibility of deriving a specific Christian view somehow from the cultus of the servants of Mithras. But then he comes in his explanation to the conclusion that this conception is apparently older than either Christianity or Mithraism, and that it had developed under the military monarchies of the Asiatic Diadochi.

In any case we presuppose that one thing is to be ruled out: that is the assumption that Christianity on its own part influenced the religious environment in general through the analogous phenomena which we have been considering. This seems to me to be ruled out by the well-known principle of Reitzenstein that it is simply inconceivable that the Christian religion could have influenced not merely one single religion but a whole array of religions in which the analogous formations are shown to be present in similar form. There is also a second reason for ruling out this assumption. The phenomena which are in question here are such as the sacrament, the supernaturalist dualistic psychology (the pneuma doctrine), the radical dualism and pes-

simism of the Pauline-Johannine Christianity, the religious goal of deification and the way that leads to it, and the vision of God. We can even add
to this list the theme of this book: the belief in the Kyrios and the cult of
the Kyrios. All these are distinctive phenomena which it would be very
difficult, and indeed even impossible, to conceive of on the soil of the Old
Testament Jewish religion or of the authentic gospel of Jesus. Or does one
wish in all seriousness to assert that the sacrament is an original creation of
the religion which began with the preaching of Jesus and was then borrowed
by the religious environment?! One would hardly be able to do this; one
would then have to join Albert Schweitzer,[3] who however has sensed the
problem here before us much more keenly than the other students who
reject *a limine* the history-of-religions approach, in deriving the Christian
sacrament from eschatology.

But, some may object, one cannot think that of all people the apostle
Paul, who had been a rabbi, was so fundamentally to be understood in
terms of the Hellenistic-Oriental milieu. Indeed Schweitzer[4] has recently
objected to the method of research of the history-of-religions school that it
makes the entire subsequent development incapable of being understood. If
Paul has brought in something so startlingly new, so the argument runs, then
it is hardly comprehensible that primitive Christianity would continue to
harbor him in its midst. If Paul has already hellenized or orientalized Christianity, then the *altum silentium* about the apostle in the subsequent development of Christianity remains incomprehensible, the development which
itself represents the hellenization of Christianity. Indeed with its theses
the history-of-religions study would lend assistance to the ultra-Tübingen
view, i.e., it would favor the thesis that with Paul one has to move from
primitive Christianity into a later period, or one has to go along with
Gunkel and Maurenbrecher in pushing the process of hellenization and
orientalization back into the Palestinian primitive community, and finally
with Drews and B. W. Smith dissolve the person and the gospel of Jesus in
this process. I can be brief here because I believe that my book presents a
running refutation of these assertions. The assertion that it remains incomprehensible how the absolutely new in Pauline Christianity according to
the history-of-religions view could have been endured in primitive Chris-

[3] *Geschichte der paulinischen Forschung von der Reformation bis auf die Gegenwart*
(1911), p. 189.
[4] *Ibid.*, pp. 179 ff.

tianity is refuted by the explanations in the third and fourth chapters of my book. If it is true that in the most important appropriation (the Kyrios cult and the sacrament) what is involved is more of an unconscious process in the life of the community, and that Paul built further on the foundation of this faith of the community and gave expression and language to what is here in unspoken form, then that rapid development becomes understandable and conceivable. The fact that the Christianity of the first half of the second century does not refer directly to Paul, and in fact passes over him in silence, becomes understandable when one sees that the "hellenizing" of Christianity in the apologists with their optimistically rational total outlook is something wholly different from its amalgamation with orientally syncretistic mysticism with its dualism and pessimism as it is found in Paul (John) and in Gnosticism. (What then emerges at the end of the second century as the culmination of the development is neither the one nor the other. We can call it the ecclesiastically tempered Paulinism, the Paulinism that has been divested of all Gnostic dangers and tendencies. It is, if we wish to choose our *termini* following a famous example, the gradual orientalizing and re-forming of Christianity into syncretism as over against the acute orientalizing in Paul and in Gnosticism.) And thus also is the *altissimum silentium* about Paul in the first half of the second century A.D. to be understood. In conclusion, we do not at all need, with the assumption of that process of "hellenizing" or orientalizing of Christianity, to go back into Palestinian primitive Christianity or into the gospel of Jesus. For the decisive turning point of Christianity, not at all to be explained away, lies just at its transition from Palestinian to Hellenistic territory. Here and only here lies the natural beginning of that stormy development which Christianity suffered at the outset.

But someone will pose the question of how one is to think that the basic ideas and attitudes of Hellenistic Oriental piety could have come to Paul, the rabbinically minded Jew. This is a question which is not easily solved. But—quite apart from the already mentioned influences of the Hellenistic primitive community—for the *personal* peculiarities of the Pauline total outlook one may point out now that Paul was a Jew of the *Diaspora*. To speak here at the outset of an impossibility then means, to put it plainly, to do violence to the facts. We also have no other former rabbi and Pharisee to point to, who knew how to use the Greek language for his purposes as Paul did. To be sure we will have to acknowledge that Paul can never have come into very intimate contact with the practical cultic piety of his time. Both the rabbinic character of Paul and even the nature of the mystery religions would forbid our assuming on his part any sort of personal knowledge of a mystery religion. But we may suppose that already in Paul's time there was a body of religious literature which had been completely separated from the connections that had to do immediately with cult and practice and thus was accessible to a wider circle. And the supposition that Paul was acquainted with such semi-literary edifying writings as they were available in the Hermetic tractates, in the edificatory, purely religious parts of the magical literature, appears to me more probable than that the apostle might have read any of the actually Greek philosophical writings. In this way, Paul the Pharisee may have stored up and meditatively thought through many particular speculations and mysterious attitudes in his innermost being, without needing in any way to fear for the purity of his inherited religion which still consisted only of plain, elementary principles and was manifested essentially in rite and practice. Then came the strong and stormy impulses which stormed in upon him from the new Christ religion. And as in a thaw the sluggish masses slide into the stream and the ice floes strike against one another and push and pile up, so now the mass of thoughts in Paul has slipped into the stream and has piled up in an amazing heap, and the result was the Pauline theology.

This is intended only as an effort somehow to make understandable a course of events which in fact is not easily understandable. In general, however, one will do well not to theorize a priori too much about possibilities and impossibilities in this area, neither on one side nor on the other. The actual historical course of events has always proved to be more strange, more diverse and richer than the theories posed in advance. The work in the history of religions certainly has not developed in this area out of preconceived theories; it has been shaped under the compulsion of the facts. And it can do nothing at all better than, in ever more intensive labor, to let the facts speak for themselves. Then the dispute over theories will clear up by itself and will come to an end. Whether in the present book I have succeeded in letting the facts speak for themselves and in approximating the actual course of events may be left to the judgment of those whose calling it is to form such judgments.

For a time I intended to write, in a work conceived on a still larger scale, on the emergence of Christianity in the milieu of the Hellenistic Roman civilization. But more and more I became aware that for such an undertaking the status of the work in this field in general and in particular my ability did not suffice. Therefore I concentrated my work on this one problem. It is true that the history and development of the belief in Christ stand so very much in the center of the general development of Christianity that in my presentation I have often approached that more general and more comprehensive task. I hope that the frequent glimpses and excursuses into the general development, however, will not crucially disturb the unity and progress of the whole, but rather will prove to be useful and even necessary. The treatment of a theme thus situated in the center of the whole opens up vistas toward the periphery in all directions. But I believe that the work still has preserved its recognizable center. In the citing of literature I have been sparing; only what has been of help to me is named. I make no claim to exhaustiveness. Larger polemics and discussions are restricted to the essential points. For such I have let the sources speak for themselves all the more extensively, particularly in the later chapters.

The perceptive study by W. Haupt, *Worte Jesu und Gemeindeüberlieferung,* as well as the essay by J. Weiss, *Das Problem der Entstehung des Christentums,* and the writing by Krebs, *Das religionsgeschichtliche Problem des Urchristentums,* only came to my attention during or after the completion of my work.

For friendly and untiring assistance with the proofs I express my hearty thanks to my young friend, *st. theol.* Nahnsen.

WILHELM BOUSSET

*Göttingen*
*September 1913*

# FOREWORD TO
# THE SECOND EDITION

It is with feelings of sadness that I let this book go from my hands. The recollection of the too-soon departed friend and colleague, the great scholar and the unforgettable teacher painfully weighs upon me and upon those who have supported me in the preparation of the new edition of his favorite work. But there is joined with this also a sense of thankfulness that it has been possible for us to give his book in the essential parts the form which he himself would have given it, if it had been permitted him to put the last touches on it. In his literary remains was found the new version of the first four chapters complete, and the assurance that these sections of his presentation, which had been most hotly disputed by the critics, would have received his imprimatur gave us the courage to venture a new edition. For even though he certainly would have put an improving hand to various aspects of the following sections in detail, it is not to be assumed that their composition would have given him any occasion for fundamental alterations. His personal copy also contained an abundance of notes which could be worked into the footnotes. In doing this I have had the most cordial assistance of my colleague, Dr. Rudolf Bultmann. The chief burden of the work, however, fell upon the two gentlemen who unselfishly undertook to give the book the clean dress in which it is presented to the readers, Privatdozent Lic. August Dell in Giessen and theological student Otto Munk from Mainz. The former supervised the work in press with active personal participation, and the latter checked the greater part of the quotations and prepared the new index. Thus we may hope that the book in its new form is not unworthy vitally to preserve the memory of the man who created it, even for a coming generation.

GUSTAV KRÜGER

*Giessen, Pentecost 1921*

# CONTENTS

# 1
## JESUS THE MESSIAH—SON OF MAN
### IN THE FAITH
### OF THE PALESTINIAN
### PRIMITIVE COMMUNITY

With the question as to the position of Jesus in the faith of the Palestinian primitive community, we stand on relatively firm ground. However disputed the questions about the so-called self-consciousness of Jesus may be, still it can be taken as fully assured that the community in Jerusalem from the very first was united on the basis of the conviction that Jesus of Nazareth was the Messiah who was to be expected by the Jewish people. Perhaps they were not altogether sure from the outset about what this Jesus of Nazareth in the time of his earthly life had been or had intended to be, but they knew that the house of Israel has either to hope for or to fear this Jesus, whom heaven now has taken up until the times of the consummation, as the one designated the Messiah from the very beginning.[1]

However, we shall have to attempt still more precisely to analyze this confession of the community that Jesus is (or will be) the Christ. For in and of itself, that statement says very little. The conceptions which contemporary Judaism had of the Messiah and with which the conceptions held by the community of Jesus' disciples were immediately connected are of a highly variegated and manifold nature.[2] They oscillate, as it were, between two poles. On the one hand, people expected—and indeed this was probably predominant in the great mass of the people—some sort of powerful king from David's tribe who, as a victorious ruler, would again establish

[1] Acts 3:20-21; cf. 2:36; etc.
[2] On the following, cf. Bousset, *Religion des Judentums,* 2nd ed., pp. 255-67, 297-308.

31

the ancient throne of David, would destroy the rule of the hated Romans and would exercise his rule from Jerusalem over the whole world in justice and holiness, so that the nations all would make their pilgrimage to the gates of Jerusalem and would pay to her their tribute. On the other hand, Jewish fantasy had created, or rather had taken over, a transcendent, idealized picture of the Messiah which, taken strictly, hardly had any more than the name in common with the former. This transcendent Messiah of Jewish apocalyptic was not to be born of woman upon earth; he is thought of as a supra-terrestrial, angel-like, and preexistent being. He was to appear from above at the end of time in almost divine splendor; indeed, he appeared plainly at the side of God as future judge of the world. The former messianic conception is somewhat comprehended in the title of the Son of David,[3] and the latter is bound up with the enigmatic and mysterious designation "the Son of Man" (i.e., the Man).[4] The Jewish messianic expectation oscillated between these two poles of interpretation, so that almost nowhere does one or the other emerge in pure form. Even where it is primarily the picture of the earthly Messiah, the king of David's lineage, that is sketched, as for example in the seventeenth Psalm of Solomon, transcendent traits are blended with this picture; and again, where the transcendent interpretation has the dominant position, as in the portraits in the Book of Enoch, there are not lacking those purely earthly traits of the king of vengeance who annihilates his adversaries with the sword.

Accordingly we pose the question: "In which sense did the Palestinian primitive community apply the idea of the Messiah of contemporary Judaism to Jesus?" Did it adopt the earthly political ideal of the Messiah as the Son of David or that strange transcendent ideal of the Messiah, or perhaps even in essence a blending of the two pictures of the Messiah?

In answering this question we shall not be able to turn to a source which appears to be the most obvious. I mean the book of Acts. The author of Acts already stands much too far from the milieu of the Jerusalem primitive community, and what he has taken over by way of source material for the presentation of the primitive community is, insofar as it interests us in this connection, of a most meager sort. The speeches in the first half of the book, which come into consideration here in a special way, are almost purely literary

[3] Ps. Sol. 17.21.
[4] Parables of Enoch; IV Ezra, *visio* 6; for a fuller treatment, see further the text, § 4 in this chap.

32

witnesses of a wholly stereotyped nature; they show frequent traces of a demonstrably later composition, and indeed, as we shall see still more specifically, that precisely in the messianic terminology.

In the answering of our question, therefore, there remain for us no other sources than our Synoptic Gospels. The gospel tradition which is deposited in them we may claim, especially in its older stratum, as a work of the Palestinian primitive community. We need not here at first engage in a painstaking preliminary investigation, with all its uncertainties, as to what of these self-witnesses is to be traced back to Jesus himself and what to the theology of the primitive community. We shall have to assume a priori that the community of Jesus' disciples has deposited in the gospel tradition its faith and its view of the messianic meaning of the person of Jesus, even when it has frequently only repeated genuine material of its master's messianic self-expressions and has not created something. For the gospel tradition is sketched from the first from the standpoint of a community of messianic faith and for the purpose of bearing witness to this messianic faith.

The Gospels, however, offer abundant and valuable material for the answering of our questions. We shall best arrange this material if at the outset we proceed from the question of which messianic titles in the first place are applied to Jesus in the gospel literature. For, as we have already seen, the substance is often bound up with the titles in the closest possible way.

1. Now it is true that a special set of conditions prevails in the investigation of these honorific designations of Jesus. The material coming into consideration here is relatively small in scope. But here we immediately strike upon a fact of fundamental importance. The entire gospel tradition (including the Gospel of John) needs, in the simple narrative, no title at all for Jesus, but only his own name, ὁ Ἰησοῦς. It never tells of the Christ, of the Son of David, of the Son of God, or the Son of Man, but simply of Jesus.[5] In all probability this is related to a fundamental conviction of the Palestinian primitive community. For it, Jesus was first the coming Messiah (παρουσία Χριστοῦ) or the one elevated by God through the resurrection to be the Messiah (Acts 2:36; Rom. 1:3); it could not at all speak so simply and objectively of the earthly Jesus as the Christ.

Thus there remain for our investigation only those cases in which Jesus is designated with messianic titles in the address of other persons, or those

---

[5] Only in the Gospel of Matthew are found the exceptions ὁ Χριστός Matt. 11:2, and even Ἰησοῦς Χριστός, 16:21; cf. also 1:1 (here also υἱὸς Δαυείδ), and 1:18. Finally also the inscription in Mark 1:1.

in which he himself speaks of himself in the third person as the Messiah. If we begin by taking cases of the former kind, it is not surprising, but probably even rests in part in good historical tradition, when here—and indeed at decisive climactic points—the most general and to Jewish messianology the most familiar title Χριστός appears: Mark 8:29 (Caesarea Philippi!); 14:61 (the question of the high priest); 15:32 (ridicule at the cross).[6] The book of Acts may also be claimed as a witness here. Harnack[7] has well observed that in this book "Christ" often appears, not yet as a proper name as it does with Paul, but in the original sense of the title. In the twenty-five passages in which the word Χριστός is assured by the manuscript witnesses, the combination Ἰησοῦς Χριστός is found eleven times, always in fixed formulas, in connection with ὄνομα and κύριος. In the other fourteen passages, however, it is used in the full sense of the Messiah title; and of these, eight belong to the first half of Acts which we are considering (2:31, 36; 3:18, 20; 4:26; 5:42; 8:5; 9:22). For all that, these observations say very little new to us. For that Jesus was the Χριστός to his first disciples is indeed guaranteed quite apart from this.

Further, the title "Son of God" in the address of other persons to Jesus is already found in a series of important Marcan passages, which are further to be discussed below in broader connections.

2. But an important observation can already be made here, namely, that the title "Son of David" is hardly found in the older stratum of the gospel tradition at all. There is no trace of it in the Logia. In Mark the address "Son of David" occurs only once, on the lips of the blind man of Jericho (10:47). But it cannot be shown from this context that any sort of special significance is attached by the evangelist to this form of address. Instead, it is characteristic that upon Jesus' entry into Jerusalem in Mark 11:10 indeed the ἐρχομένη βασιλεία πατρὸς ἡμῶν Δαυείδ is spoken of. Jesus himself, however, is introduced, not as David's son, but as ὁ ἐρχόμενος.[8, 9] In fact we find one passage in our Gospels in which there is a direct polemic

---

[6] For this reason in Mark 15:12 βασιλεὺς τῶν Ἰουδαίων is intentionally placed on the lips of Pilate: ὃν λέγετε τὸν βασιλέα τῶν Ἰουδαίων. Matt. 27:17, 22: Ἰησοῦν τὸν λεγόμενον Χριστόν. Χριστός further in Matt. 26:68; Luke 23:2 (Χριστὸν βασιλέα, expression of the Jews before Pilate); 23:39 (24:26, 46 of the Messiah generally).

[7] *Neue Untersuchungen zur Apostelgeschichte* (1911), pp. 72-73.

[8] A mysterious messianic title, developed in dependence upon Ps. 118:25-26; cf. Matt. 11:3.

[9] Otherwise in Matt. 21:9, 15, Son of David, and still elsewhere in the later passages of Matt. 12:23 and 15:22.

against the assumption of Jesus' sonship to David.[10] For that is the thrust of the remarkable dialogue in Mark 12:35-37, which is hardly to be traced back to Jesus but rather obviously bears the traces of a beginning church dogmatics; in this pericope the view of Jesus as David's son is intended to be rejected in favor of a loftier view: Jesus is not David's son but David's Lord.[11] The author of the Epistle of Barnabas has rightly understood the thrust of the passage (12:10): "Now since it was to be expected that they (the Jewish sinners) would say that Christ is a son of David, David himself, because he feared and foresaw the error of the sinners, said 'The Lord said to my Lord' " (Ps. 110). This view of the utter rejection of the ideal of the Son of David to be sure has not prevailed. In later times, as generally in the evaluation of the person of Jesus the specifically Jewish-messianic ideal receded into the background and less value was placed upon the more specific interpretation of this ideal, and as here rather all details came under the mechanical perspective of fulfilled prediction, naturally Jesus had to be the Son of David and in this respect also to satisfy the Old Testament prophecy.[12] But the almost total silence of the older stratum of the gospel tradition shows that in the primitive community people were at best indifferent and even distrustful toward the ideal of the Son of David.

3. Now this is an observation whose importance is not to be underestimated, one which leads us immediately to the kernel of the whole problem. It is illumined by the fact now to be explained, that a hitherto unexplained messianic title, namely the designation ὁ υἱὸς τοῦ ἀνθρώπου, actually dominates the presentation of our Gospels.

Of course, with this title there is a peculiar state of affairs. It is completely lacking not only in the gospel narrative but also in the address of other persons to Jesus; it is found only as a self-designation of Jesus, and indeed here again in an exclusively dominating position, so that other self-designations of Jesus alongside it almost completely disappear.[13] It is not

---

[10] On this, cf. the splendid little treatment by Wrede, "Jesus als Davids Sohn," *Vorträge und Studien* (1907), VI, 147-77.

[11] In this connection it is not the "genuineness" or lack of genuineness of this saying which concerns us. Even if the polemic against the interpretation of the Messiah as David's son did stem from Jesus himself, it would still be characteristic of the attitude of the primitive community that it would repeat this polemic.

[12] This is already Paul's evaluation in Rom. 1:3 (cf. II Tim. 2:8). The genealogies of Jesus in Matt. and Luke are constructed in this tendency. It dominates the birth legends in Matt. 1:20; Luke 1:27, 32; 2:4, 11. Cf. Acts 2:25, 29, 34; 13:34.

[13] Jesus' self-designation as the Χριστός belongs to the tertiary level of our gospel tradition. Mark 9:41, ἐν ὀνόματι ὅτι Χριστοῦ ἐστέ, is a reworking of the (Logia-)

easy to find a basis of explanation for these observations, which appear almost contradictory. However, one probably can point to the fact that the specifically transcendent-eschatological meaning of the title (*vide infra*) and perhaps also the awareness of its mysterious character made it impossible for the community tradition to have the earthly Jesus already addressed by other persons as υἱὸς τοῦ ἀνθρώπου, while in the self-designation of Jesus the character of the subjective-proleptic and of the secrecy-filled mystery remained with the term.

In any case, however that may be, only the numerous passages in which Jesus speaks of himself as υἱὸς τοῦ ἀνθρώπου offer us a more extensive body of material for answering the question about the Christology of the Palestinian primitive community, or of a thrust which came to be dominant in it. To be sure some will be inclined a priori to doubt and dispute this. Since what is involved here are self-expressions of Jesus, so the argument runs, from these to be discerned in the first place is the self-consciousness of Jesus and not a Christology of the primitive community. Accordingly we must first show, not that Jesus never used this title of himself, for that does not lend itself to demonstration with certainty, but rather that the self-designation of the Son of Man in surprisingly numerous cases does not go back to Jesus himself, but rather actually stems from the community tradition, and that here if anywhere, in the confession of Jesus as the Son of Man, we have before us the conviction of the primitive community.

One can indeed also point out a priori that this oft-repeated speech of Jesus about himself in the third person evokes the impression of a certain unnaturalness, if it is taken seriously as historical, but that on the other hand the riddle is immediately solved if we may here recognize in general a stylized form of the community's language and that in particular the oft-recurring formula ἦλθεν ὁ υἱὸς τοῦ ἀνθρώπου from the outset creates the impression of a specifically hieratic stylizing. Still this does not relieve us of the responsibility of the precise investigation of particulars.

---

parallel in Matt. 10:42, εἰς ὄνομα μαθητοῦ. Matt. 23:10, μηδὲ κληθῆτε καθηγηταί, ὅτι καθηγητὴς ὑμῶν ἐστι εἷς ὁ Χριστός is the addition of a redactor who in the preceding distich missed the reference to Christ, probably correctly, for in 23:8 the διδάσκαλος, for the sake of the parallelism, is to be referred to God. Note also in addition to πατήρ and ῥαββί the specifically Greek καθηγητής. About the title "Son (of God)" on the lips of Jesus in Mark 13:32 (mentioned in the parable in 12:6) and Matt. 11:27=Luke 10:22 (title or figure of speech), see below. The main thing here is only to make clear the small number of these exceptional cases.

I begin with the cases in which the title owes its origin to literary arbitrariness or to the special tradition of one of the later gospels.[14] Here above all belongs the framing of the question at Caesarea Philippi in Matt. 16:13: τίνα λέγουσιν οἱ ἄνθρωποι εἶναι τὸν υἱὸν τοῦ ἀνθρώπου? This awkward formulation, by which the answer is anticipated in the question, is explained by a comparison with Mark 8:27. Similarly, Matt. 16:28 speaks of the coming of the Son of Man with his Kingdom, while Mark 9:1 speaks only of the coming of the kingdom of God in power, and Luke 9:27 simply of the coming of the kingdom of God. The already dogmatic-sounding sentence, "The Son of Man has come to save the lost," is found in Matt. 18:11 and Luke 9:56 in an interpolation supported only by manuscripts of little value, and is here clearly to be recognized as a supplement to the fine conclusion of Luke 19:9 (καθότι καὶ αὐτὸς υἱὸς ᾿Αβραάμ ἐστιν), for the purpose of reinforcing the point. Again Luke, in the great community saying in 6:22, speaks of a persecution for the sake of the Son of Man, of which Matt. 5:11 still knows nothing. And this passage, Luke 6:22, is especially important because with every word it presupposes later circumstances of the community persecuted by the synagogue. This community gathers itself around the confession of the Son of Man and is persecuted on account of this confession. The concluding words of the great eschatological discourse in Luke (21:36), σταθῆναι ἔμπροσθεν τοῦ υἱοῦ τοῦ ἀνθρώπου, are not confirmed by either of the two parallels. Similarly, Luke 22:48, "Why do you betray the Son of Man with a kiss?" stands alone. To this latest stratum of gospel tradition also belongs the secondary interpretation of an already secondary parable (of the tares in the wheat field), in which the Son of Man twice appears (13:37, 41), and similarly the parable in Matt. 25:31 ff. with the large-scale portrait of the Son of Man as judge of the world. We shall speak of this more explicitly later. The dogmatic comment about the suffering and dying of the Son of Man in Luke 24:7 stands within an obviously later section which shows the clear tendency to suppress the tradition of the resurrected one in Galilee; Luke 17:22 (the days are coming when you will long to see one of the days of the Son of Man) is a transitional comment of the evangelist on the logion from Q in 17:23. A similar judgment is also indicated concerning the enigmatic and awkward appendix to the special

[14] So far as I can see, it is the achievement of Wellhausen (*Skizzen und Vorarbeiten* VI, 187-215) to have shown emphatically in how many passages the title "Son of Man" has first penetrated into the gospel tradition.

pericope in Luke 18:8*b*: When the Son of Man comes, will he find faith[15] upon the earth?

But similarly also on the basis of simple literary observation, in our *older* tradition, in Mark and in the Logia, some of the remaining passages exhibit a secondary reworking. Thus the sentence in Mark 9:12*b*: "What is written concerning the Son of Man? That he would suffer and be rejected," awkwardly interrupts the good connection between 12*a* and 13 in such a way that it must be viewed as an interpolation from Matt. 17:12*b*. Again this Matthaean passage is shown to be a secondary addition in the old text of Mark. And the command of Jesus on the descent from the Mount of Transfiguration that the disciples should tell no one of their experience is visibly a secondary addition and falls under the same judgment as does Mark 16:8 ("they told no man anything, for they were afraid").[16]

But especially deserving of attention are the passages in which, by a comparison of our oldest sources, the Logia and the Gospel of Mark, a still later insertion of the Son of Man title even into our better sources can be demonstrated. Thus in the logion about the reward for confession, Matt. 10:32-33, with its fourfold "I"—"whoever confesses me, him will I confess, and whoever denies me, him will I deny"—apparently has preserved the original wording of its source (the Logia). In Mark 8:38, with the insertion of the Son-of-Man title in the second half, this deformity has resulted: "Whoever is ashamed of me and my words, of him also will the Son of Man be ashamed." [17] This form then in turn has influenced Mark's parallels in Luke 9:26 and Matt. 16:27, and indeed within the Logia context the passage in Luke 12:8 as well. If here Mark is shown to be secondary in relation to the Logia tradition, the reverse is the case in the logion of the sign of Jonah (Matt. 12:39-40=Luke 11:29-30). Here the source common to Matthew and Luke has first brought in the Jonah clause from the following pericope and has inserted it into the saying transmitted by

[15] One should note here the later concept of faith, otherwise foreign to our gospel literature.

[16] In both cases the comments are intended to explain why the respective preceding narrative has become generally known only in a later time; thus they also contain an indication of the relatively late formation of the legendary accounts in which they occur. Cf. also with Mark 9:9-10 the simple (original?) account in Luke 9:36*b*.

[17] To assume with Wellhausen on the basis of this passage that Jesus himself spoke of the Messiah–Son of Man as a strange person means arbitrarily to suppress the most obvious explanation in favor of a very risky and more remote one. Cf. also my *Jesus der Herr* (1916), p. 10, against Wernle, "Jesus und Paulus," *Zeitschrift für Theologie und Kirche*, 1915, pp. 1-92.

Mark (8:12: εἰ δοθήσεται σημεῖον) in its original form, and then somehow has referred the sign of the prophet Jonah to the sign which the "Son of Man" is to give to this generation.[18]

One of the most important observations of synoptic criticism, which is also of special significance for our question, may be made in a comparison of Mark 10:41-45 with Luke 22:24-27. For on the basis of this comparison it is established that the logion of Mark 10:45, which is so heavily freighted with dogmatic import, "the Son of Man has not come to be ministered unto but to minister and to give his life a ransom for many," has its simple original form in the saying, "I am in your midst as a servant" (Luke 22:27).[19]

Quite evidently the logion in Matt. 12:32=Luke 12:10 about blasphemy against the Son of Man is also a later community saying. The community of the disciples of Jesus here interprets the blasphemy against the marvelous spirit at work in them (note the context) as an unforgivable sin. One may perhaps blaspheme the remote (sojourning in heaven) Son of Man, but not the presently active Spirit! In Mark 3:28 the logion appears in another context; any connection with the Son of Man is lacking.[20]

Now there remain in the Gospel of Mark as well as in the Logia a series of passages in which the Son-of-Man title appears, where it cannot be set aside for such simple reasons of external literary criticism. The observation is significant—and particularly here the doubled witness of the Gospel of Mark and of the Logia carries some weight—for it proves unequivocally that the title belongs to the oldest and primary stratum of community tradition. On the other side, however, the judgment will have to be maintained that in essence we possess even here the earliest community dogmatics and not Jesus' own self-testimony.

[18] It appears to me probable that here Luke, without expressing it, is thinking of the sign of the death and resurrection, just as does Matthew, who explicitly says it (and thus probably also their common source).

[19] Luke here represents the Logia tradition; cf. also Luke 22:29-30 and Matt. 19:28. One should note esp. the parallelism of the entire context in Mark and Luke. Mark has connected the Logia pericope 10:41-44 with the preceding by means of the artificial transition of 10:40. The dogmatic saying in Mark 10:45 has developed out of the text as transmitted by Luke through the following procedure: 1. insertion of the Son-of-Man title, 2. insertion of the current formula with ἦλθεν, 3. introduction of the contrasting clause "οὐ διακονηθῆναι ἀλλά," 4. the glossing of the διακονῆσαι by means of the reference to the sacrificial death. In *Jesus der Herr*, pp. 8-9, I have discussed doubts about the relative priority of Luke 22:24 ff.

[20] In the entire context of 3:22-30, of course, Mark appears to be altogether dependent upon the Logia (see below). In this connection, however, he has inserted the saying about the blasphemy against the Holy Spirit, which hardly belonged here originally, in an older wording than Matt. and Luke offer it.

First of all, as has been observed by many, these self-descriptions of Jesus may further be divided into two groups. In one of them Jesus speaks of his position as Son of Man as a present state; he makes himself known openly before all the people as the Son of Man, and as such he claims rights which he presently exercises. To this group the following passages would belong: the Son of Man has power on earth to forgive sins (Mark 2:10); the Son of Man is Lord of the Sabbath (Mark 2:28); the Son of Man has no place to lay his head (Matt. 8:20═Luke 9:58); the Son of Man (in contrast to John the Baptist) came eating and drinking (Matt. 11:18 ff.═ Luke 7:33-34). Here some have already long since, and altogether correctly, pointed out that it is hardly conceivable that at the beginning of his activity, openly and before all the people, without any sort of precautions, Jesus could have identified himself as Messiah with the title of the Son of Man,[21] still well known in the literature of late Judaism. Besides, this does not agree with what we otherwise know from the Gospels about the reserve which Jesus practiced in his messianic self-consciousness; in particular it does not agree with the accent which in the Gospel of Mark, whether with or without the intention of the evangelist, quite evidently rests upon the confession of Peter at Caesarea Philippi. And above all, if the Son of Man can only mean the supra-terrestrial transcendent Messiah, as now is generally acknowledged, then we cannot explain how Jesus already in the present could claim for himself the predicate and the rights of the Son of Man. Therefore there is a general inclination likewise to abandon to criticism this entire series of self-expressions of Jesus, however one may now account for the development of this community tradition.[22]

There still remains the second group of self-testimonies. In them the eschatological character of the Son-of-Man title is in fact preserved. Here Jesus speaks in the circle of those whom he trusts, and once in the final official hearing, in mysterious allusions (and therefore also in the third

---

[21] I consider the efforts to deny late Jewish literature any acquaintance with the title to have failed completely. See below, pp. 42 ff.

[22] Cf. esp. H. Weinel in the carefully weighed presentation in his *Biblische Theologie des Neuen Testaments*, 2nd ed., pp. 211 ff. It is largely customary to attempt to explain these passages as linguistic misunderstandings (ὁ υἱὸς τοῦ ἀνθρώπου═ἄνθρωπος). This appears to me to be utterly impossible for Mark 2:10 (in spite of the strange confirmation which Matt. 9:8 seems to offer for this thesis). Dogmatic reediting has much more profoundly disarranged this pericope (see below, Chap. II). The assumption appears possible to me in the sayings in Mark 2:28, Matt. 8:20═Luke 9:59, and possibly Matt. 11:19 ("a man" came, ate, and drank). M. Dibelius (*Formgeschichte des Evangeliums*, p. 76) sees in Matt. 11:18-19═Luke 7:33-34 a postscript of the community to the parable of Jesus about the self-willed children.

person), of his future position in the office of the Son of Man and of his death as the point of transition to this future position of honor. It is far from my intention here to take up the difficult and not entirely soluble question about the messianic self-consciousness of Jesus. At any rate it has in this connection only an indirect and secondary significance. I still think, however, that an investigation of the passages under consideration leads to the conclusion that we have in them an essentially later tradition, i.e., community theology. It may be generally conceded that the thrice-repeated predictions of the passion in Mark (8:31; 9:31; 10:33) in an almost stereotyped formulation, which acquire their point by means of the title "Son of Man," as we have them, create the impression throughout of a schematizing and dogmatizing reworking. The predictions of Mark 14:21, 41,[23] which bear a quite similar stamp, are subject to the same reservations. The reference to the Son of Man in Mark 13:26-27 stands among those eschatological statements which we are generally accustomed to recognizing as stemming from a Jewish or Jewish-Christian apocalypse. The only activity here attributed to the Son of Man, the gathering of those who are dispersed, fits particularly into the Jewish milieu. The threat with which, according to Mark 14:62, Jesus turns during the trial to his opponents appears as an utter surprise[24] and inharmoniously in this context, in which what is involved is a simple yes or no to the question whether he is the Christ. And even this focusing of the trial of Jesus on the Messiah question is subject to serious historical misgivings which will later engage our attention in context. There still remain the passages in the eschatological discourse of the Logia: Matt. 24:27=Luke 17:23-24; Matt. 24:37, 39=Luke 17:26, 30.[25] But here also the question arises whether we may actually hold it psychologically conceivable that Jesus could have compared his future appearing with the flashing of the lightning which shines from one end of the earth to the other, i.e., actually whether he made his own person into a myth. Here also the question may be posed which later will occupy us in

---

[23] Cf. in Mark 14:21 the wholly secondary general reference to the fulfillment of Old Testament prophecy (see below, Chap. II). 14:41 of course has its parallel in Matt. but not in Luke.

[24] Norden (*Agnostos Theos*, pp. 194-95) stresses the ecstatic character of this confession which begins with ἐγώ εἰμι and points to Celsus' portrayal of the Syrian wandering prophets (in Origen VII, 9) with their confession: ἐγὼ ὁ θεός εἰμι ἢ θεοῦ παῖς ἢ πνεῦμα θεῖον· ἥκω δέ, ἤδη γὰρ ὁ κόσμος ἀπόλλυται. . . καὶ ὄψεσθέ με αὖθις μετ' οὐρανίου δυνάμεως ἐπανιόντα.

[25] Matt. 24:44=Luke 12:40 is probably a doublet to the simpler and figurative wording in Mark 13:35.

its full import, whether Jesus himself, as it happens in the Lucan passage, could have spoken of a day of the Son of Man and therewith could have put "his" day in place of the Old Testament "day of Yahweh," or whether he actually, as Matthew records, spoke of his own parousia in the place of the parousia of the omnipotent judging God.[26]

For all that, it is not to be denied that perhaps one or another of the Son-of-Man passages could have come from the mouth of Jesus himself. But one is not able to escape the impression that on the whole, in the Son-of-Man sayings we have before us the deposit of the theology of the primitive community. That is the assured and given point of departure.

4. At this point we stand before a fact of eminent importance for the history of the belief in Christ, a point which we must now pursue further. In the end, what we have to do is to get a clear conception as to the source, meaning, and import of the title "Son of Man." On these points we can work upon a foundation which has been securely laid by varied and thorough research from the most diverse sides.

First as to the linguistic significance of the title: ὁ υἱὸς τοῦ ἀνθρώπου corresponds to the Aramaic בר אנשא (=Hebrew בן־האדם). Wellhausen's investigations in particular have shed light upon the linguistic meaning of this term.[27] According to Wellhausen, bar 'nascha in Aramaic usage means nothing other than "the man" in the definite and particular instance. אנשא is, as he has made especially clear, a word with generic meaning and signifies the species "man." If the Aramaean wishes to designate one particular man, he must either choose another word (e.g., גברא the man, אתתא the woman), or make use of that periphrastic form. As in our language the word "cattle" is generic and we may say "so many head of cattle," just so the Aramaean says "a son of man" (בר אנש), "this" or "that son of man" (ההוא בר אנשא), "sons of men" (בני אנשא); and thus must the expression, "the" son of man (בר אנשא) be explained in this context.[28] From this set of facts, Wellhausen and the other researchers who

[26] So far as I can see, there remains only the saying in Matt. 10:23: "You will not have gone through all the cities of Israel before the Son of Man comes." Because of its particularism this saying gives the impression of being very early and is to be ascribed to the Logia. But it places us in the time of the beginning missionary activity on the part of the primitive community rather than in the life of Jesus.

[27] Cf. above all his discussion with Dalman's attacks, *Skizzen und Vorarbeiten* VI, pp. V-VII, and pp. 187-215.

[28] The interpretation of the expression in the sense of "ideal man" or of man in contrast to the Jew is naturally excluded. If such an idea had been possible at all in the milieu with which we are concerned, it would have had to be expressed by the simple אנשא, and not by the term בר אנשא.

followed him[29] have drawn the conclusion that the title "Son of Man" is not to be attributed to Jesus, because such a title never existed in the region of the Aramaic language and for linguistic reasons cannot have existed. It is inconceivable how the utterly colorless "the man" (and *bar 'nascha*= ὁ υἱὸς τοῦ ἀνθρώπου means nothing more) could ever have gained the sense of a messianic title of dignity. There is rather here a misunderstanding which first arose on the soil of the Greek language through (an incorrect) translation with ὁ υἱὸς τοῦ ἀνθρώπου (for ἄνθρωπος).[30] So the argument runs.

Yet no sort of decisive proof can be conceded to this conclusion. First of all, there are reservations of a linguistic nature that arise against it. Dalman has not been able, in his sharp statements against Wellhausen,[31] to demolish the basic linguistic theses of the latter, but at one point his statements remain eminently worthy of attention. For Dalman shows that in an entire series of dialects which he investigated (with the exception, of course, of the Jewish-Galilean and the Christian-Palestinian), the expression *bar 'nasch* rarely appears and is regarded as archaic-poetic, and further, that the definite *bar 'nascha* in this language region is utterly unheard of. If this is correct, thus if here for the singular "man" (in the definite or the indefinite sense) substitute forms such as (the) man, (the) woman were customary, then the possibility is certainly given that a wholly extraordinary *bar 'nascha* could take on a terminological meaning without thereby introducing the danger of a misunderstanding.

But even if Dalman is not correct, and *bar 'nascha* in general usage first was taken as nothing but an expression for the individual (definite) man, then it is utterly beyond comprehension why a quite general term such as "the man" could not also, under certain conditions, have become a messianic term. Jewish apocalypticism loved to coin such mysterious and

[29] Especially Lietzmann, *Der Menschensohn*, 1896. Eerdmans, *Theol. Tijdschr.* 1894, pp. 165 ff.

[30] Wellhausen and Lietzmann, by placing the emergence of the title "Son of Man" in Greek-speaking territory, pass over one eminently important datum for the understanding of the messianic theology of primitive Christianity. Against this handling of the question, in my judgment, an objection is offered by the synoptic tradition, which shows that the title belonged to the original stock of the Palestinian tradition.

[31] Cf. Dalman, *The Words of Jesus*, pp. 234-41. In the general linguistic evaluation (אנש generic; בר אנש "a member of the human species"; בר אנשא the emphatic state of בר אנש; the appearance of גבר as an alternate form for the designation of an individual man), Dalman comes very close to Wellhausen's opinion, only he less definitely works out the general principles and proceeds more empirically and lexicographically. Cf. Wellhausen's reply, already referred to above.

enigmatic terms. In it we find such expressions for the Messiah as הבא=
ὁ ἐρχόμενος, the "shoot" (zemach, ἀνατολή), or even (in later tradition)
the leper! [32]

And the conditions under which this term could develop are in fact
present within Jewish apocalypticism. Here the matter must rest: the title
ὁ υἱὸς τοῦ ἀνθρώπου is to be understood out of the prophecy in Daniel
(7:13). Here the seer, after he has had the world empires appear in the
form of fearful beasts, beholds the kingdom of Israel in the image of a
man who was brought before God's throne: "And behold, there came one
with the clouds of heaven in the form of a man (כבר אנש) and he was
brought before the Ancient One . . . and to him were given power and
honor and lordship." If for Daniel himself the one in human form[33] is only
framed as a symbol for the people of Israel, the kingdom of the saints,
still for Oriental imagination it was only a short step to make out of the
symbol a concrete figure and to interpret this passage messianically. Perhaps
this step had already been taken in the translation of the LXX, which
translated the sentence, "And he came (was brought) before the Ancient
One," with καὶ ὡς παλαιὸς (!) ἡμερῶν παρῆν.[34] Such reinterpretation
certainly is present also in the so-called Similitudes of the Ethiopic Book of
Enoch. There Enoch views the one in human form as a personally preexistent being with the Ancient One in heaven (chap. 46), and this human-
figured one then takes over, in the Similitudes, the role of the Messiah. Only
one thing is still under dispute, whether in the Similitudes the coined title
"Son of Man" is already present or not. One may point to the fact that in the
Similitudes it is almost always put as "this" or "that" Son of Man.[35] And
in fact the seer seems with these pronouns constantly to point back to that
basic vision which he had had at the beginning (chap. 46). But it still is
not to be denied that along the way of such a repeated reference the title,
"the Son of Man," could have and must have arisen. And thus we find in

[32] Bousset, Religion des Judentums, 2nd ed., p. 305, n. 1.

[33] The question whether there is not underlying the Danielic, eschatological picture a
mythical, personal figure of the "man," which then in Daniel was turned into a symbol
and referred to the people of Israel, does not need to be pursued further in this context.
For our purposes it all comes out to one and the same thing, whether the personal interpretation of the human figure represents a return to a pre-Danielic myth or a simple misunderstanding. At any rate, it happened.

[34] Theodotion correctly has: καὶ ἕως τοῦ παλαιοῦ τῶν ἡμερῶν ἔφθασεν. The wording
of the LXX could of course rest upon a simple scribal error.

[35] Cf. the compilation of the passages by Beer in Kautzsch, Pseudepigraphen, p. 262.
Bousset, Religion des Judentums, 2nd ed., p. 301, n. 2.

fact also once or twice the simple form "the" Son of Man (62.7; 71.17 mss., cf. 69.27).[36] A second important witness in Jewish literature is offered by the so-called vision of the Son of Man in the Fourth Book of Ezra, which of course is post-Christian. Here also the conditions are similar. Ezra sees "one like the figure of a man" rise out of the sea, and, looking back, calls this one *ille homo* (13.3), *ipse homo* (13.12).[37] All these observations point to the fact that at least in certain apocalyptic circles[38] the title, "the" Son of Man, for the Messiah could very well have arisen. And then even our gospel literature, within which, as we have seen, the title "Son of Man" may be traced back into the earliest (i.e., the Palestinian) strata, proves beyond any doubt that that transition to the title actually did take place. So then we will best be able to paraphrase and explain the strange and enigmatic designation *bar 'nascha*, ὁ υἱὸς τοῦ ἀνθρώπου, with the term "the" (well known from Daniel's prophecy or from the apocalyptic tradition) "Man." [39]

5. Along with the title, however, the primitive community—and here we stand in the presence of a fact of most decisive importance—also

---

[36] Dalman (*Words of Jesus*, p. 243) assumes that in the Greek copy from which the Ethiopic was made perhaps a simple ὁ υἱὸς τοῦ ἀνθρώπου could already have been used everywhere. Gressmann (*Israelit. jüd. Eschatologie*, p. 355) is of the opinion that the Greek οὗτος ὁ ἄνθρωπος, ἐκεῖνος ὁ ἄνθρωπος, αὐτὸς ὁ ἄνθρωπος could go back to a simple Aramaic בר אנשא.

[37] In addition, for the distribution of the Son-of-Man idea there comes into consideration also the (already christianized) Ascension of Isaiah, Latin text XI.1; also the Jewish or Jewish-Christian apocalypse in Mark 13:26 (Matt. 24:30).

[38] It must be conceded that the use of the term did not progress uniformly. The abovementioned passages of IV Ezra still lie precisely on the same level as the parables in Enoch. And Rev. 1:13; 14:14, again more closely follows Dan. 7:13. This, however, may have been due to the dominant role of Dan. 7:9 ff. in later Jewish apocalyptic, in consequence of which the constantly repeated reference to the original figurative usage of Daniel resulted. The example of the Apocalypse of John is especially clear here.

[39] Altogether new connections, important for the history of religions, would be opened up if Reitzenstein's recently proposed combinations (his essay, *Das mandäische Buch des Herrn der Grösse und die Evangelienüberlieferung*, SAH, 1919, No. 12) were to prove valid. On pp. 22 ff. Reitzenstein constructs from the first and second tractates of the Right Ginza a little apocalypse which is supposed to have emerged in the circle of the Baptist's disciples soon after the destruction of Jerusalem. In this apocalypse the figure of a Son-of-Man-Messiah (Enos-Uthra), who is to appear in Jerusalem as a supra-terrestrial light manifestation and as judge to destroy Jerusalem, plays a dominant role. Reitzenstein believes that he can show the influence of this apocalypse on several passages in the gospel literature (Matt. 11:1 ff.; 23:34-39, and esp. on the examination of Jesus before the high priest and Jesus' Son-of-Man response). Then the Son-of-Man expectation of primitive Christianity in the broadest scope would be directly borrowed from the Baptist sect or influenced in its development from that direction. Before a comprehensive examination of the Mandaean literature I do not venture a final judgment about this bold and stimulating combination. Through this discovery my major theses would only be confirmed and supplemented.

appropriated the total contents of the representations which are connected with it. With the title "Son of Man" is bound up, to be specific, that striking transcendent view of the messianic figure to which we have already referred above. As soon as one interpreted the symbol from Daniel messianically, the Messiah had to become a supra-terrestrial figure. This Messiah–"Son of Man" indeed is not born upon earth; he appears in the clouds of heaven. Thus here already the idea of preexistence obtrudes itself. He plays some kind of role in God's great judgment of the world; his kingdom is a marvelous kingdom. In all these respects the idea of the transcendent Messiah is actually already developed most clearly in the Similitudes of Enoch. Enoch sees the Messiah in human form at the beginning of the story (46), and thus he is preexistent; his name was spoken before the sun and earth were created (48.6); he suddenly appears out of heaven; he has become the judge of the world, who in the judgment of the kings appears at the side of God, and indeed already begins to displace God.[40]

And now we can show how with the title "Son of Man" the total Jewish preformed Son-of-Man dogma enters into the theology of the primitive community. As in the vision in Daniel the "Son of Man" appears at the side of the Ancient One in the judgment of the world, as Enoch sees the one in a human figure beside God in the primeval time, just so is Jesus for the faith of the primitive community first of all the Son of Man who reigns at the right hand of God or of God's power. Only one thing is added from the standpoint of the new faith to this picture of the Son of Man enthroned in splendor, namely the conception of the *exaltation* of the earthly Jesus of Nazareth to the dignity of the Son of Man, which the Jewish Son-of-Man dogma naturally could not prefigure.[41] In the Lucan account of the trial of Jesus before the high priest this confession emerges with special clarity: ἀπὸ τοῦ νῦν δὲ ἔσται ὁ υἱὸς τοῦ ἀνθρώπου καθήμενος ἐκ δεξιῶν τῆς δυνάμεως [θεοῦ] [42] (Luke 22:69).[43] According to the account in the book of Acts, Stephen, in ecstasy before his martyrdom, sees

---

[40] *Religion des Judentums*, 2nd ed., pp. 301-2.

[41] Cf. Acts 2:36 and 5:31, and particularly John 3:14; 8:28; 12: (32), 34.

[42] Θεοῦ is a gloss on τῆς δυνάμεως and is lacking in the Old Latin mss. e and l (69: θεοῦ τῆς δυνάμεως). Cf. above the text of Hegesippus.

[43] As compared with Luke, the Marcan text appears complicated: "You will see the Son of Man sitting at the right hand of Power and coming with the clouds of heaven" (14:62). The "seeing" actually fits in only with the prophecy of the return. Obviously two different motifs are combined in Mark. Matt. 26:64 has placed ἀπ' ἄρτι, corresponding to the Lucan ἀπὸ τοῦ νῦν, before the wording of Mark and thereby has made this completely meaningless. From what source may Luke have drawn the logion, a trace of which is also found in Matthew?

the heavens open and the "Son of Man" [44] standing at the right hand of God. The Lord's brother James is said (according to Hegesippus, in Eus. CH II, 23.13) to have answered the question about what he thought of Jesus thus: "Why do you ask me about the Son of Man? He is seated in heaven at the right hand of the great power and will come again on the clouds of heaven."

Similarly, the concept of the coming of the heavenly Messiah is transferred to Jesus and his parousia. He is to appear on the clouds of heaven (Mark 14:62), in the glory of the Father, surrounded by the angels (Mark 8:38 and par., 13:26; cf. I Thess. 4:15-16). He will send forth his angels to gather the elect from all four corners of the earth (Mark 13:27; cf. Matt. 13:41).[45] Then further, connected with this is the fact that in the gospel tradition, here and there, the conception of the kingdom of God is displaced by that of the kingdom of Christ.[46] For to the Son of Man are to fall the power and honor and lordship (Dan. 7:14). So people ventured already to speak of the "day" of the Son of Man just as the Old Testament spoke of the day of Yahweh.[47] And just as the Jewish eschatology predicts the coming of God, so the Christian eschatology predicts the coming, the parousia, of the Son of Man.[48] The most momentous step in this development, however, consists in the fact that Jesus as the Son of Man also becomes the future judge of the world and therewith, appearing in God's place, already begins in the faith of the primitive community to displace God from his position. We see the dogma of Jesus as judge of the world in the gospel tradition[49] grow before our very eyes. First he becomes the witness in the judgment before the throne of God (Luke's "before the angels of God" is only a circumlocution for God) concerning those who denied him and those who confessed him (Matt. 10:32-33=Luke 12:8); then he himself, in the glory of his Father and surrounded by his angels, reckons with those who denied him (Mark 8:38), then he becomes the

[44] The fact that in the book of Acts the title "Son of Man" is found only here shows, among other things, how little this writing may be said faithfully to reflect the preaching of the primitive Christian community.

[45] The gathering together of the dispersed plays a major role in the Son-of-Man vision of IV Ezra; cf. also the parables of Enoch, 57. Mandaean apocalypse in Reitzenstein, p. 24.

[46] Cf. Matt. 13:41; 16:28; 20:21; Luke 22:29-30.

[47] Luke 17:26, 30; cf. Luke 17:22; I Cor. 1:8, and Acts 2:20.

[48] Matt. 24:37, 39; cf. 24:44; I Thess. 2:19; 3:13; 4:15, and 5:23.

[49] The attitude of Jesus himself in this respect is clearly established by sayings such as Matt. 10:28 and Luke 12:5-6, and particularly by Mark 10:40. Cf. also the dogmatic advance from Luke 12:32 to Luke 22:29.

judge of the world in general who rewards each one according to his deeds (Matt. 16:27; cf. Luke 21:36).[50] Finally, Matthew sketches, in a parable, the large-scale picture of the Son of Man who takes his seat upon the throne of his glory to divide the throngs of people as the shepherd divides the sheep from the goats.[51] And all these observations are finally reciprocally supportive; as little as Jesus proclaimed himself to be the judge of the world, as little as he spoke about his coming in the glory of the Father and about "his" kingdom, just so little also did he speak of the day of the Son of Man and of the parousia of the Son of Man in judgment. All this lies on the same line of the community's dogmatics, now so rapidly developing.

One idea which already belonged to the stock of Jewish Son-of-Man dogmas, to be sure, was hardly transferred at once to Jesus; I mean the idea of his preexistence before the world. At least in the entire tradition of our Synoptic Gospels there is hardly a trace that would suggest that one must take the obscure saying in Luke 10:18, "I beheld Satan falling as lightning out of heaven," as a reference to an experience of preexistence. Here at first the earthly life of Jesus and the lively recollection of him posed a decisive hindrance to the further development of the idea. In the beginning the opinion may well have been predominant that Jesus sojourned here upon earth as a simple man ($\pi\alpha\hat{\iota}\varsigma$ $\theta\epsilon o\hat{\upsilon}$) and was exalted to be the Son of Man only after the close of his life.[52] But certainly the time is not far off when Jesus will become a spiritual being, heavenly, preexistent, coming down from above. The development which has begun here strides forward with brazen-faced persistency.

Above all, however, it was from the standpoint of the Son-of-Man dogmatics that the enigma of the crucifixion of Jesus which so gravely troubled the souls of the disciples was solved. Now people peered deep into the marvelous dispensations of God. They recognized that suffering and death were the only possible way by which Jesus could enter upon that higher level of existence of the Son of Man. The cross became the bridge which connects the lowliness of Jesus of Nazareth with the heavenly

---

[50] One should observe that in all these passages *the same* constantly varying word of Jesus occurs.

[51] Matt. 25:31 ff.; cf. with it further Acts 10:42, "the one foreordained to be the judge of the living and the dead." II Cor. 5:10 ($\beta\hat{\eta}\mu\alpha$ $X\rho\iota\sigma\tau o\hat{\upsilon}$), *et passim*.

[52] Cf. the book of Acts: God has made Jesus the Christ, 2:36; 5:31; "Jesus of Nazareth, a man attested to you by God through miracles and signs," 2:22; cf. 10:38; $\pi\alpha\hat{\iota}\varsigma$ $\theta\epsilon o\hat{\upsilon}$ 3:13, 26; 4:27, 30. Cf. also the interpretation, to be examined more closely later on, of the significance of the baptism of Jesus in the primitive community. Acts 10:38: "God has anointed him with the Holy Spirit and with power."

splendor of the Son of Man. The inner excitement which energized the souls of the disciples when this truth came to them still vibrates clearly in the thrice-repeated predictions of the passion which resound through the Gospel of Mark like the solemn strokes of a bell: *the Son of Man must* suffer and die and on the third day rise again.[53] It is an inner necessity, a divinely ordained "must" which leads through defeat to victory, through death to glory.

6. When we survey all these details in context, the certainty of our judgment is immediately confirmed. What is present in the Son-of-Man passages of the gospel tradition is in the first place a coherent and complete community dogmatics.[54] From the details which we recognized with compelling certainty as community dogmatics (judgment of the world, consideration of the suffering on the cross) a conclusion on the whole structure is allowed and indeed demanded.

Now we see quite clearly. The first community of the disciples of Jesus viewed him as the Messiah, in that they, half-consciously rejecting the Son-of-David ideal, adapted to him the Jewish apocalyptic figure of the Son of Man. From this point all previously made observations draw their inner unity: the complete subsidence of the title of the Son of David, the polemic against the idea of Christ's being a son of David, the less frequent use of the name Christ, the dominance of the Son-of-Man title.

When and how rapidly may this development have occurred? We may suspect that the Messiah–Son of Man idea was approximately as ancient in the primitive community as the belief in Christ itself. The messianic faith of the primitive community *could* be formed after the death of Jesus in no other form than that of the ideal of a transcendent Messiah. The hope that Jesus as an earthly man would take over the role on earth of the king from David's tribe was once and for all shattered. There remained only that heavenly figure which in the Jewish tradition was indissolubly joined with the picture from the prophet Daniel and the name of the Son of Man. Very soon, after the disciples of Jesus grasped the daring faith that in spite of his suffering and death Jesus was the promised Messiah, their messianic

[53] Mark 8:31; 9:31; 10:33; cf. Luke 24:7. Only later does the idea enter that the suffering and death of the Son of Man are prophesied in the Scripture; see below.

[54] Even here I do not consider the question whether this community dogmatic view with respect to individual points could begin with authentic utterances of Jesus about himself. With this question we enter upon the area of uncertainties and subjective decisions. I have stressed in *Jesus der Herr*, p. 10, how difficult, indeed how impossible it is to derive the Son-of-Man passages, seen in their totality, from the self-consciousness of the historical Jesus.

faith will have taken on the form of the expectation of the Son of Man.

From here we look back once more at the hour of the emergence of this messianic faith. The tradition as it is given in its purest form by Paul in I Cor. 15 tells us that the disciples, particularly and first of all Peter, had a series of visions in which they saw Jesus and through which they came to the conviction that he was still alive. People on the critical side are for the most part in agreement that what is involved here is a purely spiritual event in the souls of the disciples, and they thus reject any idea of an external miracle. On the other side are those who gladly stand by the appearances of the resurrected One as ultimate inexplicable happenings, as a psychological wonder which is no longer subject to analysis. For an actually historical consideration even those visionary experiences will have to occupy a second place. The most important and most central thing in all this is and remains, however, that in the souls of the disciples the rocklike conviction arose that in spite of his death and apparent defeat, indeed precisely through all that, Jesus had become the supra-terrestrial Messiah in glory who would return to judge the world, and that this certainty made possible for them the faith in the substance of the gospel which Jesus represented. The most diverse factors worked together to form that new conviction. The driving force was the incomparable, powerful, and indestructible impression which Jesus' personality had left behind on the souls of his disciples and which was more powerful than public humiliation and death, agony and defeat. This attitude was heightened by the recently experienced shattering of all their hopes through the unexpected defeat and the sudden fall of their hero and master. It is a psychological law that such a disappointment of the most ardent hopes by brutal reality causes, or at least can cause, after a period of discouragement, a swing to the other extreme, in which the human soul, with a defiant "nevertheless," rises victorious to an outlook which makes the impossible possible. But then it was further of tremendous importance that in the contemporary apocalyptic a ready-made image of the Messiah had been created which appeared to hold the clue to the entire perplexing riddle which the disciples had experienced. The disciples of Jesus salvaged their hopes, which certainly had already been stimulated during the lifetime of Jesus,[55] by reshaping them into a loftier and more powerful form. They

---

[55] That the idea of the Messiah was thrust upon Jesus appears in my judgment to be confirmed as authentic tradition (the confession at Caesarea Philippi, the request of the sons of Zebedee, Jesus' entry into Jerusalem, perhaps also the inquiry of the Baptist). Jesus' attitude toward this remains uncertain (see Chap. II).

cast about their master the king's mantle which was ready at hand, set upon his head the loftiest crown they could secure, and confessed Jesus as the Son of Man who through suffering and death had entered into glory. The new convictions naturally did not come to be through an essentially intellectual process. It was a spiritual battle and a contest involving matters of life and death. Who will wonder at the fact that the disciples, in those days of most intense excitement, of oscillating between despair and most daring victorious hope, saw visions and felt their master to be perceptibly near? Thus the new faith was formed and opened the book of world history to its page, and its first confession ran thus: Jesus the Messiah–Son of Man.

The first Christian community was gathered around the conviction that Jesus is the Messiah–Son of Man. The confession of the Son of Man was the shibboleth which separated the circle of Jesus' disciples from the Jewish synagogue. Thus is explained the role which the Son of Man plays as judge in the words of the gospel tradition which deal with confession and denial.[56] Luke quite clearly alludes to this persecution of those who confess the Son of Man from the side of the Jewish synagogue: "Blessed are you when men hate you and thrust you out (of the synagogue) and abuse you (the synagogal ban) and blot out your name as evil (from the synagogal rolls) *for the sake of the Son of Man*" (6:22). And we still possess an echo of these conditions in the Fourth Gospel. Jesus meets the man born blind, who symbolizes the community which had been blind and had received sight, after the synagogue had expelled him (ἐξέβαλον αὐτὸν ἔξω 9:34), and asked him: σὺ πιστεύεις εἰς τὸν υἱὸν τοῦ ἀνθρώπου;[57] And the blind man finally confessed πιστεύω κύριε, κὰι προσεκύνησεν αὐτῷ. Here we already have a later touching up, particularly in the part about worshiping Jesus. *But the main thing, the separation of Judaism and the Christian community by the confession of the Son of Man, is faithfully preserved.*

It hardly needs further to be demonstrated that this confession was not only the external mark of recognition of the disciples of Jesus but also the focal point of their conviction. The thoroughly eschatological character of the primitive Christian community is indeed well enough known. But the eschatology of the disciples of Jesus was now concentrated in the expectation of the coming of the Son of Man. Everything else, indeed even the coming of God in his Kingdom as proclaimed by Jesus, could fall into the back-

---

[56] Matt. 10:31-32 (=Luke 12:9), Mark 8:38, and parallels.

[57] Most of the mss. have already inserted here the usual confession of the υἱὸς θεοῦ. Cf. further John 9:22; 12:42; 16:1.

ground by comparison. The little Christian apocalypse in Mark 13 simply holds to the portrayal of how the Son of Man sends out his angels and gathers his righteous ones. What one expects of the end is the parousia of the Son of Man. One lives in the longing even to see only one of the days of the Son of Man. And one expects him in heavenly Godlike glory, surrounded by his angels, as the judge of the world, who gathers all the peoples before his throne. In infinite majesty, yet on familiar terms with his own and acknowledging them, he was to appear. Already something of the mystical attitude of the bride who awaits her bridegroom was blended into this eschatological expectation of the community.[58] And this Son-of-Man eschatology is now no myth and no empty dream but rather living actuality. One knows who this anticipated Son of Man is, Jesus of Nazareth, in recollection presently conceivable, in hope immediately at hand. One lives according to his demands in order to receive his promises. It is still a little flock which is gathered around this Son of Man, but the message concerns the entire people of Israel. But when Israel is converted—and Israel will be converted—then God will send to his people this very Messiah whom heaven has taken up and concealed for a time (Acts 3:20-21). Indeed perhaps the Son of Man will come even before the mission of the community to Israel has been completed (Matt. 10:23).

7. The Messiah–Son of Man faith was developed along with the Palestinian primitive community, and as the primitive community lost its significance and on the other hand the Gentile Christian church was developed, this faith also again receded. Nevertheless we can follow its traces even beyond our first three Gospels. In the first place here the Fourth Gospel comes into consideration. For surprisingly this writing, which otherwise so wholly belongs to a later milieu and is based upon Pauline theology, contains the Son-of-Man dogma of the primitive community in the clearest fashion, and on its own part carries it forward. The author of the Fourth Gospel connects the Son-of-Man title and the dignity of the judge of the world most closely to each other: καὶ ἐξουσίαν ἔδωκεν αὐτῷ κρίσιν ποιεῖν, ὅτι υἱὸς ἀνθρώπου ἐστίν (John 5:27)—and shows with this one saying that he is fully familiar with the nature and character of the Son-of-Man idea. With him the title "Son of Man" is preferably used in connection with the heavenly exaltation or the ascension.[59] But it is especially characteristic that here is preserved in full clarity the idea that the death on the cross essentially and

[58] Mark 2:19-20; Matt. 25:1, 6, 10.
[59] 3:13; 6:62; 8:28; 12:34.

first of all is to be considered as the way by which Jesus was exalted to become the Son of Man. Hence the evangelist likes to play with the interweaving of Jesus' being lifted up on the cross and his heavenly exaltation; for to him the cross is in fact the exaltation: ὅταν ὑψώσητε τὸν υἱὸν τοῦ ἀνθρώπου; τότε γνώσεσθε ὅτι ἐγώ εἰμι (8:28; cf. 3:14; 12:(32)34). But most of all, he completes this whole series of ideas through the introduction of the idea of preexistence which is still lacking in the Synoptics: "No one has ascended into heaven except the one who has come down from heaven, the Son of Man" (3:13), and, "When you see the Son of Man ascend into heaven where he was before" (6:62). The connection between heaven and the Son of Man is not interrupted even during his sojourn on earth: "The angels of God ascending and descending upon the Son of Man" (1:51).

Thus the Son-of-Man dogma of the primitive community is continued in the Fourth Gospel in thoroughgoing fashion. The observation is perhaps a not insignificant hint for the estimate of the character and origin of the Fourth Gospel, but in this connection it is a new indication that in the Son-of-Man dogma of the primitive community we have before us a clearly recognizable and fixed structure of ideas which for a considerable time played a dominant role in Christian dogmatics.

Furthermore in this connection there stands the already mentioned Son-of-Man confession of Stephen in the book of Acts, and more especially that of the Lord's brother given by Hegesippus (*vide supra*, p. 47). It is also worthy of note that in the Gospel of the Hebrews the words which the resurrected One addressed to his brother, according to the tradition of Jerome (*de vir. ill.* 2), are: *Frater mi comede panem tuum, quia resurrexit filius hominis* [!] *a dormientibus*.

The later Jewish tradition, which in general has preserved for us so little usable recollection of the struggles in the breaking away of the Christian group from its native soil, has at least preserved for us a valuable notice for the history of the Son-of-Man dogma. I refer to that expression of the Amoraean Abbahu[60] (around 280 in Caesarea), which is formulated in imitation of Num. 23:19 (God is not a man, that he should break his word, nor a son of man, that he should repent): "If anyone says to you 'I am God,' he is lying—'I am the Son of Man,' he will regret it at last; 'I ascend toward heaven,'—whoever has said this will not experience it."

---

[60] Jerusalem Talmud, Taanith 65b; on this passage, cf. Dalman, *Words of Jesus*, p. 246. Lietzmann has exerted himself in vain to maintain, in the face of this passage, his thesis of the impossibility of the messianic title "Son of Man" on Palestinian-Aramaic soil.

Would it be too daring to suspect that here we have one last echo of the battles which were fought between the young Christian community and the Jewish synagogue over the confession of the Son of Man?

Still more important is another observation. In my judgment we can establish that the Son-of-Man idea continued to have its effects exactly—and exclusively—in the Jewish-Christian sects which were formed later. The earlier heresy-fighting fathers of the church, who have preserved for us only very meager notices about these Jewish-Christian movements, unfortunately paid little attention to them. They are caught on the observation that the Jewish Christians (Ebionites) denied the virgin birth and consequently, according to the fathers' opinions, explained Jesus as a mere man. From Epiphanius' account of the Ebionites and especially from the extensive source documents of that Jewish-Christian sect which are preserved for us in a heavily reworked form in the Pseudo-Clementine Homilies and Recognitions, we know of strange speculations in which Christ was interpreted as the Primal Man who appeared first in Adam and was revealed in manifold forms.[61] And a striking notice about the Jewish Christian Symmachus and his following has been preserved for us by Victorinus Rhetor: *dicunt enim eum ipsum Adam esse et esse animam generalem.*[62] If the primitive Christian community revered Jesus as the Messiah–Son of Man, i.e., as the "Man," then these latter speculations are explained as gnosticizing extensions of that originally simple faith. As the "Man," Christ was first identified in these circles in some form with the first man Adam, who is also glorified in the Haggada[63] as an almost divine figure. And to this were joined all sorts of speculations of Oriental origin about the semi-divine figure of the Primal Man who is revealed in manifold manifestations and embodiments in the world.[64] And thus again and again we are led back by various sects to the fact that the faith of the first community of Jesus' disciples was focused around the Son-of-Man concept.

[61] Bousset, *Hauptprobleme der Gnosis*, pp. 172 ff.

[62] Migne, PSL VIII, 1155, 1162; cf. Harnack, *Dogmengeschichte*, 4th ed., I, 327. On the interesting and here openly evident identification of the Primal Man with the world-soul, it is to be noted that in the accounts of the church fathers the Manichaean Primal Man also frequently appears as the world-soul. These connections cannot be pursued further here. I shall allow this and the following suggestions from the first ed. to stand and refer now to Reitzenstein's studies (*Die Göttin Psyche*, SAH 1917, No. 10, and *Das mandäische Buch des Herrn der Grösse und die Evangelienüberlieferung*, ibid., 1919, No. 12). What I said in n. 39 on p. 45 holds true here also.

[63] Cf. Bousset, *Hauptprobleme*, pp. 174-75.

[64] Ps.-Cl. Hom. 3.20, Rec. II, 22 (I, 52); cf. Hom. 17.4 (18.13-14)=Rec. II, 47. Epiphanius Haer. 30.3.

Of course Schmidtke, in his penetrating and perceptive study (*Neue Fragmente und Untersuchungen der judenchristlichen Evangelien*, 1911), has sought very sharply to separate the Jewish-Christian "Gnostic" tendency, the literature of which is found in reworked form in the Pseudo-Clementines, from genuine Jewish Christianity. The sect of the Nazarenes stood nearest to the Great Church. At the time of Epiphanius (or of his source, Apollinaris of Laodicea) the remnants of this sect, who possessed an Aramaic translation of the canonical Gospel of Matthew (Gospel of the Nazarenes) as their gospel, were still to be found only in Berea. On the one side Schmidtke tries to distinguish these from the heretical Ebionites with their Ebionite gospel, which he identifies with the Gospel of the Hebrews; these people were located in the regions east and northeast of the Sea of Galilee. On the other side he wishes to distinguish them sharply from the "Elkesaite" tendency which in particular comes to expression in the Pseudo-Clementines and in Hippolytus' statements about the Elkesaites, and which had its home in the regions east of the Dead Sea as far as the marshes of the Euphrates. Unfortunately I cannot deal in detail with these ingenious studies, but I should like to indicate briefly that I find them not altogether convincing. In particular, I do not believe that we can make such a sharp distinction between the Ebionite and the Elkesaite tendencies and, further, assign the Pseudo-Clementines unconditionally to the latter. For on the one hand there is again between the Jewish Christianity of this literary circle and the Pseudo-Clementines a considerable difference (Waitz, *Pseudo-Klementinen*, pp. 154 ff.). On the other hand, writings like the latter, in which an original Judaistic anti-Paulinism (cf. the figure of the *inimicus homo* at the end of Rec. I, then in particular Hom. XVII, 13-19, etc.) has been preserved in such clear and characteristic ways, must have stood in closer connection with the genuine development of Jewish Christianity than Schmidtke seems to assume. I still believe that it is permissible to hold to the simpler interpretation that the Judaism of the country east of the Jordan was undermined by Oriental influences very early (after the destruction of Jerusalem) and for the most part took on a Gnostic character, even though other small sect groups also continued to exist alongside it. The combinations by Epiphanius of an influence which "Elxai" is supposed to have gained over Ebion or over the various Jewish Christian sects are, as they appear in his work, confused and unusable, but they still perhaps contain a historical core. Thus I believe that for the evaluation of the intellectual development of Jewish Christianity east of the Jordan we still have our best material in the Jewish-Christian sources of the Pseudo-Clementines (not so much in the Book of Elxai [along with the more closely related phenomena, Epiphanius, Haer. 53] [65] whose Gnosticism must be regarded as essentially Oriental-pagan). For what the church fathers know of heretical Judaism in general does not go beyond some general phrases repeated in a stereotyped form and saying nothing. The above-proposed surmise of a connection between the primitive Christian Son-of-Man dogmatics and the Christ-Adam speculation of the heretical-Gnostic

---

[65] W. Brandt, in his work *Elchasai*, 1912, has in my judgment much too strongly emphasized the Jewish character of the sect.

Jewish Christianity confirms me in this judgment also. The Nazarene Jewish Christianity of Berea with its translated Aramaic Matthew, its ecclesiastical canon, and its total attitude in full agreement with the Great Church (cf. Schmidtke, pp. 108-26) I hold to be a wholly secondary and accidental phenomenon which will have had hardly anything to do with the Christianity east of the Jordan and its development. Here we have a circle of Jewish Christians who in later times, we do know know under what circumstances, fully merged with the Great Church.

# Appendix I. Resurrected on the Third Day

Here arises a particularly difficult problem which can hardly be solved with the means now at hand, namely the question whether, along with the whole idea complex of the Messiah–Son of Man dogmatics, the idea also of the suffering and death of the Messiah had already been preformed in Jewish messianology and therefore could simply have been taken over by the faith of the primitive community. This hypothesis is not a priori essential. The previously treated premises, the Jewish transcendent Messiah picture of the Son of Man and the historical experience of Jesus' suffering and death, completely suffice in and by themselves to account for the messianic faith of the first Christian community in its genesis. And most of all, one can object to those continuing conjectures in these terms: That idea of the suffering and dying Messiah cannot be shown to have been current in Jewish literature at the time of the New Testament. Whatever the original meaning of the enigmatic hymn to the Servant of God in Isaiah 53,[66] no proof can be adduced that in the New Testament period this chapter was understood and interpreted messianically within Judaism. Even an application of Zechariah 12:10 (they shall look on him whom they have pierced) to the death of the Messiah is, at least up to the present, not demonstrable for the period we are now considering. It is true that according to IV Ezra 7:28 ff. the Messiah is said to die, but his death here results from the passing away of the whole terrestrial world; there is nothing here about a suffering and a violent death. The Messiah of Samaritan eschatology also dies, but he dies a peaceful death.[67] Of course the later Jewish messianology is familiar with the theory of a defeated and dying Messiah. But again these speculations cannot be traced back into

[66] Cf. the conjectures of Gressmann in *Israelit. jüd. Eschatologie*, pp. 283 ff., and also Baudissin, *Adonis und Esmun*, p. 424.

[67] Merx, "Ein samaritanisches Fragment ü. d. Taeb," Actes du huitième congrès des Orientalistes. Sect. Sémit., Leide, 1893, pp. 117 ff. Cowley, "The Samaritan doctrines of the Messiah," *Expositor*, 1895, pp. 162-64.

the New Testament period. The fact that in them suffering and dying are attributed to a second messianic figure, to the Messiah ben Joseph or Messiah ben Ephraim, suggests the suspicion that we have to do here with a rabbinical artificial speculation. The whole combination appears to have developed subsequently on the basis of messianically interpreted scriptural passages (Zech. 12:10). Perhaps the fact that one could not escape the force of the Christian proof by means of the predictions in the Old Testament and with it the idea of the suffering and dying Messiah ben Joseph, whom people had already accepted on the basis of Deut. 33:17, also played a part.[68] It is highly worthy of note that Justin, who in his *Dialogus cum Tryphone* transmits to us such an abundance of Jewish apologetic and polemic, still shows no trace of an acquaintance with this speculation of Jewish messianology.

The conception of a suffering, dying, and again victoriously living deity must of course already at that time have been current all around Palestine in Egypt, Syria, Phoenicia, and Asia. And the possibility must be conceded that already in the New Testament period this idea could have gained some influence upon Jewish apocalyptic and therewith indirectly upon the primitive Christian faith. Most of all it must be emphasized that in the time under consideration there probably were in circulation curious speculations about the Primal Man, in which his dying and rising again, his sinking down into the realm of matter, his becoming entangled in it and his being freed again and being exalted were described.[69] And again it remains possible that these fantasies about the dying and rising Primal Man could be connected quite early with the Jewish messianic speculation about "the Man." Later we will come back to the point that in fact the fantasy of the dying and rising god, widespread in Hellenism, in all probability exercised a strong influence upon *Hellenistic* Christianity. Perhaps we will also be able to judge even more clearly with regard to Judaism and the Palestinian Christian community.[70]

Only one fact could nevertheless come into consideration in this regard and occasion a more definite assertion in this area: that is the doctrine which, so it seems, already occupied its secure place in primitive Christian dogma,

[68] Cf. the material in Dalman, *Der leidende und sterbende Messias*, 1888; J. Klausner, *The Messianic Idea in Israel*, pp. 483-501. Bousset, *Religion des Judentums*, 2nd ed., pp. 264-66.

[69] Cf. Bousset, *Hauptprobleme*, pp. 160-223, and now the above-mentioned (p. 45, n. 39) investigations of Reitzenstein.

[70] Cf. again the far-reaching studies of Reitzenstein, which are however still in a fluid state.

of the resurrection of the Son of Man on the third day or after three days.[71] For not only Paul with his testimony in I Cor.[72] speaks for it, but already the older stratum of our gospel literature. Since for a critical consideration of the resurrection tradition in Paul any explanation of that three-day time lapse in terms of some event already known to the apostle which may have happened on Easter Sunday is ruled out, we are confronted with the problem of finding another derivation of this assertion. In I Cor. 15:4 Paul points us in the direction of proof from the prophecies in the Old Testament (κατὰ τὰς γραφάς). In the Old Testament there is offered as something of a point of contact the passage in Hos. 6:2, ὑγιάσει ἡμᾶς μετὰ δύο ἡμέρας· ἐν τῇ ἡμέρᾳ τῇ τρίτῃ καὶ ἀναστησόμεθα.[73] It is beyond any doubt that in this saying, particularly on the basis of the translation in the LXX, one could have found a confirmation of the idea of the resurrection on the third day.[74] But it is extremely unlikely that this entire datum would have been derived from that one obscure passage of Old Testament prophecy. Thus the suspicion arises that in this datum we have a transferral of a mythical note to the proclamation of the resurrection of Jesus. There are parallels from the cultus of the dying and rising gods. The death of Osiris[75] falls on the seventeenth, and the festival of his discovery on the nineteenth of Athyr (thus τῇ τρίτῃ ἡμέρᾳ). In the Roman cult of Attis the observance of the death of the god fell on the twenty-second, and the celebration of his revival, the Hilaria, on the twenty-fifth of March (or more precisely on the night of March 24/25, thus μετὰ τρεῖς ἡμέρας).[76] Thus the datum of the third day

[71] As is known, the tradition varies. In all, Mark speaks up in three predictions for μετὰ τρεῖς ἡμέρας, 8:31; 9:31; 10:34, as does Matt. 12:40; for τῇ τρίτῃ ἡμέρᾳ already Paul in I Cor. 15:4 and Matt. as well as Luke in the parallels to Mark. It is difficult to say which tradition is earlier. They could have arisen side by side and need not be taken as in contradiction with one another, since "after three days" could be the more indefinite expression for "on the third day." Incapable of being reconciled with the τῇ τρίτῃ ἡμέρᾳ is only the expression used in Matt. 12:40 (τρεῖς ἡμέρας καὶ τρεῖς νύκτας).

[72] In and of itself the testimony of Paul in I Cor. 15:4 does not go back to the primitive community in Jerusalem in spite of the appeal to the tradition *alone* (see below, Chap. IV).

[73] The question as to the original meaning of the passage can stand aside here. Still, cf. the interesting conjectures of Baudissin, *Adonis und Esmun*, pp. 406-15.

[74] Perhaps the τῇ τρίτῃ ἡμέρᾳ instead of μετὰ τρεῖς ἡμέρας stems from Hos. 6:2.

[75] Plutarch, de Is. et Osir., chaps. 13, 39; cf. chap. 42.

[76] Hepding, *Attis und sein Kult*, pp. 149 ff., 167 ff.; cf. also Frazer, *Adonis, Attis, Osiris* (1906), about possible connections between the cult of Attis and the Christian Easter celebration. Baudissin considers it possible that somehow and sometime also in Phoenicia the resurrection day of Adonis was the third day after death (*Adonis und Esmun*, p. 409). He points to a celebration in Malta which is probably related to the cult of Attis, in which every year a picture was thrown out in a garden under some bean blossoms and after "about" three days of fasting was brought back again with a joyous celebration and was

could stem from the myth or the cultus of a dying and rising god. The general dogmatic datum that the dying hero rises on the third day or after three days is transferred to Christ. Then for the Palestinian primitive community a part of this myth would already have been current. And no longer avoidable would be the question whether the conception of the Messiah–Son of Man could not already have been combined in Judaism with that of the suffering and dying god, and thus the idea of a suffering, dying Messiah would have been known here.

But these suspected combinations are by no means certainties. For in the last analysis the datum of the third day could also be derived from other premises. It can be shown to have been an assumption of a widespread folk belief that the soul of the deceased still remained some three days with the corpse before leaving it. To inquire after the home and source of this view would be a rather futile effort, since it is connected with the observation of the beginning decomposition of the corpse and could have been formed everywhere spontaneously. It played a role in particular in Persian eschatology[77] and can be demonstrated also in Jewish apocalyptic and in the later Jewish literature.[78] From this also could have developed the dogmatic belief that the Son of Man had stayed three days in the tomb and thereafter had been elevated to his glory.[79] Then however we do not need the detour by way of the myth of the suffering and rising god in order satisfactorily to account for that datum of the third day.

It may further be pointed out in this connection that the question about the development of the tradition of the "third day" (or of the "after three days") is not to be complicated with the problem of the development of the celebration of Sunday. The development of Sunday has nothing at all to do with the resurrection tradition. The locus of the development of Sunday is the Christian cultus. So, just as young Christianity later changed the Jewish weekly fast days from Monday and Thursday to Wednesday and Friday, thus also the distinguishing of Sunday (cf. Justin, Apol. I, 67.7 τὴν δὲ τοῦ ἡλίου ἡμέραν) in the Christian cultus, which perhaps is already

---

set up again (pp. 129 and 409). Baudissin would like also to assume that Hos. 6:2 was written in view of a cultic resurrection festival of a god on the third day.

[77] Cf. Vendidad 19.28 and Yasht 22.2 ff. (Hadhokht Yasht).

[78] On the whole question, cf. Boeklen, *Die Verwandtschaft der jüdisch-christlichen mit der persischen Eschatologie*, pp. 28-29. Bousset, *Religion des Judentums*, 2nd ed., p. 341; and now above all Baudissin, *Adonis und Esmun*, pp. 412-16.

[79] This interpretation would be interesting also to the extent that it would allow us to see that the belief in the exaltation of Jesus by no means needs to have been bound up from the very first with the assumption of a bodily resurrection.

alluded to by Paul in I Cor. 16:2, signifies a separation from the Jewish Sabbath. Only later, certainly before the development of the Gospel of Mark in its present form,[80] is the combination then consummated, that the κυριακὴ ἡμέρα is the day on which the resurrection of Jesus took place. Two other passages of the later tradition also point to this: Ignatius warns the Magnesians (9:1): μηκέτι σαββατίζοντες ἀλλὰ κατὰ κυριακὴν ζῶντες. ἐν ᾗ καὶ ἡ ζωὴ ἡμῶν ἀνέτειλεν δι᾽ αὐτοῦ. And Barnabas establishes the Christian celebration of Sunday, not with a reference to the resurrection, but with a curious eschatological play on numbers, and then continues (15.9): διὸ καὶ ἄγομεν τὴν ἡμέραν τὴν ὀγδόην εἰς εὐφροσύνην, ἐν ᾗ καὶ ὁ Ἰησοῦς ἀνέστη ἐκ νεκρῶν καὶ φανερωθεὶς ἀνέβη εἰς οὐρανούς.[81]

# Appendix II. Descent into Hades

The acceptance of the three-day interval between death and resurrection now opened a new door to Christian imagination. People did not stop with the simple idea of rest in the tomb or of the tarrying of the soul with the corpse. There developed the fantasy of the descent of Jesus into Hades. Since the tradition about it actually is to be traced back almost to the primitive period of Christianity, it too may now be treated in this connection. If we wish to evaluate the tradition correctly,[82] we must distinguish be-

[80] See further material in Chap. II and cf. E. Schwartz, "Osterbetrachtungen," ZNW VII (1906), 29 ff.

[81] If one wishes to assume that the date of Friday for the day of Jesus' death is historical tradition, this combination could be supported by means of the tradition of "on the third day," and even the "after three days" could if necessary be interpreted in this way. Conversely, the date of Friday as the day of Jesus' death could be arrived at only out of the already fixed assumption of Sunday as the day of resurrection with the help of the τῇ τρίτῃ ἡμέρᾳ. Reservations about the historicity of the tradition of the παρασκευή in Schwartz, "Osterbetrachtungen," pp. 31-32. Of course it appears to me unlikely that the date of Friday for the day of the Lord's death first arose out of the cultic practice of fasting on Friday (Schwartz, p. 33). Matt. 12:40 is a decisive argument against thinking that both dates, Friday and Sunday, were originally matters of fact.

[82] In the following presentation I take up once again my investigations of this theme in my Hauptprobleme, pp. 65-71, in an altered form, with special regard to the objections of Loofs which he raised in his address on "Christ's Descent into Hell," delivered to the International Congress on the History of Religions in Oxford, 1910. I am indebted to Loof's careful collection of the pertinent material for the clearer explication of my position, which to be sure I must still maintain against him in all essentials. [C. Schmidt, in an excursus to his edition of the "Conversations of Jesus with his disciples after the resurrection" (Gespräche Jesu mit den Jüngern nach der Auferstehung), TU XLIII (1919), 453 ff., has raised a vigorous protest against Bousset's expositions. Cf. contra Bousset, "Zur Hadesfahrt Christi," ZNW XIX (1920), 50-66. Bousset could not be convinced of the correctness of Schmidt's presentation of the evidence. Gustav Krüger.]

tween two confluent streams: a popular one, which worked with stronger imagination and more glowing colors, and a more learnedly dogmatic one, which apparently was eager again to strip away the all too fantastic-mythological features and to accentuate the dogmatic-doctrinal ones. The latter naturally became dominant in the literary tradition. It is present in its most pregnant form in that characteristic adulterated Old Testament citation which Justin already knows as a saying from Jeremiah and whose removal from the Old Testament he makes into an accusation against the Jewish tradition, and which Irenaeus quotes six times.[83] In the tradition of Justin it runs thus: ἐμνήσθη δὲ κύριος ὁ θεὸς ἅγιος ᾿Ισραὴλ τῶν νεκρῶν αὐτοῦ τῶν κεκοιμημένων εἰς γῆν χώματος καὶ κατέβη πρὸς αὐτοὺς εὐαγγελίζεσθαι αὐτοῖς τὸ σωτήριον αὐτοῦ (Dial. c. Tryph. 72; 298 B). Irenaeus summarizes this view in the following words (IV, 27.2): *Et propter hoc Dominum in ea, quae sunt sub terra, descendisse, evangelizantem et illis adventum suum; remissione peccatorum existente his qui credunt in eum. crediderunt autem in eum omnes qui sperabant in eum, id est qui adventum eius praenuntiaverunt et dispositionibus eius servierunt, iusti et prophetae et patriarchae, quibus similiter ut nobis remisit peccata.* Since Irenaeus[84] in our passage traces this doctrine back to the Presbyter, since Justin already knows a forged Old Testament citation which contains the doctrine, and finally since Marcion[85] formulated his assertion that Christ preached to Cain, the Sodomites and the Egyptians, and the mass of other heathen but not to the patriarchs,[86] apparently in strict opposition to the church's thesis, we can trace the conception of the preaching in Hades back to the early second century.

We will be able to go still a bit further: We find the preaching in Hades witnessed to, not only in the apocryphal Gospel of Peter X.41, but we can also observe that this idea has already undergone considerable expansion in the Shepherd of Hermas.[87] For here the remarkable idea is proposed (Simil.

---

[83] Irenaeus III, 20.4; IV, 22.1; IV 33.1; IV, 33.12; V, 31.1 (cf. IV, 27.2), ἀπόδειξις. TU XXX, 1 (1907), 42. Cf. Loofs, "Christ's Descent into Hell," p. 293.1.

[84] It is worthy of note that Clement of Alexandria also, in Strom. VI, 6.45 and Adumbrations on I Pet. 3:19, operates with an apocryphal quotation, λέγει ὁ ᾅδης τῇ ἀπωλείᾳ· εἶδος μὲν αὐτοῦ οὐκ εἴδομεν, φωνὴν δὲ αὐτοῦ ἠκούσαμεν, which cannot be so simply derived from Job 28:22 and Deut. 4:12. The quotation is also found in the Naassene sermon in Hipp. V, 8 (§ 154.8); here, however, it is related not to the descent into Hades but to the descent of the Primal Man into the terrestrial world.

[85] Cf. further Celsus in Origen II, 43; also Orac. Sibyll. VIII, 310-11.

[86] Iren. I, 27.3. Epiph. Haer. 42.4.

[87] Clement of Alexandria is dependent upon Hermas in the two passages, Strom. II, 9.43 and VI, 6. 45-46. It is interesting to observe how in the latter passage he further develops the idea of the apostles' preaching in Hades.

IX, 16.5) that the apostles have preached to those who sleep in Hades.[88]

So with the idea of Jesus' preaching in Hades we approach a point very close to the older New Testament period. And yet this specific theologoumenon, *sicklied o'er with the pale cast of thought,* cannot have been the original form.[89]

For beside this view, as we have said, there stands another, popular, richer in mythological colors. What is involved here is not a harmless and peaceable preaching in Hades, but an actual battle of the prince of life with the prince (and the powers) of the underworld and of death. These popular conceptions make their way of course only later, perhaps with Origen,[90] into actual literature of note. Still they were available for that use. They led a nonliterary existence, and it is characteristic of them that they come to a breakthrough in written documents which do not exactly belong to better literature. Here belongs the apologist Melito of Sardis, one of the earliest witnesses for these conceptions. In a fragment from him extant in the Syriac[91] we read: *at quum dominus noster surrexit e mortuis et pede deculcavit mortem et vinxit potentem et solvit hominem . . .*[92] As is evident at first glance, the statements of Melito in this fragment stem from the hymnic

[88] I shall leave undecided the question whether the passages I Pet. 3:19-20 and 4:6 are to be placed in this context. If Christ's descent into Hades is at all what is being discussed here—now as previously I see no reason to deny this—the passages belong in this context insofar as what is involved here is also a preaching of Christ in Hades (according to 4:6, the idea of an announcement of the judgment is probably ruled out). The singular feature, that "the disobedient spirits in prison" appear as the recipients of the preaching, moreover has had no visible influence upon the history of the idea of the descent into Hades. Cf. the statements about the passage in 3:19 in Clem. Alex., Strom. VI, 6.45 and in the Adumbrations on I Pet. 3:19. Th. Zahn, *Forschungen*, III, 94-95.

[89] This theologoumenon of the preaching in Hades possibly has already played a role in Judaism. The Latin translation offers the addition to Sir. 24:32: "I (Wisdom) will penetrate all the regions deep beneath the earth and will visit all those who sleep and will illumine all who hope in the Lord." Thus a *preaching* in Hades by Wisdom! This could be a Christian interpolation, but that assumption is not necessary. In any case, we have here a theologoumenon behind which a more powerful myth must have stood originally.

[90] Cf. C. Clemen, *Niedergefahren zu den Toten* (pp. 180 ff.); M. Lauterburg, article on "Höllenfahrt" in *Realenzyklopädie prot. Theol. u. Kirche*, VIII, 199; Bousset, *Hauptprobleme*, p. 257. Cf. here the documentation from a later period in Origen, Lactantius (Inst. div. IV, 12.15), Firmicus Maternus (de errore prof. relig., 25); above all, the detailed portraits in the Gospel of Nicodemus (Tischendorf, *Evang. Apocr.*, 2nd ed. (1876), 329 and 392-93). One should note that the later fantasies are dependent upon Ps. 106:16 (LXX): συνέτριψεν πύλας χαλκᾶς καὶ μοχλοὺς σιδηροῦς συνέκλασεν (see below, Od. Sol. 17).

[91] Otto, *Corpus Apologet.*, p. 419, Fragm. XIII. On these Syriac fragments, cf. Harnack, *Chronologie der altchristl. Lit.* I, 518.

[92] Cf. Otto, p. 421, Fragm. XVI: et suscitavit genus Adami e profundo sepulcro.

language of the liturgy. And so then even in one of the earliest extant witnesses to the ancient Christian liturgy we encounter the myth of the descent into hell. In the so-called Egyptian Church Order there is found within the Praefation of the episcopal mass this sentence: *qui cumque traderetur voluntariae passioni, ut mortem solvat et vincula diaboli dirumpat et infernum calcet.*[93] Again in the popular literature of the apocryphal acts of the apostles these colors are especially strong. In the Acts of Thaddaeus, which appeared about 250, it is said: καὶ κατέβη εἰς τὸν "Αιδην καὶ διέσχισε φραγμὸν τὸν ἐξ αἰῶνος μὴ σχισθέντα καὶ ἀνήγειρεν νεκροὺς καὶ κατέβη μόνος· ἀνέβη δὲ μετὰ πολλοῦ ὄχλου πρὸς τὸν πατέρα αὐτοῦ (Eus. CH I, 13.20).

The mythology is still stronger in the Acts of Thomas[94]:

ἡ δύναμις ἡ ἀπτόητος ἡ τὸν ἐχθρὸν καταστρέψασα.

καὶ ἡ φωνὴ ἡ ἀκουσθεῖσα τοῖς ἄρχουσιν,

ἡ σαλεύσασα τὰς ἐξουσίας αὐτῶν ἁπάσας,

ὁ πρεσβευτὴς ὁ ἀπὸ τοῦ ὕψους ἀποσταλεὶς καὶ ἕως τοῦ ᾄδου καταντήσας,

ὃς καὶ τὰς θύρας ἀνοίξας ἀνήγαγες ἐκεῖθεν τοὺς ἐγκεκλεισμένους

πολλοῖς χρόνοις ἐν τῷ τοῦ σκότους ταμιείῳ.

But more recently a still richer body of material for all this, to be dated in a still earlier time, has been made available to us in the discovery of the Odes of Solomon.

According to the foundational studies of Gunkel and Gressmann, these Odes appear certainly to be of Gnostic origin,[95] and thus could not be employed directly as a witness for genuine Christianity. But on the other hand it has not yet been possible to ascribe the Gnosticism contained in them to a

---

[93] Latin text in Hauler, p. 106 (LXX, 12). Schwartz, *Über die pseudo-apostolischen Kirchenordnungen* (Schriften d. wissensch. Gesellsch. Strassburg, 1910, pp. 38 ff.), has presented evidence that this Church Order is closely related to Hippolytus' περὶ χαρισμάτων ἀποστολικὴ παράδοσις. Schermann, *Ägyptische Abendmahlsliturgien* (Studien z. Gesch. u. Kultur d. Altertums (1912), VI, 1-2), holds firmly to the Egyptian origin of the Church Order, but assumes with Schwartz a close relation to Hippolytus and identifies the latter as the one who has handed down the already (around 212) fixed Church Order.

[94] Chap. 10. One should note that here too a liturgically stylized prayer is present. Cf. chap. 143: οὗτος ὁ σφήλας τοὺς ἄρχοντας καὶ τὸν θάνατον βιασάμενος. Chap. 156: ὁ κατελθὼν εἰς ᾄδου μετὰ πολλῆς δυνάμεως· οὗ τὴν θέαν οὐκ ἤνεγκαν οἱ τοῦ θανάτου ἄρχοντες καὶ ἀνῆλθες μετὰ πολλῆς δόξης, καὶ συναγαγὼν πάντας τοὺς εἰς σὲ καταφεύγοντας παρασκεύασας ὁδόν.

[95] Cf. esp. Gunkel, ZNW XI (1910), 291-328. Gressmann, *Internationale Wochenschrift*, July 22, 1911. German translation by Flemming in Harnack, *Ein jüdisch-christliches Psalmbuch*, TU XXXV, 4 (1910). Ungnad and Staerk, *Die Oden Salomos* (Lietzmann, *Kleine Texte*, No. 64, 1910).

definite Gnostic sect that is known to us. Indeed it is possible that they come from a time in which what was common to Christian and Gnostic had not yet been definitely and consciously separated, and that in them simply a popular early Christianity with strong Gnostic tendencies comes to expression, the date of which we then would have to set at the latest around the middle of the second century.

A major theme of these Odes is the Messiah's descent into hell, and here we naturally find the full glowing colors of the myth, especially in Ode 42 [96]:

> Hell saw me and grew weak,
> Death spewed me out, and many others with me.
> I became gall and poison to him,
> I descended with him, deep as the depths of hell.
> His feet and his head grew weak,
> For he could not endure my countenance.
> I formed the community of the living among his dead ones.
>
> · · ·
>
> Then the dead hastened to me, called and said:
> Have mercy on us, Son of God!
> Lead us out of the fetters of darkness,
> Open the gate through which we shall ascend with (to?) you.
>
> · · ·
>
> But I listened to their voice
> And sealed them with my name upon their heads;
> For they are free men,
> And they belong to me. [97]

If through this survey our eyes have been sharpened for the myth of Christ's descent into Hades, we can follow its traces still further back. Even when Ignatius of Antioch asserts (Magn. 9.3) that Christ has awakened the prophets out of Hades (παρὼν ἤγειρεν αὐτοὺς ἐκ νεκρῶν), this actually goes beyond the boundaries of the theological idea of the descent into Hades. Both ideas, "preaching in Hades and awakening of the righteous," are also found side by side in the Excerpta ex Theodoto.[98] However, for all that, we

---

[96] The German translation here follows Gunkel-Gressmann, ZNW XI, 302.

[97] For numerous parallels in the Odes, cf. 15, 17 ("I broke iron bars, my chains became glowing and melted before me, and nothing appeared barred to me . . . and I went to my prisoners, to free them"), 22, (25), 28, 29. The question whether the "I" in the individual psalms is the Messiah or the believer who imitates the Messiah's journey to hell need not concern us here.

[98] Chap. 18.2: ὅθεν ἀναστὰς ὁ κύριος εὐηγγελίσατο τοὺς δικαίους τοὺς ἐν τῇ ἀναπαύσει καὶ μετέστησεν αὐτοὺς καὶ μετέθηκεν καὶ πάντες ἐν τῇ σκιᾷ αὐτοῦ ζήσονται.

are still in the tempered atmosphere of dogmatics. But the saying in the Apocalypse of John seems quite different (1:18): "I was dead and behold, I am alive and have the keys of Hades and of death in my hand." One who holds in his hand the keys of the rulers of the underworld has won them in victorious battle with the dread powers there below; the journey to Hades was a journey of struggle and of victory. Even the curious passage in Matt. 16:18 seems to take its light from here. "Upon this rock I will build my church, and the gates of Hades will not prevail against it (will not hold it, restrain it)." The company of the righteous who have fallen asleep also belongs to the ecclesia triumphans. The gates of Hades are opened and they no longer hinder passage to freedom.[99] When the author of Ephesians takes Ps. 68:19: "He has ascended into the heights and has led captivity captive, has given gifts to men," and interprets it (4:9) thus: τὸ δὲ ἀνέβη τί ἐστιν εἰ μὴ ὅτι καὶ κατέβη εἰς τὰ κατώτερα μέρη τῆς γῆς, it is likely that he refers the ἠχμαλώτευσεν αἰχμαλωσίαν to the victory of the prince of life over the demonic hosts of Hades, even though a hysteron-proteron results. How otherwise should he have hit upon the conception of the descent into Hades in this quotation! Matt. 27:51 will also belong in this same connection: "And the earth trembled and the rocks were shattered and the tombs were opened and many bodies of the saints that slept arose and came out of the tombs after their awakening and went into the holy city and appeared to many." This is in fact to be interpreted as the echo of the violent struggle which, about this time when the prince of life contended with Hades, raged in the underworld. Thus precisely in these earlier New Testament passages[100] we find everywhere, even if only in fragments, the strong, popular, and mythological conceptions of the struggle of Christ with the powers of the underworld, conceptions of which the theologoumenon of the preaching in Hades is only a feeble reminiscence.

---

Cf. also Tertullian, de anima 55: *in paradiso quo iam tunc et patriarchae et prophetae appendices dominicae resurrectionis ab inferis migraverint.* Apolog. 47: *et si paradisum nominemus locum divinae amoenitatis recipiendis sanctorum spiritibus destinatum.* Cf. Irenaeus V, 5.1; perhaps also Clement, Protrept. XI, 114.4, ἐξαρπάσας τῆς ἀπωλείας τὸν ἄνθρωπον προσεκρέμασεν αἰθέρι.

[99] In this context, as in Rev 1:18, there recurs the figure of the power of the keys. On the conception of celestial gatekeepers, key keepers, etc., cf. Köhler, *Archiv für Religions-wissenschaft*, VIII (1805), 215 ff. [and Dell, "Matthäus 16:17-19," ZNW XV (1914), 27 ff.].

[100] Cf. further Acts 2:24: λύσας τὰς ὠδῖνας τοῦ θανάτου, καθότι οὐκ ἦν δυνατὸν κρατεῖσθαι ὑπ' αὐτοῦ.

It really can no longer be doubted that these popular conceptions of Christ's journey into hell and of his struggle with the demons of the underworld contain a myth which originally has nothing to do with the person of Jesus but only later has been adapted to him. This myth of a redeemer-hero who descends out of the celestial heights into the depths of the underworld in order there to do battle with its demons, to break their strength, to rob them of the secret upon which their power rests, who then again is raised victorious into the heights, was not framed by Christianity. Christianity grows up in an intellectual atmosphere in which such myths are not newly created, but only taken over. Analogous motifs may be demonstrated in non-Christian areas. The well-known narrative of the journey to hell of Manda d'Hayya (Hibil-Ziwa) in the Mandaean religion certainly grew in its own soil. The beautiful half-legendary song of the king's son who goes forth to win the pearl [101] from the dragon is recognized with ever increasing certainty as of non-Christian origin. The expedition of the Primal Man in the Manichaean religious system against the demons of darkness and of the depths belongs in this context, along with so many other Gnostic redeemer fantasies, though these are a special case to be discussed a little later. In passing it may be mentioned that this myth possesses a typical and, where it is completely preserved, rarely missing characteristic, namely the feature that the hero descends into the world of demons unrecognized at first, since he is made like the lower powers, and dwells there unrecognized.[102]

The assumption that such a myth is taken over, not created, by Christianity adequately explains its early and sudden emergence in the various passages of the Christian tradition. It is a mistake to assume that one could confirm the authenticity of this conception within a religion by means of the proof of antiquity which can be adduced from the conception. A religion with such triumphant powers of development and enlistment as Christianity possessed had attracted to itself with amazing speed the most diverse patterns of thought which were proffered to it. Here in essence the sense and feeling

---

[101] Cf. Acts of Thomas, chap. 111.

[102] For further detail, cf. Bousset, *Hauptprobleme*, pp. 239 ff., and O. Pfleiderer, *The Early Christian Conception of Christ*, pp. 97-106. Incidentally, in the broader sense all the myths which treat the sun hero which sinks into the depths also belong here (*Hauptprobleme*, pp. 221-22); cf. the assembled material which H. Schmidt has compiled in *Jona* (FRLANT IX, 1907).

for style must make the judgment. There is no time limit governing the possibility of such transfers of ideas.[103]

Only after it is acknowledged that the Christian ideas about the journey to Hades gain their basic explanation in the setting of the history-of-religions connections sketched here can one raise the question of what the Christian religion has adapted to this myth out of its own possessions. And the comparison then certainly shows us the distinctive originality of the new religion at one essential point. It has the prince of life descend into Hades in order to rescue the races of men, whether all of them or with some restriction, who dwell there. All other characteristics of the myth by comparison recede in importance and become a by-product. Here the power and originality of the Christian spirit are shown. The idea of the universality of salvation, of the ecclesia which embraces all the races of mankind, radiates triumphantly from the myth. Then in the leading theological circles the myth is almost suppressed, and out of it the colorless abstraction of Christ's preaching in Hades is developed. In all this the spiritual and intellectual power of Christianity is shown. But as almost everywhere else, the way here leads from the myth to the idea and not in the opposite direction.

For the rest, here first of all it must be pointed out that this myth of Christ's descent into hell, in an interesting restructuring, has achieved a still much more intensive influence upon the pattern of Christian thought. In place of the descent of the hero into the underworld and hell there comes the appearing of Christ here upon earth. Seen from the standpoint of the heavenly world above, the earth is the place of darkness and of terror, thronged by the demons. The struggle of the redeemer-hero with the demons of the depths becomes the struggle of Christ on the cross with the devil and the "archons" of this world, and his victorious ascent becomes the ascension from earth to heaven. Thus we will encounter the myth in Paul, in the freshest, most highly original colors. Thus it is early established almost as Christian dogma, that Christ's appearing on earth and in particular his death have the ultimate aim of conquering the devil and his demons, the annihilation of death. The apologists, otherwise so rational, actually know only this mythical theory of redemption, and in particular in the systems of

---

[103] Even if it were proved that the transferral had already occurred on Palestinian soil, the above theses would not be damaged thereby. For one cannot assert a priori that such a myth must have remained remote from Palestinian Judaism (cf. what is suggested above with reference to Sir. 24.32). But that proof cannot be produced. None of the New Testament passages discussed goes this far back. Even if one sought to find the myth already in Paul (Rom. 10:7), still Paul also has non-Palestinian traditions. It is not native to the

the Gnostics, in place of the descent into hell there appeared almost exclusively the likewise mythically conceived descent, portrayed in detail, of the redeemer to earth.[104] For to the Gnostic this world of the senses is altogether essentially the place of darkness and of condemnation. We shall have to return to these connections in the following sections.

---

older gospel literature. The "risen on the third day" does not belong here in an immediate sense, nor does Matt. 12:40.

[104] The motif of the redeemer's remaining unrecognized runs through all such Gnostic representations (*Hauptprobleme*, pp. 239 ff.). But it is also found in the realm of genuine Christian literature: Paul in I Cor. 2:8 (!), Ascensio Jesaiae X-XI.

# 2
## THE FAITH OF THE COMMUNITY
## AND THE PICTURE OF JESUS OF NAZARETH
## IN THE FIRST THREE GOSPELS

The Palestinian primitive community laid the foundation for the picture of Jesus found in the first three Gospels. This was its unique work, one which hardly any other work approaches in significance in the history of Christianity. This is not the place to engage in an investigation of how this work of a "life" of Jesus as we have it in three different sketches came about. It hardly needs to be stressed that the following studies operate in general on the basis of the two-source theory (the priority of Mark, the Logia as the source for the speeches in Matthew and Luke). In addition I assume[1] that Mark somehow presupposes a collection of the Lord's words—although hardly the Logia as they are found in Matthew and Luke. A much more difficult and even more important problem is how the outline of the life of Jesus in Mark's Gospel came to be, according to what laws the oral tradition which lay behind it was reworked, how the latter was gradually assembled out of only individual fragments into larger units and was fixed in written form, until finally an outline of the "life" of Jesus and the speeches of the Logia developed. To discuss all this thoroughly would require a comprehensive treatment.[2] Finally, we do not intend here to set forth the significance

[1] *Contra* Wellhausen's famous thesis. On this question, cf. now also M. Dibelius, *Formgeschichte des Evangeliums* (1919), pp. 68 ff.

[2] Up to the present these questions have hardly been taken into account. Even the more recent investigations which have undertaken to go back of the Gospel of Mark to its prehistory and sources (e.g., J. Weiss, *Das älteste Evangelium*, 1903, and Wendling, *Urmarkus*, 1905, and *Entstehung des Markus-Evangeliums*, 1908), still are always too much oriented to literary criticism and to "source" distinctions. Here an entirely new method must be introduced, one which will proceed above all in terms of criticism of style and will be

for the history of religions which the figure of Jesus of the first three Gospels as a whole has had for the development of Christianity. That would mean a parallel undertaking to the present work which would be almost as extensive as this one. The question to be answered in this chapter is more modest and limited. To what extent and in what way did the messianic- (Son of Man-) faith treated in the preceding chapter retouch and reshape the picture of Jesus in recognizable fashion?

I. *The Messiah Dogma.* I begin the investigation with the Messiah dogmatics, specifically that in Mark, and place first the last section of the life of Jesus, the passion narrative. This passion narrative, which begins with Mark 11 (10:46-52) and is continued in 14:1 ff. after the long intervening passage which has been worked in by the evangelist, has a different style from the other parts of the life of Jesus in Mark's Gospel. Elsewhere it is generally clear that the foundation upon which "Mark" worked consisted of a series of teaching anecdotes, miracle stories, and logia, which originally stood side by side as individual pieces without inner connection, only then to be woven with light connecting threads in the literary composition into a whole. Here however there is a coherent account which hangs together, the individual component parts of which never led such a separate existence. Indeed it may be asserted with all probability that this passion narrative[3] represents the most ancient kernel of a coherent tradition of the "life" of Jesus, and that the achievement of the evangelist Mark (or of "Ur-Markus") consisted in his expanding this tradition already circulating in a number of individual items (or of small groups of stories already compiled) into a presentation of the total activity of Jesus from the baptism on.[4] The composition of his Gospel, the relatively large amount of space which the presentation of the last days of Jesus occupies in his total presentation, the way in which every-

---

oriented to the investigation of the laws of oral tradition. In his *Formgeschichte,* Dibelius has presented an initial broader attempt, in which naturally there is still much to be altered and completed. Initial steps and good observations are also to be found in Wendland, *Hellenistisch-römische Kultur,* 2nd ed., pp. 258 ff.; J. Weiss, article on "Literaturgeschichte des Neuen Testaments" in RGG, first ed. [Cf. K. L. Schmidt, *Der Rahmen der Geschichte Jesu.* Literarkritische Unters. zur ältesten Jesusüberlieferung, 1919. Krüger.]

[3] This passion narrative did not have the scope which it presently occupies in the Gospel of Mark. Much was first added by the evangelist. Luke probably was also acquainted with an outline of this narrative in addition to the Gospel of Mark, and from this he preserved many a primary tradition as compared with Mark. This cannot be discussed in detail here.

[4] Cf. also Dibelius, *Formgeschichte,* pp. 8 ff., and his attempt to understand the passion narrative as an illustration of the earliest Christian kerygma of the death and resurrection of Jesus.

thing in this Gospel presses toward this end, all these confirm this supposition about its development.

A look at the passion narrative shows us now how it is wholly dominated by the messianic idea and everything in it is placed under the rubric of the proof that this crucified Jesus is nevertheless the Messiah, the king of the Jews. This certainty rings through the whole presentation of the tragedy with a triumphant sound and gives to it the character of great inner calm and of concentrated power. It is a witness of faith of the first rank which the primitive community here gives, and as such it has had an aftereffect with a force unequaled.

The presentation begins with the triumphal entry of the Messiah into Jerusalem.[5] The anointing of Jesus also is placed in a messianic framework. To be sure it is an anointing εἰς τὸν ἐνταφιασμόν. It is the suffering and dying Messiah who is thus crowned, just as it is already the Messiah Jesus who on the sacred eve of the Passover holds the last supper with his disciples and places the solemn arrangement of the meal of the new covenant alongside or over against the Passover meal of the old covenant. The fact of Peter's denial is placed under the heading of the fulfilled messianic prediction (Mark 14:26 ff.). The scene in Gethemane closes with the reference: "Behold, the Son of Man is delivered into the hands of sinners." [6] The hearing before the high priest weightily concludes with the solemn question, "Are you the Christ?" and the equally solemn acknowledgment of the dignity of the Son of Man. The hearing before Pilate begins with the abrupt opening question, "Are you the king of the Jews?" and with Jesus' answer. The Barabbas scene, which completely dominates the trial, has a messianic thrust. The Jews have rejected the true king and have chosen in his place the ruffian and murderer. The ridicule and mistreatment by the soldiers becomes, in the light of faith, a tremendous element of irony in the event and a testimony, given against their will, of the royal glory of Jesus. The narrative works with the same tools when it sets the mocking of Jesus by the bystanders in the center of the scene at the cross, but it speaks still more clearly at the beginning: "And the superscription with his accusation read: 'King of the Jews.' " [7] And thus the ancient presentation could end quietly

---

[5] Here I take the presentation as it lies before us in the Gospels (Mark) as a unity. Certainly the evangelist must have added some further touches to the account. But he did not create its character. Therefore we can refrain here from making any separation of elements.

[6] These two traditions are not attested by Luke; they were perhaps added later.

[7] In the closing scene, the confession of the heathen centurion to the Son of God, Luke again differs (ὄντως ὁ ἄνθρωπος δίκαιος ἦν, 23:47). I have excised it above for reasons which will become clearer later on.

with the burial (*vide infra*); the night of the tomb is already illumined by the certainty of victory of the Christian kerygma: He has risen and has appeared to his disciples.

Some will object that this whole account, in its essential component parts, is simply history and not subjective testimony characteristic of the faith of the company of Jesus' disciples. And in fact it is not to be denied that historical motives are contained in this presentation. But again it is clear that the whole of the passion narrative presents a projection behind which stands the full force and daring of the faith in him who has been elevated to be Son of Man, a fiction which conceals within itself a kernel of historical truth, but still a fiction.

By a series of individual observations it may also be shown how the messianic thrust of the community tradition has rewritten history. Jesus' entry into Jerusalem is presented in this narrative as a solemn messianic proclamation. Here Wellhausen has discerningly suspected that in this scene a popular disturbance which accidentally broke out during the entry of the prophet has been reshaped into a messianic self-presentation planned by Jesus. I find the main proof of this in the pericope of the question concerning authority (Mark 11:27 ff.), which from the first will have stood in chronological context with the entry and the cleansing of the temple. If the messianic entry of Jesus into Jerusalem actually took place as Mark tells it, then the question of the scribes and elders about his ἐξουσία no longer makes sense, and Jesus' evasive answer even less. The impact of the deliberate proclamation furthermore depends essentially upon the one point in the account, that Jesus had the foal of an ass fetched by his disciples. But already by the emphasis upon the miraculous knowledge of Jesus this point is shown to be legendary; and the observation emerges that with the very same means and motives in still another passage of the Marcan account the original tradition is reworked, i.e., out of the last meal of Jesus a Passover meal is constructed (14:12-16). Moreover, in Matt. 21:10-11 (οἱ δὲ ὄχλοι ἔλεγον οὗτός ἐστιν ὁ προφήτης Ἰησοῦς ὁ ἀπὸ Ναζαρὲθ τῆς Γαλιλαίας) and 21:14-16 (=Luke 19:39-40) we seem to have a parallel account of the entry, in which in fact only one enthusiastic welcome of the prophet entering Jerusalem was being described. And finally, we may mention only in passing the fact that the Fourth Gospel expressly assures us that only later, after Jesus' glorification, did people discover the connection of the messianic prophecy in Zech. 9:9 with the entry into Jerusalem. For the Fourth Gospel is not free from a certain tendency in its presentation to oppose the emphasis that Jesus is the (Jewish) Messiah. Nevertheless, its comment remains important. Thus in all probability a relatively harmless and unimportant scene in the tradition of the community has been significantly reinterpreted. The messianic king who is to be rejected by his people solemnly enters into Jerusalem.

Furthermore, we can be quite certain that the same tendency was at work also in the shaping of the account of the trial before the Sanhedrin. W. Brandt [8] has already pointed out that the dramatic impressive scene in which the high priest, with the tearing of his garments, solemnly condemns Jesus to death because of his messianic confession, does not harmonize with the legal concept of blasphemy found in the Mishna (Sanhedrin VII, 5); and from this Brandt has perceptively drawn his conclusions. Blasphemy against God, for which the death penalty is assessed, is the explicit slandering of the sacred name of God.[9] To what extent is the assertion of Jesus that he is the Messiah supposed to be a blasphemy against God? Surely one will not seriously wish to construe blasphemy against God out of this, that Jesus as a forsaken prisoner, by his confessing to be the Messiah, has compromised God! The account in Mark 14:61b does not move upon a historical base but is a creation of Christian dogmatics. Only thus do we understand also the accusation here made of blasphemy against God. It is considered from the standpoint of the Christian faith, for which the confession of sonship to God already had a metaphysical meaning, and the assertion of sonship to God and the assertion of deity were very close together. A man who made himself out to be God (cf. John 10:33 ff.) or the Son of God without actually being such would in fact blaspheme God. It is not Jewish legal views but Christian dogma expressed here: If Jesus is not truly the Son of God then he actually has uttered blasphemy in the trial, and the solemn judgment of the high priest would be justified.

Finally, even the self-confession of Jesus as the Son of Man appears singularly uncalled-for as an answer to the question of the high priest. One also gains the impression that it is not the historical Jesus speaking here but the community which proclaims its faith in the Son of Man. In the formula given by the Gospel of Mark we already hear clearly the Christian con-

---

[8] *Die evangelische Geschichte und der Ursprung des Christentums*, 1893.

[9] Hölscher's statement (*Ausgewählte Mischnatraktate*, ed. by Fiebig, No. 6. Sanhedrin und Makkot, p. 35) that one has no right to transfer the legal views of the Mishna to the age of Jesus cannot satisfy here. For if we leave aside the Jewish tradition and the question of its age, inner logic argues against this treatment of the messianic witness of Jesus as blasphemy in the legal sense.

fession: "Seated at the right hand of God, whence he shall come again to judge the living and the dead."

Even here we cannot deny that the question of the Messiah played a part in the hearing before the high priest. One can hardly imagine that it would not have been involved. But on the other hand we will have to concede that in the Marcan account the original proceedings are concealed within the community's theology in such a way that they can hardly be recognized any longer.

One could perhaps assume that the Gospel of Luke stood somewhat nearer to the historical state of affairs with its account. Here in fact the solemn condemnation of Jesus for blasphemy against God is missing. Here the first question addressed to Jesus is simply this: εἰ σὺ εἶ ὁ Χριστός, εἰπὲ ἡμῖν. And when Luke then adds on the question about the divine sonship, this curious splitting of the issues can best be explained by the fact that that simple posing of the question had been handed on to him from a better source, and that he provided a place for the additional material of the Marcan account in a second scene that he adds; only here does he bring in the round Marcan ἐγώ εἰμι. And the restrained way in which Jesus answers the (first) question about messiahship in Luke, and the way in which he refers to his identity with the Son of Man only in an oblique manner, may still best be understood psychologically. Finally, Luke hands down the Son-of-Man saying in a simple form: ἀπὸ τοῦ νῦν δὲ ἔσται ὁ υἱὸς τοῦ ἀνθρώπου καθήμενος ἐκ δεξιῶν τῆς δυνάμεως τοῦ θεοῦ, while in Mark and all the more in Matthew, who confirms the Lucan ἀπὸ τοῦ νῦν with his ἀπ' ἄρτι, the introduction of the prophecy of the return of the Son of Man throws things into a state of confusion. But to be sure, the account of Luke as a whole is still only secondary and for its own part is obviously dependent upon Mark. In the reconstruction of an earlier source we do not get beyond certain probabilities. Only this much is clear: how here in general the community tradition has been energetically at work.

The criticism of Wellhausen (*Evangelium des Markus,* p. 136), with whom Norden, *Agnostos Theos,* p. 195, has associated himself, is further involved in the presentation. Wellhausen assumes that the accusation of blaspheming the temple, which is summarily dismissed and treated as false testimony by Mark, played the decisive role in the trial.[10] Therefore he excises Mark 14:61b-62 and

[10] Cf. the repetition of the charge in the crucifixion scene in Mark 15:29, and the later attempt at an allegorical reinterpretation of the logion in John 2:19; also the tradition in

takes the condemnatory saying of the high priest in vs. 63 as an answer to Jesus' silent acknowledgment of the charge of blaspheming the temple. Thus in the hearing before the high priest Jesus would have been condemned as one who blasphemed the temple, and the decisive messianic turn would have been added only in the community tradition. Reitzenstein (*Das mandäische Buch des Herrn der Grösse und die Evangelienüberlieferung*, SAH, 1919) has attempted to explain and historically to justify the whole account in another way. He takes as his point of departure the already mentioned (p. 45, n. 39) proof that in the first two tractates of the Ginza we have an old first-century apocalypse which goes back to the circles of John's disciples. On the basis of this source and other related witnesses he sees in the Baptist and his sect a sharply revolutionary tendency as over against the stability of Judaism and its legal-cultic institutions.[11] In these circles accordingly there was current the expectation of a transcendent mythical Messiah-"Man" (Enos-Uthra), who would destroy Jerusalem and the temple at his appearing. Already at that time there was an ancient prophecy about him: "On my left they placed a sword and a great axe. . . . I lay waste and build up again, I destroy and again establish *my palace*" (Lidzbarski, *Johannesbuch*, chap. 76.242.8).[12] Such a predictive proclamation then is actually transferred from the related baptist sect to Jesus and his following, and is rightly sensed by Jesus' disciples as false testimony. It is conceivable that the high priest, who was acquainted with the expectations of the baptist sect, when he heard that catchword about temple destruction, asked Jesus whether he was the Messiah. Thus confronted with a definite question, Jesus at any rate did not deny the awareness which he had secretly cherished that he was the Messiah. Perhaps (if one disregards the ἐγώ εἰμι in Mark 14:62) he only referred in general terms to the surely coming Son of Man but did not argue what he still believed and hoped in the deepest part of his being.[13] This then was the occasion of his condemnation, in the high priest's view, and not Jesus' acknowledging the dignity of the Messiah; the fact that he confessed to the ideal of the temple-destroying Son of Man was the blasphemy against God, worthy of death. Thus it all fits into a recognizable unity, and the trial of Jesus throughout its entire course can be grasped historically. Reitzenstein's attempt to refine out of the Mandaean literature some source pieces which put us in a position to gain a glimpse into the intellectual pattern of the baptist sects in the New Testament age appears to me to be worthy of the most careful attention. But I feel myself not in a position to render a final judgment in this matter until the sources of Mandaean and Manichaean origins which must be considered in this connection will have been made further accessible. Even

---

Codex D and the Old Latin in Mark 13:2: καὶ διὰ τριῶν ἡμερῶν ἄλλος ἀναστήσεται ἄνευ χειρῶν.

[11] Cf. also Bernoulli's interpretation in his great work on John the Baptist, 1918.

[12] With the curious expression "palace," Reitzenstein, p. 66, also compares a Manichaean fragment (T II D 18) reported to him by F. W. K. Müller: "I am able to destroy this *palace* which is made with hands, and in three days I shall make what is not made with hands."

[13] Thus according to a letter from Reitzenstein dated February 23, 1920.

conceding that Reitzenstein is correct in his view of the revolutionary character and the significance for the history of religions of the baptist sects, I would still have reservations about his reconstructions of the historical course of events in the trial of Jesus. In any case the connection which he finds here was no longer understood by the gospel accounts and must only be read between the lines. A transferral of a messianic threat against the temple to Jesus and his followers as a "false testimony" certainly lies in the realm of possibility, although even Reitzenstein (pp. 69-70) does not hide the difficulties on details. But one should expect that if the high priest was so well acquainted with the messianic expectations of the baptist community, his question in imitation of the "false testimony" would have had to be more exact. He would then have had to take up the key term "Son of Man" ("Man") thus: "Are you the Son of Man who is to destroy (Jerusalem and) the temple?" Even more difficult to understand is Jesus' answer. The difficulty does not lie in the fact that Jesus confesses himself to be the Son of Man. It is rather that without a word of reply he should have affirmed the revolutionary messianic ideal of the baptist community, while his disciples at least from a very early time onward rejected this in the most definite manner (cf. also the fundamental position of Jesus, at least as it was handed down in the community, in Matt. 5:17). Here there appear to me to be insoluble difficulties. But another combination of elements yet could present itself. It would be possible that in fact the revolutionary expectation of a temple-destroying Messiah–Son of Man of the baptist sects was transferred to the community of Jesus and the connection was made in the Jewish polemic against the latter. In the section about the "false testimony" in the trial of Jesus we would then have to see an apologetic discussion with this accusation, which would then, by its lack of connection with the whole, betray itself as a later insertion. Such an apologetic discussion would then also be present in John 2:18-19; and even in Acts 6:13 ff. it is still taken as a false testimony that Stephen is said to have proclaimed ὅτι Ἰησοῦς ὁ Ναζωραῖος οὗτος καταλύσει τὸν τόπον τοῦτον. The figure of Stephen himself and a prophecy such as Mark 13:2 on the other hand would show that that revolutionary attitude had again found sympathy in certain circles of the primitive community. For the Gospel account of the trial of Jesus it would then result that the specifically messianic passage Mark 14:60 ff. would present the original account which we could recover, which then of course on its own part would again be marked by the above-stated difficulties. The Lucan account, which does not have the episode of the false witnesses, would then most faithfully present the original account. Of course one would then have to assume that Luke 22:71, τί ἔτι ἔχομεν μαρτυρίας χρείαν, is thoughtlessly joined to Mark as against Luke's older source. In view of the difficulties present I refrain from taking a final position and content myself with having presented the various possibilities.

Now we turn to the first part of the life of Jesus in the Gospel of Mark. We may surmise at the outset that here the messianic tendency of the community tradition will be less discernible. For here we have to do not with a whole which was sketched from a definite viewpoint but with fragments of occasional oral tradition which only later were loosely strung together, in which that messianic interest can come to light here and there only in a more incidental fashion. Yet even here it is expressed in a series of individual sections quite apart from the multiple introduction of the Son-of-Man title which was discussed above in the first chapter (pp. 37 ff.).

I begin with a Son-of-Man passage which earlier had to remain unsettled, because the reworking here did not consist of a simple insertion of the title, but went much deeper than that. We have already referred to the offense which the saying in 2:10, "The Son of Man has power on earth to forgive sins," has caused to the majority of the critics. But the tradition is not set straight by the assumption of a mistake in translation or by some other simple elimination of the title "Son of Man." The dogmatic reworking of this pericope was much more profound. Most of all, it is striking in the very beginning that the scribes take offense at the simple announcement of the forgiveness of sins which Jesus here expresses as a shepherd of souls, and that in this they see a case of blasphemy, i.e., an invasion of the prerogatives of God. From the outset this looks like a dogmatic reflection which however has its counterpart in the explicit claim of Jesus as the Son of Man to forgive sins in the place of God. And we do not see how actually the comparatively small miracle which Jesus performs here is to establish his God-like claims. According to the view of those times many God-men have done miracles—and greater ones than Jesus does here. But no one has thus, on the basis of such, put himself in the place of God as does the Son of Man Jesus. Finally, it is striking that apparently according to the context of 2:9-11, which contains a conclusion *a majore ad minus,* the miracle of the healing of the sick appears as something greater than the forgiving of sins in the place of God. We will attempt the elimination of the two sentences on which the doubtful part of the narrative hangs: βλασφημεῖ· τίς δύναται ἀφιέναι ἁμαρτίας εἰ μὴ εἷς ὁ θεός; (7*b*), and ἵνα δὲ εἰδῆτε ὅτι ἐξουσίαν ἔχει ὁ υἱὸς τοῦ ἀνθρώπου ἀφιέναι ἁμαρτίας ἐπὶ τῆς γῆς (10). That produces a good and smooth connection:

Jesus . . . says to the lame man: "Child, your sins are forgiven you." And there were some of the scribes sitting there and thinking in their hearts: "Who is this who speaks thus?" [14] And Jesus recognized in his spirit that they were thinking such things and said to them: "Why are you thinking

[14] The opponents regarded the words of Jesus as idle chatter. He should rather help and heal.

such thoughts? Which is easier, to say to the lame man, 'Your sins are forgiven you,' or to say, 'Rise and take up your bed and walk' "? [15] Then he said to the lame man: "I say to you, rise, take up your bed and go to your house." [16]

It has long since been recognized that in Mark 2:19 the reference to the death of the bridegroom and even the fasting in those days is a plainly later *vaticinium ex eventu.* Moreover, Wellhausen has shown (*Markus-Kommentar, in loc.*) that along with 2:20 also the words of 2:19*b* which stand in immediate connection with this verse and the mention of the bridegroom are to be stricken out. The authentic answer of Jesus to the question about fasting originally ran: "Can wedding guests fast?" Jesus regards himself and his disciples as the guests at the wedding feast of the new in-breaking age[17]—a grand and exciting picture. It was the community that first introduced the contrast between the bridegroom and his friends, and the idea of the bridegroom's dying.

In the original answer to the first question about the Sabbath (2:23 ff.)

[15] One should note how the anticlimax in the previous text is changed into an actual climax. In Jesus' mind the forgiveness of sins is the more difficult, healing the easier of the two.

[16] The criticism of the pericope is directed in a quite similar direction by M. Dibelius, *Formgeschichte*, pp. 34-35, only that Dibelius emphasizes that the stressing of the right of the Son of Man to forgive sins has been woven into the narrative from the very beginning, as soon as the story was employed in Christian preaching, and that thus there never was an "original" narrative which can be literally determined. In addition, it has been necessary for me to consider whether the reworking which is to be assumed here has not altered the text even more profoundly, so that originally there had been only a simple miracle narrative and the entire dialogue had been added only later. We find the motif of the forgiveness of sins also in Luke 7:48, and indeed there it is better established, although of course even there it appears quite in the nature of an afterthought. In addition, there is in 7:49 a striking parallel: καὶ ἤρξαντο οἱ συνανακείμενοι λέγειν ἐν ἑαυτοῖς· τίς οὗτός ἐστιν, ὃς καὶ ἁμαρτίας ἀφίησιν; still it would perhaps be possible that this motif was only added to the original miracle story of the Marcan narrative and then further expanded dogmatically.

Here we might first point to a general observation. By and large the narrative tradition about the life of Jesus flows in two distinct streams. We have on the one hand the teaching anecdotes and on the other the miracle stories. The attention of the narrator or of the hearer is drawn either to the miracle or to the logion. Naturally this does not preclude that in a teaching anecdote a miracle of Jesus will also be mentioned, or that a logion of Jesus will stand in a miracle story, extending beyond the framework of the latter and claiming attention for itself. As a rule, however, the streams remain separate; they appear to correspond to a varied interest in the life and the person of Jesus.

[17] According to the text as we have it, the question runs: "Why do not your disciples fast?" It is very striking that an objection is made to the nonfasting of Jesus' disciples, while nothing at all is said of his own nonfasting, which must be presupposed. Originally the question will have been raised about the nonfasting of Jesus and of his disciples. With the altered answer, an alteration of the way the question is posed became necessary.

Jesus proceeds from the general principle that need knows no laws, and as an illustration uses the example of David who in an emergency ate the show-bread. Only the loosely connected continuation in 2:27-28 has introduced the idea of the lordship of the Son of Man over the Sabbath, an idea which perhaps rests on a mistaken translation. Thus now the preceding statement takes on the appearance that Jesus here intends to place himself in his messianic dignity beside King David.

The expression of Jesus in 3:27 about the binding of the strong man has likewise always caused difficulties for exegesis. People have asked in vain to what experience of Jesus himself the consciousness of having bound the devil could be related. For even the victorious overcoming of the temptations, if indeed this is a historical tradition at all, cannot be regarded as a binding of the devil. A look into the parallel tradition of the Logia makes the original meaning of the saying clear. Immediately preceding this the subject under discussion is the in-breaking of God's lordship (Matt. 12:28=Luke 11:20)! Thus it is *God* who according to this context binds the strong man. From his expulsion of the demons Jesus concludes that *God* has already conquered the devil in decisive fashion and now divides the spoil, in that he allows Jesus to drive out the demons. The context here is destroyed by Mark through an abbreviation of the text, and at the same time Jesus moves into the place which God had originally occupied.

In the logion: "Whoever will save his life shall lose it, but whoever will lose his life for my sake and the gospel's will save it" (8:35), we must rule out the addition which exalts the person of Jesus, "for my sake and the gospel's," [18] on account of the completely clear rhythm of the saying, which demands two equal and balanced parts. We find the same interpolation also in the parallels Matt. 16:25 and Luke 9:24, and even in Matt. 10:39. In the Synoptics only Luke 17:33 has remained free of it. But the Gospel of John (while Luke hellenizes) has best preserved the wording—albeit with a new, easily removed addition: ὁ φιλῶν τὴν ψυχὴν αὐτοῦ ἀπολλύει αὐτήν, καὶ ὁ μισῶν τὴν ψυχὴν αὐτοῦ [ἐν τῷ κόσμῳ τούτῳ εἰς ζωὴν αἰώνιον] φυλάξει αὐτήν (12:25).

To this category moreover belong the sayings in Mark in which already the ὄνομα of Jesus is emphasized. In the formula ἐν ὀνόματι ὅτι Χριστοῦ ἐστε (Mark 9:41) one sees immediately the later language of the community

---

[18] εὐαγγέλιον is found after all only in secondary parts of the tradition and is a word which belongs to the community, not to Jesus; Mark 1:15; 10:29; 13:10 (!); 14:9; 16:15 (cf. Wellhausen's commentary on Mark 1:15).

(*vide supra*, pp. 3-4, the comment on the title Χριστός). Here Matt. 9:42 is at least relatively more original (εἰς ὄνομα μαθητοῦ). The logion about receiving a child ἐπὶ τῷ ὀνόματί μου (10:37) again stands in a curious parallel to the saying in Matt. 10:40 (cf. Luke 10:16) about receiving the disciples of Jesus and is furthermore a doublet to Mark 10:13-16. In the parallels the saying is not about the ὄνομα of Jesus. Finally, the small pericope about the exorcist who is driving out the demons in the name of Jesus (9:38-39) is surely secondary. The expulsion of demons in the name of Jesus cannot have been discussed during his lifetime; Jesus did not qualify as a supra-terrestrial miraculous being for his environment. The pericope reflects in interesting fashion some later questions and difficulties which moved the community of Jesus' disciples.

While Luke (17:2), who here following the Logia preserves the accurate tradition, only speaks of the little ones whom one is not to offend, Mark 9:42 brings the little ones into a connection with Jesus by means of the addition "because they believe," while Matt. 18:6 still more plainly enlarges upon it: "the little ones who believe in me." [19]

In the parable of the wicked vineyard keepers (12:1-12) the sharp contrast between the servants and the son, which in fact contains a quite clear reference to Jesus' special position of honor, appears to have been inserted only later. In the form in which the parable presently lies before us it does not have the transparent character of the other parables of Jesus. As a probable thing in the course of everyday life we do not comprehend how the lord of the vineyard could send his son without protective measures to the openly revolutionary tenants who have murdered his servants, until we realize that here the entire salvation drama is supposed to be presented in an allegory. But Jesus' parables elsewhere distinguish themselves precisely by their immediate power of conviction. And moreover, nowhere else in his parables did Jesus push his own person into the foreground in such a way as here. Especially obvious is the reediting in the quotation from Ps. 118 about the cornerstone that was rejected by the builders. For in the first place, the messianic application of this passage already presupposes the well-developed proof from prophecy on the part of the community. In the second place, we see how here the interest in the idea of the Messiah emerges quite

---

[19] Matt. 18:10 again rightly speaks only of the "little ones." The same relationship exists between Mark 15:32 and Matt. 27:42. The formula "faith in Jesus" (Christ) will be treated in context in the third chapter.

one-sidedly and how it has suppressed the original point of the parable, the rejection of the keepers of the vineyard.

It has already been pointed out that the pericope on the question of the Son of David in 12:35-37 is hardly comprehensible in the mouth of Jesus and only becomes fully clear when it is understood as a deposit of the community's dogmatics. For what kind of meaning is it supposed to have had in the mouth of Jesus? Are we actually to assume that with the mysterious allusion to Ps. 110 Jesus intended to lead the scribes, even if only by intimation, into the secrets of his messianic self-consciousness, after he had refused, at least according to the Synoptics' presentation, in Jerusalem to give them any answer about his ἐξουσία (11:27-33)? Or would one wish us to believe that Jesus, quite apart from the connection with his person, intended to display to the scribes a sample of his exegetical cleverness? Even if we were willing to admit that Jesus could already have been interpreted as the κύριος of Ps. 110, and therefore allowed this conviction to be reflected in the question addressed to the scribes, still the form and manner in which he here employs this secret proud awareness to pose an insoluble riddle for the biblical scholarship of his opponents remains a useless and incomprehensible game. But it all becomes clear when we assume that here we have not the *ipsissima verba* of Jesus, but the theology of the primitive community. In this way the disciples of Jesus later disputed with the scribes about the authority of their master. Ps. 110 was one of the essential bases upon which the community theology was built. And again in this pericope the technically developed proof from prophecy is present, as then the entire artificial interpretation of the Psalm in general is conceivable only in the context of a dogmatically fixed conviction about the transcendent messiahship of Jesus. And finally the composition of Mark's Gospel confirms our judgment. This pericope in which the tables are turned seems loosely joined to a collection of genuine controversial utterances of Jesus.

The saying in Mark 13:31 which is supported by a strong self-consciousness: "Heaven and earth shall pass away, but my words shall not pass away," stands at the close of the (Jewish?) apocalypse which has been reworked by Mark. It was perhaps originally the concluding word of the prophecy of an apocalyptic ecstatic person unknown to us. The community naturally had no reservations about transferring this strong saying to the exalted Lord. Then of course later—probably under the impact of the postponed parousia —the community appended the clause in 13:32, that no one but the Father, not even the angels nor the Son, knows anything of the day and hour.[20]

In conclusion some remarks on the prehistory of the life of Jesus as we find it in the Gospel of Mark and likewise in a source of Luke and Matthew that is independent of Mark. It is clear that by means of this beginning (baptism and temptation) the entire life of Jesus is placed under the messianic perspective. All the more will we be doubtful from the outset whether we have actual history here or only the interpretation of evangelical tradition. There is the further fact that the character of the stories is explicitly legendary. When we hear that the heavens are opened, the spirit hovers in the form of a dove, a voice sounds from heaven; when the devil is introduced in conversation with Jesus, or the angels minister to him and the (wild) animals surround him, we have first to recognize the purely legendary style[21] and to ask ourselves whether here the question about historicity can even be asked at all.

Those traits which lend a certain historical dimension to the whole stem from the history of the Baptist. Even the characterization of the baptism of John as baptism by water in contrast with the Christian baptism by the Spirit presupposes the Christian sacrament of baptism and the later conviction that baptism and the bestowal of the Spirit belong most closely together,[22] as on the other hand the characteristic introduction of the Baptist with sayings from the Old Testament presupposes the developed proof from prophecy.

It is certainly historical tradition that Jesus came to the baptism of John; for to a later age, as the accounts in Matthew and in the Gospel of the Hebrews show, it was a highly uncomfortable admission. But everything else is on uncertain footing. The community fabricated the prehistory of the hero before his public appearance according to a definite schema; the hour of illumination is followed by the hour of temptation, as we find again in

---

[20] On this passage further, see p. 92, below.

[21] Gunkel (*Das Märchen im Alten Testament*, RV II, 23/26, pp. 147 ff.) has suggested the very appealing conjecture that in the baptismal account the legendary motif of the (crowning) bird, which alights upon the person who is to be chosen as the new king and thereby causes him to be recognized, plays a part. The religio-historical material on this in Bousset-Lüdtke, NGG (1917), pp. 746 ff. I add also the appearance of the dove at the election of Bishop Fabian of Rome (Eus. CH VI, 29.2) and of Polycarp in the Acta Pionii.

[22] Again, this opinion was possible only on the basis of the conviction that every Christian must possess the Spirit. But this dogmatic assumption probably stems first from the Pauline theology.

quite similar schemata in the stories of Zarathustra, Buddha, and Mohammed.[23]

Within the Logia we can make such observations generally less frequently. First of all, apart from the passages already discussed in the first chapter, we shall have to count among these Logia the citation from Mal. 3:1 (Matt. 11:10, and par.), in which by means of a bold emendation the messianic messenger of God is made into the forerunner of the Messiah, and thus the latter once again appears in the place of God.[24] Such artificial Old Testament proofs only gradually developed on the basis of the well-established messianic faith in the community of Jesus' disciples. The immediately adjacent saying (Matt. 11:11): "No one among those born of woman has arisen who is greater than John the Baptist, but the least in the kingdom of heaven is greater than he," when taken as a logion on Jesus yields no really recognizable meaning. If we assume that here as everywhere else in genuine sayings the kingdom of God has an eschatological meaning, then it is difficult to understand how Jesus, who even grants the patriarchs a rank of eminence in the future kingdom of God, could concede to the Baptist only the lowest place, in fact no place at all. The saying takes on some meaning only when we take the kingdom of God here simply in the sense of "church." But then we surely have a reworking of a genuine logion from the standpoint of the community. In genuine spiritual greatness Jesus had awarded the palm to John and had conceded to him without qualification the first place among all those born of woman. This was a saying which a believing community could not leave without some emendation. They inserted the clause: "The least in the community[25] is greater than he." And thereby at the same time they naturally elevated the figure of the Master high above that of the Baptist.[26]

But most of all the logion Matt. 11:27=Luke 10:22 demands in this context a detailed investigation. Again and again, apologetically oriented theologians, in the effort to build a bridge between the discourses of Jesus in the first three Gospels and those in the Fourth Gospel, have referred to this

---

[23] The investigation can be pursued to a conclusion only later, in the discussions of the meaning and history of the concept ὁ υἱὸς τοῦ θεοῦ. Similarly, the relation of the baptismal account to the transfiguration narrative can also be discussed only in this context.

[24] Cf. also Mark 1:2, probably an interpolation from the Logia.

[25] βασιλεία in the sense of the present kingdom (the community) certainly already in Paul, Rom. 14:17; I Cor. 4:20; Col. 1:13; 4:11.

[26] Cf. Dibelius, *Die urchristliche Überlieferung von Johannes dem Täufer*, FRLANT XV (1911), 12 ff.

passage, and not without reason. But the singular character of this saying within the synoptic tradition, rather than serving to validate the Johannine tradition, may create a suspicion as to the historicity of this saying.

Norden[27] has now recently devoted a detailed and penetrating study to this logion. He takes as his point of departure the character of the entire composition in Matt. 11:25-30. Following assertions of David Friedrich Strauss, he finds in this section a formal parallelism of composition with the prayer of thanksgiving in Jesus ben Sirach 51. In both cases there is a parallel threefold division: 1. prayer of thanksgiving; 2. the assertion of a perfect revelation granted the person speaking; and 3. an exhortation to the believers to appropriate to themselves the revelation (by union with the one proclaiming it). In this, Norden does not intend to assume a direct dependence of Matthew (or of the Logia) upon Sirach, but rather he postulates only a general literary schema, which he then pursues further (Sir. 24, Od. Sol. 33, in the Hermetic tractate Poimandres, and in the Epistle to the Romans). Accordingly, then, we would have in the logion fragment a literary composition sketched according to a definite schema and not a genuine fragment from a discourse of Jesus.

The chief doubt which exists for me against Norden's construction would be this: He proceeds from the composition in Matt. 11:25-30 as from a solid foundation, while the parallel in Luke shows that it must at least remain doubtful whether the third logion, the call to salvation, belonged to the original stock of the source. But supposing that it were proved that Matt. 11:25-30 is a literary composition according to a definite schema, along with this there still could exist the assumption that for this composition, more or less genuine Logia of Jesus are used and that even the disputed saying could belong to these genuine elements. Norden himself concedes (p. 302) that the introduction in Matt. 11:25-26 shows a different character from the following, that the way in which the gnosis here is reserved for the νήπιοι appears as a protest-like rejection of the conventional type and as an echo from the same sphere from which comes the moving logion about the children to whom the kingdom of God belongs. But that is best explained when we assume that here a genuine logion of Jesus has been reworked, and also the unconnected ταῦτα finds its simplest explanation[28]

---

[27] *Agnostos Theos*, pp. 277-308.

[28] This explanation appears to me to be simpler than the hypothesis of Norden (p. 302) that in Matt. 11:25-30, as also in Sirach, through a departure from the usual pattern, the prayer of thanksgiving has moved to the beginning and the traces of such a shifting of position have been preserved in the ταῦτα. But what is involved here, if I understand

when we assume that here is a fragment borrowed from some other context.[29]

Now the question must be taken up anew, whether there is not in the logion Matt. 11:27=Luke 10:22 at any rate a genuine tradition. Here it first of all catches our attention how sharply this logion is set off from the preceding: "All things have been given to me by my Father. And no one knows the Son except the Father, and no one knows the Father except the Son and he to whom the Son wills to reveal him." The style has been completely changed; where at first we had an inward prayer of thanks, now in this verse we are met by a dogmatic confession. In place of the "I" and the "thou," which is still maintained carefully and consistently in the "me" at the beginning, down to the transition, the discourse proceeds in the third person about the Father and the Son, which immediately reminds us of the Fourth Gospel. Thus in no case is the saying in Matt. 11:25-26 with its genuine contents able also to cover and to save the logion in 11:27. There is present here only a wholly superficial connection. And therefore we will have to test our logion quite alone and for itself.

It is first of all, as Norden (p. 287) rightly brings out, a migratory saying which is widely known even outside the synoptic tradition. It is found again in the Gospel of John (10:15): καθὼς γινώσκει με ὁ πατὴρ κἀγὼ γινώσκω τὸν πατέρα. It further became the shibboleth of a series of Gnostic sects,[30] which found in it a confirmation of their doctrine of the "unknown God." Seen in terms of the contents of the saying, there lies over it a peculiarly ardent satisfied attitude. Luke has well captured this total outlook, when he introduces the logion by portraying the situation thus: "In that hour he rejoiced in the Holy Spirit and said." A deep mystery surrounds Father and Son and separates them from the rest of the world. But this mysterious unity is based upon mutual knowledge. And this attitude has influenced the formulation of the preceding saying. The veiled mystery demands unveiling

---

Norden correctly, is only a pattern which in details is handled quite freely and not a dependence that is literal, even to the point of a ταῦτα. In addition, it is of course to be conceded that Matt. 11:25-26 has acquired its form and shading of tone—one may note the contrast of concealing and revealing—from the setting.

[29] One should note that this logion also fits into the context of the collection. Cf. Luke 10:13-15, the lament over Chorazin and Bethsaida, and Luke 10:16, the logion: "The one who hears you hears me; the one who despises you despises me." As to thought, the above-treated logion in 10:21 follows quite well after this. What comes next, of course, goes far beyond this context.

[30] It is hardly necessary here to go further into detail on the divergent form which the logion has received from these circles (ἔγνω; rearrangement of the clauses). Here there appears to be present a later reflection.

and revelation, and only the Son brings these. But upon this mystery is based the bestowal of power upon the Son: πάντα μοι παρεδόθη.[31] We cannot escape the fact that the notes sounded here are singular within the entire synoptic tradition.[32]

But we still do not wish to tarry here on the self-expression of Jesus, with which Jesus sets himself as "Son" [33] over against the Father. It will, rather, be useful for the certainty of the proof if we can bring the question of the genuineness of our passage to a conclusion without going into the detailed investigation of the origin of the Son-of-God title. Thus if we leave aside this one instance, Jesus actually nowhere in his preaching raises the claim of bringing a new, mysterious, utterly unheard-of message from God. It is the God of the fathers about whom he preaches, the God of whom the Old Testament bears witness, whom the simple and uneducated souls of the νήπιοι know. Only that this God is a living reality within one's grasp, and that one must take seriously this reality—this was his proclamation, and not a new knowledge of God.

Neither do these notes have the Old Testament ring to them. Where in the Old Testament the knowledge of God on the part of the pious is spoken of, it has to do with a simple practical recognition of his existence and lordship, with the recognition of his will and living according to his commandments, and finally with the experience of his gracious protection.[34] Where it (rarely) says that God knows his people, the pious, or makes himself known to them, it signifies that he graciously turns his attention toward them, has chosen them, surrounds them with his protection.[35] But the idea

---

[31] The interpretation of the παρεδόθη in the sense of the παράδοσις, i.e., the doctrinal tradition, mistakes the meaning of the passage. The πάντα μοι παρεδόθη is rather to be taken in the sense of Matt. 28:18; see below, p. 89.

[32] Heitmüller, in his article "Jesus Christus" in RGG, first ed., III, 375, correctly judges "that the entire way of conceiving the significance of Jesus (Revealer) which we have here corresponds little to the view of the earliest community." But the conclusion which he draws from this, that precisely for this reason we have no occasion for distrusting the essential content of the saying of Jesus as to its genuineness, I regard as very doubtful.

[33] It appears to me that it can hardly be denied that we have here more than a mere figure of speech, but rather a self-designation of Jesus as "the Son" in the sense of the title.

[34] Cf. a collection of passages in Norden, Agnostos Theos, p. 63.1. Note how γνῶσις and παιδεία (Ps. 118:66), γνῶσις and εὐθὴς καρδία (Ps. 35:10; Prov. 27:21), γνῶσις and ὁδοὶ κυρίου (Jer. 5:4) belong together. It is worthy of note how on the soil of the Jewish-Greek literature the word immediately acquires a different and a more intellectual sound: Wisd. Sol. 7:17, τῶν ὄντων γνῶσιν ἀψευδῆ; 2:22, οὐκ ἔγνωσαν μυστήρια θεοῦ; IV Macc. 1:16, γνῶσις θείων καὶ ἀνθρωπίνων πραγμάτων.

[35] Cf. Hos. 12:1, νῦν ἔγνω αὐτοὺς ὁ θεός (the Masoretic text does not make sense) καὶ λαὸς ἅγιος κεκλήσεται τοῦ θεοῦ. Amos 3:2, πλὴν ὑμᾶς ἔγνων ἐκ πασῶν φυλῶν τῆς γῆς. Ps. 47:3, ὁ θεὸς ἐν ταῖς βάρεσιν αὐτῆς γινώσκεται (through his gracious protec-

that the prophet, for instance, the leading pious one, is joined by means of his gnosis with God in a mysterious union over against the entire world and that it is his office to reveal this mysterious knowledge of God—this idea is completely alien to Old Testament experience.

In order to make this plain—I know only one passage in the literature of Judaism which can be claimed as a parallel to our passage here, and this one clearly stands in the Hellenistic milieu. I refer to the characterization of the pious man by the godless one in Wis. Sol. 2:13 ff.: ἐπαγγέλλεται γνῶσιν ἔχειν θεοῦ καὶ παῖδα κυρίου ἑαυτὸν ὀνομάζει . . . ἀνόμοιος τοῖς ἄλλοις ὁ βίος αὐτοῦ . . . καὶ ἀλαζονεύεται πατέρα θεόν . . . εἰ γάρ ἐστιν ὁ δίκαιος υἱὸς θεοῦ ἀντιλήψεται αὐτοῦ (vide infra, p. 94). Here we have an individual or probably a circle of pious ones who glories in his (their) gnosis, joins himself by means of the gnosis with God in the feeling of mysterious sonship to God (παῖς=υἱός!) and places himself in conscious contrast to all the world. The opponents of these pious ones are the godless ones who have not learned the secrets of God (2:22). Here we sense the same atmosphere as in the logion of Jesus, only that in this the whole attitude is connected to the One who as the Son stands over against the Father. But here again we are no longer on Old Testament soil.

Now, following the study made here by Norden and supplementing it, we survey the milieu which we have already reached in Wisd. Sol. 2, on the soil of Hellenistic mystery piety. There,[36] in the Hermes prayer of the magical papyrus London CXXII, 50, a magician or a mystic prays: οἶδα σέ, Ἑρμῆ, καὶ σὺ ἐμέ. ἐγώ εἰμι σὺ καὶ σὺ ἐγώ.[37] Of course we have here to do, in spite of a strong external agreement, with a very much deeper-lying level of the most primitive piety. According to the context the speaker here is a magician who glories in knowing the outward forms of God, his origin, his cultic sites, and, most of all, his sacred names (τὰ βαρβαρικὰ ὀνόματα καὶ τὸ ἀληθινὸν ὄνομα). Because he knows these mysterious names, he has the ἐξουσία[38] of God, and is identical with him: "I am thou and thou art I." And yet we discern in this prayer how out of this primitive attitude a higher personal mysticism of mysterious union with the deity can grow:

tion). Wisd. Sol. 4:1 (the virtuous woman) καὶ παρὰ θεῷ γινώσκεται καὶ παρὰ ἀνθρώ- ποις.

[36] I refer only in passing to the hymn of Amenophis IV, "No one other than your son the king knows you," as a parallel note from a quite ancient period.

[37] Cf. the text of the prayer in Wessely, *Denkschriften der Wiener Akademie* (1893), p. 55; Kenyon, *Greek Papyri*, I, 116; and in a possible reconstruction in Reitzenstein, *Poimandres*, p. 20.

[38] Cf. the conclusion of the prayer: (ἐλθέ μοι) καὶ πρᾶξον μοι πάντα.

"Come to me, Lord Hermes, as [the] children come into the bodies of [the] women," the prayer begins. Thus this mysterious motto of the dual knowledge reverberates, is gradually separated altogether from the primitive magical rites and ideas, and takes on the stamp of a personal mysticism. In Gnosticism there comes into being that mysterious connection between God and man, in which the god draws the man and the man draws the god wholly into his being in a miraculous union. We find this double note again in the mystical Hermetic literature and, most of all, also the idea that the mysterious gnosis in the first place proceeds from the deity, that man *is known* by the deity. There it is said: οὐ γὰρ ἀγνοεῖ τὸν ἄνθρωπον ὁ θεὸς ἀλλὰ καὶ πάνυ γνωρίζει (i.e., something like "he takes man into his knowledge") καὶ θέλει γνωρίζεσθαι, or in I.31 ἅγιος θεὸς ὃς γνωσθῆναι βούλεται καὶ γινώσκεται τοῖς ἰδίοις.[39] But the mystic who has gained this mysterious knowledge implores the deity for power by means of this knowledge to enlighten τοὺς ἐν ἀγνοίᾳ τοῦ γένους μου ἀδελφούς, υἱοὺς δέ σου, and concludes with the words: "The 'man' will devote himself to thee, καθὼς παρέδωκας αὐτῷ τὴν πᾶσαν ἐξουσίαν." Indeed, even in the Neo-Platonist Porphyry this mysterious double note is sounded. In the mystical epistle *ad Marcellam* he coins the expression (chap. 21)[40] εὐγνώμονα δὲ βίον κτησάμενοι μανθάνουσι θεοὺς γινώσκονταί τε γινωσκομένοις θεοῖς. Finally, especially interesting in this connection are the mystical statements of a Zosimus document[41] of the third or fourth century. Here the author describes the effects of a magic mirror upon the soul which views itself therein: It becomes itself the holy spirit, it is in possession of rest (ἡσυχία, γαλήνη), and finds itself unceasingly in the state in which one knows God and is known by him.

In any case it is clear that the apostle Paul with his well-known sayings about the dual knowledge becomes immediately comprehensible in terms of this mystical milieu. When he addresses the Galatians (4:8): "But now,

[39] Cf. further X.4, ἴδιον γὰρ ἀγαθοῦ τὸ γνωρίζεσθαι; VII.2, ἀφορῶντες τῇ καρδίᾳ εἰς τὸν ὁραθῆναι θέλοντα. The mystical catchword of "to be known," moreover, is already found in Philo, of course not connected with the deity but with the higher power of the soul which, unknown, holds sway over man: ἀλλὰ νῦν ὅτε ζῶμεν κρατούμεθα μᾶλλον ἢ ἄρχομεν καὶ γνωριζόμεθα μᾶλλον (here the meaning of the γνωρίζεσθαι is especially clear) ἢ γνωρίζομεν. οἶδε γὰρ ὑμᾶς (*sc.* ἡ ψυχή) οὐ γνωριζομένη καὶ ἐπιτάγματα ἐπιτάττει (de Cherubim § 115).

[40] Cf. also chap. 13: σοφὸς δὲ ἄνθρωπος ὀλίγοις γινωσκόμενος, εἰ δὲ βούλει καὶ ὑπὸ πάντων ἀγνοούμενος, γινώσκεται ὑπὸ τοῦ θεοῦ. Here the γινώσκεται acquires the general meaning of familiar acquaintance.

[41] Περὶ ἀρετῆς πρὸς Θεοσέβειαν (Berthelot, *La chimie au moyen âge*, II, 269 ff.). Cf. also Reitzenstein, *Historia Monachorum* and *Historia Lausiaca*, pp. 247-48.

since you have known God, or rather are known of God"; when he says to the Corinthians (I Cor. 8:3): "If anyone loves God [ἀγάπη and γνῶσις naturally belong very closely together], he is known of God"; when he portrays the hereafter in mysteriously moving tones (I Cor. 13:12): "Then I shall know even as also I am known"—he becomes a sufficient witness for the penetration of that mystical outlook into the piety of the New Testament.

One will in fact have to raise the question whether our logion of the dual gnosis of the Father and Son could not also have first emerged in the milieu of Hellenistic piety. For the πάντα μοι παρεδόθη would find in this context its fully adequate explanation, as in particular the parallel of the Hermetic Tractate I.32 καθὼς παρέδωκας αὐτῷ πᾶσαν τὴν ἐξουσίαν clearly shows. And from this it would prove that all attempts to interpret παράδοσις in the sense of "tradition" are mistaken. To be sure, apparently opposing our attempt is the fact that here is present ancient logion tradition.[42] May we nevertheless propose the bold suggestion that even the Logia already show at an essential point some traces of a Hellenistic spirit? For all that, still even the Logia, as they lie at the basis of Matthew and Luke, are a Greek work. And if this work is in large part a translation, then we will be permitted to assume that a reworking has been joined with the translating process. The possibility still remains that a dogmatic migratory saying of Hellenistic community tradition has here found an acceptance among the Logia of Jesus.

A brief survey of the further development in this direction in the later Gospels of Matthew and Luke may conclude this discussion. The note in Mark that Jesus' relatives came to take Jesus home ὅτι ἐξέστη (Mark 3:21) is suppressed in Matthew (as also in Luke). In place of the offending Marcan sentence (6:5), "he could perform no wonders there," Matt. 13:58 relates: "he did not perform many wonders there." Out of the Marcan "he healed many" (1:34) Matthew makes "he healed all" (8:16; cf. Luke

---

[42] Here Johannes Weiss (*Schriften des Neuen Testaments, in loc.*) has raised a counter-objection which ought to be noted. If the logion is actually to be understood in the sense of the mystical dual knowledge, it had to mean, "The Father knows no one (i.e., illumines by means of his knowledge) but the Son." This is correct, if one presses the established sense of the γινώσκειν in this connection. Still the γινώσκειν here also can be understood in a more general sense without our being thereby removed from the milieu which we have affirmed. The mystic (the man of God), who has full knowledge of God and the divine ἐξουσία, in this sense is for the whole world a mystery, the depth and scope of which only the deity penetrates and understands.

4:40).[43] Well known is the bold dogmatic alteration with which he blunts (19:17) the point of the logion which was intolerable for a later age, "No one is good save God alone" (Mark 10:18).

If in these passages the effort to exalt Jesus' position of honor comes to expression only in a negative way, yet in the following cases the same tendency comes more directly into operation. Matt. 7:21, "Not everyone who says to me 'Lord, Lord' will enter the kingdom of heaven, but he who does the will of the Father who is in heaven," is already, in contrast with the simple Lucan saying (6:46), stylized in consideration of the Christian cultus and the liturgy. Only the appeal "Lord, Lord" in the cultus can be thought of when the hope of gaining the kingdom of heaven—to be sure according to the logion in erroneous fashion—is connected with it (*vide infra*). The characterization of the false prophets who in *Jesus' name*[44] drive out demons and perform great wonders (7:22-23) is first introduced by Matthew (cf. Luke 13:26-27). The saying, "Where two or three are gathered together in my name, there am I in the midst of them" (Matt. 18:20) is certainly not a word of the historical Jesus, but a saying of the believing community connected with the Christian worship, with which a Jewish saying concerning the Shekinah of God is imitated.[45] From this the suspicion that the so-called Summons of the Savior in Matt. 11:28-30 is a saying which originally concerned wisdom and was transferred to Jesus takes on more probability.[46] The answer of Jesus in the scene at Caesarea Philippi to the confession of Peter has been solemnly reshaped in Matthew in the style of the later community language.[47]

On the whole the Gospel of Luke shows fewer traces of such further editing. Here may be mentioned Jesus' preaching in Nazareth, that special sec-

---

[43] Cf. further how Jesus' blunt rejection of a specific miracle in Mark 8:11-12 in the course of the literary development has become in Matt. 12:40 the reference to the great miracle of the descent into Hades of the Son of Man.

[44] Cf. what is said above, pp. 79-80, on the ὄνομα 'Ιησοῦ in Mark.

[45] Cf. Pirqe Aboth III.3. "But when two are agreed and occupy themselves with the Torah, there is the Shekinah among them." Other parallels in Wünsche, *Neue Beiträge*, p. 218 (on this passage).

[46] It is possible that the lament over Jerusalem in Matt. 23:37-39 (Luke 13:34-35) could have been originally a part of the preceding quotation (from the "Sophia of God"?). Harnack, *Sprüche und Reden Jesu*, p. 119. The unexplainable logion in Matt. 23:39=Luke 13:35 then perhaps should be understood as a farewell of Wisdom to Israel until the coming of the Messiah. This observation would serve very well to make clear how such transferrals could have taken place. Cf. with this logion now also the far-reaching religio-historical explanations of Reitzenstein, *Das mandäische Buch des Herrn der Grösse* (see above, p. 45, n. 39), pp. 41 ff. Here again I should like to reserve judgment.

[47] On the confession of the "Son of the living God" which is inserted here, see below.

tion of Luke in which Jesus already at his first appearing plainly announces himself as the Messiah (4:16 ff.). In Luke 10:23-24 the pronouncement of the disciples' blessedness because they see what prophets and kings have yearned to behold is clearly connected to the beholding of the person of Jesus, while in Matthew, in a context which to be sure is similarly secondary, the same words are uttered in connection with the mysteries of the kingdom of God.[48]

Finally, Matthew like Luke in a series of passages has already made the kingdom of God into a kingdom of Jesus (of the Son of Man, *vide supra,* p. 47), quite contrary to the original intention of Jesus. To this group belong the passages Matt. 13:41; 16:28; 20:21; Luke 22:29-30; 23:42.[49] Perhaps it is also theological reflection that in the Gospels as we presently have them Jesus indeed speaks of my Father, your Father, the Father, but never of "our" Father. Of course the Gospel of Mark hardly comes into consideration here. Here the name "Father" in general is very rare,[50] and the usage which most of all comes into consideration here, ὁ πατὴρ ὑμῶν ὁ ἐν τοῖς οὐρανοῖς, is found only one single time, Mark 11:25 (11:26 only in mss.), in a passage which looks almost like an interpolation from Matthew. In the Logia, the "your Father" (in heaven) appears already to have existed here and there: Matt. 5:48=Luke 6:36; Matt. 6:32=Luke 12:30; Matt. 7:11=Luke 11:13 (to be sure, ὁ πατὴρ ὁ ἐξ οὐρανοῦ).[51] But that usage still is carried through with evident reflection only in Matthew's Gospel (and then later in the Gospel of John). Apart from the Logia passages, Luke has the "your Father" only one time, in 12:30.[52]

Only at this point can we take up the investigation of the designation of Jesus as ὁ υἱὸς τοῦ θεοῦ which we postponed in the preceding chapter. According to the older gospel tradition it is found in the mouth of Jesus

---

[48] Still the logion-saying in Matt. 12:41-42=Luke 11:31-32 about the "greater than Jonah, greater than Solomon" originally could have had a general reference to the preaching of the kingdom of God. Only through the secondary connecting of the words with the meaning of the sign of Jonah has the personal reference become a necessity here.

[49] Cf. John 18:36; I Cor. 15:24; Col. 1:13; Eph. 5:5; II Tim. 4:1; Rev. 1:9; 11:15; II Pet. 1:11.

[50] And in fact almost wholly in demonstrably secondary connections, Mark 8:38; 13:32; the prayer in Gethsemane should be included here, too (14:36).

[51] In this passage the "your heavenly Father" naturally is given since Jesus here contrasts earthly fathers with the heavenly Father. For this reason also no conclusion about the "self-consciousness" of Jesus is to be drawn from the words, "If ye then, being evil."

[52] The "(Our) Father" explicitly appears in both evangelists, Matt. 6:9 and Luke 11:2, as a prayer which the disciples are to utter. One wonders whether the evangelists intended already thereby to indicate that Jesus did not include himself in this prayer.

most rarely. In the Gospel of Mark it appears only one time in the eschatological clause in 13:32, which is appended to a logion which certainly stems
from the community theology (*vide supra*, pp. 81-82); and in the parable
of the vineyard keepers, which in the present form is not genuine (see pp.
80-81), it is interpreted by means of the contrast between servants and Son.
Besides this we have in the Logia the one saying in Matt. 11:27=Luke
10:22. We have already discussed the critical reservations which are opposed
to the genuineness of this logion. The observation how seldom the title Son
(of God) in still somewhat older tradition appears in the mouth of Jesus
is suited for providing new confirmation of those individual studies.

In the context here another question interests us, namely whether
this title (alongside the other ὁ υἱὸς τοῦ ἀνθρώπου) was customarily used
in the primitive community. At first glance it appears that this assumption
must be made. In the temptation narrative even in the source common to
Matthew and Luke (logion) the devil twice addresses Jesus with "Son of
God." And most of all, the title plays a rather dominant role in the Gospel
of Mark. It dominates the account of the baptism of Jesus (as it after all
dominates the temptation narrative in Matthew's and Luke's common
source), and also climaxes the temptation narrative in the cry "This is my
Son"; the demon-possessed address Jesus as Son of God (3:11; 5:7); the
question of the high priest in the trial is whether Jesus is the Christ, the
Son of the Most High God, and at the end the heathen centurion confesses
the Son of God (15:39). The superscription of the Gospel in most manuscripts says, not improperly: The Gospel of Jesus Christ, the Son of God.
In the light of this therefore, it seems that we may conclude with some
certainty that ὁ υἱὸς τοῦ θεοῦ was a messianic title familiar to the first
community of Jesus' disciples. Still, strong reservations are raised against
this conclusion.

In the first place Dalman[53] has already drawn attention to the fact that
in the later Jewish literature the title υἱὸς θεοῦ can hardly be demonstrated.
In the discussion with Dalman I was able, still in the second edition of my
*Religion des Judentums* (pp. 261-62), to point particularly to IV Ezra
13:32, 37, 52; 14:9 as witnesses for the use of this messianic title. But
now it has been established that in all the passages we are not to read
υἱὸς θεοῦ but rather παῖς θεοῦ, in the sense of *'ebedh Yahweh*.[54] In this

---

[53] *Words of Jesus*, p. 269.

[54] See the new edition by Violet. The Latin (cf. the Syriac) translation reads *filius*;
on the other hand, the Arabic (and once the Ethiopic also) refers back to the Greek παῖς

Dalman is in fact correct; the use of ὁ υἱὸς τοῦ θεοῦ in the sense of the messianic title in the later Jewish literature is not provable. And his suspicion is further confirmed by an explicit testimony of Origen. Origen objects to the way in which Celsus has the Jew whom he introduces as an opponent of the Christians to speak; a Jew would not say: ὅτι προφήτης τις εἶπεν ἥξειν θεοῦ υἱόν, but rather ὅτι ἥξει ὁ Χριστὸς τοῦ θεοῦ (I. 49).

One could object that here an *argumentum e silentio* of an accidental character has been too heavily exploited. But the observation has a still more profound reason. For upon closer reflection we see plainly that the title "the Son of God" does not at all fit in with the sensitivities of Old Testament piety. It has a much too mythical ring which stands in contradiction with the rigid monotheism of the Old Testament. When in the Old Testament simply "sons of God" are the topic, supra-terrestrial being are meant thereby, and it is an echo of the primitive mythical outlook which has already become wholly alien to later Judaism. It is characteristic that the LXX almost everywhere in such a case translates it with ἄγγελοι θεοῦ.[55] In lofty and figurative discourse Israel is given (in the salutation) the honorific title "Son (of God)," [56] and the Israelites "Sons of God," [57] but the cases are seldom. Never does the designation occur in a simple narrative. It is especially characteristic that even the king or the messianic ruler never receives the solemn title "the Son of God" in the Old Testament. In the address in Ps. 2:7 it does say: "Thou art my son, this day have I begotten thee." Or it is said of the king in Ps. 89:26: "He will call to me, my father art thou" (cf. II Sam. 7:14). But if the "kiss *the* Son" in Ps. 2:12 actually stands assured in the text, then this objective use of the title would be unique in the entire Old Testament. However it is probably now generally conceded that here we have to do with a corrupted text. It is, in fact, a long way from the lofty poetic address "Thou art my Son" to the simple title

---

(*puer*). The redactional work of the editor already becomes most clearly evident in 7:28: Latin *filius meus Jesus*; Syriac *filius meus Messias*; Ethiopic *Messias meus*; Armenian *Messias Dei*; Arabic[2] *Messias*. In 7:29 the Ethiopic reads "my servant the Messiah." A confirmation of "my servant" which is probably to be presupposed throughout is afforded by the related Syriac Baruch Apocalypse 70.9, "my servant the Messiah." On the passage Ethiopic Enoch 105.2, cf. *Religion des Judentums*, 2nd ed., p. 261.

[55] Cf. Gen. 6:2; Job 1:6; 2:1; Dan. 3:25, 28 (LXX 3:92, 95), here everywhere ἄγγελοι θεοῦ. Exceptions in Ps. 29 (28):1; 89 (90):7; also Ps. 81 (82):6: υἱοὶ ὑψίστου.

[56] E.g., Exod. 4:22 (Israel is my firstborn son). Hos. 11:1 (but textually not assured; LXX ἐξ Αἰγύπτου μετεκάλεσα τὰ τέκνα αὐτοῦ. Jer. 31:19 (Is Ephraim my dear son?).

[57] Deut. 14:1 (You are sons of Yahweh, your God). [In 32:5 the text appears to be corrupted. LXX οὐκ αὐτῷ τέκνα (not υἱοί)]. Mal. 1:6. But cf. further Ps. Sol. 17.27 γνώσεται γὰρ αὐτούς (the pious Israelites), ὅτι πάντες υἱοὶ θεοῦ εἰσιν αὐτῶν.

"the Son." And here we see quite clearly the limits which are never over-stepped by Old Testament piety. From this point now it becomes also all the more clear how alien within the Old Testament milieu is the portrayal, already discussed (p. 87), of the pious person(s) in Wisd. Sol. 2:13 ff. When in this passage it is offered as a characteristic of the pious simply that καὶ παῖδα Κυρίου ἑαυτὸν ὀνομάζει . . . ἀλαζονεύεται πατέρα θεόν . . . εἰ γάρ ἐστιν ὁ δίκαιος υἱὸς θεοῦ, in my judgment the entering of a new mysterious element into Jewish piety is clearly discernible.[58]

Once again I shall take up the main theme. It is now clear of what great importance is the observation that the whole of later Jewish apocalypticism was unacquainted with the messianic title "Son of God." We now see that this was no accident but rather is grounded in the nature of Israelite-Jewish piety. If this is so, it demonstrates the legitimacy of our critical question whether we may ascribe the creation of this title already to the Palestinian primitive community. The question is not easy to answer, and I confess that here I have wavered and still waver. In my discussion with Wernle,[59] who has referred me to the double occurrence of the title within the temptation narrative in the source common to Matthew and Luke, I have at one time considered the possibility that here we could be faced with a new creation of the primitive community in dependence upon the well-known messianic passages (Pss. 2:7, 89:27). More recently Wetter[60] has taught me that at least the messianic ideal which is opposed as a false one in the second (or third) temptation becomes comprehensible precisely in the Hellenistic milieu. The notion that the Messiah must prove his sonship to God or his deity by means of a miracle of flight indeed plays the leading role in the Simon Magus tradition.[61] When Jesus here rejects the temptation to venture such a miraculous flight as the chosen Son of God, this could point to a dispute of the community of Jesus' disciples with the Simon Magus sect and the ideal of their redeemer-hero. I would add to this the fact that among the miracles which are attributed to Simon in the Pseudo-Clementines Hom. II, 32 (cf. Rec. IV, 9), the changing of stones into bread is told (ἐκ λίθων ἄρτους ποιεῖ). And Wetter rightly brings out that in the third (or second) temptation, which alone can be understood as a dispute with the Jewish

---

[58] Cf. also the specifically Hellenistic sentiment in 2:23, ὅτι ὁ θεὸς ἔκτισεν τὸν ἄνθρω-πον ἐπ' ἀφθαρσίᾳ καὶ εἰκόνα τῆς ἰδιότητος ἐποίησεν αὐτόν.

[59] Wernle, "Jesus und Paulus," ZThK XXV (1915), p. 13, and Bousset, Jesus der Herr (1916), pp. 4-5.

[60] Wetter, Der Sohn Gottes (1916), pp. 139-40.

[61] Wetter, pp. 102-3, 87.

messianic milieu, even the title υἱὸς τοῦ θεοῦ is lacking. Accordingly Wernle's proof appears to me to lose its compelling force.

On the other hand, of course, in the Gospel of Mark, as was brought out earlier, the title appears already to have such a secure place that in fact it is difficult to assume that it was not already at home in the Palestinian primitive community. Nevertheless here also a series of reservations arise. The confessions of the demon-possessed to the Son of God probably stem from the special theory of the messianic secret, whose originator will have been the evangelist Mark himself.[62] In the question of the high priest the superfluous and, in the mouth of the high priest, utterly impossible addition, "the Son of the Most High God," could likewise be an ornamentation of the evangelist's last editing, who introduced the title here just as Matt. 16:16 [63] added the ὁ υἱὸς τοῦ θεοῦ τοῦ ζῶντος to the simple ὁ Χριστός of Mark 8:29. Luke on the other hand (22:66 ff.) with his characteristic separation of the question of the Χριστός and that of the υἱὸς τοῦ θεοῦ perhaps still points to the more nearly original tradition. Finally, when the Gospel of Mark places in the mouth of the Gentile captain the confession of the Son of God, still the υἱὸς τοῦ θεοῦ here cannot be understood in the sense of a confession to the Jewish Messiah. Instead, we see clearly that for the evangelist [ὁ] υἱὸς τοῦ θεοῦ was here the great formula in which the nature of Jesus Christ was summarized for the faith of the Gentile Christian community.

There remains as a fixed bit of material the twice-occurring voice of God at the baptism and in the transfiguration scene: "Thou art my Son"— "This is my Son." And even though the legendary (mythical) character of both stories is plainly evident, still it can hardly be disputed that in their essential contents[64] these already were in circulation in the Palestinian primitive community. Both have in the present structure of Mark's Gospel a dominant position and will surely have exerted the most lively influence upon the imagination of the primitive community. Nevertheless, we must here emphasize that it is still a long way from the form of address which we have before us here to the title ὁ υἱὸς τοῦ θεοῦ, a way which Old Testament piety has not traversed. May we, without further ado, assume that already the first community of Jesus' disciples had taken the daring

---

[62] One should observe that Mark 1:24 still offers the general ὁ ἅγιος τοῦ θεοῦ. Cf. John 6:69.

[63] Matt. has also inserted the title in 14:33 and 27:40.

[64] Yet cf. here the conjecture, further discussed below (p. 97, n. 70) as to the original wording of the baptismal utterance.

step and had creatively formed the title "the Son of God," which the Old Testament and the messianic faith of late Judaism did not know, out of Old Testament beginnings (Ps. 2:7) and the tradition about Jesus' baptism and transfiguration? Or did this title ultimately develop first on Greek soil, in the Greek language?

For the answering of this question some further points of contact come into consideration. We only mention the fact that the book of Acts has the title "Son of God" only one single time, namely where it characterizes the preaching of Paul in a comprehensive way (9:20).[65] But we must especially emphasize that the earliest community usage yields still another title which would conflict with that of the υἱὸς θεοῦ, namely παῖς θεοῦ[66] or 'ebedh Yahweh. This term, which would at once suggest an early influencing of primitive Christian messianology by Deutero-Isaiah, is found within our gospel literature of course only in one passage in a quotation borrowed from Isa. 42:1 ff. (Matt. 12:18). But it is demonstrable in a series of the earliest liturgical fragments of primitive Christianity, thus in the hymn of the community in Acts 4:27, 30 (cf. 3:13, 26); in the Lord's Supper prayers of the Didache (9:2-3, 10:2-3); in the great Roman community prayer in I Clem. 59.2, 3, 4; in the prayer in the Martyrdom of Polycarp (14:1, 3; cf. 20:2), which perhaps is dependent upon the primitive Christian liturgy.[67] Indeed in the bishop's prayer of the eighth book of the Constitutions (chap. 5) the concluding doxology runs: διὰ τοῦ ἁγίου παιδός σου Ἰησοῦ Χριστοῦ τοῦ θεοῦ καὶ σωτῆρος ἡμῶν.[68] Further, it is important that the

---

[65] Cf. somewhat further Acts 13:33. In addition, the title υἱός is lacking also in James and in I Peter. In the book of Revelation it is found only in 2:18.

[66] Wernle, "Jesus und Paulus," p. 13, has raised against me the objection that this observation does not mean much, since παῖς can also mean υἱός and is simply equivalent in meaning to υἱός. This is true in general for the purely Greek language area (cf. further Wisd. Sol. 2.13 παῖς=2.18 υἱός), but not in the Palestinian language area. For here παῖς θεοῦ (κυρίου) is just a translation of 'ebedh Yahweh.

[67] Still a number of important passages should be cited here: in Diognetus 8.9; 9.1; Barnabas 6.1; 9.2, this title appears in two Old Testament passages which have suffered a Christian interpolation. Celsus (Origen, Contra Cels. VII, 9) is acquainted with Christian (?) prophets who in ecstasy cry out ἐγὼ ὁ θεός εἰμι ἢ θεοῦ παῖς ἢ πνεῦμα θεῖον (cf. with this Corp. Herm. XIII, 14 Θεὸς πέφυκας καὶ θεοῦ παῖς; cf. XIII, 2, 4). Magical papyrus (Wessely) from the fourth century, Χριστός=ἠγαπημένος παῖς (cf. with this Schermann, Griech. Zauberpapyri, TU XXXIV, 3). Docetists in Hippolytus, Philosophumena (ed. Duncker, p. 420.51), ὁ μονογενὴς παῖς. Acta Pauli et Thecl. 17.24. Acta Justini 2. Athenagoras 12, τίς ἡ τοῦ παιδὸς τὸν πατέρα ἕνωσις. Celsus (Origen, Contra Cels. I, 67; II, 9), σωτῆρα νομιζόμενον καὶ θεοῦ τοῦ μεγίστου παῖδα. V, 2, θεὸς μὲν καὶ θεοῦ παῖς οὐδεὶς οὔτε κατῆλθεν οὔτε κατέλθοι. V, 52; VI, 42; VI, 74; VIII, 14; VII, 56, ἐβούλετο ἡμᾶς μᾶλλον Σίβυλλαν ἀναγορεῦσαι παῖδα θεοῦ ἢ Ἰησοῦν.

[68] Cf. therewith the Epitome, διὰ τοῦ παιδός σου Ἰησοῦ Χριστοῦ, and the Latin text of the so-called Egyptian Church Order, per puerum tuum Jesum Christum (ed. Hauler,

title can be shown precisely in the tradition of later Jewish Christianity. Epiphanius judges (Haer. 29.7) concerning the so-called Ebionites: καταγγέλλουσι τὸν τούτου παῖδα ᾽Ιησοῦν Χριστόν. In the fragments of a Nazarene exposition which Jerome reports in his commentary on Isaiah, it is said with a clear connection with Acts 3:13-14: *qui peccare faciebant homines in verbo dei, ut Christum dei filium* (thus=παῖδα) *denegarent* (on Isa. 29:20-21), and *qui consilio pessimo dei filium denegastis* (on Isa. 31:6-9).[69]

But now these two observations, that the term παῖς θεοῦ has a firm place in liturgical usage in which very often the most ancient material of all is contained, and that on the other hand it can be shown to be Jewish Christian, secure a very high antiquity for the title. Indeed we must reckon with the possibility that the designation of Jesus as the Isaian Servant of God (in the messianic sense) can be traced back to the earliest community. From this then a new reservation against the antiquity of the title "Son of God" would be raised. For it cannot be denied that the two designations stand in particular tension with each other and will hardly have developed in the same milieu.[70]

Here the investigation must, for the time being, be broken off. For now it is shown on the other hand that where the title "Son of God" comes to undisputed dominance, that is, in the area of popular conceptions in the Gentile Christian church and in that of the Pauline-Johannine Christology, there are bound up with it conceptions of a kind in part primitively mythological, in part speculatively metaphysical; and these simply have nothing more to do with Jewish-primitive Christian messianology. And there

---

pp. 104-5). If Schwartz (Schriften d. wissensch. Gesellsch. Strassburg VI, 38 ff.) is correct, we have here the Church Order of Hippolytus. This would coincide nicely with Hippolytus' Contra Noetum 5 (Lagarde 47.20), οὐδεὶς εἰ μὴ μόνος ὁ παῖς καὶ τέλειος ἄνθρωπος καὶ μόνος διηγησάμενος τὴν βουλὴν τοῦ πατρός (cf. further Lagarde 49.8, 10; 51.15).

[69] Cf. the passages in Schmidtke, *Neue Fragmente und Untersuchungen zu den judenchristlichen Evangelien*, TU XXXVII, 1 (1911), 108-10, and with this p. 114 (also p. 64).

[70] Yet a conjecture may at least be indicated here. Could not the voice of God in the baptismal account after all have been originally σὺ εἶ ὁ παῖς μου ὁ ἀγαπητός, ἐν σοὶ εὐδόκησα? The connection with Isa. 42:1 then would be complete. Cf. the translation in Matt. 12:18 which differs from the LXX: ἰδοὺ ὁ παῖς μου ὃν ᾑρέτισα, ὁ ἀγαπητός μου, ὃν εὐδόκησεν ἡ ψυχή μου. The epithet ἀγαπητός μου in Mark 1:11, like the other ὁ ἐκλελεγμένος μου in Luke 9:35 appears to point in this direction (cf. ἠγαπημένος παῖς in the magical papyrus. Diognetus 8.9; ἠγαπημένος also in Barn. 3.6; 4.3, 8 and in numerous places in the Ascensio Jesaiae, the epithet of the "elect one" especially frequent in the similitudes of Enoch). The changing of παῖς into υἱός in the baptismal account in Mark then would signify the first step in the development which reached its culmination in the introduction of the total wording of Ps. 2:7.

once more the question of the religio-historical origin of the designation will have to be discussed.

II. *Miracle*. The faith of the community not only inserted into the traditional picture of the life of Jesus the much stronger stress upon Jesus' person and upon the messianic idea. It also above all surrounded this picture with the nimbus of the miraculous. Here also we can still follow the development in part in its individual segments. We are still able to see clearly how the earliest tradition of Jesus' life was still relatively free from the miraculous. It is characteristic that the older part of the evangelical tradition, as over against the narrative portion, was probably a collection of the words of the Lord (or a gospel consisting essentially of the Lord's words), in which miracle naturally played no role. At the most, here and there a catena of Logia was joined to a briefly told miracle story (e.g., the Beelzebub saying). Certainly when the Logia were collected there were many miracle legends of the life of Jesus already in circulation. But people did not consider these things to be the truly important and decisive matters.

Moreover, it is striking that the passion narrative, apparently the earliest sketch of a part of the history of Jesus, has remained almost completely free of the miraculous. For the bizarre miracle of the blighted fig tree was probably a literary addition of the evangelist Mark and was inserted by him into a ready-made context.[71] Otherwise, the miraculous figures only in two brief remarks in the narration, both of them inserted in the crucifixion scene: one about the ensuing darkness and one about the rending of the temple veil.[72]

Still more important is the observation that the historical tradition of Mark's Gospel is divided into two streams which flow side by side in almost total separation. Beside the teaching anecdote, which on the whole is almost lacking the miraculous, there stands the miracle story. Beside pieces in which the teaching and controversial sayings dominate stand others which are simply filled with miracles: 4:35–5:43 and the parallel series of narratives which are grouped around the doublets of the miracles of feeding. Indeed even the narrative style appears here and there to change. For the observa-

---

[71] Note the "nested" system in the narrative which appears here as so often and seems to be peculiar to Mark. The account interrupts the story of Jesus' appearance in the temple and is itself in turn broken apart. Luke does not know the narrative.

[72] But one should observe how Mark 15:38 is inserted almost as a literary gloss in the context of 15:37, 39.

tions[73] which have been made about the changes between a short, compressed, paradigmatic style of narrative and a more expansive, colorful, storylike style in Mark's Gospel are divided almost wholly between these two adjoining areas of the teaching anecdote and the miracle story. We can formulate the state of affairs thus: There are narratives which in addition to a great miracle contain a logion of Jesus transcending the immediate situation and capturing the attention by reason of its general contents. This double point introduces a certain lack of unity and keeps the attention of the hearer unsettled. These narratives however form a rare exception and arouse the suspicion that they are a later composition (or reworking). A good example is offered by the pericope of the healing of the lame man, in which the powerful logion about the right of the Son of Man to forgive sins is joined with the miracle. And precisely in this narrative we already (p. 40) have had to assume, for other reasons, a profound (dogmatic) reworking. A good example is offered also by the pericopes which deal with Jesus' healing on the Sabbath: Mark 3:1-6 (and par.), Luke 13:10-17; 14:1-6. A comparison of these stories with one another shows how here three different great miracles (the healing of the withered hand, of the crippled woman, and of the man suffering from dropsy) have been fitted to one and the same logion of Jesus (or to a series of such). The original tradition must have reported about Jesus' healing on the Sabbath only in quite general terms and in the same terms connected the controversial utterance with the account. Perhaps the two narratives of the centurion of Capernaum (the sole miracle story which only Matt. and Luke have in common) and the Syrophoenician woman may also be placed here. They obviously belong in the series of didactic narratives and yet both are climaxed with the great miracle of healing performed at a distance. It is nonetheless noteworthy that in the gospel account such miracles performed at a distance are described only in cases where Jesus is dealing with Gentiles. Would it be too daring to suppose that at one time both narratives told that Jesus had gone into the house of Gentiles in order to give help? The reworking[74] then would have eliminated the offense and introduced the great miracle.

Thus the streams are ever more clearly separated, and we can indeed observe how in the miracle narratives a special (and naturally a later)

---

[73] Cf. Wendling, *Die Entstehung des Markus-Evangeliums,* 1908, and M. Dibelius, *Die Formgeschichte des Evangeliums,* 1919.

[74] One should observe how in the pericope of the centurion of Capernaum just at the end the witnesses completely diverge.

stratum of tradition of the life of Jesus is present. But of course very early the conviction must have arisen in the community of his disciples that the miracles of Jesus belonged to the most important portion of his life.[75] The historical reality of this life itself, in fact, affords a certain point of contact. For it cannot be denied that in his lifetime Jesus exercised the gift of healing the sick, and that healing the sick and "driving out the demons" belonged to the characteristic traits of his itinerant life. On the other hand, there was also at work the dogmatic conviction that miracles belonged to the imminence of the kingdom of God proclaimed by Jesus and were its most certain witnesses.[76] Thus the tradition of the life of Jesus plunged deep into the really miraculous and therewith went far beyond the simple healing and expelling of demons by Jesus.

On the question about the emergence[77] of the miracle reports of the life of Jesus, one will do well not to work too much with Old Testament prototypes and reflections of Old Testament narratives. I shall later show that here and there the Old Testament has influenced the narrative of Jesus' life, that the proof from prophecy has created some history. But one will not do justice to the popular miracle fiction with this assumption alone; this miracle fiction does not bear a scribal character. Instead, the fabrication of miracles in the life of Jesus probably took place as such a procedure usually takes place. People transferred to Jesus all sorts of stories which were current about this or that wonderworker and decorated gospel narratives that were already at hand with current miraculous motifs. Proof of the latter is most easily adduced. That the healed sick man is brought on a bed (a litter) and

---

[75] Cf. the characteristic summary of Jesus' activity in Acts 10:38 (healings, expulsion of demons) and heightened in 2:22: δυνάμεις, τέρατα, σημεῖα.

[76] Cf. Matt. 12:28=Luke 11:20; Matt. 11:2-6=Luke 7:18-23; Matt. 11:20-24= Luke 10:13-15. For the attitude of the community these sayings are at any rate characteristic. Some of them of course, in spite of Mark 8:11-12, may go back to Jesus, a question which cannot be decided here. Some question marks may be permitted. Matt. 12:28=Luke 11:20 (Jesus' expulsion of the demons an indication of the imminence of the kingdom of God) stands in sharp contrast of attitude to Matt. 12:27 (Luke 11:19). The answer to the envoys from the Baptist cannot stem from Jesus in the form in which we have it. Moreover, cf. with this logion an interesting Mandaean parallel and on this the comments of Reitzenstein, *Das mandäische Buch des Herrn der Grösse* (see above, p. 45, n. 39), p. 60. The situation in which Jesus spoke the woes against Capernaum, Chorazin, and Bethsaida is not clear. We learn nothing elsewhere of a final break with these places for his work such as these words presuppose. Perhaps the woes reflect the break of the primitive community with its Galilean home. They are preserved in the Logia within the missionary address which also contains many other late elements.

[77] The prehistory in Matthew and Luke should not at all be adduced in this connection. It apparently belongs to non-Palestinian territory, at least as far as the central legend of the miraculous birth is concerned.

then immediately gets up and walks, even takes his bed on his shoulders and carries it home;[78] that the physician who brings healing appears at the head of the bed; that the physician meets the bier on which the dead is borne;[79] that the futility of the efforts of the physicians is stressed before the wonderworker comes and heals;[80] that the suddenness of the accomplishment of the miracle[81] and its extraordinariness[82] are emphasized; all these are migratory motifs which are also utilized in the narratives of the life of Jesus. Moreover, it is worthy of note that we can still demonstrate from profane sources how a story of the identification of an apparent death by a famous physician is transformed in later sources into the miracle of an awakening of the dead.[83] That at the prayer of a pious person in the ship a mighty storm is suddenly calmed is a migratory Jewish legend. It is told of Rabbi Gamaliel II (Baba mezia 59b) as well as of an anonymous Jewish boy (jer. Berachoth IX, 1).[84] In the Gospels it appears before us somewhat more highly stylized: Jesus threateningly commands storm and sea, and adjures the latter as one adjures a demon! A parallel to the walking on the sea is found in Lucian, Philopseudes 13.[85] So also other narratives may have migrated over into the life of Jesus, even where definite proof is lacking and we are left to conjectures. The clearest case is that of the story about the Gadarene demoniac, which judged by its level as a whole appears at first glance as an alien element in the gospel history. What we have here is an amusing story of poor deluded devils who against their wills do what they most earnestly wish to avoid doing. Such a little story was told of some expeller of demons and then was transferred to Jesus. Even the place name of Gadara or Gerasa may have been attached originally to this itinerant story. Perhaps it occasioned the account of Jesus' journey to the east shore of the Sea of Galilee. But even then the information as to place takes on

[78] Cf. Weinreich, *Antike Heilungswunder*, pp. 173-74. Lucian, Philopseudes 11: "And Midas took his bed on which he had lain and hurried forth and went to the fields."

[79] The famed physician Asclepiades meets a funeral procession and discovers life in the body of the one who is apparently dead: Pliny, hist. nat. VII, 124; Celsus II, 6; Weinreich, p. 173.

[80] Weinreich, p. 195.

[81] *Ibid.*, p. 197.

[82] *Ibid.*, p. 198.

[83] See above, n. 79: The same story which is found in Pliny and Celsus in its original form is told by Apuleius, Flor. 19, as an absolute miracle. Asclepiades awakens the dead: *"confestim spiritum recreavit."*

[84] Fiebig, *Jüdische Wundergeschichten des neutestamentlichen Zeitalters*, pp. 33, 61.

[85] I owe the reference to J. Weiss, RGG, first ed., III, 2188. Cf. in general the statements by Weiss about the style of the miracle narratives.

its difficulties and has impelled copyists and exegetes to make all sorts of conjectures. Jesus never traveled either to Gadara or to Gerasa.

Similarly the narrative of Jesus' transfiguration appears, in terms of its total style, as a foreign element in the gospel narrative. If the story just discussed lies beneath the gospel's level, this one lies, as it were, above it. Even the gospel accounts of the appearances of the resurrected One have not thus elevated the figure of Jesus into the purely spiritual and supernatural as is done here. We note especially the expression μετεμορφώθη. The clothes which glisten indescribably are the attribute of a supra-terrestrial being. Moreover there are in the narrative some rudimentary elements which still are not understood. Among these is the mention of the two men who appear beside Jesus and who obviously quite artificially and without more specific reason are identified as Elijah and Moses. To this category also belongs the utterly unexplainable cry of Peter: "It is good to be here; let us build three tabernacles here." What can have served here originally as the prototype of the gospel narrative? Some theophany on a high mountain in which three divine figures appeared? And is the building of tabernacles perhaps to be connected with the preparation of a place (a tent) for the appearing deity? [86]

In this connection still another great miracle, which to be sure belongs to the Johannine account, may be mentioned, because with it we do not have to stop with simple conjecture and with reasons of internal probability. I refer to the miracle of the wedding at Cana. This miracle with its style also actually fails to fit into the gospel narrative. When people again and again have taken offense at this story from the side of asceticism and opposition to alcohol, and have tried to eliminate it through all sorts of reinterpretations, they have not been so far wrong. There is a demonstrable parallel to this miracle from the cult of Dionysos, which can be traced

---

[86] In Mark's Gospel the transfiguration miracle appears to be inserted into an older literary context. Mark 9:11-13 (the question about Elias) follows closely the logion in Mark 9:1. Those parts of Mark's Gospel in which the three disciples Peter, James, and John play a role belong in general to the secondary stratum of the evangelical tradition; cf. 5:37 (raising of Jairus' daughter) and 13:3 (introduction to the following apocalypse). The same must be true of the depicting of the scene in Gethsemane in 14:33. Secondary tradition has a tendency to conceal itself behind prominent names. Cf. further the little secondary pericope in which John again appears as spokesman in Mark 9:38. We may further refer to the possibility that in the transfiguration scene there could be present an appearance of the resurrected One which has been back-dated into the life of Jesus. The introductory scene of *Pistis Sophia* is sketched on the basis of our narrative, but here it has become a transfiguration of the resurrected One by means of the garment of light which was sent to him from heaven. Also to be noted is the motif that the manifestation takes place on the mountain (cf. Matt. 28:16).

back into the New Testament period. On the island of Andros, so it is told, a temple fountain of Dionysos is said to have flowed with wine instead of water all year long. A similar thing is told of the sacred place of Dionysos in Teos. In Elis on the eve of the beginning festival, in the presence of prominent men people used to place three empty jugs in the sacred place of Dionysos; then the doors were locked, and the next morning they found the jugs filled with wine. Here, we may surmise, is the genesis of the wine miracle of Cana! People set the epiphany of the new God over against the epiphany of the god Dionysos and its miracle: And he revealed his glory and his disciples believed on him.[87]

Perhaps in a similar way the emergence of the legend of the feeding of the five thousand may be illuminated. It bears similar characteristics of style. The modest parallels of the Old Testament (II Kings 4:42-44) and the echo of the Christian celebration of the supper do not suffice to account for the development of this story. Here again a cultic myth may be present. A god rules over his own, reveals his glory and bestows his gifts.[88]

Thus did the community of Jesus' disciples fictionalize and surround the picture of Jesus with the glitter of the miraculous. Or, otherwise expressed, the personal image of Jesus begins to work with magnetic power and to draw to itself all possible materials and narratives which were at hand in his environment. But even where they are quite alien in character, the high power of gospel fabrication so amalgamated them that this process is recognizable only to the more discerning eye.

But most of all in this connection we still have to direct our attention to the supernatural climax which the presentation of the close of Jesus' life has maintained by means of the legends of the empty tomb and of the bodily resurrection of Jesus.

A series of clues points to the fact that the dogma of the bodily resurrection and a definite reflection about the whereabouts of Jesus' body were at first alien to the faith of the first community in the exalted Lord. Indeed,

[87] Cf. Pliny, hist. nat. II, 103 (XXXI, 13); Diodorus III, 66; Pausanias VI, 26.1-2; Athenaios I, 61. Nilsson, *Griechische Feste,* pp. 291-93. It is highly significant that January 5 (or more precisely the night of January 5/6) is given as the date of the beginning of this festival of Dionysos, i.e. the date of the early Christian festival of Epiphany, and that already in the early Christian liturgy the sixth of January also was recognized as the anniversary of the wedding at Cana. I intend to deal with this further in its larger context in a special essay.

[88] Perhaps one could make some advance here if one should pose the question of where else in the cultus of a deity bread and fish played a role as sacred food. Cf. the Abercius inscription and Dölger, ʼΙχθύς, p. 147: Brot und Fisch im Kult der Taanit.

if we were correct in the surmise which we have already (p. 59) discussed among others, about the development of the interval of three days out of the assumption that the soul tarries with the body for three days, then that would lead to the conception of an independent continuing life of the soul without the body. The word of Jesus to the thief (Luke 23:43): "This day you will be with me in Paradise," [89] which of course belongs to a later tradition, seems to point in the same direction. Moreover, it is not easy to answer the question how Paul conceived of the resurrection in general and the resurrection of Jesus in particular. That he could have thought of a resurrection of "this" body which is laid in the earth is (even for the resurrection of Jesus) ruled out by I Cor. 15:50. The figure which he chose of the "naked" grain of wheat which is laid in the earth (I Cor. 15:36-37) may not be somehow interpreted in the sense of an organic springing forth of the new body out of the old one. For the apostle a miracle is performed here, and he clearly holds fast only to the two ideas, that the old body must pass away and that God gives *a new body* by means of a miracle. Only with such a view is compatible the fact that in another passage (II Cor. 5:1) the apostle conceives of the new body as already present with God in heaven.[90] If we wished to take it strictly, we should have to say that according to Paul actually nothing arises out of the grave; and it is only to be regarded as the preservation of a traditional word when Paul speaks of resurrection and even of a making alive (awakening) of our mortal body (Rom. 8:11), somewhat as we still speak naturally of the sun's rising and setting. But Paul will surely have conceived of the "resurrection" of Christ after the analogy of the general resurrection. And thus we could conceive that the apostle could be fully convinced of the (pneumatic) bodily reality of the exalted Christ without in any way reflecting about the fate of the sarkic body of Jesus. In the most detailed passage in which Paul describes the being and essence of Christ from his preexistence down to his final exaltation, Phil. 2:6 ff., he does not mention the resurrection at all, but only the exaltation.[91]

[89] Of course it would be possible that Paradise should be taken as a *status intermedius* (still in the underworld). The same question arises again in the Lazarus pericope.

[90] However one might otherwise interpret the passage, this clearly expressed conviction cannot be explained away. It matches the conception in the Ascensio Jesaiae IX, 1-2, 9-13, of the clothes (bodies) of the pious which are in heaven; cf. also the Slavonic Enoch (ed. Bonwetsch) 22.8 ff. Bousset, *Religion des Judentums*, 2nd ed., p. 319.

[91] Thus also in the Gospel of John the ὑψωθῆναι of Jesus is found emphasized exclusively. Once in an obviously secondary addition ἐκ νεκρῶν ἀναστῆναι (20:9). Similarly in 2:22 ὅτε οὖν ἠγέρθη ἐκ νεκρῶν appears to be an addition; cf. further in the appended chapter, 21:14.

Neither should the primitive community be assumed, without further ado, to have imagined a personal continuing life of Jesus only under the assumption that Jesus had arisen out of the tomb with his body. The conception of the resurrection of the flesh is indeed in the Jewish-Palestinian eschatology of the time of Jesus on the way to dominance, but it did not by any means completely achieve this dominance. We may assume that the conceptions and imaginations in this area were still in an extremely lively and fluid state.

Thus also the rise and growth of the legend along with the ultimate miracle of the empty tomb may still be traced out within our gospel literature, without our laying claim to the *argumentum e silentio* of the Pauline resurrection account (I Cor. 15). In fact it appears probable that the story of the women at the empty tomb at one time circulated by itself and was first artificially connected by Mark with the kernel of the passion narrative, which originally ended with the burial. Of decisive significance[92] here is the point that the women first come to the grave to anoint the body of Jesus on Sunday (the third day). With the climatic conditions of the Near East this is so utterly inconceivable[93] that we are compelled to assume the entire structure of this narrative was not sketched as a unity, but that a compiler has painstakingly bound together traditions of diverse origins. The point that the women came to the tomb to anoint the body of Jesus belonged to a separate tradition which was first connected by Mark to the older presentation of the passion narrative and is squeezed into the order of a chronology (day of death on the παρασκευή, resurrection on the μιᾷ τῶν σαββάτων)[94] to which it did not at all fit.

Other observations confirm this judgment. For all that, it remains curious that the thought of the crucial hindrance to their plan to anoint the body

[92] On the following, cf. E. Schwartz, "Osterbetrachtungen," in ZNW VII (1906), 1-33.

[93] It is noteworthy that Matt. 28:1 has again removed this feature and that the writer of the Fourth Gospel pretty clearly offers a polemic against it in 19:39-40. Moreover, the interpretation which the story of the anointing at Bethany has already found in Mark 14:8 (προέλαβεν μυρίσαι τὸ σῶμά μου εἰς τὸν ἐνταφιασμόν) stands in a certain tension with the above motif.

[94] On the possibility that this dating of the death and the resurrection likewise belongs first to the tradition, see above, pp. 59-60. Schwartz, "Osterbetrachtungen," p. 31, correctly points out that in the older account in Mark 15:42 about the burial the datum ἐπεὶ ἦν παρασκευή is inserted altogether inorganically (Luke 23:54 smooths out the account; in Matt. the datum stands in another place in 27:62; only in the later legends of the Gospel of Peter vs. 5 [vss. 23, 24] and John 19:31, 42, does the explanation of the hasty burial of Jesus have its fixed place). There remains the possibility that it was the evangelist Mark who first inserted the Pauline τῇ τρίτῃ ἡμέρᾳ into the historical presentation of the life of Jesus.

of Jesus, the stone before the door of the tomb, occurred to the women who hurried to the tomb only on the way there. The stone before the door of the tomb belonged to the most ancient tradition. Once again in this passage a seam is clearly visible. Further, the composite character of Mark's Gospel is plainly shown in the outline of the concluding story. In preparatory fashion the "women" are already introduced before the burial, at the cross of Jesus (15:40-41). Then they emerge again only at the end of the story of the burial, in which they play no role (15:47). This is the well-known nested style of composition with which the evangelist Mark works and connects sources of varied origins. Under this presupposition also the enigma of the abrupt and inartistic ending of Mark's Gospel with the ἐφοβοῦντο γάρ, which is so little in harmony with the entire pattern of the older passion narrative, which is artistic to a high degree, is solved. Here Mark was tied to the traditional material; the appearance of the resurrected One to his disciples still was not available to him as historical narrative but as simple kerygma. The above-mentioned concluding verse of the narrative, "And they told no one, for they were afraid," is furthermore of completely obvious tendency. It is supposed to give an answer to the question why the story of the women at the empty tomb remained unknown for so long.[95] Thus it remains to be shown that the legend of the women at the empty tomb did not yet belong to the older gospel narrative of the close of the life of Jesus. The narrative was formed independent of that report; on the other hand it is still closely bound to the authentic tradition that Jesus appeared to his *disciples* in Galilee, in the assumption that only women saw the empty tomb.

Thus at this main point the ultimate miracle was introduced into the Christian community faith and the personal image of Jesus of Nazareth; the faith in the exaltation of the Son of Man acquired the tangible form that Jesus had awakened (arisen) from the tomb of the third day.[96]

III. *The Messianic Secret.* With this heavy stress on the manifest messianic glory in the life portrait of Jesus and the retouching of this portrait with

[95] It is highly noteworthy that the transfiguration legend in Mark 9:9 also has acquired a quite similar suspicious addition. Might the evangelist Mark himself have been at work here? The pen of the evangelist perhaps is shown also in Mark 16:7. For the same tendency which obliterates or glosses over the disciples' flight to Galilee is visible in Mark. 14:27-28.

[96] With one exception (I Thess. 4:14; cf. 4:16), Paul has the passive ἐγερθῆναι. Perhaps it is no accident that in the solemn predictions in 8:31 (9:9-10); 9:31, and 10:34 Mark already everywhere uses ἀναστῆναι (cf. the Apostles' Creed). In Gal. 1:1 Marcion probably read Ἰησοῦ Χριστοῦ τοῦ ἐγείραντος ἑαυτὸν ἐκ νεκρῶν.

the miraculous, a certain difficulty arose, however. Opponents of the gospel could raise the objection: If Jesus thus openly presented himself to all the people as the Messiah–Son of Man sent from God, if he performed such miracles, how does it happen that the people to whom he was sent by God in the first place did not believe on him? How is the evident failure of his preaching to be explained? The response to this question, if we see correctly, within the gospel tradition lies with the theory of the messianic secret,[97] which already permeates the entire Gospel of Mark.[98] And the answer runs thus: Jesus did not at all intend that the Jewish people should come to believe. Therefore he indeed revealed his messianic glory, but just as often and just as decidedly he again concealed it. This tendency is manifested in various forms, most of all in the constantly recurring schematic conception that Jesus expelled the demons because they recognized him (1:23, 34; 3:11 ff.; 5:19).[99] This interpretation cannot be historical. Quite apart from the unacceptable basing of Jesus' healing activity on this recognition, our rejection of it as historical stems from the fact that this assumption, that Jesus' messiahship was constantly and basically recognized from the side of the possessed ones, rests upon an obvious dogmatic assumption: The demons which are at work in the sick perceive the holy emissary of God before a suspicion of it comes to any man. Unfortunately this stubbornly maintained tendency has gravely distorted the picture of Jesus' expulsion of the demons in the Gospels and almost emptied it of all clear traits.[100] On the same line lie the numerous cases in which Jesus performs miracles of healing the sick and then commands them not to make this miracle known (1:44; 5:43; 7:36; 8:26). The command of silence in the miracle stories of the raising of Jairus' daughter and of the healing of the blind man of Bethsaida best show how the narrator here has lost all sense of the possible and the actual and is only following a schematic tendency. And again in the same line lies the theory set forth in Mark's Gospel that Jesus intended by his speaking in parables to harden the people and that by interpreting these parables he

[97] In the following section I follow Wrede's splendid proof in his *Messiasgeheimnis*. With regard to the facts which he has disclosed I acknowledge his correctness in almost every respect. It is in weighing these facts where I differ with him, as will be evident from the discussion.

[98] Mark can hardly have created this, yet he has followed it consistently.

[99] This theory of veiling is also found in 5:19: "Go to your house and tell it (only) to your own people."

[100] The strange and characteristic expression in Mark 9:29, τοῦτο τὸ γένος ἐν οὐδενὶ δύναται ἐξελθεῖν εἰ μὴ ἐν προσευχῇ, taken precisely, stands in contradiction with the otherwise everywhere portrayed exorcistic procedure of Jesus, in which there is nowhere a trace of prayer.

communicated especially to the disciples the deeper secrets of the divine wisdom which lie hidden in the parables. The evangelist Mark places great value upon this theory. He has placed it in the center of his presentation of Jesus' parabolic discourses (4:10-12, 34). He artificially sets the stage for the whole tendency by telling first of the thronging of the people to Jesus (3:7-12), and then of the calling of the disciples to the mountain (3:13-19), then has Jesus separating himself even from his relatives (3:20-21, 31-35), in order to set his relation to the masses and to his disciples in sharp contrast. That all this is mere theory, which agrees neither with Jesus' relation to the people in general, nor with his character as popular orator, nor with the nature of the parable,[101] should today require no further proof.[102] The theory recurs only one more time in Mark's Gospel, namely in Mark 7:17, where the disciples of Jesus ask him about the meaning of the παραβολή: "Nothing that comes from without to man can make him unclean"—and he gives to them alone[103] a further explication of this paradox (Maschal).

Surely we are justified in bringing together this theory of hardening the people with the reports of the concealing of Jesus' miraculous deeds in this fashion. Here the theory comes to expression, while there it was only referred to. Jesus intends to harden the Jewish people, therefore he conceals his messianic glory in word and work. Judaism's failure to believe was no failure of Jesus and no fate suffered by him, but his own free will. After all this, to be sure, we can hardly help conjecturing that the tendency of the messianic secret has also colored the scene at Caesarea Philippi. That does not mean that, as Wrede was inclined to assume, the whole scene is fabricated. The messianic confession of Peter will have to stand as historical. But unfortunately, through the retouching tendency of the evangelist, the answer of Jesus has been lost to us.

This tendency is crossed by another, not identical, yet related one, namely the emphasis upon the constant lack of understanding on the part of the disciples. It is clearly suggested in the strange section 8:14-21 (misunderstanding of Jesus' saying about the leaven). In this pericope, which is completely secondary because it already presupposes the doublet of the miracle of feeding the five thousand, everything except the logion of Jesus, to which

---

[101] Mark 4:10-12 also conflicts with 4:13, which must already have belonged to the (reworked) source of Mark.

[102] The fact that at one time Jesus also states in a quite definite case that he is ready to cause offense (Matt. 15:12 ff.) belongs in an entirely different realm and proves nothing at all against what is said above.

[103] Cf. 7:17, ὅτε εἰσῆλθεν εἰς οἶκον with 4:10, κατὰ μόνας.

it connects, is unhistorical and embellished tendentious material. From this perspective also such passages as 4:13 (?); 6:52; 9:10, 19, 32, and perhaps also the depiction of the Gethsemane scene in 14:37-41, are illumined. The depth of the mystery which surrounds the person of Jesus corresponds to the fact that even the disciples, although his glory is revealed to them, understood nothing of it. Only after death and exaltation did this mystery open up to a believing community.

IV. *Prophecy.* Closely connected with miracle belongs prophecy. Miracle and prophecy are the confirmation of everything divine upon earth. Thus the theory of fulfilled prophecy of the Old Testament was imposed upon the image of Jesus, and in various respects it reshaped that image.

It is generally acknowledged that the primitive Christian community laid the foundation for the proof from Old Testament prophecy which played such a significant role in later history. The individual stages of this process still may be traced out in some measure. Not only the Gospels can serve as sources here, but with the stability of the tradition also the book of Acts and even Paul, if we disregard the peculiarities of his Old Testament proof which resulted from the particular character of his gospel (doctrine of justification, attitude toward the law, the coming of salvation to the Gentiles, the hardening of Israel).

In the first place, naturally the proof from prophecy at the outset was directed to the two great events at the end of Jesus' life, first to his exaltation (resurrection), then to his death. In fact, one Old Testament passage, the prophecy in Dan. 7:13, had already worked in a decisive manner in the development of the Son-of-Man dogmatics. But elsewhere also it will have been easy for the community to demonstrate the portrait of the exalted Messiah in the Old Testament. Most of all here Ps. 110 has stimulated the Christian imagination. We can demonstrate its effect on numerous passages of the earliest Christian literature.[104] It lent support to the earliest (still free of any idea of bodily resurrection) conviction: "From henceforth the Son of Man sits at the right hand of the power of God." In I Cor. 15:26

---

[104] Mark 12:35 ff. (see above, p. 81), Luke 22:69 (cf. Mark 14:62); I Cor. 15:25; Heb. 1:3; 10:13; 12:2. Cf. Acts 7:56, the confession of James in Hegesippus according to Eus. CH II, 23.13. Moreover, it is worthy of note that Acts 7:56 describes the Son of Man as ἐκ δεξιῶν ἑστῶτα τοῦ θεοῦ, and that Mark 14:62 and Luke 22:69 instead of at the right hand "of God" have τῆς δυνάμεως (θεοῦ in Luke 22:69 is probably an explanatory addition), and Hegesippus has τῆς μεγάλης δυνάμεως. Is popular mythology expressed in these stereotyped variations? Cf. the ἑστώς and the μεγάλη δύναμις in the tradition of Simon Magus. See in Chap. III further about the doubled Kyrios in the psalm.

Paul connects the reference to Ps. 8 with the quotation from Ps. 110 (πάντα ὑπέταξεν ὑπὸ τοὺς πόδας αὐτοῦ). Indeed Ps. 8 also was probably quite early applied to Jesus because it could be understood as a hymn to the Son of Man. From Paul, precisely because he no longer placed any value upon the title "Son of Man," we can deduce the use of the Psalm in the primitive community, although we do not find its traces in the Gospels and the book of Acts.[105] At the beginning of the book of Psalms the Christians found further that powerful song of triumph which in every word invited a messianic interpretation. Therefore the saying with which the Psalm reached its climax: "Thou art my Son, this day I have begotten thee," was connected with the exaltation of Jesus.[106] In the messianology of Judaism Ps. 118 already played a special role; the association of its words: "Blessed is the one who comes in the name of the Lord," with the Messiah was so general that out of this saying developed a *terminus technicus* for the Messiah (הבא, ὁ ἐρχόμενος),[107] which the evangelical tradition presupposes as such. Specifically Christian, on the other hand, is the application to Jesus of the figure of the cornerstone rejected by the builders.[108] Indeed it appears almost as if already in the earliest time people possessed a collection of passages in which the Messiah was described as a stone (cornerstone, precious stone, stone of stumbling).[109] In view of all that has been said, it may be clear that the exposition of Ps. 16:8-11 (Acts 2:25 ff., repeated in 13:35) with its clear connection with the bodily resurrection belongs only to a secondary stage of community dogmatics and of proof from prophecy. The proof from prophecy then here already has a particularly artificial and reflective character (2:29-31).[110]

From Paul (I Cor. 15:4) we further learn explicitly that the community before him had already employed the proof for the necessity of Christ's suffering and dying. We may with great probability trace this tradition back to the Palestinian primitive community. For if here at first the necessity of

---

[105] Cf. the explicit citation in Heb. 2:6.

[106] Acts 4:25-26; 13:33-34; Heb. 1:5; 5:5. In the gospel tradition then the psalm is already connected with the baptism of Jesus, perhaps has first reshaped the wording of the pronouncement of the heavenly voice at the baptism, which stems from Ps. 42:1, and then in a later tradition (Luke in D, vet. lat. Justin) completely supplanted it (cf. above, p. 97, n. 70).

[107] Cf. Jesus' entry into Jerusalem and the query of the Baptist.

[108] Mark 12:10 shows the age of the interpretation; cf. Acts 4:11.

[109] Cf. I Pet. 2:6-8 and the curious combination of Isa. 28:16 and 8:14 in Rom. 9:32-33.

[110] The use of Hos. 6:2 for the "risen on the third day" (I Cor. 15:4) is also reflective, if this connection is to be assumed as assured.

Christ's death was differently understood, and thought of as an inner necessity in that people conceived of it as the necessary passageway to glory (*vide supra*, p. 49), still the proof from prophecy confirms anew the view that here it is not human wickedness and chance that prevailed, but rather the long-planned and predestined counsel of God (Acts 2:23). It will be shown later that again there were some psalms in particular which had a strong effect upon the community, especially Ps. 22 and 69. Elsewhere also people have often found the Messiah in various ways in the suffering and dying righteous man of the psalms.[111]

Further, the obscure saying in Zechariah (12:10): "They shall look on him whom they have pierced," must have been influential, all the more since in the quotation familiarity is shown with the Masoretic text as opposed to the LXX.[112] A second famous saying from Zechariah (13:7) has influenced the passion narrative of Mark (14:27). It is curious that the great fifty-third chapter of Isaiah on the suffering and dying servant of God appears at first to have had so little effect upon the Christian imagination. The application of this chapter to the suffering Messiah must indeed have been unheard of in all the Jewish messianology. In all his letters Paul shows no substantial traces of an influence from this chapter. It is also highly significant that still in Matt. 8:17 the passage in Isa. 53:4 is connected, not with the vicarious atoning death of Jesus, but with the healing of the sick. The ancient formulas about the "lamb of God" in the Fourth Gospel and the Apocalypse, which perhaps stem from the primitive Christian liturgical language, need not—at least not all of them—necessarily stem from Isa. 53. Of the older writings only I Peter[113]—and that to be sure in the strongest fashion—was influenced from that source. Also in Acts (8:22) we find one explicit quotation from that chapter.

This is all the more remarkable since on the other hand the picture which Deutero-Isaiah sketches of the servant of God appears from the outset to have been influential in the Christian community in the shaping of the picture of Jesus. Here I refer to what was said above (pp. 96-97) about Jesus' title παῖς θεοῦ and its secure place in the earliest Christian liturgy. Elsewhere also the influence of Deutero-Isaiah is shown in a series of passages of

[111] Ps. 41:10; John 13:18; Ps. 40:7; Heb. 10:5; cf. the incorrect reading σῶμα (instead of ὠτία) κατηρτίσω μοι.

[112] Matt. 24:30; Rev. 1:7 (in both passages the curious joining of Dan. 7:13 and Zech. 12:10); John 19:37.

[113] Cf. I Pet. 1:19-22=Isa. 53:7; 2:24=53:12; 2:25=53:6; cf. Luke 22:37=53:12.

earlier Christian literature.[114] Most of all this prophet's work influenced the shaping of the account of Jesus' baptism. Less frequently are seen the traces of Moses' prophecy about a prophet like himself whom God would send (Acts 3:23; 7:37), although already before Jesus the messianic interpretation of the passage appears to have been popular.[115]

The proof from prophecy was applied with special preference to the forerunner of Jesus. In daring fashion people applied to him the voice in the wilderness of Isa. 40:3 and, with violent alteration of the text, the prediction of God's messenger in Mal. 3:1[116] (Mark 1:2; Matt. 11:10=Luke 7:27).

In this entire presentation we have presupposed without further ado that even the words of Jesus which contain such a well-formed proof from prophecy are on the whole to be attributed to the theology of the community. The justification of this arises from the general consideration that, as we have seen in this connection, the proof revolves around the facts, which lie beyond the actual life of Jesus, of his death and exaltation (resurrection). For most of the passages coming under consideration, moreover, the evidence of their inauthenticity has already been presented.[117] And we may refer to the fact that in the entire Logia tradition actually only one such example appears, namely the bold reinterpretation of Mal. 3:1 in Matt. 11:10=Luke 7:27 (cf. Mark 1:2), which has already been discussed (p. 83). And it may still further be mentioned that while in Mark 14:21 Jesus speaks of the passing of the Son of Man "as it stands written of him," Luke 22:22 offers the expression κατὰ τὸ ὡρισμένον, and that similarly

---

[114] Matt. 12:18 ff.=Isa. 42:1-4; Luke 4:18-19=Isa. 61:1 ff.; cf. Acts 10:38 with Isa. 61:1; 13:47 with 49:6; 3:13 with 52:13.

[115] Cf. Mark 6:15; 8:28.

[116] Other instances: the preaching in Galilee in Matt. 4:15=Isa. 8:23; 9:1; healing of the sick in Matt. 8:17=Isa. 53:4; speaking in parables in Matt. 13:35=Ps. 78:2; hardening of the people in Mark 4:12=Isa. 6:9-10; flight of the disciples in Mark 14:26=Zech. 13:7; betrayal by Judas in Matt. 27:9=Zech. 11:12-13; Acts 1:20=Pss. 69:26; 109:8; John 13:18=Ps. 41:10; cf. John 17:12. The last-named passages show how people preferred to solve enigmas and difficulties by means of reference to the Old Testament prophecy.

[117] On Mark 9:12b, cf. p. 38 (when, in the following verse, it is said of Elias: "They have done to him as they would, as it is written concerning him," two different motifs collide here. The reference to the Scripture appears to have been inserted); on Mark 12:6-7, 12:35 ff., pp. 80-81; on Mark 14:27-28, p. 106, n. 95; on Mark 14:62, pp. 73-74. Few directly messianic interpretations of Old Testament passages can be traced back to Jesus. I mention as conjecture the relating of Elias to the Baptist (Mark 9:12) and the reference to the wonders of the messianic age in Matt. 11:15=Luke 7:22 (?). The later Gospels continue the proof from prophecy in the mouth of Jesus; cf. Luke 4:17 ff.; 18:31 (the "third" prediction of the passion); Luke 22:37 (Isa. 53:2), particularly 24:27, 44; John 13:18; 17:12.

the general allusion to the fulfillment of Scripture in Mark 14:49 is not confirmed by Luke 22:53.

The community not only placed in the mouth of Jesus a series of Old Testament prophecies, but it also represents him as predicting almost all particulars of his passion. A whole series of individual traits of the passion narrative are found again thus doubled in the prophecy: the ascent to Jerusalem, the betrayal by Judas, the arrest, the flight of the disciples, the hearing before high priest and scribes, Peter's denial, the delivery into the hands of the Gentiles, the mockery, the scourging, the violent death, the resurrection on the third day,[118] the appearance to the disciples in Galilee.

With this survey, even those prophecies which one would be psychologically inclined to regard as possible (the betrayal by Judas, Peter's denial) become critically doubtful. Here also "prophecy and miracle" are the driving force in the expansion of the gospel narrative. And at the same time people presented Jesus as the one who, fully the master and lord of his own fate, in clear consciousness strides into the night of death.

But now, through the proof from prophecy, the story of Jesus' life has been further elaborated and retouched. People not only found prophecy fulfilled in the life of Jesus; the proof from prophecy has itself made history. At one point in particular the Old Testament and fulfilled prophecy had to serve for the retouching of history, where historical recollection was very defective and full of gaps: in the account of the crucifixion and death of Jesus. How many features of the crucifixion scene harmonize with the song about the suffering of the righteous man in Ps. 22: the division of Jesus' clothing among the soldiers in Mark 15:24=vs. 19 (this connection with Ps. 22 is already explicitly set forth in the Fourth Gospel 19:24, and at the same time the historical account is accordingly expanded in a clearly recognizable fashion); further, the mockery by the passers-by in 15:29= vs. 8 (cf. the still stronger reminiscences in the account of Matt. 27:43= vs. 9 and also=Wisd. Sol. 2:13, 18-20); Jesus' cry of agony on the cross in 15:34=vs. 2. In addition there is in the Fourth Gospel the word of Jesus on the cross, "I thirst" (19:28), with an express allusion to Ps. 22:16; also the tradition that Jesus was fastened to the cross with nails (20:20, 25, 27) can be derived from Ps. 22:17. Justin (Apol. I, 35) already sets forth this connection between prophecy and fulfillment. This is such a series

[118] Cf. the three predictions of the passion in Mark 8:31 and 9:30 ff., and particularly 10:33-34; further 9:9, 12b; 14:8; 14:19-21, 27-30.

of agreements that it is forbidden on this basis in every individual case to find accidental agreement of prophecy and actual history. Here we see before us the embellishing community which borrows the colors for its painting from the Old Testament. Besides the twenty-second, then, the sixty-ninth Psalm also has influenced the passion narrative: From it comes the feature that Jesus was given vinegar to drink (Mark 15:36=Ps. 69:22) (cf. John 15:25=Ps. 69:5; John 2:17=Ps. 69:10). Thus even the conjecture that the crucifixion of Jesus between two malefactors is spun out of Isa. 53:12 [119] appears not impossible. Still against this, one could raise the objection that Isa. 53 appears only relatively late to have attracted to itself the interpretative imagination. Finally, we find in Isa. 50:6: "I have given my back to scourging and my cheeks to smiting," perhaps the seed of the accounts of Jesus' scourging and mistreatment.[120] Likewise here we should refer to the stereotyped feature, which also corresponds to the prophecy, of Jesus' silence, which however would again stem from Isa. 53. In the later Gospels the process continues. Besides the examples already cited we should also refer to Luke 23:46=Ps. 31:6 (Father, into thy hands I commend my spirit) and to John 19:37 (the piercing with the lance, following Zech. 12:10). And the surmise is still possible that the dating of Jesus' death in John is accomplished with a view to the interpretation of Jesus as the Old Testament paschal lamb (cf. John 19:36).

To be sure, otherwise the Old Testament has exerted only a scant influence on the forming of history. We have already mentioned that at first Isa. 42:1 and then Ps. 2:7 influenced the report of Jesus' baptism. Jesus' entry into Jerusalem may have been reshaped, with the help of the prophecies in Zech. 9:9 and Ps. 118:25-26, out of a relatively insignificant event into a messianic triumphal entry. And possibly the writer of the Fourth Gospel in his presentation still shows a knowledge of the original situation, while Matthew, on the basis of the Zechariah passage, has further embellished it and, under a misunderstanding of the Hebrew parallelism, has substituted two asses for the one. Thus we can also refer in the narrative of the miraculous feeding to an Old Testament example (*vide supra*, p. 103) (II Kings 4:44), and in

---

[119] Cf. the explicit reference to this prediction in mss. of Mark at 15:28 and in another place at Luke 22:37.

[120] Still the scene of the ridiculing by the soldiers may have another origin than the Old Testament prediction. Cf. H. Reich, *Der König mit der Dornenkrone*, 1905; H. Vollmer, *Jesus und Sacäenopfer*, 1905; esp. Wendland, "Jesus als Saturnalienkönig," *Hermes*, XXXIII (1898), 175-79; E. Klostermann, commentary on Mark 15:16 ff. (HNT); there more bibliography.

still many other passages one suspects Old Testament influences. But in almost all cases it has remained a matter of conjecture.[121]

V. *The Significance of the Death.* In a subordinate way the question may be handled whether the primitive community has already placed its master's death under the perspective of sacrificial death. The decision is not easy; Paul's testimony that he has taken it over from the tradition that Christ died for our sins according to the Scripture does not reach back unconditionally to the Palestinian primitive community, but leads first of all to the tradition of the Hellenistic community. In the speeches of the disciples in the first half of the book of Acts the idea of sacrifice plays no role. We can also point to the fact that in the theology of the primitive community we have already found a double reason for the necessity of the crucifixion, first as a passageway for Jesus from earthly lowliness to the glory of the Son of Man, and then as a fulfillment of Old Testament prophecy. The question arises whether the primitive community already has added to it this third reason. At any rate it is not to be denied, the idea of sacrificial death lay extraordinarily near to the Palestinian primitive community, rooted as it was in Old Testament soil. The sacrificial idea which dominated the Old Testament cultus must have been thrust by inner necessity into the consideration of the death of Christ. On the other hand in the Old Testament and the Jewish tradition the picture of the suffering and dying righteous one and the view of the atoning and vicarious significance of martyrdom are offered. Here the fifty-third chapter of Isaiah may not have been at all influential at first. The idea of martyrdom and of its significance had again become vital in the Maccabaean age. In the prayers of the Maccabaean martyrdom the idea of satisfaction is expressed with all sharpness; already the ἱλαστήριος θάνατος of the righteous ones is spoken of.[122] The two patterns of thought blend and are interwoven. Here one must not look for clarity of thought. Thus already the primitive community may have formed the idea ὅτι Χριστὸς ἀπέθανεν ὑπὲρ τῶν ἁμαρτιῶν ἡμῶν κατὰ τὰς γραφάς.

The evidential material in our Gospel which comes into consideration here

---

[121] I shall not go into the birth legend in greater detail, because its formation did not occur on the soil of the Palestinian primitive community. Cf. the birth of Jesus in Bethlehem according to Mic. 5:1, the flight to Egypt (Hos. 11:1), perhaps the slaughter of the infants in Bethlehem in Jer. 31:15, although naturally the narrative cannot be derived from that source.

[122] Bousset, *Religion des Judentums*, 2nd ed., pp. 228-29.

is, to be sure, only limited in scope. But in two passages in the older evangelical tradition the sacrificial idea has already entered into the community tradition of the words of Jesus. Out of the simple logion transmitted by Luke (from the Sayings source ?) in the original form: "I was in your midst as one who serves," the solemn saying in Mark has emerged: "The Son of Man came not to be ministered unto but to minister and to give his life a ransom for many" (*vide supra,* p. 39). And likewise the "shed for many" (for the forgiveness of sins) has entered into the tradition of the Lord's Supper sayings in Mark-Matthew. The symbolism of the Supper originally had no connection with the death on the cross. The breaking of the bread is nothing more than the preparation for eating. And if Jesus had intended to symbolize his death with the symbol of the cup, then the action corresponding to the shedding of blood would have been the pouring out of the wine.

Therewith the idea was still in no way grasped in its full import. Christ still is not *the* sacrifice, beside which all other sacrifices come to nothing, or the *one* righteous one who suffers vicariously for the world. He is a ransom "for many," his blood is shed "for many." The full import is first given to the idea by Paul. But the images are at hand. And when Paul considers Christ as the passover lamb (I Cor. 5:7) or when he considers the sacrifice of Christ as a sacrifice for sin (II Cor. 5:21) or speaks of the death of Christ as a means of atonement (Rom. 3:25), he probably has not himself coined these images and symbols—they were no more than this at first—but only repeated them.

VI. *Conclusion.* Thus did the community embellish and decorate the life portrait of its master. But by doing so it accomplished more than that: it preserved a good bit of the authentic and original life. It preserved for us the beauty and wisdom of his parables in their crystalline form—a Greek community would no longer have been able to do this. It bowed down before the stark heroism of his ethical demands which were rooted in an equally daring faith in God, and it took practically nothing away from them; it faithfully preserved the picture of the great battler for truth, simplicity, and plainness in religion against all false virtuousness; it dared to repeat without weakening it his devastating judgment on the piety of the dominant and leading circles; it basked in the luster of his trust in God, of his regally free, careless way with respect to the things and the course of this world;

it steeled itself to his hard and heroic demand that they fear God and not man; with trembling and quaking soul it repeated his preaching of the eternal responsibility of the human soul and of God's judgment; with jubilant rejoicing it proclaimed his glad message of the kingdom of God and the duty of fellowship in righteousness and love and mercy and reconciliation.

It has become fashionable to say that the whole proclamation contains nothing at all new and special, nothing that had not previously been vital in many places here and there in the surrounding world. As if it all depended on the new and unheard-of in religion! As if it did not depend upon the age-old, somehow, though concealed, yet germinally present, i.e., the eternal and universally valid; and most of all upon the plainness and the clarity, the wholeness and integrity with which this Eternal shines forth anew and comes to consciousness, as well as upon the compelling force and passion with which it grips the heart.

But in this connection we should most of all observe how only in this peculiar combination of the historical figure of Jesus and the proclamation of the community that picture of Jesus was created which became so tremendously influential for the history of Christian piety. Only in that behind the gospel of Jesus the community placed the figure of the heavenly Son of Man, the Lord and Judge of the world, and let his glory, half veiled and concealed by his history, shine through in transparent fashion; only in that it sketched the picture of the wandering Preacher on the gold background of the miraculous, wove around his life the luster of fulfilled prophecy and surrounded it with the charm of the half-disclosed secret; only in that it thus placed him in a great divine salvation history and had him appear as its crown and completion; only thus did the community make this picture of Jesus of Nazareth influential. For the purely historical actually is never able to have an effect, but only the vitally contemporary symbol in which one's own religious conviction clarified is presented. And an age which by no means lived solely on the simply ethical and simply religious, but on all sorts of more or less fantastic eschatological expectations, on faith in miracle and prophecy, on an imminent, unprecedented, special intervention of God in the course of nature and of history, on all sorts of means of salvation and messiahs, on devils and demons and the early triumph of God and his people over these inimical powers—such an age needed this very picture of Jesus as the first disciples of Jesus created it, and accepted the Eternal in it in the colorful wrappings of temporal clothing. This drama of the creation of a picture of Jesus drawn by faith will unfold for us once again from the standpoint of a purer and higher, a more universal and more generally valid faith; indeed it actually repeats itself infinitely often throughout the entire course of Christian history.

# 3

## THE GENTILE
## CHRISTIAN PRIMITIVE COMMUNITY

Between Paul and the Palestinian primitive community stand the Hellenistic communities in Antioch, Damascus, and Tarsus. This is not always adequately considered.[1] The apostle Paul's connections with Jerusalem were of a most meager kind.[2] Without the messianic faith of the primitive community which Saul the persecutor in his security and his pride came to know, the conversion at Damascus remains psychologically incomprehensible. But then the definite personal testimony of the apostle tells us that the connection with the primitive community has been limited to a minimum of a fourteen-day association with Peter and James, however strange that may appear. In

---

[1] On this point I take pleasure in the agreement with W. Heitmüller in his splendid essay, "Zum Problem Paulus und Jesus," ZNW XIII (1912), 320-37. Cf. Heitmüller's pointed formulation on p. 330: "Paul is separated from Jesus not only by the primitive community, but also by another stage. The course of development runs: Jesus–primitive community–Hellenistic Christianity–Paul." With respect to Wernle's (see above, p. 38, n. 17) vigorous attack directed against our view, it is sufficient to refer to the discussion in *Jesus der Herr*, pp. 39 ff.

[2] In the first edition at this point I doubted the fact that Paul ever appeared as persecutor of the Palestinian primitive community, and attempted to have him begin as opponent of the Christian movement in Damascus. I no longer believe that Gal. 1:22 justifies so decisive a criticism. Of course the account of Acts about Saul as persecutor of the primitive community is not compatible with that passage. We shall have to assume that the prominent man probably kept himself more in the background during the action (cf. moreover Gal. 1:23, ὁ διώκων ἡμᾶς ποτε). It is obvious that the explanation of Saul's journey to Damascus in Acts 9:1 is unhistorical. But this still is no reason to reject the journey altogether.

any case the apostle experienced his development as a Christian on the soil of the Hellenistic community. He did not create this Hellenistic community, nor did he determine its individual character from the beginning. It is one of the most important established facts that the universal religious community of Antioch, consisting of Jews and Hellenes, developed without Paul (Acts 11:19 ff.). Alongside this appears as equally important a second fact, that the great Roman community, equally universal in its orientation from the first (as appears in the Epistle to the Romans), was not established by Paul or even by one of his pupils. The full current of the new universal religious movement was already at flood level when Paul began his work, and even he was at first carried by this current. When the apostle so stoutly asserts his absolute independence of flesh and blood, and the individuality and originality of his proclamation, it is always the authorities in Jerusalem that he has in view in so doing. He does not think seriously of denying that his Christianity stands in vital connection with that of the congregations in Damascus, Tarsus, and Antioch. It is of course true that Paul often represents himself as a pneumatic who knows no tradition at all, whose certainty rests upon personally experienced revelation received in a state of ecstasy. He says that he went to Jerusalem on the basis of a revelation (Gal. 2:1), and we know from the book of Acts that a solemn decision of the congregation sent him thither. But along with this he is acquainted also with a fixed tradition (I Cor. 15:1 ff.), however seldom it comes out. But where the apostle thus appeals to the tradition, it is, according to all that is said, not the tradition of Jerusalem but first of all that of the Gentile Christian community in Antioch (only indirectly that of the Jerusalem community). And when Paul speaks of a τύπος τῆς διδαχῆς of the congregation in Rome (Rom. 6:17), we may add as the hidden contrast the τύπος τῆς διδαχῆς of the congregations in the East.

We apply these general observations also to the account of the development of the primitive Christian faith in Christ, and thus pose the question: What may the attitude of those Gentile Christian communities toward Jesus of Nazareth have been? It certainly appears that we would have to refrain from answering this question because the sources of it are completely lacking to us. For the account of Luke[3] in Acts gives us the most scanty material

---

[3] Heitmüller (p. 331) wishes to adduce for the pre-Pauline Hellenistic Christianity above all the "acknowledged good Hellenist source" of Acts 6, 7, 8, and 11. But the Hellenistic tendency on Palestinian soil is again not to be so simply identified with the Hellenism in Antioch, Tarsus, and Damascus. And the account in Acts 11 does not offer

for Christology, and moreover this material may be used from the pre-Pauline period only with caution. And yet we possess a source, though difficult to us, of the highest authentic value, namely the genuine epistles of the apostle himself. Out of the epistles of Paul we can distill what he presupposed as basic conviction in the Hellenistic congregations, by separating what is his special and personal property. This is of course a difficult task, one which cannot be achieved without a very keen feeling for style and, for many areas of Pauline piety and theology, not at all with certainty.[4] Yet I think that precisely for Christology, standards can be set up for the separation of the elements that have been taken over and those that are personal and individual with Paul.

I. *The Title Kyrios.* Here also we begin with an investigation of the title which Jesus of Nazareth receives in the Pauline letters. Here we at once encounter some observations of fundamental importance. We see that the old titles which have dominated the community's faith in Christ almost completely disappear. In the Pauline era the title "Christ" is about to change from a title into a proper name. To be sure a sensitivity for the titular nature of the term still appears to hold sway in that Paul almost always says Χριστὸς ᾽Ιησοῦς (the Christ-Jesus) and only rarely ᾽Ιησοῦς Χριστός, and that where a second title appears, he places the name "Jesus" in the middle: κύριος ᾽Ιησοῦς Χριστός, υἱὸς (θεοῦ) ᾽Ι. Χρ.[5] But basically the title "Christ" in Paul no longer has an independent life. Of still greater import and significance is the fact that Paul no longer uses the designation "the Son of Man," on which, as we have seen, the dogmatics of the primitive community hinged. That he knew the title appears perhaps from the use of the Son-of-Man psalm κατ᾽ ἐξοχήν (Ps. 8) and its messianic interpretation in I Cor. 15:26, as well as from his speculations about Christ as the second pneumatic man. But he did not use the title, or better said: the title was not taken over from the Hellenistic primitive Christian community,

much for our purposes (with the exception of the one statement about the name Χριστιανοί in 11:26).

[4] Heitmüller (pp. 331-32) has the task more precisely in mind. He suggests that we start out from I Cor. 15 and then particularly from Romans, or more exactly, from what we can conclude from the latter epistle about the spiritual conditions of the Hellenistic Roman community. These are noteworthy counsels. Still, for the present task, in which matters are somewhat simpler, they do not come so much into consideration.

[5] Paul observe these rules throughout all his letters with such regularity and with so few execptions that on the basis of this fact we can frequently make a decision in the case of textual variants.

because in this sphere it had already become incapable of being understood. It is a remarkable drama of an extremely rapid development. Robes and garments which had just been woven around Jesus' figure were taken off again, and new robes and garments were woven. But if we ask the question, which was "the" new title for the person of Jesus in the Pauline epistles, there can be no doubt as to the answer. It is the designation κύριος[6] which holds the dominant position here.

The designation κύριος is in fact something new, for this title is not used, apart from a few exceptions, in the older evangelical literature. Here we meet a fundamental observation with which, because of its importance, we must tarry somewhat longer.

In our more precise investigation we must note at the outset that there is a fundamental distinction between the vocative form κύριε and the full title ὁ κύριος. In the New Testament the address κύριε has already attained a much wider scope. With this title, in addition to God and Christ, other heavenly beings also are addressed,[7] but it is also customary among men, with the servant addressing his lord,[8] the son addressing his father,[9] or a man addressing his superior[10] or any honored person.[11] Only thus can the term ὁ κύριος come into consideration here.

The title ὁ κύριος is found in Mark's Gospel only one single time,[12] namely

---

[6] Here again I am pleased to be in agreement with Heitmüller (p. 333): "This title (Lord) for Jesus Christ may be characteristic for our Hellenistic Christianity and may indeed have arisen in it."

[7] Cf., e.g., Rev. 7:14.

[8] Matt. 13:27; 25:11, 20, 22, 24; Luke 13:8; 14:22; 19:16 ff.

[9] Matt. 21:30; cf. I Pet. 3:6.

[10] Matt. 27:63.

[11] John 11:21; 20:15; Acts 16:30.

[12] In Mark 5:19 ὁ κύριος (on Jesus' lips) is evidently=God. But the pericope Mark 12:35-37 (Christ the Lord of David) also does not belong here. Some have indeed sought to put exceptionally heavy stress upon it (cf. Wernle, "Jesus und Paulus," passim, and on this my statements in Jesus der Herr, pp. 15-16) and said that it shows that the primitive community already gave a messianic interpretation to Ps. 110, and accordingly had to find in this passage the κύριος standing alongside Yahweh (the Lord said to my Lord). Thus the emergence of the title could be accounted for, without remainder, in the Palestinian milieu. I agree with Wernle on the point that actually in this passage we have the theology of the primitive community. But in his presentation of the proof he has forgotten that this community did not read the psalm in the wording of the LXX with the important doubled κύριος, but in the Hebrew (Aramaic) wording. And in this we have the characteristic nuance of Yahweh and Adoni (ne'um Yahweh l'Adoni): Here the title Adoni still has an explicit profane character and not a religious one (cf. I Sam. 24:7, 11: my lord, Yahweh's anointed one). What the pericope is all about is not at all the title ὁ κύριος, but only the demonstration that Jesus is not the son but the lord of David and the latter is his servant. From here to the solemn religious title it is still a long way. Even when it is said in 12:37,

within the rearranging of Jesus' entry into Jerusalem, which as we have shown above (pp. 71 ff.) is secondary: ὁ κύριος αὐτοῦ χρείαν ἔχει (11:3).[13] But the address κύριε is also found only once, and perhaps it is not by chance that it occurs in the mouth of the *Syrian* woman (7:28). In the Logia the title ὁ κύριος is nowhere found.[14] The address κύριε in Luke 6:46: "Why call ye me Lord (=Master) and do not the things that I say?" which is fully explained by the context, has no force of proof at all.[15] Whether the κύριε in Matt. 8:8=Luke 7:6 is to be traced back to the Logia must remain doubtful, since the derivation of the entire pericope (the centurion from Capernaum) from the Logia is disputed.

On the whole the Gospel of Matthew follows the speech usage of its sources. It has ὁ κύριος only in the parallel to Mark 11:3=21:3.[16] On the other hand the address κύριε appears in a series of passages.[17]

Ὁ κύριος is found much more frequently in the Gospel of Luke. And here first the Χριστὸς κύριος in 2:11 calls for a special discussion. Since it is likely that the first two chapters of Luke stem from an Aramaic source,

---

αὐτὸς Δαυεὶδ λέγει αὐτὸν κύριον, and here κύριος apparently stands as an absolute, still one must again keep in mind the fact that we have to do with a translation of an Aramaic wording. And Dalman, *Words of Jesus*, p. 329, asserts correctly that in the original Aramaic text which is to be assumed for this, the "Lord" cannot possibly have stood without a suffix. According to the context of the sentence it must originally have read: "David himself calls him *his* Lord." It is the Greek translation with the doubled ὁ κύριος (εἶπεν ὁ κύριος τῷ κυρίῳ μου)—naturally first on the soil of the Hellenistic community—that first become so uncommonly important for the history of the Kyrios title in the religious sense. Luke and Acts 2:36, καὶ κύριον αὐτὸν καὶ Χριστὸν ἐποίησεν, use the Greek Bible and stand on Hellenistic soil.

[13] In the entire parallel account in Mark 14:12 ff. it is, strangely, ὁ διδάσκαλος λέγει (on this designation, cf. further John 11:28; Mark 5:35=Luke 8:49; Matt. 9:11). Heitmüller (p. 334, 1) prefers not to understand the expression ὁ κύριος in Mark 11:3 "in the technical sacral sense."

[14] Matt. 24:42 ("you know not what day your Lord comes") is not confirmed by Luke 12:40 (the Son of Man). In Mark 13:35 the original imagery of this sentence (the coming of the lord of the house) still shows up clearly.

[15] The expansion of the saying in Matt. 7:21 will be discussed further below. In Matt. 8:21 the second of the disciples who profess to follow Jesus addresses him as κύριε. In the parallel in Luke 9:59 κύριε is found only in a group of mss. (Matt. 8:19 has διδάσκαλε).

[16] There is some uncertainty about the text in Matt. 28:6, ὅπου ἔκειτο ὁ κύριος.

[17] In parallels which Matt. has in common with Mark, 8:2 (=Luke 5:12), Mark lacks an address; 8:25 (Mark διδάσκαλε, Luke ἐπιστάτα); 17:4 (Mark ῥαββεί, Luke ἐπιστάτα—syr. sin. omits the address in Matt.); 17:15 (syr. sin. om. Mark and Luke διδάσκαλε); 20:30, 31 κύριε υἱὸς Δαυείδ (κύριε is lacking in 30: ℵ D vet. lat. syr.; 31: e.—Mark: υἱὸς Δαυείδ); 20:33 (=Luke 18:41; Mark ῥαββουνεί); 26:22 (Mark without an address, Matt. 26:25 ῥαββεί). In addition there are the cases in which Matt. stands alone or has an entirely divergent text: 8:6, 13:51 (mss.); 14:28, 30; 15:22, 25; 18:21; 25:37, 44.

this Χριστὸς κύριος would thus become very significant and could yield a proof that the title was present in the Palestinian primitive community. But precisely when we make the assumption of an Aramaic source, the surmise immediately arises that Χριστὸς κύριος is an incorrect translation of the formula current in the Old Testament, "the anointed of the Lord," משיח יהוה. A similar mistake in translation, or an emendation introduced by a Christian editor, is in all probability found also in the Χριστὸς κύριος in Ps. Sol. 17:32 [18] and certainly in the LXX Lam. 4:20 (Our life's breath, Yahweh's anointed, was seized: LXX πνεῦμα προσώπου ἡμῶν Χριστὸς κύριος συνελήφθη). But in any case Luke himself has inserted the title κύριος in 2:11, and then he uses it more than a dozen times.[19] κύριε is also found more frequently.[20] Thus with Luke the period of the later usage of language begins.

It is further especially characteristic that in the few verses of the inauthentic ending of Mark ὁ κύριος is also found twice (16:19-20). If we then add the fact that in the fragments of the Gospel of the Hebrews[21] and most of all in the Gospel of Peter[22] the use of κύριος gains the predominance, then we have a clear picture of the increasing penetration of the title into the later gospel literature. Especially interesting here is the usage of the Fourth Gospel. Here the address κύριε is of course very common (in some 30 passages); but in the first 19 chapters ὁ κύριος does not occur a single time in the authentic text.[23] Only in the last two chapters is the word found several times,[24] though never in the mouth of the evangelist, but always

---

[18] Ps. Sol. 18.5 has it explicitly *"his* anointed one" (Χριστοῦ αὐτοῦ). The doubled genitive in the superscription of Ps. 18 and in 18:7 (Χριστοῦ κυρίου) naturally is also to be interpreted in this sense. Cf. Kittel *in loc.* in Kautzsch, *Pseudepigraphen*. Böhlig, "Zum Begriff κύριος bei Paulus," ZNW XIV (1913), 26-27, correctly points out that the title κύριος never occurs for the Messiah in the Jewish literature. Though he refers to Test. Benj. 6 as an exception, in my judgment it cannot be shown why the κύριος which occurs here frequently should not be referred to God (cf. 11.2 concerning the Messiah: ἀγαπητὸς κυρίου).

[19] Luke 7:13*; 10:1, 39*, 41*; 11:39; 12:42; 13:15*; 17:5, 6; 18:6; 19:8 (31 and 34= Mark 11:3) [22:31 ℵ A D]; 22:61 (twice); 24:3*, 34 (passages with strongly attested ms. variants are indicated with the *).

[20] Besides the passages already mentioned: Luke 5:8 (cf. Matt. 14:28, 30); 9:54, 61; 10:17, 40; 11:1; 12:41; 13:23; 22:33, 38, 49.

[21] Preuschen, *Antilegomena*, 2nd ed., 1905, pp. 4.24, 35; 6.11, 25; 8.4, 9.

[22] Cf. vss. 2, 3 (twice), 6, 8, 10, 19, 21, 24 (35 κυριακὰ ἡμέρα), 50 (twice), 59, 60. In addition, σωτήρ only in vs. 13, υἱὸς θεοῦ vss. 6, 9, 45-46.

[23] In John 4:1 the text is obviously confused and not even assured in the mss.; ℵ D vet. lat. syr. cu. read Ἰησοῦς; in 6:23 εὐχαριστήσαντος τοῦ κυρίου is lacking in D a e vet. syr.; 6:11 is an awkward gloss, as conceded by many critics. On John 13:13, see below.

[24] John 20:2, 13, 18, 20, 25 (28); 21:7 (twice); 21:12.

in the conversation of the disciples speaking of Jesus. The fact that the *Johannine epistles also are not acquainted with the title* proves that this complete absence—apart from the last two chapters[25]—is no accident. An explanation of this state of things will be attempted below.

One will not be able to oppose these observations with the argument that the preaching of the κύριος ᾿Ιησοῦς in the Palestinian primitive community is attested in the book of Acts in many passages, as for example Peter summarizes his first sermon with the words: ἀσφαλῶς οὖν γινωσκέτω πᾶς οἶκος ᾿Ισραήλ, ὅτι καὶ κύριον αὐτὸν καὶ Χριστὸν ἐποίησεν ὁ θεός (2:36). However one may evaluate the book of Acts, it may be taken as assured that its testimony cannot match the plain facts within the gospel tradition. Above all, the speeches in Acts are compositions of "Luke," in which he perhaps may have used this or that ancient element of the tradition, and also perhaps may have artificially read something into the attitude of the primitive community—but not any sort of authentic documents. The use of κύριος in Acts is accordingly to be judged in the same terms as is the penetration of the κύριος title into the Gospel. Indeed, it even appears likely that the occurrence of the title κύριος in the first half of Acts can be used as a means for precisely distinguishing the reworking done by Luke from the older sources which he used.[26]

Some have maintained that these observations still actually can prove nothing.[27] Since the title κύριος first occurred after the exaltation of Jesus, its use in the Gospels cannot at all be expected. In the early times people still were aware that κύριος is a predicate of the exalted One and not of the historical Jesus. Just as our Gospels never tell of ὁ Χριστός, ὁ υἱὸς τοῦ ἀνθρώπου, so also they avoided, with a certain historical fidelity, the title ὁ κύριος. Its absence in the gospel literature therefore would not indicate that it was still absent from the community's usage. Here however perceivable differences are present. Even those (later) gospel sources (the Gospel of Luke, of the Hebrews, of Peter; the inauthentic ending of Mark) which introduce the title κύριος without hesitation hold fast to the rule that

---

[25] One could be tempted, on the basis of these observations, to assume in chap. 20 a redactional reworking, through which the title has entered here for the first time. Perhaps the parts in 20:2-10, 18, 20, 24-29 belong first to a reworking of the Gospel, and precisely here are found the κύριος passages (exception in 20:13). Chap. 21, as an appended chapter, does not come into consideration.

[26] Cf. Bousset, "Der Gebrauch des Kyriostitels als Kriterium für die Quellenscheidung in der ersten Hälfte der Apostelgeschichte," ZNW XV (1914), 141-62.

[27] Cf. Wernle, *Jesus und Paulus*, pp. 20 ff., and Althaus, "Unser Herr Jesus," *Neue kirchliche Zeitschrift* XXVI, (1915), 455 (p. 17 in the separate ed.).

in the narrative they *never* speak of ὁ Χριστός, ὁ υἰὸς τοῦ ἀνθρώπου, but always only of ὁ Ἰησοῦς. Conversely we never find ὁ κύριος (with the exception of Mark 11:3; on this, *vide supra*) as a self-designation of Jesus, while the designation ὁ υἰὸς τοῦ ἀνθρώπου (here and there also ὁ Χριστός) in this way has entered into the gospel literature as a mysterious proleptic self-revelation of Jesus. The reason for this lies deeper. The community which handed down the Gospels did not avoid the honorific descriptions of Jesus as Χριστός and υἰὸς τοῦ ἀνθρώπου for reasons of historical fidelity, but because they had the lively conviction that these titles had specifically eschatological meaning and quite properly applied only to the future one, to the one who would appear in glory. In the specifically eschatological designation of Jesus as the υἰὸς τοῦ ἀνθρώπου this perception was of decisive force. But this hindrance was absent in the case of the title κύριος, since from the very beginning this title had no actual eschatological significance, but rather first of all described the present Lord of the community. Therefore no other word could so easily take its place in the gospel literature alongside the simple "Jesus." And thus conversely, in my judgment, the conclusion remains compelling that the absence of this title in the older Palestinian gospel narrative points to its absence from the usage of the community. And we may expect that in the opposite case at least one would have to be able to demonstrate the title κύριος more often in the mouth of Jesus as a self-designation.

The entire study finally also acquires a strong confirmation from a linguistic consideration. We must ask the question: Presupposing that the title κύριος can be traced back to the Palestinian primitive community, what then was its original meaning, and what was the corresponding Aramaic word? Here the investigators who attempt to keep the κύριος in the Palestinian milieu come to the parting of the ways. Some[28] assume that the designation of Jesus originally had its roots in the term Mar (more precisely Mari, Maran)＝teacher, rabbi; and that then out of this simple title of the rabbi the solemn and religious designation of Jesus as the Lord of his community could have been shaped. Against this attempt it may first be pointed out that, even if it were valid, the actual problem would not be solved, namely how the specifically religious significance of κύριος for Paul and the Pauline communities could have been formed out of the inoffensive

---

[28] Esp. Dalman, *Words of Jesus,* pp. 324 ff. (cf. also pp. 179 ff.). By and large, Althaus, "Unser Herr Jesus," p. 532 (p. 38), follows him; against him, cf. my statements in *Jesus der Herr,* p. 17.

title Mar=rabbi. But apart from that a series of reservations may be raised against the correctness of this derivation. First, it is not proved that the title Mar=rabbi, which certainly was current in the later Talmudic Judaism,[29] was already customary in the time of Jesus. It is strikingly absent in Jesus' discussion of the passion for titles in Matt. 23:6, where we evidently have an enumeration of honorary titles (rabbi, abba)[30] customary at that time. Further, if Jesus had actually used the title κύριος, it would remain utterly incomprehensible that the simplest and most obvious translation κύριος is not actually found more frequently alongside ῥαββί, διδάσκαλος (ἐπιστάτης) in the oldest gospel literature. Finally, it may be objected that in Aramaic usage the simple Mara (מרא) without a suffix is quite unusual, and only the form Mari or Maran (my lord, our lord) is found.[31] But in the later gospel literature, with the exception of John 20:13, 28, there are always found the absolute ὁ κύριος and the absolute vocative κύριε.

This derivation, then, must be rejected,[32] and here also one cannot appeal to the nevertheless noteworthy passage in John 13:13-14: ὑμεῖς φωνεῖτέ με· ὁ διδάσκαλος καὶ ὁ κύριος, καὶ καλῶς λέγετε. For the source of this Johannine logion can be demonstrated with certainty. It stems from the Synoptic saying which is immediately afterward cited (13:16) and which we find again in Matt. 10:24: οὐκ ἔστιν μαθητὴς ὑπὲρ τὸν διδάσκαλον οὐδὲ δοῦλος ὑπὲρ τὸν κύριον αὐτοῦ. From here the author of the Fourth Gospel has borrowed the title which he otherwise avoids. But conversely, the synpotic saying is evidence that for the older usage the designations διδάσκαλος (its opposite μαθητής) and κύριος (its opposite δοῦλος) are not synonyms.

It is still less possible to understand the designation κύριος in the religious sense and thus as a transferral of a divine title to Jesus. Wernle (p. 20) simply refers to the "Mar" of Daniel 2:47 and 5:23. But he has not noticed

[29] Concerning King Jehoshaphat, for example, it is reported in the Babylonian Talmud Maccoth 24a, Kethuboth 103b, that he greeted every learned man with "Rabbi, rabbi, mari, mari." Dalman, p. 325.

[30] On the title "Abba," see Dalman, pp. 339-40. The Καθηγητής which stands in third place is of course pure Greek; ibid., p. 340.

[31] Dalman, pp. 326, 339. In the case of the title "rabbi," of course, the sense of the suffix has been completely lost, as the translation with διδάσκαλος or ἐπιστάτης shows. Dalman, p. 335. But this does not mean that the same must have been the case also with the modern "Mari."

[32] Even Dalman, p. 328, takes this path only hesitantly and must assume that the Lucan ὁ κύριος must have been used in the form "Maran," in order to correspond to the character of the Aramaic language.

that there the absolute title Mar, or Mara, is not present at all, but rather God is described as the Lord of the kings, Lord of heaven. And the observation which we could make with reference to the passages in Daniel may be generalized. On the basis of the most thoroughgoing research, Dalman (pp. 179-80) judges: "The significant transition from the divine name 'Jahve' to the divine name 'Lord' did not take place in the region of Hebraic Judaism. It is rather a peculiarity of Jewish Hellenism, and from that source found its way into the language of the Church, even of the Semitic-speaking part of it. For מריא in the Syriac of Edessa and for מרא in the Christian Palestinian there is no Jewish parallel." Even the replacement of the name of Yahweh in the public reading of the holy scriptures with Adonai, which after all for its own part is always taken as a personal name, not a title, is (according to Dalman)[33] indeed to be assumed for the age of Jesus, but it had not passed into the usage of everyday life. Here people rather replaced the name of God in their quotations of scripture with השם, while among the Samaritans it was the custom always to replace the name of God with שמא, even in public scripture reading. In spite of all that, it still is not ruled out that God could sometimes be described in Jewish literature as the "Lord" of someone. Yet the instances are rare (*vide supra* the Daniel passages and Dalman, pp. 180-81). But from this to the title "the Lord" is a long way.

Thus if the "significant" transition to the divine name "the Lord" first took place on Greek soil (under the influence of the LXX), it is all the more proved that ὁ κύριος in the religious sense for Jesus is conceivable only on the soil of the Hellenistic communities.

For this should be emphasized once more. What is involved in Christian usage in general is the absolute ὁ κύριος. Not only, as has already been emphasized above, in the gospel literature (and Acts), so far as the title has made its way into these, but also in Paul, who comes into consideration here especially because with him now ὁ κύριος undoubtedly has a religious significance. Paul without exception uses—and here we possess extensive

---

[33] I should still regard even this as questionable. The note in the Mishna (Tamid VII, 2, Sota VII, 6) to the effect that in the temple one utters the name of God as it is written, but in the provinces (thus in the synagogues) by a substituted word, appears indeed to presuppose the substitution of the name Adonai already for the time of the temple; but whether we may go back into the *time of Jesus* with the custom remains doubtful. Geiger, *Nachgelassene Schriften*, III, 261, judges that the above-mentioned Samaritan custom was also the originally Jewish usage, and that only later did people introduce the substitute formula Adonai in imitation of the Hellenistic κύριος. This of course cannot be proven (Dalman, p. 182), but can serve as a likely conjecture.

evidence—κύριος standing alone without μοῦ or ἡμῶν.[34] If with him in this connection the formula ὁ κύριος ἡμῶν Ἰησοῦς Χριστός is likewise stereotyped,[35] in this apparently liturgically stylized usage probably only reasons of euphony are involved. How precisely things are measured here following the laws of euphony is shown in the complex formulas ἀπὸ θεοῦ πατρὸς ἡμῶν καὶ κυρίου (without ἡμῶν) Ἰησοῦ Χριστοῦ (thus almost always in Paul) or ἀπὸ θεοῦ πατρὸς καὶ Χριστοῦ Ἰησοῦ τοῦ κυρίου ἡμῶν (in the Pastorals). I consider extremely significant the observation that Paul for his own part, where he is not influenced by liturgical usage, always prefers the absolute ὁ κύριος. If a "Maran" or "Mari" had been put in his mind and memory by the primitive community, why then does he never say ὁ κύριος ἡμῶν or ὁ κύριός μου?

There remains as the only counter-instance the formula Maranatha, with which Paul is already acquainted in I Cor. 16:22. It then emerges again in the Lord's Supper prayer in Didache 10 beside an ἀμήν and its Greek equivalent probably is present in Rev. 22:20, ἀμήν, ἔρχου κύριε Ἰησοῦ. Here to be sure we have to do with an old cultic formula. But still the possibility cannot be dismissed that the Maranatha formula could have developed not on the soil of the Palestinian primitive community but in the bilingual region of the Hellenistic communities of Antioch, Damascus, and even Tarsus.[36] And since the Maranatha remains as the only counter-instance against all the propositions that have been set forth, one will have to reckon seriously with this possibility.[37]

II. *The Cultic Significance of the Kyrios Title.* Now it follows that the bestowal upon Jesus of the name ὁ κύριος involves not only a new title. With the word a new fact, a new unique relationship of the community to its κύριος is given. This must first appear in more thoroughgoing investigation of the original meaning of the designation. And here will be involved the difficult task first of all to disregard all the expressions in which Paul

---

[34] On this and the following, cf. the more precise demonstration in my *Jesus der Herr*, pp. 20-21.

[35] With the formula ὁ κύριος Ἰησοῦς (ἡμῶν) the usage varies.

[36] In my *Jesus der Herr* (p. 22) I considered whether Maranatha could not have been a formula of confirmation and oath-taking with reference to God which has nothing to do with the Jesus cult. In view of the Greek parallel formula in Rev. 22:20 and the above-emphasized rare designation of God with Maran in the Palestinian milieu of the earlier period I prefer not to hold to the suggestion.

[37] Althaus, p. 23, also concedes this possibility as such and points out that precisely in Tarsus the divine name Mar is found alongside that of Baal.

represents his individual relation to the κύριος, most of all the formula ἐν κυρίῳ (εἶναι), which will later appear more clearly as a purely personal bit of property, and to discover those utterances in which the apostle gives expression to the common Christian consciousness.

Paul once characterizes the Christians as οἱ ἐπικαλούμενοι τὸ ὄνομα τοῦ κυρίου ἡμῶν ʼΙ. Χρ. (I Cor. 1:2).[38] What we have here is no personal confession; the apostle is speaking rather of an objective state of affairs. This is the distinctive mark of the Christians in general, that they call on the name of the Lord. And what is involved here is not the personal relation of an individual to the exalted Christ, but the community which in its worship does this invoking of the name. Most of all, as will be more precisely shown in the course of the investigation, the stress upon the name points to the common *cultus* of the Christians. Indeed in this periphrase for those who belong to the community of Christians it appears anyway that we have a formula widely used and not first coined by Paul. It is found also in Rom. 10:13, II Tim. 2:22, and in characteristic connections in Acts 9:14, 21; 22:16. This name has already been established in the age of Paul in such a way that people altogether without embarrassment applied to the Christian community[39] the well-known passage in Joel: "Whoever calls on the name of the Lord [Yahweh!] will be saved" (3:5). Immediately before quoting that passage, Paul says "The same Lord over all is rich unto all who call upon him" (Rom. 10:12). For him it is self-evident that the κύριος in this context is the Lord Christ.

Now we shall attempt to gain from Paul an understanding as to wherein this ἐπικαλεῖσθαι τὸ ὄνομα κυρίου took place and how this relationship of Jesus as Lord to the community is presented.

Already in Paul's time confession and baptism stood at the beginning of the Christian life. Paul explicitly tells us that the Christian confession is summarized in the confession of the κύριος ʼΙησοῦς: "If thou shalt confess with thy mouth the Lord Jesus and shalt believe in thy heart that God hath raised him from the dead" (Rom. 10:9).

Moreover it is well known that baptism in the Pauline age was a baptism in the name of the Lord Jesus. One can read this between the lines in I

---

[38] In his commentary on the Corinthian epistle, J. Weiss prefers to deny this expression to the apostle. I cannot find the reasons given for this compelling. The difficulty which is actually involved in the ἐν παντὶ τόπῳ αὐτῶν καὶ ἡμῶν can perhaps be eliminated by striking out the καὶ ἡμῶν (with A 77: a liturgical addition with which the liturgist related the apostolic greeting to his own community).

[39] Rom. 10:13; Acts 2:21.

Cor. 1:13 (ἢ εἰς τὸ ὄνομα Παύλου ἐβαπτίσθητε). The apostle says it explicitly in I Cor. 6:11: ἀλλὰ ἀπελούσασθε, ἀλλὰ ἡγιάσθητε, ἀλλὰ ἐδικαιώθητε[40] ἐν τῷ ὀνόματι τοῦ κυρίου 'Ι. Χρ. καὶ ἐν τῷ πνεύματι τοῦ θεοῦ ἡμῶν.[41] The washing in the baptism of Christians takes place for him in the calling on[42] the name of the *Lord* Jesus. Once again the cultic element, which lies immediately present in the stress upon the name, emerges. The book of Acts confirms this interpretation of the Pauline passage: ἀναστὰς βάπτισαι καὶ ἀπόλουσαι τὰς ἁμαρτίας σου ἐπικαλεσάμενος τὸ ὄνομα αὐτοῦ.[43] The author of the Epistle of James speaks of "the good name which is invoked over you" (2:7).

Upon baptism the Christian enters into the life of worship. He may participate in the sacred meal of the Christians. And this meal is already in Paul's writings a δεῖπνον κυριακόν (I Cor. 11:20), it is a participation at the τράπεζα κυρίου (I Cor. 10:21).[44] Jesus is the κύριος about whom as host, and we might even say as cultic hero, the community is gathered in its common meal, just as the followers of the Egyptian Serapis come to the table of the Lord Serapis (*vide infra,* pp. 142-43). Indeed, still more, the Supper is κοινωνία τοῦ αἵματος καὶ τοῦ σώματος τοῦ Χριστοῦ, i.e., a fellowship with the body and blood of the (exalted, experienced-as-present) Lord which, communicated through food, is not purely spiritual, but even has an effect in the body, and yet again is also a spiritual fellowship.[45]

And again, Christian worship is determined and characterized by the invoking of the name of the Lord Jesus. From the development in later times we may judge that the formulated, solemn community prayer of Christian worship in general was still addressed to God,[46] that here at least under the influence of the Jewish liturgy and of the Lord's Prayer the boundary between God and Christ was observed. Paul testifies to us of a

[40] ἡγιάσθητε (ye are sanctified) and ἐδικαιώθητε (ye are justified) are, along with ἀπελούσασθε, parallel expressions for the grace which the Christians received in baptism. On ἐδικαιώθητε, cf. Reitzenstein, *Hellenistische Mysterienreligionen,* pp. 100 ff. [2nd ed., pp. 112 ff.].

[41] ὄνομα and πνεῦμα are the two effective factors in the sacrament of baptism.

[42] Heitmüller, *Im Namen Jesu,* pp. 88 ff. I Cor. 1:13 and the symbolism of Rom. 6 show that, in addition to the formula ἐν ὀνόματι, Paul also was acquainted with the other εἰς τὸ ὄνομα.

[43] Acts 22:16; cf. (2:38); 8:16; (10:43); 19:5.

[44] With the expression τράπεζα κυρίου, cf. LXX Mal. 1:7, 12 (Mal. 1:7-12 is moreover, as is well known, later the classic prophetic passage for the eucharist).

[45] Heitmüller, *Taufe und Abendmahl bei Paulus* (1903), pp. 23 ff.

[46] Community prayer to Jesus probably in Acts 1:24 (σὺ κύριε καρδιογνῶστα) in a matter which esp. concerned the Lord.

personal prayer to the Lord; he has prayed to him for deliverance from his sickness: ὑπὲρ τούτου τρὶς τὸν κύριον[47] παρεκάλεσα (II Cor. 12:8). But it is still worthy of note that here he does not use one of the technical words (προσεύχεσθαι, δεῖσθαι), but rather παρακαλεῖν: he has exhorted the Lord, as he exhorts his congregation. On the other hand, in the Pauline age the custom of prayer in the name of Jesus must already have appeared. The brief allusion in II Cor. 1:20, διὸ καὶ δι' αὐτοῦ τὸ ἀμὴν τῷ θεῷ πρὸς δόξαν δι' ἡμῶν, points to the fact that the doxology connected with the Amen at the close of the prayer was somehow connected with a naming of the name of Jesus. In this context a passage in Colossians is particularly instructive: "The word of Christ is to dwell in you richly; in all wisdom you are to teach and admonish each other; with psalms, hymns and spiritual songs sing in your hearts to God in thankfulness; and *all that you do in word or in deed, do it all in the name of the Lord Jesus*, giving thanks to God the Father through him." [48] We clearly see how in this admonition: "Do all that you do in the name of the Lord Jesus," Paul is thinking essentially about what goes on in the worship life of the Christians. The proceedings received their special Christian character, according to Paul, through the invocation of the name. And not only the special prayer is made in the name of Jesus, but also the exhortation and preaching in worship. The preachers, the inspired prophets, are conscious of speaking in the name of the Lord,[49] and they give expression to it: διὸ παρακαλεῖτε ἀλλήλους καὶ οἰκοδομεῖτε εἰς τὸν ἕνα (I Thess. 5:11).

The formulated and detailed Christian community prayer was, as stated, probably from the first addressed to God (in the name of Jesus Christ). But alongside this we rightly have to think, in connection with ἐπικαλεῖσθαι τὸ ὄνομα τοῦ κυρίου, of brief outcries of prayer, sighs of the oppressed and overflowing heart which in worship were addressed directly to Jesus. To

---

[47] κύριος is in Paul (apart from Old Testament quotations) almost always to be referred to Christ. Cf. the prayer of Stephen in Acts 7:59: κύριε 'Ιησοῦ δέξαι τὸ πνεῦμά μου.

[48] Col. 3:16-17; cf. the parallel passage in Eph. 5:20.

[49] The formulas in Paul stem from the Christian worship: εὐχαριστῶ . . . διὰ 'Ιησοῦ Χριστοῦ, Rom. 1:8. χάρις τῷ θεῷ διὰ 'Ιησοῦ Χριστοῦ τοῦ κυρίου ἡμῶν, Rom. 7:25 (Eph. 5:20); I Cor. 15:57. καυχᾶσθαι διὰ τοῦ κυρίου ἡμῶν 'Ιησοῦ Χριστοῦ, Rom. 5:11. Cf. 15:17; Phil. 3:3; II Cor. 10:17; I Cor. 1:31. παρακαλῶ ὑμᾶς διὰ τοῦ ὀνόματος (note the stress upon ὄνομα) τοῦ κυρίου ἡμῶν 'Ιησοῦ Χριστοῦ, I Cor. 1:10; cf. Rom. 15:30; II Cor. 10:1. ἐν Χριστῷ λαλοῦμεν, II Cor. 2:17; 12:19; Rom. 9:1. ἀσπάζεσθαι ἐν κυρίῳ, I Cor. 16:19; Rom. 16:22.

this category belongs the already discussed formula Maranatha (our Lord, come). The eschatological outlook of the primitive community, the yearning for the Lord who is to come, forcibly set precedents in such ecstatic cries. The not altogether clear statements of Paul in I Cor. 12:1-3 presuppose that in the Corinthian community the cry κύριος Ἰησοῦς was a sign and identifying mark of the ecstatic discourses of the prophets in rapture. "No one can (in rapture) say κύριος Ἰησοῦς except by the *Holy* Spirit." [50]

A particularly distinctive example of the invoking of the name of the Lord is given to us by Paul in the letter to the Corinthians on the occasion of the advice which he offers the Corinthians in the case of the incestuous person (I Cor. 5:4-5). The congregation—so the apostle advises—in solemn assembly is to deliver this man to Satan, i.e., to bring about his death by means of prayer. But they are to do this ἐν τῷ ὀνόματι τοῦ κυρίου Ἰησοῦ, συναχθέντων ὑμῶν καὶ τοῦ ἐμοῦ πνεύματος σὺν τῇ δυνάμει τοῦ κυρίου ἡμῶν Ἰησοῦ. In the solemn assembly of the Christians the *name* of the Lord Jesus is to be invoked, the *power* of the Lord Jesus is to be present. The name of the Lord is the powerful instrument of the cult through which the presence of his power is guaranteed. Thus the name of Jesus governs the miracle in Christian worship.

One feature which certainly must have played a large role in the Pauline age, though of course we search for it in vain in Paul, is exorcism in Jesus' name. Here the examples from the earlier Christian literature are so abundant and so clear that on this point we may indeed supplement the picture gained from Paul. The Gospel of Mark already knows of exorcism in Jesus' name in that interesting pericope, which we could not accept as historical, of the man who is driving out demons in Jesus' name, without believing on him (9:38-39). Matthew, in his editing of the Sermon on the Mount (7:22) knows of wandering prophets who in the name of the Lord prophesy, drive out demons, and perform many wonders (δυνάμεις). In the false ending of Mark Jesus promises his believers that "in his name" they are to drive out demons, speak with new tongues (languages), be protected against snakebite and poison, and heal the sick by laying hands on them (16:17-18). Characteristic also is the story in Acts of the sons of Sceva

---

[50] This calling on the name of the Lord in worship has already entered into Jesus' language in Matt. 7:21. The folly, opposed here, of assuming that one might enter into heaven by means of his saying "Lord, Lord," naturally takes on meaning only when we think of the calling upon the name of Jesus in worship, in the cultus. The authentic and simple word of Jesus in Luke 6:46 has been liturgically stylized here.

who began (certainly in imitation of the Christian community's custom) to drive out demons in the name of the Jesus whom Paul proclaimed (19:13). In view of this it presumably is only accidental [51] that in his epistles Paul passes over these instances of exorcism, if he did not actually intend them in his mention of the ἐνεργήματα δυνάμεων beside the χαρίσματα ἰαμάτων (I Cor. 12:9-10).

In all these events, the miracle and the expulsion of demons in Jesus' name, we again have to do in the first place with the Christian cult and the structuring of worship. To be sure they also play their great role in the private life of the Christians, but the assembly of the Christian community represents their chief locus. In the fellowship the Christians perform the mightiest wonders in the name and in the power of the Lord Jesus. And these wonders again characterize the worship of the first Christians. The portrayal of that worship by Paul in I Cor. 12:9 [52] can leave no doubt at all on that score.

What the κύριος signified for the first Hellenistic Christian congregations thus stands before us in bright and living colors. It is the Lord who holds sway over the Christian life of fellowship, in particular as it is unfolded in the community's worship, thus in the cultus. Around the κύριος the community is gathered in believing reverence, it confesses his name, under the invocation of his name it baptizes, it assembles around the table of the Lord Jesus; it sighs in the fervent cry "Maranatha, come, Lord Jesus"; to the Lord, we can further add, already now the first day of the week is dedicated, and very soon people begin to identify it as κυριακὴ ἡμέρα; under the invocation of his name people perform miracles and drive the demons out! Thus the community is gathered as a σῶμα around the κύριος as its head, to whom it pays veneration in the cultus. Where Paul speaks of the Christian community as a σῶμα whose κεφαλή is Christ, this community gathered for worship [53] is always in view for him. He thinks of it

---

[51] But perhaps the conjecture is here suggested that Paul may have been deliberately rejecting these lower, all-too-popular naïve views.

[52] Cf. also the juxtaposition of prophecy, exorcism, and the working of miracles in Matt. 7:22; exorcism and speaking in tongues in Mark 16:17.

[53] I Cor. 12. (Cf. esp. the expression in 12:13, εἰς ἓν σῶμα ἐβαπτίσθημεν). In I Cor. 10:17, ὅτι εἷς ἄρτος, ἓν σῶμα οἱ πολλοί ἐσμεν is thought of altogether in a cultic sense. Rom. 12:5-8 (note how here the whole portrayal acquires a definite context when one interprets it from the standpoint of the Christian community's worship, esp. the conclusion, ὁ μεταδιδοὺς ἐν ἁπλότητι, ὁ προϊστάμενος ἐν σπουδῇ, ὁ ἐλεῶν ἐν ἱλαρότητι. In the first and third phrases, the gifts of Christian brotherly love at the time of worship are in the author's mind). Also in the following verses, Rom. 12:9-13, the special consideration

first of all when he speaks of the οἰκοδομή, the ναός of God,[54] when he poses the οἰκοδομή[55] as the obligation and as the goal of the believers.

And this is only natural enough. For here in the gatherings of the fellowship, in worship and cult, there grew up for the believers in Christ the consciousness of their unity and peculiar sociological exclusiveness. During the day scattered, in the vocations of everyday life, in solitariness, within an alien world abandoned to scorn and contempt, they came together in the evening, probably as often as possible, for the common sacred meal. There they experienced the miracle of fellowship, the glow of the enthusiasm of a common faith and a common hope; there the spirit blazed high, and a world full of wonders surrounded them; prophets and those who speak in tongues, visionaries and ecstatic persons begin to speak; psalms, hymns, and spiritual songs sound through the room, the powers of brotherly kindness come alive in unexpected fashion; an unprecedented new life pulses through the throng of the Christians. And over this whole swaying sea of inspiration reigns the Lord Jesus as the head of his community, with his power immediately present in breathtaking palpable presence and certainty. This cultic veneration of Jesus in worship Paul summarizes in the great bold words (Phil. 2:9 ff.): "Wherefore God has also highly exalted him and has given to him *the name above all names,* to the end that at the name of Jesus[56] every knee should bow, of celestial and terrestrial and sub-terrestrial beings, and every tongue should confess that *Jesus Christ is Lord,* to the

---

of the Christians' worship echoes again and again. When Paul says of the Corinthian community, ἐπλουτίσθητε ἐν αὐτῷ (I Cor. 1:5), he is thinking there quite essentially of their worship. In what follows he speaks of the λόγος and of the Gnosis which receives this Logos, of the μαρτύριον Χριστοῦ, which has taken firm root among the Christians, and of the χαρίσματα. Cf. Col. 2:19; Eph. 4:5 (εἷς κύριος, μία πίστις, ἐν βάπτισμα, see below, Chap. VII); 4:11-16.

[54] I Cor. 3:9; I Cor. 3:16-17; II Cor. 6:16.

[55] The connection with worship is quite clear in I Cor. 14:3, 5, 12, 26 (14:4, 17), perhaps also in II Cor. 10:8; 13:10. Cf. Eph. 4:12 (οἰκοδομὴ τοῦ σώματος τοῦ Χριστοῦ); in 4:16 the ἐπιχορηγία κατ' ἐνέργειαν ἐν μέτρῳ ἑνὸς ἑκάστου μέρους—through which the αὔξησις τοῦ σώματος ποιεῖται εἰς οἰκοδομήν (from Christ)—is connected with the gifts of the Spirit which are effective in the worship. From this perspective then Col. 2:19 with its somewhat more colorless expressions also is illumined.

[56] Here the προσκύνησις of Jesus is already indicated. It is no accident that the προσκυνεῖν still is not found in the earlier gospel literature. In the Gospel of Mark only one time, in 5:6 (the demon-possessed man from Gadara [Gerasa] in Gentile territory); here Luke 8:28 also has προσπίπτειν; Mark 15:19 does not come into consideration. But the Gospel of Matthew already uses the word προσκυνεῖν ten times! The formulas which are found in Mark, προσπίπτειν, πίπτειν πρὸς τοὺς πόδας, γονυπετεῖν, are of a more indefinite kind and do not go as far as προσκυνεῖν. For more detailed discussion, cf. particularly Chap. VII.

glory of God the Father." This is once more an illumination of the state of things of fundamental importance. The sacred cult-name of Yahweh, which holds sway over the cult in Jerusalem, here appears to be transferred to the new Kyrios, and the solemn confession of Deutero-Isaiah (45:23) to the omnipotent God is directed to Jesus.

All this is incorporated in the title "Kyrios." It is of eminently practical significance; it characterizes the new veneration of Jesus in Christian worship; the name Kyrios and the cult of Christ belong immediately together. In almost all the expressions which bear witness to the cult of Christ in the first communities we encounter at the same time the κύριος title.[57]

But then at the same time it is clear that we were correct in seeing in the interpretation of Jesus as the Kyrios of the community, not the special work of the apostle, but the basic conviction of the Christian community which is simply repeated by him. Here we have to do not at all with a notion, an idea which is thought up and then propagated by one individual, but rather with something that lies much deeper, with a conviction which stems from the immediacy of the religious feeling. The correlate to the κύριος Χριστός is, in all the enumerated expressions of primitive Christian piety, not the individual but the community, the ἐκκλησία, the σῶμα τοῦ Χριστοῦ, and in fact first of all the particular community organized for worship. What we have here has erupted from the depths of a community consciousness which is formed and comes to expression in the common cultus. It is not the personal deed of an individual but the instinctive will of the group which is expressed in the κύριος Ἰησοῦς.

It is, in fact, the *Hellenistic* community in which this development so important for the history of religions took place, through which, out of the future Messiah Jesus, the present cult-hero as Kyrios of his community came into being. Here first of all with the new title a new set of facts is given. Some of course have vigorously disputed this and have thought that at least the fact of the living and present cultic connection of the community to the exalted Lord was already present in the Palestinian primitive

---

[57] So far as I can see, it is the merit of Deissmann to have been the first to point out emphatically that the Christology of primitive Christianity and of the early church must be comprehended from the standpoint of the Christ cult; cf. his coherent statements in his *Light from the Ancient East*, pp. 386 ff. The connections between κύριος veneration and Christ veneration were well stated in J. Weiss, *Christus* (RV I, 18, 19), pp. 24-25. Only, this κύριος veneration may not be transferred back, as Weiss seeks to do, into Palestinian primitive Christianity with a reference to the Aramaic formula "maranatha." Against Weiss, see also Böhlig, "Zum Begriff κύριος bei Paulus," ZNW (1913), 28.

community. Wernle lent expression to this contravention with especial agitation (p. 55): "How could we seriously believe the legend of the Christ sitting at the right hand of God in inactivity and without contact with his community!"

Now it is not to be denied that certain beginnings toward this development were already present in the Jerusalem community. Among these in the first place is the exorcism in Jesus' name—although this practice is reported strangely enough in the earlier sources of just those circles which did not belong to the legitimate community and were regarded by the latter as doubtful (*vide supra*, p. 80; Mark 9:38; Matt. 7:22; Acts 19:14-15; and the figure of the Jacob from Kephar Zephaniah who is frequently mentioned in the rabbinical tradition). But still, we probably may assume that the word of the returning disciples, τὰ δαιμόνια ὑποτάσσεται ἡμῖν ἐν τῷ ὀνόματί σου, though of course it first emerges in Luke 10:17,[58] nevertheless echoes an experience which the primitive community already had had. And with the exorcism in Jesus' name there is given a certain presence of his ὄνομα and a certain cultic association.

We would advance still further if we could, without any further ado, transpose back into the primitive community the sacred actions, baptism and the Supper, in the form in which we encounter them in Paul or in the Pauline communities. But here of course we are treading on most uncertain ground. As concerns the sacrament of baptism, in another place[59] I have developed the reasons on the basis of which I am inclined to assume that it first emerged in Hellenistic soil. And even if one wished to assume that a custom of baptism—in conjunction with the community of the Baptist—had existed in the community of Jesus' disciples from the very beginning, it still remains quite doubtful as to when and where the specifically Christian custom of baptism "in the name of Jesus" developed. That Paul received Christian baptism is, to be sure, an assured starting point; but whether any weight is to be put upon the details in the account in Acts must remain doubtful, in view of the specifically legendary character of that account.

As concerns the Supper, only this much seems to me to be assured: that the disciples of Jesus from the first possessed a solemn common meal, "the breaking of bread." We cannot even decide when and where an Anamnesis of Jesus' last meal with his disciples (which cannot originally have had the

---

[58] One should note that in the important logion in Mark 9:29 nothing is said about an exorcism in Jesus' name.

[59] Cf. Bousset, "Der Gebrauch des Kyriostitels" (see above, p. 125), pp. 155-56.

meaning of a fixed institution) was somehow connected to this common meal. The eucharistic celebration of the Didache still does not show, except perhaps in the brief liturgical formulas appearing at the end of chap. 10, any trace of such expansion of the original celebration of the meal. In any case we can definitely deny that this common meal in the primitive community has acquired the meaning of a κοινωνία with the exalted Lord or with the body and blood of the exalted Lord and thus has taken on the specific character of the Pauline κυριακὸν δεῖπνον. Thus we must reject the attempt to gain, with utterly uncertain inferences from the status of baptism and the Supper in the Pauline communities, some evidence for the living communion of the primitive community with the exalted Lord. There remains as a somewhat assured fact only the exorcism in Jesus' name.

III. *The Religio-Historical Source of the Title.* Consequently we must now pose the question whether there are not analogies to be found in the history of religions to the Christ cult and the Kyrios name, by which each could explain the other or at least could shed some light.

For a long time already the analogy which the Kyrios cult of the Christians possesses in the Roman cult of the Caesars has been pointed out. In the cult of the Caesars the Romans took possession of the inheritance of the Orient.[60] The Orientals' sense of the profound distinction between ruler and subject created this cult; in Egypt from most ancient times there was an active belief that the king was the son or the incarnation of the highest deity; Persian religion disseminated the idea that the king was in possession of the divine celestial fire (Hvarenô) which gave and assured victory and lordship to him. All these motifs are then blended by Alexander the Great and his successors with others of Greek origin. In Egypt the Ptolemies developed an entire system of veneration of the rulers, so that the series of the gods to be venerated began with Alexander and ended with the current sovereign and his wife-sister. The Seleucid rulers were not backward in claiming veneration as divine. When then, after the irrepressible disorders which had afflicted the Orient in the last centuries, the powerful figures of the Roman generals and imperators appeared in the East, when Caesar and then especially Augustus again shaped an ordered world out of the

[60] On the general statements, cf. Wendland, *Hellenistisch-römische Kultur*, 2nd ed., pp. 123 ff., 142 ff., 149 ff. and the literature indicated there; Harnack, *Dogmengeschichte*, 4th ed., I, 137.1; Wilamowitz-Moellendorff, *Geschichte der griechischen Religion*, Jahrbuch des freien deutschen Hochstifts, 1904; Deissmann, *Light from the Ancient East*, pp. 338 ff.

seething chaos of the οἰκουμένη, and golden peace, happiness, and prosperity settled upon the peoples of the earth with the Roman *imperium*—then the Orient devoted its ardent religious reverence to the Roman rulers. And Byzantinism and a servile disposition in no way formed the mainsprings of this emperor cult. Anyone who assumes that has grasped little enough of this last offshoot of the history of religions, the cult of the emperors. However often those phenomena may have been introduced into the company of this cult, yet the honest impression has not been completely lacking that they contained a genuine outburst of religious longing. The prudent Emperor Augustus knew how to use this enthusiasm which he found in a skillful way and to shape and form it while preserving the different peculiarities of the West, which was reserved and unaccustomed to this belief, and the enthusiastic East. Thus the cult of the ruler was gradually developed into a dominant power in religious life, indeed into the central point of the religion of late antiquity, at least in the eastern part of the Roman Empire. In it state and religion joined hands in an unprecedentedly close connection; the state in its epitome in the *Dea Roma* and the *Divus Augustus* offered itself as the object of religious devotion, as the only object having a fixed and firm stability in the flooding current of things and events; in its organs it watched and held sway over the life and prosperity of religion. And religion became, with an immediacy it was never again to have, religion of the state; it surrounded the state and the ruler who stands at the head of the state with the nimbus of divinity. New momentous ideas are woven together with this ruler cult: faith in the power of the deity which saves, heals all injuries and infirmities, and is bestowed upon the man personally; a power which is in some way incarnate in the divine savior of the world, the emperor; the idea of a return of the golden age, the end of the old and the beginning of a new world epoch which is supposed to come with the new god; the conviction that in the ruler one has to see the ἐναργὴς ἐπιφάνεια (the *Deus Manifestus*), the deity that has become visible and tangible on earth. All these are motifs which show a strong analogy to the formation of the Christian faith in the Kyrios, and in a later section we shall have to demonstrate how in this respect fertile influences have passed over into the Christian religion.

The main thing here is that the title Kyrios had a dominant role in this ruler cult. Already the paean which (according to Athenaios VI, p. 253) the Athenians are said to have sung to the victorious Demetrios Poliorketes upon his entry, and in which they celebrate him as the bodily present deity, concludes with the words: "Therefore we pray to you; give us peace, for you are *the Lord.*" [61] Then in a later time particularly in Egypt the title can be demonstrated in connection with the cult of the ruler.[62] To be sure, on the famous inscription of Rosetta (196 B.C.)[63] to Ptolemy Epiphanes the absolute κύριος is not found; we find the title only in conjunction with characteristic genitives.[64] But for the first century B.C. our sources are more productive. On an inscription from the year 62 B.C. it is said with reference to Ptolemy XIII: τοῦ κυρίου βασιλέος θεοῦ,[65] and on another from 52 B.C. from Alexandria Ptolemy and Cleopatra are called κύριοι θεοὶ μέγιστοι.[66] Even for the kings of the Herodian house the title "Lord" is repeatedly demonstrable.[67] On an inscription of Abila in Syria Tiberius and Livia are called the Lords Augusti.[68] Under Caligula, Claudius, and Nero the witnesses for the title κύριος begin to multiply.[69] The report of Josephus that the Jewish martyrs were executed because they refused to call Caesar "Lord" [70] shows how firmly this terminology was fixed. The Roman governor asks the martyr Polycarp what would be so bad about saying Kyrios Caesar! [71] Already under Domitian the title *"dominus et deus noster"* appears to have at least a semiofficial standing.[72]

In fact, even the word κυριακός, which we encounter in the Kyrios cult of the Christians in the terms κυριακὸν δεῖπνον and κυριακὴ ἡμέρα, is, as it appears, prefigured in the language of the ruler cultus. Already on an Egyptian inscription (Edict of the prefect T. Julius Alexander of Egypt)

---

[61] Even if there should not be an immediate tradition here, still the paean is extraordinarily important for the mood of the cult of the ruler.

[62] On the following, cf. Deissmann, pp. 338 ff.

[63] Dittenberger, *Orientis Gr. Inscr.*, No. 90. In summary also in Wendland, *Hellenistisch-römische Kultur*, pp. 406-8.

[64] κύριος βασιλειῶν, lord of the thirty-year period. The former expression also demonstrable for Ptolemy IV, Philopator. Deissmann, p. 352, n. 4.

[65] Dittenberger, *Orientis Gr. Inscr.*, No. 186.

[66] SAB, 1902, p. 1096.

[67] Deissmann, p. 353, n. 1.

[68] Dittenberger, No. 606.

[69] Deissmann, p. 353. Deissmann calls attention to the fact that under Nero the title occurs for the first time also in Greece (Acraephiae in Boeotia). Dittenberger, *Sylloge*, 2nd ed., No. 376. Cf. with this the matter-of-factness with which Festus speaks of Nero as ὁ κύριος in Acts 25:26.

[70] Bellum VII, 418-19 (here, of course, the formulas Καίσαρα δεσπότην ὁμολογεῖν, ἐξονομάζειν).

[71] Martyrdom of Polycarp 8.2.

[72] Suetonius, Vit. Domit. 13. Of course it was Aurelian who first was officially proclaimed as *dominus ac deus.* Wendland, *Hellenistisch-römische Kultur*, p. 150. Deissmann (p. 356) calls attention to the fact that from the time of Domitian onward the title "our Lord" also appears.

from July 6, A.D. 68, in the temple of El Kargeh the imperial finances (ταῖς κυριακαῖς ψήφοις) and the imperial treasury (τὸν κυριακὸν λόγον) are spoken of.[73]

But after all this, in spite of all the factual and linguistic analogies, it would be a mistaken and hasty judgment if we sought to bring the Christian Kyrios cultus and its development into immediate connection with the cultus of the Caesars. In the time and in the areas in which the Kyrios-Jesus cultus emerged, the ruler cult will hardly have already had so dominant a role that one may assume that the worship of Jesus as the Lord has developed in conscious opposition to it.

And if we look more carefully, the Oriental ruler Kyrios cult is only a partial manifestation in a much more comprehensive setting. In order to recognize this we now pose the question of the distribution of the religious term κύριος in Hellenistic culture. Of course in this investigation there first of all emerges a characteristic negative result. Upon specifically Greek soil, in national Greek religion, the title κύριος hardly played a role worthy of mention. This is shown[74] in the literature, where the designations δεσπότης, δεσπότις, δέσποινα occur much more frequently (particularly in poetry, less frequently in the prose writers), as well as in the inscriptions. Here, it is true, κύριος and κυρία are more frequently found (more frequently than δεσπότης, etc.). But when we look closer, we see that it has its own state of affairs governing this. For we can venture the assertion in general that wherever on inscriptions an apparently Greek deity is identified with that title, either an alien (Oriental) god is hidden behind the Greek figure or else at least influences of alien origin are in operation.

For example, the surname κύριος for Zeus[75] is found essentially in Thrace and Syria; further, when in an inscription at Comana (Cappadocia) Apollo is designated with this title, or in Galatia, Helios, we can be sure that behind both some Oriental sun deity is concealed. Thus in Transjordania the

---

[73] Dittenberger, No. 669; cf. with this Deissmann, p. 357. Later testimonies in Deissmann, *Bible Studies*, pp. 217-18. Deissmann, *Light from the Ancient East*, pp. 358 ff., also cites the custom of dedicating to the emperor a certain day (or certain days?) of the month with the name "Sebaste": "But the more I regard this detail in connexion with the great subject of 'Christ and the Caesars,' the more I am bound to reckon with the possibility that the distinctive title 'Lord's Day' may have been connected with conscious feelings of protest against the cult of the Emperor with its 'Augustus Day'" (p. 359).

[74] Cf. the splendid assembling of the material in Roscher's mythological lexicon; see on Kyrios by Drexler. Only here the attempt is nowhere made to set temporal limits for the emergence of the Kyrios title.

[75] For the evidence, where it is not explicitly given, see the article in Roscher; there the material is alphabetically arranged according to the gods' names.

Kyria Athena is the Arabian Allât, and the Kyrios Dionysos who can be demonstrated there is the Arabian Dusares. It can also occasion no surprise that the Kyrios title is found precisely with deities who only in the later Hellenistic religion come to enjoy a broader distribution and a more general veneration, deities such as Hecate and Asclepius.[76]

Three enclaves in particular may be shown for the use of the term: Asia Minor, Egypt, and Syria. We can deal quickly with Asia Minor as not coming much into consideration here. I might only mention that Artemis of Ephesus receives this address, and most of all, that the title appears to have been customary in the cultus of the Magna Mater (Cybele) and of Zeus Sabazios.[77]

In *Egypt* the title κύριος (in Egyptian approximately Neb) does not correspond to ancient indigenous usage.[78] Naturally there is here also a great difference between κύριος with the genitive and the absolute κύριος.[79] The latter usage, so far as I can see, can first be documented for the first century B.C. Most of all, we possess as witnesses for the addressing of Isis as κυρία a whole series of inscriptions from Philae from the last Ptolemaic period, the earliest of which stems from the reign of Ptolemy Alexander.[80] Beside Isis of Philae is placed Hermes-Thoth of Pselkis in Nubia with numerous inscriptions—only from the time of the Roman Caesars, it is true—the oldest of which, so far as I can see, stems from the time of Tiberius (A.D. 33).[81] This observation also is important, for we shall again encounter the

[76] Cf. also, e.g., London magical papyrus CXXI, 706: κύριε 'Ασκλήπιε; 934, 937: κυρία Σελήνη (Wessely, Denkschr. der Akademie, Vienna, 1893, pp. 44, 51). κυρία Ἑκάτη; the great Paris magical papyrus 1432; cf. 2499, 2502.

[77] Documentation in Cumont, *Les mystères de Sabazius et le Judaisme* (Comptes rendus des séances de l'Acad. des Inscr. et Belles Lettres, 1906), pp. 63 ff.; separate printing, p. 6. Esp. important is Servius, ad Aeneid., III.113 (=Varro!): *Dominam proprie matrem Deum dici.* For Sabazius the inscription: θεᾶς 'Ιδείας μεγάλης μητρὸς Διὶ Ἡλίῳ μεγάλῳ κυρίῳ Σαβαζίῳ ἁγίῳ (Roscher, I c, col. 1762). Cumont would see in this and other epithets perhaps Jewish influence. But what we have here are much more extensive connections.

[78] According to information given by my colleague Sethe.

[79] Cf., *e.g.*, in the famous inscription on the Rosetta stone, κύριος τῶν βασιλειῶν, κύριος τῆς τριακονταετηρίδος.

[80] C. I. Gr. 4897 (99-90 B.C.). The text of the inscription is not assured. Still it appears possible (see also the appendix to the Corpus) to establish a several-times-repeated παρὰ τῇ κυρίᾳ Ἴσιδι. Then there follow a whole series of testimonies in 4897 b (before 72 B.C.): ἥκω πρὸς τὴν κυρίαν Ἴσιν; 4898 (69 B.C.); 4899 (55-52); 4904 (Ptolemy Auletes?); 4905; 4917 (before 73 B.C.); 4931-32 (25 B.C.); 4939 (Augustus?); 4940 (A.D. 22). Further in the supplement to the volume: 4897 c (before 71?; cf. 4897 d, e, f); 4930 b (before 71): τὴν μεγίστην θεὰν κυρίαν σώτειραν Ἴσιν.

[81] C. I. Gr. 5101 (cf. further 5080, 5082, 5088, 5092, 5093, 5095, 5101, 5105, 5108 c, d). The Hermes of Pselkis corresponds to the Thoth of Pnubis, whose name Παῦτνουφις

Kyrios name for Hermes in the Hellenistic-Egyptian literature. Also an inscription from A.D. 14 with the title for the god of Coptos Min-Pan can be shown.[82] By way of contrast with this, it can only be accidental that Serapis, who is so closely connected with Isis in the cult, appears as κύριος only in the later inscriptions, and so far as I can see only in the second Christian century, on inscriptions or papyri. Especially important for our purposes are the two papyrus witnesses: ἐρωτᾷ σε Χαιρήμων δειπνῆσαι εἰς κλείνην τοῦ κυρίου Σαράπιδος ἐν τῷ Σαραπείῳ and ἐρωτᾷ σε Ἀντώνιος Πτολεμαίου διπνῆσαι παρ' αὐτῷ εἰς κλείνην τοῦ κυρίου Σαράπιδος.[83] The fact that for Osiris[84] practically no evidence is found is probably adequately explained by the fact that in the age of the Diadochi Serapis begins decisively to drive Osiris out of the practical cultus.[85]

Thus Plutarch, in his essay *De Iside et Osiride*, correctly represents the general state of affairs when again and again he introduces Osiris and Isis with the designation κύριος and κυρία.[86]

In general we may conclude concerning Egypt that the absolute ὁ κύριος is demonstrable in connection with divine figures just as early as, and even earlier than, its use in the ruler cult. This would at the same time show that we have to regard κύριος as a designation in the ruler cult as one particular instance of the general religious practice of calling the gods κύριοι. And thus the above-cited witnesses from the ruler cult are to be employed also as witnesses to this general usage.

(Παότνουφις) on two of these inscriptions, 5087 and 5096, perhaps also appears together with κύριος.

[82] C. I. Gr. 4716 d [1] (cf. d [13, 16]): παρὰ τῷ κυρίῳ Πανί.

[83] Oxyrhynchus Papyri I, 110; III, 523 (from the 2nd Christian cent.). Letter of the soldier Apion in Deissmann, *Light from the Ancient East*, pp. 179 ff.; letter of Antonis Longos to his mother, *ibid.* pp. 187 ff. (both from the 2nd Christian cent.). Inscriptions: C. I. Gr. 4684 (Alexandria, undated); 3163 (Smyrna, A.D. 211); 5115 (Nubia, A.D. 232; cf. 5110). παρὰ τοῦ κυρίου Σεράπιδος τοῦ ἐν Ἀβύτου, inscription from Abydos, 2nd cent. A.D.? (Preisigke, *Sammelbuch griech. Urkunden* (1913), I. Heft, No. 171).

[84] In Roscher's lexicon, only the Paris magical papyrus 2355 f is referred to.

[85] Otherwise I mention further the inscriptions τῷ θεῷ καὶ κυρίῳ Σοκνοπαίῳ (24 B.C., at Soknopaiu-Nefos in the Fayyum. Dittenberger, *Or. Gr. Inscr.* 655). κύριος Βησᾶς (Preisigke, Nos. 1065, 1066, 1068, 1069). The inscription of Dababiyeh: τῶν κυρίων θεῶν Πριώτου θεοῦ μεγίστου καὶ Ὠρεγέβθιος καὶ Ἴσιδος Ῥεσακέμεως (A.D. 232, Preisigke, No. 239). παρὰ τ. κυρ. Θ Ἀσκληπιῷ καὶ Ἀμενώθη καὶ Ὑγιείᾳ (*ibid.*, No. 59), παρὰ τοὺς κυρίους (!) Ἀνούβις θεούς (*ibid.*, No. 240, A.D. 212).

[86] Chap. 6 (Osiris) τοῦ κυρίου καὶ βασιλέως ἐφορῶντος. Chap. 10 τὸν γὰρ βασιλέα καὶ κύριον Ὄσιριν ὀφθαλμῷ καὶ σκήπτρῳ γράφουσιν. Chap. 12 ὁ πάντων κύριος (cf. μέγας βασιλεὺς εὐεργέτης). Chap. 35 πάσης ὑγρᾶς φύσεως κύριος καὶ ἀρχηγός. Chap. 49 ὁ τῶν ἀρίστων πάντων ἡγεμὼν καὶ κύριος Ὄσιρίς ἐστιν. Chap. 40 (Isis) ἡ κυρία τῆς γῆς θεός, *et passim*.

It is more difficult to settle upon a conclusion as to the time when the Greek Kyrios title appeared in *Syria* and its environs. Nevertheless we can probably conclude a priori that the usage must have been widespread here very early. Here indeed the local deities of the different places are explicitly the lords of the tribes and the districts. I recall in brief the Semitic designations Baal, Adon (of Byblos), Mar, Mar 'Olam, and also the Phoenician Baalsamin (in Philo of Byblos=κύριος τῶν οὐρανῶν). The tradition of Greek inscriptions reflects this same state of affairs.

Thus it is only natural that above all the great Syrian goddess, the Atargatis of Hieropolis, receives the title κυρία. On an inscription at Kefr Havar,[87] one Lukios, who glories in his begging pilgrimages in honor of his goddess, the θεᾶ Συρία Ἱεραπολιτῶν, is called the δοῦλος of the goddess πεμφθεὶς ὑπὸ τῆς κυρίας ['Α]ταρ [χ]άτη[ς]. In Batanaea, Trachonitis,[88] and Auranitis we encounter in a whole series of places the Arabic Allât as the κυρία Athena. Associated with her is Marnas on an inscription at Kanatha[89]; Zeus in Batanaea and Auranitis,[90] and also in Damascus.[91] On an inscription from Abila (from the time of Tiberius) Kronos received the title κύριος.[92] Also Dionysos Dusares[93] and the Baal Markod[94] appear in this series of gods who receive the surname of veneration.

Finally, to the area of Syrian mixing of religions[95] belong some important observations which the tradition of the church fathers about Gnostic sects

---

[87] Ch. Fossey, *Inscr. de Syrie* (Bulletin de correspond. hellén., XXI [1897], 60).

[88] Batanaea: Lebas Waddington III, 2203 a, b (Tharba); 2216 (Nela); 2345 (Kanatha). Trachonitis: 2453 (Dama); 2461 (Harrân). Cf. also in Batanaea 'Αρτέμιδι τῇ κυρίᾳ (perhaps the indigenous moon goddess, the double-horned Astarte): Schürer, *Gesch. des jüd. Volkes*, 4th ed. II, 46-47.

[89] Lebas Waddington III, 2412 g: Διὶ Μάρνα τῷ κυρίῳ.

[90] Waddington III, 2288, 2290 (C. I. Gr. 4625), 2413 b (C. I. Gr. 4558). Let me also call attention to the interesting inscription (Ma'ad near Byblos, Renan, *Mission d. Phénicie*, p. 242): τῷ κυρίῳ Διὶ κὲ κυ[ρί]ῳ Οαου (?) [Σέλ]ευκος [θε]οῦ Σατρά[που] ἱερεὺς ἐποίησε.

[91] Waddington III, 1879 (C. I. Gr. 4513).

[92] Dittenberger, No. 606; cf. in Deissmann, p. 353, the same inscription, on which Tiberius and Livia are mentioned as the κύριοι Σεβαστοί; see above, p. 140, n. 68. The North African Saturnus, who corresponds to Kronos, is also called *Deus Dominus* (*Berliner philolog. Wochenschr.* XXI, col. 475).

[93] Waddington III, 2309 (C. I. Gr. 4617) προνοίᾳ κυρίου κτίστου Διονύσου (A.D. 171).

[94] Mitteil. d. D. A. Instituts, Athens, X (1885), 168-69: κυρίῳ Γενναίῳ Βαλμαρκῶδι.

[95] I might further mention that in the so-called "Mithras liturgy" Helios appears as κύριος τοῦ οὐρανοῦ καὶ τῆς γῆς (Dieterich, *Eine Mithrasliturgie*, p. 10.30) while the Most High God Mithras is addressed by the initiates who appear before him as κύριε. In Dio Cassius II, 253, Tiridates addresses Nero thus: "I am your servant, my lord; I have come to you, my God, to pray to you as I do to Mithras."

allows us to make. Hippolytus tells about the followers of Simon Magus that they reverenced Simon in the form of Zeus, Helena in the form of Athena, τὸν μὲν καλοῦντες κύριον, τὴν δὲ κυρίαν.[96] This very interesting notice is explicitly confirmed by the account of the Pseudo-Clementine Homilies.[97]

According to the explicit report of Irenaeus this phenomenon is repeated in striking fashion among the Valentinians. Irenaeus takes offense[98] at the fact that this sect expressly reserves the title κυρία for the Sophia Achamoth, while they do not call Jesus κύριος but only σωτήρ.[99] According to all probability, however, the worship of Achamoth among the Valentinians goes back to Syrian Gnosticism.

While Gnosticism received its shape in principle in the area of religious syncretism in Syria, the many-branched syncretistic literature which goes under the name of Hermes is of specifically Egyptian origin, and here also we encounter the religious Kyrios title with surprising frequency. σὺ πάτερ, σὺ ὁ κύριος, σὺ ὁ Νοῦς—thus speaks the mystic here at the high point of the mystery in the prayer of dedication (XIII, 21).[100]

The survey shows that the title κύριος spans an area in the history of religions which can still be fairly precisely delimited. It penetrated Hellenistic-Roman religion from the East; Syria and Egypt are its actual home territories. That it plays the leading role in the Egyptian-Roman worship of the ruler is only a local phenomenon within this general context. Indeed the Greek translation of the Old Testament, with its translation of the name

[96] Hippolytus, Ref. VI, 20. Cf. Irenaeus I, 23.4. Still here the designation of κύριος or κυρία is not mentioned.

[97] II, 25: Ἑλένην κυρίαν οὖσαν ὡς παμμήτορα, οὐσίαν καὶ σοφίαν. XVIII, 12 (Peter, repeating the teaching of Simon): ἐκ τῆς μεγάλης δυνάμεως ἔτι τε καὶ τῆς κυρίας λεγομένης.

[98] Adv. Haer. I, 1.3; 5.3 (They call the Μήτηρ: Ὀγδοάδα καὶ Σοφίαν καὶ Γῆν καὶ Ἰερουσαλὴμ καὶ ἅγιον Πνεῦμα καὶ Κύριον ἀρσενικῶς.

[99] Dölger (Ἰχθύς, RQ, Supplem. XVII, 409-10) has appropriately pointed out that this statement corresponds to the state of things not only in the letter of Ptolemaeus to Flora (ὁ σωτήρ eleven times: cf. Harnack, *Mission and Expansion of Christianity*, I, 103, n. 2), but also in Heracleon's Commentary. Finally, in this conclusion we must mention the note about the Basilidians in Theodoret, Haer. fab. I, 4, τὸν δὲ σωτῆρα καὶ κύριον Καυλακαύαν ὀνομάζουσι (Hilgenfeld, *Ketzergeschichte*, p. 197, n. 319).

[100] Cf. V, 2: εὖξαι πρῶτον τῷ κυρίῳ καὶ πατρὶ καὶ μόνῳ καὶ ἑνί. . . . ἄφθονος γὰρ ὁ κύριος—Asclepius (Ps. Apuleius) 8 (p. 43.2): dominus et omnium conformator; 22 (p. 58.9): deus pater et dominus; 26 (p. 63.16): dominus et pater, deus primipotens (cf. chap. 23, p. 60.11; 29, p. 67.12 *et passim*). Stobaeus (Ecl. I, 744) ὁ μὲν κύριος καὶ πάντων δημιουργός. Κόρη Κόσμου, *ibid.*, p. 944: τῶν ὅλων κύριον καὶ θεόν. p. 996: κυρία μῆτερ Isis. Cf. ὁ κύριος ἡμῶν Ἑρμῆς in a horoscope from the first year of the Emperor Antoninus, in Reitzenstein, *Poimandres*, p. 119.

of Yahweh by means of κύριος, now also enters into this context. The translation emerged just on the soil in which this most general designation of God (besides θεός) was customary and was understood. Thus Judaism with its Bible acknowledged the κύριος to whom alone it paid reverence.[101]

But we now make a second, still more important observation. It appears as if the title κύριος was especially given to the deities which stood in the center of the cultus of the fellowship involved. Thus it is hardly an accident that those deities in the worship of whom late Egyptian religion was likewise concentrated, whose cultus also passed for the characteristic feature of Egyptian piety throughout the Oikoumene, attract to themselves the title κύριος more than do all other deities: I mean Osiris, Isis, and Serapis. That Syrian "mendicant monk" speaks plainly of his Kyria (Atargatis) in whose honor he undertook his begging pilgrimages. But especially striking here are the analogies of the Gnostic sects. The Simonians gather themselves around the κύριος Simon and the κυρία Helena. The Valentinians worship the Sophia Achamoth and not Jesus as their Kyrios. To this corresponds the fact that, as can clearly be demonstrated, almost the entire sacramental cultus of these Gnostics is connected with Achamoth (or with the Μήτηρ; the doubling of the heavenly Μήτηρ and the fallen Achamoth is only later introduced).[102] Achamoth (Μήτηρ) is the cult-heroine of the Valentinians or of the earlier Gnostics whose cult they appropriated. Therefore she is κύριος. Likewise the Hermetic sects to which the Hermetic writings are to be traced gather themselves around the worship of the Kyrios–Nous–Hermes.

It was in this atmosphere that Antiochene Christianity and that of the other primitive Christian Hellenistic communities came into being and had their growth. In this milieu the young Christian religion was shaped as a Christ cultus, and out of this environment then people also appropriated the comprehensive formula κύριος for the dominant position of Jesus in worship. No one thought this out, and no theologian created it; people did not read it out of the sacred book of the Old Testament. They would hardly have dared without further ado to make such a direct transferral of this holy name of the almighty God—actually almost a deification of Jesus. Such proceedings take place in the unconscious, in the uncontrollable depths of the group psyche of a community; this is self-evident, it lay as it were in

---

[101] It is worthy of note that Josephus does not follow this usage and almost never uses the title κύριος. (Schlatter, "Wie sprach Josephus von Gott," BFcT XIV, No. 1, 9-10).

[102] Cf. Bousset, *Hauptprobleme*, pp. 63 ff.

the air, that the first Hellenistic Christian communities gave the title κύριος to their cult-hero. Just as the translators of the Old Testament simply applied to the holy God of the Israelite people the Kyrios title widely used in the Oriental world, in order to present him as the κύριος κατ᾽ ἐξοχήν of all the world; as the almost contemporary Gnostic sects gathered around the κύριος Simon, the κυρία Helena, the κυρία Μήτηρ, the κύριος Νοῦς-Hermes; as the Egyptian religion was concentrated in the cultus of the lords Osiris, Isis, and Serapis; so also is young Christianity comprehended in the cultus of the Lord Jesus. "For even if there are so-called gods, whether in heaven or on earth, just as there are gods many and lords many, still we have one God the Father . . . and one Lord Jesus Christ" (I Cor. 8:5-6). With these words the apostle Paul places his seal under this whole context. The young Christian religion, with unprecedented one-sidedness and with daring obstinacy, opposed to the many lords of the Hellenistic cults the one Kyrios Jesus Christ. Kyrios faith and Kyrios cult present that form of Christianity which it has taken on in the setting of Hellenistic piety. And when Paul parallels the position of θεός and of κύριος in the Christian community with that of the πολλοὶ θεοί and πολλοὶ κύριοι in the Gentile religions, the connections are comprehensible and clear. For in that the apostle with the help of the Kyrios concept on the one hand places his Lord directly at the side of God and yet on the other hand subordinates him in definite fashion, he believes that he finds, in the Hellenistic cult, analogies for this gradation within the divine essence,[103] and is convinced that on this basis he is understood with his confession εἷς θεός, εἷς κύριος.

Now it becomes clear that it was no accident that we did not encounter the title Kyrios on Palestinian soil in the gospel tradition. Such a development would not have been possible here. This placing of Jesus in the center of the cultus of a believing community, this peculiar doubling of the object of veneration in worship, is conceivable only in an environment in which Old Testament monotheism no longer ruled unconditionally and with absolute security.

[103] Incidentally, it is not completely clear what the apostle may have been thinking of when he assumed the difference in worth between the concepts θεός and κύριος to be well known. One wonders whether he felt a contrast between the Greek θεοί and the Oriental κύριοι, and in the subordination of the latter to the former was following a Greek opinion. Or did he have in mind κύριοι who, like Adonis, Attis, Dionysos, and even Isis-Osiris, as highly venerated cultic deities nevertheless stood somewhat lower than the highest gods?

One could in fact attempt at this point to infer some Jewish cult of angels as a prefiguring analogy for the Christ cult of the first Christian communities.[104] But at least for the Palestinian milieu this attempt may be shown to be impossible. What can be proved in this connection for the earlier time in genuinely Jewish territory is limited to faith in the angels as mediators of prayers. Such an idea is perhaps already suggested in Job 5:1; 33:23. In the Book of Tobit (Codex B) the seven archangels are explicitly characterized as mediators of prayers.[105] The Jerusalem Talmud (Berachoth IX, 13a) forbids an actual prayer to the angels (Michael and Gabriel). Midrash Mechilta and Jerusalem Targum oppose the worship of angels (pictures of angels) in the exposition on Exod. 20:23; sacrifices to Michael (!) as to sun, moon, and stars are similarly opposed in some other passages in the Talmud.[106] The repeated prohibitions probably prove the existence of such abuses. But here a later time is involved. And further, we see that official Judaism constantly rejected actual veneration of angels as an abuse. The general intimations of Jewish angel worship in the apologist Aristides (XIV, 4) and the Kerygma of Peter (Clem. Alex. Strom. VI, 5.41) are, as clearly emerges in the Aristides passage, only an awkward bit of inference-drawing from the sanctity of the Sabbath, new moons, and other festival days in the Jewish cultus.[107]

The indications which we find in the New Testament for the assumption of a certain distribution of the angel cultus carry more weight. The Apocalypse clearly has polemics against prayer to angels;[108] in the Epistle to the Colossians a heretical (Jewish Christian-Gnostic) angel cult is opposed.[109] Perhaps we should include in the same connection the effort in the first chapters of Hebrews to prove Christ's superiority to the angels.[110] But from this no conclusion with reference to Palestinian Judaism (and primitive Christianity) is permitted, but possibly only with reference to certain (heretical) currents in the Judaism of the Diaspora. And we will hardly be able to invoke such a conjecturally assumed Jewish angel worship for the *explanation* of the Kyrios cult of the Hellenistic communities. The concentration of the religion in the worship of the one Kyrios is still something quite different from occasional invocation and veneration of Jewish angels. Nevertheless one may with good reason see a certain analogy in traces of the angel cult that exist here and there within the Jewish Diaspora. What is involved in some cases is a certain softening and veiling of Old Testament monotheism.

[104] On the following, cf. the material in W. Lueken, *Michael,* 1898.

[105] Tobit 12.15; cf. 12.12. Eth. Enoch. 9.2 ff.; 15.2; 40.6; 47.1-2; 104.1. See more material in Lueken, p. 7.

[106] Aboda Sara 42 b, Chullin 40 a, collected passages in Lueken, pp. 6, 7. For angel litanies from a much later time, cf. *ibid.,* p. 11 b.

[107] The comments of Celsus are to be judged in the same way (Origen I, 26, V, 6). Origen rightly defends the Jews (V, 8): οὐκ ᾽Ιουδαϊκὸν μὲν τὸ τοιοῦτον, παραβατικὸν δὲ ᾽Ιουδαισμοῦ ἐστιν.

[108] Rev. 19:9-10; 22:8; with these, cf. Ascensio Jesaiae VII, 21. Characteristic is the rejection of the κύριος title by the angel (VIII, 4-5): ego non sum dominus tuus, sed socius tuus sum. Further parallels in Lueken, p. 63.1.

[109] 2:18-19, 23; cf. 2:8, 15.

[110] We perhaps have a defense of the veneration of angels in Jude 8-10; II Pet. 2:10-11.

IV. *Further Consequences.* This view of Jesus as the Kyrios has certain consequences. I have already disputed that people in the Hellenistic primitive communities had read the title κύριος out of the Old Testament. It certainly has its own roots. But after this designation for Christ had once been adopted, people naturally read it into the Old Testament and connected the sacred name of God with Jesus of Nazareth. Thus alone does this curious process become fully clear and understandable. And now in turn this interpretation of the Old Testament heightens the veneration of the Kyrios; indeed it leads in the direction of beginning gradually to obliterate all boundary lines between the Old Testament God and the Christ.

Already Paul [111] offers us here an abundance of examples. He is already familiar with the connection of the passage in Joel, "whoever calls on the name of the Lord will be saved," with Christ.[112] The term for the Christians: οἱ ἐπικαλούμενοι τὸ ὄνομα τοῦ κυρίου (*vide supra*) may stem from this. In Rom. 11:34 Paul connects the saying of Deutero-Isaiah (40:13): τίς ἔγνω νοῦν κυρίου . . . ὃς συμβιβᾷ αὐτόν, with God, but in I Cor. 2:16, on the other hand, obviously and clearly with Christ. It is still more significant that the great confession: "As I live, says the Lord, every knee shall bow to me and every tongue shall confess God" [113] (Isa. 45:23), which in Rom. 14:11 he connects with God, in the great passage in Philippians he employs for characterizing the new position of Jesus Christ as Lord. Even the word in which Old Testament piety is so simply and classically expressed: "Whoever glories, let him glory in the Lord" (Jer. 9:22-23), is twice simply transferred by Paul to Christ (I Cor. 1:31; II Cor. 10:17).[114] Paul can find the κύριος in the Old Testament wherever he wishes. Already with him we find the influential idea that Christ has already held sway over the fate of the people of Israel in their past. He is the miraculous rock that followed them, that accompanied the people through the wilderness (I Cor. 10:4). To him Moses turned when he went to the holy place and laid aside the veil (II Cor. 3:13 ff.). Probably related to this is the theologoumenon that Christ was the mediating cause through which God created the world (I

---

[111] We have already referred above (p. 122, n. 12) to the significance of Ps. 110 with its doubled κύριος. In I Cor. 15:25 Paul shows a familiarity with this passage.

[112] Rom. 10:13; cf. Acts 2:21.

[113] LXX ℵ read τὸν κύριον.

[114] Perhaps the κύριος in I Cor. 10:26 (τοῦ κυρίου γὰρ ἡ γῆ καὶ τὸ πλήρωμα αὐτῆς) is also to be referred to Jesus. This reference in II Cor. 3:16 is assured by the context: ἡνίκα δὲ ἐὰν ἐπιστρέψῃ πρὸς κύριον, περιαιρεῖται τὸ κάλυμμα (Ex. 34:34). Cf. II Thess. 2:8-9.

Cor. 8:6). But in all these interpretations of the Old Testament Paul hardly led the way. He only followed an interpretation of the Old Testament which naturally had to be introduced once the connection of the title κύριος to Jesus was fixed.

One further consequence is joined with this attribution of the position of Lord to Jesus. In his being honored as Lord, Jesus also became the object of Christian faith. Once again it is one of the most significant observations that the concept of faith in Jesus (Christ) in the actual religious sense is still not found at all in the older gospel tradition and only begins to enter in some passages of recognizably later origin.[115]

Here we cannot yet go into the matter of the Pauline proclamation of faith in Christ and of the way in which Paul makes this faith the central point of the new religion. But I must already point out that with his statements about faith Paul appears to presuppose the general conviction of the community that faith in the Lord Jesus Christ belongs to being a Christian. Paul's own contribution must have been the personal penetration and spiritualizing of "faith" as the center of all religious life, or at least the introduction of this knowledge into the religion of Christianity.[116] But he appears in his statements already to presuppose a formulated confession of faith of the community: "If you confess with your mouth *the Lord Jesus* and believe in your heart that God has raised him from the dead, you will be saved" (Rom. 10:9-10). The formula: "Believe in God who has raised Christ from the dead" could already have been handed down to him.[117] Already for the Judaism of the Diaspora the concept of faith (in the sense of faith in the one God) had moved into the center of the religious life. The πρῶτον πίστευσον, ὅτι εἷς ἐστιν ὁ θεός became a mark of identification

---

[115] Mark 9:42 (τῶν μικρῶν) τῶν πιστευόντων and Matt. 18:6 τῶν πιστευόντων εἰς ἐμέ are additions, as a comparison with Luke 17:2 shows (see above, p. 80). Even with Mark 15:32, ἵνα ἴδωμεν καὶ πιστεύσωμεν (note Matthew's addition of ἐπ᾽ αὐτόν), the formula "believe on" still is not given. Moreover, Luke does not have this scene, and in the Marcan text, vss. 31-32 are a doublet to 29-30. Even the expression πιστεύετε ἐν τῷ εὐαγγελίῳ in Mark 1:15 is obviously late. Further, the sayings in Luke 8:12 (μὴ πιστεύσαντες σωθῶσιν); 8:13 (πρὸς καιρὸν πιστεύουσι) and 22:68 are later additions; probably also 18:8 (will the Son of Man find faith on the earth?). Otherwise, it is well known that we have examples of πιστεύειν and πίστις simply with reference to belief in the wonder-worker (Mark 2:5; 4:40; 5:34, 36; 9:23; 10:52; 11:23; Matt. 8:10 [=Luke 7:9]; 9:29; 15:28; 17:20; Luke 18:42), or to belief in prayer, which however is almost identical with belief in miracles: Mark 11:23-24, Luke 17:5-6. Of course the formula is used by Luke in a larger sense: ἡ πίστις σου σέσωκέν σε, 7:50; 17:19; cf. 22:32.

[116] See the following chapter.

[117] In addition to Rom. 10:9-10, cf. Rom. 4:24; 8:11; I Cor. 6:14 (I Cor. 15); II Cor. 4:14; Gal. 1:1; Col. 2:12; I Thess. 1:10 (II Tim. 2:8).

in the Judaism in the dispersion.[118] Now, as the peculiarity of the Christian community there was added to this the confession of the Lord Christ or the faith in the God who had raised him from the dead.

All this constituted further developments of tremendous significance. One may ever so sharply sense the doubtful aspects of this development, the burdening and complicating of the simple belief in God through the introduction of the cultic worship of the Kyrios Christos, and yet one will have to concede that it came about with an inner necessity. Infant Christianity in its environment *had* to assume this form of the κύριος faith and the κύριος worship; it could not at all turn out otherwise. In an age in which people honored the ruler with the solemn religious title of κύριος and prayed to him in the cult as κύριος, in a time in which there were many "lords" in heaven and on earth, the Hellenistic Christian communities also had to set this crown upon the head of their Lord and address him as "our Lord." But on the other hand new and unprecedented, not to be derived and explained in terms of the times and the milieu, is the sublime determination with which the Christian community opposed its faith in the Lord to all other faith. "Even if there are many lords, we have one Lord, Jesus Christ." Here is shown the grandiose force and unanimity of the young religion and its unique strength. The spirit of unconquerable and stalwart Old Testament monotheism is transferred to the Kyrios worship and the Kyrios faith!

And along with it, the Kyrios of the Hellenistic Christian community becomes a present, tangibly alive entity. The *Son of Man* of the primitive community stems from Jewish eschatology and remains an eschatological entity. Indeed in the Easter days when the new faith emerged, the immediate disciples had beheld him in their presence. But now the heavens have taken him up until the restoration of all things (Acts 3:21). He is the future Messiah who is to come in glory, and the fundamental attitude of his disciples is the fervent expectation of his coming. But the *Kyrios* of the Hellenistic primitive community is a being who is *present* in the cult and in the worship. He permeates and surrounds his community in worship with his presence, and fills them from heaven with his miraculous powers. Only now is it said: "Where two or three are gathered together in my name, I am in the midst of them."

In this presence of the κύριος in worship, in the experiences of his tangible actuality which people have here, there grew up from the outset a powerful

---

[118] Bousset, *Religion des Judentums*, 2nd ed., pp. 223 ff., 345 ff.

opponent to primitive Christian eschatology. Of course the opposites still lie within one another, and the tensions have not yet appeared. The boundary lines of present and future become blurred and run together. The end is near, and the Son of Man will soon come. What one experiences of the tangible reality of the Lord is a foretaste of the blessedness which the end brings. The Spirit with his gifts which the Lord gives to his community is only "first fruits" and "pledge" of the promised blessed benefits of the future, a first greeting from heaven, the reddening sky of the coming day. Meanwhile, in this present possession one can quietly await the future; wholly imperceptibly, quite gradually, the center of gravity begins to shift from the future to the present. Kyrios cult, worship service, and sacrament become the most dangerous and most significant opponents of the primitive Christian eschatological outlook. Once the former become fully developed, the latter will have lost its impetus that carries everything along with it. But that will be the development: the Son of Man will be more or less forgotten and will remain as an indecipherable hieroglyph in the Gospels. The future belongs to the Kyrios present in the cult.

# 4

## PAUL

The personal Christ piety of the apostle Paul arose on this foundation of the Kyrios faith and the Kyrios cultus in the Hellenistic primitive Christian communities. It came into being and grew in the milieu of a community in whose center the Kyrios worship stood. For the apostle, the Lord who is worshiped in the Christian community is a reality which he presupposes as self-evident and given. But all this of course now becomes for him only the point of departure for a further development. In the Christ piety of Paul there now sounds one entirely new note, and it becomes the dominant: the intense feeling of personal belonging and of spiritual relationship with the exalted Lord. This feeling of the relationship goes far beyond the ἐπικα-λεῖσθαι τὸ ὄνομα τοῦ κυρίου which we infer from Paul as the general Christian possession. In glowing passion Paul embraces the κύριος Χριστός as the one presently living, governing his life. When the apostle calls himself the δοῦλος of this Lord Jesus, he is thinking not only, and not even in the first place, of cultic relationships; he is experiencing this Lord as a present power, in whose service he places his whole personal life. To the Lord belongs all strength and power which is revealed in the apostle's deeds; to Paul himself belongs only what is weak therein (II Cor. 12:9). Whatever in Paul's life was wrong is charged to him; whatever he has performed and achieved—more than all the others—was the grace of the Lord. For him Christ is the Triumphator, who travels through the world in his chariot of victory; before him walks the apostle as a conquered one and a captive, while all around, the incense aroma of the new knowledge of God rises into the air (II Cor. 2:14-15). It is the apostle's pride when his body is consumed in the service of this Lord, when the death of Jesus becomes visible in his own body which has been used in Jesus' service (II Cor. 4:9-10). Christ is "the" Lord and Paul "the" slave.

I. *Christ Mysticism and Cultic Mysticism.* Thus for Paul Christ becomes the supra-terrestrial power which supports and fills with its presence his whole life. And this Christ piety of the apostle is summed up for him in the one great ever recurring formula of ἐν κυρίῳ (Χριστῷ) εἶναι. We must first of all attempt to insert this formula and along with it the Christ mysticism characterized by it into the previous context—a much disputed problem.

At least it is now fairly generally acknowledged that it would be wrong to relate the ἐν Χριστῷ of Paul to what we call the ethical-religious personal image of Jesus of Nazareth, whether one assumes a mediation of this personal image by the Christian Palestinian primitive community, or whether one construes out of II Cor. 5:16 a personal acquaintance of the apostle with Jesus which somehow conditioned the subsequent development. All these combinations are untenable and even false. The state of affairs as it is set forth in the Pauline epistles enters a veto against them. It can be definitely asserted that what we call the ethical-religious personal image of Jesus was of no influence or significance at all for the piety of Paul. It is useless[1] to adduce as arguments against this the various items from Jesus' life with which Paul is supposed to have been acquainted. This does not lead any further than the proposition that for Paul Jesus of Nazareth was a historical figure. To be sure, Paul cited a series of sayings of the Lord, but how rarely and on how relatively restricted questions: on the question of the apostle's legitimate claim to support by the community (I Cor. 9:14) and on a detail of eschatological hope (I Thess. 4:15); indeed, even the command about the indissolubility of marriage (I Cor. 7:10, 12) still does not belong to the bases of the Apostle's proclamation.[2]

The picture which Paul actually sketches of the κύριος Ἰησοῦς is not taken from the earthly life of Jesus of Nazareth. The Jesus whom Paul

---

[1] Cf. Heitmüller, "Zum Problem Paulus und Jesus," ZNW XIII (1912), 321.

[2] For I Cor. 11:23-25, it remains doubtful whether there is present here a logion of the earthly Jesus or (according to Paul's view) a revelation of the exalted Lord.

knows is the preexistent supra-terrestrial Christ who was rich and for our sake became poor, who was in the form of God and took on the form of a servant, the Son of God whom the Father gives as a sacrifice, the one who fulfills the prophecies, the one who accomplishes the promises. Into *this* "personal image" of Jesus all the individual features which Paul brings out here and there are fitted: his humility, his obedience, his love, his truthfulness, his faithfulness even to death on the cross.[3] The subject of all these predicates is not the "historical" Jesus. Paul no longer has a place at all in his proclamation of the gospel for one basic feature of the personal picture of Jesus, indeed for its foundation, namely his piety and his faith in God: Paul does not proclaim the faith of Jesus, but faith in Jesus. How then does one propose still to speak of a personal image of Jesus in our sense in the thought of Paul?

We misunderstand the phrase ἐν Χριστῷ εἶναι of Paul if we somehow mean by it the historical Jesus in our sense. Of course one exception is to be made to this statement. At least one fact of that earthly life is foundational also for Paul's image of Christ: his death. But this can only be discussed below in a broader context. Against this, one has repeatedly and correctly brought out that precisely the relative lack of familiarity with which Paul encounters the historical person of Jesus explains how for him, and for him in particular, the Christ could be sublimated into the abstract entity of the Pneuma, into the principle of the new Christian life. However, this does not positively account for the emergence of the Christos–Pneuma view.

The attempt to derive Paul's Christ mysticism from his conversion experience at Damascus is very widespread. In this experience the Christ is supposed to have appeared to the apostle as a purely supra-terrestrial, divine (II Cor. 4:6) being detached from all earthly connections. There Paul experienced him as a new and present power who from now on should determine his life. This combination is very often proposed with great certainty, and it is amazing with what boldness some claim to be able to penetrate the mystery of Paul's conversion and set forth their knowledge of it at great length. Over against this we should recall that Paul himself spoke of his experience only in a few brief allusions, and always only when it was a matter of establishing his right and his authority as an apostle. We should also remember that he treated his Damascus vision as an extraor-

---

[3] Phil. 2:6 ff.; II Cor. 5:14; II Cor. 1:19-20.

dinary and unique fact, not as the first in a series of visions of Christ out of which then his mysticism could have developed, and that therefore in his own testimony he does not afford us a handle for grasping the entire combination. Also, one must ask how it is to be explained that Paul alone developed his peculiar piety of ἐν Χριστῷ εἶναι, with which even in the following period he still stands alone, while according to his own testimony all the original disciples of Jesus had had the same visionary experience of the appearance of the exalted Lord.

It may nevertheless be acknowledged that this derivation of Pauline Christ mysticism, even though it is not proved, still cannot be entirely refuted, and that the special way by which Paul was led to faith in Christ can yield a certain point of contact for the special form of his Christ piety. But this piety is not derived and grasped in its actual roots thereby. It does not become understandable and conceivable until we keep in mind that behind Paul's mysticism of the ἐν Χριστῷ εἶναι there stands the living experience of the Kyrios Christos present in worship and in the practical life of the community. The fire of his Christ piety was ignited, not at the historical Jesus, nor in the first place at the Christ who appeared to him near Damascus, but rather at the powerful reality of the Kyrios as Paul experienced it in the first Hellenistic communities.

We have already seen how intensely Paul lived in this cult mysticism. On the basis of his letters, in fact, we could sketch such a lifelike portrait of the significance of the Kyrios for the Hellenistic groups of Jesus' disciples. The chief witness for it is that picture, dominating all his thought and his piety, of the body of the community, whose head is Christ, a picture which he never grows weary of painting, filling in details in ever new expressions (I Cor. 12; Rom. 12; Colossians[4]): καὶ αὐτός ἐστιν ἡ κεφαλὴ τοῦ σώματος τῆς ἐκκλησίας. For him this is more than a figure; it is a tangible reality. And when he speaks of this reality, Paul is always thinking in the first place of the community gathered in worship, active in the cultus. Here the body of Christ was actually present; here the individual ceased to be, merged into the whole, and felt himself to be only a member of the body; here the new and blessed life force overflowed from the head through all the members and bound them together with unbreakable bonds. This the apostle has experienced, however much he also felt himself to be the leader of this fellowship, experienced in vital reality. It is not comprehensible how it does

---

[4] Cf. also the less mystical image of the building and temple of the community.

any injury to his dignity and originality when one strongly underscores this motif in his piety.

Indeed, when we start the consideration at this point, in my judgment the uniqueness and significance of the apostle's personality comes out all the more in a clear light. For it is just his achievement to have re-formed into individual mysticism, ethicized, and transposed out of the cult into the total personal life that cultic and community mysticism, in the ardor of experience. And the Pauline letters give us the opportunity to listen in on this intimate process, so significant for the history of religions, of the development of personal mysticism out of cultic mysticism. We shall attempt to trace out the clear and tangible evidences of this.

The sixth chapter of Romans is especially forceful as evidence in this respect. It is quite clear that here Paul connects one of the most characteristic presentations of his Christ mysticism to cultic events and representations which were bound up with the sacrament of baptism. One cannot escape the impression that here Paul proceeds from a conviction, already present in the communities,[5] of the cultically sacramental intimacy of the Christians with Christ which is accomplished in baptism. The belief must already have been present that baptism as an act of initiation is a dying and coming to life again, somehow comparable to Christ's death and resurrection. Analogous views in the ancient mysteries will be discussed below. Here Paul begins, and in sublime exposition he frees that cultic experience, which had been understood only in the mood of a mystery, from its gloomy ties, reorients it to the personal, interprets it spiritually-ethically, and enlarges it. Thus emerges the canticle about the Christians' living and dying with Christ. Perhaps here we can still see the exact point at which the change from the mysticism of community and sacrament into Paul's personal mysticism took place. The figures of speech which Paul employs in his explanations are in conflict. At first he speaks of being baptized into Christ's death, of being buried with Christ in baptism, all this in close conjunction with the baptismal rite. But then with verse 5 the figurative language changes: "knowing this, that our old man was crucified, that the body of sin might be destroyed, that we might no longer serve sin." This cross mysticism which begins here has, precisely taken, nothing more to do with the sacrament of baptism. These are new, unprecedented imaginations which now emerge

---

[5] Heitmüller, "Zum Problem Paulus und Jesus" (see above, p. 119, n. 1), p. 355, rightly points out that Paul assumes that the sacramental view of baptism is well known even in the Roman congregation which has not been under his spiritual influence.

out of the soul of the apostle. It is as if here a mysticism of a more personal note struggles free and flies upward with freer strokes of the wings. But it did take its point of departure from the community's cult and sacrament.[6]

As in Rom. 6:1 ff., so also in Gal. 3:26-27, Paul ties a brief series of mystical thoughts to the sacrament of baptism: "For you are all sons of God through faith in Jesus Christ. For as many of you as have been baptized have put on Christ." Here the apostle proceeds from a baptismal mystery. For him baptism serves as an act of initiation in which the mystic is merged with the deity, or is clothed with the deity (for parallels, *vide infra*). Thus in baptism the Christians have become one with the Son, and hence themselves have become sons. How curiously this brief allusion stands out in contrast with the surrounding thought-world in the Galatian epistle! Elsewhere the statements of the apostle about sonship and servanthood, about the inheritance of Abraham, about God's free gracious will, his relation to the law, and his acceptance through faith are almost dominated by a sober judicial rigor. Now here suddenly a mystical note sounds: sonship through the miracle of the sacrament, and the sacramental union with Christ! This is indeed a sound from another world. But the cultic mysticism which is present here is again interwoven in peculiarly free fashion with the purely intellectual ideas of the apostle about faith and divine sonship, and in a similar way is separated from the soil on which it has grown up.[7]

In Col. 3:5 ff. Paul presents to us in solemn and pregnant formulas a bit of his personal speculative mysticism, which we shall discuss more in detail a little later. Here he speaks of putting off the old man and putting on the new man . . . according to the image of the one who created him, where there is neither Greek nor Jew, neither circumcision nor uncircumcision, neither barbarian nor Scythian, slave nor free man, but Christ is all and in all! Who is this new man whom Paul has in view? None other than the community, the body whose head is Christ, and indeed first of all the community assembled in worship: "And let the peace of Christ rule in your hearts, to which you also are called in *one body*. The word of Christ is to dwell in you richly, in all wisdom you are to teach and admonish each other, singing [in your hearts?] with psalms, hymns, and spiritual songs; and

---

[6] In the above I follow the valuable suggestions which Dibelius (*Die Isisweihe bei Apulejus,* SAH 1917, No. 4, pp. 45 ff.) has given, only that I do not altogether agree with his interpretation of the complete independence of Paul's cross mysticism as over against the cult mysticism of the community.

[7] Cf. further the statements about baptism in Col. 2:11 ff.

all that you do in word or in deed, do it all in the name of the Lord Jesus, giving thanks to God the Father through him" (3:15-17).

The apostle sounds an especially mystical note in the sentence in II Cor. 3:18: "But we all with unveiled face reflect the glory of the Lord, being changed from one δόξα to another, since it all comes from the Lord who is the Spirit." I shall demonstrate later how strongly the language of Hellenistic piety (μεταμορφοῦσθαι! δόξα!) dominates in this sentence. Here I shall only point out that even in writing down this sentence Paul has in mind the experience of Christian worship. For here he evidently sets this over against the worship of the synagogue. Twice in the preceding context he has referred to the latter. "Down to the present day the same veil lies over the reading (in worship services) of the old covenant." "Until today, when Moses is read the veil lies upon their hearts" (3:14-15). Then when he continues: "But *we* all reflect[8] with unveiled face the glory of the Lord," it is clear that in the "we" he is thinking of the community assembled for worship. In the worship service of the Christians the Lord fills the believers, who like a mirror take upon themselves the splendor of his light, with his presence. But of course this idea then is expanded in the apostle's thought to include the whole of the Christian life.

For the apostle, the eucharist is a κοινωνία τοῦ αἵματος καὶ τοῦ σώματος Χριστοῦ (I Cor. 10:16). What Paul so painstakingly develops in this context can hardly have been a simple community idea. For the popular view, the Supper must have been simply an eating and drinking of the body and blood of the Lord, a *mysterium tremendum*. Now Paul introduces into the mystery of the cultus a mystical idea. The eucharist is κοινωνία, a mystical personal union of the community with its head; as the community blends into a miraculous unity, a body, through participation in the one bread— so the apostle presents it—just so does it also experience κοινωνία with the exalted Lord. But it is of course a miraculous κοινωνία τοῦ αἵματος καὶ τοῦ σώματος, a union with the exalted Lord which extends even to include corporeality. But again now this idea goes beyond cult and sacrament: "God is faithful, through whom you were called to the κοινωνία of his Son Jesus Christ our Lord" (I Cor. 1:9; Phil. 3:10).

In conclusion we may still refer to a detail. In Rom. 5, in his portrayal of the life of the Christian who is reconciled with God, Paul repeatedly speaks of

---

[8] The remarks of Corssen, ZNW XIX, 1919/20, pp. 2 ff., against Reitzenstein's statements in the *Historia Lausiaca*, pp. 243 ff., prompt me to hold to this translation rather than Reitzenstein's interpretation (κατοπτρίζεσθαι=to be reflected in).

his καυχᾶσθαι as a special characteristic feature: καυχώμενοι ἐν τῷ θεῷ διὰ Ἰησοῦ Χριστοῦ. Should not the rejoicing of the worship services in the Christian communities have been uppermost in his mind here also? The phrase in Phil. 3:3, οἱ πνεύματι θεοῦ λατρεύοντες καὶ καυχώμενοι ἐν Χριστῷ Ἰησοῦ renders this conjecture highly probable. In this connection we also think of the portrayal in Acts of the Christians' worship in Jerusalem (2:46 ἐν ἀγαλλιάσει) and in Antioch (11:28, Codex D: ἦν δὲ πολλὴ ἀγαλλίασις; cf. I Pet. 1:6). And since we are already discussing Rom. 5, it may be pointed out that it is a cultic idea when Paul speaks of our having προσαγωγή through Christ, the same idea which then in Hebrews moves into the central position with its statements about the ἀρχιερεὺς τῆς ὁμολογίας ἡμῶν. Thus the cultus and the whole Christian life for Paul lie everywhere interwoven with each other. But everywhere the apostle pushes out above and beyond the piety of the cultus and the sacrament which surrounds and envelops him, to the purely ethical-religious, to the intellectual-personal!

Thus we can get a glimpse into the coming-to-be and the growing of the Pauline Christ mysticism and of the formulas of ἐν Χριστῷ or ἐν κυρίῳ εἶναι which summarized it. All this first of all grew out of the cultus; the Lord who governs the entire personal life of the Christian has developed out of the cultically present Kyrios.

II. *The Identification of* κύριος *and* πνεῦμα. This derivation and explanation of the Pauline Christ piety out of the community cult and cult mysticism now becomes even more convincing through the fact that we can point to a second wholly parallel process in the formation of Paul's thoughts.

It is in fact generally known how there is a second formula immediately parallel and analogous to the Pauline formula of ἐν κυρίῳ (Χριστῷ) εἶναι: it is the ἐν πνεύματι εἶναι. The two formulas coincide so completely that they can be interchanged at will. The Christian is ἐν Χριστῷ as he is ἐν πνεύματι.[9] As the Spirit dwells in the believers, so also Christ dwells in them.[10] And all the manifestations of the new Christian life can be traced back by Paul in similar fashion to the Spirit or to Christ.[11]

---

[9] Rom. 8:9; cf. with I Cor. 1:30; II Cor. 5:17; Rom. 8:1, and 16:11.

[10] Rom. 8:9; I Cor. 3:16; cf. with Rom. 8:10; II Cor. 13:5, and Gal. 2:20.

[11] ἀγάπη ἐν Χριστῷ, I Cor. 16:24; Rom. 8:39; ἐν πνεύματι, Col. 1:8; δικαιωθῆναι ἐν Χριστῷ, Gal. 2:17; ἐν πνεύματι, I Cor. 6:11; δικαιοσύνη ἐν πνεύματι ἁγίῳ, Rom. 14:17; δικαιοσύνη ἐν αὐτῷ (sc. Χριστῷ) II Cor. 5:21; life wrought by the Spirit, Rom.

But the two formulas are also related in that they have a similar genesis. As the ἐν κυρίῳ εἶναι of Paul grew out of the worship experience and the cult mysticism of the community, thus also his doctrine of the Pneuma emerged through a grand reworking of a popular view which has its roots essentially in the living experience of the community, especially its experience of worship. Let us imagine this popular view of the Spirit and of his actions. According to it the Pneuma is the completely supernaturally regarded divine power which seizes man in ecstasy and makes him capable of miracles.[12] The ecstatic glossolalia (speaking in tongues) as well as its interpretation; prophecy, ranging from the inspired utterance of the prophet who proclaims heavenly mysteries to soothsaying and mind reading[13]; ecstatic prayer, healing of the sick and driving out of demons; immunity to snakebite and all sorts of poisons; visions and ecstatic trances; indeed ultimately all sudden and unexplained impulses of human psychical life—all this is the sphere of influence of the Spirit.[14] Behind this popular view there stands clearly visible a still more primitive one, which breaks through even in Paul when he speaks of πνεύματα in the plural. As there are evil demons, so according to this view there are good spirits,[15] and both classes of spirits surround man with their powers. There is only a value distinction between possession by a good spirit and by an evil one. But this bare animism to be sure is overcome in large measure in the milieu of the New Testament communities. It is the one, the holy Spirit, the Spirit of God, who is active in his various gifts.

But most of all it must be emphatically pointed out that the effects of the Spirit become vital and come to actualization in essence in the community gathered for worship. Prophets, those who speak in tongues, wonder-workers, exorcists pursue their work above all in the Christians' worship (I Cor. 12). Through them worship acquires its characteristic mark; the pneumatics are the leaders of the cultic community life. According to the account in

---

8:2, 11, 13; Gal. 6:8; life in Christ, Rom. 6:23; cf. 6:11; I Cor. 15:22, etc. Cf. Deissner, *Auferstehungshoffnung und Pneumagedanke bei Paulus* (1912), p. 93; Gunkel, *Die Wirkungen des Geistes,* pp. 97 ff.

[12] It is the merit of Gunkel, *Die Wirkungen des heiligen Geistes* (1888), to have taught us this. Cf. also Weinel, *Die Wirkungen des Geistes und der Geister im nachapostolischen Zeitalter bis auf Irenaeus* (1899). On this, my review in GGA, 1901, No. 10, pp. 753-76.

[13] I Cor. 14:24-25; cf. 2:15.

[14] Cf. esp. I Cor. 12-14 and the pneumatic passages in the book of Acts; also Mark 16:17 ff., although nothing is said about the Spirit here.

[15] I Cor. 12:10; 14:12; 14:32 (πνεύματα τῶν προφητῶν! With this, cf. Rev. 22:6). In 14:12 and 14:32, some mss. have emended the text by removing the plural.

Acts the Spirit comes over the community assembled in worship (4:31). In the sacrament of baptism he descends upon the one being baptized (Acts 10:44; 19:6). The hymns and songs of the community are prompted by the Spirit (ᾠδαὶ πνευματικαί, Col. 3:16). Later witnesses far into the second century can here be adduced. Most of all the classic portrayal of prophecy in the eleventh Mandate of Hermas is recalled [16]: "Now when the man who possesses the Spirit of God comes into the assembly of righteous men who have faith in the Spirit of God, and prayer goes up to God from the assembly of those men, then the angel of the prophetic spirit fills the man; and the man, filled with the spirit, speaks to the throng as the Lord wills." In contrast to this, it is a mark of the false prophet that he avoids the assembly of the pious. The intimate connection between pneumatic experience and community cult cannot come out any more clearly than this. Naturally it would be foolish to assert that this was the only source of ecstatic experiences for the early Christians. Obviously individual ecstasy played its role in the life of the early Christians; for this it suffices simply to refer to the person of Paul.[17] But the observation still stands that in earliest Christianity the Spirit most powerfully and effectively blazed up in the community gathered for worship, and that until far into the second century the activities of the Spirit were a characteristic possession of the cultic community life. Only in the assembled community was the δύναμις Χριστοῦ effective, which enabled it to hand over to Satan the evildoer; Paul, who intends to be present with his spirit from a distance, feels himself a link in the chain (I Cor. 5:4-5).

But now what has Paul made out of these simple and naïve conceptions! Although he himself still partly lives in the middle of them, glories in his

[16] Cf. further the portrayal of the prophets in the congregation at Antioch in Acts 12:28, Codex D, and of Ignatius' ecstatic behavior in the congregation in Philad. V, 7. Above all, Irenaeus II, 31.2; II, 32.4 in Eus. CH. V, 7.2: miracle of raising the dead διὰ τὸ ἀναγκαῖον τῆς κατὰ τόπου ἐκκλησίας πάσης αἰτησαμένης μετὰ νηστείας καὶ λιτανείας πολλῆς. V, 7.5, οὐκ ἔστιν ἀριθμὸν εἰπεῖν τῶν χαρισμάτων, ὧν κατὰ παντὸς τοῦ κόσμου ἡ ἐκκλησία παρὰ θεοῦ λαβοῦσα ἐν τῷ ὀνόματι 'Ιησοῦ Χριστοῦ τοῦ σταυρωθέντος ἐπὶ Ποντίου Πιλάτου ἐκάστης ἡμέρας . . . ἐπιτελεῖ. Esp. interesting is the note in Tertullian, de anima 9, about Montanist prophecy, which regularly occurs during the congregation's worship in a state of ecstasy. For a long time the exorcists form a class of the minor church officers.

[17] It appears almost as if Paul emphasizes individual ecstasy more strongly than does his environment. His opinion that glossolalia is to be essentially a transaction between the individual and his God, and one is to employ this gift in the congregation only under precautions, contradicts the analogy of the by far most common phenomena of speaking in tongues, as the background of which an ecstatically stimulated congregation almost always appears.

signs and wonders as apostolic attestations,[18] is proud of his speaking in tongues[19] and his visions,[20] and ascribes to his spirit even pneumatic effects from a distance,[21] he goes far beyond these conceptions. He makes the Pneuma into the element of the entire new Christian life, not only on its specially miraculous side but in its total ethical and religious attitude. As its fruits he enumerates all the virtues of the Christian life (Gal. 5:22-23). The great gracious gift of Christian liberty is the work or the life-expression of the Spirit (II Cor. 3:17). This is a complete μετάβασις εἰς ἄλλο γένος. According to the popular view the Spirit works in speaking in tongues, healing of the sick, prophecy, exorcism of demons, ecstasies; according to the view of Paul which is built upon these he works peace, joy, love, patience. In the popular view the spirit is the power of God which for a moment or at least only for a specific time rests upon a man, only then to leave him again. Paul speaks of a constant walk in the Spirit, through whom the law of God is fulfilled and the lust of the flesh is restrained (Rom. 8:4; Gal. 5:16, 25); of a continuing mind (φρόνημα) of the Spirit; of his dwelling in man (Rom. 8:6, 9, 11). In the popular view the Spirit comes upon some few favored ones whom people know by name, the bearers of the Spirit who lead the worship of the Christians. But Paul decrees that the Spirit belongs to the necessary stock of possessions of each Christian life. Whoever does not have the Spirit of Christ does not belong to him (Rom. 8:9)! Indeed, this Spirit is given to every individual Christian at the very outset along with faith and baptism (Gal. 3:2, 5; I Cor. 12:13). In the popular view the Spirit stands most of all in connection with worship and cultus; according to Paul it is the great basic reality of the Christian life.

Now we can draw the parallel. We have seen that behind the Christ mysticism of the apostle stands the Kyrios who is active in the cult of the community with his miraculous powers and his fullness of life. And behind the Spirit mysticism of Paul stands the living reality of the pneumatic experiences which again are most abundantly and powerfully unfolded in the worshiping assembly. No wonder when in Paul the two entities κύριος and πνεῦμα, though not everywhere and not completely, begin to merge, when for him the Spirit becomes the Spirit of Christ, and he can finally say: ὁ δὲ κύριος τὸ πνεῦμά ἐστιν (II Cor. 3:18).

[18] II Cor. 12:12; Rom. 15:19.
[19] I Cor. 14:18.
[20] II Cor. 12:1 ff.
[21] I Cor. 5:3-5.

III. *Religio-Historical Estimate of Paul's Christ Mysticism*. Before we spin out these threads further, a general religio-historical evaluation of the apostle's Christ mysticism must be attempted. For this Christ mysticism of Paul, the genesis of which we are surveying to some extent, is a religio-historical phenomenon of high and general significance. It resounds a quite special note of personal sentiment and of fervent mystical mood. This striking interweaving of abstraction and the personal, this binding together of a religious principle with a person who has walked here upon earth and has suffered death here, is a phenomenon of unique power and originality. It unmistakably gave to Pauline Christianity a great part of its impetus and its striking force. In this Christ mysticism the element of deity appears visible and palpable to the believing soul in a manner previously unheard of. And once again the strong sense of man's distance from the divine is maintained.

This becomes especially clear when we raise the question about direct parallels to Paul's Christ mysticism in the realm of Hellenistic religion. We see at first glance that it is not altogether easy to find such parallels at all. The religious mysticism of declining antiquity moves along a similar and yet characteristically different line. The goal of Greek (orientally conditioned) piety, as has been ever more clearly shown, is deification: In the sacred devotion the man dies and the new god is born.[22] This conviction comes to expression concisely and clearly in Poimandres: τοῦτό ἐστι τὸ ἀγαθὸν τέλος τοῖς γνῶσιν ἐσχηκόσι θεωθῆναι (§ 26). The wide distribution of this ideal of deification and its dominance in the piety of late antiquity is to be discussed in context later on. The main thing here is essentially to bring out one side of this idea: This Greek mystery piety does not so much concern a life in the deity, with the deity, but rather a mystical identity with the deity. When at the high point of the Isis mystery, as Apuleius[23] has portrayed it for us, the initiate is clothed in a costly coat which reaches to the ankles and is adorned with rich designs, "which the initiates call the Olympian stole"; when he then, with brightly burning torch in his hand and with a halo of palm leaves upon his head, "adorned like the sun," is

---

[22] In the portrayal of the Isis mystery in Apuleius, Metamorph. XI, 21 (cf. chap. 23), the initiation is correspondingly called *voluntaria mors*. The other initiates present farewell gifts to the person who is to be initiated, as one offers them to a dead person. Reitzenstein, *Hellenistische Mysterienreligionen*, pp. 110 ff. [2nd ed., pp. 132 ff.].

[23] Cf. Metamorphoses XI, 24; Reitzenstein, pp. 28 ff. [2nd ed., pp. 28 ff.].

presented like a statue to the worshiping people[24] when the curtain is suddenly drawn back—all this signifies nothing other than that in this moment the initiate serves as the incarnate deity of the mystery.[25] When in the Attis initiation the initiate, following the example of his cult-hero, performs on himself the fearful act of emasculation, he himself thereby becomes Attis and experiences with him his death and his return from death. We possess a still later witness for this view which follows from the meaning of the ceremony itself. In the account of Damascius about the entrance into the cave of Hierapolis it is said [26]: ἐδόκουν ὄναρ ὁ Ἄττης γενέσθαι καί μοι ἐπιτελεῖσθαι παρὰ τῆς Ματρὸς τῶν θεῶν τὴν τῶν Ἱλαρίων[27] καλομένην ἑορτήν. ὅπερ ἐδήλου τὴν ἐξ ᾅδου γεγονυῖαν ἡμῶν σωτηρίαν.

Partly transformed into the magical realm, yet in such a way that the originally religious character still everywhere shines through, these conceptions appear in the Hermetic prayers and other religious witnesses which Reitzenstein[28] has collected from the literature of magic as the closest parallels to the piety of the Corpus Hermeticum. There, *inter alia,* appears the following: σὺ γὰρ εἶ ἐγὼ καὶ ἐγὼ σύ. ὃ ἂν εἴπω, ἀεὶ γενέσθω. τὸ γὰρ ὄνομά σου ἔχω ὡς φυλακτήριον ἐν τῇ καρδίᾳ τῇ ἐμῇ.[29] There an initiate prays: "Come to me, Hermes, as children come into the body of women. . . . I know you, Hermes, and you know me. I am you, and you are I." [30] Or again: "For you are I and I am you. Your name is mine and mine is yours. I am your image (εἴδωλον)." [31]

[24] Nothing is said here directly about praying. It says only: "The people hung on my appearance." Still, cf. the portrayal of the taurobolium (Attis mystery?) in Prudentius, Peristephan. X, 1046 ff. (Hepding, *Attis,* p. 66), where it is said at the end, when the initiate climbs out of the pit: *omnes salutant atque adorant eminus.*

[25] The god with whom the initiate is identified here is, as it appears, Serapis, who in later interpretations is frequently identified with the sun-god, whose attribute is the halo. (Papyrus XLVI, Brit. Mus. V. 5, ἐπικαλοῦμαί σε Ζεῦ Ἥλιε Μίθρα Σάραπι. Zeus Helios Sarapis is a title of the god frequently found on inscriptions.)

[26] Vita Isidori in Photius, Cod. 242, p. 345 a, ed. Becker.

[27] About the Hilaria (resurrection) festival, cf. Hepding, *Attis,* pp. 167 ff.

[28] *Poimandres,* pp. 15 ff.

[29] *Poimandres,* p. 17. Here mysticism and magic are completely intertwined. The idea of the *unio mystica* is connected with the other, that the magician possesses the powerful name of God. But this *Onoma* again is felt as a present spiritual force.

[30] Cf. *Poimandres,* p. 20. With this, cf. a curious Christian parallel from a later time. In Symeon, the "new theologian," is found the sentence: μακάριος ὁ τὸ φῶς τοῦ κόσμου ἐν ἑαυτῷ μορφωθὲν θεασάμενος, ὅτι αὐτὸς ὡς ἔμβρυον ἔχων τὸν Χριστὸν μήτηρ αὐτοῦ λογισθήσεται (Holl, *Enthusiasmus und Bussgewalt,* p. 71). The Hellenistic piety is also transmitted in its fantastic imagery.

[31] *Poimandres,* p. 21. The term εἴδωλον is significant. Thus one sought to explain the duplication of the deity by having the pious person be related to the deity as to its εἴδωλον

This *unio mystica* takes on a completely pantheistic, speculative color in the prophetic consecration of Hermes. To the question of what kind of form the reborn one will have, the mystical answer is given: τὸ πᾶν ἐν παντὶ ἐκ πασῶν δυνάμεων ἐνεστώς (XIII, 2). And after the ceremony is completed, we read: πάτερ τὸ πᾶν ὁρῶ καὶ ἐμαυτὸν ἐν τῷ Νωΐ (§ 13). Finally, after the great pantheistic confession: σὴ Βουλὴ ἀπὸ σοῦ, ἐπὶ σὲ τὸ πᾶν, the mystic concludes his hymn with the words: Βουλῇ τῇ σῇ ἀναπέπαυμαι[32] (§ 19).

A passage of Asclepius (Ps.-Apuleius) which may be presented here in conclusion shows how startlingly every distinction between divine and human appears erased in this entire religious attitude. Here it is said that man has the ability through the magical consecration of pictures (picture-magic) to make gods. As a parallel and analogy to this idea there is drawn the idea that in the consecration he himself becomes a god: *"Et non solum inluminatur*[33] (in the mystery religion consecration) *verum etiam inluminat, nec solum ad deum proficit, verum etiam conformat deos"* (chap. 23).

There is no doubt that Paul with his formula of ἐν Χριστῷ εἶναι takes a distinctive position as contrasted with these views. In him the plain and bare formula that the believer becomes the Christos himself is never uttered. Paul rather instinctively shrinks back from this formula just as he shrinks from explicitly calling Christ God. The distance between the believers and the Christos is maintained. Christ remains the surpassing element, the spiritual being who takes the believers into himself. The piety of the mystery system is absolutely individualistic, eudaemonistic, egoistic; the individual mystic achieves for himself the blessed state of deification. The divine is completely absorbed into the human. These perils are avoided in Paul. Christos remains the *Kyrios*. The believer is taken up into his being, but this is not inverted.[34]

---

To this corresponds the identification of the young Ptolemy god as εἰκὼν ζῶσα on the Rosetta inscription, and the designation of the ruler as ἐναργὴς ἐπιφάνεια of the deity. The designations of Christ as εἰκών, ἀπαύγασμα, χαρακτήρ of God the Father belong in part to this context (on all this, see below, Chap. VII); Paul nowhere says quite directly that the believers are εἰκών of Christ; II Cor. 3:18, τὴν αὐτὴν εἰκόνα μεταμορφούμεθα, comes nearest to it; Rom. 8:29 is probably, and I Cor. 15:49 is certainly conceived eschatologically (cf. further Col. 3:10).

[32] A similar pantheistic mysticism in Corp. Hermet. XI, 20-21.

[33] Inluminari=φωτίζεσθαι (!) here has the immediate meaning of deification.

[34] Of course at one point within Hellenistic mystery piety there is a certain analogy to the Pauline conception. I refer to the significance which the god Nous-Hermes has in certain parts of the Corpus Hermeticum, particularly in the Poimandres. Here, within a clearer mysticism, he appears of course as does the pneuma in Paul, as the higher element

A second great basic feature of Pauline mysticism is joined with this. In the apostle, strictly conceived, it is not the individual believer who appears as the actual correlate to Christ, but the community, the σῶμα Χριστοῦ.

When Paul feels the eucharist to be κοινωνία τοῦ αἵματος καὶ τοῦ σώματος Χριστοῦ, he immediately connects it in his thinking with the body of the community which is nourished and united through the one bread (I Cor. 10:16-17). Thus where the apostle speaks of the whole of the community's life, this image of the body urges itself upon him with intense power and in all its consequences (vide supra, p. 156), until the ideas are joined for him in the late Epistle to the Colossians in the sublime confession: καὶ αὐτός ἐστιν ἡ κεφαλὴ τοῦ σώματος τῆς ἐκκλησίας (1:18). The false teacher is then characterized as οὐ κρατῶν τὴν κεφαλήν. And the mysticism reaches a climax in the sentence ἐξ οὗ πᾶν τὸ σῶμα διὰ τῶν ἀφῶν καὶ συνδέσμων ἐπιχορηγούμενον καὶ συμβιβαζόμενον αὔξει τὴν αὔξησιν τοῦ θεοῦ (2:19).

Thus the Christ mysticism becomes for the apostle the foundation of a new sociological view. On this point there arises for him a sense of community of an unprecedented power and intensity: ἡ ἀγάπη τοῦ Χριστοῦ συνέχει ἡμᾶς, "so that those who live should no longer live unto themselves, but unto him who for their sakes died and is risen again" (II Cor. 5:14-15).

Quite certainly something of this feeling of belonging together and of these social instincts had become vivid in the piety of the Hellenistic mysteries. Participation in the common initiation often led to a closer association of life in general; here in this milieu, as we know, the designation of the participants in the same cultus as brother and sister[35] arose inde-

---

of life of the pious and believing persons. The ultimate goal of deification is maintained (I, 26), but actually this ideal of deification divests itself of its naturally eudaemonistic character; it means the surrender to the new (supernatural) life element and the absorption in it. I, 21: "But tell me, o Nous, how can I enter into life? And my god said: 'The man who exists in the Nous will come to know himself. . . . I myself, the Nous, am present with the holy and good and pure and merciful and those who live in piety. And my presence becomes a help, and at the same time they perceive all things and conciliate the father in love, and praise and thank and honor him, devoted to him in love.' " X, 21: "The Nous enters into the pious soul and leads it to the light of knowledge." Cf. also the prayer in Reitzenstein, Poimandres, p. 17: εἰσέλθοις τὸν ἐμὸν νοῦν καὶ τὰς ἐμὰς φρένας εἰς τὸν ἅπαντα χρόνον τῆς ζωῆς μου. The mysticism in the initiation of the prophets, on the other hand (see above), has a completely natural, sacramental character; yet cf. here also XIII, 3: ἐγεννήθην ἐν Νῷ. § 13: τὸ πᾶν ὁρῶ καὶ ἐμαυτὸν ἐν τῷ Νοῖ. Nevertheless the Nous here is everywhere an utterly bloodless abstraction, and there is lacking the personal element which appears in the ἐν κυρίῳ of Paul.

[35] Reitzenstein, Poimandres, p. 154. Dölger, ᾽Ιχθύς, p. 135.

pendent of the appearance of Christianity. Here the mystic began to identify the mystagogue as "father," and the latter to call the former "son." [36] Here, in the tight little circle which often felt itself misjudged and scorned by all the world, an intensive life of fellowship could develop.[37] But we may not overlook the obverse side of the matter. In this connection less weight is to be placed upon the defective exclusiveness of these religions and consequently the sharp fluctuation of their adherents who frequently tried out now one group and then another and often were members of several societies at the same time. On the contrary the viewpoint already mentioned above comes quite significantly into account here. Since the goal of the religious mystery initiation is the individualistically eudaemonistic goal of deification, here all sense of fellowship was overrun by the aristocratic self-consciousness of the individual mystic who has found fulfillment in the initiation. Thus on this soil is developed the characteristic figure of the religious leader. The authentically Greek aristocratic interpretation of the wise man[38] as the θεῖος ἄνθρωπος who alone stands firm in a tottering world, who is leader and savior, pastor and pedagogue for his environment, is transferred to the new θεῖος ἄνθρωπος, the mystagogue.[39] With the gradual spiritualizing of the mystery religions and their development from the purely cultic to the religious and moral, this person becomes at the same time preacher of a new religious-philosophical world view and of a morality connected with it. But this new leader feels himself to be on a solitary aristocratic height, to which he gradually draws only some elect ones to himself, while the majority even of the fellow members of the mystery cult, who achieve only the lower degrees of initiation, remain far beneath. As the ἄνθρωπος θεοῦ he is elevated above the entire lower world in self-satisfied dignity and seclusion.

In contrast to all this, Paul's preaching of the ἐν Χριστῷ (ἐν κυρίῳ) εἶναι means a new world. It means the ministering absorption of the individual will in one great surpassing, world-embracing will which is expressed

---

[36] Dieterich, *Mithrasliturgie*, pp. 153 ff.

[37] Cf. the beautiful portrayal of mood in Corp. Herm. IX, 4.

[38] Cf. the splendidly comprehensive portrayal of this figure in Holl, "Die schriftstellerische Form des griechischen Heiligenlebens," *Neue Jahrbücher für das klassische Altertum*, XXIX (1912), 418. Esp. pertinent material is found in the Alexandrian Philo.

[39] On the image of this new leader, cf. the close of the Poimandres and No. XIII of the Corpus Hermeticum (the initiation of prophets); further the source drawn by Reitzenstein from the Paris magical papyrus Mimaut, in *Poimandres*, pp. 147 ff. (ποίησόν με ὑπηρέτην τῶν ἀνὰ σκιάν μου); the confession of the Gnostic, Valentinus (Clem. Alex., Strom. IV, 13.89). Most of all, also, Od. Sol. 10, 15, 17, 20, 28, 29, and 36. The fact that it often remains unclear whether in these psalms it is the messiah or the initiate (mystagogue) who is spoken of is precisely the characteristic thing.

in the totality of a comprehensive fellowship, the triumphant awareness of being incorporated into a power that moves from victory to victory ("Here there is neither Jew nor Greek, neither bond nor free, neither male nor female. For you are all one in Christ Jesus"); the victorious confidence given therewith as to the purpose and meaning of their own work—"we are God's fellow-laborers." It signifies a much stronger stressing of the ethos, the moral obligation, a deliverance of religion out of its individualistic erroneous ways into which it had gone astray with the collapse of the national religions, and thus out of weakness and aimlessness.

Nevertheless we must not overstress the opposites which here come to light. The different worlds touch and the threads run this way and that. It can hardly be denied that here and there Paul, with his high sense of the pneumatic who leads his life ἐν Χριστῷ, ἐν κυρίῳ, approaches the just described aristocratic high sense of the θεῖος ἄνθρωπος (the mystagogue). It is true that the explicit idea of deification is still remote from the apostle. He never said: ἐγώ εἰμι ὁ Χριστός. But expressions are found in him in which he touches upon this idea. In heightened mysticism he can say of himself: καὶ ἀνταναπληρῶ τὰ ὑστερήματα τῶν θλίψεων τοῦ Χριστοῦ ἐν τῇ σαρκί μου ὑπὲρ τοῦ σώματος αὐτοῦ, ὅ ἐστιν ἡ ἐκκλησία (Col. 1:24). Denials of his truthfulness and trustworthiness are for him a blasphemy against his Lord and *his* truthfulness (II Cor. 1:19; 11:10). Doubts of his fitness and probity are directed against Christ himself: ἐπεὶ δοκιμὴν ζητεῖτε τοῦ ἐν ἐμοὶ λαλοῦντος Χριστοῦ (II Cor. 13:3). This consciousness often gives to his battles the character of passionate animosity and irritation. In his opponents he sees opponents of the pneuma which governs him. For him they easily become servants of Satan and their motives prompted by an evil will, deliberate wickedness.

He sharply draws the boundary between the pneumatic and the ordinary man, the man who has only a psyche. The pneumatic, who has come to know the depths of the Deity, lives in a completely different sphere and leaves the world of the psychic person far beneath him.[40] And as a pneumatic, the apostle boldly breaks all the historical connections that are burdensome to him, rejects the authorities in Jerusalem, and intends no longer to know Ἰησοῦς κατὰ σάρκα.[41] All this has something grand and powerful about it; it alone placed Paul in a position to burst open the fetters

---

[40] I Cor. 3:1-3; 2:10 ff.
[41] Gal. 1:16; II Cor. 5:16.

which still hampered the victorious march of the young religion that was striving toward universalism. Yet in other places, especially in Rome, the same development took place along more peaceful lines and without this violence. Surely a developing church fellowship must have been threatened by peculiar perils[42] through such a subjectivism full of new and unprecedented revelations, whose legitimations rested wholly upon themselves. It was not wholly unjustified that the opponents accused Paul of preaching himself (II Cor. 4:5).

And finally, in this picture of the pneumatic also belongs the heightened consciousness of the perfection of his present Christian estate, with all the recognition of the corruption and wickedness of the earlier condition out of which God has redeemed him through Christ. The daring word which Paul hurls at his Corinthian community, οὐδὲν ἐμαυτῷ σύνοιδα (I Cor. 4:4) may be born out of the attitude of the moment, and in the following clause (ἀλλ᾽ οὐκ ἐν τούτῳ δεδικαίωμαι) it acquires some limitation, but in general we still may say that Paul experiences sin in his life only as an exceptional state[43]; he never enumerated it among the inimical powers which are able to separate the Christian from his God.[44]

It is the religious superman, the θεῖος ἄνθρωπος, who at least in part is stirring in Paul, in all his sublimity and with all his perils. Thus there remains a certain affinity between the Pauline Christ mysticism and that mystery piety portrayed above. But the other side of the matter hardly needs to be stressed once again. One needs only to call to mind the picture of how Paul as organizer held sway in his churches in order to see that he knew how to overcome the dangers of an individualistic and eudaemonistical nature mysticism. The fact that he could do this has its basis in the peculiarity of his Christ mysticism. Basically Christ always remained for him the element far surpassing and embracing his own life, the higher law of his "I."

Finally, this Christ mysticism that is peculiar to Paul became significant for the history of mysticism in general. The ἐν Χριστῷ of the apostle

---

[42] Cf. the splendid comments of Reitzenstein, *Hellenistische Mysterienreligionen*, pp. 203-4 [2nd ed., pp. 234-35].

[43] One should note esp. the relation of the clauses in Gal. 2:19 and 20: after the plerophoric Ζῶ δὲ οὐκέτι ἐγώ, ζῇ δὲ ἐν ἐμοὶ Χριστός—the reluctant admission: ὃ δὲ νῦν ζῶ ἐν σαρκί.

[44] Rom. 8:37-38; Phil. 3:12; the goal which Paul pursues and with respect to which he senses his imperfection is not the liberation from sin and guilt but the ἐξανάστασις ἐκ νεκρῶν (3:11). Cf. II Cor. 4:7 ff.; 12:7. Paraeneses like Rom. 6:12 ff. are not characteristic of Paul's own Christian consciousness. Nevertheless even here the thought is expressed that sin has actually already disappeared from the Christian's life and must still be opposed only on the periphery.

became for the Christian religion a stage out of which the God mysticism was to be developed. It is extraordinarily characteristic that, as often as he speaks of an εἶναι ἐν Χριστῷ and of a dwelling of Christ in us, he knows almost nothing at all of the expressions εἶναι ἐν θεῷ, or θεός ἐστι (οἰκεῖ) ἐν ἡμῖν. It is true that once, if the Colossian epistle is authentic, Paul uses the mystical expression of the life of the Christians which is hidden in God (3:3; cf. Eph. 3:9). And here and there one can perhaps point out expressions which contain a certain God mysticism.[45] But in comparison with the large amount of space which Christ mysticism occupies in his thought, all this hardly comes into consideration. In Paul a note like the saying in Acts 17:28, ἐν αὐτῷ γὰρ ζῶμεν καὶ κινούμεθα καὶ ἐσμέν, is not actually sounded.

But even in the territory of Hellenistic piety this God mysticism is not at home. This is shown by the very scanty and fragmentary parallels which Norden was able to adduce in his *Agnostos Theos*[46] in his investigation of this passage, in spite of his being well-read in the field. Deissmann also, a long time ago, on the occasion of his study of the formulas ἐν Χριστῷ (εἶναι) and ἐν θεῷ, expressed the judgment: "Nothing decisive can be ascertained out of analogies in profane literature, for strictly speaking these are completely lacking." [47]

If now on the other hand we can make the observation that already in the Johannine writings the God mysticism has been fairly richly developed, the judgment can be ventured that, in the history of the Christian religion, God mysticism developed out of Christ mysticism. The mood of the ἐν θεῷ

[45] The καυχᾶσθαι ἐν θεῷ in Rom. 2:17 and 5:11 does not at all belong here, and the same judgment is to be made about the παρρησιάζεσθαι ἐν θεῷ in I Thess. 2:2. The formula of greeting ἐν θεῷ in I and II Thess. is avoided by Paul in the other epistles. Further to be mentioned are such expressions as ζῆν τῷ θεῷ in Rom. 6:10-11. Yet note that the bare formula is used here only of Christ, and that it is said of the Christians: ζῶντας δὲ τῷ θεῷ ἐν Χριστῷ Ἰησοῦ; cf. Gal. 2:19. θεὸς γάρ ἐστιν ὁ ἐνεργῶν ἐν ἡμῖν, Phil. 2:13. Distinctive also is the expression in I Cor. 3:16: ὅτι ναὸς θεοῦ ἐστε καὶ τὸ πνεῦμα τοῦ θεοῦ ἐν ἡμῖν οἰκεῖ.

[46] Cf. pp. 21-23. It is worthy of note that among the few parallels, one is provided by the Corpus Hermeticum: XI, 18: πάντα ἐστὶν ἐν τῷ θεῷ οὐχ ὡς ἐν τόπῳ κείμενα· ὁ μὲν γὰρ τόπος καὶ σῶμά ἐστιν καὶ ἀκίνητον, καὶ τὰ κείμενα κίνησιν οὐκ ἔχει (cf. IX, 6). Norden further draws a comparison with Marcus Aurelius IV, 23: ἐν σοὶ (the personified φύσις) πάντα. Cf. also the statements of Reitzenstein, "Die Areopagrede des Paulus," *Neue Jahrb. f. d. klass. Altertum*, XXXI (1913), 397, and also esp. about the passage in Dio Chrysostom in the Olympic discourse, §§ 27 ff., περὶ τῆς πρώτου τοῦ θεοῦ ἐννοίας. The question as to how far a certain personality mysticism already springs up in Hellenism out of natural pantheistic mysticism demands renewed investigation.

[47] Deissmann, *Die Formel "in Christo Jesu"* (1892), p. 94. The judgment is perhaps too sharp; see Norden, *Agnostos Theos*, p. 23, n. 4.

εἶναι, which is not so simply offered and is not so self-evident, arose out of that of the ἐν Χριστῷ εἶναι.

IV. *The Christ–Adam Theology.* A highly individual and not easily understandable Christ speculation is bound up with the Christ mysticism in the apostle. The Kyrios Christos who is present, from whom the new exalted life of the Christians emanates, becomes for him the δεύτερος Ἀδάμ, the second man, in comparison with the first Adam higher in essence, the creator and head of a new and by nature exalted humanity. Just as Paul's Christ mysticism stands in closest connection with the pneuma mysticism, so also one cannot understand his Christ speculation without going into his whole doctrine of the Spirit and the great contrast of πνεῦμα and σάρξ which dominates the Pauline theology. The apostle himself points us to this larger context when in I Cor. 15:45 he defines as the nature of the first Adam the ψυχὴ ζῶσα, and that of the second Adam the πνεῦμα ζωοποιοῦν (cf. II Cor. 3:17, ὁ κύριος τὸ πνεῦμά ἐστιν); and when he calls the first man χοϊκός (he could also have said σαρκικός), the second ἐπουράνιος.

This time we will even do well to proceed from the Pauline πνεῦμα–σάρξ doctrine, in order then on this broader basis first to comprehend in its total import Paul's speculation about the first and the second man, for which there are not so many witnesses at our command.

In this context, only the basic features of the Pauline pneuma doctrine can be taken into account. Two things must be especially emphasized: (1) the stark, supernatural basic outlook which dominates the whole, and (2) the strong natural trait with its intermingling of the spiritual and the sensual which characterizes the Pauline speculation.

1. The starkly supernatural total outlook: one would not rightly understand the apostle if one were to speak of his pneuma doctrine as a component part of his psychology or anthropology. Strictly speaking[48] one cannot even speak of the pneuma as a psychological possession of man in Paul's sense. In the actual meaning of the word there is only one divine spirit.

Where Paul speaks of a "spirit" of man, he is expressing himself imprecisely and not terminologically. But this happens on the whole very

---

[48] Holtzmann, *Lehrbuch der neutestamentlichen Theologie,* 2nd ed., II, 19: "Strictly speaking, what is said leads to the conclusion that in Paul's anthropology it is highly improper to speak of a spirit of man as original endowment of man."

seldom.[49] Otherwise the spirit belongs to God and stands in sharp contrast to this world (I Cor. 2:12, πνεῦμα τοῦ κόσμου). Man has it only as a gift of divine grace.

The natural man stands over against this spirit of God in utter isolation. The natural human nature is flesh (σάρξ). The nature of the flesh, however, is in all respects determined by its absolute opposition to the spirit. The nature of the flesh is alienation from God, enmity against God (Rom. 8:7). All moral evil springs from this enmity against God; it is the root of the radically evil in human nature. The flesh is not subject to the law of God, and indeed it cannot be (Rom. 8:7). Therefore spirit and flesh are the two great antagonistic powers striving against each other: "The flesh lusts against the spirit" (Gal. 5:17). Flesh and sin are thus bound indissolubly together. Sin rules in the flesh, or rather the flesh is bound to sin by its nature.[50] Therefore the final end and tendency (φρόνημα) of the flesh is death (Rom. 8:6). All fleshly nature is excluded from the higher heavenly world in principle (I Cor. 15:50). But the ethical task of the Christian life is the mortification of the flesh: νεκρώσατε τὰ μέλη (Col. 3:5); εἰ δὲ πνεύματι τὰς πράξεις τοῦ σώματος θανατοῦτε, ζήσεσθε (Rom. 8:13).

But the σάρξ embraces the whole man, not only his bodily, material nature to which the expression σάρξ appears at first glance to refer. To be sure Paul speaks with special emphasis of the law of sin which rules in his members (7:23), or of the sinful passions in our members (Rom. 7:5), or he warns that sin is not to be allowed to rule in our mortal bodies.[51] But at the same time the inner side of man also belongs wholly to the realm of

---

[49] In I Cor. 2:12, "spirit" means just the inner life of man, and the choice of the expression is occasioned by the parallelism between man and God. Elsewhere also Paul quite generally designates the inner life of man, in contrast to the physical life, by use of the word πνεῦμα (σῶμα, σάρξ; the latter concept then likewise is not terminological): Rom. 1:9; 12:11; I Cor. [5:3?]; 7:34; 16:18; II Cor. 2:13; 7:13; Col. 2:5. Quite unique is Rom. 8:16: "God's Spirit bears witness with our spirit." Here, if one is not satisfied with the assumption of an imprecise manner of speaking on the part of the apostle, "our spirit" is the general element of all Christian life experience, from which then the special ecstatic-enthusiastic experience in the life of prayer (πνεῦμα κατ' ἐξοχήν) is distinguished. The expression μολυσμὸς πνεύματος in II Cor. 7:1 (if it is Pauline, then here too πνεῦμα is simply the inner aspect of man) is strange and is generally recognized as being odd. The trichotomous formula in I Thess. 5:23 likewise cannot be considered for the real terminology of Paul (cf. Phil. 1:27). Perhaps Paul's formula of farewell μετὰ τοῦ πνεύματος ὑμῶν in Gal. 6:18; Phil. 4:23, and Philemon 25 also belongs among the exceptions. In his *Evangelium des Paulus*, Holsten has reckoned the ratio of passages in which "the Spirit" or the (supernatural) Spirit of God which is immanent for man is spoken of to those where πνεῦμα signifies the human spirit, as ninety-one to twelve.

[50] Rom. 7:14, 17-18; 8:3: σάρξ ἁμαρτίας.

[51] Rom. 6:12; cf. Col. 3:5; Rom. 8:10-13.

the lower sarkic world. Where he speaks terminologically, Paul identifies this inner life of the natural man with the term ψυχή. And in the most definite fashion he places the ἄνθρωπος πνευματικός in opposition to the ψυχικός. Anyone who possesses only this natural life of the soul (ὁ ψυχικός means this) lives in a different world from the pneumatic (I Cor. 2:14). The first Adam, in contrast to the second, pneumatic man, is (only) ψυχὴ ζῶσα (I Cor. 15:45). So then as expressions of the σάρξ not only the sexual, specifically bodily sins come in consideration, although the apostle usually names these first in his catalogs of vices, but also all kinds of sins of the soul. Thus he speaks of a mind (φρόνημα) of the σάρξ and its tendency to enmity against God (Rom. 8:6 ff.). Indeed in this context he does not hesitate to speak of a human νοῦς which in contrast with the divine spirit belongs to the natural equipment of man,[52] indeed even stands in opposition to the spirit and also has the corruptible tendency of the flesh.[53] For the apostle the pneumatic who is filled with the Spirit of God and the old man are completely separated from one another, different beings, who have almost nothing in common save the name; only the way of the divine miracle leads from the one to the other. For Paul the ἄνθρωπος πνευματικός is in truth a being of another and a higher category than the natural man. Over against him the sarkics are just simply (plain) men (I Cor. 3:3; cf. 15:32), "only" souls (ψυχικοί), upon whom the pneumatic looks down from his unattainable heights (2:14-16). Just as the ecstatic has ceased to be himself and feels himself seized by an alien force, so also is this the case with Paul's pneumatic Christian: the natural being has completely died in him. In unsurpassed lively fashion the apostle himself, in fact, has expressed this double consciousness of the ecstatic in II Cor. 12:2 ff.: "I know a man in Christ who fourteen years ago—whether in the body or out of the body I do not know; God knows—was caught up into the third heaven. And I know such a man—whether in the body or out of the body I do not know; God knows—who was caught up into Paradise and heard unspeakable words, which it is not lawful for a man to utter. Concerning such a man[54] I will glory, but concerning myself I will not glory except in my weaknesses." This is the divided state of the consciousness in the ecstatic experience. But this now is the striking thing: Paul has extended this manner of thought

[52] I Cor. 14:14-15 (14:19).

[53] φυσιούμενος ὑπὸ τοῦ νοὸς τῆς σαρκός, Col. 2:18; ἀδόκιμος νοῦς, Rom. 1:28 [ματαιότης τοῦ νοός, Eph. 4:17]; cf. also Rom. 12:2, ἀνακαίνωσις τοῦ νοός.

[54] On the translation, cf. Reitzenstein, *Hellenistische Mysterienreligionen,* p. 54 [2nd ed., p. 60].

to the entire life of the Christian; for him it stands under a higher power which slays his "I": for I no longer live, but Christ (the Spirit) lives in me.

Up to this point the matter is completely clear. We see that the supernaturalism of Paul is so strong that it threatens completely to break apart the unity and continuity of the human "I." The Pauline Christian, like the ecstatic, has lost his "I," not temporarily but permanently. The "I" of man is nothing, the powers which determine this "I," whether spirit or flesh, are everything.

But here now enters a somewhat different and moderating view of Paul, which however is not carried through to the point of clarity. Here and there, when he reflects more precisely, he has made the attempt to hold more firmly to the unity of the human "I." This is already basically the case when he sets the "I" in the middle, as it were, between πνεῦμα and σάρξ,[55] so that it now can be affected from one side or the other. But the apostle has conceded most to this human "I" in the great exposition in the second half of Rom. 7. Here he definitely distinguishes it from the power of flesh and sin which dominates it.[56] And it is highly noteworthy that precisely in this context, and elsewhere, so far as I can see, only once,[57] he chooses for this "I" of man, which is not absorbed in the sensual nature of the σάρξ, a term that is curiously reminiscent of the terminology of Platonic idealism, namely the concept of νοῦς. He speaks of the Nous of man which serves the law of God, of the ἔσω ἄνθρωπος[58] which rejoices in the law, of the competing laws of the Nous and his members. Clearly, Paul speaks here of man as he is by nature, and thus of the Nous as a possession of the natural man. Anyone who thinks that with this picture of dividedness and wretchedness the apostle intends to portray the condition of the converted Christian simply has not understood him at all. Nevertheless, that this passage was able to evoke a long, still continuing dispute over its correct interpretation is due to a basically correct impression. For actually this exposition occupies

---

[55] Cf. Gal. 5:17 (the human "I" alongside the powerful forces of the Spirit and the flesh as a third—of course wholly powerless—factor).

[56] Rom. 7:14, ἐγὼ δὲ σάρκινός εἰμι, πεπραμένος ὑπὸ τὴν ἁμαρτίαν. 7:17, ἡ ἐνοικοῦσα ἐν ἐμοὶ ἁμαρτία. Cf. Rom. 8:4 ff.

[57] Rom. 12:2, ἀλλὰ μεταμορφοῦσθε τῇ ἀνακαινώσει τοῦ νοός and also I Cor. 14:14-15 do not belong here. Here νοῦς in the sense of the conscious intellectual life appears in contrast to an ecstatically pneumatic condition. In I Cor. 2:16, however, νοῦς Χριστοῦ is exactly equivalent to the supranatural Pneuma. This terminological deviation is occasioned by the Old Testament.

[58] Even the concept of ἔσω (ἐντός) ἄνθρωπος is ultimately Platonic. Bonhöffer, *Epiktet und das Neue Testament*, pp. 115 ff.

a singular and distinctive position within the Pauline world of thought. Never did the apostle make as many concessions to the natural "I" of man as here. Nowhere did Paul so closely approximate a platonizing manner of thought.

Yet even here the "I," the ἔσω ἄνθρωπος, remains only a phantom, only a shadowy figure, without its own initiative and condemned to utter powerlessness, endowed only with a longing after the better which is condemned to perpetual weakness, and with an awareness of its wretched situation, not much different from the ball in the Galatian epistle which is kicked back and forth between the two opposing powers of the σάρξ and the πνεῦμα.

Thus these beginnings toward another view, which could do justice to a genuine psychological consideration, cannot obscure the basic outlook of Paul. Such incongruences and inconsistencies *must* occur in the Pauline world of thought. The determined standpoint of ecstatic piety, the view of a complete transformation of the human nature through its contact with God cannot be unconditionally maintained by one who extends this manner of viewing things (as the apostle does) from particular moments of special ecstatic experience to the whole of the Christian life. For actually from that bluntly supernatural standpoint any coherent psychology has become an impossibility. But in spite of all concessions, the Pauline supernaturalism on the whole does not deny its origins.

2. The second basic characteristic of the Pauline pneuma doctrine can be treated more briefly. This is its natural basic feature, the interweaving of spiritual and natural views. We have just seen how Paul, when he speaks of σάρξ, thinks not only of the material quality of man, and how for him the σάρξ has an inner side, a ψυχή, so that the concepts σαρκικός and ψυχικός become identical. But conversely, the pneuma for him is not something purely spiritual which could exist as such permanently and without a somatic foundation for itself. This comes to expression most clearly in his eschatology. He cannot at all conceive of it otherwise than that the pneuma will be given a bodily basis in its eschatological perfection. Thus is explained his hope in the σῶμα πνευματικόν (I Cor. 15:44; cf. Rom. 8:10-11, 19, 23; II Cor. 5:1 ff.). When in this connection he speaks of the δόξα of the future body, it must be acknowledged that with him this concept oscillates between a more spiritual interpretation (glory, honor, in I Cor. 15:40, 43) and a natural one (splendor). But it can hardly be denied that with reference to δόξα he thinks again and again of the fine celestial substance of light as

it is native to the stars.[59] To him it is obvious that the exalted Lord possesses a heavenly corporeality, a σῶμα τῆς δόξης. He has seen this δόξα of God once, near Damascus, in the face of Christ (II Cor. 4:6), and in the consummation the Christians are to become σύμμορφοι τῆς εἰκόνος τοῦ υἱοῦ (Rom. 8:29; Phil. 3:21). This view of the apostle is not limited to eschatology alone. He speaks in mysterious fashion of a somatic basis of the new pneumatic life in this world. It is already said of the believers: μεταμορφούμεθα ἀπὸ δόξης εἰς δόξαν καθάπερ ἀπὸ κυρίου πνεύματος, and for him the eucharist is a κοινωνία αἵματος καὶ σώματος with the exalted Lord. It is difficult for us to transport ourselves into this close interlacing of spiritual and natural in the thought of the apostle. This is an alien world which however is to become clearer and plainer to us by means of the parallels from the history of religions yet to be introduced.

First of all, of course, it is necessary on this basis to grasp the apostle's speculation about the first, psychic man and the second, pneumatic man, in its full import. Here, also, the heaviest stress is to be placed upon the supernaturalistic, dualistic character of the speculation. The first and the second man appear in Paul in the same detachment and isolation with respect to each other as do the world of the πνεῦμα and that of the σάρξ. Just as the Christian as pneumatic is related to the psychic or the ordinary man, so Christ stands in the same relationship as the creator and originator of the new humanity.

This relationship is a metaphysical one, ordained from the beginning, not one that has come to be historically. The psychic, lower nature of Adam is determined and established from the outset by the creative act of God: ἐγένετο ὁ πρῶτος [ἄνθρωπος] Ἀδὰμ εἰς ψυχὴν ζῶσαν (I Cor. 15:45). Even the statements which Paul makes in Rom. 5:12 ff. are not in contradiction with this. For in this context Paul has not turned his attention at all to the question about the source of man's condition (which led him into sin). Here, quite in agreement with Jewish theology as it appears in IV Ezra and the Syriac Book of Baruch,[60] he has only the one interest, to show how death as destiny has dominated from Adam outward and onward to include the whole human race. The apostle did not think in the slightest degree about the strange assumption that the determination of the nature

---

[59] I Cor. 15:41; cf. II Cor. 4:17, αἰώνιον βάρος τῆς δόξης. Col. 3:4, φανερωθήσεσθε ἐν δόξῃ.

[60] On the doctrine of Adam in these writings, cf. Bousset, *Religion des Judentums*, 2nd ed., pp. 467 ff.

of the first man was wrought through a historical event and a free act. Christ then in his higher pneumatic being (πνεῦμα ζωοποιοῦν) appears (in the fundamental statements of the Corinthian epistle) in contrast with the lower being of the first Adam; it makes no difference whether Paul conceived this characterization from the standpoint of the preexistence and of the original Jesus Christ or from the standpoint of the exaltation— if indeed it is proper in Paul's mind even to formulate this question so sharply.[61]

This however is the noteworthy and characteristic thing about this theologoumenon of Paul: The relation between the first and the second Adam is that of blunt opposition. The first man and the second actually have nothing in common but the name. And this commonality of the name is purely external. Paul by calling Christ ἄνθρωπος in no way intended to indicate that the two men are bound together by the common essence of humanity. Rather, the term "man" for the Messiah probably was handed down to the apostle through the tradition. With him, so it appears, behind the idea of the pneumatic man, there stands the Jewish dogma of the Messiah–Son of Man, only he has divested it of its Jewish-Aramaic linguistic clothing. And behind that there probably[62] already stands the widespread Hellenistic myth of the Primal Man, only Paul transposes this myth from the primeval age into the end time. And perhaps even in the expression in I Cor. 15:46, ἀλλ' οὐ πρῶτον τὸ πνευματικόν, ἀλλὰ τὸ ψυχικόν, ἔπειτα τὸ πνευματικόν, we may glimpse an argument with that myth of the pre-existent Primal Man.

But be that as it may, any idea of intending to express, by the sharing of the name, an actual community of nature between Adam and Christ is utterly alien to the apostle. In the thought of Paul the relation between the first and the second Adam may in no way be thought of in the sense of an evolution. In every respect Christ is the exact opposite of the first man. He is πνεῦμα ζωοποιοῦν, the first man is ψυχὴ ζῶσα (only a living being); he is ἐπουράνιος (in his nature he stems from the higher world), the latter

---

[61] The latter is the more probable, for in his christological experiences the apostle proceeds from the present experience of exalted Lord. On the other hand, the idea is far from him that the metaphysical destiny of Christ was ethically earned in his earthly life. His exaltation to be the Son of God with power happened κατὰ πνεῦμα ἁγιωσύνης, on the basis of the Holy Spirit of God which was at work in him from the very first (Rom. 1:4).

[62] This will be treated more precisely in Chap. X in the context of Irenaeus' doctrine of recapitulation. In Paul the material is too slight for an investigation. On the broad religio-historical connections which perhaps are relevant here, cf. Bousset, Hauptprobleme, pp. 160-223.

is χοϊκός; from Adam the entire stream of death and of sin has gone out into the world, from Christ, the second man, the stream of life and of righteousness. These are radical opposites. To the apostle Christ is not the consummation of the first man but the death of natural humanity.

At the same time also the other parallel between the πνεῦμα-σάρξ doctrine and the speculation about the first and the second man obtrudes; I mean their natural connection. In the first place of course there are here also great spiritual opposites which stand before the apostle's eyes. From the first man the stream of unrighteousness and sin, of condemnation and death, has been poured into the world, while from the second proceed righteousness, deliverance, and life. But all this is based upon a foundation in nature. The first man and the second are different and separated basically in their nature. The connection of the first man with all the members of natural humanity is simply natural, i.e., determined by physical birth and ancestry. Thus the first humanity represents a somatic relation. Paul can speak of a σῶμα τῆς ἁμαρτίας. When he breaks out in the moving cry of longing for redemption: τίς με ῥύσεται ἐκ τοῦ σώματος τοῦ θανάτου τούτου, he is not thinking primarily of the body of the individual man, but of the body of death which includes all humanity, of the νόμος ἐν τοῖς μέλεσιν which holds sway over the individual (Rom. 7:23-24). The old man, whom one is to put off, has his members on the earth, and the exhortation runs: νεκρώσατε οὖν τὰ μέλη τὰ ἐπὶ τῆς γῆς. Spiritual vice, unchastity, impurity, passion, lust, and covetousness (Col. 3:5, 9) correspond to these members. But the new man and the new humanity also represent a spiritual-bodily unity. They are of heavenly material (ἐπουράνιοι), as the first man and the first humanity are of earthly material (ἐκ γῆς, χοϊκοί) (I Cor. 15:47-48). The new man is indeed the κύριος Χριστός whose body is the ἐκκλησία and whose members are the believers. As one puts on Christ in the sacrament of baptism, so are the believers to put on the new man, and to this mystical union corresponds the overflowing with love, mercifulness, goodness, humility, gentleness, patience.

In this coherent basic view with its sharp opposites and its astounding mixture of spiritual and natural aspects the mystical view of Jesus' death and resurrection which is peculiar to Paul takes its place.

Here also, two words of Paul may be placed at the beginning, words in which his outlook is crystallized, as it were: "One died (for all [63]), therefore

---

[63] In this passage, of course, taken precisely, there are two patterns of thought which flow together for Paul. Into the idea of dying with Christ is blended the other, that Christ

all are dead" (II Cor. 5:14). "As in Adam all die, even so in Christ shall all be made alive" (I Cor. 15:22). What is involved here is the idea of the significance of Jesus' death and resurrection as a type, indeed actually a prototype. The two events are not one-time events; what took place here happens again and again, and it happens repeatedly because it happened once in prototypical power.

Now we shall attempt more exactly to analyze these strange and daring ideas of the apostle. We must begin with the idea that according to Paul death is an event which has a strong significance for Christ himself. This conception is concisely and clearly summed up in the clauses of Rom. 6:10-11: "In that he died, he died to sin once for all; in that he lives, he lives unto God." In his earthly existence, which Paul indeed actually considers only in the perspective of humiliation and emptying,[64] Christ was related to sin; with one part of his being he was at home in this lower world (Rom. 1:1 ff., κατὰ σάρκα). Here is a fearful mystery which Paul summarizes in the paradoxical words that God has sent his Son ἐν ὁμοιώματι σαρκὸς ἁμαρτίας (Rom. 8:3). This Christ, the Son of God, took upon himself sinful flesh, flesh which by its nature was necessarily sinful! [65]

Thus for Christ himself death acquires the value of a great deliverance from the power of sinful flesh which clings to him, even if only outwardly. And this deliverance is a final one; he has now been raised into the higher sphere where the σάρξ ἁμαρτίας cannot follow him: "Christ raised from the dead dies no more, death has no more dominion over him" (Rom. 6:9).

And this deliverance and triumphant exaltation over the entire sphere of this world of death, flesh, and sin is now likewise of prototypical significance for all who belong to Christ. They have already died and risen with Christ; in Christ's crucifixion the old human nature (ὁ παλαιὸς ἄνθρωπος, Rom. 6:6) was thoroughly destroyed, sin was condemned to death in and with the flesh (8:3).[66] The process is a real, tangible, corporeal one: τὸ σῶμα τῆς ἁμαρτίας is destroyed in him (Rom. 6:6). It takes place

---

has acquired us as his own possession by means of his sacrificial death, so that we now no longer have any claim upon our own life.

[64] Phil. 2:6 ff.; II Cor. 8:9.

[65] The ἐν ὁμοιώματι is by no means meant to negate the fact that even Christ's flesh, like all flesh, was necessarily sinful. Flesh without sin is an inconceivable thought for Paul. It is rather meant to indicate that in Christ the σάρξ did not play the dominant role as elsewhere in human nature. It was only outwardly assumed and could not be a match for the Spirit of God which was dominant in Christ.

[66] κατακρίνειν, to pronounce final judgment, to condemn to death, occurs in this context almost as equivalent to ἀποκτείνειν. Perhaps here also we have to assume a penetration of the juristic set of ideas into the mystical.

through the body of Christ and its death (Rom. 7:4, ἐθανατώθητε διὰ τοῦ σώματος τοῦ Χριστοῦ; cf. Rom. 8:3); Paul bears the νέκρωσις τοῦ Ἰησοῦ in his weak and mortal body (II Cor. 4:10); this ἀπέκδυσις τοῦ σώματος τοῦ σαρκός is even compared to bodily circumcision (Col. 2:11). It is as though Paul could hardly be satisfied with this radical realism. The death of the old nature and the new life is for the apostle no deed of the believer; strictly taken one can hardly even speak of a process in the life of the believer; it is a fact accomplished once and for all. The old man is put to death, the newness of life is here. The Christians have only to walk therein as one strolls about in springtime sunshine (Rom. 6:4). The first half of Rom. 6 contains no ethical paraenesis[67] but the great good news of the freedom of the Christian life from sin through Christ's death and resurrection. The Christians (through their becoming Christians) *have* nailed their flesh to the cross (Gal. 5:24), or rather the world is crucified to them and they to the world (Gal. 6:14). The great break lies behind them. The exhortation to put aside the old leaven is limited by the clause: καθώς ἐστε ἄζυμοι. The Christian life means the celebration of a festival (I Cor. 5:7-8). It is extraordinarily characteristic that Paul, where he speaks of being dead and resurrected with Christ in broad context, does not refer to the free ethical act of Christians but to the sacrament of baptism. The supernatural redemption through death and resurrection is continued in the sacrament or is appropriated in the sacrament. The Lutheran idea of a daily, never ceasing battle with the old Adam, always being repeated with the same intensity, is not Pauline. Paul's entire ethic stands, not under the sign of the stern "Thou shalt," but under the motto "Thou must because thou canst not do otherwise." "If one died, then were all dead." [68]

V. *The Source of the Pneuma Doctrine.* We now attempt to arrange in order the powerful and remarkable conceptions of the apostle in a larger context, and we begin with the most comprehensive of his speculations, the

---

[67] In the context of the Pauline ideas it almost becomes a problem of how to fit in the paraenesis which is yet so necessary. Naturally here the praxis with its tasks is much too strong for Paul for it not to penetrate the theory. Especially distinctive is the transition in Rom. 6:12 ff. It is the Christian's *task* above all to conquer the body which because of its sarkical nature is irreformable and as *sarkical* body excluded from redemption, and to place it in the service of God, even against its will. Cf. Rom. 8:10; 8:13 (!); 12:1; 13:14; I Cor. 9:27, etc.

[68] Cf. also I Cor. 6:11, καὶ ταῦτά τινες ἦτε (after the enumeration of the list of vices): ἀλλὰ ἀπελούσασθε, ἀλλὰ ἡγιάσθητε, ἀλλὰ ἐδικαιώθητε. Rom. 5:1, δικαιωθέντες οὖν ἐκ πίστεως εἰρήνην ἔχομεν πρὸς τὸν θεόν (under no circumstances is it to be read ἔχωμεν; this would be to miss the entire meaning of the passage).

πνεῦμα–σάρξ doctrine. Its essential content may be summed up in two sentences. Paul asserts on the one hand the simply supernatural character of the divine pneuma and its contrary position as over against all human, natural being. But he asserts on the other hand that this pneuma is not a possession of the few individual favored ones, so that others had to acquiesce in their lack, but that it is necessary for every Christian man, indeed that it is the substance of his higher life before God. Thus the highest and best in man, without which he actually is not man, or at any rate has no standing before God, is yet an alien thing, something given to him from above out of grace, something brought to him from without. That upon this foundation the uniqueness of Pauline religion as a religion of redemption is built has perhaps already become clear here, but we shall more fully discuss it later on.

Where in Paul's environment do we find a similar one-sided view? When we frame the question so definitely and sharply, two authorities are ruled out from the start. These are the religion of the Old Testament and the gospel of Jesus. Not only that the powerful religion of the Old Testament and of the gospel is not generally included in this reflectively wrought-out and tortuously artificial framing of the question, so that we are not permitted to seek what would be a direct answer to it here; they also show no traces of such a view even indirectly. In particular it is important to see this clearly with regard to the gospel of Jesus and of the Palestinian primitive community. In Jesus' preaching and in that of the primitive community the simple idea of the forgiveness of sins plays a central and dominant role, and in the assured interpretation of the gracious, forgiving God, there are perfected here beginnings which were given in the Old Testament religion and particularly in the religion of late Judaism. But not even the slightest trace is found of the supernaturalism of the Pauline religion of redemption, of the principle that the best and highest must only be given to man from above and from without, or that the natural sensual being of man has nothing of that best and highest. If we wish to formulate it sharply,[69] we could say that the gospel of Jesus presents the (ethical) religion of the forgiveness of sins, while first in Paul Christianity is reconstructed into a "redemption" religion in the supernatural sense.

But the spirit of Greek philosophy also is utterly alien, indeed diametrically opposed to the *Pauline* fundamental outlook, judged wholly in general terms.

---

[69] In his *Paulus* (RV I, 5, 6), in spite of a formulation which perhaps is too sharp in some particulars, Wrede has correctly sensed the chief difference between Jesus and Paul (cf. pp. 90 ff.).

Of course the two have in common with each other the fact that both here and there such comprehensive views and penetrating reflections are undertaken, that the religious and the moral life are viewed under comprehensive conceptual categories. One also cannot fail to recognize that in later Platonism, insofar as it further developed the pessimistic aspect of Plato's world of thought, certain motifs of a redemption faith came to have currency. But in the entire territory of genuine Greek philosophy down to Neo-Platonism, the idea is and remains unprecedented and unheard-of, that the best and highest, the goal of all human life is not even found in the human soul but is in fact something alien, against which the soul strives with a native tendency. What would a Greek philosopher have been able to do with the principle that the first man is a less worthy being because he is only "soul"! And equally foreign to him is the assumption of a redemption from without and from above. It remains the fundamental conviction of the Greek sage, insofar as he is idealistically oriented, that he holds his life and his fate firmly in his own hands, that he finds the foundation of his life when he himself reflects upon himself and descends into the depths of his own being. In this process the religious consideration can function more or less powerfully, the higher can be intimated with lesser or greater strength as the divine in man, the conflict of the lower human nature with the higher can be sensed with more or less liveliness; still the thought world of Greek philosophy remains separated by a gulf from the radical Pauline dualism and pessimism.

Is it accordingly to be assumed that Paul solitarily blazes his own trail as creator of a religion of redemption in the strict sense of the word, and that he has given to Christianity this powerful new direction out of his own resources?

Upon closer examination we find some parallels in the religio-historical milieu surrounding Paulinism. We shall have to turn our gaze toward those mixed formations in which philosophy and orientally conditioned belief, intellectual reflection and ancient mystery practice, speculation and religious-ecstatic mysticism are intertwined to form a strange new creation.

In this milieu the first tangible figure to come before us is that of the Jewish theologian Philo.[70] Even in him we encounter a total outlook which

---

[70] In order not to encumber the present study too much, I shall present the detailed evidence on the statements about the religio-historical connections of the Pauline doctrine of the pneuma in another context, but refer here above all to the splendid presentation of Bréhier, *Les idées philosophiques et religieuses de Philon d'Alexandrie*, 1908, Cf. particularly pp. 207 and 225 (295 ff.).

is completely and in its innermost essence alien to the Greek-philosophical outlook even though it appears wholly clad in Greek garments.[71] We must not let ourselves be deceived by his dependence upon Stoic-Platonic idealism; inwardly Philo stands over against this idealism as totally alien. He knows no greater and more dangerous enemy of true piety than the spirit of Greek philosophical autarchy, the sense of the sage who feels his life and his soul to be in his own hands and under his own control. As much as he borrows again and again from this spirit, yet on the other hand he never grows weary of opposing it.[72] The pious person who wishes to find his God must leave behind him this entire world of the "I" which is conscious of his own self; he must not only renounce his lower existence of the body and the soul, but he must also give up his λόγος and his νοῦς if he is to attain to God.[73] Even in Philo religious speculation grows out of the experiences of ecstatic piety. The nature of man in itself belongs only to the lower, earthly sphere. Philo also can speak of the φίλαυτος and ἄθεος νοῦς (Leg. Alleg. I, 49), of the γήϊνος νοῦς Ἀδάμ who is driven out of Paradise (de plantatione 46). A higher element, one given freely by God and not belonging to the actual equipment of man, must be added in order for man to be endowed with his ultimate worth. Philo calls this higher element by various names. One time it is the divine Nous (in contrast to the lower, human Nous); another time, when it is nurtured on Old Testament reminis-

[71] In the form of his ideas Philo certainly is through and through dependent upon the later Stoic tendency which is characterized by a strong Platonic flavor and of which Poseidonius may be regarded as the chief representative. But one does not understand the center of philosophical piety and basic outlook, the supernaturalist mysticism peculiar to him, which is bound up with a strong inclination toward a dualistic pessimism in anthropology, if one takes his point of departure in Poseidonius. Just as little, and even less, is Philo to be understood as a Jew in terms of Old Testament piety. The posing of the question in the form "either Greek or Jewish" is highly inadequate and does not see the various possibilities on this already syncretistic soil. Something relatively new comes to life here. Clement of Alexandria, in a not incorrect impression, calls Philo a Pythagorean (Strom. I, 15.72; II, 19.100). One will have to seek for analogies within the movement which is usually called Neo-Pythagoreanism. For the present, however, this territory is much too little worked out for one to be able to be surefooted here.

[72] Cf. the polemic against the φίλαυτος, ἄθεος, αὐτοκράτωρ, νοῦς, de conf. ling. 125; against the φίλαυτον δόγμα of the wisdom of Cain, quod det. pot. 32; against the pernicious folly that man is the measure of all things, de posterit. Caini 35-38. Philo is the first *apologist* to oppose philosophical idealism with the weapons of skepticism, in order to capitalize from it for theology.

[73] From the numerous passages coming into consideration, here only one esp. distinctive one: In Quis rer. div. haer., after it is stated how the soul has to divest itself of the body, sense perception, and the logos (§ 69), it is said: ἀλλὰ καὶ σεαυτὴν ἀπόδραθι καὶ ἔκστηθι σεαυτῆς—τὸν αὐτὸν δὴ τρόπον, ὅνπερ τῶν ἄλλων ὑπεξελήλυθας, ὑπέξελθε καὶ μεταναστηθι σεαυτῆς (cf. *ibid.*, §§ 263-65).

cences, the divine Pneuma.[74] It is a special and favored class of men with whom that divine gift is shared. This class is much more widely separated from ordinary men than by the gulf which according to the philosophical view separates the wise man from the common herd. It is the ὁρατικὸν γένος, the race of men destined for the blessed vision, who have nothing more to do with those who stem from the γήϊνος νοῦς Ἀδάμ, and are elevated above them as in Paul the pneumatics are elevated above the psychics.[75]

The Hermetic circle of writings offers, now in the area of pure Hellenistic piety, still closer connections with the basic Pauline outlook. This body of writings occupies a quite solitary position within Greek literature. Even if only a few fragments and bits were still extant of that movement which we are used to summing up under the general name of Neo-Pythagorean philosophy but which is less a philosophy than a half-religious movement, then it would probably become more clearly evident how close were the connections between Hermeticism and Neo-Pythagoreanism, and these writings would be subject to a more certain placing within a larger intellectual context.[76]

Be that as it may, there emerges here even more clearly than with Philo that psychological supernaturalism. The Nous is a divine, personally conceived, supernatural power. He dwells in the pious and good, the pure and merciful, bestows upon them correct knowledge, brings it to pass that they become lord over the influences of the lower, corporeal life.[77] But he leaves the evil to the τιμωρὸς δαίμων who likewise is regarded as the one who leads astray into all passions and as the fiery demon of punishment and

---

[74] On this compromise in the language of Philo, cf. Reitzenstein, *Hellenistische Mysterienreligionen*, pp. 144 ff. [2nd ed., pp. 168 ff.].

[75] The more exact documentation in Reitzenstein, p. 145 [2nd ed., p. 169], and below in Chap. V.

[76] In my judgment, Reitzenstein (*Poimandres*) is correct when he dates the earliest stratum of the literature which is present in the Corpus Hermeticum up somewhere in the first Christian century. I cannot go into the more specific proof in this connection and can only indicate in general that with these writings we stand in the springtime of the great Gnostic movement. At any rate, so far as I can see, the *Tractates* show themselves to be free of any influence by Christianity, while, to be sure, here and there traces of the influence of the Greek Old Testament can be shown. Agreement between the Hermetica on the one hand and Paul and John on the other points to the common soil of piety in which they are rooted. Unfortunately, our quotations (apart from those fragments published by Reitzenstein) must still follow Parthey, *Hermetis Trismegisti Poemander* (Berlin, 1854). In addition there are the Asclepius (Pseudo-Apuleius) in the works of Apuleius III, ed. by Thomas (Teubner) and the important fragments in the Eclogai of Johannes Stobaeus (quoted according to the page numbers of the *editio princeps*).

[77] Cf. Corpus Hermeticum I (Poimandres), 22; X, 21; XII, 4.

vengeance.[78] Therefore the question whether all men have the Nous is answered with a stout negative.[79] It does not belong to the human equipment as such. The pious receive it as a gift of grace.[80] Still, the Nous is necessary to the perfection of the human nature. Men who do not have it do not rise very far above the level of the nonrational animals.[81] Thus there are two completely different classes of men: those who possess Nous,[82] the few, who stand in contrast to an entire world; who, ignored, oppressed, and persecuted, yet stand over against the dull and sluggish masses who do not possess the Nous,[83] with the full self-assurance of men who are the recipients of divine grace. And here also, as in Paul, only still more in the background, there stand behind this supernaturalism the sacrament and the sacramental outlook. Once there is even mention of a baptism with the Nous (IV, 4). In ecstasy, in the divine vision, man experiences his exaltation into the world of the divine element or, in other words, his deification.[84]

With regard to the Hermetic writings and the *Oracula Chaldaica* related to them, one can even speak of a Hellenistic, purely Gentile "Gnosticism" in the technical sense of the word. Also in the Hermetic writings themselves the catchword "Gnosis" occurs now and again: The pious are those who have knowledge (Gnosis),[85] those who are in Gnosis.

Indeed, the whole colorful world of Christian Gnosticism stands in this same line. Here we encounter the specific religion of redemption as we find it in Paul (and John), carried out to the most one-sided consequences and distortions, furnished with a variegated mythological apparatus and with a much stronger sacramental emphasis in contrast to the former. Here is found in remarkable fashion also the Pauline terminology (πνεῦμα, ψυχή, σάρξ) in prolific development and logical arrangement. In Philo (in part) and particularly in the Hermetic writings, on the other hand, Greek philosophical language predominates, and the Nous, not the Pneuma, appears as

---

[78] I, 23; cf. X, 21, 23 (end).

[79] IV, 3; IX, 5; X, 23 f.; cf. Asclepius, chap. 7 (ed. Thomas, par. 42.5 ff.); 9 (44.26); 18 (53.1); 22 (57.20).

[80] IV, 4 (baptism with the Nous); XIII, 14 (οὐσιώδης γένεσις); somewhat differently, X, 19 (ψυχὴ ὅλη νοῦς γίνεται; cf. X, 6).

[81] IV, 2-3; X, 24; XII, 4.

[82] I, 21 (ὁ ἔννους ἄνθρωπος); IX, 5 (ὁ ὑλικός and ὁ οὐσιώδης ἄνθρωπος); cf. on the concept οὐσιώδης, I, 15; XIII, 14; X, 6 (οὐσία θεοῦ); Asclepius 7, par. 42.14; X, 19 (εὐσεβὴς ψυχή—ἀσεβής). Stobaeus Ecl. I, 136 (οἷς θεοπτικὴ δύναμις οὐ πρόσεστι).

[83] IX, 4; cf. Stobaeus Ecl. I, 708-10.

[84] See particularly chaps. I and XIII.

[85] I, 26; IX, 4.

the higher supernatural power which operates in human life. At this point one could object that the Gnostics are simply dependent upon Paul, as the coinciding technical language proves. And certainly in many respects a directly Pauline influence can be demonstrated. But that conclusion still would be hasty; it can hardly be assumed that the few and difficult-to-understand terminological statements of Paul which are found scattered through his epistles should have had such a powerful effect upon the most diverse Gnostic systems.[86] And the specific language usage of this religious psychology (distinction between πνεῦμα and ψυχή) can be traced to the very center of the purely Hellenistic literature.[87] But it may also be demonstrated in general that "Gnosticism" in its foundations is a pre-Christian phenomenon; and to these foundations belongs, as the agreement of their Hellenistic and their Christian aspects shows, this radical dualism of anthropology and its related stark supernaturalism in a belief in redemption.

Thus the Pauline doctrine of the Pneuma with all its consequences stands in a broad context. In his gloomy anthropological pessimism,[88] in the dualistic-supernatural development of the doctrine of redemption, Paul follows a contemporary mood which had already at that time seized many minds.

[86] See below, Chap. VI, for the evidence in detail.

[87] Extraordinarily significant here is the beginning of the so-called Mithras Liturgy (rev. text in Reitzenstein, p. 109). The seer prepares to leave his body and expects to behold the ἀθάνατος Aeon ἀθανάτῳ πνεύματι. But his soul also will remain behind ἀρτίας ὑπεστώσης μου πρὸς ὀλίγον τῆς ἀνθρωπίνης μου ψυχικῆς δυνάμεως, ἣν ἐγὼ πάλιν παραλήμψομαι. . . . I am pleased to see that Johannes Weiss (*Kommentar zum ersten Korintherbrief*, pp. 371-72), referring to Reitzenstein, places the Pauline terminology in this context of mystery religion. Then however Gnosticism also, seen on the whole, becomes an independent witness to this intellectual world. It is significant that the Pauline terminology is found also in James 3:13 and Jude 19 (Reitzenstein, *Hellenistische Mysterienreligionen*, pp. 151 ff. [2nd ed., pp. 176 ff.]).

[88] It can safely be conceded that in his *terminology* Paul possibly is dependent in part on the Greek Old Testament. The fact that he consistently denotes the higher aspect of man by πνεῦμα, not by νοῦς, may be explained in these terms, just as on this point the Old Testament influence on language is evident also in Philo (see above, p. 184). On the other hand, we may have here simply the popular Christian usage. In any case, the question must remain altogether an open one, as to whether the view of the πνεῦμα as a higher spiritual element was alive in the popular usage far beyond the language region which was under the influence of the Septuagint. The language usage of Gnosticism, insofar as it is to be propounded as independent of Paul, would indicate this, and in addition there are numerous other observations to be made in the territory of Hellenism (Reitzenstein, *Hellenistische Mysterienreligionen*, pp. 136 ff. [2nd ed., pp. 159 ff.]). Still more, one could be inclined to derive the *terminological* contrast of πνεῦμα or σάρξ (not the thing itself, the sharp dualism) from the Old Testament, all the more since in Gnosticism this terminology is not dominant. On the other hand, one cannot possibly derive the terminological *contrast* of πνεῦμα and ψυχή from the Old Testament *differentiation* between *ruach* and *nephesh;* and the adjectival form ψυχικός is even less comprehensible in those terms. But in the present context all this can only be mentioned. The large connections in substance, not the terminology, form the decisive element here.

VI. *Religio-Historical Analogies.* However, one can hardly escape the impression that this entire theory of redemption and redemption piety of Paul grew up in the soil of Hellenistic piety. The myth of the suffering, dying, and rising god was extraordinarily widely distributed in the Hellenistic religious life, strongly conditioned by the Orient. Above all it belongs to the characteristic features of almost all the so-called mystery religions. It will not be worth our while here to list all the gods who die and come back to life and to analyze their myths in detail. I may refer here to the Babylonian Tammuz, the Syrian Adonis (Esmun), Asia Minor's Attis, whose cultus had already assumed a fixed form in Rome at the time of the Emperor Claudius, the Egyptian Osiris, who in union with the closely associated figures of Isis and Serapis spread over the whole oikoumene in the age of the Diadochi (and even earlier), the Dionysos of the Orphic mystery religion (the Orphic "Phanes" also belongs here), and finally to Melkart of Tyre and Heracles Sandan of Tarsus.[89]

More important than all these individual observations is the fact that, long before the Pauline era, people had become aware of the kinship of all these divine figures to one another. The Babylonian Tammuz and the Phoenician figures of Adonis and Esmun indeed after all grew up in the same soil and perhaps have a common root, as Baudissin's study most recently has shown anew with a comprehensive consideration of all the possibilities. That their figures also are later mixed with one another cannot surprise us.[90] The identification of the Egyptian Osiris with the Adonis of Byblos[91] probably goes back to early antiquity. At least since the age of the Diadochi the identification of Osiris-Dionysos is well established and has become common property. In the Hellenistic basic document which Reitzenstein[92] has extracted from the Gnostic Naassene Preaching and which probably goes back

[89] Cf. the compilations of M. Brückner, *Der sterbende und auferstehende Gottheiland,* 1908 (RV I, 16). O. Pfleiderer, *Das Christusbild des urchristlichen Glaubens* (1903), pp. 55-89. Further, the specialized works: Baudissin, *Adonis und Esmun, eine Untersuchung zur Geschichte des Glaubens an Auferstehungsgötter und an Heilgötter,* 1911. Hepding, *Attis und sein Kult,* 1903. For Dionysos and the Orphic mysteries: Rohde, *Psyche,* 2nd ed., II, 38 ff., 103 ff. On Sandan of Tarsus: Böhlig, *Geisteskultur von Tarsos* (1913), pp. 24-51. A ceremony of ἔγερσις of the Tyrian Melkart is attested by Menander in Josephus' Ant. VIII, 146 (cf. II Macc. 4:18-20). Traces of the suffering and dying God in the Old Testament: Gressmann, *Israelit. jüd. Eschatologie,* pp. 328 ff.; Baudissin, *Adonis und Esmun,* pp. 403 ff. Perhaps even Marduk was a dying and rising god: Zimmern, *Keilinschr. und AT,* 3rd ed., pp. 370-71; Baudissin, *Adonis und Esmun,* p. 107.

[90] Baudissin, *ibid.,* pp. 345-84.

[91] *Ibid.,* pp. 185 ff.

[92] *Poimandres,* pp. 83 ff.

to the first Christian century, indeed already in the Attis cult-song to which
that "Preaching" is only a commentary, there stand the three deities that
here particularly concern us beside each other as ultimately identical: Attis,
Adonis, and Osiris. And with Osiris naturally the Dionysos who is closely
bound up with him joins the circle. This is the μυστικὴ θεοκρασία, of which
the Neo-Platonist tradition later speaks: (Attis) ὃν Ἀλεξανδρεῖς ἐτίμησαν
Ὄσιριν ὄντα καὶ Ἄδωνιν κατὰ τὴν μυστικὴν θεοκρασίαν.[93]

Thus there grows up beyond the individual divine figures the one figure
of the suffering, dying, and rising god. No more does the individual divine
figure with its specific myth come so much into consideration; in all these
figures is manifested the one idea which seizes Hellenistic superstitious piety
with mystical power, the idea of the dying and rising, salvation-bringing
deity. And this idea gradually acquires a philosophical dress; the myth becomes religious speculation. The suffering and dying god is the deity which
has its real home in the ideal world, the κόσμος νοητός, and now, for the
purpose of creation, to bring into flux the sluggish masses of matter, has
descended into the lower and dirty world of matter. This deity has thereby
been lost to this lower world of the senses, held prisoner in it, torn and
broken, and yet has not lost the capacity again to be raised out of the sunken
condition of death to the divine world.

Thus has one source[94] of Plutarch already interpreted the Osiris myth.
Osiris is the Logos, whose figures and ideas the goddess Isis τὸ τῆς φύσεως
θῆλυ takes up into herself (chap. 53). Only his soul is imperishable, immortal. For the Abiding and Rational and Good is stronger than perishable-
ness and change. His body however is frequently torn and destroyed by
Typhon; that is, what enters into this corporeal world from that ideal
world, like a seal in wax, has no permanence and falls victim to the disordered and destructive power of the evil element (chap. 54). But when
Typhon destroys these likenesses of the imperishable Being, Isis grieving takes
them up into herself and preserves them for the coming of a new world.
In similar fashion Plutarch (or his source) refers the two great world
cycles of the Stoic theory of world periods to Apollo and Dionysos. For

---

[93] Damascius, Vita Isidori, § 242, ed. Becker, p. 343 a 20; Migne, PSG CIII, 1292; cf.
Suidas s. v. Heraiskos, I, 873, ed. Bernh.: τὸ ἄρρητον ἄγαλμα τοῦ Αἰῶνος ὑπὸ τοῦ θεοῦ
κατεχόμενον, ὃν Ἀλεξανδρεῖς ἐτίμησαν Ὄσιριν ὄντα καὶ Ἄδωνιν ὁμοῦ κατὰ μυστικὴν
ὡς ἀληθῶς φάναι θεοκρασίαν.

[94] The section beginning with chap. 45 comes into consideration. Cf. Heinze, *Xenokrates*,
pp. 31 ff., whose tracing of this section back to Xenocrates I regard as improbable. Cf. also
Reitzenstein, *Hellenistische Mysterienreligionen*, p. 93 [2nd ed., p. 104].

him Apollo represents the time when everything had gone up in fire, but Dionysos Zagreus with his destiny of διασπασμός and of διαμελισμός represents the contemporary world age with its becoming, suffering, and passing away.[95]

Especially characteristic are the interpretations of the Attis myth in the already mentioned Naassene Preaching.[96] The various names of God are interpreted: He is called Necys as the one buried in the dungeon of the body; God, when he has again been changed into his original nature; Akarpos, when having entered into flesh he pursues the desires of the flesh; Polycarpos, as the one freed from earthly appetite. When the mother of the gods emasculates him, the supra-terrestrial, eternal and blessed world calls the masculine power of the soul, its better part, back to itself. The whole creation in heaven and on earth and under the earth entreats him that he will let the disharmony (ἀσυμφωνίαν) of the world cease (παῦε), and therefore he is called Papas.[97]

In briefer survey form, the ascription of the meaning of this myth to the mother of the gods appears in the fifth discourse of the Emperor Julian which also provides the conclusive proof of the non-Christian origin of the basis of that Gnostic Naassene Preaching and with it goes back to an earlier source of Stoic-Platonic origin[98]: Attis is the creative divine primal power which works upon matter. Against the advice of the mother of the gods he oversteps the Milky Way and enters the cave of the nymph to marry her, and this signifies the sinking down of the divine primal power into the lower world. Through the emasculation inflicted upon him the mother of the gods brings to a halt the power that has gone wild in an unrestrained urge to create, and calls it back to the heavenly home.

In the middle of these fantasies there emerges moreover a curious figure of Oriental origin: namely the Primal Man (Anthropos) who sinks down into matter and is again liberated from it.[99] Behind this figure stands an ancient myth, never yet satisfactorily explained as to its meaning or as to its history, of the slain (and again living) Primal Man. In Hellenistic syncretistic territory he has come to be an entity of speculation, a cosmogonic power.

---

[95] de Ei apud Delphos, chap. 9.

[96] On the following, cf. Reitzenstein, *Poimandres*, and Wendland, *Hellenistisch-römische Kultur*, 2nd ed., pp. 178-79.

[97] Hippolytus, Ref. V, 8.22, 31, 36, ed. Wendland.

[98] Wendland, p. 179. Cf. the brief summary of the theory of Julian in Sallust, de diis et mundo, chap. 4. The material in Hepding, *Attis*, pp. 51-58.

[99] Cf. the chapter on the Primal Man in my *Hauptprobleme*, pp. 160-223.

This figure comes out most clearly and most purely in the first Tractate of the Hermetic collection.[100] The Anthropos, the favorite child of the god Nous, in his urge to create breaks through the lower spheres of the demiurge and bowing down he beholds Physis, who blissfully smiles at him in all her beauty. Drawn downward by the compulsion of love, he is embraced and held fast by Physis. Here the myth breaks off, but its end, the story of the liberation of the Primal Man from matter and his elevation into the heavenly world, can easily be completed from the second, paraenetic half of the Tractate. For in the believers there is accomplished only that which has occurred by way of prototype in the fate of the Anthropos.

In most Christian-Gnostic systems the myth of the Anthropos has already become a fragment which is not understood.[101] On the other hand in the Naassene Preaching (perhaps already in its Hellenistic basis which was untouched by Christian influence) he is merged with the figures of Attis, Adonis, Osiris, and related deities, into the already discussed one great figure of the dying and rising God, the God who sinks down into matter and again emerges from it. Thus his figure appears here at the very beginning in a broadly sketched statement and has pushed into the background the figure of Attis which apparently played the leading role in the cult song and in the original commentary; thus it represents the advancing process of orientalizing of the syncretistic Hellenistic literature.[102]

This myth of the dying and suffering god or of the divine power which sinks down into the world of matter and is again raised out of it, however, as we have already seen in part, takes a generally anthropological and practically paraenetic turn. The god with his fate in victory and defeat becomes the type for the destiny of the pious. *What occurs here is not a once-for-all fact of the past; it happens ever anew.*

If we look more closely, we find that just those *speculations* about the dying and rising god and his cosmic significance grew up out of the *cultus and the experiences of the believers in the cultus.*

Already in the cultus of the god who dies and awakens to new life the way is paved for this *unio mystica* of the believers with the god. For this is

---

[100] I regard the system of Poimandres as early Gnostic, pre-Valentinian, and thus as belonging to the first Christian century.

[101] On the other hand the figure of the Primal Man once again dominates the specifically oriental system of Manichaeism and here also already has the speculative cosmogonic character, only that the myth again appears in a more disordered and grotesque form.

[102] Reitzenstein, *Poimandres*, pp. 102 ff., has collected further parallels to the Anthropos myth in the Zosimus literature and in Iamblichus (revelation of Bitys).

the evident meaning of the cultic celebrations of all the dying and again rising vegetation deities, that the participant in the cult actively and imitatively takes part in the destiny of the god in frenzied grief and exuberant joy. Even in a later time these connections remained constantly in the consciousness of the observants.

In characteristic manner the liturgical fragment which probably stems from the Attis cult, and which Firmicus Maternus has preserved for us in *de err. prof. relig.* XXII, 1, summarizes this outlook:

> Θαρρεῖτε μύσται τοῦ Θεοῦ σεσωσμένου
> ἔσται γὰρ ἡμῖν ἐκ πόνου σωτηρία.

In the Roman cultic celebration of Attis which had acquired its definitive form in the times of the Emperor Claudius, the day of mourning, which bore the distinguishing name of Sanguis (March 24), was followed after a vigil by the festival of Hilaria (March 25).[103] And Macrobius (Saturnal. I, 21.10) summarized the meaning of the Adonis cult in these words: *simulationeque luctus peracta celebratur laetitiae exordium.* The εὑρήκαμεν συγχαίρομεν of the Osiris-Isis mysteries points in the same direction.[104] An ancient cultic saying from this religion clearly illuminates this context: "As surely as Osiris lives, he also will live; as surely as Osiris is not dead, he also will not die; as surely as Osiris is not destroyed, he also will not be destroyed." [105] Thus generally mystical speculation and religious practice appear most closely related. And even where the sacramental cultus has already been dissolved and the piety has been elevated into a more spiritual atmosphere, the connection remains. In Poimandres the proto-typical character of the Primal Man who sinks down into matter is strongly emphasized. The human race stems from this union with Physis. "And for this reason man, in contrast to all other living things, has a dual nature, mortal because of the body, immortal on account of the 'essential' man. He is immortal and has power over all things and yet he suffers, as befits mortal beings, and is subject to fate" (§ 15). For this reason the admonition applies to him to recognize that he stems from the world of light and of life (§ 21).

---

[103] Cf. Cumont, *Oriental Religions in Roman Paganism,* p. 57.

[104] Seneca, Apocol. 13. Firmicus, De errore prof. relig. II, 9. Dieterich, *Mithras-Liturgie,* p. 216.

[105] Cumont, *Oriental Religions in Roman Paganism,* p. 100. Erman, *Die ägypt. Relig.* (1905), pp. 96-97. Cf. also the already mentioned conclusion of the so-called Mithras liturgy (see above, p. 164, n. 22), and the *voluntaria mors* in the Isis mysteries of Apuleius, also mentioned there.

He is to devote himself to the Nous, the leader of his soul, is to hate and abhor his life of the senses (§ 22) and thus is to find the way back to the homeland of light and of life. Fallen from celestial heights, as once upon a time the Primal Man; having fallen through the planetary spheres and being clothed with shameful garments, as he was; men are to ascend as he did to the highest heaven of the Father God.[106] Thus throughout the entire Preaching of the Naassenes there runs this idea: The Anthropos is only a type of the race of pneumatics. Like him they have fallen and like him they are to arise: The current which flowed from heaven hither is to flow upward again; the race which has wandered into exile in Egypt is again to find the homeland, Mesopotamia.

The Stoic-Platonist source which the Emperor Julian follows (*vide supra*, p. 190) interprets the Attis myth in the same way. "And what he (the god) has experienced and suffered is universal experience and fate. This admonition, to turn from the lower and toward the higher, applies to us all. And after the god's emasculation, the trumpet calls not him alone but all of us upward, we who share with him a heavenly origin and an earthly fall. The gods bid us also do away with the lack of restraint, ascend to the limited, the unified, the one, with Attis as redeemed ones celebrate the festival of joy." [107]

One will not be able to avoid the impression that here is given the spiritual atmosphere within which the Pauline dying-with-Christ and rising-with-Christ is located. The peculiar nuances of the Pauline interpretation naturally can still be present. Obviously one cannot speak of a fall of the divine in Christ; with him indeed it is all the mercy of the redeemer. Nevertheless there is found the peculiar idea that through his humiliation into fleshly existence Christ enters into a connection which is equally contrary to nature, and that for Christ himself death signifies a deliverance, even, as we have seen, in Paul's view. Paul did not envisage the idea of a preexistence of souls and of a fall from the supra-terrestrial world. For him the death of the redeemer does not have the meaning of doom and submergence into the lower realm, but precisely that of liberation. Yet the parallel again becomes quite close when we set the Pauline "in Adam die, in Christ be made alive" over against the falling and rising with the divine hero in Hellenistic piety.

And the main idea is the same. The pious person experiences in mystical

---

[106] The cultic element which in the Poimandres is almost wholly spiritualized appears even more clearly and palpably in the Krater (IV) and in the consecration of the prophets (VIII).

[107] Wendland, *Hellenistisch-römische Kultur*, p. 180.

fellowship the same thing which the divine hero previously and fundamentally has experienced in exemplary power. The experience of the believers
is only the consequence, victoriously being worked out, of the once given
beginning. One simply closes the switch and the electrical current flows
through.

This parallel, however, becomes even closer when we note that, as those
Hellenistic speculations developed out of the cultus of the dying and rising
god, so also behind Paul's statements about dying and rising with Christ
there stands quite plainly and clearly (cf. Rom. 6; Gal. 3:26-27) the
sacrament. In the general discussion above of the connections of the Kyrios
faith with the cultus it has already become apparent to us that even before
Paul, and not created by Paul, in the community's faith the conviction
was dominant that baptism as the initiatory act of Christianity is a dying
and a rising analogous to the death and resurrection of Christ. The connections discussed here are suited for giving to those conjectures an essential
confirmation. The links in the chain of religio-historical comparison are
joined. As especially in the Poimandres of the Corpus Hermeticum (but in
part also in other named sources) the sacramental-cultic mystery of rebirth
appeared raised into the sphere of personal-spiritual experience and religious
speculation, so also in Paul a fully analogous case was present. Even Paul
has made a spiritual experience out of the baptismal mystery of the community religion, an experience which in its fundamental significance dominates the whole life of the Christian and gives to it a victorious power and
a unique impetus.

And yet, if we consider all this, the incomparably greater moral-religious
power and the spiritual originality of the apostle would emerge into a clear
light. The Hellenistic piety, even the spiritualized form, experiences in this
dying and rising with the deity first of all the liberation from the world
of perishability, of death, and of gloomy fate (εἱμαρμένη); its gifts of grace
are immortality (ἀφθαρσία) and eternal life. But for Paul there stands in
first place here the thought of *deliverance from sin and guilt*: "In that Christ
died, he died unto sin, once for all; in that he lives, he lives unto God. Thus
then you conclude that you *are dead for sin* but alive for God." Through all
the mystery beliefs and mysterious speculations the ethos of the gospel is
articulated.

However, not only the apostle's mysticism of cross and sacrament but
also his far-reaching and comprehensive speculations about the first and the

second man are to be placed in a larger religio-historical context. We have already seen how among the dying (sinking down into matter) and rising-to-life deities in widespread speculations there emerges the enigmatic figure of the (god) Ἄνθρωπος, the Primal Man. Would the conjecture be too daring that in Paul the contrast of the first and the second man does not represent a simple speculation drawn from the Old Testament, but that in the conception of the idea of a higher pneumatic man he followed a myth already known to him, already at hand? Reitzenstein has correctly pointed out that in I Cor. 15:45 the sentence ὁ ἔσχατος Ἀδὰμ [εἰς] πνεῦμα ζωοποιοῦν appears curiously unmediated.[108] One can in fact hardly imagine how Paul could have so simply spun this bold idea out of Gen. 2, if the doctrine of a heavenly spiritual and divine being Ἄνθρωπος had not already lain before him so that he could interpret this into the biblical word. To be sure the question arises whether our witnesses for its existence go so far that they are able to give the conjecture an adequate certainty. They are all either considerably later than Paul or else cannot yet be dated with certainty. In Jewish apocalyptics we do meet the figure of the Ἄνθρωπος, but here it is first a purely eschatological entity and it lacks that speculation about the dying and sinking down of the man into matter and his being raised out of it. The same is true in the many Jewish legends; in them Adam appears as a lofty divine being, even in the Pseudo-Clementines and their doctrine of the Adam who travels through the aeons as revealer. On the other hand the astonishingly wide distribution of the myth[109] at least since the second century can be pointed out. The figure of the Anthropos not only shows up in numerous Gnostic systems, where it appears, moreover, obviously as a frozen remnant of older comprehensive speculations. It has also passed over into Hellenistic mysticism and appears here in the core of the Corpus Hermeticum, the Poimandres. The Naassene Preaching has behind it a long prehistory which points to the fact that in Gentile-Gnostic circles, which were connected with mysteries of the Attis cult, people had already assimilated the figure of the Ἄνθρωπος to Attis.[110] Thus in fact the conjecture arises that the apostle was already acquainted with an Oriental myth of the redeemer-god Anthropos which had one time sunk down into

---

[108] *Hellenistische Mysterienreligionen*, p. 172 [2nd ed., p. 198]. The textual emendation proposed here, ὁ ἔσχατος Ἀδὰμ [εἰς] πνεῦμα ζωοποιόν, would in fact eliminate difficulties that can be otherwise overcome.

[109] On this and the preceding, cf. the documentation in my *Hauptprobleme*.

[110] Cf. the evidence in Reitzenstein's *Poimandres*.

matter and a redemption mysticism connected with the myth (perhaps through the mediation of Judaism?) and that he connected with this his speculation about the ἔσχατος ᾿Αδὰμ πνεῦμα ζωοποιοῦν.

Of course the differences are everywhere evident. In the Oriental myth the Primal Man is at the same time the one who has sorrowfully sunk down into matter, is defeated and vanquished, and is mightily raised up again, the one in need of redemption and the redeemer-god who redeems himself for his people, both in one. Paul on the contrary allots the roles to two different persons, the first and the second Adam. The thought of an actual fall of the ῎Ανθρωπος πνευματικός is far from him and must be far from him. The dying or sinking down of the Primal Man signifies his defeat and loss, the dying of the Christos signifies his liberation and exaltation. In the Oriental myth the Primal Man is first of all a figure of the primeval age, the development of the world begins with his fall; for Paul the second man stands at the end of the development, and with his death and resurrection the last act of the drama begins. At any rate, a powerful reshaping has taken place. Indeed it appears almost as if Paul is conscious of this and that he refers to it with the strange statement which would then be illumined from this angle: ἀλλ᾿ οὐ πρῶτον τὸ πνευματικόν, ἀλλὰ τὸ ψυχικὸν ἔπειτα τὸ πνευματικόν. If at last the myth of the Primal Man in fullness of detail and surrounded by an abundance of other myths appears at the center of the Manichaean religion, we may now say, particularly after the many new items of information gained through the Turfan find, that on the whole Mani is only the reproducer, not the creator, of the wholesale mythologeme and of the bizarre fantasies which are united in his system into a picture of bewildering variety. The Mandaean religious documents which at many points are closely akin to Manichaeism likewise know the figure of the Primal Man,[111] even though it is here completely overshadowed by the related but still different figure of the Manda-d'Hayya (Hibil Ziwa) who triumphantly descends into hell and vanquishes the demons.[112]

But still with all these fundamental differences one may not overlook the similarities here and there. Even in Paul the idea is intimated that this

[111] Cf. Brandt, *Mandäische Religion*, p. 199, as well as the interesting fragment in Lidzbarski, *Johannesbuch der Mandäer*, pp. 55-56, which has recently been treated by Reitzenstein, *Die Göttin Psyche*, SAH, 1917, pp. 9 ff. In this we find once again Mani's entire central myth of the Primal Man. Of course the question arises as to how far borrowings have taken place on the part of Manichaeism.

[112] The apostle is also acquainted with this myth. See the excursus on the descent into Hades.

appearing of the Christos in this world means an almost contra-natural joining of his pneumatic divine nature with the σὰρξ ἁμαρτίας and for this reason a burden from which only death and resurrection deliver him. If in the apostle's thought the appearing of the δεύτερος 'Αδάμ is an eschatological fact which stands at the end of the world, on the other hand it is also a basic feature of Oriental mysticism and speculation that the (re-) appearing and final ascent of the Primal Man after the completed reassembling of all his lost elements of light is the sign of the end and of the collapse of the world.[113] And in conclusion we may only briefly refer to the fact that that particular interweaving of natural and spiritual which we encounter in the speculation of Paul in so characteristic a manner finds its complete parallel, indeed the larger, explanatory context, in that Oriental mysticism. Here the Primal Man is clearly a cosmic power,[114] with whose sinking into matter the great world development, the dissolution of the unnaturally mixed good- and evil-natured elements of the world begins. The process of the liberation of believing and pure souls is only a partial process of the great natural-spiritual event through which the world of light and life is separated from the darkness. The individual light-souls, however, are nothing other than parts of the fallen Primal Man, entirely included within a great natural-spiritual whole and a natural-spiritual general process; the Primal Man's fall is their fall, his exaltation their exaltation. Here we have at least parallel

[113] This is especially clear in Manichaeism. In the portrayal of the beginning of the future world it is said (in the Fihrist, in Flügel, *Mani*, p. 101): "Then the Primal Man comes from the world of the polar star." Cf. also the parallels in the Turfan fragments in F. W. K. Müller, SAB, 1904, p. 20 (the god Ormuzd from the upper northern region). Incidentally, it is already stated in the old Persian religion that at the great resurrection of the dead first of all Gayomart (the Primal Man) appears. The Jewish apocalyptic, as it appears, preserved this motif of the myth, the appearing of the man at the end of things (while the Jewish legend is acquainted only with the first half of it, the pre-terrestrial Primal Man [Adam]). In Mandaeism Enos-Uthra (the Man) appears at the end of time.

[114] This and all the following is particularly clear and obvious in Manichaean speculation. As is known, the five higher elements form the equipment of the Primal Man, and then the five spiritual powers correspond to these. The consequence of the conquering of the Primal Man is the mixing of the five elements of light with those of the darkness. Darkness and light are intertwined, like two great powerful bodies, two trees from different roots, etc. Here, as is evident, the doctrine of redemption is almost overgrown with this naturalistic view. The Primal-Man myth in the Poimandres and in the Naassene Preaching is conceived less in cosmogonic terms and more in anthropogonic terms. Here the spiritual element predominates. But the interweaving of the spiritual and the naturalistic is also clearly present here. The Primal Man sinks and descends with the abundance of light and life through the spheres of the planets down into Physis. Then there develops that miserable mixing of the higher and lower elements and the struggle between the two, which is continued and operative in every human soul.

formations of ideas which all the more clarify and open up to us the essence of the Pauline mystical speculation.

Thus it can hardly be denied that the total mystical speculation of Paul about the world of the πνεῦμα and of the σάρξ, about Christ, the second Adam, about the destruction of the σῶμα τῆς ἁμαρτίας of the old man, about the believers' living and dying with him, stands in a larger religio-historical context. It was an unbelievably daring deed of the apostle that he introduced this thought-world to the gospel and interpreted the appearing, suffering, dying, and rising of the Christos from this perspective and took this as the central point of a cosmic event which begins with the creation and ceases with the consummation in the hereafter. The cultic veneration of the κύριος 'Ιησοῦς Χριστός in the Hellenistic communities and the personal Christ mysticism which rests upon that veneration gain their conceptual grounding and their systematic structure. Jewish-primitive Christian eschatology is finally overcome thereby. The appearance of Jesus upon earth, his death and his resurrection now no longer serve as something preliminary, as the first stroke; they become the actually decisive thing in the great cosmic process. Out of a religion of the future and of pure yearning develops a religion of blessed fulfillment and certainty. And what within it is still future and still yearning nevertheless appears as a necessary consequence of what has already happened.

On the other hand we cannot overlook that with his speculation the apostle is treading perilous paths. A foreign element here is pressed upon the gospel; a strong supernaturalism, a gloomy dualism and pessimism, which does not stem from the world of the Old Testament and of the gospel. With the apostle, spirit and flesh become absolute opposites; the higher life of the Christian stands in contradiction with his natural disposition and only through a miracle has been submerged in the latter from above and from without. Thus now the κύριος appears as πνεῦμα in absolute opposition to all natural human disposition. The first man as he came forth from God's hand possessed, in contrast to him, a fundamentally less-worthy being; he was "only a living being." No bridge of development leads from the first to the second man. The appearance of the second man here upon earth comes wholly under the category of humiliation, his dwelling ἐν ὁμοιώματι σαρκὸς ἁμαρτίας is a difficult enigma, and his death is both a liberation for him and the solution of the enigma. Those who are his are to follow him on this way of death and of deliverance from the lower and natural existence.

Christ is not the fulfillment but the death of the natural man. Creation and redemption threaten to tear apart completely, and this sharp division is continued through the whole world in which the redemption has become a reality. Like someone who comes from another sphere, the pneumatic appears over against the psychic. The world of man threatens to split into two classes. Here then we see all the dangers of this Pauline mysticism more clearly rear their heads, and here also the gate of invasion for all specific sacramental beliefs and all "natural" cult practices is given. And yet once more the opposite side of the consideration must be brought out. At one point Paul has still maintained the continuity with the past and the gospel. In unprecedentedly bold fashion he has set the death of Jesus, the cross, a historical event in the middle of the world of oriental speculation. To be sure, this death of the Christos no longer appears only as a unique happening; it is the creative beginning of a great event which is continued in the believers until the great consummation. But still the idea is combined with a historical reality. The myth is transferred from the primeval age into the present and is bound up with history. And with the death a fixed place is given to the actual and genuine appearing of Jesus of Nazareth. And even if for Paul the entire life of Jesus has significance almost solely in view of this death, *still it is the death of a real man* with his humility and his obedience even up to the cross which here acquires such a powerful world-encompassing significance. Here the boundary is given which basically separates the apostle from Christian Gnosticism with which he still has so much in common; here is the point at which the divergent ways divide. On the one side the myth will further seize the Christian religion and will completely overrun and choke the historical gospel, the idea will entirely set aside the unique historical event of the cross and the reality of the earthly Jesus (Gnosticism). On the other side, along with his death, the entire earthly life of Jesus will take on a new and unprecedented significance (Gospel of John). On the one side the contrast between the world of the πνεῦμα and that of the σάρξ will be developed to the ultimate consequence, so that thereby the Jesus of the gospel is removed without a trace and is re-formed into a myth; the worlds of creation and redemption are torn apart. On the other side this contrast is moderated to such an extent that the Christos no longer appears as the death and annihilation of the natural man, the first Adam, but as his reproduction, crown, and fulfillment, and that between the world of creation and that of redemption a harmony is established

(Irenaeus and the ecclesiastical theology). As much as Paul seeks to conquer the idea of the pneumatic superman in the service of the community, and as strongly as he spiritualizes the sacramental, the dangers from that side are a constant threat.

Thus emerges Paulinism in all its utter sublimity, with the ardor and inwardness of its mysticism, but also with all the dangers that are specifically peculiar to it, as a one-sided religion of redemption alongside Jesus' gospel of the forgiveness of sins.

VII. *Consequences.* With all this the Pauline religion is concentrated and crystallized in the *faith in Christ,* the πίστις κυρίου Ἰησοῦ Χριστοῦ. We have already shown how the actual "faith in Jesus" was still foreign to the gospel tradition and therewith to the Palestinian primitive community, and how then probably the confession (the *fides quae creditur*) of the κύριος Jesus Christ became the foundation of Hellenistic Christianity. It can hardly be doubted that with the apostle Paul the faith (in the form of faith in Christ) first appears as the inner center of the religious life. The religious concept of faith has a fairly long prehistory. It first emerges within the history of religions at the point where the religions are released from the national soil, strive for universalism, and begin to lead their own life outside and beyond the national cultures. So long as the religion is predominantly nationally conditioned, it is quite essentially bound to the stock of the national life, to mores, usage, and custom; only with the separation of nation and religion does that which we call faith, the personal conviction of the individual, come into its own. Thus it is understandable that the well-defined concept of religious faith is first found above all in Hellenistic Judaism of the Diaspora.[115] The Jewish philosopher Philo is the first theologian of faith, the first who develops a detailed psychology of faith.

But even in Philo the concept of faith and its comprehension in its central necessity has a prehistory which leads back into Greek philosophy. One recognizes this when one notices how often Philo defines faith as the sure and dependable conviction.[116] Thus he characterizes faith as ἀκλινὴς καὶ βεβαία ὑπόληψις[117] or as ὀχυρωτάτη καὶ βεβαιοτάτη διάθεσις.[118] Of

---

[115] On this, cf. Bousset, *Religion des Judentums,* pp. 235 ff., 514-15.
[116] On the following, cf. Bréhier (see above, p. 183, n. 70), p. 223.
[117] περὶ ἀρετῶν, 216.
[118] De conf. ling., 51.

Abraham's attitude toward the divine prediction it is said: τὸ δὲ ὅτι γενήσε-
ται, πάντως κατὰ τὰς θείας ὑποσχέσεις βεβαίως κατείληφεν.[119]

These definitions, however, are borrowed from Stoic philosophy. The firm
and unshakable conviction which is based upon knowledge (ἐπιστήμη)
belongs to the ideal of the Stoic sage. Thus Plato in the Stoic sense defines
knowledge as κατάληψις ἀσφαλὴς καὶ βέβαιος ἀμετάπτωτος ὑπὸ λόγου.[120]
In the great ideal portrait of the Stoic sage which is in Stobaeus, Ecl. II,
6. 6, p. 232, we find also the word "faith" bound up with the concept of
a firm conviction: τούτοις δὲ ἀκολούθως οὐκ ἀπιστεῖν. τὴν γὰρ ἀπιστίαν
εἶναι ψεύδους ὑπόληψιν, τὴν δὲ πίστιν ἀστεῖον ὑπάρχειν, εἶναι γὰρ
ὑπόληψιν ἰσχυράν, βεβαιοῦσαν τὸ ὑπολαμβανόμενον, ὁμοίως δὲ καὶ τὴν
ἐπιστήμην ἀμετάπτωτον ὑπὸ λόγου. διὰ ταῦτά φασι μήτε ἐπίστασθαί τι
τὸν φαῦλον μήτε πιστεύειν.

This Stoic ideal now in Philo is transferred into the religious realm in a
characteristic and peculiar fashion. The imperturbability of the conviction is
no longer the highest good of the wise man who trusts in himself and is self-
contained, but of the pious person who finds the certainty and irrefutability
of his life and his conviction in the omnipotent God. In the statements of
Philo about faith there still often resounds, particularly under the influence
of Gen. 15:6, the Old Testament idea that faith is confidence in the fulfillment of the divine prophecy. But basically almost everywhere for him this
confidence is expanded into the permanent frame of mind in which a man
turns from perishable things and finds the substance of his life in the
eternal, unwavering, and only dependable God. "Friend, do not rashly take
from the wise the praise that is due to him, and do not ascribe to the unworthy the most perfect of virtues, *faith*. . . . You will know assuredly
that on account of our kinship with mortal nature to which we are closely
bound, which persuades us to trust in money and honor and lordship and
pleasure, health and strength of body and much else, it is not easy to believe
God without any other support. But this, to abandon everything and to
mistrust the creature which is in itself undependable, but to trust God

---

[119] Q. rer. div. haer., 101. Cf. also the contrast of belief and unbelief, de ebr., 40, 188.
[120] De congr. erud. causa, 141 (cf. q. deus s. immut., 22: τὸ μὴ τοῖς πράγμασι
συμμεταβάλλειν ἀλλὰ μετὰ στερρότητος ἀκλινοῦς καὶ παγίου βεβαιότητος ἅπασι τοῖς
ἁρμόττουσι χαίρειν). Clement of Alexandria (Strom. II, 2.9.4) explicitly says τὴν
γοῦν ἐπιστήμην ὁρίζονται φιλοσόφων παῖδες ἕξιν ἀμετάπτωτον ὑπὸ λόγων (on this,
cf. the note in Stählin's edition, I, 117). In general we may also compare Clement's statements which are dependent upon Philo. For him belief is πρόληψις ἑκούσιος; θεοσεβείας
συγκατάθεσις (then follows a reference to Heb. 11:1); ἀφανοῦς πράγματος ἐννοητικὴ
συγκατάθεσις, ἐπιστήμη θεμελίῳ βεβαίῳ ἐπερηρεισμένη (Strom. II, 2.8-9; cf. II, 5.24;
6.27).

alone, who in truth alone is true (faithful=πιστός),[121] is the work of a great and Olympian reason." [122]

God alone is the Ἐστώς, who stands firm while all else in the world wavers.[123] But whoever has found God learns likewise to stand firm, as Philo again and again emphasizes that Moses *stood* before God: εἴρηται γὰρ σὺ δὲ αὐτοῦ στῆθι μετ' ἐμοῦ (Deut. 5:31), ἵνα ἐνδοιασμὸν καὶ ἐπαμφοτερισμόν, ἀβεβαίου ψυχῆς διαθέσεις, ἀποδυσάμενος τὴν ὀχυρωτάτην καὶ βεβαιοτάτην διάθεσιν πίστιν ἐνδύσηται.[124]

Thus is achieved in Philo this transition, which cannot be overestimated in its significance, of the concept "faith" (=firm conviction) from philosophical into religious language. From this perspective it is understood how then from the outset the concept plays such a central and dominating role in religion. Even here the thought-forms for the universal religion are prefigured. There, in Greek philosophy, the ideal is set up: the firm, unshakable conviction, disturbed by nothing, in theory as in practical life. When philosophy began to doubt the attainability of this ideal: δυσεύρετον σφόδρα τὸ τούτων ἐστὶ γένος,[125] religion answered by affirming it confidently: The pious finds in God the unshakable footing for his life.

Now one will no longer marvel over the fact that this religious concept of faith occurs also, although not so frequently and dominantly, in the Hermetic writings, which show so many affinities with Philo. Here we find the splendid word: τὰ μὲν γὰρ φαινόμενα τέρπει, τὰ δὲ ἀφανῆ δυσπιστεῖν ποιεῖ. φανερώτερα δέ ἐστι τὰ κακά, τὸ δὲ ἀγαθὸν ἀφανὲς τοῖς ὀφθαλμοῖς (IV, 9). In Poimandres we read at the end: διὸ πιστεύω [126] σοι καὶ μαρτυρῶ, εἰς ζωὴν καὶ φῶς χωρῶ (32). Especially significant and fruitful here is the

---

[121] Philo likes to use the predicate πιστός with reference to God. Bréhier (*Les idées philosophiques* . . .) considers the translation "believing" (in the sense of a firm conviction) to be possible, appealing to Leg. All. III, 204; de mut. nom., 182.

[122] Q. rer. div. haer., 91 ff.; cf. de Abrah., 268-69.

[123] Leg. Alleg. II, 83 (89): διασυνιστάντος αὐτόν τε καὶ τὴν γένεσιν τοῦ δεσπότου, ἑαυτὸν μὲν ὅτι ἀκλινὴς ἕστηκεν ἀεί, τὴν δὲ γένεσιν, ὅτι ταλαντεύει καὶ πρὸς τἀναντία ἀντιρρέπει. III, 38; De post. Ca., 19, 23: τὸ μὲν οὖν ἀκλινῶς ἐστὼς ὁ θεός ἐστι τὸ δὲ κινητὸν ἡ γένεσις· ὥστε ὁ μὲν προσιὼν θεῷ στάσεως ἐφίεται. In the section following, 23-31, cf. the reference to Gen. 18:22-23 (Abraham), ἑστὼς ἦν ἔναντι κυρίου. Deut. 5:31 (Moses) στῆθι μετ' ἐμοῦ. De gigant., 48 ff.; de plantat., 135.

[124] De conf ling., 31; cf. 106.

[125] De post. Ca. 43; cf. Seneca, ep. 42 (*virum bonum*) ille . . . *fortasse tamquam Phoenix semel anno quingentesimo nascitur* (cf. Holl, N. Jahrb. f. klass. Philol. XXIX [1912], 419).

[126] πιστεύω is used here altogether in the technical sense. Perhaps I, 21 also is to be read thus: ἐὰν οὖν μάθῃς σεαυτὸν ἐκ ζωῆς καὶ φωτὸς ὄντα καὶ πιστεύσῃς, ὅτι ἐκ τούτων τυγχάνεις, εἰς ζωὴν πάλιν χωρήσεις (cf. Reitzenstein's reconstruction of the text).

end of the ninth chapter (§ 10): "This may appear true to you, Asclepius, if you consider it rationally, and if you are ignorant, unbelievable: τὸ γὰρ νοῆσαί ἐστι τὸ πιστεῦσαι, τὸ ἀπιστῆσαι δὲ τὸ μὴ νοῆσαι. . . . For the Nous led by the Logos (Word) up to a certain point, attains to the truth, and having considered everything (testing it) and finding it agreeing with what is proclaimed by the Logos, 'he becomes a believer' and finds his rest in the glorious 'faith' " (IX, 10). After all that has preceded we can conceive of how such a manner of speaking could arise on this half-philosophical, half-religious soil. And now when we find even the sentence: "Be baptized (the καρδία is addressed), if you can, in this vessel, since *you believe* that you will ascend to the one who has sent down the 'Krater,' since you recognize for what purpose you have come to be" (IV, 4), we see how the religous concept of faith is bound up with the mystery tendency and the idea of the sacrament.[127] And once again, even in the later Asclepius writing, it is said of the pious: *fiducia credulitatis suae tantum inter homines, quantum sol lumine ceteris astris antistat* (chap. 29).[128]

We see clearly how Paul with his stressing of the significance of faith for religion takes his place in a large context. In him also it is not difficult to demonstrate the fundamental concept of faith. In the forceful saying, "whatever is not of faith is sin" (Rom. 14:23), the original significance of faith in the sense of firm conviction breaks through clearly.

In this sense the apostle pictures the faith of Abraham: εἰς δὲ τὴν ἐπαγγελίαν τοῦ θεοῦ οὐ διεκρίθη τῇ ἀπιστίᾳ. ἀλλὰ ἐνεδυναμώθη τῇ πίστει . . . πληροφορηθείς (Rom. 4:20), even though here the firm conviction is onesiddly connected with the fulfillment of the divine promise.

Moreover it is at once clear that with Paul, just as with Philo, the religious implication of the concept appears brought fully to its culmination. With Paul the object of faith is God, faith occurs as directed toward God. Not only in the sense that he recognizes the existence of God, but in the deeper and fuller sense, that he relies upon God, or, better, finds in God the support

---

[127] Reitzenstein, *Hellenistische Mysterionreligionen*, p. 85 [2nd ed., p. 95], refers to Apuleius XI, 28. After his second initiation Apuleius says: *plena jam f i d u c i a germanae religionis obsequium divinum frequentabum.* The sentence on the Inscription of Abercius, πίστις πάντη δὲ προῆγε καὶ παρέθηκεν τροφὴν πάντη, in itself therefore is no decisive argument against the pagan-Hellenistic source of the inscription (Reitzenstein, p. 86 [2nd ed., p. 95]).

[128] Cf. further Themistios in Stobaeus, Florilegium IV, p. 107 M: ἐφορῶν ὄχλον ἐν βορβόρῳ πολλῷ καὶ συνελαυνόμενον . . . φόβῳ δὲ θανάτου τοῖς κακοῖς ἀπιστίᾳ τῶν ἐκεῖ ἀγαθῶν ἐμμένοντα. Dieterich, *Mithraslit.*, p. 164.

of his whole life.[129] Of course one cannot call the apostle a psychologist of faith to the extent that this is true of Philo. Even in the New Testament the *locus classicus* for the actual religious concept of faith is found not in Paul but in the Epistle to the Hebrews. For Paul it is less important to say what faith actually is than what faith is worth. The alpha and omega of his proclamation is that man's standing before[130] the gracious God, his δικαιο-σύνη, rests upon religious faith. Thus the Pauline idea of faith in general is narrowed; the forgiveness of sins (almost=δικαιοσύνη θεοῦ) appears quite essentially as the correlate of faith. The duty of the Christians becomes πιστεύειν ἐπὶ τὸν δικαιοῦντα τὸν ἀσεβῆ (Rom. 4:5). But in this narrowing and abbreviating, "faith" is comprehended by Paul with a previously un-heard-of energy as the center of the religious life in general.

*With all this it becomes all the more significant that for Paul Jesus Christ appears as the object of this faith,* or that for him faith becomes πίστις Χριστοῦ Ἰησοῦ (in the sense of the objective genitive). The formula in question[131] to be sure is not as frequently found in the Pauline epistles as, by way of comparison, in the Johannine literature; but it stands precisely at the climactic points of the Pauline expositions: in the conclusion which crowns the presentation of the doctrine of justification (Rom. 3:22-26), in the dispute with Peter in Antioch (Gal. 2:16-20),[132] and finally in the passage in which the apostle most explicitly explains the real essence of faith: Rom. 10:6-14.[133]

The object of faith for the apostle has thus been doubled in a peculiar way. Faith is for Paul in the same sense and to the same extent faith in Christ Jesus as in God. Jesus moves into the very center of religious contemplation. We can hardly explain this unique complication of the idea of faith, which in the apostle appears with such self-evident character, other than again under the assumption that here he is dependent upon an already well-defined conviction of the community. I have already pointed out (p. 150) that Paul himself confirms this surmise. In his fundamental statement about

[129] Rom. 4:17, 24; 10:9; I Thess. 1:9.

[130] I deliberately hold to the translation of δικαιοσύνη θεοῦ as "righteousness before God" (unless the genitive everywhere should be taken as subjective: righteousness as an attribute of God). Linguistic analogies to this (Semitic) genitive in Ps. 51:19: זבחי אלהים (LXX, of course, has θυσίαι θεῷ); John 6:28-29, τὰ ἔργα, τὸ ἔργον τοῦ θεοῦ.

[131] πιστεύειν (πίστις) εἰς Χριστὸν Ἰ.; πίστις with the genitive.

[132] It is noteworthy how here also belief in the Son of God immediately comes into connection with the forgiveness of sins.

[133] Cf. further Phil. 1:29; 3:9; Col. 2:5.

faith he points quite clearly to an already formulated confession of faith of the community. Jesus' position as Lord (κύριος ᾿Ιησοῦς) and his resurrection appear to have been the contents of this confession[134] whose validity the apostle presupposes also for the Roman congregation. In this context faith takes on even for him almost the significance of agreement to a formulated confession.

But here once again one sees clearly how with Paul the spiritual-religious grows out of the cultic. For him faith is deepened and spiritualized—and this will certainly have occurred in part under the influence of the above-sketched Hellenistic thought-world—into a continuing vital relationship to God, into the center of all religious life. But in these deepened and spiritualized contexts the person of Jesus maintains its fundamentally significant position which it already had in the simple confession of the community, only that here it becomes in a wholly different sense a living presence which dominates and fills the personal Christian life. For the Christian, faith, the πίστις εἰς Χριστὸν ᾿Ιησοῦν, becomes the organ with which he grasps the present reality of the πνεῦμα–κύριος.

VIII. *Theology.* As conceivable as this whole development is, and as much as it appears to have occurred with an immanent necessity, still it signifies a remarkable complicating and burdening of that simplicity and plainness of religion which appears at the high points of Old Testament religion and in the gospel of Jesus. For the object of religious faith as of veneration in worship now is presented in a peculiar thoroughgoing duplication. The figures of God and of Christ appear to the eye of faith closely fitted together. How did Paul, who from his Old Testament monotheistic past must have had a sensitivity for these difficulties, come to terms with them?

First of all we must note that Paul is concerned, in an almost consistently followed terminology, to keep the two figures altogether separate from each other—at least outwardly. For him God is always θεός (πατήρ) and Jesus always κύριος. In fact, in one passage as we have already seen, it even appears as though the apostle intends with these formulas to emphasize a vigorous subordination of the figure of Christ to God in a fundamentally formulated manner. This is the passage where he contrasts the confession of the one God and the one Lord of the Christians with the belief of the Gentiles in many gods and many lords (I Cor. 8:5-6). He apparently proceeds from the awareness that even according to the Gentiles' impression the many

---

[134] Cf. Acts 17:18: ὅτι τὸν ᾿Ιησοῦν καὶ τὴν ἀνάστασιν εὐηγγελίζετο.

"lords" occupy a subordinate position in relation to the class of θεοί.[135] This would of course once again show upon what dangerous paths these reflections of Paul are moving. For they finally come out at a point of letting Christ as a divine being appear at a level below God; as a half-god, if we wish to put it crudely.[136]

Such a speculation about the relation between God and Christ is also shown where in Paul's writings the Kyrios appears as εἰκὼν θεοῦ[137] or even absolutely as εἰκών.[138] This term, which could stem from Gen. 1:26 (and then of course from the speculation about the heavenly Anthropos), recalls on the other hand that already on the oldest inscription which gives us information about the ruler cult, the ruler is called εἰκὼν ζῶσα of the deity.[139] And in a later section we shall see still more precisely how people sought to make conceptually clear the relation of the god-ruler to the deity by using the image of the ἐναργὴς ἐπιφάνεια, the *deus manifestus*.

Yet the possibilities can only briefly be considered, since only some brief allusions of Paul are available to us for comparison. The actual title for Jesus with which the apostle evidently seeks to overcome this difficulty is in any case that of the υἱὸς τοῦ θεοῦ. To be sure this title likewise (like the concept of πιστεύειν) appears much less frequently in the Pauline epistles than in the Johannine literature. Yet on the other hand we find it here at the climactic points of the presentation. Thus in the monumental introduction to the Epistle to the Romans Paul several times summarizes his proclamation as the gospel of the Son of God (1:3, 4, 9). What comforts him and lifts him above the still present imperfection of his life as a Christian in the flesh is faith in the *Son of God* (Gal. 2:20). That God sent his *Son* (Gal. 4:4), did not spare his own *Son* (Rom. 8:32), is the core of his preaching. The only place where the author of the book of Acts uses the title ὁ υἱὸς τοῦ θεοῦ occurs in the summary of the Pauline preaching (9:20).

We have already given reasons for our doubting whether the title "Son of God" at all stems from Jewish messianology and accordingly from Palestinian primitive Christianity. If the doubts are valid, then the possibility

[135] See above, p. 147. Cf. J. Weiss, *Kommentar zum ersten Korintherbrief, in ioc.* With Weiss I should refrain from connecting the κύριοι exclusively with the emperor cult.

[136] In the energy with which Paul stresses the *one* Lord Jesus Christ, the apostle of course stands out, noticeably distinguishing himself from the milieu in which he moves. Here the full force of Old Testament monotheism is at work.

[137] II Cor. 4:4; Col. 1:15.

[138] Rom. 8:29.

[139] Dittenberger, Or. Gr. Inscr., 90 (at the beginning): εἰκόνος ζώσης τοῦ Διός.

must be reckoned with that here we have to do with an independent creation of Paul. This possibility could be supported by the consideration that according to its nature the term ὁ υἱὸς τοῦ θεοῦ points to theological reflection (not, like the title κύριος, to cult and praxis), since in it obviously the *relation* of the two beings, God and Christ, is in view.

But we shall not go into that further here. Whether with the designation of Jesus as the υἱὸς τοῦ θεοῦ Paul reached back to an older messianic title or not, in any case with him it receives a new imprint which has nothing more to do with Jewish messianology. In Paul the Son of God appears as a supraterrestrial [140] being who stands in the closest metaphysical connection with God. The idea of a selection on the basis of moral worthiness [141] and an ethical fellowship of will are in no way under discussion. With the term "Son" two things are intended: The heavenly nature of Christ on the one hand is to be pushed as close as possible to God the Father, and on the other hand is still to be particularly distinguished from him. One cannot escape the impression that Paul chose precisely this concept, while he completely avoided the term ὁ υἱὸς τοῦ ἀνθρώπου, in order to make clear to his Hellenistic congregations, in a formula current among them, how the relation of God the Father and Christ was to be grasped conceptually. The idea of a son of the deity [142] was current among them. The assumption of a divine triad consisting of Father, Mother, and Son appears to have been widespread on the soil precisely of Syrian (and Egyptian) religion. It appears as if Paul could make a connection, in the milieu surrounding him, not only with the vague and general concept of sons of gods, [143] but also with the more definite idea of a son deity. [144] With this assumption, which after all still remains possible if the term should stem from Jewish messianology and the

[140] Rom. 1:4: τοῦ ὁρισθέντος υἱοῦ θεοῦ ἐν δυνάμει.

[141] κατὰ πνεῦμα ἁγιωσύνης. Rom. 1:4 had to do not with the moral confirmation of Jesus in the earthly life, but precisely with his original metaphysical state. The supraterrestrial Pneuma is the effective factor in the resurrection, Rom. 8:11.

[142] I should not wish to bring the title in Paul into too close a connection with the imperial cult and the well-known formula *Divi Filius* (θεοῦ υἱός; cf. Deissmann, *Bible Studies*, pp. 166-67; *Light from the Ancient East*, pp. 346-47), since the cult of the emperor had hardly assumed such a dominant position in the time of Paul, and since the title θεοῦ υἱός=*Divi filius* does have a very concrete and well-defined content; cf. the considerations set forth by Dölger ('Ιχθύς, RQ, Supplement XVII (1910), 389-403) and the material assembled there.

[143] Mark 15:39 quite evidently refers to such a general conception of sons of God.

[144] The material is well assembled in Baudissin, *Adonis und Esmun*, p. 16.1. Cf. Usener, *Dreiheit*, Rhein. Museum, New Series LVIII (1903), 32-33. Bousset, *Hauptprobleme*, pp. 333 ff., 71, *et passim* (see *Trias* in the Index).

theology of the primitive community, the power and originality of the new proclamation would then come to expression in the vigor, as well as in the persuasiveness, with which Paul associates the one Son with the one Father.

This conception of the Son of God is connected in Paul, in the first place and almost altogether, with the figure of the present Kyrios. This is indeed understandable from the outset. For it was just this position of the Kyrios beside God in the actual church worship that above all demanded an explanation. And this explanation ran thus: the Kyrios is ὁ υἱὸς τοῦ θεοῦ; on the one hand, as the Son he stands close by the side of the Father, yet on the other hand he is still a being in his own right, separate from the Father. Therefore the content of the apostle's gospel is the ὁρισθεὶς υἱὸς θεοῦ ἐν δυνάμει κατὰ πνεῦμα ἁγιωσύνης ἐξ ἀναστάσεως νεκρῶν. And it is almost always this exalted Son of God upon whom Paul focuses.[145] The earthly sojourn of the Son of God is for him a presupposition for his present place of honor, which he briefly alludes to here and there: "God sent his Son." But Paul has hardly reflected upon the manner in which the divine being has appeared here upon earth. The real birth of Jesus[146] (from father and mother) he simply assumes; indeed he even stresses Jesus' descent from David's tribe, following the community's tradition which had come down to him. It almost appears here and there as if Paul intends to make a certain reduction of the plain reality of Jesus' manhood in fleshly lowliness. He speaks of God having sent his Son ἐν ὁμοιώματι σαρκὸς ἁμαρτίας (Rom. 8:3), who assumed the form of a servant, was found in his outward appearance (σχῆμα, habitus) as a man, and again had come ἐν ὁμοιώματι[147] ἀνθρώπων (Phil. 2:7). For him the humanity, the "sinful flesh" of Jesus is after all a difficult puzzle, the solution of which is the crucifixion (vide supra, p. 198). All these are beginnings which could lead into Docetism. But Paul only passes over such conceptions; he never seriously applied his reflection to the enigma of how the divine pretemporal essence in Jesus had been joined to a human actuality. Indeed for him this problem is still completely veiled, since in connection with the earthly reality of Jesus he thinks exclusively of the σάρξ, the external sensual corporeality. In fact, in this entire earthly manner of existence of Jesus, it is only the death that actually

---

[145] Cf. Rom. 1:3-4, 9; 8:29; I Thess. 1:10; I Cor. 1:9; 15:28; II Cor. 1:9; Gal. 1:16; 2:20 (faith in the Son); 4:6 (Spirit of the Son); Col. 1:13 (βασιλεία).

[146] Rom. 1:3; Gal. 4:4.

[147] ὁμοίωμα however is intended each time to express both aspects of the idea: the similarity which is heightened to the point of identity and yet a certain difference.

interests him. Thus he stresses that God did not spare his own *Son,* that we were reconciled through the death of his Son (Rom. 8:32; 5:10). All speculations about the significance of the baptism for the entrance of the heavenly essence into Jesus or even about a miraculous birth lie outside the thought-world of the apostle. Even less transparent are the conceptions which Paul forms of the preexistent essence of the Son of God. It cannot even be demonstrated whether he already connects the term "Son of God" with the preexistent one, although it is likely, since he does speak of the earthly Jesus as the "Son." He speaks with reference to the preexistent one of a πλούσιον εἶναι (II Cor. 8:9), an ἐν μορφῇ θεοῦ ὑπάρχειν (Phil. 2)[148]; he connects with this term an allusion to a myth which has not been unraveled up to the present time (οὐχ ἁρπαγμὸν ἡγήσατο τὸ εἶναι ἴσα θεῷ [149]); he identifies πνεῦμα ἁγιωσύνης as if it were the higher essence of the Son, in consequence of which he now is the Son of God in power (Rom. 1:4); but even all these conceptions he mentions only in passing.

When he speaks of the Son of God, it may once more be stressed, he has in view the present exalted Lord whom the Christians venerate in the cultus. He seeks to clarify for himself and his Hellenistic communities this enigma of a κύριος alongside the θεός by means of the concept of ὁ υἱὸς τοῦ θεοῦ, which places the Kyrios very close to God and yet holds Father and Son apart from each other.[150] Thus the Pauline proclamation becomes the gospel of the ὁρισθεὶς υἱὸς θεοῦ ἐν δυνάμει. At the same time the content of the preaching of Jesus is remarkably transformed. The Father in heaven whom Jesus proclaimed becomes the Father of our Lord Jesus Christ. The

[148] I cannot convince myself that in I Cor. 15:45 (ὁ ἔσχατος 'Αδὰμ εἰς πνεῦμα ζωοποιοῦν) Paul is thinking of the preexistence of Christ and not simply of his heavenly exaltation, no matter how appealing the construction may be that in his speculations about the preexistence of Christ he could have started out from the mythologoumenon of the Primal Man (υἱὸς τοῦ ἀνθρώπου!). If Paul referred to these speculations, he did so in a polemical fashion; cf. I Cor. 15:46.

[149] In passing I should like to refer to a certain parallel in the Oracula Chaldaica (Kroll, p. 12). Here it is said of the most high God: ὁ πατὴρ ἑαυτὸν ἥρπασεν οὐδ' ἐν ἑῇ δυνάμει νοερᾷ κλείσας ἴδιον πῦρ. "The Father withdrew himself (made his being inaccessible) and did not share his own fire even with his supra-terrestrial δύναμις." Thus Christ did not regard his deity as something which he must preserve for himself by ἁρπαγμός! But whence might the unusual expression in Paul and the Oracles stem?

[150] It is not correct when one represents the formula "God in Christ" with all the possibilities of a spiritualizing softening as Pauline. II Cor. 5:18 does not justify this: In Christ God was reconciling (ἦν . . . καταλλάσσων) the world to himself. Moreover, the worship of God in Christ is not a correct formula for Pauline Christianity: In the Pauline communities the veneration of the Kyrios stands alongside the veneration of God in an unresolved actuality.

belief in God the Father remains in the center, but it is narrowed in a characteristic manner.

After all this one still may not actually speak of a deity of Christ in the view of Paul. He evidently avoids the expression θεός, just as he also keeps his distance from the idea of a deification of the believers. However Rom. 9:5 is to be read and interpreted, it should be generally acknowledged that Paul is not to be credited with a doxology to Christ as ὁ ὢν ἐπὶ πάντων θεός. He still speaks naturally of the God and Father of our Lord Jesus Christ,[151] describes God as the head of Christ in the same sense as Christ is the head of man (I Cor. 11:3), and sets Christ in dependence upon God as he sets the community in dependence upon Christ (I Cor. 3:22-23).[152] The God who has awakened Christ from the dead (*vide supra*, p. 150) appears as the object of Pauline faith. And in almost startling strength Old Testament monotheism emerges in the apostle when he moves in the lines of eschatological thought. At the end Christ, after he has conquered and subjected all enemies, will give the rule back to the Father, and then God is to be all in all and Christ the firstborn among brethren (I Cor. 15:25 ff.; Rom. 8:29).

And yet the dogma of the deity of Christ is on the march. Nowhere may we forget that behind the personal piety of Paul and his theology there stands as a real power and a living reality the cultic veneration of the κύριος in the community. But what people worship in the cultus must stand wholly and unconditionally on the side of God. If Paul, following Old Testament instincts, still avoids the predicate of the deity of Christ and seeks to maintain a boundary line between θεός and κύριος, yet the massive faith of the community will ride smoothly over this careful distinction. It will consciously express the great mystery of the deity of Christ and place it in the center of the Christian religion. For it unconsciously has that mystery already in cult and praxis.

---

[151] II Cor. 1:3; 11:31; cf. Eph. 1:3; I Pet. 1:3.

[152] Cf. I Cor. 8:6. God the original source and the ultimate goal, the Kyrios the mediating cause. Of course Col. 1:16 already εἰς αὐτὸν ἔκτισται.

# 5

## THE BELIEF IN CHRIST
## IN THE JOHANNINE WRITINGS

We pass at once from Paul to the Johannine writings (Gospel and Epistles),[1] because here on the one hand we encounter once more in the development of genuine Christianity a singular, relatively original formation, rooted in its own soil, which yet on the other hand stands in the line of Pauline Christianity.

I. *Designations of Title and Dignity.* Here also the discussion may begin on the periphery with the question of the titles and designations of honor which are ascribed to Jesus in the Johannine writings.[2] Here are offered at once two startling and almost paradoxical facts. The first is this: The designation κύριος, which plays so decisive a role in Hellenistic Christianity, disappears here almost completely. I have already pointed out that in the first nineteen chapters of the Gospel—thus in the actual life of Jesus—the title is completely absent,[3] and that it appears only in the resurrection narrative. One could be tempted to explain this with the assumption that

---

[1] I shall treat the Johannine literature as a unit, in spite of the fact that I do not believe it is a literary unity. But religio-historically it forms a unity, apart from some few points which will be brought out in the presentation.

[2] The Logos concept will not be treated until Chap. IX. The evangelist has made use of it only in passing.

[3] Passages such as 12:21 and 20:15 prove that the frequently used address κύριε does not lie in the same line with ὁ κύριος.

the author of the Fourth Gospel intended to apply the designation of κύριος, not to the Jesus who walked upon earth, but only to the exalted Lord. *But against this there is the fact that* κύριος *is completely lacking also in the Johannine epistles.* In addition an internal reason can be shown why the Johannine literary circle actually on the whole avoids the title κύριος. The Gospel has Jesus say: "You are my *friends* (φίλοι)[4] if you do what I command you. I no longer call you servants (slaves), for the servant does not know what his lord is doing; but I have called you friends, because I have told you all that I have heard from the Father" (15:14-15), and: "The Father loves you (φιλεῖ), because you have loved him and have believed that I have come forth from God" (16:27). Correspondingly in III John the author extends greetings in the name of the circle of φίλοι.[5] These apparently trivial observations allow us at once to gain a profound insight into the nature and peculiarity of Johannine piety. The Christ mysticism peculiar to the Johannine writings,[6] which will be treated more precisely later on, leads these pious ones (φίλοι) so close to Jesus that they solemnly—perhaps there is here a latent opposition to Paul—reject the predicate of servants of Christ for themselves and for this reason apparently also avoid the title κύριος. It is the circle of these friends of God and friends of Christ who speak in the Johannine writings.

Equally paradoxical is the other fact that the Fourth Gospel has retained the old title of Jewish messianology which stands at the center of the dogmatics of the Palestinian primitive community, the title ὁ υἱὸς τοῦ ἀνθρώπου. And it has not merely preserved the word here and there accidentally, but it uses the term with full insight into its nature and its significance. Precisely as Son of Man Jesus is for this Gospel the judge of the world (5:27), the preexistent one, the one who has come from heaven, the one ascended and exalted to heaven (3:13; 6:62), above whom already during his earthly sojourn the heavens opened up so that the angels

---

[4] An investigation of the history of this predicate might be rewarding. I call attention to the wise men who are called φίλοι θεοῦ, Epictetus II, 17.29 and IV, 3.9; Abraham as φίλος τοῦ θεοῦ in Philo and in James 2:23. The fellow cultists in the much-disputed Abercius inscription are φίλοι (Hepding, *Attis*, p. 84, 1. 15). Further material in Holl, *Enthusiasmus und Bussgewalt*, p. 129.

[5] The words of Jesus in 13:13-14 appear to contradict these observations: ὑμεῖς φωνεῖτέ με ὁ διδάσκαλος καὶ ὁ κύριος, καὶ καλῶς λέγετε· εἰμὶ γάρ. Here, however, the Fourth Gospel is dependent upon Synoptic reminiscences; see above, p. 127. 13:16 (οὐκ ἔστιν δοῦλος μείζων τοῦ κυρίου) is a quotation from Matt. 10:24.

[6] The Apocalypse stands in sharp contrast with its prevailing designation of Christians as δοῦλοι θεοῦ.

descended upon the head of the Son of Man, then again to ascend (1:51). His suffering and his death—here also a primitive Christian motif is clearly maintained in the face of later reflection—appear only under the perspectives of exaltation and glorification.[7] It is the exalted Son of Man who, present in the sacrament, gives to his own people his flesh and blood to eat (6:53). In the confession of him the faith of the Christian community, which appears under the symbol of the man born blind now healed, is summarized in contrast to the synagogue (9:35).

If there is anything that argues for the view that the author of the Fourth Gospel still has some connections with Palestine and the Palestinian primitive community, it is this observation. At the same time, of course, the evangelist, while he took over the concept with its entire contents and all its individual consequences, yet spiritualized and reinterpreted it in a grandiose fashion. He completely separated the Son of Man from Jewish eschatology and apocalypticism and from the ardent expectation of his return in popular Christianity. In the same moment in which he faithfully explains the ancient meaning of the title, that God has given the judgment to Jesus because he is the Son of Man, he spiritualizes and makes contemporary the great "works" of the resurrection of the dead and the judgment in such a way that he falls into the danger of completely eliminating the primitive Christian eschatology. In this manner the title "Son of Man" becomes for him the comprehensive designation of the preexistent and eternal glory of Jesus which surpasses everything earthly, in comparison with which the earthly sojourn of Jesus is only an episode.

But the actual title with which John paraphrases Jesus' position of honor is ὁ υἱὸς τοῦ θεοῦ. In a manner quite different from that of Paul the Johannine writings set it at the center of the proclamation. The Christian confession is summarized in the solemn sentence that Jesus (Christ) is the Son of God,[8] the confession with which the Gospel also concludes. There can be no doubt at all that this title has here a metaphysical significance quite alien to all Jewish messianology. Christ is the supra-terrestrial Son of God who is in the Father's bosom and for this reason is in a position to reveal the divine secrets,[9] who testifies of what he beheld and speaks what

---

[7] In addition to the already discussed (above, p. 53) peculiar view of the ὑψωθῆναι in 3:14, 8:28, and 12:34, there is the usage, which is in the same line, of δοξασθῆναι in 12:23 and 13:31 (always in connection with the title "Son of Man").

[8] John 3:36; 11:27; 19:7; 20:31.

[9] John 1:18. Again, the present tense shows that the earthly life of Jesus is for the evangelist only an episode.

he has heard,[10] whom the Father has sent into the world,[11] in order to give eternal life to the believers, who has come forth from the Father into this world and returns out of this world to the Father,[12] who alone is from above, while all others are from below,[13] the Son to whom the Father has given all his works, even including the greatest of them, judgment and resurrection.[14] To him God gave the Spirit without measure; him God has consecrated and sealed.[15] Christian faith is fully and totally faith in him (πιστεύειν εἰς τὸν υἱόν, εἰς αὐτόν).[16]

A solemn adjective for the υἱός is the title Monogenes. We encounter it in the Gospel as well as in the First Epistle.[17] In the post-apostolic literature, so far as I can see, it is very seldom used.[18] Its acceptance into the old Roman baptismal confession perhaps came about under the influence of the Fourth Gospel. Among the Valentinians the Monogenes appears as a figure of the Ogdoad, who however also appears again under another name as πατὴρ τῆς ἀληθείας.[19] This, like the adoption of the term Logos, which usually appears inserted between the πατὴρ τῆς ἀληθείας and Anthropos though these belong together, perhaps already indicates a direct influence of John's Gospel. Wobbermin[20] pointed out that the names of the other aeons (βύθιος, ἀγήρατος, αὐτοφυής, ἀκίνητος) point to Orphic theology and find their parallels in the Orphic literature, and that the Monogenes also stems from there. In particular Monogenes appears to have been an adjective applied to Kore.[21] I would add that the name of the Arabian God Dusares is interpreted in a remarkable fashion in Epiphanius, Haer. 51.22, as μονογενὴς δεσπότου. This is noteworthy because in this context Dusares appears at the same time as the miraculously born son of a virgin goddess (παρθένος) and people celebrated his birthday, like that of the curious Alexandrian aeon, on January 6! (Vide infra, Chap. VII.) As to the meaning of the word, the parallels indeed show that the term μονογενής in this connection has a deeper and fuller sound than in its usual connection, in which

[10] John 3:11, 32; 5:30 (5:37-38); 6:46; 8:26, 38, 40; 15:15.
[11] John 3:16; I John 4:9-10, 14-15.
[12] John 16:28.
[13] John 8:23.
[14] John 5:19 ff.; 10:37-38; 14:10.
[15] John 3:34-35; 6:27; 10:36.
[16] Belief in the Son is "the" work which is acceptable to God, 6:28-29. It is the "commandment" of God, I John 3:23; 5:4.
[17] John 1:14, 18; 3:16, 18; I John 4:9.
[18] Cf. the doxology in Mart. Polyc. 20.2: διὰ παιδὸς αὐτοῦ τοῦ μονογενοῦς 'Ι. Χριστοῦ; the trinitarian formula in Acta Apollon. 46; the Greek text of the Acta Perpetuae 21.11. I Clem. 25.2 calls the phoenix μονογενής.
[19] The πατὴρ τῆς ἀληθείας will have stood originally at the head of the system; in the promotion of Bythos he then becomes μονογενής.
[20] Religionsgeschichtliche Studien, pp. 117 ff.
[21] Proclus in Tim. II, 13.9, καὶ γὰρ ὁ θεολόγος τὴν Κόρην μουνογένειαν εἴωθε προσαγορεύειν. Cf. Hymn. Orphic. 29.2. For other documentation for Monogenes in the Orphic usage, cf. Wobbermin, p. 118.

in fact it means nothing more than "only." [22] In this usage it stems from the mystery religion and in fact is supposed to have a mysterious sound. It is something different whether one asserts the "Monogenes" of some man or of a god.

Now the practical, cultic point of view also clearly emerges. It is to the Son of God just as *the Son* that the *same honor* comes as to the Father. "All should honor the Son as they honor the Father." [23] The author of the Fourth Gospel stands in conscious opposition to Judaism. The synagogue of his time attacks this cultic equation of the Son with the Father as blasphemy against God (10:33). The evangelist defends this doubling of the object of the Christian cultus. Indeed, one honors the Father by honoring the Son. "The Father and the Son are one" (10:30).[24] The Father has given to him his holy name,[25] i.e., in the cultus of the Christians the name of Jesus plays the same role as the name of the Old Testament Yahweh. Therefore all faith is a faith in the *Name* of the Son of God,[26] every prayer is a prayer in his name, and the holy new commandment, in the fulfilling of which the essence of Christianity consists, is a commandment of the Son.[27] Thus for him the concepts "Sonship to God" and "deity" move very close together.[28] A deep mystery lies hidden in the term "Son of God." As the Jews accuse Jesus in the trial of making himself the Son of God, it is said: ὅτε οὖν ἤκουσεν ὁ Πειλᾶτος τοῦτον τὸν λόγον, μᾶλλον ἐφοβήθη (19:8). And the charge is turned back threateningly on the synagogue: "Whoever does not honor the Son does not honor the Father who has sent him" (5:23).

Thus the evangelist sums up in the concept of the υἱὸς τοῦ θεοῦ all that is included in the title κύριος in Paul and in Hellenistic popular Christianity.

II. *The Reconstruction of the Life of Jesus.* But with all that, we still have not touched upon what is the really special and peculiar thing about the faith in Christ, particularly that of the Fourth Gospel. This is the picture

---

[22] Luke 7:12; 8:42; 9:38; Heb. 11:17. The Latin translation of the Roman symbol "unicus." Ignatius, Rom., Proem: Ἰησοῦ Χριστοῦ τοῦ μόνου υἱοῦ αὐτοῦ.

[23] John 5:23 (cf. 12:26).

[24] Conversely it is said in this specific polemical sense: "I (the Jesus who is revered in the community alongside the Father) honor the Father, you (the Jews) dishonor me" (8:49). Cf. I John 2:22-23.

[25] John 17:11-12. This is perhaps a borrowing from Paul, Phil. 2:9 ff. Yet the evangelist makes a much more emphatic use of this viewpoint.

[26] John 1:12; 2:23; 3:18.

[27] For fuller treatment, see below, Chap. VII.

[28] John 10:33-36 (see below, Chap. VII).

of Jesus sketched by the evangelist on the basis of his faith. We shall now try to imagine the situation in which this picture of Jesus emerged.

It has been pointed out how little Paul's preaching of Christ was oriented to the picture of the historical Jesus; how for him the present πνεῦμα–κύριος is so much the one and all, that in bold defiance he even refuses any longer to know Jesus κατὰ σάρκα; how for him the sarkic nature was regarded almost as something alien (σάρξ ἁμαρτίας) which Jesus bore in his humiliation, and death as a liberation from this lower nature. In all these *theories*, of course, within genuine Christianity Paul stood fairly alone. But popular Christianity also, which was developed on Hellenistic, Oriental soil, stood at quite a distance from the life of Jesus. For this kind of Christianity he is the exalted Lord who draws near in the worship of his community, who in the sacrament, particularly in the sacrament of the eucharist, is tangibly present, in whose name one prays, drives out demons, or performs miracles (*vide infra,* Chap. VII). In this milieu the historical recollection of the Jesus of Nazareth who sojourned on earth had little meaning at first. The fact that the Gospels, and precisely the Synoptic Gospels, nevertheless played so large a role in the earliest church, that they became sacred books for reading aloud immediately alongside the Old Testament, is plainly a problem, the solution of which can only be given later, and a proof that there were at work in the formation of the church other forces with which we have not yet become acquainted. But how strong the estrangement from the person of Jesus of Nazareth had already become is most clearly shown by a phenomenon which we can demonstrate precisely in the surroundings of the Johannine circle: I refer to the so-called Docetism. It is among the heretical phenomena in Christianity which may be demonstrated earliest; and it appears by no means at first only to have been a characteristic of the emerging Gnostic tendency in the proper sense of the term, but to have extended its influence deep into the genuine Christian circles. The Johannine epistles, Ignatius of Antioch, and Polycarp of Smyrna fought it explicitly, and the Gospel of John forms a front against it indirectly.[29] Syria and Asia Minor appear to have been its home. But what is Docetism, the doctrine that Jesus has not appeared ἐν σαρκί, that he has walked on earth as a phantom, other than the definitive separation of the Christian religion from the earthly life of Jesus of Nazareth!? Out of the figure of Jesus of Nazareth there had just been formed the myth or the dogma of the πνεῦμα–κύριος, the Son of God, who descended from the heights of heaven, into this world,

---

[29] For fuller treatment, see below, Chap. VII.

in order again to depart and to ascend into the heights of heaven—and now the myth begins to turn against history and makes the attempt completely to eliminate it and to put itself alone on the throne.

We can imagine that our Synoptic Gospels would no longer suffice for such an age. The figure of Jesus of Nazareth as it is here portrayed was much too earthly and concrete, much too human-Jewish and limited, much too little dissolved into miracle and idea. The comparison of our Gospels with one another shows how many offenses here were to be eliminated. But working on details and minutiae hardly sufficed any longer. One could do it as the Gnostics were soon to do, and begin to allegorize even the life of Jesus in the Synoptics, as people had already learned to do with the Old Testament. Then came the author of the Fourth Gospel and attempted it with a grand new construction.

The great idea which he conceived, naturally not consciously but instinctively, was to carry myth and dogma all the way back into the history. This had already happened in small measure, when the primitive community transferred its Son-of-Man dogma and its proof by miracle and prophecy back into the life of Jesus; but now it became a matter of wholly dissolving history into myth and allowing it to become transparent for myth.

This was accomplished by the author of the Fourth Gospel. What he sketches in his new life of Jesus is the Son of God, or God, sojourning upon earth. His first appearance is the epiphany of his glory and omnipotence which causes water to become wine. The commonplace miracles of healing and exorcisms have disappeared. Jesus performs the miracles for his and the Father's glory. They have become spectacle miracles, revelations of his glory. He lets his friend die in order to call him forth again from the grave by means of his word. And his words also belong to his miraculous works. When the ῥήματα of Jesus appear in the Gospel almost as a parallel concept to the ἔργα (especially clearly in 14:10 ff.), this does not prove that the ἔργα of Jesus in the view of the evangelist are to be connected not to the supernatural wonders[30] but to his ethical-personal conduct. Rather conversely, the words of Jesus are drawn to this supernatural perspective. These words of his are, as it were, divine oracles of miraculous and mysterious profundity. The timid masses stand helpless, completely without understanding before these oracles, as does Nicodemus before the word on the new

[30] ἔργα=σημεῖα, 5:36; 7:3, 21; 9:3-4; 10:25, 32-33, 37; 15:24. In 5:20 ff. also the ἔργα τοῦ πατρός are first of all the great wonders of the resurrection and the judgment, which then of course are spiritually reinterpreted. (It is a different story with τὸ ἔργον in 4:34 and 17:4.)

birth, as does the Samaritan woman before the proclamation of the heavenly water of life, as does the multitude in Galilee before the preaching of the heavenly manna and the enigmatic saying about the σάρξ of the Son of Man.[31] One of these words suffices to cause his persecutors to fall to the ground before him; but to those who keep these words of wonder, he promises that they shall not taste death for eternity (8:51). Thus in miraculous saying and work he travels about the earth. And from the beginning onward the miraculous streams of the sacrament flow about him. He appeared in water and blood (I John 5:6 ff.), he intends to bestow everlasting living water and to give his flesh and blood to men, he is the bearer óf the rebirth from spirit and water. Out of the body of the crucified flow the life-streams, water and blood. The one who has seen it bears witness to it, and his word is true! From the very beginning Jesus appears in public matured, introduced by John as the Lamb of God who bears the sins of the world, hailed by his disciples as the Messiah, suspected by Nathanael as something loftier, towering far beyond the boundaries of Galilee and Nazareth, hailed by the Samaritans as Savior of the world. Prayed to as Son of Man by the one born blind and now seeing, confessed by Martha as Son of God, sought by the Gentiles who had come to the feast, revealed in conversation with Pilate as the king whose kingdom is not of this world; free, from the beginning on he was master of his fate and his life. The souls and thoughts of all men lie transparent before his eyes. The nature of the betrayer is clear to him from afar, and he even includes the betrayal in his plan. Out of free omnipotence he gives and takes his life. His death is exaltation, a revelation of his glory; the trembling and fearful Jesus of Gethsemane has disappeared, and in triumph the Son of Man strides into the night of death. In unapproachable eminence he confronts all his enemies and assailants. Gone is the burning agony with which Jesus of Nazareth contends for the soul of his people. That he does not win this people is no failure and no disappointment; it is the foreordained counsel of God, the judgment which the judge—Son of Man executes upon this impenitent people. In the same sublimity, however, he is separated from everything human in general; he repulses his mother and his brothers; they live in another sphere. For him the boundary between God and creature disappears. Even prayer

[31] All this is not a case of awkwardness on the part of the evangelist in the constructing of the dialogue. It simply belongs to his technique. Every word of mystery of the divine revelation is underscored by the emphasis upon the lack of understanding in the hearers. With respect to them there also is no dispute and no explanation, but only the simple repetition of the mystery.

to his Father already creates difficulties; the author explicitly says once or twice that this communication in prayer occurs for the sake of Jesus' surroundings.[32] He utters the word on the cross, "I thirst," for the sake of the fulfillment of Scripture.

And yet, at least if we put ourselves in the setting of the outlook current at that time, the human element has not completely vanished and been swallowed up in the divine. The position is still to be maintained that "the Word became flesh." There is still just enough of the human left over so that it provides a certain setting for the divine, and with great skill the impression is achieved that, when the whole of the picture is seen, the magical and phantasmal does not arise. It is yet a human life here upon earth. This is first of all accomplished with external means. A definite chronology is placed at the base of the life and its course, surpassing the earlier Gospels in this respect. The Fourth Gospel is richly furnished with geographical details, far beyond the synoptic example. It runs its course, to be sure no longer in Galilee—there only exceptionally—but still in this specific corner of the earth, Palestine. The concrete figure of the Baptist continues to stand at its threshold. A multitude of concrete situations are sketched, an abundance of figures press around Jesus' figure. To be sure, the concrete portrayals remain mostly fragments which are arbitrarily broken off; of course the secondary figures are mostly silhouettes and remain in the background, but the one lighted figure stands out all the more radiantly against the varied background. And the few human features appear especially striking in the flood of divine light. *This* Jesus thirsts and asks the Samaritan woman for water, he tarries at the joys of the wedding feast, he weeps at the tomb of Lazarus, he kneels and washes his disciples' feet. At the cross he gives the son to the mother and the mother to the disciple. He is actually betrayed and denied, arrested and tried, he himself bore his cross to the place of execution,[33] he is actually crucified. And most of all, this Logos full of divine splendor condescends to his disciples in friendly familiarity. He speaks to them without parables, in complete openness. He calls them friends, not servants, he leaves behind for them his testament, the commandment of love. Even they are not able to grasp all that he has to say to them. But he

[32] John 11:42; 12:30. It may be, however, that one or the other of the passages used here and elsewhere in the presentation in which the "tendency" is excessively urged owes its existence to an unspiritual redactor of the Gospel, but basically almost all of this is wrought out by a single mind.

[33] Some have correctly seen in the elimination of the figure of Simon of Cyrene and in the emphasis that Jesus himself bore his cross a direct polemic against Docetism.

promises them that the Spirit whom he will send is to teach them all things, and as the exalted One he breathes his Spirit upon them. Throughout the Gospel sounds the note that what the Son has, he has from the Father, and the Father is greater than the Son.

"And the Word became flesh"; the evangelist has carried through with his program. What he pictures is the Logos–God who sojourns on the earth, and yet from the same Gospel there sounds forth again and again the note: *ecce homo*. He has taken the Pauline proclamation of the πνεῦμα Χριστός and his own proclamation of the supra-terrestrial Son of God (the Logos) out of abstraction and brought them to living vividness. He has preserved and shaped the little bit of humanity in the picture of Jesus which was still to be kept on the basis of this total outlook. He has reconciled the myth with history, so far as that was at all possible. Indeed, he did still more, or better said, in addition he achieved a success which he did not intend. He, or the school which speaks in this writing, thought of the work, so far as we can see, not as a supplement but as a substitute for the Synoptic Gospels. But fortunately the Fourth Gospel did not suppress the first three; they had already sunk roots too deeply into the primitive Christian community life. But now, since the Fourth Gospel has been associated with the first three, the latter could be read and understood in the light of the former. And some generations later, the church regarded "the" Fourfold Gospel as an intrinsic necessity, as necessary as the four directions of the heavens and the four winds.[34] Thus the Fourth Gospel has not only rescued this small amount which it preserved itself of the life of Jesus; it has also prevented a discrepancy between the synoptic picture of Jesus' life and the early church's proclamation of the Kyrios Christos from arising in the consciousness of the Christians. This significance of the Fourth Gospel for the development of the Christian religion has been dimly perceived by the church's tradition: "But John, last of all, since he saw that the bodily matters (σωματικά) had been made known in the gospels, urged by his acquaintances and lifted up by the Spirit of God into the heights, has written the pneumatic gospel."[35]

III. *Fading of the Pauline View of the Pneuma*. But what does the Son of God or God–Logos who sojourns on the earth mean for the piety of the Fourth Gospel? And how is the personal relationship of the believer to that

---

[34] Irenaeus III, 11.8.

[35] Clement of Alexandria, Eus. CH VI, 14.7, and related passages (Irenaeus III, 1, 11 *et al.*) in Corssen, *Monarchianische Prologe*, p. 103 (80).

supra-terrestrial being, who walked the earth in Jesus of Nazareth, struc-tured? Here we first of all make an observation of fundamental importance in a negative sense. The author of the Johannine writings, who in so many respects is the closest spiritual kinsman of Paul, does not take over Paul's view of the κύριος–πνεῦμα. There is a deep-seated reason for this. He has not at all taken over the total πνεῦμα–σάρξ speculation which was so funda-mental for Paul, as he likewise is no longer familiar with the foundation of this speculation, the pneumatic enthusiasm. Only once does a note from the great Pauline thought-world sound forth: "What is born of the flesh is flesh,[36] what is born of spirit is spirit." But the idea is here already narrowed and purely sacramentally structured. Elsewhere also the spirit either appears in a definite connection with the sacrament [37] or has become for John a speculative entity: the Paraclete whom the Father or the Son sends. As such—here, too, a sharp limitation of his nature has taken place—he is the bearer of the divine *supernatural revelation,* who at this point continues the work of the Son[38]: τὸ πνεῦμα τῆς ἀληθείας.

The concept σάρξ is found only in some few general expressions[39] and then in the favorite ideas[40] of the Johannine writings, that Christ has come in the flesh, and that he gives his flesh in the sacrament; and this heavy stressing of the flesh of Christ is even un-Pauline.

Thus at this point the fire of Pauline Christ mysticism has almost com-pletely disappeared. The Spirit has become the Spirit of the sacrament, Spirit of the office and of the confession, third person in the Godhead; the impetuous fire of elementary experience has burned down to slag. Neverthe-less, Christ mysticism remained an integrative and determinative part of Johannine piety. It only seeks its own new paths. Its individuality may be

[36] John 3:6. The statement in the following section about the inexplicable character of what is spiritual also has a Pauline ring to it; cf. I Cor. 2.

[37] John 1:32-33; 3:5; I John 5:6-8. The obscure saying in 6:63 also is probably, for all its spiritualizing, to be understood in terms of the effect of the Spirit in the sacrament. The Spirit which the resurrected One breathes upon his disciples is the Spirit of office which enables them to forgive sins; 20:22.

[38] John 14:17, 26; 15:26; 16:7 ff. It is from this perspective also that the expression "in spirit and in truth" is to be understood. Here the spirit has become an abstraction, almost the principle of the rational piety that is free from all that is low or base. In I John the Spirit appears—this is once again an externalization—as the bearer of the true confession, 4:2-3, and as such the Spirit of truth stands in opposition to that of falsehood, 4:6. In I John 3:24 (perhaps only a transition to 4:1) and 4:13 there are quite general reminiscences of Pauline origins, to which the author himself appears to have given little thought.

[39] John 1:13 (θέλημα σαρκός); 8:15; I John 2:16 (ἐπιθυμία τῆς σαρκός).

[40] John 1:14; 6:51-56, 63; I John 4:2; II John 7.

summed up in the one word: "This is the will of my Father, that everyone who *beholds* the Son and *believes* in him should have eternal life" (6:40). We shall understand this saying only on the basis of another saying which, to be sure, does not contain Christ mysticism but a direct God mysticism. "Beloved, now are we children of God, and it does not yet appear what we shall be; but we know that when he appears we shall be like him, for we shall see him as he is" (I John 3:2). This is a quite singular note of curious and mysterious God mysticism which must first be understood. The idea which is expressed here may be summarized very shortly *"deification through vision of God."* Here of course the idea appears in eschatological garb. Deification through vision of God is postponed to the blessed future. But it is obviously independent of eschatology and can even be separated from it.

On what soil may this high-strung mysticism have grown? We look in vain for parallels in Old Testament religion. It is in harmony with ancient, widespread belief and with the spirit of the Old Testament cultus when here the basic impression predominates that man cannot look upon the face of Yahweh without dying.[41] In the psalms, to be sure, it is frequently said that the pious behold God's face. "I shall behold thy face in righteousness, I shall be satisfied when I awake in thy likeness."[42] "In the Old Testament God hides his face from his people when he is not caring for them, and shows it to them when he is working righteousness and saving."[43] But these simple pictorial expressions still do not in any way come up to this idea of deification through the vision of God.

In the Gospel one passage would come to mind: "Blessed are the pure in heart, for they shall see God." It also probably lies in the line of the passages in the psalms just discussed.[44]

[41] Exod. 33:20, 22, 23. H. Gressmann, *Mose und seine Zeit,* p. 227 (224.5). An earlier and altogether naïve period is of course still free from this trembling fear in the presence of deity; cf., e.g., Exod. 24:1 ff. Moses and the ancients "beheld the God of Israel," "thus they beheld God, ate and drank." But that certainly does not belong in this context.

[42] Ps. 17:15; cf. 11:7; 22:25 (140:14). Cf. also Exod. 33:14, where we read that the face or countenance of Yahweh will go with the Israelites (Gressmann, p. 222).

[43] Wellhausen, *Kommentar* on Matt. 5:8. But could not this vision of God perhaps stem from cultic language? One beholds God when one seeks him in his temple. Of course the Israelite cult does not suggest such ideas. [Cf. Graf W. Baudissin, on the origin of the formula "to see the face of Yahweh," in the Festschrift celebrating the twenty-fifth anniversary of the founding of the theological students' association in Berlin. Also, by the same author, "Gott schauen in der alttestamentlichen Religion," *Archiv für Rel. Wiss.,* XVIII (1915), 173-239. Bultmann.]

[44] If Matt. 5:8 should already be understood in the sense of an actual religious mysticism (cf. the commentary of Klostermann, *in loc.*), this would be a still surer proof that this

Thus we are once again compelled to look for parallels outside the Old Testament and the genuinely Christian milieu. And these are in fact afforded us on the soil of Hellenistic piety, where two sources of this mysticism are demonstrable which then unite into a common stream. The one source is in particular the piety and the worship praxis of the mystery religion. It is recognized and has long been deservedly emphasized that the climax of all mystery celebrations and of all mysterious rites of consecration is *epopteia*.[45] After long preparations, fasts, purifications, penances, the mystic achieves the climax of the dedicatory rite, where he beholds the deity himself. Originally this was simply achieved, e.g., by causing the sacred pictures of the god, at a given moment, to shine forth in the midst of darkness in a magical light through some sort of secret lighting effect.[46] Later, this originally naïve and crude proceeding must often have been refined. They apparently used the means of artificially induced ecstasy, had the initiates behold the deity, and many times believed in reality behind these proceedings.

In the Isis mystery, the course of which Apuleius has preserved for us in his Metamorphoses (XI, 23), the initiated one, who through the consecration apparently is elevated to deity, reports: "I went to the boundary of death, I trod Proserpina's threshold, and after I passed through all the elements, I turned back again: *at midnight I saw the sun shining with a bright white light, I came before the lower and the most high gods face to face, and prayed to them from near at hand.*" We see how here in part a magical lighting effect still plays its role in the consecration, and yet at the same time everything is elevated to the spiritual-personal level. Hence the rites of consecration have acquired the name of φωτισμός.[47] There the initiate

---

saying belongs to the latest tradition (or to Matthew himself), and indeed this is, in and of itself, not improbable.

[45] Cf. the material particularly in Anrich, *Das antike Mysterienwesen* (1894), esp. p. 30, but also pp. 63 ff. De Jong, *Das antike Mysterienwesen* (1909), pp. 15 ff. (Eleusinian mysteries), esp. pp. 313 ff.

[46] De Jong, pp. 313 ff. (Light effects in the Egyptian cults and in the Mithras service). [G. P. Wetter, *Phos* (ΦΩΣ), Uppsala (1915), pp. 7 ff. Bultmann.]

[47] On these connections, cf. Wobbermin, *Religionsgeschichtliche Studien*, pp. 154 ff. Wobbermin has already correctly derived thence the designation of Christian baptism as φωτισμός, φώτισμα, φωτίζειν. Cf. the usages "illustrari" and "illustratus" in Apuleius, Metamorph. XI, 27, 29; on this, see also Reitzenstein, *Hellenistische Mysterienreligionen*, pp. 30, 77-78, 106 *et passim* [2nd ed., pp. 31, 118] (see index under φῶς, φωτίζειν). Similarly De Jong, *Mysterienwesen*, pp. 313 ff. Cf. Apuleius, Metamorph. XI, 23, p. 425 below. It belongs directly in this same connection when in the apocryphal acts of the apostles Christ appears to the believers in a bright light at the initiatory act of baptism or at the eucharist. Actus Petri Verc., chap. 5 (baptism); Acta Thomae, chaps. 27, 153

then probably hailed the manifested deity with χαῖρε νύμφιε, χαῖρε νεὸν φῶς.[48] Clement, who at the end of his Protrepticus clothes himself in the garb of the mystagogue and imitates the solemn language of the mysteries, admonishes the Christians: τὸν ὄντως ὄντα θεὸν ἐποπτεύσωμεν ταύτην αὐτῷ πρῶτον ἀνυμνήσαντες τὴν φωνήν· Χαῖρε φῶς. φῶς ἡμῖν ἐξ οὐρανοῦ . . . ἐξέλαμψεν[49] ἡλίου καθαρώτερον.

This vision of God serves at the same time as deification of the initiate. It may be presupposed as well known that deification or at least the elevation of the initiate into the blessed life of the deity is always regarded as the ultimate aim of the initiatory rites in the later mystery religions.[50] This context again immediately confronts us, as has already been pointed out, quite clearly in the Isis mysteries. For after the initiate is led to that climax of the revelation, he is adorned with the robes of the deity, has the halo of the god placed on his head, and is thus presented to the assembled people, who bow in respect at his appearance.[51] This is deification through the vision of God: the closing prayer of the Hermetic tractate Asclepius (Logos teleios) sums it up in brief: χαίρομεν, ὅτι ἐν σώμασιν ἡμᾶς ὄντας ἀπεθέωσας τῇ σεαυτοῦ θέᾳ.[52]

A second beginning point for this ecstatic mysticism is found in a place where we should not at first expect it, namely in the astronomic-astrological religion which dominated the period.[53] Since Plato, the stars had been the visible gods throughout all the religiosity of the philosophically educated. People derived the name θεός even from θεῖν, "to run," or from θεᾶσθαι, "to be seen."[54] Thus the science of astronomy and the pseudo-

---

(baptism); Actus Petri, chap. 21 (Agapé). To this group also belong the light manifestations at the baptism of Jesus, and the baptism of fire in some Gnostic sects.

[48] Firmicus Maternus, de err. prof. relig. 19.1. Cf. the reference in 2.4-5: nec ostensi tibi luminis splendore corrigeris. See also p. 166.

[49] Protrept. XI, 114. Clement also follows the language of the mysteries when he interprets the nature of baptism as φώτισμα, δι' οὗ τὸ ἅγιον ἐκεῖνο φῶς τὸ σωτήριον ἐποπτεύεται, τουτέστιν δι' οὗ τὸ θεῖον ὀξυωποῦμεν, Paidagogos I, 26 (cf. the entire exposition in 20-28).

[50] See above, pp. 164 ff. Cf. also Reitzenstein, Hellenistische Mysterienreligionen, passim (cf. index under ἀποθεοῦσθαι, θεοῦν); further, the statements below in Chap. X.

[51] See above, pp. 164-65.

[52] Reconstruction of the text in Reitzenstein, Hellenistische Mysterienreligionen, pp. 113-14 [2nd ed., pp. 136-37].

[53] On the following, cf. the good summary statements of Cumont in his Astrology and Religion Among the Greeks and Romans (New York & London, 1912), Lecture V, and particularly his special essays on "Le mysticisme astral dans l'antiquité" (Extraits des Bulletins de l'Academie royale de Belgique, 1909. Printed separately in Brussels, 1909, where pp. 26-33 have a number of valuable documents representative of this piety) and "La théologie solaire du paganisme romain," Paris, 1909.

[54] Onatas in Stobaeus, I, 49, ed. Wachsmuth: τοὶ δ' ἄλλοι θεοὶ οἱ θέοντές ἐντι κατ'

science of astrology are at the same time religion and theology. The astronomer, who studies the paths of the stars reflectively, observes the ways of the gods; the astrologer investigates their wills which govern all things. But the wise man, who becomes truly absorbed in the heavenly world above, this cosmos full of radiant beauty and unfailing order and harmony, at the same time experiences a *unio mystica* with those divine powers. He feels himself lifted out of the petty and everyday affairs of the earth, the busy ant heap here below, caught up, elevated to the free and beautiful, the eternal and blessed world of the gods which is relieved of all confusion and restlessness. His soul, which indeed comes from above, which, born of the sun, is sunlike itself, akin to the stars, an ἀπόσπασμα of ether and light, experiences ever anew in the heavenly vision this its kinship with the deity. This too is deification through the vision of God.

The platonizing Stoic Poseidonius of Apamea appears above all to have been the enthusiastic proclaimer of this world view. In Cicero's *Somnium Scipionis* there is a classical witness to this heaven mysticism, as also to some extent in Seneca's *Consolatio ad Marciam*. Pliny boasts of Hipparchus, the pioneer in astronomical science: *numquam satis laudatus, ut quo nemo magis adprobaverit cognationem cum homine siderum animasque nostras partem esse caeli* (Hist. Nat. II, 85). "I well know that I am mortal and am of a day's duration, but when I trace out the closely pressed orbits of the stars, I no longer touch the surface of the earth with my feet, but feast with Zeus himself on celestial ambrosia" [55]—thus, much later, does the creator of the Ptolemaic world system still confess.

One of the most prominent witnesses to this astronomical world view is the Alexandrian Jewish philosopher Philo.[56] For him still astronomy is a divine science. Among all the senses which are lent to men, he most highly praises the ability to see. For by means of the eye man beholds the starry heavens. "For as soon as the sight, drawn upward by the light, perceived the nature and the harmonious movement of the stars, the well-ordered

---

οὐρανόν. Plutarch, de plac. philos. I, 6, p. 880 b (Poseidonius): βλέποντες δὲ τοὺς ἀστέρας ἀεὶ θέοντας αἰτίους τε τοῦ θεωρεῖν ἡμᾶς ἥλιον καὶ σελήνην θεοὺς προσηγόρευσαν. De Is. et Os. 60, p. 375 c: ὥσπερ τοῖς θεοῖς πᾶσιν ἀπὸ δυεῖν γραμμάτων τοῦ θεατοῦ καὶ τοῦ θέοντός ἐστιν ὄνομα κοινόν. Clement of Alex., Protrept. 26.1, p. 19.14 ff., ed. Stählin: τῶν ἀστέρων τὰς κινήσεις ἐπιθεώμενοι ἐθαύμασάν τε καὶ ἐξεθείασαν, θεοὺς ἐκ τοῦ θεῖν ὀνομάσαντες τοὺς ἀστέρας. Evagrius Ponticus 633, ed. Frankenberg: ἀπὸ τοῦ πᾶν τεθεικέναι καὶ θεᾶσθαι ὠνόμασται ὁ θεός. Cf. F. Boll, "Aus der Offenbarung Johannis" (Στοιχεῖα I) 42.1: θεοί=ἀστέρες.

[55] Anthol. Pal. IX, 577. Boll, *Studien über Claudius Ptolemäus* (Leipzig, 1894), pp. 74 ff.

[56] The most important passages are collected in Cumont, "Le mysticisme astral," pp. 28 ff.

revolutions of the fixed stars and the planets, . . . it offered to the soul an ineffable joy and rapture, and the more the soul feasted upon the sight of the manifestations, . . . the more insatiable was its longing for spiritual vision. Then it went further and explored what then is the nature of these visible things. . . . Out of the investigation of these things emerged philosophy, the most perfect good that has entered into human life." [57]

At the same time we clearly see in Philo the transition whereby this still very rationally determined enthusiasm of astronomical origin is gradually dissolved into a mysticism of the vision of God, which then rests wholly upon itself. It is well known and cannot here be explicitly proved how the totality of Philo's piety reaches its peak in the mysticism of the vision of God. The followers of this God mysticism are again and again characterized by Philo as the ὁρατικὸν γένος,[58] as the ὁρατικοὶ ἄνδρες,[59] as the φιλοθεάμονες καὶ τὰ ἀσώματα ὁρᾶν γλιχόμενοι,[60] as the θίασος ὀξυωπέστατα ὁρῶν.[61] He speaks of an ὀπτικὴ ἐπιστήμη.[62] In his thought these ὁρατικοὶ ἄνδρες appear over against the run-of-the-mill, lower human race, the γήϊνος νοῦς Ἀδάμ.[63] He demands: τὸ δὲ θεραπευτικὸν γένος βλέπειν ἀεὶ προδιδασκόμενον τῆς τοῦ ὄντος θέας ἐφιέσθω . . . μέχρις ἂν τὸ ποθούμενον ἴδωσιν.[64] It is this entire mystical piety which is rooted, as we can still see precisely, with one root in the piety of the mysteries, to the style and language of which Philo has adapted himself throughout, and with the other in astronomical enthusiasm.[65]

This God mysticism, separated from all cultic and technical-astronomical elements, is particularly clear and evident in the Hermetic tractates. In the "Krater" we find the beautiful expression: "For the vision of God has about it something peculiarly its own. It holds fast those who attain to the vision, as the magnet holds fast to the iron" (IV, 11).[66] In the "Κλεῖς" the prophet extols the divine vision: "It is full of all immortality; those who

---

[57] De opificio, § 54; cf. 69 ff., 77 (Cohn's translation); cf. esp. the great confession in de spec. leg. III, 1-6; also 185-94; de Abrahamo § 58, 110; de spec. leg. I, 39-40, 49, 207 ff., II, 45; etc.

[58] De migrat. § 18; de fuga § 140; q. rer. div. haer. § 36, 78-79.

[59] De plantat. § 36.

[60] De ebr. § 124.

[61] De plantat. § 58.

[62] De spec. leg. III, § 100.

[63] De plantat. § 46.

[64] De vita contemplativa chap. 2, ed. Mangey, II, 473.

[65] See a similar transition from astronomy to the mystical vision of God in the Hermetic fragment in Stobaeus, Ecl. I, 480.

[66] Cf. § 6: αὕτη ἡ τοῦ νοῦ ἐστιν ἐπιστήμη, τῶν θείων ἐντορία καὶ ἡ τοῦ θεοῦ κατανόησις.

have experienced it (Uranus and Kronos!) are often drawn out of the life of the body to the blessed vision: εἴθε καὶ ἡμεῖς ὦ πάτερ" (X, 4-5). "For it is possible that the soul, still to be found in the body of the man, is deified when it has beheld the beauty of the good" (§ 6). "But I stood up, penetrated by his power and instructed in the nature of the universe and of the *highest vision*" [67] (I, 27).

IV. *The Peculiarity of Johannine Piety.* All this is deification through the vision of God, and this is the milieu in which that great mystical saying of the Johannine epistle from which we started out becomes understandable. The fact that all is here eschatologically reshaped does not affect the substance of the matter. The mystery of the vision of God already experienced here is indeed, even in the mystery religion, only an anticipation of the blessed final goal in the beyond. Moreover, Paul also stands on this base with the mystical conclusion of I Cor. 13 and with his rapture into the third heaven and into Paradise (II Cor. 12:1 ff.) [68]; only here mere fragments of this mysticism become visible, while in the Johannine writings all appears set in a broad context.

For this is the peculiar and original outlook of the Fourth Gospel. *This vision, which deifies men occurs in the image of the Son of God who has appeared on earth.* "This is the will of my Father, that everyone who beholds the Son and believes on him should have eternal life" (6:40). One can object that, apart from that passage in I John from which we started out, the Johannine writings never speak of *deification* of the believers. But one will have to realize that the concepts of eternal life and deification are correlative concepts. What deity has by way of an advantage over man is precisely eternal life, ἀθανασία, ἀφθαρσία. And the men who have the

---

[67] Immediately preceding it is the famous sentence: καὶ τοῦτό ἐστι τὸ ἀγαθὸν τέλος τοῖς γνῶσιν ἐσχηκόσι τὸ θεωθῆναι (I, 26). The concluding prayer of Asclepius has already been quoted above, p. 224.

[68] To me it appears probable that in II Cor. 4:6 Paul portrays his foundational vision of Christ with colors which he has borrowed in part from the language of the mysteries: ὁ θεὸς ὁ εἰπὼν ἐκ σκότους φῶς λάμψει (to this point of course there is a reminiscence of Gen. 1:3), ὃς ἔλαμψεν ἐν ταῖς καρδίαις ἡμῶν πρὸς φωτισμὸν τῆς γνώσεως τῆς δόξης τοῦ θεοῦ ἐν προσώπῳ Χριστοῦ. Just as the initiate beholds the radiant deity in the *epopteia*, so has Paul seen the divine *doxa* in the face of Christ. The whole is φωτισμός, and γνῶσις is the result. The idea of the δόξα of the believer which is produced thereby is lacking here. It can easily be completed from II Cor. 3:18. This verse is saturated with mystical piety. Out of the mysterious words we hear the great theme sound forth quite clearly: deification (τὴν αὐτὴν εἰκόνα μεταμορφούμεθα ἀπὸ δόξης εἰς δόξαν) through the vision of God (τὴν δόξαν κυρίου κατοπτριζόμενοι). Cf. also Rom. 8:29-30 (δοξάζειν!). How the concepts δόξα and δοξάζειν are native to this milieu has been shown particularly by Reitzenstein, *Hellenistische Mysterienreligionen, passim* (see index).

salvific blessing of eternal life are thereby elevated into the sphere of deity. It is extraordinarily characteristic that in the concluding prayer of Asclepius (chap. 41), in place of the Greek sentence: χαίρομεν ὅτι ἐν σώμασιν ἡμᾶς ὄντας ἀπεθέωσας τῇ σεαυτοῦ θέᾳ,[69] the Latin tradition (Ps.-Apuleius) puts the sentence: *quod nos in corporibus sitos aeternitati fueris consecrare dignatus.* Thus the evangelist could avoid the term "deification," from which an instinctive feeling must still have held him back, and yet could say quite the same thing to his readers with the concept "eternal life."

The whole Gospel must be read anew in the light of these connections. Only now does the saying in the prologue emerge in its full weight and significance: "The Logos became flesh, and *we beheld* his Doxa, a Doxa as of the only begotten of the Father, full of grace and truth." "And of his fullness (his Pleroma, the upper heavenly world,[70] which came down with him) have we all received, grace for grace." [71] The apostles and eyewitnesses of the life of Jesus have experienced the vision of God in this image of God, and are now themselves flooded by the utter abundance of the powers of the upper world. They have beheld the Father in the Son (14:9), and thus the Father has taken up residence among them (14:23). With the Son they are taken up into the sphere of the divine eternal life: "The world beholds me no more, but you *behold* me, for I live and you shall live" (14:19). And this vision is to be perfected in eternity (17:24).

Moreover, the hearing of the miraculous word of God corresponds to this vision of God (*vide supra*, p. 217). With complete correctness the judgment has already been expressed that in the Fourth Gospel Jesus appears as the mystagogue who with his marvelous word leads his people toward the goal. Where the prologue speaks of the revelation of the Μονογενής, it characterizes this activity by use of the term "which the Greeks use of priests and soothsayers when divine secrets are made known to them":

---

[69] On the Greek tradition, see Reitzenstein, Arch. für Rel.wiss., VII (1904), 393, and *Hellenistische Mysterienreligionen,* pp. 113-14 [2nd ed., pp. 136-37].

[70] In spite of Reitzenstein's statements in his *Poimandres,* pp. 26-27, the explanation and origin of the concept πλήρωμα still appears to me to be a riddle. [On this, cf. now K. Müller, *Beiträge zum Verständnis der valentinianischen Gnosis,* NGG, 1920, pp. 179 ff. Krüger.]

[71] In this context Charis is the divine nature which has appeared in visible and tangible form, and which is bestowed upon men as saving gift. The concluding prayer of Asclepius begins: χάριν σοι οἴδαμεν ὕψιστε· σῇ γὰρ χάριτι τοῦτο τὸ φῶς τῆς γνώσεως ἐλάβομεν. In the same way the concept passes over into the language of the sacraments; Did. 10:6: "Let grace come, and the world pass away." In the epiclesis of the Marcosians (at the eucharist?), Charis is called down into the chalice. Irenaeus I, 13.2 (cf. 13.3).

ἐξηγεῖσθαι.[72] Therefore the word (the Logos) of Jesus has such a miraculous and mysterious power.[73] This power engenders belief (4:41, 50). It is the ruin of the Jews that this "Logos" has no place in them, that they are not able to hear it (8:37, 43; 5:38). For his people, however, everything depends upon their keeping (τηρεῖν) the "word" of Jesus or their abiding in the word (8:31). With the reason that τὸν λόγον σου τετήρηκαν Jesus commends them to the Father (17:6).

It mediates to them the highest blessings of salvation; it accomplishes in them the mysterious purification: καθαροί ἐστε διὰ τὸν λόγον ὃν λελάληκα[74] (15:3; cf. 13:10). Fellowship with the word corresponds exactly to fellowship with Christ: ἐὰν μείνητε ἐν ἐμοὶ καὶ τὰ ῥήματά μου ἐν ὑμῖν μένει (15:7). On the other hand the word takes them out of the world, the world hates them because they have received the word (17:14). The Father will love the one who keeps the word and will make his abode with him (14:23). Indeed, this word has the power that conquers death and produces eternal life: "Whoever hears my word . . . , has eternal life and does not come into judgment, but has rather already passed from the realm of death to that of life" (5:24). "If one keeps my word, he shall not taste death forever" (8:51). Only from this perspective is it explained that the word appears plainly as the judge who judges unbelief (12:47-48).[75] The secret word of the mysteries becomes a personified, independent, divine potency (a Logos alongside the Logos in the special sense). For this secret word is finally God's own word itself. The Son declares what he has heard (seen) in eternity with the Father.[76] He bears his holy word of mystery well pre-

---

[72] Holtzmann, *Neutest. Theol.*, 2nd ed., II, 423-24; cf. Walter Bauer (Commentary on John 1:18 in the *Handbuch zum NT* by Lietzmann): Pollux VIII, 24: ἐξηγηταὶ δ' ἐκαλοῦντο οἱ τὰ περὶ τῶν διοσημιῶν καὶ τὰ τῶν ἄλλων ἱερῶν διδάσκοντες.

[73] This is not true of the Epistle of John, where the Logos of Jesus is usually more prosaically identified with the ἐντολή. On the other hand, this concept of the λόγος (alongside μαρτυρία 'Ιησοῦ) echoes again in the Revelation: 1:2, 9; 3:8, 10; 6:9; 20:4; 22:7, 9, 18-19 (otherwise in 12:11; and in 12:17, ἐντολή and μαρτυρία).

[74] Probably a reminiscence of the catharsis in the mysteries. Holtzmann, II, 424. Cf. esp. Corpus Hermetic. XIII, 15: καλῶς σπεύδεις λῦσαι τὸ σκῆνος· κεκαθαρμένος γάρ. Cf. Philo, de somn. I, 226, p. 654 squ. M.: purification and fructification of the soul by the Logos which bestows the truth.

[75] Bréhier has expressed and ingeniously followed through the conjecture that the Logos in Philo is in part the personified mystery word (*Les idées de Philon,* pp. 101-7). We would have here a fitting analogy for such a transition. This will be discussed again in Chap. IX in broader context.

[76] John 1:18; 3:11, 32; 7:16; 8:26, 28, 38, 47; 12:49; 14:10. The concepts of seeing and hearing merge into one another. The alternation of ἃ ἐγὼ ἑώρακα and ὑμεῖς οὖν ἃ ἠκούσατε in 8:38 is probably accidental; cf. 8:26, 28. (Or is beholding to be placed above hearing here?)

served within himself: ἀλλὰ οἶδα αὐτὸν καὶ τὸν λόγον αὐτοῦ τηρῶ (8:55). And it is the word of the Father which he has given to his people; it binds together Father, Son, and community: τὰ ῥήματα ἃ ἔδωκάς μοι δέδωκα αὐτοῖς, καὶ αὐτοὶ ἔλαβον καὶ ἔγνωσαν (17:8).[77]

But however strongly the significance of the word is stressed, one will hardly be able to avoid the impression that the evangelist[78] speaks of the high points of his Christian experience when, in the prologue and in the farewell discourses, he proclaims the heavenly *vision of God* which takes place in the Logos. The eyewitnesses of his life now at last repeat both, the holy vision of God and his holy word of mystery. In his farewell prayer Jesus speaks of all those who will come to faith διὰ τοῦ λόγου αὐτῶν. And the Epistle solemnly begins: "That which was from the beginning, which we have heard and have seen with our eyes, which we have *beheld* and our hands have handled, of the Logos of life . . . , what we have seen and heard, that we declare to you." The evangelist places his whole Gospel under this ultimate aim. The community is to experience this vision of God in the image of Jesus. It can come to communion with God in many ways: in worship, in listening to the preaching, and in participation in the sacrament, but, above all, this book is to assist them, "that you may believe that Jesus Christ is the Son of God and that *believing* you may have *eternal life* through his name."

Here we have the center around which the ideas of the evangelist and his religion revolve.[79] *Faith* in the sense of the Fourth Gospel is nothing other than this looking upon the likeness of Jesus in his divine Doxa, with the evidences of the omnipotence and omniscience bestowed by God, in his marvelous deeds and words, with the streams of sacramental grace flowing about him; upon this likeness, which shone forth in a definite time and at a definite place, but now is eternally present. Faith and vision are correlative concepts: πᾶς ὁ θεωρῶν τὸν υἱὸν καὶ πιστεύων εἰς αὐτόν (6:40). Faith is not a belief in this or that, in specific facts such as death and resurrection

[77] It is noteworthy that once in the Gospel the words of Jesus are equated with the entity of the πνεῦμα: τὰ ῥήματα ἃ ἐγὼ λελάληκα ὑμῖν πνεῦμά ἐστιν καὶ ζωή ἐστιν (6:63). In similar fashion, 3:34 brings ῥῆμα and πνεῦμα together. One can still see here how the concept of the miraculous Word is suppressing and supplanting the Pauline concept of the wonder-working Pneuma.

[78] Holtzmann (2nd ed., II, 424) seek ingeniously to discern in the Gospel a graded ascending scale of initiation. "Purification is introduced as the preliminary stage of the initiation, . . . *vision* (ἐπόπτεια) *as the height of perfection.*" He also employs to this end the fact that alongside the disclosures given in the present, reference is made to the completion of the revelation in the future by the Spirit (16:10, 13).

[79] I John 1:1 ff.; cf. 4:14, ἡμεῖς τεθεάμεθα καὶ μαρτυροῦμεν.

(the Pauline theology of saving facts disappears again almost completely), but a submergence of oneself into the whole, in the fullness of his being, a πιστεύειν εἰς ᾽Ιησοῦν Χριστόν. As Moses lifted up the serpent in the sight of all the people, so has God now lifted up the Son of man visibly, so that in believing contemplation of this divine symbol all might gain eternal life. In this sense (not in the sense of the sacrificial death) it is said that God gave his Son, namely as the object of faith and of vision (3:14-16; 8:28).[80]

And the *Gnosis* of the Fourth Gospel rests upon the mystical vision and upon faith. In the emphasis upon γινώσκειν, γνωρίζειν, intellectualism in the strict sense of the word cannot at all be what is meant. The "knowledge" of the Johannine writings is altogether mysterious knowledge which rests upon the vision of God, indeed consists of it. θεωρεῖν and γινώσκειν are used almost synonymously and are interchanged with each other, and likewise the concepts γινώσκειν and πιστεύειν.[81] Knowledge rests entirely upon the revelation of God and of Jesus. The believers know, because God and Jesus have known them, because they are known.[82] Thus ἀλήθεια, which is given to the believers out of the fullness of the incarnate Logos, appears as a correlative concept to Charis (1:14). And this truth is a divine, living power; it makes man free and brings ἐλευθερία (8:32). It is the truth which the initiate receives in the consecration: *consecrate* them with thy truth, thy *word* is truth (17:17).[83] All this again is rooted in the soil of Hellenistic, Oriental piety. This no longer needs detailed proof.[84] For example, a look into the concluding prayer of the *Logos teleios* of Asclepius suffices to reveal this interweaving of grace, knowledge, vision of God, deification, eternal life, in full comprehensibility and clarity.

We also possess still another saying of the evangelist in which this mysticism of his is most admirably summarized. It is the great confessional saying: "Herein is *eternal life,* that they *know* Thee, the only true God, and Jesus Christ whom thou hast sent." Here we have once again the interlocking of mysterious Gnosis and life; here the orienting of the Gnosis to the one

[80] Cf. I John 4:9-10, although here of course the idea of sacrifice is introduced with the ἱλασμὸν περὶ τῶν ἁμαρτιῶν ἡμῶν.

[81] Cf. John 14:19-20; 17:6-8; 6:69.

[82] John 10:14-15; 15:15 and the parallels (Matt. 11:27) discussed above (pp. 88-89), particularly in Paul, I Cor. 13:12 and 8:2-3.

[83] Cf. 14:6, ἡ ἀλήθεια καὶ ἡ ζωή. In this context Christ appears as ἡ ὁδός. On this, cf. the view of the Nous as ὁδηγός of the soul in the Hermetic literature X, 21. Reitzenstein, *Poimandres*, p. 23.5. πνεῦμα and ἀλήθεια in John 4:23; πνεῦμα τῆς ἀληθείας in 14:17, 15:26, and 16:13.

[84] Reitzenstein, *Hellenistische Mysterienreligionen*, pp. 112 ff. [2nd ed., pp. 135 ff.].

sent from God, Jesus Christ; here also the avoidance of the concept of deification and the use of the substitute formula for it, eternal life.

V. *The Son of God the Light.* Finally, these connections emerge still more clearly and understandably when we consider one last concept which like no other one gives Johannine mysticism its character; I mean the term φῶς, and along with it the pair of concepts φῶς and σκότος. Right through the prologue there sounds this solemn note: "The life was the light of men." "And the light shined in the darkness." Indeed, when it is so definitely stressed that the Baptist was not the light, that he was only to bear witness to the light, it almost appears as if φῶς is a disputed predicate of honor which here is ascribed to Jesus with great definiteness. Again and again at the high points of the Gospel this motif echoes: The separation among men, the great judgment, occurs in the position they take with reference to the light (3:19-20). Twice Jesus solemnly makes the claim: ἐγώ εἰμι τὸ φῶς τοῦ κόσμου (8:12; 9:5). In his farewell words he exhorts the people to walk in the light[85] so long as the light is with them (12:35-36, 46).

With this term "light" there is a peculiar set of circumstances. As obvious as the application of this concept to God and to the divine essence appears, the realm in which it plays a dominant role may be fairly definitely delimited. In Old Testament usage, so far as I can see, the designation of God as light is not common. The concept of light is frequently associated with God. He is the creator of the light, but also of the darkness (Isa. 45:7), he clothes himself in light (Ps. 104:2), is a lamp to the way of the righteous (Ps. 119:105); the source of life is in him, and in his light we see light (Ps. 36: 10). But the simple formula that God in his essence, in the absolute sense, is light[86] is not found there.[87]

---

[85] It is worthy of note that in the Epistle the predicate "light" is ascribed explicitly only to God, 1:5, 7. Cf. I John 2:8-10; James 1:17 (πατὴρ τῶν φώτων); I Pet. 2:9; I Tim. 6:16.

[86] Cf. Pss. 5:6; 36:9; 38:10, and 89:15. A passage which would most definitely come into consideration for comparison is Isa. 10:17: "The light of Israel will become a fire, and his Holy One a flame" (RSV). Only if we go out of the actual territory of the Old Testament do we find the saying of Wisdom 7:26: ἀπαύγασμα γάρ ἐστι φωτὸς ἀϊδίου. *Here we have the language of Hellenistic mysticism.* Cf. Test. Asher 5.2 (ζωή--θάνατος, ἡμέρα—νύξ, φῶς—σκότος), 3 (πᾶσα ἀλήθεια ὑπὸ τοῦ φωτός ἐστιν): Gad 5.1; Naph. 2.7, 10 (οὐδὲ ἐν σκότει ὄντες δύνασθε ποιεῖν ἔργα φωτός); Levi 4.3 (φῶς γνώσεως), and 18:3; Zeb. 9.8 (ὁ κύριος φῶς δικαιοσύνης); Jos. 20.7 (κύριος ἐν φωτί . . . Βελίαρ ἐν σκότει); Benj. 5.3 (ὅπου γὰρ ἔνι φῶς εἰς διάνοιαν καὶ σκότος ἀποδιδράσκει), and 11.2. Cf. Bousset, *Religion des Judentums*, 2nd ed., p. 385.

[87] One could point out that in fact even in the Gospel of John one reads "light of men" and "light of the world," and that this could only be an expansion of the Old

Moreover, in the language of all earlier Greek philosophy (perhaps excepting Neo-Pythagoreanism), so far as I can see, this characterization of the deity hardly appears. This is all the more remarkable since the Stoa, which indeed quite particularly influenced the religious language of broad segments of the educated populace, brought into currency a series of parallel descriptions, drawn from nature, for the deity: πῦρ, πνεῦμα, αἰθήρ (πνεῦμα πυρῶδες, πῦρ αἰθέριον, etc.).

On the other hand, this designation can be localized within a quite specific milieu. One needs only to take a look into the Gnostic literature, which here comes into consideration in both its branches, the specifically Christian as well as the Hellenistic,[88] in order to see how the view of the light nature of the celestial worlds and its inhabitants dominated the total representation and language of Gnosticism. This observation alone, that such a definitely limited area for the light symbolism can be demonstrated,[89] would in my judgment suffice to provide a new proof of the dependence of the language of John's Gospel upon this milieu of Hellenistic mystery piety.[90] Suffice it here to say that in this area the figure of the saving deity (the Soter)

---

Testament "light of Israel" and "light on the pathway of the righteous." But that would by no means cover the absolute expressions of 1:4 (τὸ φῶς ἐν τῇ σκοτίᾳ φαίνει); 1:7-9, 12:35-36 (υἱοὶ φωτός!), and 12:46; cf. also I John 1:5, 7 (God=light).

[88] The *Corpus Hermeticum* comes into consideration here first of all; in the Oracula Chaldaica, on the other hand, the divine nature is thought of predominantly in terms of its nature as πῦρ.

[89] Scattered traces of this view are already to be found in Paul: Rom. 13:12, ὅπλα τοῦ φωτός; I Thess. 5:5, υἱοὶ φωτός; II Cor. 11:14, ἄγγελος φωτός; Col. 1:12, τοῦ κλήρου τῶν ἁγίων ἐν τῷ φωτί; II Cor. 6:14, τίς δὲ κοινωνία φωτὶ πρὸς σκότος. Cf. Eph. 5:8-9.

[90] One might read the statements of the Barbelo Gnostics in the Coptic source (trans. by Schmidt, *Philotesia Kleinert* (1907), pp. 315 ff.), particularly the beginning, and the excerpt of Irenaeus I, 29.1 (cf. I, 30.1), the account of the Docetists (VIII, 9-10) and the Sethians (V, 19 ff.) in Hippolytus' Refutation (cf., e.g., p. 124, 10 W, ἡ τοῦ καταμεμιγμένου τῷ ὕδατι φωτὸς [ἀκτίς]); the account of the achievement of redemption among the later Basilidians (*ibid.*, VII, 26; cf. p. 374.69), the Valentinian Ptolemaeus in Epiphanius' Haer. 33.7, p. 457.6 H, τοῦ δὲ πατρὸς τῶν ὅλων τοῦ ἀγεννήτου ἡ οὐσία ἐστὶν ἀφθαρσία τε καὶ φῶς αὐτοόν, ἁπλοῦν τε καὶ μονοειδές. The Pistis Sophia is filled with this light symbolism (Bousset, *Hauptprobleme*, p. 88). The basic Pseudo-Clementine writing contained all sorts of speculations about the *virtus immensae et ineffabilis lucis,* of which the Recognitions have preserved some fragments for us (II, 49, 57, 61, 67, 70; III, 14-15, 75). To go into Manichaeism here would lead us too far afield. ([Cf. Wetter, *Phos*, pp. 98 ff.] On the other hand we may refer particularly to the early-Gnostic or half-Gnostic Odes of Solomon. Of the Corpus Hermeticum, the Poimandres, the Initiation of the Prophet, and the Kleis come particularly to mind. One characteristic feature which moreover fits most of these writings of course does not recur in the Fourth Gospel; I mean the contrast of φῶς on the one hand and, on the other, πῦρ as the less worthy demonic element. The Johannine writings do not speak at all of πῦρ (in the religious sense).

acquires the actual title or the proper name φῶς,[91] just as does the Logos in the prologue in the context of a definite rejection of such a claim of the Baptist. For at this point a still much more eye-catching and compelling parallel draws our attention. If there is anything that is characteristic and has always been sensed as characteristic of the Fourth Gospel, it is the powerful double note with which it begins: καὶ ἡ ζωὴ ἦν τὸ φῶς τῶν ἀνθρώπων. This pair of concepts emerges again in the Corpus Hermeticum and here dominates in particular the presentation in the Poimandres. Here the essence of the most high God is defined as light and life (ζωὴ καὶ φῶς ὑπάρχων, § 9); his favorite child, the Primal Man, is like him in essence (§ 12).

[91] Valentinians in Epiphanius 31.4, p. 388.11 H (of the redeemer born of Mary): εἶναι δὲ αὐτὸν φῶς ἀπὸ τοῦ ἄνω Χριστοῦ καὶ διὰ τοῦτο πατρωνυμικῶς καλεῖσθαι φῶς διὰ τὸ ἄνω φῶς. Excerpta ex Theodoto 34, 40, 41, repeatedly calls the savior, the Nymphios of Achamoth, φῶς. Irenaeus I, 29.1 (summarizes correctly, while the Copt relates lavishly): Barbelon . . . generasse simile ei (the most high God) lumen . . . et videntem Patrem lumen hoc unxisse illud sua benignitate . . . hunc autem dicunt esse Christum (an interesting assimilation of the two names φῶς and Christ; cf. also Iren. I, 30.1: esse quoddam primum lumen in virtute Bythi). Ophites in Celsus VI, 31 ἔνθεν εἰλικρινὴς πέμπομαι φωτὸς ἤδη μέρος υἱοῦ καὶ πατρός. According to the traditions of Bitys (who again appeals to the authority, which is demonstrable among the Gnostics, of Nicotheos) the Primal Man is said to have borne the name of φῶς: ἀφ' οὗ καὶ φῶτας παρηκολούθησε λέγεσθαι τοὺς ἀνθρώπους (Reitzenstein, Poimandres, p. 104). I suspect that here we should read φῶς and not φώς following all the parallels which are adduced, in spite of the inappropriate combination of the traditor concerned (cf. further below on Reitzenstein, p. 105: πνευματικὸς καὶ φωτεινὸς ἄνθρωπος). Finally, one might compare also Od. Sol. 36.3: "I was called the brilliant light, the Son of God" (also Acta Thomae 48: Ἰησοῦ ἡ δεξιὰ τοῦ φωτός. 80: σὺ εἶ τὸ ἀπόκρυφον φῶς). Thus in a series of passages there emerges with steady regularity the term φῶς, understood fully as a title, for the saving deity. But the analogies lead us still further. We recall now further that Firmicus Maternus has handed down to us as a symbolum of a mystery religion (of Dionysos?) the saying, χαῖρε νυμφίε, χαῖρε νέον φῶς (de err. prof. rel. 19. 1, p. 47.4 Z). Clement of Alexandria appears to be acquainted with this mystical saying when the Protrept. XI, 114, imitating the language of the mysteries, calls: τὸν ὄντως ὄντα θεὸν ἐποπτεύσωμεν ταύτην αὐτῷ πρῶτον ἀνυμνήσαντες τὴν φωνήν· χαῖρε φῶς (Wobbermin, Religionsgeschichtliche Studien, pp. 159 ff.; see above, p. 224). Related to this is another mystery saying which Cumont has found in Cosmas of Jerusalem: ἡ παρθένος ἔτεκεν, αὔξει φῶς (Cumont, "Le Natalis Invicti," Extraits des comptes rendues de l'Ac. des Inscr. et Belles Lettres (1911), pp. 292-93; cf. ibid. the remark in the Calendarium of the astrologer Antiochus on December 25: ἡλίου γενέθλιον αὔξει φῶς and the analogous tradition in Epiphanius, Haer. 51.22: ἡ Κόρη ἐγέννησε τὸν Αἰῶνα). Finally, the φωστὴρ τέλειος μέγας mentioned in the Naassene Preaching and the cultic saying ἱερὸν ἔτεκε πότνια κοῦρον Βριμὼ Βριμόν (Hippolytus, Ref. V, 8.39, p. 96.18 W) also belong here. The parallels are all significant. Do the ever-recurring descriptions of the savior-god as φῶς perhaps stem from the mystery cult and refer to the divine manifestation of light at the climax of the initiation ceremony? (Cf. what was said above about epopteia and photismos.) In any case, Norden, by whose comments I have been prompted to assemble this material, is right when he points to the fact that an investigation of the semasiology of φῶς is urgently desirable (Agnostos Theos, pp. 299, 395). [Cf. the study by G. P. Wetter mentioned on p. 223, n. 46. Bultmann.]

Therefore man is of his essence: ὁ δὲ ἄνθρωπος ἐκ ζωῆς καὶ φωτὸς ἐγένετο εἰς ψυχὴν καὶ νοῦν (§ 17). Man is therefore to reflect upon himself, is to recognize that he comes from the world of light and life (§ 21), is to put off the baser garments of his soul which the soul has brought hither from the spheres of the planets, and return to the higher world of light and life. The initiated mystic rejoices: διὸ πιστεύω σοι καὶ μαρτυρῶ, εἰς ζωὴν καὶ φῶς χωρῶ (§ 32).[92] In the Initiation of the Prophet then light and life even appear as divine hypostases, of whom it is said: ζωὴ καὶ φῶς, ἀφ' ὑμῶν εἰς ὑμᾶς χωρεῖ ἡ εὐλογία (XIII, 18), and finally: σῷζε ζωή, φώτιζε φῶς, πνευμά[τιζε] θεέ (§ 19).[93]

Associated with this is the broader observation that here again we encounter the Johannine contrast of φῶς and σκότος in sharp articulation. One needs only to read the beginning of the Poimandres, whose cosmology of course is more dualistically structured than is that which the Johannine prologue indicates, in order to be convinced of this. Similarly the admonition of Tractate VII contains this dualism: here we hear of the gates of knowledge, ὅπου ἐστὶ τὸ λαμπρὸν φῶς, τὸ καθαρὸν σκότους. Here the hearers are admonished to cast off the body ὃν φορεῖς χιτῶνα . . . τὸν σκοτεινὸν περί-βολον, τὸν ζῶντα θάνατον (§ 2). Similarly it is said again in the Poimandres: Anyone who loves the body which comes from the error of love remains in darkness (§ 19).[94]

With all that, the formation of ideas in the *Corpus Hermeticum* is so original that a dependence upon the Fourth Gospel cannot be considered even a remote possibility, just as little as can a dependence in the other direction. What we have here is the common soil of the language of a mystical piety. After all that has preceded we can presume that this association of light and life and the setting in opposition of light and darkness stem from this common linguistic soil, whether this language now may be explained in terms of the astronomical-astrological piety which found light and life yonder above with the radiant gods and for which this lower world beneath

[92] The parallel tradition of the concluding prayer of the Poimandres in the Berlin papyrus 9794, cols. 2, 3, 42 ff., which was discussed by the first editors (Berliner Klassikertexte VI) as a Christian prayer, begins: ἅγιος ὁ θεὸς ὁ ὑποδείξας μοι ἀπὸ τοῦ Νοὸς ζωὴν καὶ φῶς. To be compared with this is the concluding prayer of Asclepius (Reitzenstein, *Hellenistische Mysterienreligionen*, p. 114 [2nd ed., p. 137]): ἐγνωρίσαμέν σε ὦ φῶς. . . . ἐγνωρίσαμέν σε ὦ ζωή.

[93] Cf. XIII, 9: τὸ ἀγαθὸν . . . ἅμα ζωῇ καὶ φωτί . . . . § 12: ζωὴ δὲ καὶ φῶς ἡνωμέναι εἰσίν, ἔνθα ὁ τῆς ἑνάδος ἀριθμὸς πέφυκε τοῦ πνεύματος. Here and in the text above the Pneuma occurs curiously as a third entity alongside light and life.

[94] Cf. § 20, τοῦ ὑλικοῦ σώματος τὸ στυγνὸν σκότος. In § 28 perhaps we should read ἀπαλλάγητε τοῦ σκοτεινοῦ (σώματος· τοῦ) φωτὸς μεταλάβετε τῆς ἀθανασίας.

the moon became a world of darkness, or whether it rests upon happenings of the mystery initiation, in which the mystic with the *epopteia* (the φωτισ-μός) had the experience of σωτηρία, of life.

Thus the Johannine writings with their view that one acquires life by means of the vision, with their concepts of the miracle-working word, of faith, knowledge, truth, light and darkness, light and life, are rooted in the soil of Hellenistic mysticism. This does not belittle the originality of the evangelist. Indeed only from this perspective do we grasp the sublime conception of his proclamation: "Whosoever beholds the Son has eternal life." For the author has this new thing to say to his environment: One does not gain eternal life, elevation into the world of the deity, by gazing into the starry heavens, into their pleroma, the abundance of splendid godlike beings that wander there, nor by means of the vision of deity which the mystic experiences at the climax of the sacred initiation. *Here* is the fullness of grace, here is light and life, here is perfect Gnosis: "Whosoever beholds the Son and believes on him has eternal life."

This explains, at the same time, yet another phenomenon in the Fourth Gospel, namely the pointed form and manner with which the author asserts the immediate presence of the blessing of eternal life imparted by the Son. In constantly repeated expressions the evangelist emphasizes that anyone who believes on the Son already has eternal life, does not come into judgment, has passed from death to life, shall not see death, shall live even though he was dead, and that the great judgment which the Son of Man accomplishes consists in the separation between belief and unbelief.[95] The connection is clear; the mysticism which lives by the present comes into conflict with the eschatology which is dominant in Judaism and primitive Christianity. The simple Kyrios cult of the Christian community, although it already had sharply shifted the center of gravity from the future into the present, was capable of being reconciled with the eschatology. The Lord who is present in the cultus can yet at the same time be expected as the future judge of the world who comes from heaven. In a wholly different measure the Pauline view of the κύριος, who as πνεῦμα is the source of power for the new Christian life, has already actually made present and spiritualized the goods of salvation of the new religion. Yet the Pneuma is and remains an eschatological entity, and the prophecy of his being poured out belongs to Jewish-primitive Christian eschatology. Thus with Paul the view of the

---

[95] Cf. John 3:17-21; 5:1-27 (8:15-16); 8:51; 11:25-26; 12:46-50. At this point the Epistle diverges from the Gospel. Such expressions are hardly to be found in the Epistle.

Spirit as ἀρραβών and ἀπαρχή of all future blessings of salvation could develop. The religious mysticism of the Gospel of John, however, makes a clean sweep of the eschatology. The few expressions which still preserve the eschatology no longer stand in organic connection with the basic conviction of the Gospel; they were perhaps first added by a redactor who "ecclesiasticized" the Gospel.[96]

Thus in the Gospel the goods of salvation are almost totally transposed out of the future into the present. The ideas of eternal life, resurrection, and judgment are spiritualized in grandiose fashion. This spiritualizing is most strongly exhibited where a primitive Christian eschatological motif has been kept visible. I have earlier pointed out how in the Fourth Gospel Jesus remains the Son of man to whom all judgment is given. But in the same moment also the great reinterpretation appears. The judgment consists in the great separation of the spirits, which the Son of Man accomplishes in the present. And since this judgment is achieved altogether immanently, it can also be said that the Son of God judges no one. From an eschatological entity the Son of Man has become a presently effective power (*vide supra*, p. 213).

VI. *Christ Mysticism and God Mysticism.* We saw earlier that the mysticism of Paul remains in essence a Christ mysticism, but that it has the significance of leading from a Christ mysticism to a God mysticism. This transition to a God mysticism is achieved in the Johannine writings. In this development it is clearly shown that Jesus mysticism is the way to God mysticism.

Here the material is more abundantly present in the Epistle than in the Gospel. While in the Gospel Christ is presented as the light of men, the First Epistle begins its proclamation thus: "God is light—and if we walk in the light as he is in the light, we have fellowship with him" [97] (1:5-7). To be understood similarly, then, is the sentence: "Whoever loves his brother abides in the light" (2:10). The prologue of the Gospel of John also speaks in allusory fashion of birth from God (1:13), but this theme is treated much more explicitly and more frequently in the Epistle: "Whoever is born

---

[96] Cf. the vss. 5:28-29 which totally disrupt the connection and the addition which in its stereotyped recurrent form is lifeless, καὶ ἀναστήσω αὐτὸν ἐν τῇ ἐσχάτῃ ἡμέρᾳ, in 6:39, 40, 44, 54 (12:48; in 11:24-25 the clause appears as a saying of Martha which is corrected by Jesus). The first epistle of John is marked by more impartiality with respect to eschatology; cf. I John 2:28; 4:17; 5:20, and even 3:2; still the idea of the Parousia stands in the Gospel also, at least in its present form; 14:2-3; cf. 21:22.

[97] Following Codex A this should read μετ' αὐτοῦ (instead of μετ' ἀλλήλων).

of God does not sin, because his seed [98] remains in him" (3:9).[99] "Everyone who loves is born of God and knows God" (4:7). "The one who is born of God keeps himself (pure) and evil does not touch him" (5:18). The Epistle also speaks more frequently than does the Gospel of τέκνα θεοῦ.[100] To this corresponds the ὑμεῖς (ἡμεῖς) ἐκ τοῦ θεοῦ ἐστε (contrast: the false doctrine ἐκ τοῦ κόσμου) I John 4:4, 6.[101] Connected with the "born of God" is the abiding in God or God's abiding in us. And these formulas also are used by the author of the Epistle almost exclusively in connection with God,[102] while in the Gospel the great motif: "Abide in me and I in you," is struck essentially in connection with Jesus. Thus the Epistle coined the great sayings: "No man has ever seen God; if we love one another, God abides in us" (4:12). "God is love, and the one who abides in love abides in God and God in him" (4:16). And as the recognizable sign that God dwells in the believers and they in him, he has given to them his Spirit (4:13; 3:24).[103] To be sure, the conclusion of the Epistle touches upon this connection in a curious way: "And he (the Son of God) has given to us a mind that we might know the true one, and we are in the true one, in *his Son Jesus Christ*. This is the true God and eternal life. Little children, guard yourselves from idols." Here the surmise arises that the words "in his Son

---

[98] The great theme of rebirth from God cannot be treated in detail here. It has been proven that the conception stems from the piety of the Hellenistic mystery religions (cf. Reitzenstein, *Hellenistische Mysterienreligionen*, Index, see ἀναγεννᾶσθαι, ἀνακαινοῦσθαι, γένεσις, μεταγεννᾶσθαι; Dieterich, *Mithrasliturgie*, pp. 157 ff. Perdelwitz, *Die Mysterienrel. und das Problem des I. Petrusbr.* [1911], pp. 40 ff.). The image of the σπέρμα in I John is especially strong and evident.

[99] Cf. I John 5:1, 4; 5:18; on 2:29, see below.

[100] I John 3:1-2; 3:10 (contrast of τέκνα τοῦ διαβόλου; cf. John 8:44); 5:2; John 1:12; 11:52.

[101] Cf. with 4:2-3 the ἐκ τῆς ἀληθείας εἶναι in 3:19.

[102] Cf. 2:6, ὁ λέγων ἐν αὐτῷ (God) μένειν ὀφείλει καθὼς ἐκεῖνος (Christ) περιεπάτησεν καὶ αὐτὸς οὕτως περιπατεῖν; hence the ἐν αὐτῷ εἶναι in 2:5 is to be referred to God also. 2:24, καὶ ὑμεῖς ἐν τῷ υἱῷ καὶ τῷ πατρὶ μενεῖτε is explained from the context (confession of the Father and the Son). 2:27, καθὼς ἐδίδαξεν ὑμᾶς μένετε ἐν αὐτῷ, is to be referred to the *chrisma* and its teaching; ἐν αὐτῷ is neuter. Then, 2:29, ἐὰν εἰδῆτε ὅτι δίκαιός ἐστιν, γινώσκετε ὅτι καὶ πᾶς ὁ ποιῶν τὴν δικαιοσύνην ἐξ αὐτοῦ γεγέννηται, certainly (cf. the τέκνα θεοῦ that follows in 3:1) refers to God; probably also the παρουσία αὐτοῦ that precedes in 2:28 (cf. 3:19-21) and the μένειν ἐν αὐτῷ. In 3:17 (in spite of the context) it is said expressly: πῶς ἡ ἀγάπη τοῦ θεοῦ μένει ἐν αὐτῷ; in 3:24, according to the context, the corresponding double expression ἐν αὐτῷ μένειν and μένει ἐν ἡμῖν is to be referred to God; cf. further 4:15. 3:6 forms the *only remaining exception*.

[103] See what is said above about the Gospel.

Jesus Christ," through which the assertion of Christ's full deity is introduced into the context, first came to be a part of the text as a gloss.[104]

But in the Gospel also the great theme of the God mysticism is sounded, even if only in the farewell discourses and in such a way that in a wholly different manner the Son appears as the mediator and fellowship with Christ appears as the condition of fellowship with God. "If one loves me, he will keep my word, and my Father will love him, and we will come to him and make our abode with him" (14:23). "The one who loves me will be loved by my Father, and I will love him and will manifest myself to him" (14:21). "If you keep my commandments, you will abide in my love, just as I have kept my Father's commandments and abide in his love" (15:10). "The Father loves you because you have loved me and have believed that I came from the Father" (16:27). And this full harmony of the triad then sounds through the entire seventeenth chapter: "The glory which thou hast given to me I have given to them, that they all may be one as we are one, I in them and thou in me, so that they may be perfected in one" (17:22-23). Thus is the God mysticism in the Gospel wholly bound to the Christ mysticism, while in the Epistle it appears separated from the latter and at the same time rooted in its own soil.[105]

However, in spite of this transition to God mysticism, the Son of God remains the dominant figure, particularly in the Gospel, and in part also in the epistles. With the ever-recurring ἐγώ εἰμι, which is simply drilled into the ear of the reader, he is presented to the world as its salvation: ἐγώ εἰμι ὁ λαλῶν σοι, Jesus responds to the question of the Samaritan woman about the Messiah in 4:26; ἐγώ εἰμι ὁ ἄρτος ὁ καταβὰς ἐκ τοῦ οὐρανοῦ (6:41); ἐγώ εἰμι ὁ ἄρτος τῆς ζωῆς (6:48); ἐγώ εἰμι τὸ φῶς τοῦ κόσμου (8:12); ἐγώ εἰμι ἡ θύρα (10:7, 9); ἐγώ εἰμι ὁ ποιμὴν ὁ καλός (10:11, 14); ἐγώ εἰμι ἡ ἀνάστασις καὶ ἡ ζωή (11:25); ἐγώ εἰμι ἡ ἄμπελος ἡ ἀληθινή (15: 1, 5); ἐγώ εἰμι ἡ ὁδὸς καὶ ἡ ἀλήθεια καὶ ἡ ζωή (14:6). These solemn tones sound through the entire Gospel. In them is speaking the Son of God,

---

[104] 5:11, καὶ αὕτη ἡ ζωὴ ἐν τῷ υἱῷ αὐτοῦ ἐστιν, is to be interpreted differently. Here the Son is the mediator of life (through faith, 5:12-13), but is not himself the life.

[105] It is difficult to say whether the development moves from the Epistle to the Gospel or the other way around. If we take the Pauline Christ myticism as starting point, there results a certain probability for the latter assumption. From general considerations, one could on the other hand be inclined to the conclusion that the stronger stress upon Christology is the later one. The author of the Epistle of James also is acquainted with a strong God mysticism even up to the idea of birth from God: βουληθεὶς ἀπεκύησεν ἡμᾶς λόγῳ ἀληθείας, 1:18, and similarly I Pet. 1:3: εὐλογητὸς ὁ θεὸς ὁ κατὰ τὸ πολὺ αὐτοῦ ἔλεος ἀναγεννήσας ἡμᾶς.

to whom the Almighty God has given his name (17:12) and his dignity. In all the expressions we are reminded of the revelation of Yahweh in the Old Testament, and in part also of the hieratic style in which the self-revealing god is introduced in the documents of Hellenistic piety.[106]

VII. *John and Paul.* Thus the Johannine piety is presented as an original formation of powerful uniqueness within the Christian religious history. "John" of course stands on the shoulders of "Paul." Here as there religion has become Christ piety, here as there it is summed up in faith in the Son of God; here as there Christ is a spiritually personal power who is present in every moment; the cultically sacramental is thrust into the background and is swallowed up by the personally spiritual, but it does not disappear; it remains the self-evident presupposition upon which a freer spirituality is erected. Here as there on the foundation of the community cultus a spiritual, personal religion has been erected. Here also the Son of God appears as a figure who stands altogether on the side of God; Father and Son are one (10:30); one sees the Father in the Son (14:9); the cultic veneration which one pays to the Son at the same time honors the Father (*vide supra*, p. 215). And yet a differentiation is made between Father and Son: the Father is greater than the Son (14:28); the Father is always the one who gives,[107] the Son the one who receives. No one in the world can snatch anything out of the Father's hand, therefore the Son also holds fast to those who are his (10:29). Conversely, the Son has only to keep what the Father has entrusted to him (6:39-40; 17:10, 12), and over the redemption accomplished through the Son the predestinating counsel of God holds sway (6:37 ff., 44 ff., *et passim*).[108]

And yet again, what a difference between the Pauline and the Johannine Christ mysticism! It is noteworthy that even though both, Paul as well as "John," proceed in their outlook from the exalted, present Christ, the accent here shifts perceptibly. The evangelist much more decisively dwells upon the pre-temporal nature of the Son of God. To the evangelist, he is the Son of Man who ascends to heaven, from whence he once came,

---

[106] On these connections, cf. now Norden, *Agnostos Theos*, pp. 177-201, esp. pp. 184 ff.; also Reitzenstein, *Poimandres*, pp. 244 ff.

[107] Cf. particularly 3:34 (οὐ γὰρ ἐκ μέτρου δίδωσιν τὸ πνεῦμα); 3:35 (πάντα δέδωκεν ἐν τῇ χειρὶ αὐτοῦ). 5:19-30; 6:37 ff., 44 ff.; 7:17, 28; 8:16, 28-29, 38, 54-55; 10:32, 36 ff. (ὃν ὁ πατὴρ ἡγίασεν); 12:4, 9-10.

[108] On the relationship of the Father and the Son, see above, pp. 213 ff.; on Christ mysticism and God mysticism, pp. 237 ff.; further, on prayer in the name of Jesus and on the commands of Jesus (commands of the Father), see below, Chap. VII.

who came into the world in order once again to leave the world, who came from the glory of the Father in order to return again to the glory of the Father, the Logos who became flesh. And yet he also dwells, with completely different devotion and intensity, upon the picture of the Jesus who has appeared upon earth. Paul wished to know nothing of Jesus κατὰ σάρκα. In the Fourth Gospel John sketches his glorified picture. And even if with him the idea of the exalted Christ provides the dominant note, even if the Christ of the Fourth Gospel is no longer the past one but the present one, who speaks to today's generation, even if often here the earthly sojourn appears as an episode between preexistence and ascension, yet the gaze, having become calmer, sweeps over this majestic whole: ἐξῆλθον ἐκ τοῦ πατρὸς καὶ ἐλήλυθα εἰς τὸν κόσμον. πάλιν ἀφίημι τὸν κόσμον καὶ πορεύομαι πρὸς τὸν πατέρα (16:28).

Here we stand at the threshold of the great difference in basic attitude which opens between Paul and John. If Paul came with the roaring of the violent storm, with volcanic fire and earthquake, behind him comes the quiet and sublime calm of the Fourth Evangelist. For Paul, Christ was the power of the pneuma which storms out of heaven, seizes man in the breath of the storm, thoroughly shakes him and stirs him to the deepest roots of his being, shatters the old man and shapes a new, jubilant creation out of the chaos. For John, Christ is the gentle, illuminating, warming, and fructifying light, in the vision of which, full of reverence, he becomes absorbed, the great mystagogue to whose mysterious word with its miraculous, death-destroying power he listens devoutly. For Paul, coming to this Christ means the death of the old man, a complete break, a painful-blessed experience of being rent and divided. For John it is a simple joyous experience of being lifted up, a vision of the glory of the Son of God, a constant receiving from his fullness. The wholly supernaturalistic-dualistic speculation of Paul about the struggle between spirit and flesh has disappeared except for one isolated echo, disappeared in such a way that John without embarrassment speaks of the necessity of partaking of the σάρξ of the Son of Man. In John we hear no longer of the absolute opposition between the first and the second man.

The reflection that the old man must be destroyed in those who come to Christ is not found. The outlook has become quite calm: To those who accept him, he gives power to become children of God; to those who hear his words, he gives eternal life. Like comes to like, those who love the light come to the light. From step to step Jesus leads his own into the secrets of the celestial world. He will not call them servants, they are to be his friends, he is no longer the Kyrios, he is the confidant of their souls. In John the saying about the mutual knowledge of the Father and the Son, which separates men from the Father and the Son, is supplemented: "I know my own and my own know me" (10:14). Thus in the great farewell prayer he has in view as the main theme this great mystery: God, Christ, and the fellowship of believers, a unity which was willed by the Father from all eternity and is perfected unto all eternity.

To be sure, with all this the Pauline supernaturalism and dualism has not vanished, but it is moved to another place. The cleft no longer runs, as with Paul, between Adam and Christ, between the entire old human nature and the new creation, so that every human soul is painfully aware of it; instead it runs between Jesus and his community on one side and the unbelieving world on the other side. Here the new cleft opens up, in a similar fashion in the Gospel as in the epistles: here light, there darkness; here God, there world; here truth, there falsehood; here children of God, there children of the devil; here church, there synagogue; here pure confession, there false doctrine. In many respects this dualism is harsher and sharper than that of Paul. For while Paul in his burning missionary zeal, with his love for his lost people, boldly pushes across this chasm and seeks to overcome it, John appears in an almost shocking manner to be content with these contrasts. In both of them the idea of predestination enters in at this point. But while Paul struggles with this thought in ever-recurring efforts and finally conquers it with the resplendent "from God, through God, to God are all things," the Johannine Christ speaks of it as of a fact about which one is no longer agitated.[109] And yet those who belong to God and to Jesus are even more sharply separated than in Paul from the world of corruption, sin, and guilt. If Paul places a strong accent upon the thought that Christ in his sacrificial death has borne the expiation for the totality of past sins; if for him the recollection of the sins still present in the Christian life emerges at least on the periphery, yet on the whole these groups of ideas are alien to Johannine piety, in spite of individual formal expressions which are found in I John. For this piety, the death of Christ is

---

[109] John 6:37 ff., 44 ff.; 8:37, 43, 44 (an almost dualistic refashioning of the idea of predestination); 10:26. While the predestination first of all refers to unbelieving Judaism, what is said about it in the Gospel naturally also concerns the entire world. As in Paul (Rom. 9–10), so also in John (3:19; 1:11; 7:17) the emphasis upon individual guilt appears alongside the idea of predestination.

the beginning of his exaltation and glorification[110]; in it we search almost in vain for the term "forgiveness of sins" [111]; on the contrary, we find the Pauline assertion of the sinlessness of the Christian life heightened to an almost shocking bluntness in the great confession in I John 3:4-10: "Whoever is born of God does not sin."

But if the practical dualism of the Johannine writings is harsher and more blunt than the Pauline, yet the theoretical dualism appears much less precisely constructed. The opposites which obtrude themselves into John's thought from his piety in fact do not actually concern human nature as such, as they do in Paul, who sets Christ against Adam. Basically they are first of all of an empirical nature; the practical polemic against Judaism, unbelieving world, heresy, stands behind them. Ultimately, even the Christians belong to the cosmos created by God, although it stands over against God so bluntly and inimically. From this perspective is explained the continual changing of attitude in the Johannine writings with respect to the way the κόσμος is regarded. Thus can the author on the one hand speak of the judgment of this world, of the prince of this world,[112] of the world's hatred toward God's people,[113] and can have Jesus refrain from praying for the world[114]; and on the other hand he can coin the solemn saying, "God so loved the world," can speak of the saving of the world by the Son, of the Savior of the world.[115] How much more unified is the Pauline doctrine of the σάρξ in comparison with the cosmos view of the Johannine writings! In a way quite different from that of Paul, the chasm between creation and redemption, which only temporarily yawns in John's thought, is closed again.

Still, with all that, the Johannine piety, like the Pauline, is a religion of redemption in the one-sided sense of the word, only that in Paul the redemption is more closely connected with the old human nature and thus is understood more inwardly, while in John it concerns the external inimical power of the world. But it remains redemption: The children of light were helpless

[110] The ἔδωκεν in John 3:16 (cf. I John 4:9) is not to be understood in the sense of the sacrificial idea.

[111] In John 20:23, the institution of the ecclesiastical forgiveness of sins is meant.

[112] John 12:31; 14:30; 16:11.

[113] John 15:18; 17:14.

[114] John 17:9; other dualistic expressions: 7:7; 8:23; 13:1; 14:17, 19, 22, 27; 15:18-19; 16:8, 20, 33; 17:15, 16. This view of the world is predominant in I John (cf. the few exceptions in the following footnote).

[115] John 3:16 (I John 2:2; 4:9); 3:17; 12:47; 4:42 (I John 4:14); cf. further (besides the many passages in which κόσμος is used quite neutrally) 1:10; 1:29; 6:33, 51; 8:12; 9:5 (14:31; 17:21, 23?).

243

in captivity; there is the one great light, the life and the savior of the world who has come into this sphere of darkness, falsehood, and the devil, *toto genere* different from the whole human race, he alone in every respect from above; and he has drawn to himself the scattered elements of light, his own, who were given to him by the Father, with miraculous power: ὁ ἄνωθεν ἐρχόμενος ἐπάνω πάντων ἐστίν (3:31).

In spite of the fact that he wrote a fourth Gospel, John is basically somewhat further removed from the preaching of Jesus than is Paul. The gospel of the forgiveness of sins as Jesus proclaimed it has still further disappeared. In its place appears the message of redemption and the redeemer; in place of the savior of sinners stands the one who is the friend of his own people, to whom the friends yield themselves in calm and radiant frame of mind as to the one who has for them the words of eternal life.

# 6
## GNOSTICISM

I. *Intellectual Foundations.* Gnosticism[1] is first of all a pre-Christian movement which has its roots in itself. It is therefore to be understood in the
first place in its own terms and not as an offshoot or a by-product of the
Christian religion.

The basic feature in the character of this movement is a sharp dualism
and a radical pessimism toward this lower, natural world, closely bound up
with that dualism. In it, motifs which stem from Greek philosophy of a
Platonist or Neoplatonist tendency are combined with specifically Oriental,
mythologically determined dualism. From the platonizing philosophy which
had begun extensively to dominate the basic attitude of the educated
world in the later age of the Diadochi, Gnosticism borrowed the great
contrast of the lower sensual-material world and the spiritual-ideal world.
But this contrast, which there, in spite of all the gloomy attitudes, still
always preserves the character of a graded distinction of lower and higher,
is now here, precisely under Oriental (Persian) influences, further developed
into the assumption of an absolute opposition. However, there is lacking in

[1] On the following, cf. my *Hauptprobleme* and my articles on "Gnosis" and "Gnostiker"
in the Pauly-Wissowa *Real-Enzyklopädie*. Wendland, *Hellenistisch-römische Kultur*, 2nd ed.,
pp. 163-87. Up till now the material is found most fully in Hilgenfeld, *Ketzergeschichte*,
1884.

the Oriental dualism as determined by Persian religion the more profound opposition between the world of the spirit and the world of matter, between that which is visible and that which is invisible. The battle of the good god (Ahura-Mazda) and the evil god (Angra-Mainyu) takes place within this visible world. On the side of the good god stand the light and the day, all beneficent natural forces, good men, useful animals, healthful plants; on the side of the evil god, darkness and night, the pernicious forces in nature, evil men, harmful animals, poisonous plants. Into these naïve and popular contrasts is projected the great Greek basic idea of the conflict of spirit and matter, visible and invisible. And thus the sharp dualism and the radical pessimism of the Gnostic world view first come about: Spirit and matter, invisible world and visible world [2] are two antagonistic forces which stand over against each other in almost total alienation.

On this point Gnosticism was sensed to be specifically non-Greek even by the latest representatives of genuine Hellenism. For this we have a fully qualified witness in no less than the head of the Neoplatonist school, Plotinus. In his great discussion with the Gnostics he maintained, against their doctrine of the "bad world," [3] "Further, one may not admit that the world is created evil because there is too much mischief in it. For this means to attribute too much worth to it and to confuse it with the spiritual world, of which it is only a likeness. But is there indeed a finer likeness of that world? What fire would be a better likeness of the celestial fire than the fire here . . . , and after the sun in that realm, what sun would be better than the one visible to us?" (Ennead II, 9.4).[4] Clement of Alexandria also saw this. In his discussion with Marcion he concedes that even before Marcion Plato apparently had called this world evil, and in the *Phaedo* he spoke of the better men who sought to be freed from the places here on earth as from a prison and to gain the pure dwelling place above. But in the reference to other Platonist passages he sums up as a concluding judgment:

---

[2] Cf., e.g., Tertullian, adv. Marc. I, 16: *consequens est, ut duas species rerum visibilia et invisibilia duobus auctoribus deis dividant et ita suo deo invisibilia defendant.*

[3] I follow the splendid translation in *Plotin, Enneaden in Auswahl*, trans. by O. Kiefer, Jena & Leipzig, 1905.

[4] "This world also has its being through God and looks toward him. . . . It proclaims the nature of that God to men." (Ennead II, 9.9). "Now if there is another, better world than this, where is it? If the existence of the world is necessary, but there is no better one than this one, then this one affords the true image of the spiritual world" (II, 9.8). "Is it a God-fearing view that *providence* does not extend to the matters of this world, not even to anything?" (II, 9.16).

καὶ συνελόντι εἰπεῖν (τοῦ) κακὴν λογίζεσθαι τὴν ὕλην ἀφορμὴν οὐ παρέσχε τῷ Μαρκίωνι (Strom. III, 3.18-19; cf. III, 22.1).[5]

At one point in particular the distinction between Gnosticism and the later Hellenic world view and piety is shown most clearly. Along with the entire visible world the Gnostics also interpreted the world of the stars and of the visible heavens as evil and demonic. In this connection we need only to point to the role which the seven planetary powers,[6] the lower hebdomad, played for the Gnostics. The demonized planetary powers are the actual opponents and enemies of the believing Gnostic. That the soul of the pious should have an assured ascent through the world of the seven after death is by far the highest good [7] of this piety, the final goal which all the secret initiations, the sacraments, the magically powerful formulas and symbols serve. But it is not only the planetary powers from which the Gnostic hopes to be freed by his religion; he desires to be redeemed in general from the collective power of the starry world. Liberation from Heimarmene becomes the great watchword which we encounter in all its areas, in its purely pagan as well as in its specifically Christian branches. In this visible world, the power of the stars governs in Heimarmene, and man, so far and so long as he is connected with this visible world, is subjected to this stern dominion. But this is the new gospel which Gnosticism proclaims: The pious can become free from the power of fate.[8]

In this, Gnosticism comes into conflict with everything that had validity in Hellenistic piety.[9] For since Plato's time the stars serve as the actual gods precisely in the religion of the educated. The figures of the folk-gods begin to disappear from thence; people begin to feel the veneration of the starry forces and of all the powers holding sway in the heavens (in addition to the great elemental and basic forces of nature) as the truth in all religion. The stars are the visible gods. That upper world where these luminous beings wander is the really divine world. Here on earth with its dark and gloomy

---

[5] The misunderstanding of Plato also emphasized by Plotinus, II, 9.6. Cf. Tertullian, adv. Marc. I, 13: *ut ergo aliquid et de isto huius mundi indigno loquar, cui et apud Graecos ornamenti et cultus non sordium nomen est; indignas videlicet substantias ipsi illi sapientiae professores, de quorum ingeniis omnis haeresis animatur, deos pronuntiaverunt.*

[6] *Hauptprobleme*, pp. 9 ff.

[7] W. Anz, *Zur Frage nach dem Ursprung des Gnostizismus*, TU XV (1897), 5.

[8] A selection of the exceedingly numerous examples of this basic attitude in Reitzenstein, *Hellenistische Mysterienreligionen*, pp. 129 ff. [2nd ed., pp. 153 ff.]. Wendland, *Hellenistisch-römische Kultur*, 2nd ed., p. 157.

[9] For the following connections, cf. above all the splendid lectures by Cumont, *Astrology and Religion among the Greeks and Romans* (American Lecture on the History of Religion, 1912), pp. 54 ff., *et passim*, particularly Lectures III and IV.

atmosphere, in the world beneath the moon with its incalculable accidents and capricious phenomena, misfortune and wickedness may have their seat. But above, where in unvarying order the blessed, visible gods move, where everything happens in foreseeable, inviolable, and steady continuity, is the world of beauty, goodness, and harmony, the cosmos in the true sense of the word. All human life and prosperity are dependent upon it. Those celestial powers determine the life of men; and they are not merely dead, cold forces, they are gods, to which people believe—in blithe inconsistency— they can lift up their hands and pray. But man, with the best part of his nature, stems from that world; his higher Ego is a part of that ethereal light above; his spirit is sun-born, akin to the stars.[10] Thither also the soul of the wise and pious returns after death, wanders in the circle of the stars and feasts on the inexpressible beauty of that radiant world of light. At last, the astronomer, who, searching and calculating, attempts to penetrate the mysterious eternal orders of the celestial worlds, or the astrologer who undertakes through his "science" to investigate the counsel of the gods, feels himself full of mysterious rapture lifted up out of the gloomy little earth into the great free world of the gods, senses his soul's kinship with that world, and experiences in blessed ecstasy a sort of *unio mystica,* the marriage of his soul which stems from the light with the sparkling, luminous powers above.

There can hardly be a greater contrast between this sidereally determined piety of wide circles of hellenistically educated people and Gnosticism. There the stars as gods—here demonic powers; there the humble submission to the destiny sent from the gods—here the Heimarmene as the curse-evoking demonic power from whose harsh dominion the pious long to escape; there as the final goal the ascent of the soul to the luminous stars— here the chief concern of the mystic how his soul after death may escape the evil enemies, the planets; there the blessedness experienced in the vision of the starry heavens—here the striving to get beyond the entire visible world; there as the highest deities the stars and the luminous visible heavens themselves—here the great yearning for the "Agnostos Theos." [11]

Once again we find this contrast most sharply formulated in Plotinus:

---

[10] See the statements above on pp. 224 ff. Cf. Cumont, *Astrology and Religion* . . . , Lecture V, pp. 139 ff.; also *Théologie solaire,* 1909, and the essay, already mentioned several times, on "Le mysticisme astral dans l'antiquité" (see above, p. 224, n. 53).

[11] Cf. *Hauptprobleme,* pp. 83 ff.; Norden, *Agnostos Theos,* pp. 62 ff.

"What a contradiction, that they call their own souls immortal and divine, even those of the worst men, while they deny that the heavens and the stars in them, which yet consist of much finer and purer elements, have any part in the immortal soul; and still they see therein that things there are well-formed and well-ordered, but they rebuke the disorder here upon earth" (II, 9.5). "But if you wish to see beyond them (the gods) and boast as if you were not wicked, I give you something to consider: the better someone is, the more modestly he conducts himself toward gods and men; one may be proud of his dignity only in moderation, one may only go so far as our nature is able to ascend, . . . and may not surrender to the foolish dream that *one belongs alone in the immediate entourage of God*" (II, 9.9). "Of course the Gnostics do not shrink from addressing the most reprobate man as brother, but, mad as they are, they hesitate to give this name to the sun and other gods of heaven and the world-soul itself" (II, 9.18).

There we have in every word the protest of the Greek spirit against the unrestrained Promethean insolence of Gnosticism, which demonizes this entire beautiful world and the powers that hold sway over it, and is extended far and above beyond it to the one unknown, invisible God.

Thus the Gnostic religion is a religion of redemption in the sharpest and most one-sided sense of that term. Redemption here is not the ascent from the lower to the higher but wholly the liberation from the absolutely inimical, the absolutely different. At the very beginning of the development of the world an unlawful mixing of elements that do not belong together took place, whether it was that the elements of darkness seized elements of light, or that a primal being—the Anthropos[12] or the fallen goddess Sophia Prunicos, Achamoth[13]—sank down into matter. Thus did world and human nature develop κατά τινα τάραχον καὶ σύγχυσιν ἀρχικήν.[14] The hoped-for redemption consists, then, in the disentanglement and separation of the unlawfully and unnaturally mixed worlds.

Therefore the Gnostic feels homeless, an alien in an alien world. Again and again this key word of alienation sounds through the deepest and most personal confessions of the Gnostics: καὶ ἐντεῦθεν ξένην τὴν ἐκλογὴν τοῦ κόσμου ὁ Βασιλείδης εἴληφε λέγειν ὡς ἂν ὑπερκόσμιον φύσει οὖσαν,

---

[12] On Anthropos, cf. *Hauptprobleme*, pp. 160 ff.

[13] *Hauptprobleme*, pp. 58 ff.

[14] Basilides in Clement, Strom. II, 20.112.

so Clement of Alexandria (Strom. IV, 26.165.3)[15] tells us. The Marcionites[16] proclaim a ξένη γνῶσις, they desire οὐδὲν ἴδιον καταλιπεῖν in this alien world of an alien God, and for this reason they forbid marriage. The libertine Gnostics, the followers of Prodicos, regard themselves as the natural sons of God, the βασίλειοι, who have come into this alien world.[17] Again Valentinus speaks of the favored race of the Gnostics (διάφορον γένος) which has come down from above into this world in order to destroy death.[18] Among the Marcosians, the soul ascending to heaven confesses that it traces its race (κατάγειν τὸ γένος) to the preexistent God and that it returns again to its own (εἰς τὰ ἴδια) after it tarries here on earth ἰδεῖν τὰ ἀλλότρια.[19] Heracleon speaks of the property of the Father (οἰκεῖον τῷ πατρί) which has been lost in the very deepest Hyle of error.[20] And again we encounter the same confession in purely Hellenistic Gnosticism: "For this reason the Gnostics do not please the masses, and the masses do not please them. They appear to be mad and attract ridicule, they are hated, scorned and even killed. For wickedness necessarily dwells here below as in its own place." [21]

And the Gnostics' belief in God corresponds to this. Recently Norden[22] has admirably shown how the theme of the Agnostos Theos dominates the Gnostic systems. To the Gnostic's basic feeling of "strangeness" corresponds the proclamation of the alien, unknown God. With Marcion in particular this proclamation emerges in all its bluntness and harshness. At a definite point in time in the fifteenth year of the Emperor Tiberius, suddenly and without preparation, the *spiritus salutaris*,[23] Christ Jesus (for Marcion,[24] God, Father and Son, almost coincide in one[25]) appeared in the

---

[15] Cf. Clement's polemic, *ibid.*: καὶ οὐκ ἄν τις εἴη φύσει τοῦ κόσμου ξένος μιᾶς μὲν τῆς οὐσίας οὔσης ἑνὸς δὲ τοῦ θεοῦ, ἀλλ᾽ ὁ ἐκλεκτὸς ὡς ξένος πολιτεύεται.

[16] Clement III, 3.12.3: τήν τε ξένην γνῶσιν εὐαγγελίζονται.

[17] III, 4.30.1; 31.3: εἰς ξένον τὸν κόσμον ἀφιγμένοι.

[18] IV, 13.89.4 (cf. 90.3); cf. Heracleon in Origen, *in Joann.* XIII, 10-11 (Hilgenfeld, *Ketzergeschichte*, p. 483.5-6), περὶ φύσεως αἰνιττόμενος ὡς διαφερούσης.

[19] Irenaeus I, 21:5: the qualifying comment is added, καὶ τὰ ἴδια· καὶ οὐκ ἀλλότρια δὲ παντελῶς ἀλλὰ τῆς ᾽Αχαμώθ.

[20] Origen *in Joann.*, in Hilgenfeld, *Ketzergeschichte*, p. 487.1 ff.

[21] *Corpus Hermeticum* IX, 4. Cf. how the Primal Man, sinking down into the material realm, is allured by the desire to behold (the alien) τὴν τοῦ δημιουργοῦ κτίσιν, I, 13.

[22] *Agnostos Theos*, pp. 62 ff.

[23] Tertullian, adv. Marc. I, 19.

[24] [Bousset's representation of Marcion's principal doctrines has evoked a contradiction from Harnack. Cf. the latter's *Marcion* (Leipzig, 1921), pp. 350 ff. Krüger].

[25] *Immo, inquiunt Marcionitae, deus noster, . . . per semetipsum revelatus est in Christo Jesu* (*ibid.*). The teaching of the Marcionite Prepon (in Hippolytus, VII, 31) which views Jesus as μέσον ὄντα κακοῦ καὶ ἀγαθοῦ cannot be genuine.

alien world of the creator of the world in a phantom form, in order, as Tertullian[26] repeatedly maintains, to seize for himself the creatures who belong to the alien God.

Marcion proclaims *the new God* with special emphasis. *Primo supercilio stuporem suum aedificant Marcionitae, quod novum Deum proferunt.*[27] Tertullian appears to have seen correctly. Here in the proclamation of the *novus Deus* the basic attitude of the Marcionite piety is expressed. The polemic against the unjust, evil, and cruel Creator-God of the Old Testament occupies only a subordinate place and is an auxiliary construction by which the superiority of the new God should be placed in a clear light.

In this proclamation of the ξένη γνῶσις of the new God, which after all is common to Gnosticism and only emerges especially strongly and clearly in Marcion, a widespread basic attitude of Hellenistic piety is given expression. It is the yearning for the wholly new[28] and unheard-of in general. All old forms of religion have basically lost their fortunes. People expect salvation from an absolutely new beginning. All the deities coming from the east appear as the new gods over against the crowd of the old Olympians. With the new aeon, the golden age, the new god-savior (θεὸς σωτήρ)[29] "appears," so the mystical theories connected with the ruler cult proclaim it.[30] The more massive language of the apocryphal acts of the apostles proclaim the new God Jesus Christ; as emissaries of the new God the apostles travel through the lands. "What (new) then has the Lord brought to us through his appearing?" the Marcionites asked the adherents of the Great Church.[31]

---

[26] Tertullian, adv. Marc. I, 17: *o deum majorem, cuius tam magnum opus non potuit inveniri, quam in homine dei minoris!* I, 23: *quid enim injustius, quid iniquius et improbius, quam ita alieno benefacere servo ut domino eripiatur.* Hasn't Tertullian gone too far in his polemic here? It is difficult to believe that Marcion should not have shared the speculation of all the Gnostics about the supra-terrestrial origin of the human soul. Tertullian himself (de resurrect. 5) ascribes to Menander and Marcion the doctrine that the corporeality of man stems from the evil angels. Marcion's pupil Apelles openly taught that human souls are enticed by the *deus igneus* into their bodies by means of a lure (de carne Chr. 8.23; Hilgenfeld, *Ketzergeschichte*, p. 538, n. 892).

[27] Adv. Marc. I, 8; cf. I, 2 *nova et hospita* (!) *divinitas.*

[28] Cf. Marcion in Tertullian, III, 2: *subito filius et subito missus et subito Christus.* In III, 4 Tertullian sneers: *novus nove venire voluit.* In general Tertullian objects (III, 2): *atquin nihil putem a deo subitum, quia nihil a deo non dispositum.*

[29] See above, pp. 138-39, and below, Chap. VII.

[30] Inscription from Assos (A.D. 37) on Caligula's ascending the throne: ὡς ἂν τοῦ ἡδίστου ἀνθρώποις αἰῶνος νῦν ἐνεστῶτος (Dittenberger, *Syllog.* 364). Cf. the famous inscription of the Asiatic Greek cities (Priene, etc.) with the decision to move the beginning of the year to the birthday of the Emperor Augustus (Dittenberger, *Or. Gr. Inscr.* II, 458); in the introductory letter of the proconsul: γενέθλιος ἡμέρα, ἣν τῇ τῶν πάντων ἀρχῇ ἴσην δικαίως ἂν εἶναι ὑπολάβοιμεν (l. 5). Cf. also Vergil's Fourth Eclogue, *et al.*

[31] Irenaeus IV, 34.1.

It must have been difficult for the emerging church to escape this intoxication. In all this the unrestrained yearning for redemption of an age tending toward bankruptcy is expressed: a yearning for redemption which, moreover, clearly has its basis in polytheism with its receptivity for changing figures of gods. Tertullian rightly sensed this when in a trembling rage he objects to it thus: *quis deus novus nisi falsus. . . . Non habet tempus aeternitas. omne enim tempus ipsa est* (adv. Marc. I, 8).

We have already surmised that the great saying of our Gospels: "No one knows the Son except the Father, and no one knows the Father except the Son and he to whom the Son wills to reveal him," with its sound that is utterly unheard-of in the Synoptic literature, is rooted in this soil of Hellenistic piety. It is almost as if only now, since the content of the attitude of this piety in its entire scope has become clear to us, could we understand this saying also in its full import. However that may be—at any rate this logion became the Shibboleth of the Gnostics, to which they refer again and again. And again and again the church fathers must argue with their opponents on this point. Their arguments altogether, however, show how uncongenial and uncomfortable to them this logion was, and in what a dilemma they found themselves with respect to it.[32] For even if that saying and the tearing apart of the Creator-God and the Agnostos Theos on the part of the Gnostics were not identical, still we detect the pulse of a similar basic outlook: this yearning for the absolutely new, the unprecedented and completely different.

Basically Gnosticism is the native soil of all bluntly supernaturalistic theory of revelation. It is a fairly generally recognized fact that "Gnosis"[33] does not signify knowledge in our sense of the word, and that the Gnostics were no theoreticians of knowledge and philosophers of religion. Gnosis is rather mysterious wisdom which rests upon secret revelation; one might better call the Gnostics Theosophists. Gnosticism is the world of vision, of ecstasy, of secret revelations and mediators of revelation, of revelational literature and of secret tradition.[34] The light actually must shine into this world from above, out of the higher region which is totally separated from this wretched world of darkness; the sparks of light (σπινθῆρες; *vide infra*) which have been lost in the region of darkness are not able of themselves

---

[32] The chief passages, Irenaeus I, 20.3; IV, 2.2; IV, 6-7; Tertullian, adv. Marc. IV, 25; Ps.-Clem. Recog. II, 47-57; Homil. III, 2-7, 38; XVII, 4-5; XVIII, 1-2. Norden, *Agnostos Theos*, p. 76.

[33] Cf. the comprehensive investigation of the concept in Reitzenstein, *Hellenistische Mysterienreligionen*, pp. 112 ff. [2nd ed., pp. 135 ff.].

[34] Cf. Liechtenhan, *Die Offenbarung im Gnostizismus*, 1901.

to be fanned into brightness; left alone, they would miserably die out. And further, the sacrament must be related to the revelation; indeed the supernatural revelation, which pioneers in vision and ecstasy, is itself already a sacrament.[35] Where in this radical way people simply refuse to hear anything of innate powers growing out of the creation, the soil is always well prepared for sacraments[36] and for the view that the best comes to men in impersonal ways, through the influx of supernatural and yet natural powers.

Thus at last this Gnosticism with its dualistic-pessimistic way of looking at the world and its one-sided redemption piety is presented as the most decided antithesis to the Old Testament–Jewish monotheism and belief in creation. In this connection we cannot further treat the question whether this discussion with the Old Testament and Judaism first took place through the medium of Christianity, or whether—as from the outset lies within the realm of possibility—pre-Christian Gnosticism had already come into conflict with the proclamation of the synagogue in the Diaspora. Various reasons argue for the view that Gnosticism's polemic against the Old Testament and Judaism has deeper roots in its own total outlook than the contacts with Christianity.[37] In any case this attitude of Gnosticism may not be understood as further developed and thoroughgoing Paulinism. The Gnostics in their argument with the Old Testament and the Old Testament God quite essentially proceeded from cosmological motifs, while Paul proceeded from the question of the universality of salvation and of the justification of the Gentile mission. The Gnostics first attacked the Creator-God and his creation, and then—and this is altogether hellenistically conceived—the Warrior-God of Jewish people whom the world hates[38]; the opposition to law and legalist piety was first connected with Gnosticism in its later branches. Marcion appears here to form an exception. But if one looks closely, even in Marcion the cosmological basis of his entire system is quite clearly revealed. Under Pauline stimulation Marcion first built the contrast of the *deus bonus* and the *deus justus* into the more comprehensive opposites of the known and the unknown, the new and the old God, the creator and

---

[35] What we possess from the Gnostics of their own literature often bears the stamp of ecstatic, mysterious language. Cf. the fragments of Valentinus: Hippolytus, Refut. VI, 37; Clement, Strom. II, 20.114; IV, 13.91; the Valentinian fragment in Epiphanius 31.5; the famous, almost certainly Gnostic hymns of the Acta Thomae; also large parts of the Coptic Gnostic writings (Apocryphon Joannis, Pistis Sophia, the Books of Jeu); the Odes of Solomon, etc.

[36] On the sacrament among the Gnostics, cf. *Hauptprobleme*, pp. 267-319.

[37] *Hauptprobleme*, pp. 324-25. Article, "Gnosis" in Pauly-Wissowa, 1524.

[38] *Hauptprobleme*, p. 325.

ruler of the world and the redeemer-God.[39] But it is clear that in Marcion's polemic against the Old Testament, in the "separatio legis et evangelii," Pauline shoots are grafted onto an alien stock. Throughout his polemic against the *deux judex* again and again sounds the note of a much sharper dualism, for which the *deus judex* is actually the *deus malus*[40] and the stout adversary of the good God. One certainly does not understand the whole Marcion if one sees in him an advanced Paulinist. The dualism of Marcion, like that of other Gnosticism, rests upon its own foundations; in Marcion, stripped of almost all mythological by-products, it only stands out all the more starkly.

II. *Gnosticism and Paul.* To be sure, if we pose the question how it happens that this great Gnostic movement, which in its beginnings and in its foundation has nothing to do with Christianity, was placed so close to the latter and was so intimately bound up with it that we know it with few exceptions only as a subsidiary movement of Christianity, the answer must be: It is the form which *Paul* gave to Christianity that drew the Gnostic circles to it as would a magnet. It was most of all the pattern of Christianity as a one-sided religion of redemption and the connection of the redeemer myth with the figure of Jesus of Nazareth which, introduced by Paul into Christianity, exerted this great drawing power. For what was here preached as a mood, without regard to the broader consequences, in free inventive intuition, in inspired discourse of prophet and missionary, the Gnostic movement believed to be able to provide the foundation and the general background in terms of a world view. Thus did Gnosticism choose the great apostle as its doctrinal master. In a time when in the church itself— probably precisely as a result of this alliance of Gnosticism with the apostle—some drew back from him and attempted indeed not to oppose him but to silence him completely,[41] in Gnostic circles people read, collected,

---

[39] One may not appeal, for the reverse order, to Tertullian I, 19: *separatio legis et evangelii proprium et principale opus Marcionis* (then follows a reference to Marcion's Antitheses). The church fathers naturally noticed above all the generous use by Marcion of Pauline motifs; this was most unacceptable to them.

[40] Cf. the epithet which the *deus judex* receives in Tertullian I, 6: *ferus bellipotens.* To this corresponds Irenaeus I, 27.2: *malorum factorem et bellorum concupiscentem.* Tertullian II, 11: *judex et severus et quot Marcionitae volunt saevus.* I, 17: *malitia creatoris;* cf. I, 22: *saevitiae eius;* II, 24. Cf. also the application of Isa. 45:7, *ego sum qui condo mala,* to the Creator-God, and the application of the parable of the good tree and the corrupt tree to the relationship of the two gods (I, 2). All this is not exaggerated and misconceived Paulinism, but Oriental dualism of a robust sort.

[41] See below, Chaps. IX and X.

and commented on his epistles and took their stand on the authority of the apostle.[42]

It is true that Gnosticism had to bend Paul violently in order to make him useful for its purposes. And yet again these people were not entirely without justification when they appealed to him. The threads run in both directions.

Thus it appears at first glance as if the Gnostics absolutely could not appeal to Paul for their demonizing of the visible, natural world and for their opposing the Creator-God, to the Paul who in good Stoic orthodoxy bases his accusations against impenitent paganism on the basic presupposition that God has clearly revealed himself to men in his creation (Rom. 1:18 ff.; cf. I Cor. 1:21 [43]). But on the other hand, the thoroughly pessimistic doctrine of the σάρξ, which of course at first is thought of in essentially anthropological terms but then here and there (cf. Rom. 8:22-23) is extended to include the entire earthly-sensual creature, as well as the pneumatic eschatology which is connected with it, pushes Paul into the paths of Gnosticism. But going beyond Paul, people raised the question of whence then comes the absolutely inimical and alien aspect of the lower sensual nature of man; how it then happens that τὸ φρόνημα τῆς σαρκὸς ἐχθρὰ εἰς θεόν, that the first man by virtue of his creation is an essentially less-worthy being (only ψυχὴ ζῶσα); what then is to be thought about the origin of the sarkic world whose destruction and elimination Paul makes the quintessence of his eschatological hope. And as soon as one even posed these questions, one already stood with one foot on the soil of dualistic Gnosticism. Paul on his own part had dared to speak of the devil as the θεὸς τοῦ αἰῶνος τούτου. And one may detect in Irenaeus how inconvenient this word of the apostle was for ecclesiastical Christianity and with what exegetical violence the church fathers sought to render the expression harmless.[44]

---

[42] Here I refer only to the two most important facts, that Marcion's canon consisted of a Gospel and the epistles of Paul, and that the earlier schools of the Valentinians quoted, as their only authority besides the σωτήρ, the ἀπόστολος. See the material on this, particularly from Irenaeus I, 8 and Excerpta ex Theodoto, in C. Barth, Die Interpretation des N. T. in der valentinianischen Gnosis (TU, XXXVII [1911], 3), 28 ff. E. Schwartz, Aporieen, GGN, 1908, pp. 136 ff.; my review of C. Barth's work in TLZ, 1912, col. 397. It probably is not accidental that the anti-Marcionite presbyter whom Irenaeus (IV, 27.1–32.1) follows (cf. Harnack, Philotesia Kleinert, pp. 1-38) makes such abundant use of the κύριος and the Apostle (in addition to these only one reference to the Apocalypse) as his authorities.

[43] [On this and the following, cf. J. Weiss, Urchristentum, pp. 472-79. Bultmann.]

[44] Adv. haer. III, 7.1. Irenaeus connects τοῦ αἰῶνος τούτου with τὰ νοήματα τῶν ἀπίστων, and thus by ὁ θεός he understands God and not the devil.

In the apostle's polemic against the law the Gnostics could also find a confirmation of their dualistic views. In particular with his statements in Galatians about the inferior mediatorial powers with whose help God gave the law, about our ransom from the curse of the law, about the fundamentally similar inferiority of Jewish legal worship and pagan worship, Paul actually stands with one foot on the soil of Gnosticism. It is as if he himself foresaw the dangerous consequences of his daring theses, when he posed the question: "Is the law now against the promise?" (3:21) in order then of course to demur with a μὴ γένοιτο. But in the Epistle to the Romans also the Gnostics found the statements that the law brings the knowledge of sin (3:20) and produces wrath (4:15), and the question whether the Nomos is sin (7:7). The thesis that the law was given by hostile powers or by one hostile power is actually not very far from Paul in his statement of Gal. 3:19. When in that connection the Gnostics rejected the ingenious but still contrived argumentation with which he tried to escape those evil consequences, they may in fact have been of the opinion that they were only drawing the hidden conclusions of apostolic doctrine.[45]

One can further see clearly in the third book of Clement's Stromateis how vigorously all the Gnostics, who in consistent elaboration of their dualism rejected marriage, employed Paul's statements in I Cor. 7. And it must be admitted that here they were not in the wrong and that in this chapter beginnings and tendencies of an ascetic dualism actually are present.

Further, the apostle's spiritualizing doctrine of the resurrection here comes into consideration. With his assumption of the σῶμα πνευματικόν, it is only with difficulty that he stays on the borderline between the late Jewish and early Christian materialistic hope of the resurrection of the flesh and the spiritualism of Hellenistic religion. According to his total basic outlook he apparently stood closer to the latter. In the forthright and clear sentence: "Flesh and blood cannot inherit the kingdom of God," the Gnostics had a powerful weapon. One can again discern, from repeated lengthy expositions by the church fathers of precisely this passage, how inconvenient for ecclesiastical Christianity was Paul's joining in the rejection of the fleshly resurrection, an alliance which Gnosticism asserted here with a perfect right.[46]

---

[45] Cf. Clement, Strom. II, 7.34.4, οὐκ ἀγαθὸς ὁ νόμος πρός τινων αἱρέσεων λέγεται ἐπιβοωμένων τὸν ἀπόστολον λέγοντα, διὰ γὰρ νόμου γνῶσις ἁμαρτίας (cf. III, 2.7.2; 8.61; 11.76; IV, 3.9.6).

[46] Cf. all the lengthy statements in Irenaeus V, 7-15. The hinge on which they turn is the interpretation of I Cor. 15. Further Tertullian, adv. Marc. V, 10: *Hoc enim dico,*

Finally, we may here refer to a fact which lies somewhat beneath the surface and yet is especially characteristic for the connection between Paul and the Gnostic world. I pointed out above that the special peculiarity of the dualism of Gnosticism comes to expression in the demonizing of the starry powers, which in later Hellenistic piety served as the real gods for the educated people, and in the interpretation of redemption as liberation from the Heimarmene which is governed by the starry powers. In Paul's angelology there is a striking parallel to this basic outlook.[47] It is extraordinarily characteristic that on the whole, apart from some few passages[48] in which he is operating within the framework of customary language usage, Paul really knows no good angelic powers. For him the angelic powers, whose various categories he is accustomed to enumerating in the well-known stereotyped manner, are intermediate-echelon beings, in part of a pernicious kind. The archons of this aeon brought Christ to the cross, at the cross he battled with the angels and powers and wrested from them their weapons.[49] Angels and men watch the drama which the apostle, despised and scorned by all, offers with his life (I Cor. 4:9). Lascivious angels are a danger for unveiled women (I Cor. 11:10). Paul is buffeted by an angel of Satan (II Cor. 12:7). The Christians will someday have the judgment over the angels (I Cor. 6:3). The world of the angels, like the human world, needs the atonement (Col. 1:20). It is especially characteristic how Paul employs the tradition of the proclamation of the law through angels, which the Jewish tradition had framed in order to glorify the law, without hesitation and as though it were obviously in order to degrade the law: The law is given "only" through angels (Gal. 3:19).[50]

Then we have the pneumatic Gnostic, who is proudly elevated above all the mediating powers and is reckoned "alone in the immediate entourage of God" (*vide supra*, p. 249). The post-Pauline writings go into this somewhat further when they speak of the fact that only through the church

---

*fratres, quia caro et sanguis regnum dei non possidebunt, o p e r a scilicet carnis et sanguinis, solitus et alias substantiam pro operibus substantiae ponere, ut cum dicit eos qui in carne sunt deo placere non posse.* A splendid example of the art of reinterpretation of early ecclesiastical exegesis!

[47] On the following, cf. Dibelius, *Die Geisterwelt im Glauben des Paulus*, 1909.

[48] Cf., e.g. (I Cor. 13:1); II Cor. 11:14 (in Gal. 4:14 ἄγγελος is simply "emissary"); I Thess. 3:13 (ἅγιοι=angels in the train of the returning Lord; cf. II Thess. 1:7); I Thess. 4:16.

[49] I Cor. 2:6 ff.; Col. 2:15.

[50] In Gal. 1:8, it is at least assumed as possible that an angel could proclaim false doctrine.

has the πολυποίκιλος σοφία of God been made manifest even to the angelic powers, and that the angels, full of longing, desire to see the glory which now at the end of the ages has been allotted to the Christians.[51]

Thus also in Paul, the particularly Gnostic view of redemption as liberation from Heimarmene is not completely lacking, even though it is true that only limited allusions to it are found. At least in his statements about the enslavement of pre-Christian humanity under the dominion of the στοιχεῖα this note clearly sounds throughout. The stars, and perhaps also the great elemental forces of nature, are the stern lords under which humanity groans, and from which Christ has ransomed men.[52] In the great chapter on redemption where Paul names the powers which still separate the Christian from his God, he enumerates in the first place the angelic powers, the ἄγγελοι and ἀρχαί (ὕψωμα and βάθος) (Rom. 8:38). Christ's task in the interregnum will be to make a clean sweep of the strength of the world-dominating powers (I Cor. 15:24).

Nowhere does it become clearer than here how closely related are the thought-worlds of Paul and of Gnosticism. The difference is that in Paul, in the face of the original and intellectually powerful religious conceptions which he scatters about, unconcerned about all the consequences, this thought-world remains decidedly in the background, while among the Gnostics with their strong interest in a world view—of course not in the form of philosophy but of myth—it is thrust into the very foreground.

Still if we leave aside all these details, it is, as we have said, again and again the one thing that binds the apostle Paul and Gnosticism most closely together: the one-sided elaboration of religion as a religion of redemption in the bluntest sense of the term.

III. *Pauline and Gnostic Anthropology.* This phenomenon is shown above all in the anthropology of both sides. We have already mentioned the fact that our further encounters with the peculiar Pauline anthropology, with its blunt opposing of a higher divine element (the Pneuma) to the whole scope of the natural being (including ψυχή and νοῦς), are almost exclusively on Gnostic soil. Of course this terminology does not dominate Gnosticism throughout. To characterize the alien higher element in man, the Gnostics very often make use of other terms. Above all, they like to

---

[51] Eph. 3:10; I Pet. 1:12.
[52] Gal. 4:3, 9; Col. 2:20.

speak of the divine sparks of light in favored men,[53] or perhaps of the ξένον, the ἄνωθεν, the διάφορον γένος of the Gnostics (*vide supra*, p. 250). Especially preferred also is the self-designation as those who are in possession of the σπέρμα, above all of the maternal deity (the parallelism of language usage in I John immediately comes to mind)[54]; their nature represents an ἀπόρροια[55] of the highest deity (the Mother). Or it is emphasized that

[53] Cf. Satornilus in Irenaeus I, 24.1 (scintilla vitae); Epiphanius, Haer. 23.2.2, p. 250.11 H, εἶναι δὲ αὐτοὺς τοὺς ταύτης τῆς αἱρέσεως τοὺς ἔχοντας τὸν σπινθῆρα τοῦ ἄνωθεν πατρός 23.1.9, p. 249.13 H: the ἄνωθεν δύναμις sends the σπινθήρ into the men who were created by the angels: καὶ τούτου ἕνεκα πάντως δὴ τὸν σπινθῆρα σωθῆναι, τὸ δὲ πᾶν τοῦ ἀνθρώπου ἀπολέσθαι (cf. Hippolytus, Ref. VII, 28.3, p. 209. 1 W). Ophites, Epiph. 37.4: καὶ ἀποστεῖλαι ἀπ᾽ αὐτοῦ (*sc.* the ἄνω Μήτηρ by Jaldabaoth) σπινθῆρα ἐπὶ τὸν ἄνθρωπον; cf. 37.6. Sethians in Epiph. 39.2: σπέρμα τῆς ἄνωθεν δυνάμεως καὶ τὸν σπινθῆρα τὸν ἄνωθεν πεμφθέντα. Sethians in Hippolytus V, 19.6, p. 117.16 W: τὴν λαμπηδόνα καὶ τὸν σπινθῆρα τοῦ φωτός; cf. V, 21.2, p. 123.9. Exc. ex Theod. 1:3: τὸ ἐκλεκτὸν σπέρμα φαμὲν καὶ σπινθῆρα ζωπυρούμενον ὑπὸ τοῦ Λόγου, 3.1: ἐξῆπτεν τὸν Σπινθῆρα (*sc.*, the Soter). Cf. Simon Magus: Hippolytus VI, 17.7, p. 144.1. In the Pistis Sophia this higher element in the Gnostic is frequently (see the Register in Schmidt) described as the "light-man" dwelling in him. As is known, in general the language of the Gnostic sects is dominated by the contrast between φῶς and σκότος (see above, pp. 235-36).

[54] The Valentinians describe a person who does not believingly adhere to their preaching as "*non habentem de superioribus a matre sua semen.*" Iren. III, 15.2. Iren. I, 5.6: τὸ δὲ κύημα τῆς μητρὸς αὐτῶν Ἀχαμώθ. I, 7.3: τὰς δὲ ἐσχηκυίας τὸ σπέρμα τῆς Ἀχαμὼθ ψυχὰς ἀμείνονας λέγουσι γεγονέναι τῶν λοιπῶν. I, 6.4: σπέρματα ἐκλογῆς. Excerpta ex Theod. 1.1: πνευματικὸν σπέρμα. 1.3: ἐκλεκτὸν σπέρμα (cf. 40, 41, 42, *et passim*). Hippolytus V, 8.28, p. 94.14 (Naassenes); VI, 34.6, p. 163.16 (Valentinians): λόγοι ἄνωθεν κατεσπαρμένοι ἀπὸ τοῦ κοινοῦ τοῦ πληρώματος Καρποῦ καὶ τῆς Σοφίας εἰς τοῦτον τὸν κόσμον κατοικοῦντες ἐν σώματι χοϊκῷ μετὰ ψυχῆς.

[55] The Gnostics in Celsus speak of the effluences by which the earthly community is formed (ἀπορροίας ἐκκλησίας ἐπιγείου, VI, 34; in VI, 35 the saying probably is not altogether correctly understood by Origen) and accordingly of a Προυνικοῦ τινος ῥέουσα δύναμις παρθένου. Peratae in Hippolytus VI, 17.4, p. 114.26: ὁμοίως δ᾽ αὖ καὶ ἀπὸ τοῦ υἱοῦ ἐπὶ τὴν ὕλην ῥερευκέναι τὰς δυνάμεις. Sethians V, 20.7, p. 122.13, τὴν ῥύσιν ἄνωθεν τοῦ φωτός. Lecanomancy of the priest Nephotes, Parisian magical papyrus ll. 154 ff. (Reitzenstein, *Hellenistische Mysterienreligionen*, p. 69 [2nd ed., p. 74]): συνεστάθην σου τῇ ἱερᾷ μορφῇ, ἐδυναμώθην τῷ ἱερῷ σου ὀνόματι, ἐπέτυχόν σου τῆς ἀπορροίας τῶν ἀγαθῶν (afterward it speaks of the ἰσόθεος φύσις which the initiate has achieved). The expression ἀπόρροια is probably of astronomical-astrological origin. The theory that the stars with their emanations of light are the originators of all the structures and organizations here on earth is expressly set forth in the teaching of the Peratae (Hippolytus V, 15-16). More material in Reitzenstein, *Poimandres*, p. 16.4; there also on the speculations on the subject by the Harranian Ssabians, pp. 72, 169 ff.; cf. p. 263.4; Dieterich, *Abraxas*, p. 196.4: οὗ αἱ ἀγαθαὶ ἀπόρροιαι τῶν ἀστέρων εἰσὶν δαίμονες καὶ Τύχαι, Μοῖραι. From this beginning then the conception is expanded: The creation of the world in general comes about through the ἀπόρροιαι of divine powers. The juxtaposition of the two conceptions: Hippolytus V, 15.3, p. 110.23: κατὰ τὸν αὐτὸν τρόπον ὡς γέγονεν ὁ κόσμος ἀπὸ τῆς ἀπορροίας τῆς ἄνω, οὕτως τὰ ἐνθάδε ἀπὸ τῆς ἀπορροίας τῶν ἀστέρων γένεσιν ἔχειν καὶ φθορὰν λέγουσι καὶ διοικεῖσθαι. More material for that interesting transition: Reitzenstein, *Poimandres*, p. 16.4; cf. particularly the evidence from Plutarch, Isis and Osiris, 38, 53, 58 (49 should be added). I regard it as unnecessary here with Reitzenstein to assume a specifically Egyptian doctrine. It is all explained in terms of the underlying astronomical

they are φύσει sons of God,[56] and in this connection we encounter for the first time within Christianity the great catchword ὁμοούσιος.[57]

The use of the term "Nous" to designate the higher constituent part in the nature of the believer is very rare in Gnostic language.[58] This philosophical concept does not fit into this world of strong supernaturalism and

---

outlook. *This outlook has then been changed once again in Gnosticism. Here the* ἀπόρροιαι *become the overflowings of the supra-terrestrial deity into an alien world* (cf. incidentally in this connection also the Wisd. Sol. 7.25; ἀπόρροια in an obscenely mystical sense in Epiphanius, Haer. 26.8, 13).

[56] Valentinus in Clement, Strom. IV, 13.89: φύσει γὰρ σωζόμενον γένος ὑποτίθεται . . . ἐμφερῶς τῷ Βασιλείδῃ. The Basilidians, *ibid.*, III, 1.3.3: ἡ ἔμφυτος ἐκλογή. The Prodicians in Clement, III, 4.30: υἱοὺς μὲν φύσει τοῦ πρώτου θεοῦ λέγοντες ἑαυτοὺς . . . ὑπεράνω παντὸς γένους πεφυκότες βασιλεῖοι. Cf. II, 16.74.1: ὁ θεὸς δὲ οὐδεμίαν ἔχει πρὸς ἡμᾶς φυσικὴν σχέσιν ὡς οἱ τῶν αἱρέσεων κτίσται θέλουσιν. Heracleon, Origen, in Joann. IV, 24, Hilgenfeld, *Ketzergeschichte*, p. 487.20-21: καὶ γὰρ αὐτοὶ (*sc.* οἱ πνευματικοί) τῆς αὐτῆς φύσεως ὄντες τῷ πατρὶ πνεῦμά εἰσιν. Cf. Hilgenfeld, p. 491.8; *ibid.*, p. 492.29: τὴν ἄφθαρτον τῆς ἐκλογῆς φύσιν καὶ μονοειδῆ καὶ ἑνικήν. P. 496.5, 497.10-11 (οἱ φύσει τοῦ διαβόλου υἱοὶ οἱ χοϊκοί).

[57] Irenaeus I, 5.6: τὸ δὲ κύημα τῆς μητρὸς αὐτῆς τῆς Ἀχαμώθ . . . ὁμοούσιον ὑπάρχον τῇ μητρί (cf. I, 5.5). Exc. ex Theodoto 42.3: ἦρεν οὖν τὸ σῶμα τοῦ Ἰ. ὅπερ ὁμοούσιον ἦν τῇ ἐκκλησίᾳ (cf. 50, 53, 58). Clement, Strom. II, 16.74: εἰ μή τις μέρος αὐτοῦ καὶ ὁμοουσίους ἡμᾶς τῷ θεῷ τολμήσει λέγειν. Origen against Heracleon in Joann. V, 24; Hilgenfeld, p. 487.24: ἐπιστήσω μὲν δέ, εἰ μὴ σφόδρα ἐστὶν ἀσεβὲς ὁμοούσιον τῇ ἀγεννήτῳ φύσει . . . λέγειν τοὺς προσκυνοῦντας ἐν πνεύματι. Hilgenfeld, p. 488.1: ἡ πνευματικὴ φύσις ὁμοούσιος οὖσα τῇ ἀγεννήτῳ. Cf. p. 496.31. Ptolemaeus to Flora, Epiph. 33.7.9, p. 457.13 H; Hippolytus, Ref. (Peratae), p. 196.16; 198.3: τὸ ἐξεικονισμένον τέλειον γένος ὁμοούσιον; cf. V, 8.10, p. 915 (Naassenes); VII, 22.7, 12, p. 198.26; 199.19; X, 14.2, p. 274.25 (Basilides). Finally, Corpus Herm. I, 10. The word appears to have been common in Orphic circles: Abel, *Orphica Fragmenta* 76, p. 182; 307, p. 270. Wobbermin, *Religionsgeschichtliche Studien*, pp. 103-4.

[58] One should also observe the frequent self-description of the Gnostics as τέλειοι. Iren. I, 6.4; I, 13.6. Naassenes in Hippolytus V, 8.9, 29, p. 90.24, 94.24 (γνωστικοὶ τέλειοι), 30, p. 94.27. Cf. V, 17.10, p. 115.24; Epiph. 31.5.6, p. 391.10 H. The word belongs to the language of the mysteries and is to be taken in the sense of "initiated ones." Most clearly Corpus Herm. IV, 4: ὅσοι μὲν οὖν συνῆκαν τοῦ κηρύγματος καὶ ἐβαπτίσαντο τοῦ νοός, οὗτοι μετέσχον τῆς γνώσεως καὶ τέλειοι ἐγένοντο ἄνθρωποι τὸν νοῦν δεξάμενοι. Cf. Philodemus, περὶ θεῶν (edited by Diels, AAB, 1915, Phil.-Hist. Kl., no. 7, published 1916), I, 24.11: οὐδὲ τὸν τε[λείως] τέλειο[ν οἱ θεοὶ π]άντες ἅμα [φοβεῖν] γε[ν]ομίζονται=according to our belief all the gods together cannot frighten the perfectly matured. "τέλειος is the artificial expression of the Epicureans, borrowed from the language of the mysteries, for the perfect man in contrast to the rabble," Diels, *op. cit.*, p. 93.1. Cf. also the term τέλειος λόγος (word of initiation, title of a Hermetic tractate); in Irenaeus, I, 5.6, the seed of Achamoth ready *ad susceptionem perfectae rationis* (in the Greek text stands only τελείου; λόγου is to be added). Clement, Paid. I, 6.26, hands down to us as names for Christian baptism the words χάρισμα, φώτισμα, τέλειον (means of initiation), λουτρόν. The Basilidians believed themselves to be permitted to sin διὰ τὴν τελειότητα (Clem., Strom. III, 1.3.3). Cf. even Justin, Dial. 8, p. 225 D: ἐπιγνόντι σοι τὸν Χριστὸν τοῦ θεοῦ καὶ τελείῳ γενομένῳ. Hist. Laus. 93.2 Butler: οἱ δὲ τέλειοι νομοθεσίας χρείαν οὐκ ἔχουσιν.

anthropological dualism. Only in the Hellenistic Gnosticism of the Hermetic writings did it have (*vide supra*, pp. 185-86) the dominant position, and indeed the almost exclusively dominant position.[59]

Along with all this, however, we now find the full scope of the Pauline terminology again in the Gnostic conceptual world and almost exclusively here (cf. *ante*, pp. 186-87): the stark opposition of πνεῦμα and σάρξ, the still more distinctive opposition of πνεῦμα and ψυχή, the formulas ψυχικός and χοϊκός (for the latter frequently the preferred expression ὑλικός), indeed even the conception of the σῶμα πνευματικόν.[60]

Especially worthy of note is the recurrence of the terminological distinction between πνεῦμα and ψυχή, with which we must occupy ourselves in more detail. For the Gnostic terminology has here gone through a development through which the original was in part obscured. When the Valentinians[61] chose the well-known threefold division of men into pneumatics, psychics, and hylics (sarkics, choics), this no longer corresponded to the stark Pauline dualism in which the ψυχή falls altogether into the world which is in opposition to the spirit of God. What we have here is explicit mediation theology, with which these Gnostic schools confronted the Great Church

[59] In the Hermetic source of Zosimus (in the Book Omega) the ἄνοες stand over against the πνευματικὸς ἄνθρωπος. Reitzenstein, *Poimandres*, pp. 102-3. Cf. Sethians in Hippolytus V, 19.14, 15, p. 119.3, 7.

[60] To be remembered here are the well-known speculations of the Valentinians (also those of Marcion's pupil Apelles, cf. Hilgenfeld, *Ketzergeschichte*, p. 539) about the miraculous body of the redeemer, formed κατ' οἰκονομίαν (see below); and above all Epiph. Haer. 31.7.10, p. 397.19 H.: τὸ δὲ ἑαυτῶν τάγμα πνευματικὸν ὃν σώζεσθαι σὺν σώματι ἄλλῳ, ἐνδοτέρῳ τινὶ ὄντι, ὅπερ αὐτοὶ σῶμα πνευματικὸν καλοῦσι φανταζόμενοι. It is intriguing how Epiphanius here ridicules as heretical a teaching which is fundamentally Pauline but which he naturally does not recognize as such. Cf. further the speculations about the *corpus animale* and *spirituale* (of the risen Christ) among the Gnostics, Irenaeus I, 30.13-14. Cf. Corpus Herm. XIII, 13 and the beginning of the so-called Mithras Liturgy, and finally the interesting allusion to an ἀγγελικὸν σῶμα in a burial inscription found on the Via Latina (Dölger, Ἰχθύς, RQ, Supplem. XVII, 78). Cf. ZNW XV (1914): "Eine frühchristliche Schrift . . ." (edited by Reitzenstein), p. 82, l. 216: *qui corpus et spiritum caelestium servat.*

[61] From the fragments which we have, it is not certain whether Valentinus was already making use of the Pauline terminology. He uses other expressions. Also in Exc. ex Theodoto 51 there is exhibited a definitely un-Pauline usage (cf. θεία ψυχή—ὑλικὴ ψυχή—ζιζάνιον συμφυὲς τῇ ψυχῇ). The Basilidians spoke of πνεύματα προσηρτημένα τῇ λογικῇ ψυχῇ; Clement, Strom. II, 20.112. According to the Valentinians in Hippolytus VI, 34.6, p. 163.14, man is a κατοικητήριον sometimes for the soul alone, πότε δὲ ψυχῆς καὶ δαιμόνων, πότε δὲ ψυχῆς καὶ λόγων (cf. Valentinus in Clement, Strom. II, 20. 114). On this entire anthropology, cf. *Hauptprobleme*, pp. 361 ff. Cf. the fragment of the Sophia Jesu Christi translated in Hennecke–Schneemelcher–Wilson, I, 243 ff. Also un-Pauline is, e.g., Hippolytus V, 34.7, p. 163.22: κατοικῆσαι τὸν Χριστὸν εἰς τὸν ἔσω ἄνθρωπον τουτέστιν τὸν ψυχικόν, οὐ τὸν σωματικόν.

in order to avoid a break with it.[62] Under this perspective then the pneumatics and psychics move together almost as a unity over against the hylics who are unconditionally consigned to damnation. But we can still adduce the evidence that the Valentinians originally also knew the purely dualistic opposition of πνεῦμα and ψυχή. Irenaeus formulates their eschatology in the sentence: τοὺς δὲ πνευματικοὺς ἀποδυσαμένους τὰς ψυχὰς καὶ πνεύματα νοερὰ γενομένους . . . νύμφας ἀποδοθήσεσθαι τοῖς περὶ τὸν Σωτῆρα ἀγγέλοις.[63] The Marcosians spoke in their sacramental prayers of the Gnostic's traveling to his homeland, ρίψαντα τὸν δέσμον αὐτοῦ, τουτέστι τὴν ψυχήν.[64] And this usage must have been extended far beyond the Valentinian sects. We meet it in particular in the numerous source documents of a Gnosticism which certainly had already degenerated, which Hippolytus excerpted in his *Refutatio*. Above all, the Baruch Gnosticism of Justin with an almost unprecedentedly sharp contrasting of πνεῦμα and ψυχή is worthy of note here. Here Elohim represents the pneumatic element, the Edem the psychical one, so that it can be said directly: ἡ ψυχὴ κατὰ τοῦ πνεύματος τέτακται καὶ τὸ πνεῦμα κατὰ τῆς ψυχῆς (Hippolytus, p. 226.98). The redeemer leaves his earthly part to the Edem with the words: γύναι ἀπέχεις σου τὸν υἱόν, τουτέστι τὸν ψυχικὸν ἄνθρωπον καὶ τὸν χοϊκόν.[65] Also in the statements of the sect of the Naassenes, among whom Pauline terms are extraordinarily frequently[66] found and who like the Valentinians appear to be acquainted with three races, the ἄγγελοι, ψυχικοί, and χοϊκοί,[67] the concepts ψυχικός and σαρκικός are again taken together as a unity over against πνευματικός.

An interesting and again more mediating view is found in the secondary Basilidian system transmitted by Hippolytus. According to it the pneumatic elements came down into this lower world in order to improve and to perfect the psychical elements:[68] υἱοὶ δέ ἐσμεν ἡμεῖς οἱ πνευματικοί, ἐνθάδε

---

[62] Cf., e.g., Iren. I, 6.1; Exc. ex Theod. 54, 57; Heracleon in Origen (Hilgenfeld, *Ketzergeschichte*, p. 496.30-31).

[63] Iren. I, 7.1; cf. Exc. ex Theod. 64.

[64] Iren. I, 21.5; cf. I, 21.4: the sacrament of Apolutrosis (the sacrament of redemption) is neither σωματικά nor ψυχική, ἐπεὶ καὶ ἡ ψυχὴ ἐξ ὑστερήματος καὶ τοῦ πνεύματος ὥσπερ κατοικητήριον.

[65] Hippolytus V, 26.32, p. 131.32; cf. 27.3, p. 133.9.

[66] Cf. πνευματικοί—σαρκικοί in Hippolytus, p. 88.23; 90.15; 92.16; 93.18; 96.22; 97.15 *et passim*.

[67] Hippolytus V, 6.7, p. 78.21. The passage does not belong to the actual kernel of the Naassene writing.

[68] Hippolytus V, 8.44, p. 97.14: into God's house comes no one unclean, οὐ ψυχικὸς οὐ σαρκικός, ἀλλὰ τηρεῖται πνευματικοῖς μόνοις, ὅπου δεῖ γενομένους βαλεῖν τὰ

καταλελειμμένοι διακοσμήσαι καὶ διατυπῶσαι καὶ διορθώσασθαι καὶ τελειῶσαι τὰς ψυχὰς κάτω φύσιν ἐχούσας μένειν ἐν τούτῳ τῷ δαστήματι.[69]

Here, on the soil of Gnosticism, we look into a rich and diverse imaginative world. But in broad areas[69] we still encounter specifically Pauline terminology (it is highly noteworthy that according to Clement, Strom. IV, 13.93.1, even the Montanists described those who adhered to the Great Church as ψυχικοί), whether it is that the Gnostics here are already dependent upon a few passages in the Pauline epistles or—as in any case is more probable—that Paul is already affected by a more widely distributed language usage which also penetrated into Gnosticism (*vide supra*, pp. 186-87).

Most of all, however, the same *substance* is present here as with Paul. Whether the higher aspect of man is characterized as σπινθήρ, λαμπηδών, or φῶς; as χαρακτήρ, σπέρμα, or φύσις θεοῦ; as θεία ψυχή, or πνεῦμα— essentially it arrives at the same thing, at plain anthropological dualism: The highest and best in man appears as something simply set in opposition to his (lower) nature, and the unity of man's personal life is dispersed. Therefore, as for Paul human nature is already divided into two different classes of men, that of the pneumatics and that of the psychics, and the man of ordinary stripe for Paul stands in contradictory opposition to the pneumatic man, so also Gnosticism rests altogether upon the basic presupposition of two metaphysically different classes of men. This principle is already found expressed in Satornilus in the sharpest formulation: δύο γὰρ πεπλάσθαι ἀπ' ἀρχῆς ἀνθρώπους φάσκει, ἕνα τὸν ἀγαθὸν καὶ ἕνα τὸν φαῦλον. ἐξ ὧν δύο εἶναι τὰ γένη τῶν ἀνθρώπων ἐν κόσμῳ, ἀγαθῶν τε καὶ πονηρῶν.[70] And Gnosticism in all its manifestations holds fast to this contrast, only that in the Valentinian schools it is moderated in favor of the "ecclesiastics," into the well-known threefold division. Here it is connected with the well-defined attitude of the mystery- and sacramental piety, so that the naïve contrast between initiated and uninitiated now appears to be based upon a metaphysical foundation.

Nevertheless, in one respect the Gnostics go far beyond Paul. The dualism of Paul is more an attitude than a reflective world view. For him the radical difference between the pneumatic and the psychic or sarkic man is

---

ἐνδύματα καὶ πάντας γενέσθαι νυμφίους ἀπηρσενωμένους διὰ τοῦ παρθενικοῦ πνεύματος.

[69] Hippolytus VII, 25.2, p. 202.26. Cf. Valentinus' own statements in Clement, Strom. IV, 13.89.2 (Irenaeus I, 6.1, ἅλας καὶ φῶς τοῦ κόσμου). Heracleon in Origen in Joann. IV, 39, Hilgenfeld, 492.26-27.

[70] Epiphanius, Haer. 23.2. Cf. in Irenaeus I, 24.2: cf. also the Sethians in Epiph. 39.2.

practically given. He does not reflect further upon the "whence" of this manifestation of two essentially different classes of men. When he does reflect upon it, he retreats to the inscrutable counsel of God and the mysteries of predestination and of eternal election. He does not reflect upon how the unity of the human ego can be maintained if the innate human nature stands in sharp opposition to the divine world and the higher existence of the pneuma is wholly a gift of divine grace. For him the human ego at best becomes a pattern empty of any content, which receives its distinctive character altogether from without, from the powers of the σάρξ or of the πνεῦμα (Χριστός). He revels in contradictions and paradoxes: "I no longer live, but Christ lives in me."

With the Gnostics Paul's fragmentary views come together into one large continuous whole. The dividedness of human nature acquires a metaphysical background. The favored Gnostics are sparks of light from another world which have sunk down from above into this darkness—whether the originally pure light has been lost to the darkness, or whether by means of an attack the darkness has stolen some elements of light from the upper world. They are the seed (σπέρμα) or emanation (ἀπόρροια) of the most high divine Mother, who could not keep the fullness of her love to herself but let some of it sink down into the lower world, or who herself fell from the upper world and with her children longs for liberation. They are by nature sons of God who have lost their homeland; they are of the essence (ὁμοούσιοι) of the enigmatic and mysterious Primal Man, who once sank into matter and entered into an unnatural connection with it, or who was taken captive by the demons of darkness. This new metaphysics of Gnosticism is worked into the Mosaic account of the creation of man.[71] Paul had already proclaimed that the first man had come forth from the hand of God as an inferior being, that he was *only* ψυχὴ ζῶσα. The Gnostics now understand it more precisely. Original Jewish fantasies[72] spun out of Gen. 1:26 about the participation of angelic powers in the creation of man are drawn in, as is the creation myth in Plato's *Timaeus*. Thus emerges the doctrine that half-demonic angelic powers or the demiurge created the lower nature of man, but that the higher heavenly powers, whether the Mother or the

[71] Cf. *Hauptprobleme*, pp. 12, 17, 19-21, 27, 34, 48, *et passim*.

[72] On the Jewish tradition, cf. Ginzberg, *Die Haggada bei den Kirchenvätern und in der apokr. Literatur* (1900), pp. 19-21; see there also the passages from the church fathers which ascribe the doctrine now to the Jews, now to the heretics. In circles of the Jewish Diaspora (Slavonic Enoch, Recension A 30.8; Pseudo-Clem. Hom. XVI, 11-12) the passage was applied to Wisdom; then in the church to the Spirit or to Spirit and Son (see below, Chap. X).

Primal Man or the Logos, deposited in this helpless creature the higher spark of light, the heavenly sperma, with the help but without the knowledge of the intermediate demonic powers, and thus a spark of divine essence is present in humanity.

The pneuma doctrine of Gnosticism now also appears in this context. The Gnostics are pneumatics because from the very first they possess the gift of the pneuma. The πνεῦμα is the same as the spark of light which has sunk into the darkness, as the σπέρμα or the ἀπόρροια of the φωτεινὴ μήτηρ. τὸ δὲ κύημα τῆς μητρὸς αὐτῆς τῆς ᾽Αχαμώθ . . . ὁμοούσιον ὑπάρχον τῇ μητρί, πνευματικόν, or: τὸ δὲ σῶμα ἀπὸ τοῦ χοὸς καὶ τὸ σαρκικὸν ἀπὸ τῆς ὕλης, τὸν δὲ πνευματικὸν ἄνθρωπον ἀπὸ τῆς μητρὸς τῆς ᾽Αχαμώθ (Iren. I, 5.6).

IV. *Pauline and Gnostic Doctrine of Redemption.* One cannot fail to recognize that with all this the *specific, stark theory of redemption,* as it is found in Paul, actually suffers a certain weakening. If the divine higher nature is from the first something native to the elect, then to a certain degree the absolute necessity of a redemption occurring at a definite time disappears. At least no longer is something absolutely new introduced into the human race by means of the redemption. It can only involve an awakening of the divine soul which has sunk down into this earthly world, a fanning and igniting of the heavenly spark which was nearly extinguished. Indeed, it could almost appear as if Gnosticism were an extension of the basic Platonic outlook.[73] As the Greek sage reflects upon the better part of his soul, which comes from above, the soul of his soul, and thus regains the way to the celestial homeland, so also Gnosis would be the self-reflection of the pious one upon the divine element of light in him, upon its origin and its destiny: ἐστὶν δὲ οὐ τὸ λουτρὸν μόνον τὸ ἐλευθεροῦν ἀλλὰ καὶ ἡ γνῶσις, τίνες ἦμεν, τί γεγόναμεν, ποῦ ἦμεν, ποῦ ἐνεβλήθημεν, ποῦ σπεύδομεν, πόθεν λυτρούμεθα, τί γέννησις, τί ἀναγέννησις.[74] Carpocrates

---

[73] Cf. the characteristic formulas: ἐλθὼν οὖν ὁ Σωτὴρ τὴν ψυχὴν ἐξύπνισεν, ἐξῆψεν δὲ τὸν σπινθῆρα . . . τὸν μὲν χοῦν καθάπερ τέφραν ἀπεφύσα καὶ ἐχώριζεν, ἐξῆπτε δὲ τὸν σπινθῆρα καὶ ἐξωοπύρει (Exc. ex Theod. 3); further, the statements of the Naassenes (Hippolytus V, 7.30, p. 86.3) on the soul-awakening God Hermes-Anthropos (ψυχὰς . . . τῶν μνηστήρων . . . τῶν ἐξυπνισμένων καὶ ἀνεμνησμένων). The Sethians in Hippolytus V, 21.9, p. 124.9: ἡ τοῦ . . . φωτὸς ἀκτὶς οἰκείου χωρίου ἐκ διδασκαλίας καὶ μαθήσεως μεταλαβοῦσα σπεύδει πρὸς τὸν λόγον τὸν ἄνωθεν ἐλθόντα (cf. Peratae in V, 17.6, p. 115.1; 17.8, p. 115.6, τοὺς ἐξυπνισμένους). Hermet. XIII, 2: τοῦτο τὸ γένος ὦ τέκνον οὐ διδάσκεται ἀλλά, ὅταν θέλῃ ὑπὸ τοῦ θεοῦ ἀναμιμνήσκεται.

[74] Exc. ex Theod. 78; cf. Hippolytus VII, 26 (self-awareness of the "Archon" of the Basilidians in similar formulas); VI, 32 (self-awareness of the Sophia among the Valen-

and his followers taught, in fact, that Jesus, because he had a "firm and pure soul," was able to remember all that he had seen in the higher world, and that for this reason God had sent to him a power with which he could scorn the creators of the world and make his way through their spheres to the upper world. The same happened to those who had received a soul like that of Jesus: *animas ipsorum ex eadem circumlatione devenientes et ideo similiter contemnentes mundi fabricatores, eadem dignas habitas esse virtute et rursus in idem abire.*[75] Here everything—apart from the passing mention of the power sent from God—is rational and is thought out in the style of platonizing philosophy. Circles of the Valentinians and the Basilidians also appear to have approached this rational attitude. At least the polemic of Clement of Alexandria, in a context in which he speaks of the φύσει σώζεσθαι of the Valentinians and the φύσει πιστὸς καὶ ἐκλεκτός of the Basilidians, seems to point to this: ἦν δ'ἂν καὶ δίχα τῆς τοῦ σωτῆρος παρουσίας χρόνῳ ποτὲ ἀναλάμψαι δύνασθαι τὴν φύσιν. εἰ δὲ ἀναγκαίαν τὴν ἐπιδημίαν τοῦ κυρίου φήσαιεν, οἴχεται αὐτοῖς τὰ τῆς φύσεως ἰδιώματα.[76]

But all this is still only appearance or the most extreme consequence here and there. Fundamentally Gnosticism remains—this was already earlier brought out—a radical religion of redemption. It is not the opinion of the Gnostics that the half-extinguished spark could, from its own nature and power, again be fanned and burst into flame. The elements of light, the fallen Sperma, the ἀπόρροιαι are in hopeless captivity here below. A redemption is required that comes down from above and comes in from without. Gnosis is not the reflection of the intellect or of the better spiritual ego upon itself; Gnosis is mysterious revelation and redemption brought about in vision and ecstasy through initiation and sacrament. It is not the philosopher who is the guide of the Gnostics but the mystagogue, and it is not philosophical study that saves the soul but participation in the mystery society and the initiation.[77]

---

tinians). Acta Thomae chap. 15 (τίς ἤμην καὶ τίς καὶ πῶς ὑπάρχω νῦν, ἵνα πάλιν γένωμαι ὃ ἤμην). Zosimus in Reitzenstein, *Poimandres*, p. 103: πορεύεσθαι (τὸν πνευματικὸν ἄνθρωπον) δὲ διὰ μόνου τοῦ ζητεῖν ἑαυτὸν καὶ θεὸν ἐπιγνόντα κρατεῖν τὴν ἀκατονόμαστον τριάδα. On these world view formulas, cf. Norden, *Agnostos Theos*, pp. 102 ff. Cf. also I Clem. 38.3; II Clem. 1.2.

[75] Irenaeus I, 25.1-2; cf. Epiph. 26.10, 4 (Gnostics), Χριστὸν . . . δείξαντα τοῖς ἀνθρώποις ταύτην τὴν γνῶσιν.

[76] Strom. V, 1.3.3.; cf. also IV, 13.91.2.

[77] How easily the concept of "Gnosis" can turn into that of magic is shown by Epiphanius 31.7.8, p. 397.9 H.: τὸ δὲ τάγμα τὸ πνευματικὸν ἑαυτοὺς λέγουσιν. ὥσπερ καὶ

However, with this supernatural character of the religion of redemption, the idea of a redemption wrought at a definite point in history is by no means given. Indeed, if one keeps his eyes on the main thing, one can first of all formulate the judgment: *in Gnostic redemption theology, myth everywhere takes the place of the historical.* The development which began with Paul is completed here with uncanny speed. *If Paul has already woven a redemption myth around the historical figure of Jesus of Nazareth, here now the historical is altogether swallowed up by the myth.*

For the Gnostic, redemption is not something which is at one time and at one point perfected, but something which happens repeatedly and in all ages. Ever since the primeval times in which the unnatural mixing of light and darkness took place, the Gnostic soul strives upward out of the depths of darkness toward the eternal home of light. And it is the same (basically taken, independent of all history) process of liberation, the same way which leads it to the goal, now and always: the separation from the lower sensual elements of existence and the surrender to the higher celestial world. Under these circumstances, can any concretely and historically given divine redeemer figure at all have direct significance for redemption? It can in particular in one connection, insofar as its myth, which it has itself experienced, becomes of exemplary or prototypical significance for the Gnostic soul and is relived by the soul in sacred, sacramental actions.

Specific examples will make this clear. One such myth of prototypical significance is the Primal-Man doctrine which is widespread in Gnosticism. The myth relates[78]: In primeval times, in the beginning of the world, a divine being, charmed by the beauty of Physis, fell from the highest world through the spheres of the planets, which shared with him their unhealthful or lower, sensual gifts, into matter, and lost to it a part of his being.[79]

---

γνωστικούς, καὶ μηδὲ καμάτου ἐπιδεομένους ἢ μόνον τῆς γνώσεως καὶ τῶν ἐπιρρημάτων τῶν αὐτῶν μυστηρίων. Of course in the Zosimus text adduced by Reitzenstein, *Poimandres*, p. 103, the πνευματικὸς ἄνθρωπος expressly rejects magic. But the renunciation shows how much Gnosis and magic are used to being bound up together.

[78] Cf. therewith the statements already given in Chap. V about the dying and rising God. The above sketch reproduces something of the doctrine of redemption of the Poimandres. On the broader religio-historical connections, see *Hauptprobleme*, pp. 160-223.

[79] This sinking down into matter and thus the beginning of creation begins with the Anthropos being reflected in matter and being inflamed with love for his own image. Traces of this view are widespread in Gnosticism: cf. the beginning of the Apocryphon Joannis; my statements about the Gnostics of Plotinus (*Hauptprobleme*, p. 188); Naassenes in Hippolytus V, 8 (particularly p. 91). It might be rewarding to explore the further ramified connections of this myth (cf. also *Hauptprobleme*, p. 205.1). [Cf. Bousset, ZNW XIX (1919/20), pp. 50 ff., and Reitzenstein, *Das mandäische Buch des Herrn der Grösse*, SAH, 1919, No. 12, pp. 25 ff. Bultmann].

Only with great effort he was again lifted up out of matter, stripped off the lower nature of matter, and restored to the planetary powers what belonged to them. *And we, it is said, are the race of this Primal Man.* With one part of his nature man stems from the higher, divine world and is immortal; with the other part he is mortal, has come under slavery to the planetary powers, and is subject to Heimarmene. But he is to be aware that he comes from the world of light and life, and under the leading of Nous is to make his way upward into the world of radiant light. Then after death his spirit will pass through the planetary spheres, will lay aside the hateful garments which come from those worlds, and, singing songs and hymns, will enter into the world of the highest deity. Indeed, in the mystery in the sacred initiation, he can even now, while he is still living, experience this heavenward journey of the soul and its being taken up into the deity.

This is still halfway pure Platonism, and yet it is already Gnostic redemption theory. The myth has developed its force; the figure of a mythical deity, to be sure a pale and abstract one, stands before the soul of the Gnostic. The soul does not find the way to the homeland by itself; it must be united with its prototype, the pre-terrestrial Anthropos; it is to learn to feel itself a part of his being and of his power; it is to know that what once took place in the primal beginnings now has validity for all times; and from all this, it is to draw power and blessed assurance: The Gnostic does not stand alone but in great, powerful connections taking place with an inner necessity, which bear him beyond the faintness and weakness of his own solitary striving.

A second great Gnostic myth runs as follows[80]: the Gnostics are sons (seed, σπέρμα, *vide supra,* p. 259) of the celestial Mother. Once this Mother-goddess, in an impetuous impulse of love, left the upper heavenly worlds; she lost her celestial bridegroom (Syzygos) and sank down into the dark world of matter. For a long time she tarried in lostness and imprisonment, surrounded by dark demonic figures. Then a most high celestial god, a Soter, approached her and redeemed her from her loneliness and lostness and freed her from the demons. Full of shame, when she saw her rescuer, the lonely one covered herself, but then she hurried toward him rejoicing, went with him into the bridal chamber, and consummated the ἱερὸς

---

[80] We find the myth already among the "Gnostics" who are to be regarded as the fore-runners of Valentinianism (Iren. I, 30, also probably Apocryphon Joannis; Pistis Sophia, were already further elaborated); then esp. pronounced and characteristic in the Valentinian schools.

γάμος.[81] What took place here as a prototype takes place ever anew. Thus every Gnostic soul has its Syzygos, is the bride of a heavenly double, its angel.[82] As surely as the Μήτηρ has found her Soter, so will the soul embrace its bridegroom and by means of this union be lifted up into the higher world, freed from the lower one. The goal of the soul is the celestial wedding. In the sacrament, in the sacred consecration of the bridal chamber it can, even here on earth, have a foretaste of that holy union and in shivers of rapture experience the mystery: "We must be united into a single being. First of all receive grace through me and from me. Adorn yourself as a bride who awaits her bridegroom, so that I may become you and you I. Let the seed of light be deposited in your bridal chamber. Receive from me (the mystagogue) the bridegroom; receive him and let yourself be received by him. Behold, grace has come down upon you." [83] Thus once again the myth has become full of prototypical, redemptive power. The Gnostic does not gain redemption only by beholding himself and reflecting upon his own self. He must be joined in faith with the Μήτηρ, must be aware of himself as a part, as σπέρμα and ἀπόρροια of her essence, must let himself be borne by the powers of redemption which stem from her and are at work in her, must unite with her in the sacrament of the ἱερὸς γάμος; only thus does he gain salvation. The Gnostics are οἱ πνευματικοὶ ἄνθρωποι, οἱ τὴν τελείαν γνῶσιν ἔχοντες περὶ θεοῦ καὶ (οἱ) τῆς Ἀχαμὼθ μεμυημένοι [δὲ] μυστήρια (Iren. I, 6.1).

[81] Evidence in *Hauptprobleme*, pp. 267 ff. The myth of the ἱερὸς γάμος is esp. clearly recognizable in Hippolytus VI, 34.

[82] This theory emerges esp. clearly in the Excerpta ex Theodoto; cf. particularly chaps. 21, 22, 35-36, 64; but see also Iren., I, 7.1 and the evidence about the sacrament of the bridal chamber in the following footnote. The entire school of Valentinus appears to have been dominated by this basic idea. Cf. *Hauptprobleme*, pp. 315 ff.

[83] Irenaeus I, 13.3 (Sacrament of the Marcosians); see the evidence in *Hauptprobleme*, pp. 315-17. In addition, the following passages: Irenaeus, in III, 15.2, sarcastically tells of the mystic who has been initiated: *neque in caelo neque in terra putat se esse, sed intra Pleroma introisse et complexum jam angelum suum*. I, 6.4: δεῖν αὐτοὺς ἀεὶ τὸ τῆς συζυγίας μελετᾶν μυστήριον. Clement III, 4.27: οἱ γὰρ τρισάθλιοι τὴν σαρκικὴν καὶ συνουσιαστικὴν κοινωνίαν ἱεροφαντοῦσιν καὶ ταύτην οἴονται εἰς τὴν βασιλείαν αὐτοὺς ἀνάγειν τοῦ θεοῦ. Cf. Heracleon (according to Origen) in Hilgenfeld, pp. 483.20; 492.6, 16; 493.1-2. Epiph. Haer. 31.7. We would be glad to know more details about the course of events in the sacrament. Irenaeus says (I, 21.3) that among the Valentinians a νυμφών was prepared for the initiate. Tertullian indicates (adv. Valent. 1) that the symbol of the phallus played a role in the ceremony. To think of an actual achievement of sexual union (by the mystagogue with the initiate), which the account in Iren. I, 13.3 could suggest, is forbidden at least for the Valentinians by the explicit explanation of Clement III, 4.29.3 (πνευματικὴ κοινωνία). But precisely in comparison with the Valentinians he accuses another Gnostic sect of σαρκικὴ καὶ συνουσιαστικὴ κοινωνία (see above); cf. the obscene mysteries which Epiphanius 26.4 relates of the Gnostics.

A third myth[84] relates: In the very beginning a divine redeemer hero journeyed down out of the heights of heaven into the deepest depths of Hades and of hell. There below he had to struggle with the powers and demons; it was necessary to outwit them and to seize from them the secret of their strength. Unrecognized, he first descended into the lower worlds, took on many different forms in order to deceive the demons, and became like them. But after the great work was done and the power of the demons was broken, he ascended victorious and now, in his own radiant glory so that all who see him marvel, has returned to the heavenly heights.

This redemption myth has of course first of all an objective meaning. That the demons were vanquished is a once-for-all fact that lies in the past, which as such has its value and its import. But here also the once-for-all event becomes a symbol that serves as an example. The believer is united with the saving deity and experiences with the deity all the terror of the journey to Hades and all the triumph in the victory over the demons; with the redeemer god the believer also experiences the heavenward journey, the glorious transformation into a radiant light-being of the higher world, the appearance before God's throne, the triumphing and rejoicing in heaven. An especially good example of this is now provided for us in the Solomonic Odes. In them the question as to the "I" who is speaking in them is often so difficult to solve because here in fact the "I" of the pious singer frequently is completely merged with the Messiah, so that in a particular case one hardly knows who is spoken of. The theme, however, which above all is being sung here is the heaven-and-hell pilgrimage, whether of the pious initiate or of the Messiah.[85]

It has already been shown that with all this the Gnostics' doctrine of redemption has its closest parallel in the idea, specifically peculiar to the

---

[84] We have already dealt with this myth and its origin in the sections on the descent into Hades (Chap. I, Appendix) and on Paul's doctrine of redemption. The conversion of the idea of the descent into Hades into the appearance of the redeemer here on earth, already presumed for Paul, is present in Gnosticism in an especially clear form. For Gnosticism indeed this earth and even the lower celestial spheres are the realm of darkness and of evil matter. Documentation for the idea of the descent of the redeemer through the lower world, his transformation, and the maintenance of the incognito: *Hauptprobleme*, pp. 238 ff. The best sources are the half-Gnostic pieces: Ascensio Jesaiae and the "Pearl," Acta Thomae 111 (for this, cf. the work of F. Haase, *Zur bardesanischen Gnosis* (1910), pp. 53 ff.; this work is comprehensive and gives a good discussion of all the possibilities of interpretation); within Gnosticism above all the Mandaean myth of the descent into hell of Hibil-Ziwa (Manda d'Hayya, Ginza r., 6th and 8th Tractates). Here the scene again is placed in the underworld. About the religio-historical connections, Dibelius, *Die Geisterwelt im Glauben des Paulus* (1909), pp. 203 ff. Hans Schmidt, *Jona* (1907), pp. 172 ff.

[85] Cf. particularly Ode 36, then Odes 11, 15, 17 (Messiah?), 20, 21, 22 (?), (25), 35, 38.

apostle Paul, of the Christian's dying and rising with Christ. Here too the unique historical event—without its reality being attacked by Paul and without its objective worth being canceled—has become a prototypical symbolic myth of present significance. Suffering, dying, and rising now signify for the redeemer the same as for all those who follow him, who are merged with him into a unity and, borne and moved by his power, experience what he experiences. And as in Gnosticism, this experience is thought of as in part yet to come, being perfected in the future, but again in part as tangibly present, occurring in the sacrament (of baptism).

V. *The Connecting of the Figure of Jesus of Nazareth with the Gnostic Redeemer Myths.* Now at last we can understand the special Christology of the Gnostics. It emerges in the fact that somehow, however well or poorly it is done, the figure of Jesus of Nazareth is connected with these mythical redeemer figures or with these redeemer myths.

Especially distinctive is the form and manner in which, among the Valentinians and the sects related to them, the redeemer figure is worked into the myth of the redeemer's ἱερὸς γάμος with Sophia. There can be no doubt at all: For all these sects the actual redemption mystery lay in the union of the Soter with Sophia, which simply has nothing at all to do with the history of Jesus of Nazareth, and in the similar experience of the Gnostic in the sacrament of the bridal chamber. Now people combine the figure of that savior-deity in some way, however slight, with Jesus and superficially attach the story of Jesus' appearing on earth to that myth. Thus[86] the Gnostics whose system Irenaeus (I, 30) has handed on to us asserted that Sophia in her loneliness had appealed to her heavenly mother, and the latter had sent the Christ to her. Unrecognized, he hurried down through all the seven heavens: *et descendentem Christum in hunc mundum induisse primum sororem suam Sophiam et exultasse utrosque refrigerantes super se invicem; et hoc esse sponsum et sponsam definiunt.* Then however the Christ thus united with Sophia descended upon the already prepared Jesus (I, 30.12). And now begins the account of the sojourn of this miraculous being upon earth, though of course the account is compressed into a small space (for here nothing essentially new happens in addition except the proclamation of the heavenly mysteries).

Similarly, in the Pistis Sophia the appearing of Jesus on earth is only

---

[86] See the more detailed evidence in *Hauptprobleme,* pp. 260 ff.

artificially woven into the narrative of the liberation of the goddess. In its present form the narrative falls into two halves. First is told how in the primordial age the redeemer (now Jesus) has freed the Pistis Sophia from her oppression in the world ruled by the demons. But this liberation was only provisional. The final redemption comes only after the completed earthly life and the victorious ascension of Jesus. Thus the narrative moves in tiresome and monotonous repetitions. Originally the entire myth naturally took place in the primordial times. Now the earthly life of Jesus appears as an episode of the myth, surrounded and bracketed by the myth on both sides, altogether merged into it.[87]

The establishment of this connection is still more painstaking among the Valentinian sects. In Hippolytus' presentation[88] it is explicitly said that the Valentinians know three Christs: first the Syzygos of the ἅγιον πνεῦμα in the world of the thirty Aeons, then the common offspring of the world of the Aeons, the ἰσόζυγος τῆς ἔξω σοφίας (thus the hero of the myth of the ἱερὸς γάμος), and third, the one born of Mary εἰς ἐπανόρθωσιν τῆς κτίσεως τῆς καθ' ἡμᾶς. Also in the system described by Irenaeus (I, 6.1) the one who appeared on earth (although he is called Soter here) seems not to be identical with the heavenly bridegroom of Sophia. He is in general a more subordinate being. Indeed it is shown here quite clearly that for the pneumatics themselves this redeemer possesses only slight significance. It is expressly stated here—one is almost shocked by the plainness—that the hylics are incapable of redemption, that from their origin the pneumatics are already the light and the salt of the earth, that therefore a decision is involved only for the psychics: καὶ τὸν Σωτῆρα ἐπὶ τοῦτο παραγεγονέναι τὸ ψυχικόν, ἐπεὶ καὶ αὐτεξούσιόν ἐστιν, ὅπως αὐτὸ σώσῃ. The Valentinian Gnostic does not need the earthly Jesus and his appearing; his heart and his piety are attached to the myth of the marriage of the Soter and Sophia. The speculation about the figure of Jesus also, then, as it is presented in this connection, appears after all entirely to correspond to this. It is here stated that Jesus received his pneumatic essence from Achamoth, that he furthermore had put on the psychic Christ from the Demiurge, and that finally he had received the psychic body ἀπὸ τῆς οἰκονομίας. Nothing is said here of a higher essence which was then bestowed upon Jesus at his baptism. This latter, still more complicated view, i.e., the hypothesis of a fourfold division

---

[87] *Hauptprobleme*, pp. 271 ff.
[88] Ref. VI, 36.

of his nature, is explicitly attributed in I, 7.2 to another tendency in Valentinianism. In the statements of Irenaeus in I, 6.2 an older source is present[89] which in part recurs with the same wording in the Excerpta ex Theodoto 58-59.[90] In the corresponding presentation of this conclusion in the Excerpta, Achamoth (Sophia) is even described as the τεκοῦσα[91] of Jesus. Thus he appears as an altogether subordinate spiritual being who in his essence does not extend beyond the sphere of the fallen Sophia.[92] It is precisely this Jesus who, for the sake of the psychics, the "ecclesiastics," has been thus accepted into the great system of aeons. Then they gradually went further in the compromise and Jesus was allowed, as it were, to be moved up in the ranks of the system of aeons. Now either he is in some fashion identified with the Soter,[93] the common offspring of the world of aeons, who joins with Achamoth in the ἱερὸς γάμος, or it is asserted that a higher essence had descended upon this tripartite Jesus only at his baptism.[94] But along with it the older view is stubbornly maintained, that Jesus received the higher pneumatic element from Sophia, so that now there enters an unnecessary doubling of this higher nature in Jesus, first from Sophia, then from the aeon which descends upon him at his baptism. This again gave occasion to new combina-

---

[89] Cf. the evidence best in C. Barth, *Die Interpretation des N. T. in der valentinianischen Gnosis* (1911), pp. 12-18. The common source, however, is not, as Barth assumed, Ptolemaeus (Iren. I, 8.5), but a writing to which Ptolemaeus appears to have supplied an appendix (exposition of the Johannine prologue). Schwartz, *Aporieen*, GGN, 1908, p. 137.

[90] Exc. ex Theod. 60-61 with the complicated Christology do not belong here. We find no trace of a parallel in Irenaeus.

[91] Jesus has taken to himself τὴν ἐκκλησίαν (τὸ ἐκλεκτὸν καὶ τὸ κλητόν). 58: τὸ μὲν παρὰ τῆς τεκούσης τὸ πνευματικόν, τὸ δὲ ἐκ τῆς οἰκονομίας τὸ ψυχικόν. 59: σπέρμα μὲν οὖν πρῶτον (τὸ) παρὰ τῆς τεκούσης ἐνεδύσατο. (Or, as I do not assume, should the τεκοῦσα only be connected here with the τὸ πνευματικόν?) Should not τῆς μητρὸς οὖν μετὰ τοῦ υἱοῦ καὶ τῶν σπερμάτων εἰσελθούσης εἰς τὸ πλήρωμα in 54.2 also be connected with Jesus? Note that in 34 as in 59 the demiurge is identified as τόπος.

[92] In chap. 58 Jesus appears as ὁ μέγας ἀγωνιστής. On this and on the view of Jesus as the son of the "Mother," cf. the hymn in Acta Thomae, chap. 49: ἐλθὲ ἡ κοινωνία τοῦ ἄρρενος, ἐλθὲ ἡ κοινωνοῦσα ἐν πᾶσι τοῖς ἄθλοις τοῦ γενναίου ἀθλητοῦ, . . . ἐλθὲ ἡ ἀπόκρυφος μήτηρ.

[93] Exc. ex Theod. 41, τὸ φῶς ὃ πρῶτον προήγαγεν τουτέστι τὸν Ἰησοῦν ὁ αἰτησάμενος τοὺς αἰῶνας Χριστός. Cf., e.g., Exc. ex Theod. 23 and 35.

[94] For more details, see below. Here, incidentally, the real crux of the dispute between the Anatolian and Italian branches (Ptolemaeus, Heracleon) appears to lie; Hippolytus tells of this dispute in VI, 35. Hippolytus connects the whole question at issue with an apparent *Quisquilium* of whether the σῶμα of Jesus was πνευματικόν or ψυχικόν. In actuality it involved the question of whether the one born of the virgin was already a pneumatic being, or whether the higher element had only entered into Jesus at the baptism. Note the sentence in 165.6: ψυχικόν φασι τὸ σῶμα τοῦ Ἰησοῦ γεγονέναι, καὶ διὰ τοῦτο ἐπὶ τοῦ βαπτίσματος τὸ πνεῦμα ὡς περιστερὰ κατελήλυθε, τουτέστιν ὁ λόγος ὁ τῆς μητρὸς ἄνωθεν τῆς Σοφίας (cf. VI, 36.4, p. 166.12, τῆς ἔξω Σοφίας).

tions[95] which we cannot pursue here. It is sufficient that one sees clearly how here the figure of Jesus gradually permeates an already existing mythological system.[96]

Finally even the mythical figure of the Primal Man which we have already discussed was amalgamated with the figure of Jesus,[97] to be sure only in some few Gnostic systems, most of all in the Naassene Preaching, and likewise

[95] According to Irenaeus I, 7.2, the Soter, who appears in the form of the dove, brings τὸ ἀπὸ (read thus instead of αὐτὸ) τῆς ᾿Αχαμὼθ σπέρμα πνευματικόν down with him. According to Exc. ex Theod. 26 (cf. 1-2) the visible (!) aspect of Jesus is said to have been ἡ Σοφία καὶ ἡ ᾿Εκκλησία τῶν σπερμάτων τῶν διαφερόντων; the invisible, however, was the "Name" (which descended upon Jesus at the baptism; cf. with this 22.6; 31.4). The complicated Christology of the Pistis Sophia also belongs here. According to it Jesus, who himself by nature belonged to the world of the highest aeons, took a power (i.e., his pneumatic essence) from the Barbelo (=Sophia), a soul from Sabaoth the Good (i.e., the demiurge), and put all this into the body of Mary, in order to be born through her body; chap. 8, 64.

[96] Here we may incidentally refer to another mythological fantasy which is readily connected with the assumption of such a multiple division of the nature of the redeemer. Cf. Reitzenstein, *Historia Monachorum*, p. 200. According to the statements of the Gnostics in Irenaeus, the redeemer must assume to himself the nature of all those whom he has come to redeem. This theme enjoys great favor in the Gnostic circles. It was enlarged into the idea of the redeemer who is in various forms and is capable of being transformed, who pervades everything and is found everywhere; and then new motifs of explicitly mythological character are adapted to it. Basilides, Iren. I, 24.4: *quoniam enim virtus incorporalis erat et Nus innati Patris, transfiguratum, quemadmodum vellet, et sic ascendisse ad eum, qui miserat eum.* Cf. *Corpus Herm.*, Asclep. 56.4 (omniformis). (On the various transformations of Jesus during his descent with the aim of escaping the attention of the demons, see Bousset, *Hauptprobleme*, pp. 239 ff.) The ability of the redeemer to transform himself is a favorite motif in the apocryphal acts: Act. Petri Verc. 20; Acta Jo. 82, 90-93, 98; Acta Thomae 10 (ὁ ἐν πᾶσιν ὢν καὶ διερχόμενος διὰ πάντων); 48, ὁ πολύμορφος (cf. 44, the πολύμορφος δαίμων); 80 (Syriac translation); 153. In the apocryphal Gospel of the Gnostics in Epiphan. Haer. 26.3, a saying of the redeemer runs thus: ἐγὼ σὺ καὶ σὺ ἐγώ, καὶ ὅπου ἐὰν ᾖς, ἐγὼ ἐκεῖ εἰμι καὶ ἐν ἅπασίν εἰμι ἐσπαρμένος· καὶ ὅθεν ἐὰν θέλῃς συλλέγεις με, ἐμὲ δὲ συλλέγων ἑαυτὸν συλλέγεις. This pantheistic tendency is found also in some of the famous logia of Jesus of Behnesa (discussed in this connection in Reitzenstein, *Poimandres*, pp. 239 ff.; see there also the parallels from the Hermetic literature XIII, 11; XI, 20). On the basis of the revelations of Bitys, Zosimus quotes the saying of Hermes: φησὶ γὰρ ὁ Νοῦς ἡμῶν· ὁ δὲ υἱὸς τοῦ θεοῦ πάντα δυνάμενος καὶ πάντα γινόμενος, ὅ τι θέλει ὡς θέλει,φαίνει ἑκάστῳ (Reitzenstein, *Poimandres*, p. 105; cf. Naassenes, Hippolytus V, 9.4, p. 98.14). In all these statements there appears to be present a widespread mythical (legendary) motif. It also plays a part in the narrative of Simon Magus, Pseudo-Clem. Recog. II, 9, Hom. II, 32. Especially interesting is the note in Martyr. Petri et Pauli, chap. 14, ed. Lipsius-Bonnet, I, 132: ἐνηλλάττετο (sc., Simon) γὰρ τῇ τε ὄψει καὶ τῇ ἡλικίᾳ διαφόρους μορφὰς καὶ ἐβάκχευεν ὑπουργὸν ἔχων τὸν διάβολον. (For this reason Nero takes Simon to be the υἱὸν θεοῦ.) The curious ἐβάκχευεν leads to the myth of the various transformations with which Dionysos seeks to escape from the Titans pursuing him (Nonnus, *Dionysiaca*, VI, 155 ff.). The myth of the battle of the Primal Man with the demonic powers as told by the Manichaeans exhibits a surprising parallel; cf. Baur, *Das manichäische Religionssystem*, pp. 53-54.

[97] Here the old title ὁ υἱὸς τοῦ ἀνθρώπου appears to have given rise to new combinations, Iren. I, 30.1; Hippolytus V, 7 on the Naassenes.

when in Jewish-Christian Gnosticism (the Pseudo-Clementines)[98] Jesus is interpreted as the primeval Adam and accordingly it is taught that this Adam (the prophet) appeared in the most diverse bearers of revelation, in order at last to come to rest in Jesus.[99] And in this connection it once again becomes especially clear how also the early Christian hymn to Jesus as the conqueror of Hades means nothing more than the transferral of a myth to the historical figure of Jesus.

VI. *Jesus' Earthly Appearing.* If Gnosticism thus succeeded in creating a place somehow and somewhere in its systems for the redeemer figure of Jesus of Nazareth, yet there remained for it an almost insoluble difficulty. For its basic outlook the idea was indeed unendurable that Jesus had lived as a real man in a genuine human existence. Such a contact of the upper celestial world and of an aeon stemming from that world with the filth of lower matter must have appeared to them once and for all impossible.

The most ancient answer which the Gnostics gave to this question was simply to cut the knot. It was roundly declared that Jesus on earth had possessed only an illusory form. This view of Docetism was one of the earliest manifestations of actual Christian heresy. The Johannine and the Ignatian writings show its wide distribution (*vide supra*, p. 216). Renowned leaders of the Gnostics like Satornilus,[100] the Basilides whom Irenaeus has portrayed for us[101] (though hardly the genuine one; *vide infra*), and above all Marcion, were representatives of this view. The foundation which Marcion gave to his Docetism is characteristic: διὰ τοῦτο ἀγέννητος κατῆλθεν ὁ Ἰησοῦς, ἵνα ᾖ πάσης ἀπηλλαγμένος κακίας.[102] For establishing his view of the *caro putativa* Marcion also referred to the appearances of angels in the Old Testament.[103] Marcion's pupil Apelles has already somewhat moderated the blunt Docetism of his master, in that he assumed that Jesus had come into the

---

[98] *Hauptprobleme*, pp. 171 ff.

[99] The mythological theme of the multiformity of the redeemer appears essentially to be native to the Primal-Man myths.

[100] Iren. I, 24.2.

[101] Iren. I, 24.4.

[102] Hippolytus VII, 31.6, p. 217.13. What follows is incomprehensible and is hardly based upon good information: ἀπήλλακται δὲ καὶ τῆς τοῦ ἀγαθοῦ φύσεως, ἵνα ᾖ μεσότης ὥς φησιν ὁ Παῦλος (Rom. 8:3?) καὶ ὡς αὐτὸς ὁμολογεῖ (Mark 10:18). The view probably coheres with the immediately preceding assertion of Prepon, already discussed above, that Jesus is μέσος κακοῦ καὶ ἀγαθοῦ.

[103] Tertullian adv. Marc. III, 9; cf. the Peratae in Hippolytus V, 16.10, p. 112.24: οὗτός ἐστι . . . ὁ ἐν ἐσχάταις ἡμέραις ἀνθρώπου μορφῇ φανεὶς ἐν τοῖς χρόνοις Ἡρώδου; yet V, 17.6, p. 115.2: ἐνθάδε σωματοποιηθείς. The Sethians in Epiph. 39.3: Χριστὸς Ἰησοῦς οὐχὶ κατὰ γέννησιν ἀλλὰ θαυμαστῶς ἐν τῷ κόσμῳ πεφηνώς.

world with a different kind of body, one taken from the stars and the elements (?).[104] We shall encounter this assumption again among the Valentinians in connection with the dogma of the miraculous birth.

It is then highly characteristic that the further efforts of the Gnostics to attribute a greater significance to the earthly form of Jesus' existence are very frequently connected with the baptismal story of our Gospels. This story must have once played a quite special role in the formation of christological ideas, and the conviction must have been widely prevalent that the baptism had a decisive significance for the forming of Jesus' person.[105] The Gnostics sided with this conviction. The most important fact which we encounter here is the report[106] that the Basilidians knew a celebration of Jesus' baptism on the eleventh or the fifteenth of Tybi (January 6 or 10).[107] The baptism of Jesus probably still had for them the significance of his epiphany.[108] We know from other sources that they assumed that in the baptism the διάκονος (as they called the Spirit) descended upon Jesus in the form of a dove.[109] From this fact we may conclude with some certainty that the report of the church fathers since Irenaeus about the blunt Docetism of Basilides is not to be trusted, all the less since Basilides, like no other Gnostic, emphasized the humanity of Jesus and even argued for the assumption of a remnant of sinful nature in him.[110]

But otherwise also the utilization of the baptismal narrative for Christology in Gnosticism is extraordinarily widespread, namely as the assumption that in the baptism a higher being, usually the Christ, descended upon the earthly Jesus. The First Epistle of John (2:22) already opposes the rending of Jesus Christ into a Jesus and a Christ. According to Irenaeus (I, 30.12), the Gnostics taught that the Christ who was united with Sophia had de-

---

[104] Tertullian, de carn. Christ. 6: *de sideribus inquiunt et de substantiis superioris mundi mutuatus est carnem*; adv. Marc. III, 11: *carnem utpote de elementis*; de res. carn. 2: *aut propriae qualitatis secundum haereses Valentini et Apellen.* Cf. Hilgenfeld, *Ketzergeschichte*, p. 539, n. 897.

[105] Since some common Christian conceptions are involved here, the investigation can be brought to a conclusion only in the next chapter.

[106] Clement, Strom. I, 21.146.

[107] Further see below, Chap. VII. It is to be noted that according to the Pistis Sophia the fifteenth of Tybi is the day of Jesus' ascension, also a sort of epiphany. It is the merit of Usener to have been the first to see the connections (*Weihnachtsfest*, pp. 18-19).

[108] [On this, cf. now Holl, *Der Ursprung des Epiphanienfestes*, SAB 1917, p. 425. Krüger.]

[109] Exc. ex Theod. 16. Clement, Strom. II, 8.38, καὶ παρέλκει ὁ διάκονος αὐτοῖς καὶ τὸ κήρυγμα καὶ τὸ βάπτισμα.

[110] Clement, Strom. IV, 12.83.

scended upon Jesus. Cerinthus[111] made use of this doctrine in order to connect with it the strongly accentuated rejection of the premise of a miraculous birth; he had the Christ descend upon Jesus, the son of Joseph and Mary.[112]

Especially characteristic in this connection is a reflection of the Gnostics in Irenaeus I, 30.13: *descendente autem Christo in Jesum tunc coincepisse (coepisse?) virtutes perficere et curare et annuntiare incognitum Patrem et se manifeste filium primi hominis confiteri.* A striking parallel to this statement is offered on the one side by Cerinthus,[113] and on the other side by that curious and much disputed fragment of Melito on the incarnation of Christ[114]: τὰ γὰρ μετὰ τὸ βάπτισμα ὑπὸ Χριστοῦ πραχθέντα καὶ μάλιστα τὰ σημεῖα τὴν αὐτοῦ κεκρυμμένην ἐν σαρκὶ θεότητα ἐδήλουν. With that assumption that the baptism represents a turning point of fundamental importance in the life of Jesus, the Gnostics stood on common Christian ground. Therefore their speculations here were also difficult to refute.

Finally, we have already mentioned that most of the Valentinian schools seized upon this doctrine of the significance of Jesus' baptism in order to be able to attribute to Jesus the redeemer a higher place in their system than he had possessed according to the more original and earlier view. Thus here the already very complicated Christology is still further complicated by the hypothesis that at the baptism the Soter[115] or the Christ[116] or the Logos[117] or the "Name"[118] or even the pre-temporal Anthropos[119] descended upon the already variously compounded Jesus.[120] The source which Irenaeus follows in I, 7.2 appears in this connection explicitly to have emphasized that Jesus

[111] On the baptismal narratives in the Jewish Christian Gospels, see below, Chap. VII.

[112] Irenaeus I, 26.1: *Jesum autem subjecit non ex virgine natum (impossibile enim hoc ei visum est).* This view is still further rationalized when a δύναμις is said to have come down from God upon the Jesus of Carpocrates (see above, p. 266), or when in Justin's Book of Baruch the angel of revelation Baruch comes to the man Jesus who is born of Joseph and Mary "in the days of Herod" (cf. the beginning of the Ebionite Gospel; Epiph. Haer. 30.13) and communicates to him the heavenly secrets (Hippolytus V, 26.29, p. 131.17), or when in the further developed Basilidian system the light which gradually illumines the whole world also comes to Jesus (here of course already the son of Mary): καὶ ἐφωτίσθη συνεξαφθεὶς τῷ φωτὶ τῷ λάμψαντι εἰς αὐτόν (*ibid.*, VII, 26.8, p. 205.14).

[113] Iren. I, 26.1: *et tunc annuntiasse incognitum Patrem et virtutes perfecisse.*

[114] Otto, Corpus Apolog. IX, par. 415., Fragm. VI.

[115] Iren. I, 7.2.

[116] Iren. III, 11.3; I, 15.3 (Marcosians).

[117] Hippolytus VI, 35.6, p. 165.8.

[118] Exc. ex Theod. 21.6; 26; cf. 31.4; Marcosians, Iren. I, 15.3 (end).

[119] Iren. I, 15.3.

[120] Note the explicit mention of this uncertainty about the nature of Jesus already in the ancient system (stemming from Valentinus himself?) in Iren. I, 11.1; 12.4. Exc. ex Theod. 61.6 is speaking simply of the spirit which descended upon Jesus at the baptism.

accordingly is a *fourfold* compounded being, who in addition to the miraculously prepared body has a share also in the Soter, Sophia, and the Demiurge. At last the Gnostics were even reconciled to a certain degree to the dogma of the miraculous birth. However, this applies almost exclusively to the Valentinian schools, their immediate forerunners, the Gnostics in Irenaeus I, 30, and some other, in part later, offshoots of Gnosticism[121]—one more proof for the late emergence of that dogma in the Christian church.

The Gnostics whose system Irenaeus has excerpted for us in I, 30[122] are the first, it appears, to connect in a noticeable fashion the doctrine of the Christ who is united with Jesus at the baptism with the idea of the miraculous birth: *Jesum autem quippe ex virgine*[123] *per operationem Dei generatum, sapientiorem et mundiorem et justiorem hominibus omnibus fuisse; Christum perplexum Sophiae* (*vide supra*, p. 271) *descendisse et sic factum esse Jesum Christum* (I, 30.12).

While the genesis of this Christology is clearly evident—here the one born of the virgin simply appears in place of the man Jesus with whom the Christ is united—the doctrine of the Valentinians here is also more complicated and more diverse, so that, especially with the confused reports of the church fathers, it is not easy to arrive at a clear understanding of it. At first glance it appears as if that theory upon which they place the greatest value and which best corresponds to their system develops without regard to the dogma of the miraculous birth. This is the doctrine, already discussed above, of the tripartite nature of the redeemer. In addition to the pneumatic element, which Jesus possessed from Achamoth, and the psychic, which he received from the Demiurge, there appears here as the third part the preexistent

---

[121] The Basilidian system in Hippolytus VII, 26.8, p. 205.13 (Jesus the son of Mary). System of the Pistis Sophia (see above, pp. 271-72). The Sethians speak of an entering of the ἄνωθεν τοῦ φωτὸς τέλειος λόγος εἰς τὴν ἀκάθαρτον μήτραν (Hippolytus V, 19.20, p. 120.16, εἰς μήτραν παρθένου, 120.22), and say that for this reason the redeemer had to cleanse himself of this impurity by a sacrament (19.21, p. 120.25, ἀπελούσατο καὶ ἔπιε τὸ ποτήριον ζῶντος ὕδατος ἁλλομένου) (on this, cf. Justin, Baruch-Gnosticism, V, 27.3, p. 133.11).

[122] The two systems in I, 29 and 30 are closely related. In I, 29 Irenaeus has suppressed the second half of the account which comes into consideration for us here and which is now preserved for us in the Coptic Apocryphon Joannis, because he was aware of this relation (cf. C. Schmidt in *Philotesia Kleinert*, p. 334). This Barbelo Gnosticism (in its simpler form in I, 30) is obviously a forerunner of Valentinianism (the idea of the fallen Sophia!). This is said directly by Irenaeus or at least by his source in I, 11.1 (ἀπὸ τῆς λεγομένης γνωστικῆς αἱρέσεως τὰς ἀρχάς . . . μεθαρμόσας Οὐαλεντῖνος).

[123] Cf. the Gnostics in Epiph. 26.10.5, p. 287.13, μὴ εἶναι δὲ αὐτὸν Μαρίας γεγεννημένον, ἀλλὰ διὰ Μαρίας (see below, Chap. VII) δεδειγμένον. σάρκα δὲ αὐτὸν μὴ εἰληφέναι, ἀλλ' ἢ μόνον δόκησιν εἶναι.

miraculous corporeality, prepared in heaven: σῶμα ψυχικὴν ἔχον οὐσίαν, κατεσκευασμένον δὲ ἀρρήτῳ τέχνῃ πρὸς τὸ ὁρατὸν καὶ ψηλάφητον καὶ παθητὸν γεγενῆσθαι. (This body is also readily described as ἀπὸ τῆς οἰκονομίας.) [124] One would hardly have taken this trouble to invent the miraculous body of the redeemer and to connect it with the premises of the doctrinal system if one had already accepted the dogma of the miraculous birth. Here we have rather a modified Docetism, similar to that which we were able to show above in Marcion's pupil Apelles. Further, there is the fact that in the old and valuable account from which we took our point of departure,[125] any mention of the virgin birth appears still to be absent.

However, the dogma of the miraculous birth is then later taken over by the Valentinian schools and is united with the older view by means of the hypothesis that that miraculous body had passed through the womb of Mary as through a tube, without taking on anything earthly from her.[126] In this speculation about the birth of Jesus people in many cases followed the presentation of Luke 1:35.[127]

Thus we can demonstrate how the Christology of Gnosticism gradually approached that of the Great Church, or went through a development parallel to the latter. A recognizable line of development runs from outright Docetism to the hypothesis that a celestial spiritual being had descended upon Jesus at his baptism, then to the hypothesis of the miraculous birth. The history of the Christology of Gnosticism will therefore be able to render good service to us in the understanding of the parallel development in the Great Church, to which we turn in the next section.[128]

[124] Iren. I, 6.1; 7.2; cf. Clement, Strom. III, 17.102: διὰ ταῦτα ἡ δόκησις Κασσιανῷ, διὰ ταῦτα καὶ Μαρκίωνι καὶ Οὐαλεντίνῳ τὸ σῶμα τὸ ψυχικόν.

[125] Iren. I, 6.1=Exc. ex Theod. 58, 59. In Irenaeus the parallel to Exc. 60 (reference to Luke 1:35) is lacking. Of course Valentinus himself appears already to have assumed the miraculous birth; cf. his vision of the ἀρτιγέννητος παῖς, who is announced to him as the Logos: Hippolytus VI, 42 (if we are actually to think of Jesus of Nazareth here in connection with the child-Logos).

[126] Iren. I, 7.2: τὸν διὰ Μαρίας διοδεύσαντα καθάπερ ὕδωρ διὰ σωλῆνος ὁδεύει (according to another source than I, 6.1). III, 11.3: *quidam quidem eum, qui ex dispositione est, dicunt Jesum, quem per Mariam dicunt pertransiisse, quasi aquam per tubam.* Hippolytus VI, 35.3, p. 164.18, διὰ Μαρίας τῆς παρθένου.

[127] They tended to refer the πνεῦμα to the Sophia, and the δύναμις ὑψίστου to the Demiurge (Hippolytus VI, 35). One should observe how here the old view of Jesus as a son of Sophia (see above, p. 273) is kept. Other interpretations in Exc. ex Theod. 60 and particularly Iren. I, 15.3 (Marcosians). Should the baptismal account in the so-called Gospel of the Hebrews, in which the Spirit appears as the mother of Jesus, be related to these?

[128] It has been the achievement of Usener to be the first to set the development of ecclesiastical Christology in these larger connections. This should not be forgotten, no matter how much of the details of his propositions may be subject to attack; cf. *Weihnachtsfest*, 2nd ed. (1911), pp. 101 ff., 111 ff., 130 ff.

VII. *Summary*. Once more we survey the whole situation. In Gnosticism a decidedly dualistic-pessimistic and for this reason specifically un-Hellenic mental tendency, which also stands in strict opposition to the Old Testament and Judaism, has been attached to Christianity. Considered in terms of its religious aspect, it is presented as a religion of redemption of the most pronounced and forthright one-sidedness. In its aspirations it tends to the absolutely different and the totally alien to all human nature, the unprecedentedly new. For this reason it completely pulls apart the ideas of creation and redemption. To it creation becomes a wrong which is made good through redemption. This movement was attracted with magical force by the form which Christianity had acquired in Paulinism. It believed that it discovered in the apostle the basic outlook of its own piety. In fact, it could begin with his radical anthropological dualism and pessimism and develop it further. It also found many other affinities with him: his theory about the inferior nature of the first man, his demonizing of almost the entire world of spirits, the tendency of his ethic to a dualistic asceticism, his spiritualistic doctrine of the resurrection, his anthropological terminology. It gathered all this into a system or systems which Paul certainly would not have recognized as his own. Most of all, it left little room for the idea of a unique redemption taking place at one point in history; this was done in that it offered an undergirding in terms of metaphysics and a world view for the contrasts, which are found in Paul only as an attitude and practically, between the old and the new human natures, and between the two classes of the pneumatics and the psychics. Thus, above all, redemption becomes for it altogether a myth. What once took place as a prototype in the primeval times takes place repeatedly and ever anew: the descent of the celestial man into matter and his painstaking elevation of himself again, the fall of the goddess and her liberation, the ἱερὸς γάμος of the lost bride with the god-savior, the victory of the hero over the demons of the depths. Only with difficulty and gradually was Gnosticism able to draw the figure of Jesus of Nazareth into its mythological basic outlook, and one clearly senses, throughout, the compromise character of the resultant view. For this reason Jesus has a surprisingly limited significance for the practical piety of many Gnostic sects, as is best evidenced in the ancient Valentinian source document in Irenaeus and in the *Excerpta*. Indeed, in general one cannot ignore the fact that in the cult, in the sacramental praxis, and often in the basic attitude of piety, the "mother" has a much greater significance than has he. The "mother," not

Jesus, is the κύριος (the cult heroine) of the Gnostic.[129] Nevertheless the lines of connection with Paulinism are not completely broken off. The basic form of religion remained similar; it is experienced as redemption from natural reality which came to be through creation. And even in Paul the historical redemption was already on the way to developing into a myth, into a process which once occurred as prototype but becomes vital ever anew in the copy of that prototype.

Gnosticism shows the dangers with which one side of the Pauline piety threatens the further development of the Christ piety. How did it happen that the authentic development of the Christian church did not take place along these lines? There must have been factors other than Paulinism at work in the formation of the Christian religion. The next sections will show what these were.

---

[129] Cf. *Hauptprobleme*, pp. 58 ff.; article "Gnostiker," in Pauly-Wissowa's *Real-Enzyklopädie*, cols. 1535-37.

# 7

## THE CHRIST CULT
## IN THE POST-APOSTOLIC AGE

I. *Fading of the Pauline Doctrine of the Spirit and of the Pauline–Johannine Christ Mysticism*. When we approach the Christ faith of the post-apostolic age (apart from Gnosticism), we first have to make clear to ourselves that one must forget the whole broad projection of Pauline (and Johannine) total outlook if one wishes to understand the much simpler and more naïve thought-world of non-Pauline Christianity. Almost nothing remains of the total πνεῦμα–σάρξ outlook of Paul; of the bold enlargement of the pneuma concept and its reshaping from the cultic into the religio-ethical; of his stubborn dualistic supernaturalism which is grounded in this concept and which tends to be a world view; of the radical psychological pessimism; of the peculiarly inward and dominant position which he gives to the Christos in this connection; of the ingenious way in which he interprets from this perspective the independence of Christianity as the new pneumatic religion of the spirit and of freedom over against Judaism, and Christ as the end of the law; of all this, I say, almost nothing is left. Already the epistles in the New Testament which one particularly—and with a certain right—senses as paulinizing at first glance show clearly that they are not at home in the real center of Pauline outlook. Paul would never say, as does the author of I Peter, that the fleshly lusts στρατεύονται κατὰ τῆς ψυχῆς (2:11).[130] He would hardly say with the author of Ephesians: "No one

---

[130] On specific reminiscences of Pauline terminology in Jude 19 and James 3:13, see above, p. 187, n. 87.

hates his own flesh (σάρκα) but nourishes and cherishes it, as Christ does the church" (5:29).[131] And one must never be confused by the many individual echoes of Paul's religious language; we indeed hear Paul's voice, but we no longer find his spirit. The total outlook of the apostle is lost; it probably never found footing in any broader genuinely ecclesiastical circles at all.

Moreover, it has long been acknowledged and demonstrated how even that popular, enthusiastic-ecstatic view of the Pneuma, from which the Pauline view stems and upon which it rests in part, disappears in a gradual transition. In place of the spirit appears the office, and in place of the community of the pneumatics appears the organized church. The literary documents in which the enthusiastic pneumatic element is still strongly emphasized can be counted on one's fingers. Above all (apart from the apocalyptic literature), there comes into consideration here the book of Acts or at least certain source elements of this writing (in the first half as well as in the second).[132] Ignatius also is personally a pneumatic ecstatic. The statements in Rom. 7 and Philad. 7 belong to the best documents for the peculiarity of the pneumatic nature. But in him this element of ancient Christianity stands in an odd and inorganic connection with the strong emphasis upon the church organized under the monarchical episcopate. The enthusiasm which martyrhood stimulates apparently has maintained or has revitalized here as in other places that factor in primitive Christian community life.[133] It is further characteristic that those passages in the literature of the post-apostolic age which best furnish us with a look into the ever-present current of enthusiasm in the post-apostolic age, namely, the statements in the Didache (chap. 11) about prophets and the eleventh Mandate of Hermas (about false prophets), already manifest a sharply critical attitude toward it and allow it a validity only with all sorts of provisos and with the application of strict precautionary regulations.

And to the extent that the Spirit ceases to be the supernatural factor who

---

[131] The utterly un-Pauline μέλη ἐσμὲν τοῦ σώματος αὐτοῦ ἐκ τῆς σαρκὸς αὐτοῦ καὶ ἐκ τῶν ὀστέων αὐτοῦ in 5:30 is not certainly attested by the manuscripts (it is lacking in B ℵ A cop). But the certainly ancient variant reading is characteristic of the usage of the post-Pauline era.

[132] Cf. A. Harnack, *Beiträge zur Einleitung in das Neue Testament*, III, *Die Apostelgeschichte* (1908), pp. 111-25.

[133] Perhaps it may be pointed out that Luke or Luke's sources point to Antioch, the home of Ignatius (cf. Codex D on Acts 11:26-28 and precisely here also the stressing of the pneumatic element). The Didache is likewise of Syrian origin. Cf. the portrayal of the prophets in Phoenicia and Palestine which Celsus gives (in Origen VII, 9).

functions in the miracles of the Christian life and its ecstatic phenomena, he emerges in new—or in old, recurring—connections. For one thing, he remains the bearer of Old Testament revelation and as such is again strongly emphasized, so strongly that later, in the apologetic literature, τὸ προφητικὸν πνεῦμα or τὸ ἅγιον προφητικὸν πνεῦμα becomes the dominant term.[134] In this way above all the Spirit establishes his connection with the cultic life of Christianity. For the books of the Old Testament are indeed first of all the holy Scriptures which are read during the Christians' worship and upon which that worship in large part rests. In these holy Scriptures the Spirit speaks to the community.[135] Moreover, from the first the Spirit enters into a definite connection with the sacrament, at least with the sacrament of baptism, and this connection is much more strongly emphasized than Paul had done (vide infra). Thus the bond with the Christian cultus is still more closely formed. Now it is said that "there are three that bear witness upon earth, the Spirit, the water, and the blood, and these three are one" (I John 5:7-8). The concept of the Spirit finally begins to win a fixed place in the developing confession of the Christian church. On the basis of a series of Pauline expressions in which the Spirit appears alongside the Father and the Son, the trinitarian baptismal formula emerges and begins gradually to displace (vide infra) the older one (ἐν ὀνόματι κυρίου). And then theological speculation begins, though only hesitatingly and timorously, to be connected with this confession.

This may be further illuminated by a series of literary documents. We have already discussed (p. 221) in context the view of the Spirit in the *Johannine writings*. In the *Pastoral Epistles* the correlative concept to Pneuma is found: σάρξ not at all (apart from the hymn in I Tim. 3:16, which has probably been incorporated; here beside πνεῦμα). Pneuma is found in I Tim. only one other time, where a *prophecy of the Spirit* is spoken of (4:1); in II Tim. 1:14 and Tit. 3:5 with a definite reference to the sacrament of baptism; finally in a wholly general expression (πνεῦμα δειλίας—πνεῦμα δυνάμεως) in II Tim. 1:7. *I Clement* mentions only at the beginning the πλήρης πνεύματος ἁγίου ἔκχυσις in the Christian community (2:2, cf. 63.2). The trinitarian formula is found twice (46.6; 58.2). Otherwise it is the Spirit who taught in the prophets in the Old Testament. The apostles possessed it (42.3), and Paul wrote πνευματικῶς (47.3). The formulation that Christ has given his σάρξ for our σάρξ, his ψυχή for our ψυχή, is not Pauline. Specifically non-Pauline is the expression in II Clem. 14:5: τοσαύτην δύναται ἡ

[134] Cf. I Pet. 1:11.

[135] With the formula ὁ ἔχων οὖς ἀκουσάτω, τί τὸ πνεῦμα λέγει ταῖς ἐκκλησίαις the apocalyptist stamps his writing as a sacred book to be read in worship services (cf. 1:3).

σάρξ αὕτη μεταλαβεῖν ζωὴν καὶ ἀφθαρσίαν κολληθέντος αὐτῇ τοῦ πνεύματος τοῦ ἁγίου. The author of the *Epistle of Barnabas* knows almost only the Old Testament Spirit of God, except for the fact that in the beginning, like Clement, he speaks of the χάρις τῆς δωρεᾶς πνευματικῆς and then of the ἐκκεχυμένον . . . πνεῦμα ἐφ᾽ ἡμᾶς (1.2-3), and one time exhorts the Christians: γενώμεθα πνευματικοί, γενώμεθα ναὸς τέλειος (4.11). (We can hardly include in this connection 7.3: the σάρξ of Jesus σκεῦος τοῦ πνεύματος, *vide infra;* and particularly 19.7: ἐφ᾽ οὓς τὸ πνεῦμα ἡτοίμασεν.)

Especially worthy of note is the state of affairs in the *Ignatian epistles.* We find a series of formulas which are strongly suggestive of Pauline usage. Remarkable, for example, is the contrast of ἀνθρωπίνη and πνευματικὴ συνήθεια (Eph. 5.1; cf. Philad. 7.1, 2; on the other hand, ἄνθρωπος for man in the higher sense, Rom. 6.2), also the more general contrast of σάρξ and θεός, Magn. 3.2; κατὰ σάρκα— κατὰ γνώμην θεοῦ, Rom. 8:3; κατὰ σάρκα ἐκ γένους Δαυίδ, ὁ Χριστὸς κατὰ σάρκα (Eph. 20.2; Smyrn. 1.1, κατὰ σάρκα, *passim*). Characteristic is the identification: ἀδιάκριτον πνεῦμα ὅς ἐστιν ᾽Ιησοῦς Χριστός (Magn. 15; cf. Smyrn. 13.1: ἐν δυνάμει πνεύματος). But, if after all this, we might be of the opinion that with the sentence οἱ σαρκικοὶ τὰ πνευματικὰ πράσσειν οὐ δύνανται we are standing on specifically Pauline ground, we get corrected when Ignatius immediately thereafter says: "But what you do in the flesh is spiritual, for you do all in Jesus Christ" (Eph. 8.2). The un-Pauline basic outlook of Ignatius further emerges in numerous expressions where he speaks of the uniting of the Christians as regards flesh and spirit. ἕνωσις πνευματικὴ (πνεύματος) καὶ σαρκικὴ (σαρκός) is the great slogan of his epistles. The Christians are said to be nailed, with flesh and spirit, to the cross of their Lord Jesus Christ (Smyrn. 1.1). They are said to hope in him σαρκί, ψυχῇ (Philad. 11.2). They are to remain in Jesus with flesh and spirit (Eph. 10.3); Jesus is ἰατρὸς σαρκικὸς καὶ πνευματικός (Eph. 7.2; cf. Magn. 1.2, ἕνωσιν . . . σαρκὸς καὶ πνεύματος ᾽Ιησοῦ Χριστοῦ. 13.2; Smyrn. 12.2; Rom. Proem; Smyrn. 13.2: ἀγάπη σαρκικὴ καὶ πνευματική; cf. Ign. ad Polyc. 1.2; 2.2). Paul simply would not thus formulate all this. Moreover, it is specifically un-Pauline, and belongs in the line of the development already stated in John, when in the statements about the sacrament the σάρξ of Jesus is so strongly emphasized (Trall. 8.1; Rom. 7.3; Philad. 4; Smyrn. 7.1: the false teachers deny that the eucharist is Jesus' σάρξ; cf. Smyrn. 12.2). And to this corresponds the fact that in the statement about the resurrection of Jesus the σάρξ once again is so heavily stressed: ἐγὼ γὰρ μετὰ τὴν ἀνάστασιν ἐν σαρκὶ αὐτὸν οἶδα; the disciples are convinced of his resurrection: κραθέντες τῇ σαρκὶ αὐτοῦ καὶ πνεύματι (Smyrn. 3).

A peculiar state of affairs prevails with the *Shepherd of Hermas.* For here we have to do essentially with reworked material stemming from the synagogue. Thus we may seek specifically Christian views only in a few parts, in the thin veneer of Christian reediting. To this category belongs, above all, the already mentioned eleventh Mandate with its lively portrayal of the appearance of the bearer of the Spirit in the Christian worship. At the close of the ninth Similitude, it is said of the Christians that they receive from the Spirit of the Son, and that the apostles have received the Spirit (IX, 24.4; 25.2). Joined with this then, actually, are only the old speculations in Sim. V, 5.2; 6.5-7; 7.1-2, 4 (cf. IX, 1.1-2), in which the pre-temporal Son of God is identified with the Spirit (*vide infra*). If one excepts the singular Mandate XI, the Spirit does not mean much for the piety of the Christian editor of the Corpus Hermae.[136]

With all this, the peculiar Christ mysticism of Paul (and also of John), the ἐν Χριστῷ in its peculiar power and vitality, on the whole disappears. Naturally the formula is occasionally maintained, though for a long time not in as frequent use as one would think, but just as formula. When I Clement speaks of εὐσέβεια, παιδεία, ἀγάπη, πίστις, ἀγωγή, κλέος, or κλῆσις ἐν Χριστῷ, this hardly means anything other than *Christian* piety, discipline, love, *Christian* faith, conduct, praise,[137] or calling to Christianity (to the Christian community). The author, in his rational and sober manner, is not at all interested in the genuine Christ mysticism. In this entire period, I find ardent, mystical Christ piety outside of John only in Ignatius. And here of course, in this mysticism's own powerful melodies there often sound

---

[136] Curious and interesting views are found, however, in the (probably) Jewish sources. The Spirit who carries away the seer is still really the natural force of the wind (Vis. I, 1.3; II, 1.1). On the other hand, in a number of passages the Spirit is simply the inward aspect of man (Vis. I, 2.4; III, 8.9; 11.2; 13.2; Sim. IX, 14.3). Especially worthy of note are the statements about the Spirit in the closely related Mand. V, IX, and X (III is also to be compared with these). Here the Holy Spirit is nothing but the good disposition dominant in man, and standing in contrast with it is the evil spirit (spirit of the devil), the evil disposition. Or taken more exactly, there are several good and evil spirits which dwell in man. Thus there is a spirit of truth (Mand. III, 1, 2, 4), a spirit of patience and of wrath: ἐν γὰρ τῇ μακροθυμίᾳ ὁ κύριος κατοικεῖ, ἐν δὲ τῇ ὀξυχολίᾳ ὁ διάβολος. ἀμφότερα οὖν τὰ πνεύματα ἐπὶ τὸ αὐτὸ κατοικοῦντα . . . (V, 1.3); a spirit of faith and one of doubt (IX, 11). The various good "spirits" (also in Paul, I Cor. 12:10; 14:12, 33; Rev. 22:6) of course usually are treated as the one "holy" Spirit. Christian editing may perhaps have been operative here. In any case this ethic is most vividly reminiscent of the Jewish basic document of the Testament of the Patriarchs. (One should also note the specifically Jewish statements about good and evil desires [Yetzer ha-ra' and yetzer ha-tov] in Mand. XII, 2). Related to this is the view set forth in Sim. IX of the twelve virgins as the twelve (virtuous) "spirits," the "powers" (of the Son) of God, with which the pious must be united (clothed) (IX, 13.2, 5, 7; 15:6; 16.1; 17.4; 24.2). One should note that in this connection, the "spirit" is not spoken of in the portrayal of the pious (IX, 17.4: μίαν φρόνησιν ἔσχον καὶ ἕνα νοῦν; IX, 18.4: ἔσται ἡ ἐκκλησία τοῦ θεοῦ ἓν σῶμα, μία φρόνησις, εἷς νοῦς). All this recalls in striking fashion the fantasies about the personified powers of the virtues in Corpus Hermeticum XIII. A comprehensive religio-historical investigation would be required to separate the various religious strata in the Corpus Hermae from one another.

[137] See the compilation in Harnack, *Der erste Klemensbrief*, SAB, 1909, p. 49.6. Accordingly I cannot agree with Harnack in holding this formula to be characteristic of the Christianity of the Epistle of Clement. The author's regarding the believers as τὰ μέλη τοῦ Χριστοῦ and his ἴδιον σῶμα (chap. 46) is likewise hardly more than reminiscence.

Pauline notes, but the whole still stands on a completely different base and in another context, as is further to be shown below.

II. *The Title Kyrios.* In one respect, however, the continuity with the past was preserved. *Afterward as well as before, Christ remains the* κύριος *of his community.* The title κύριος asserts his dominant significance, which he already had in the Pauline communities, in almost the whole body of post-apostolic literature.

The Johannine literary circle forms the only exception, which we have already touched upon and explained. Here the mystically inclined circle of "friends," it appears, rejected the title κύριος for Jesus and the name "servants of Jesus" for themselves. But the Johannine enclave did not have an influence beyond its borders.

In the rest of the literature, κύριος even becomes the title κατ' ἐξοχήν for Christ in such a way that, as we were already able to observe in Paul, it is hardly at all used for God any longer. In a detailed investigation we shall first have to disregard the appearance of the title in Old Testament citations, as well as the frequently used introduction to such citations, (ὁ) κύριος λέγει. Of course these citations, too, demand close investigation as to whether in them the name of God and what was said of him had not already been transferred to Christ. But we do not have the space here to discuss that in detail.

The facts of the case are tidiest in I Clement. Some twenty-five times we find the adjective δεσπότης for God,[138] never for Christ, while with κύριος, almost without exception only Jesus is designated.[139] One exception, which only confirms the rule, is formed by the address κύριε directed to God three times in the great prayer of the congregation (60.1; 61.1, 2, along with δέσποτα in 61.1, 2). For this prayer was hardly formulated by Clement himself, but stems from the Christian, and ultimately from the Jewish, liturgy. Apparently the change is made from one designation to the other in quite deliberate fashion: e.g., 24.1: ὁ δεσπότης ἐπιδείκνυται διηνεκῶς

---

[138] δεσπότης connected with Christ is a singularity in II Pet. 2:1 and Jude 4 (κύριος καὶ δεσπότης!). Connected with God, it appears in Rev. 6:10 and Barn. 1.7 and 4.3 (it is uncertain in II Tim. 2:21).

[139] I Clem. 43.6 should probably read, with A lat. only τοῦ ἀληθινοῦ καὶ μόνου (C + κυρίου; S cop. + θεοῦ). In any case κυρίου, even following the other usage, is impossible. 53.5 can hardly serve as an exception, because of the general term (κύριος alongside θεράπων!). From this evidence we must decide in passages where the reading is not altogether certain in favor of connecting the term with Christ. For this is assured by about twenty unequivocal passages.

ἡμῖν τὴν μέλλουσαν ἀνάστασιν ἔσεσθαι, ἧς τὴν ἀπαρχὴν ἐποιήσατο τὸν κύριον Ἰησοῦν ἐκ νεκρῶν ἀναστήσας. 49.6: ἐν ἀγάπῃ προσελάβετο ἡμᾶς, ὁ δεσπότης, διὰ τὴν ἀγάπην . . . τὸ αἷμα αὐτοῦ ἔδωκεν ὑπὲρ ἡμῶν Ἰ. Χρ. ὁ κύριος ἡμῶν.[140]

In Luke's Acts of the Apostles, so far as I can see, the distinction between θεός and κύριος (again, naturally apart from Old Testament passages) is similarly almost purely maintained. The use of κύριος is here, as is known, an extraordinarily frequent one. In numerous passages[141] the connection with Christ is fully assured. On the other hand, I know only a few passages in which the reference to God is demanded[142]: 3:20, ὅπως ἂν ἔλθωσιν καιροὶ ἀναψύξεως ἀπὸ προσώπου τοῦ κυρίου καὶ ἀποστείλῃ τὸν προκεχειρισμένον ὑμῖν Χριστὸν Ἰησοῦν; 4:29,[143] the address in prayer to κύριε ἔπιδε (cf. the context in 4:30); probably also 8:22, δεήθητι κυρίου (HLP Min. Vulg. Iren. θεοῦ!), and 8:24, δεήθητε πρὸς τὸν κύριον (D fu. syr. pesh. θεόν!).[144]

In the remaining cases, in which no absolutely sure and direct decision is possible, from the context and from internal reasons an opinion can still be brought to a level of high probability, or often even to that of certainty. In particular there come into consideration all those passages in which the κύριος appears in a close connection with his community.[145]

[140] Note in 48.1 the petition to God: προσπέσωμεν τῷ δεσπότῃ καὶ κλαύσωμεν ἱκετεύοντες.

[141] I count 37 quite certain instances (among these, 15 times κύριος Ἰ. [Χρ.]), apart from the many that are almost certain, which are discussed in the following.

[142] 17:27 is to be read as ζητεῖν τὸν θεόν (B ℵ A 61 vg).

[143] The reference of κύριε καρδιογνῶστα in 1:24 therewith also becomes uncertain; but what is involved here is a specific congregational affair (selection of an apostle).

[144] In the book of Acts, prayer (etc.) is as a rule addressed to God. Cf. μεγαλύνειν τὸν θεόν in 10:46; αἰνεῖν in 2:47 and 3:8-9; δοξάζειν in 4:21; 11:18; 21:20 (12:23); ὑμνεῖν (προσεύχεσθαι) in 16:25; αἴρειν φωνήν in 4:24; δεῖσθαι in 10:3; εὔχεσθαι in 26:29; προσευχὴ πρός in 12:5. On the other hand only ἐμεγαλύνετο τὸ ὄνομα τοῦ κυρίου Ἰ. in 19:17; λειτουργεῖν τῷ κυρίῳ in 13:2 (probably, because it involves the calling of apostles and because of the less definite expression, to be referred to Christ); 21:14, τοῦ κυρίου τὸ θέλημα γινέσθω, on account of 21:13, has to do with Jesus.

[145] Later on I shall discuss in context the fact that in the book of Acts the ὄνομα is always connected with the name of Jesus (the only exception, ὄνομα θεοῦ in 15:14, is explained by the Old Testament quotation that follows; cf. 15:17). This settles with complete certainty 9:28 (παρρησιάζεσθαι ἐν τῷ ὀνόματι τοῦ κυρίου; cf. 14:3, παρρησιαζόμενοι ἐπὶ τῷ κυρίῳ). It is no accident, moreover, that the book of Acts always connects πιστεύειν, πίστις, πιστός with κύριος. (An exception only in 16:34, πεπιστευκὼς τῷ θεῷ; this is most strange following 16:31; perhaps the correct reading is that of d and sah, τῷ κυρίῳ; the πιστεύω in 27:25 is not used in the sense of the Christian saving faith.) That Jesus is meant by this κύριος is absolutely certain: (3:16); (10:43); 11:17; 16:31; (19:4); 20:21; 24:24; (26:18). That settles the matter also for 5:14; 9:42; 14:23; 16:15; and 18:8. In the vision the κύριος Ἰ. Χρ. speaks; the κύριε is referred to him (apart from

A number of passages naturally remain completely uncertain. Still, here the connection of the title with God is nowhere a compelling probability. Thus it can be decided here also with a certain probability following the overwhelming majority of the passages that are beyond question.[146]

Matters are similar but perhaps not altogether so clear in the Pastoral Epistles,[147] in Jude[148] and in II Peter.[149] The title occurs more rarely in I Peter[150] and in Hebrews,[151] yet the rule is maintained here also.

---

the accounts of Paul's conversion, where the state of things is clear) in 10:4, 14, and 11:8 (cf. the fact that in 10:15 God is spoken of in the third person); that explains the τὰ προστεταγμένα ὑπὸ τοῦ κ. from 10:33. Further, the "Lord" appears to the apostle in a dream as in 23:11 (absolutely assured) as well as in 18:9 (cf. 9:10). The κύριος (probably Jesus) frees the apostles from prison through his angel: 5:19; 12:7, 11; cf. 8:26 (of course the ἄγγελος κυρίου also smites Herod in 12:23; in 7:30 the reading should be only ἄγγελος). In 16:14, σεβομένη τὸν θεὸν ἧς ὁ κύριος διήνοιξεν τὴν καρδίαν: the proselyte, whose heart the Lord (Jesus) first opens to full knowledge. In 11:20 we read εὐαγγελιζόμενοι τὸν κύριον Ἰησοῦν. That assures the connection of 11:21: χεὶρ κυρίου . . . πολὺς ἀριθμὸς . . . ἐπέστρεψεν πρὸς τὸν κύριον (in the conversion of Gentiles, Acts prefers elsewhere θεός; 14:15; 15:19; 26:18, 20; on the other hand, in 9:35, κύριος in the conversion of Jews); further in 11:23, προσμένειν τῷ κυρίῳ, and in 11:24, προσετέθη ὄχλος ἱκανὸς τῷ κυρίῳ (similar expressions in 2:47 and 14:23, relation of the Lord to the community!). In 20:28 we are quite certainly to read ἐκκλησία τοῦ κυρίου (not, with B ℵ, θεός, which is impossible because of the following τὸ αἷμα τὸ ἴδιον); cf. 9:31, ἐκκλησία πορευομένη τῷ φόβῳ τοῦ κυρίου—18:25, τὴν ὁδὸν τοῦ κυρίου (ἐδίδασκεν ἀκριβῶς τὰ περὶ τοῦ Ἰησοῦ). 15:40, παραδοθεὶς τῇ χάριτι τοῦ κυρίου (B ℵ A D). 20:32, παρατίθεμαι ὑμᾶς τῷ κυρίῳ καὶ τῷ λόγῳ τῆς χάριτος αὐτοῦ (15:11, χάρις τοῦ κυρίου Ἰησοῦ, but in 11:23, 13:43, 14:26, and 20:24, χάρις θεοῦ). 20:19, δουλεύειν τῷ κυρίῳ.

[146] πνεῦμα κυρίου, 5:9; 8:39. 13:10, τὰς ὁδοὺς τοῦ κυρίου τὰς εὐθείας (quotation from Hos. 14:10?), then also χεὶρ (yet cf. the preceding footnote on 11:21), 13:11 and διδαχὴ κυρίου in 13:12 not wholly assured. It is worth noting that the book of Acts does not distinguish between λόγος (ῥῆμα) θεοῦ and κυρίου. λόγος θεοῦ some fourteen times (13:48 attested by B D cop); λόγος κυρίου: 8:25; 13:49; 15:35-36; 19:10, 20 (in 11:16 and 20:35 certain words are quoted as τοῦ κυρίου Ἰησοῦ).

[147] Enigmatic is I Tim. 1:14, ὑπερεπλεόνασεν δὲ ἡ χάρις τοῦ κυρίου ἡμῶν (immediately before this we have Χρ. Ἰ. τῷ κ. ἡμῶν and then) μετὰ πίστεως καὶ ἀγάπης τῆς ἐν Χρ. Ἰ. 6:15, κύριος τῶν κυριευόντων hardly counts as an exception; otherwise in I Tim. the rule holds. Highly noteworthy is II Tim. 1:18, δῴη αὐτῷ ὁ κύριος εὑρεῖν ἔλεος παρὰ κυρίου (the change from ὁ κύριος to κύριος (=God) appears intentional; κύριος without the article also in the Old Testament quotations in 2:19). 2:14 is probably to be read ἐνώπιον τοῦ θεοῦ (ℵ C F G). 4:17, ὁ δὲ κύριός μοι παρέστη, is in all probability to be referred to Jesus, who gives help to his apostle on trial, but then also 4:18 (cf. 3:11), ῥύσεταί με ὁ κύριος (cf. βασιλεία αὐτοῦ and, with this, 4:1), and then finally what should be esp. important, even the doxology! According to 4:8, 14, the judge will be Jesus (cf. 4:1); 2:7 remains undecided. All in all the number of the assured passages runs to a good dozen. The title is absent from the epistle to Titus!

[148] An exception in vs. 5 (vs. 9 is a quotation).

[149] Here alongside a number of assured passages only scattered uncertainties in 2:9 (11); 3:8, 9.

[150] κύριος (outside of Old Testament quotations) only in 1:3; 2:13, and 3:15 (κύριον δὲ τὸν Χρ. ἁγιάσατε). Only in 2:13 is the connection not wholly certain.

[151] Except in Old Testament quotations, reference to Jesus in 2:3; 7:14; 12:14 (?), and 13:20.

The Ignatian epistles again provide a richer yield. Theodor Zahn has collected the material in the index to the larger edition of the Apostolic Fathers. In a great many passages the connection of the title with Jesus is thoroughly assured.

Even among the passages in which Zahn indicates that the reference is uncertain,[152] there is not one that must necessarily be referred to God. Thus Ignatius probably strictly carries through the distinction between κύριος and θεός, except that he already frequently designates Jesus as θεός. In Polycarp's epistle to the Philippians there is perhaps an important exception to the rule to be noted: εἰ οὖν δεόμεθα τοῦ κυρίου, ἵνα ἡμῖν ἀφῇ, ὀφείλομεν καὶ ἡμεῖς ἀφιέναι. ἀπέναντι γὰρ τῶν τοῦ κυρίου καὶ θεοῦ ἐσμὲν ὀφθαλμῶν (6.2). In what immediately follows, to be sure, again the βῆμα Χριστοῦ is spoken of. In the homily that goes under the name of Clement, once again, "the Lord" is applied to Jesus so uniformly that from the outset this reference has to be acknowledged even in doubtful passages.[153] And finally, there comes into consideration here the Didache with a consistent testimony for this use of κύριος.[154]

We may close this long series of witnesses with the Epistle of Barnabas. In it the investigation is somewhat more difficult [155] because its presentation

[152] See Index to his edition of the Ignatian epistles on Eph. 20.1 (present revelation of the Lord, probably Jesus). 21.1 (εὐχαριστῶν τῷ κυρίῳ). Philad. 11:1 (ἐδέξασθε αὐτοὺς ὡς καὶ ὑμᾶς ὁ κύριος). To Polycarp 4.1 (μετὰ τὸν κύριον σὺ αὐτῶν [τῶν χηρῶν] φροντιστὴς ἔσο). Also Polyc. Phil. 4.1 ἐντολὴ κυρίου. The decision concerning Philad. 8.1, πᾶσιν οὖν μετανοοῦσιν ἀφίει ὁ κύριος, ἐὰν μετανοήσωσιν εἰς ἑνότητα θεοῦ καὶ συνέδριον τοῦ ἐπισκόπου, would be most important. It does seem to me that here also the reference to Jesus is necessary.

[153] The ὁ κύριος λέγει with which the quotations of Isa. 52:5 in 13.2 and of Isa. 66:18 in 17.4 are introduced is, according to the context, probably to be applied to Jesus. Conversely, in 13.4 a saying of Jesus is introduced with "God says." Terms such as commandments of the Lord, instructions of the Lord, 17.3 (cf. 8.4: will of the Father—commandments of the Lord, and then "for the Lord says in the gospel"), what the Lord has prepared for his elect, 14.5, certainly refer to Jesus.

[154] The first chaps. (1–5) naturally do not come into consideration here, since they probably are borrowed from a Jewish writing, the Two Ways. It is noteworthy that Harnack in his construction of the *Jewish* basic document (*Die Apostellehre und die jüdischen beiden Wege* [1886], p. 56) brackets the sentence in 4.1, τιμήσεις δὲ αὐτὸν (the teacher) ὡς κύριον· ὅθεν γὰρ ἡ κυριότης λαλεῖται, ἐκεῖ κύριός ἐστιν as doubtful.

[155] Assured passages are 5.1, 5; 6.3; 7.2; 14.4-5; 16.8. Reference to Jesus very probable in 1.1 (ἐν ὀνόματι κυρίου τοῦ ἀγαπήσαντος ἡμᾶς); 1.3 (Spirit of the Lord); 1.4 (the Lord my companion on the way); 1.6 (hope, righteousness, love; δόγματα κυρίου); 2.1 (δικαιώματα κυρίου; cf. 2.6, ὁ καινὸς νόμος τοῦ κυρίου ἡμῶν Ἰησοῦ Χριστοῦ); therefore also 2.3 (remain unspotted before the Lord); 4.12 (the Lord judge of the world, that is, Jesus, although in 4.11 God is spoken of; cf. 5.7; 7.2; 15.5); correspondingly 4.13, βασιλεία τοῦ κυρίου (cf. 8.5); 5.3 (revealer of the past, present, future, in spite of 1.7, where the same formula is applied to δεσπότης=God, on the basis of the assured passages 5.1, 5); 6.10 (the "Lord" who has given us wisdom and understanding; the prophet of the Old

is wholly dominated by references to the Old Testament and Old Testament quotations. But the difficulty lies in the fact that the κύριος title is to be referred to Christ even in places where we would be inclined to refer it to God, i.e., in the middle of Old Testament references, rather than in any reverse observations.[156] On the other hand, certain parts of the epistle again show the opposite state of affairs.[157] In one passage it is shown quite clearly how the author, whether consciously or unconsciously, makes a distinction between the titles: εἰ ὁ κύριος ὑπέμεινεν παθεῖν περὶ τῆς ψυχῆς ὑμῶν, ὢν παντὸς τοῦ κόσμου κύριος, ᾧ εἶπεν ὁ θεὸς ἀπὸ καταβολῆς κόσμου (Gen. 1:26 follows).

As powerfully convincing as is this strong agreement of almost all the testimonies under consideration, to which I might add above all the acceptance of the κύριος title in the old Roman baptismal confession—the exceptions to be noted, for all that, are equally interesting. There are, in the first place, three: the Shepherd of Hermas,[158] the Epistle of James[159] and

Testament *means* the "Lord"; loving the "Lord"); in 6.14, 15, 16, the reference to Jesus is assured, precisely also in the Old Testament quotations, and hence we are probably also to refer to Jesus the εἶπεν δὲ ὁ κύριος in 6.12 before Gen. 1:28 and the λέγει δὲ κύριος before the quotation of unknown origin in 6.13 (with the excision of the glosses ταῦτα πρὸς τὸν υἱόν—πρὸς ἡμᾶς λέγει). 6.19 (διαθήκη κυρίου); 7.1 (ὁ καλὸς κύριος); 7.3 (the "Lord" speaks in the Old Testament; connection with Jesus necessary because of 7.2: ὁ υἱὸς τοῦ θεοῦ ὢν κύριος and 7.5); 14.3 (the Lord who speaks in the Old Testament in the giving of the law, applied to Christ; evidence in 14.4); 16.6 (the temple of God which is built in the name of "the Lord"; proof in 16.8).

[156] The Epistle of Barnabas provides a particularly good testimony as to how quickly people found Jesus in the κύριος in many passages of the Old Testament; cf. the passages in part already mentioned in the preceding note, 6.12*b*, 13, 14, 16; 14.3; 16.6. Passages in which Barnabas finds the Lord Jesus in the Old Testament alongside God: Gen. 1:27 (5.5; 6.12); Ps. 110 (12.10); Isa. 45:1, εἶπεν κύριος τῷ Χρ. μου κυρίῳ! (12.11); Isa. 42.6-7 (14.7); Ps. 22:23 (6.16). Direct insertion of Jesus into the text of the Old Testament (the παῖς θεοῦ): 6.1 (Isa. 50:8-9); 9.2 (Ps. 34:13); (υἱὸς θεοῦ): 12.9 (Exod. 17:14); 11.5 (Isa. 33:16 ff., φόβον κυρίου). Justin later offers us the most abundant testimonies; see below, Chap. IX.

[157] In the entire section 8.7–10.12 the application of κύριος to God appears to be assured in 8.7; 9.1-3; 10.10, 11, 12 (11.1?). This however is (along with 2.4–3.5) a section in which we are most probably to assume a direct borrowing of (Jewish allegorical) statement; cf. further 15.4 (16.2?).

[158] In the Shepherd of Hermas κύριος and θεός alternate probably some one hundred times. In the first place God is always meant. Only in the specifically Christian parts (particularly in the interpretations of Vis. III, Sim. VIII and IX, Mand. IV, 2.1–3.7 [Sim. V does not come into consideration here], etc.) is the transferral of the title Lord used. The unusual character of the language comes out esp. well in an expression such as Vis. II, 2.8, ὤμοσεν γὰρ κύριος κατὰ τοῦ υἱοῦ αὐτοῦ.

[159] Here the reference to God is dominant almost throughout. An exception: the superscription, and 2:1 (κύριος ᾽Ι. Χριστός). Even the (original) reference of 5:7-8 (παρουσία κυρίου) and 5:14-15 (anointing in the name of the Lord) appears to me not to be assured. One may note the quite unprecedented expressions: 3:9, κύριος (the later manuscripts emend to read θεός) καὶ πατήρ; 5:4, κύριος Σαβαώθ (a quotation?).

the Apocalypse.[160] But these are precisely the writings in which we have good reason to assume the use on a broad scale of Jewish sources or Jewish traditional materials, so that this investigation is suited for placing in the scales a new and heavy weight in favor of the hypotheses which tend in this direction.

III. *The Kyrios Cult in the Post-Apostolic Age.* This κύριος–Jesus, as was already true in the Pauline communities, is in the first place the cultic hero of the young Christian community. That may be proved here on the basis of much broader evidence with still much greater certainty.

1. Above all, one will do well to observe in this connection the emphasis upon the *name* of the "Lord" Jesus in the most varied contexts. The Christians are still always characterized, as in the Pauline age, by the fact that they call upon the name of the Lord Jesus.[161] They (gladly) bear the name of the Son of God,[162] have accepted the name of the Son of God,[163] have come to know it,[164] and are called by the name of the Son of God.[165] They suffer[166] and die[167] for the name, and confess the name[168]; Ignatius wears his chains ὑπὲρ τοῦ κοινοῦ ὀνόματος.[169] The bad Christians deny the name,[170] the heretics use the name with evil cunning (εἰώθασι . . . δόλῳ πονηρῷ τὸ ὄνομα περιφέρειν).[171]

The name determines the fellowship of the Christians. In the community, people are to accept everyone who comes there in the name of the Lord.[172]

---

[160] The reference to God predominates; cf. the frequent formulas κύριος παντοκράτωρ, κύριος ὁ θεός, the simple κύριος (to be sure in a quotation) in 11:4 and 16:5, and then quite unprecedented, 11:15: τοῦ κυρίου ἡμῶν καὶ τοῦ Χριστοῦ αὐτοῦ. Along with this, the simple κύριος referring to Jesus: 11:8; 14:13; 22:20 (κύριος κυρίων in 17:14; 19:16).

[161] Acts 9:14, 21; 22:16; therefore also Acts 2:21, κύριος in the quotation (Joel 3:5) to refer to Jesus. II Tim. 2:22.

[162] Hermas Sim. VIII, 10.3; IX, 13.2-3; 28.5 (IX, 16.3).

[163] Sim. IX, 12.4, 8; 13.7.

[164] Sim. IX, 16.7.

[165] Sim. VIII, 1.1; IX (14.3), 17.4.

[166] Acts 5:41, 9:16; Herm. Sim. IX, 28.2, 5-6; Vis. III, 1.9; 2.1; 5.2.

[167] Acts 15:26; 21:13.

[168] Rev. 2:13; 3:8.

[169] Eph. 1.2.

[170] Herm. Sim. VIII, 6.4; cf. II Clem. 13.1-2: the name is blasphemed. In spite of the following Old Testament quotation, this probably refers to the name of Jesus.

[171] Ignatius Eph. 7.1. This can also refer to the name Christian (Χριστιανός). Χριστιανός in the New Testament: Acts 11:26 (Antioch!) and 26:28; I Pet. 4:16 (to be persecuted as a Christian). Ignatius uses the term four times, Χριστιανισμός five times (cf. Χριστιανὴ τροφή in Trall. 6.1). Mart. Polyc.: Χριστιανός four times, Χριστιανισμός once. Cf. Ign. Magn. 10.1: whoever is named with another name (than μαθητὴς Ἰησοῦ or Χριστιανός) does not belong to God.

[172] Did. 12.1. Ign. Rom. 9:3, δέξασθαι εἰς ὄνομα Ἰ. Χρ.

The name is the central point of the Christian proclamation.[173] *Philip proclaims to the Samaritans the kingdom of God and the name of Jesus Christ* (Acts 8:12). The speaking and proclaiming of the apostles takes place upon the basis of (ἐπί) this name.[174] For the "name" the Christian teachers have gone out (III John 7). The Christian faith is summed up in the faith in the *name* of the Son of God (or of the Lord).[175] In the book of Acts Paul describes his persecution of the community of Jesus as a πρὸς τὸ ὄνομα 'Ιησοῦ τοῦ Ναζαραίου πολλὰ ἐναντία πρᾶξαι (Acts 26:9).[176]

All this is more or less cultically interpreted. Christianity is, in the first place, a cultic society, which acquires its definition by means of the name (of the Lord Jesus). This is the way people regarded the matter in that time. The Athenians receive the impression from the preaching of Paul: ξένων δαιμονίων δοκεῖ καταγγελεὺς εἶναι: ὅτι τὸν 'Ιησοῦν καὶ τὴν ἀνάστασιν εὐηγγελίζετο (Acts 17:18), i.e., that he is proclaiming new divine names. Gallio says to the Jews: εἰ δὲ ζητήματά ἐστιν περὶ λόγου καὶ ὀνομάτων καὶ νόμου (18:15). Here is reflected the popular impression of the Hellenistic milieu. Thousands upon thousands brought this impression to the young religion. And even if all this was being naturally explained and clarified in Christianity, still some of that basic attitude was preserved. In the so-called high-priestly prayer Jesus prays: "Keep them in thy name which thou hast given me—I have kept them in thy name which thou hast given me" (John 17:11-12). As the cohesiveness and the knowledge of God of the old covenant were conditioned and determined by the sacred name of Yahweh, so is the unity of the new religious fellowship dominated by the name of Jesus. In this sense it is meant that the Father has given his name to the Son. It is conceived in this same way when the Epistle to the Hebrews[177] speaks of the διαφορώτερον ὄνομα which the Son, in comparison with the angels, has received. And in Eph. 1:21 it is said still more plainly that Christ is exalted to the right hand of God above every power *and above every name* that is named (i.e., that is venerated in the cultus), both in this aeon and in the aeon to come.

---

[173] Acts 18:15; 17:18.

[174] Acts 4:7, 17, 18; 5:40; παρρησιάζομαι ἐπί in 9:27-28 (somewhat differently παραγγέλειν ἐν in Ign. Polyc. 5.1); 9.15, βαστάσαι τὸ ὄνομα (*sc.*, to the heathen).

[175] Especially in the Johannine literature: John 1:12; 2:23; 3:18 (cf. 20:31, ζωὴν ἔχειν ἐν τῷ ὀνόματι); I John 3:23; 5:13.

[176] Yet cf. Clem. Recogn. I, 53: *ut de nomine eius veritate quaereretur.* Didache 10 (Lord's Supper prayer). Act. Jo. 22, 31, 85 (use of the name in the Agape), 109 (in the Eucharist).

[177] Heb. 1:4; cf. I Clem. 36.2 (quotation).

Therefore the church rests upon this name. "The tower is grounded by means of the word of the all-powerful and glorious *name,* but it is maintained by the invisible power of the Lord." [178] "The name of the Son of God is great and incomprehensible, and it supports the whole world" (Sim. IX, 14.5).[179]

2. Here also we seek to comprehend in detail the relations of the κύριος and his ὄνομα to the Christian cultus and worship. At the threshold of worship already stand the miracles, healings, and expulsions of demons which are performed in the name of Jesus. For these healings and exorcisms will for a long time have played a role precisely in the Christian worship, even though they naturally also took place outside the worship service. In the assembled community the Spirit of God and the ὄνομα unfolded their most powerful effects. Above all the canonical book of Acts affords us an effective insight into the faith of earliest Christianity in the wonder-working power of the name of Jesus. We can best realize the quite massive view in the story of the healing of the lame man ἐν τῷ ὀνόματι Ἰ. Χρ. τοῦ Ναζωραίου . . . ἐν τούτῳ οὗτος παρέστηκεν ἐνώπιον ὑμῶν ὑγιής (4:10). καὶ ἐπὶ τῇ πίστει τοῦ ὀνόματος αὐτοῦ τοῦτον. . . . ἐστερέωσεν τὸ ὄνομα αὐτοῦ; (then spiritualized) ἡ πίστις ἡ δι' αὐτοῦ ἔδωκεν αὐτῷ ὁλοκληρίαν (3:16).[180] Alongside this stand the exorcisms of demons, which are performed in the power of the name by the believers, but also by the unbelievers (16:18; 19:13). To this category perhaps also belong the later[181] gospel accounts of the exorcism of demons in the name of Jesus. That finally the apocryphal acts of the apostles provide an uncommonly rich yield for

---

[178] Herm. Vis., III, 3.5, τῷ ῥήματι τοῦ παντοκράτορος καὶ ἐνδόξου ὀνόματος. In spite of the παντοκράτωρ the reference to Jesus appears to me to be assured because of the parallel in Sim. IX (cf. also the reference to baptism immediately preceding). ῥῆμα is not the proclamation but the word which consists in the name (genitivus epexegeticus); cf. Eph. 5:26, λουτρὸν τοῦ ὕδατος ἐν ῥήματι.

[179] It is worthy of note that in I Clement the ὄνομα is referred almost exclusively to God: 43.6, τὸ ὄνομα τοῦ ἀληθινοῦ καὶ μόνου; in the community prayer in 59.2 and 59.3 (τὸ ἀρχέγονον πάσης κτίσεως ὄνομα); 60.4 (τῷ παντοκράτορι καὶ παναρέτῳ ὀνόματι). Therefore certainly also immediately preceding this, 58.1 (πανάγιον καὶ ἔνδοξον ὄνομα—ὁσιώτατον μεγαλωσύνης αὐτοῦ ὄνομα); likewise 45.7 (λατρεύειν τῷ παναρέτῳ ὀνόματι), 64.1 (τὸ μεγαλοπρεπὲς καὶ ἅγιον ὄνομα). Hence perhaps also 47.7 (1.1, name of the Christians; 36.2, quotation from Heb. 1:3). Cf. Ign. Philad. 10.2. In Heb. 13:15 the reference is not clear. This attitude of the epistle of Clement is unique. Contrasting with it is the fact that in Acts the name refers in dozens of cases to Christ, and only one single time to God, and this exception is occasioned by an Old Testament quotation (15:14, 17). *Here it is Acts, not the epistle of Clement, that reflects the language of the post-apostolic age.*

[180] Cf. 3:6; 4:7, 12.

[181] Thus not Mark 9:38-39 (surely developed on Palestinian soil); but cf. in Matt. 7:22 the portrayal of the false prophets, and Mark 16:17: everywhere a stressing of the ὄνομα.

this mass faith of primitive Christianity is well known and requires no further proof. In the life of faith of the first and second Christian centuries these exorcisms in the name of the κύριος Ἰησοῦς played an uncommonly significant role. The pagan Celsus concerned himself explicitly with the Christian exorcists, and even for the enlightened apologist Justin, the fact that at the utterance of Jesus' name the demons depart is a proof of the divine power of the Logos Christos, to which he returns again and again.[182]

3. At the beginning of the Christian life stands baptism. It is still essentially a baptism ἐν ὀνόματι κυρίου, as it was in the Pauline era. The book of Acts witnesses to this formula in numerous passages[183]; even the Didache, which next to Matthew offers the earliest witness to the trinitarian baptismal formula, in its statements about the eucharist still speaks quite simply of "all those who are baptized in the name of the Lord" (βαπτισθέντες εἰς ὄνομα κυρίου). It is said, more precisely, that baptism takes place during the invocation of the name of the Lord Jesus Christ: "Rise and be baptized, and wash away your sins, calling upon the name of the Lord" (Acts 22:16).[184]

Corresponding to this is the saying about the καλὸν ὄνομα τὸ ἐπικληθὲν ἐφ᾽ ἡμᾶς (James 2:7). The passage in Joel, καὶ ἔσται πᾶς ὃς ἐὰν ἐπικαλέσηται τὸ ὄνομα τοῦ κυρίου, in the book of Acts (as already by Paul) is referred to Christ and baptism (2:21). The name of Jesus is plainly the means of grace effective (along with water) in baptism. In Eph. 5:26 this view is briefly summarized: τὸ λουτρὸν τοῦ ὕδατος ἐν ῥήματι.

Indeed, perhaps there is a connection between the practice of naming the name of Jesus over the baptizand and the fact that baptism acquired the title of σφραγίς.[185] The uttering of the name is probably only a

---

[182] See below, Chap. IX.

[183] Acts 2:38, ἐπὶ τῷ ὀνόματι Ἰησοῦ Χριστοῦ. 8:16, εἰς τὸ ὄνομα τοῦ κυρίου Ἰησοῦ. 19:5, εἰς τὸ ὄνομα τοῦ κυρίου Ἰησοῦ. 10:48, ἐν τῷ ὀνόματι Ἰησοῦ Χριστοῦ. Cf. also 10:43, ἄφεσιν ἁμαρτιῶν λαβεῖν διὰ τοῦ ὀνόματος αὐτοῦ πάντα τὸν πιστεύοντα. Quite similarly, Herm. Sim. IX, 28.5: ἵνα τοῦτο τὸ ὄνομα βαστάζετε καὶ πᾶσαι ὑμῶν αἱ ἁμαρτίαι ἰαθῶσιν.

[184] Cf. I John 2:12: ἀφέωνται ὑμῖν αἱ ἁμαρτίαι διὰ τὸ ὄνομα αὐτοῦ. Barn. 16.8: λαβόντες τὴν ἄφεσιν τῶν ἁμαρτιῶν καὶ ἐλπίσαντες ἐπὶ τὸ ὄνομα ἐγενόμεθα καινοί, πάλιν ἐξ ἀρχῆς κτιζόμενοι. Cf. also Barn. 16.7-8. Kerygma Petri (Clem. Strom. VI, 43.3): ἐὰν μὲν οὖν τις θελήσῃ τοῦ Ἰσραὴλ μετανοήσας διὰ τοῦ ὀνόματός μου πιστεύειν ἐπὶ τὸν θεόν, ἀφεθήσονται αὐτῷ αἱ ἁμαρτίαι. Acta Pauli et Thecl. 34.

[185] A suggestion perhaps already in Eph. 1:13 and 4:30 (cf. II Cor. 1:22), σφραγισθῆναι τῷ πνεύματι. Here of course two conceptions are joined in an unclear fashion. σφραγίς has nothing to do with the Spirit or the water.

weakened sacramental form for the more original, more robust custom of branding or etching upon the person being initiated the sign (name, symbol) of the appropriate god, to whom he was consecrated.[186] The meaning of this religious action is in fact simple and clear. The member of the cult who is furnished with the brand, the sign, and is thereby declared to be the property of the deity thereby stands under the protection of his deity and is immune against all attacks that come from the infernal powers.[187] This is what σφραγίς (στίγμα also) means and signifies.[188] However, if the naming of the name over the baptizand is now to be regarded as a weakening of the more original custom of branding with the sign or name of the god,[189] it would in fact also explain how the title σφραγίς could have been attached to baptism.

The earliest source which gives us a clear and undisputed witness for this labeling of baptism at the same time confirms for us the correctness of this combination. In the *Shepherd* of Hermas it is said explicitly: "Before man bears the *name* of the Son of God, he is dead; but when he has received the *seal*, he lays aside mortality and receives life" (Sim. IX, 16.3).

---

[186] Cf. on this the extraordinarily thorough compilations in Dölger, *Sphragis* (SGKA. 1911, V, 3-4), particularly pp. 39 ff. The most important documentations for the custom of religious branding in the milieu surrounding Christianity are Diodorus XIV, 30.7 (barbarians from Pontus); Lucian, de Syr. dea, chap. 59 (stigmatizing among the Syrians; also a witness from the time of Euergetes II, a warrant for a runaway slave from Bambyke-Hierapolis: ἐστιγμένος τὸν δεξιὸν καρπὸν γράμμασι βαρβαρικαῖς (see Dölger, p. 41.4). Cult of Magna Mater and of Attis: Prudentius, Peristephanon X, 1076 (*quid cum sacrandus accipit sphragitidas?*). Cult of Dionysos: III Macc. 2:29-30. Cult of Mithras: Tertullian, de praesc., chap. 40 (*signat et illic in frontibus milites suos*). Gnostic sects of the Carpocratians: Irenaeus I, 25.6; Epiphanius, Haer. 27.5; Heracleon in Clement, Ecl. proph. 25 (branding of the candidates for initiation on the right earlobe). Still important for the language usage is Joh. Laurentius Lydus, Liber de mensibus IV, 53: καὶ Αἰθίοπες δὲ τὰς κόγχας τῶν γονάτων τῶν νέων σιδηρῷ καυστικῷ σφραγίζουσι τῷ Ἀπόλλωνι. Acquaintance of the Old Testament with the religious custom: the sign of Cain; Isa. 44:5; Exod. 13:9; Lev. 19:28; Ezek. 9:4, 6. In the New Testament: Rev. 7:2 ff.; 9:4. Sign (etc.) of the beast: 13:16, 17; 14:11; 15:2; sign of the lamb: 14:1. Cf. Heitmüller, *Im Namen Jesu*, pp. 143, 173-74, 234, 249.1. [Also in *Neutest. Studien für Heinrici* (1914), pp. 40-49.]

[187] Dölger rightly refers to the splendid explanation in Herodotus II, 113: Ἡρακλέος ἱρόν, ἐς τὸ ἢν καταφυγὼν οἰκέτης ὁτευῶν ἀνθρώπων ἐπιβάληται στίγματα ἱρά, ἑωυτὸν διδοὺς τῷ θεῷ, οὐκ ἔξεστι τούτου ἅψασθαι.

[188] See the preceding note and Dölger, pp. 46 ff.; the στίγματα Ἰησοῦ in Gal. 6:17.

[189] A cultic practice which, considered religio-historically, lies between branding and the naming of the name is the custom of signing the baptizand with the sign of the cross (also done with oil or water). The earliest witness, so far as I can see, is the ἐσφράγισεν before the baptismal act in Acta Thomae, Ch. 27 (cf. Dölger, p. 96, and for later times pp. 171 ff.). The label σφραγίς could also stem from this. Yet the label, it appears, is earlier than this baptismal custom.

Here the parallels, seal—name, emerge quite clearly[190]; the designation of baptism as a seal depends upon the pronouncing of the name.[191]

In the Acts of Peter (*Actus Vercellenses,* chaps. 5-6, Bonnet I, 51.7) it is said after the baptism of Theon that God (that is to say, Christ) has held Theon to be worthy of his name: "O God Jesus Christ, *in thy name*[192] I have spoken, and he has been marked with *thy holy sign.*"[193] An especially good introduction to the meaning of this sealing with the name in the *Excerpta ex Theodoto* 80: διὰ γὰρ πατρὸς καὶ υἱοῦ καὶ ἁγίου πνεύματος σφραγισθεὶς[194] ἀνεπίληπτός ἐστιν πάσῃ τῇ ἄλλῃ δυνάμει καὶ διὰ τριῶν ὀνομάτων πάσης τῆς ἐν φθορᾷ τριάδος (?) ἀπηλλάλη.[195] In all this it is the significance of the holy name of the κύριος Ἰησοῦς, uttered in baptism, which is quite clearly in view. The baptizand over whom his name is pronounced now stands under the protection of this high Lord as his possession. With the miraculous power of his name he shields him against all enemies and opponents, above all against the supra-terrestrial might of the spiritual powers, angels and demons.[196] Indeed for this reason it is also a great

---

[190] Cf. also the parallels: βεβηλοῦν τὸ ὄνομα and εἰληφότες τὴν σφραγῖδα καὶ τεθλακότες αὐτὴν καὶ μὴ τηρήσαντες ὑγιῆ, Sim. VIII, 6.2-3; further the kindred expressions in IX, 12.8; 13.2-3; 28.5 (to receive the seal, to come to know, to bear the name of the Son of God).

[191] We must not be deceived by the explanatory gloss which follows immediately after the above sentence: ἡ σφραγὶς οὖν τὸ ὕδωρ ἐστίν. Cf. Act. Pauli et Thecl. 25: σφραγίς= ὕδωρ. This is not a definition of σφραγίς. The sentence rather proposes to interpret to the reader the apparently less customary designation σφραγίς by the more common ὕδωρ. *The "seal" originally has nothing to do with the water.* Unfortunately Dölger (p. 72) has taken his point of departure for his reflections precisely at this sentence and consequently fails to reach his goal with his otherwise so praiseworthy investigation.

[192] Note how these statements do not fit in with the earlier mentioned trinitarian baptismal formula at all. Here also the new stands beside the old.

[193] "*signatus est sancto tuo signo.*" The expression is referring to the sign of the cross. But it remains characteristic that the naming of the name and the sign of the cross are mentioned in immediate parallelism.

[194] On the σφραγίς, cf. also the characteristic statements in Excerpta 86. Like a coin the Christian bears the inscription of the name of God. As the dumb animal shows by its σφραγίς whose property it is, οὕτως καὶ ἡ ψυχὴ ἡ πιστὴ τὸ τῆς ἀληθείας λαβοῦσα σφράγισμα "τὰ στίγματα τοῦ Χριστοῦ" περιφέρει.

[195] Cf. Act. Thom., chap. 26 (II, 2, p. 141.17); 54 (p. 170.11).

[196] I regard these conceptions as proven by Heitmüller's statements (*Im Namen Jesu,* pp. 275-331). Esp. abundant documentation for the conception that baptism (the sacrament) liberates from the demons is offered by the Gnostic traditions (*Hauptprobleme,* pp. 295-96): Marcosians in Irenaeus I, 13.6: διὰ γὰρ τὴν ἀπολύτρωσιν ἀκρατήτους καὶ ἀοράτους γίνεσθαι τῷ κριτῇ. Exc. ex Theod. (besides the passage discussed in the text above), 22, 81, 83. II (Coptic) Book of Jeu 44, 48; Pistis Sophia 111, 131-33; Acta Thomae 157. From this perspective one can easily understand how very soon (and perhaps even earlier in the praxis than one can prove literarily) exorcism was indissolubly connected with baptism. Indeed, strictly speaking, baptism was from the very beginning a kind of

comfort for the Christians that his name is greater ὑπεράνω πάντος ὀνόματος ὀνομαζομένου (Eph. 1:21). On the other hand, this name obligates one to service. It is the task of the Christian life "to keep the seal pure and undefiled." Woe to one who shames the name and breaks the seal.

4. The Christian confession is connected as closely as possible with baptism. The earliest Christian confession for a long time has to do quite exclusively with the person of the Kyrios Jesus.[197] In the Pauline communities it probably was simply κύριος 'Ιησοῦς. This is also reflected in the history of the baptismal formula. Almost wherever we meet the trinitarian baptismal formula, the older cultic tradition still clearly shines through. We have already treated the baptismal formula of the Didache and the fact that in the *Actus Vercellenses Petri* the trinitarian baptismal formula stands in utter contradiction to its environment (*vide supra*, p. 297). Though we found this form in the *Excerpta ex Theodoto* (76.3; 80.3), yet in the same work an older baptismal formula of the Valentinians runs: ἐν λυτρώσει τοῦ ὀνόματος τοῦ ἐπὶ τὸν 'Ιησοῦν ἐν τῇ περιστερᾷ κατελθόντος (22). In the Pseudo-Clementine writings the mention of the trinitarian formula is extraordinarily frequent,[198] but in Recog. I, 39 the original still shines through, and in Recog. IX, 11 only the invocation of "the" holy name is spoken of.[199] Cf. I, 73: Peter baptizes *in nomine Jesu*. In the Acts of Thomas the trinitarian formula in the act of baptism occurs no less

---

exorcism. (On the history of exorcism, cf. now Dölger, SGKA III, 1-2). As opposed to Dölger's statements (p. 9), however, I prefer to see in Exc. ex Theod. 82 the earliest trace of the act of exorcism. The mention of the ὕδωρ ἐξορκιζόμενον in addition to the baptismal water remains at least very strange. On the other hand, in Acta Thomae, chap. 157, I do not see an act of exorcism but an actual baptism (baptism with oil) (see below).

[197] Trinitarian phrases (salutations, etc.) naturally are found more frequently, apart from the baptismal formula. Indeed Paul has led the way here with expressions such as II Cor. 13:13; I Cor. 12:4-5; cf. (Eph. 2:22; 3:16); I Pet. 1:2; Rev. 1:4; Ignat. Eph. 9; Magn. 13; I Clem. 46.6; 58.2.

[198] Cf. Iren. I, 21.3, ἄλλοι (Marcosians . . .) ἐπιλέγουσιν οὕτως· τὸ ὄνομα τὸ ἀποκεκρυμμένον ἀπὸ πάσης θεότητος. . . . ὃ ἐνεδύσατο 'Ιησοῦς ὁ Ναζαρηνός. . . . Χριστοῦ ζῶντος διὰ πνεύματος ἁγίου. Cf. with this Iren. I, 21.2, τὸ μὲν γὰρ βάπτισμα τοῦ φαινομένου 'Ιησοῦ εἰς ἄφεσιν (instead of ἀφέσεως following the Latin) ἁμαρτιῶν, τὴν δὲ ἀπολύτρωσιν τοῦ ἐν αὐτῷ Χριστοῦ κατελθόντος εἰς τελείωσιν; cf. the trinitarian reshaping of 21.3: εἰς ὄνομα ἀγνώστου Πατρὸς τῶν ὅλων, εἰς 'Αλήθειαν, Μητέρα πάντων, εἰς τὸν κατελθόντα εἰς 'Ιησοῦν. On the other hand, the second formula handed on in the transcription in the same place closes with 'Ιησοῦ Ναζαρία; cf. the ostensible translation with ὀναίμην τοῦ ὀνόματός σου Σωτὴρ ἀληθείας. The baptismal formula of the Elkesaites given by Hippolytus in Ref. IX, 15.1, p. 253.14 W is in two parts: ἐν ὀνόματι τοῦ μεγάλου καὶ ὑψίστου θεοῦ καὶ ἐν ὀνόματι υἱοῦ αὐτοῦ, (τοῦ) μεγάλου βασιλέως. Cf. Gressmann, ZNW XVI (1915), 191-95. [K. Müller, NGG, phil.-hist. Kl. (1920), pp. 188-200. Krüger.] On two-part formulas in Rev. 14.1 ff., Brandt, *Elchasai*, p. 90.

[199] Cf. Heitmüller, *Im Namen Jesu*, p. 295.

than five times (27, 49, 121, 132, 157), but the beginning of the baptismal prayer in chap. 27 runs: ἐλθὲ τὸ ἅγιον ὄνομα τοῦ Χριστοῦ τὸ ὑπὲρ πᾶν ὄνομα.[200] And in the baptismal prayer in chap. 157 it is said: ἐν ὀνόματί σου ’Ι. Χρ. γινέσθω ταῖς ψυχαῖς ταύταις εἰς ἄφεσιν ἁμαρτιῶν καὶ εἰς ἀποτροπὴν τοῦ ἐναντίου. Further, it may be regarded, in my judgment, as highly probable that in all the passages named the baptismal confession together with the act of water baptism (alongside the sealing with oil) owes its existence[201] only to a later redaction.[202] The testimony for the wide distribution of the simple baptismal formula down into the second century is so overwhelming[203] that on this basis Conybeare's surmise acquires high probability, that even in Matt. 28:19 the trinitarian formula was only later inserted and that Eusebius had actually read an older text which ran: πορευθέντες μαθητεύσατε πάντα τὰ ἔθνη ἐν τῷ ὀνόματί μου.[204]

To this corresponds the fact that the gradually developed confession of early Christianity, even apart from baptism, long remained exclusively a confession of Christ. The Gospel of John[205] offers such solemn confessions in several passages. According to it the synagogal ban follows the ὁμολογεῖν

---

[200] The following appeal to the maternal deity is thoroughly Gnostic. The prayer is christianized by the quoted first sentence and by the mention of the ἅγιον πνεῦμα at the end. Cf. Act. Thom., chap. 7, p. 110.19 B., and chap. 39, p. 157.16 B. *Hauptprobleme*, pp. 333 ff. On the triad of gods: Usener, Rhein. Mus. 58 (1903).

[201] In Act. Thom., chap. 26, a water baptism does not appear. The first mentioned ἐσφράγισεν αὐτούς is connected simply with the act of signing with the cross (Dölger, *Sphragis*, p. 96). The following ἐπισφράγισμα τῆς σφραγῖδος is the baptism with oil, and a further act does not follow. In all the following passages (see below) water baptism is attached to the explicitly described sealing with oil only in one short sentence. According to chap. 120 Mygdonia brings a small amount (according to S; G κρασίς?) of water along with bread (for the eucharist) and oil (for the sealing). After this it suddenly speaks of a fountain of water for baptism. What need is there then of the vessel with water that is to be brought? Again in chap. 132 it is said, "and he had a tub (σκάφην) brought and baptized them in the name . . . ." What an awkward interruption of the sacred rite! The redactor was in a dilemma as to how he should subsequently render a baptism with water possible. In chap. 152 Thomas is called a sorcerer who has bewitched men with oil (baptism), water and bread (eucharist).

[202] Cf. further Act. Pauli et Thecl., chap. 34 ("in the name of Jesus Christ I baptize myself"). Martyrdom of Paul (Bonnet, I, 104 ff.), chap. 7: "They gave him the seal in the Lord."

[203] Still in the Canones apostolorum No. 50 a baptism εἰς τὸν θανατὸν τοῦ κυρίου in place of the triple immersion in the name of the Father, Son and Holy Spirit is forbidden. Cf. Sozomen, VI, 26.24, and E. Schwartz, *Über die ps. apost. Kirchenordnungen* (Schriften der wiss. Ges. in Strassburg, VI, 1910), p. 13; baptism into Jesus' death. Ps. Cypr., de rebapt., ch. 3, p. 73.17; ch. 5, p. 75.30 Hartel: baptism only into Jesus. Cf. Schermann, *Die allgem. Kirchenordnung* II (1915), pp. 304-308.

[204] Conybeare, ZNW II (1901), 275 ff.; *contra*, Riggenbach, BFcT VII, 1.

[205] 9:35 ff. (Son of man); 11:27 (Son of God); 20:28 (God and Lord).

τὸν Χριστόν.[206] The Epistle to the Hebrews calls Christ the high priest "of our confession" and admonishes the readers to hold fast to this confession.[207] In the early textual emendation of the book of Acts the eunuch answers the question of belief: πιστεύω τὸν υἱὸν τοῦ θεοῦ εἶναι τὸν Ἰησοῦν (8:36-37). Polycarp's confession still sounds quite Pauline: οἵτινες μέλλουσι πιστεύειν εἰς τὸν κύριον ἡμῶν Ἰ. Χρ. καὶ τὸν πατέρα αὐτοῦ τὸν ἐγείραντα αὐτὸν ἐκ νεκρῶν (Phil. 12.2). Indeed, Christ himself rendered a good confession (to his Sonship to God) before Pontius Pilate himself (I Tim. 6:13). From this perspective we may infer the content of the καλὴ ὁμολογία which Timothy gave before many witnesses.[208] Further, the Christ hymn in I Tim. 3:16, which is introduced as the confessedly great mystery of the church of the living God, bears a confessional character. And in the μνημόνευε τὸν Χριστὸν ἐγηγερμένον ἐκ νεκρῶν ἐκ σπέρματος Δαυείδ (II Tim. 2:8) there is the begining of a simple christological confession. We encounter this character in especially clear form in Ignatius' many confession-like statements which point to a traditional schema. The short ὁμολογία Χριστοῦ has grown into a christological kerygma, but it has remained a ὁμολογία Χριστοῦ.[209] And finally, Harnack[210] concerning Justin judges that from him we may draw only a confessional formula to the one Creator-God and in addition an explicit fixed christological confession. There is, then, in fact in the tripartite and detailed Roman baptismal confession a distinct and at first probably quite individual modification.[211] Still,

---

[206] John 9:22; 12:42; cf. the ὁμολογία directed against Docetism in I John 2:23; 4:2-3, and 4:15.

[207] Heb. 3:1; 4:14; 10:23. The ὁμολογεῖν τῷ ὀνόματι αὐτοῦ in 13:15 appears to refer to God (or perhaps—see the preceding δι᾽ αὐτοῦ—to Christ?).

[208] I regard as unnecessary and indeed unlikely the conclusion of a two-part confession of faith in the Creator God and the μαρτυρήσας Χριστὸν Ἰησοῦν under Pontius Pilate (Harnack, Chronologie, I, 525). How the context is to be understood is indicated above.

[209] The chief passages are Eph. 7.2; 18.2; (19.1); 20.2; to Polyc. 3.2; above all the anti-docetically coined long formulas in Trall. 9 and Smyrn. 1.1-2. In another connection we shall treat the characteristic marks of the Ignatian confessions (ἐκ γένους Δαυίδ in Eph. 18.2; 20.2; Trall. 9.1; Smyrn. 1.1; baptism of Jesus in Eph. 18.2; Smyrn. 1.1; also the miraculous birth in Eph. 18.2; Trall. 9; Smyrn. 1.1). One should note that Eph. 7.2 closes with the solemn "Ἰησοῦς Χριστὸς ὁ κύριος ἡμῶν," Smyrn. 1.1 begins with ὁ κύριος ἡμῶν, while in Eph. 18.2 the ὁ θεὸς ἡμῶν has already come in.

[210] Chronologie, I, 525.

[211] I still agree completely with Harnack's judgment about the old Roman baptismal confession (Chronologie, I, 524-32). Though its existence is attested by Tertullian before the definitive dispute with Gnosticism, it still cannot be traced back far beyond the middle of the second century. This remains true in the face of Norden's interesting assertions (Agnostos Theos, pp. 263 ff.). Yet we cannot get at the problem with investigations that are essentially oriented to literary form. The hieratic-Oriental style of the confession is no hindrance to its late dating, though it naturally contains earlier formulations. [Cf. now the

even if here the κύριος Χριστός has had to give up his all-exclusive position, yet the christological kerygma now is accepted as the core of this confession, and the confession of Jesus Christ (his only-begotten Son) our Lord assumes its central position. All that we have discussed up to this point is actually already summarized in lapidary style by the author of the Ephesian epistle: εἷς κύριος, μία πίστις, ἓν βάπτισμα.

5. When the baptizand is accepted into the Christian community, he is therewith admitted to the eucharist. Baptism and the first participation in the eucharist form a single act of worship. We have already emphasized that this second sacrament, which dominates the cultus, stands in immediate connection with the κύριος Χριστός. It is δεῖπνον κυριακόν, and whatever may have been the view of the Supper in particular, the Pauline idea remained dominant: the Supper is κοινωνία τοῦ αἵματος καὶ τοῦ σώματος Χριστοῦ. According to the Gospel of John, the exalted (6:53, 62) Son of Man gives his flesh and blood for eternal life (6:54) and for enduring fellowship with himself (6:56). And both are correct: It depends upon the partaking of flesh and blood, but again it is a fellowship in which the Spirit remains the effectual force (6:63). Or at least the more general conception dominates, that in the sacred meal the Lord himself is present. Here the conclusion of the portrayal of the eucharist in the Didache 10.6 speaks quite clearly. There it is said: "Let grace come, let the world pass away." Then the community greets the present Lord with "Maranatha" and with "Hosanna to the God of David." [212] Already in Didache 14.3 the well-known passage in Malachi is connected with the Supper, and now it is said of the Lord Jesus: ὅτι βασιλεὺς μέγας εἰμί, λέγει κύριος (!) καὶ τὸ ὄνομά μου θαυμαστὸν ἐν τοῖς ἔθνεσιν. With perfect clarity the Acts of Thomas places the eucharist under the perspective of the Pauline κοινωνία[213]: ἄρτον κλάσας καὶ λαβὼν ποτήριον ὕδατος κοινωνὸν ἐποίησεν αὐτὴν τῷ τοῦ Χριστοῦ σώματι καὶ ποτηρίῳ τοῦ υἱοῦ τοῦ θεοῦ (chap. 121). Jesus is invoked upon the eucharist: ἰδοὺ τολμῶθεν προσέρχεσθαι τῇ σῇ εὐχαριστίᾳ καὶ ἐπικαλεῖσθαί σου τὸ ἅγιον ὄνομα· ἐλθὲ καὶ κοινώνησον ἡμῖν (chap. 49). From above is heard a voice which answers the eucharistic prayer with a ναὶ ἀμήν (chap. 121). According to chap. 133, the name of

---

works of Holl, Harnack, and Lietzmann in the SAB, 1919, and Haussleiter, *Trinitarischer Glaube und Christus-Bekenntnis*, BFcT, 1920, XXV. Krüger.]

[212] It is worthy of note that this part of the eucharistic liturgy has been preserved in all the later great ecclesiastical liturgies and almost always in the decisive position, immediately before the act of communion.

[213] Cf. Act. Joh., chap. 86.

Jesus is pronounced over the bread of the eucharist. And then it is said: ἐλθάτω δύναμις εὐλογίας καὶ ἐνιδρύσθω ὁ ἄρτος. Precisely corresponding to this is the conception[214] which is demonstrable later in church fathers and in ancient liturgies to a large extent, that in the Supper the Logos himself is invoked by means of the solemn epiclesis,[215] settles upon the elements of the eucharist and fills them with his essence. This is still always the spiritual-bodily presence of the κύριος in the Supper; only gradually is this pneumatic view replaced by the crudely magical view of the transformation of the elements on the one hand, and on the other by the idea of the repeated sacrifice.[216]

6. At the center of Christian worship stands prayer. Here now, to be sure, the development we are considering found its limits. The official prayer of the community continued to be directed to God. The Roman prayer handed down to us by Clement, the eucharistic prayer of the Didache and Justin's portrayal of Christian worship all prove this. Here on the one side the influence of the Jewish synagogue (I Clem. 59 ff. and Didache 9–10 are altered Jewish synagogue prayers), and on the other side the example which Jesus left behind in the Lord's Prayer probably had all too powerful an aftereffect. The massive and naïve community faith however insisted upon praying to Christ. The apocryphal acts of the apostles, which reflect as do no other sources the popular belief of the masses of ordinary Christianity, show this adequately. Here prayer to Christ has become the rule throughout. And yet Origen, with a direct appeal to the Lord's Prayer, rejects prayer to Christ,[217] which clearly shows that the latter was already a widespread custom. He speaks of a division, since some pray to the Father, and others to the Son. In typical fashion he calls the latter: ἰδιωτικὴν ἁμαρτίαν κατὰ πολλὴν ἀκεραιότητα διὰ τὸ ἀβασάνιστον καὶ ἀνεξέταστον ἁμαρτανόντων τῶν προσευχομένων (16.1).

---

[214] I can only indicate this in passing. For the present I refer for the Egyptian liturgical tradition to Schermann, *Ägypt. Abendmahlsliturgien* (SGKA VI, 1–2), 1912, pp. 75-78. In Justin's Apol. I, 66, the τὴν δι' εὐχῆς Λόγου τοῦ παρ' αὐτοῦ εὐχαριστηθεῖσαν τροφήν should be translated "the food which is consecrated by the prayer for the Logos." Cf. esp. Iren. V, 2.3 and IV, 18.5.

[215] To be compared with this is the epiclesis by which, according to the Hellenistic conception, the divine power is invoked into the images of the gods. Cf. de Jong, *Mysterienwesen*, pp. 102 ff. Characteristic here above all are the conceptions in the Hermetic tractate Asclepius (Ps.-Apuleius), chaps. 23 and 38. Cyril of Jerusalem (Catech. XIX, 7) suggested the comparison in regard to the epiclesis in pagan sacrificial meals. Cf. related Gnostic conceptions: Iren. I, 13.2 (Marcosians: λόγος τῆς ἐπικλήσεως).

[216] The development has already begun with Ignatius, Eph. 20 (φάρμακον ἀθανασίας).
[217] περὶ εὐχῆς 15, 16.

However, the κύριος nevertheless attains a firm position in the Christian community prayer. This becomes a prayer in his name (under invocation of his name). As a solemn, ever-repeated legacy, the Johannine Jesus leaves to his community prayer in his name.[218] The community prayer of Acts 4:25 ff., the Roman community prayer in Clement, the eucharistic liturgy in the Didache, and the prayer of the martyr Polycarp (chap. 14; cf. 20) are fully valid evidences for the prayer of the Christian community to God διὰ τοῦ (ἁγίου) παιδός σου. As strongly as Origen (περὶ εὐχῆς) emphasizes that prayer is to be directed only to God, just as strongly does he place stress upon the fact that no prayer occurs without Christ, that one is to pray to God in the name of Jesus.

Also in the doxologies, in the community's liturgy as in the literature, the κύριος, as in prayer, has a firm position. Here the dominant formula must have been first something like διὰ 'I. Χρ. δι' οὗ σοὶ ἡ δόξα εἰς τοὺς αἰῶνας τῶν αἰώνων.[219] Of course alongside this there appears in the literature —and certainly just as early in the community's usage—the direct doxology to Christ.[220] A compromise formula, which presupposes the simple doxology to Christ, is found already in the prayer of Polycarp (Mart. Polyc. 14.3), which appears in its language to be closely related to the eucharistic liturgy, δι' οὗ σοὶ σὺν αὐτῷ καὶ πνεύματι ἁγίῳ δόξα καὶ νῦν καὶ εἰς τοὺς μέλλοντας αἰῶνας. Cf. 22:1: 'I. Χρ. μεθ' οὗ δόξα τῷ θεῷ. Again a glance at the earliest liturgies shows us that such compromise formulas for a long time predominated, until they yielded to the simple trinitarian doxologies.

7. It became of much more far-reaching significance that the hymnody in worship was concentrated upon the person of the κύριος. It is characteristic that the later manuscripts[221] change the ᾄδοντες τῷ θεῷ in Col. 3:16 into

[218] 14:13, 14; 15:7, 16; 16:23, 24, 26; cf. I John 5:14-15. Eph. 5:20, εὐχαριστεῖν ἐν ὀνόματι τοῦ κυρίου ἡμῶν. At the same time passages like 14:13-14, 26, show how prayer in Jesus' name still can easily turn into prayer to him (ἐγὼ ποιήσω).

[219] Cf. I Clem. 20.11 ff.; 58.2; 61.3 (close of the congregation's prayer); 64; 65.2 (without the mediation, 32.4; 38.4; 43.6; 45.7; I Tim. 1:17); Jude 25. The reference of I Pet. 4:11 (cf. 5:11), ἵνα δοξάζηται ὁ θεὸς διὰ 'Ιησοῦ Χριστοῦ ᾧ (=God) ἐστιν ἡ δόξα, etc., cannot be determined with certainty; similarly Heb. 13:21 and I Clem. 50.7. The formula in Eph. 3:21, αὐτῷ ἡ δόξα ἐν τῇ ἐκκλησίᾳ καὶ ἐν Χριστῷ 'Ιησοῦ is singular; it then has its echo in the oldest liturgies known to us, the so-called Egyptian Church Order (Hippolytus? cf. the conclusion of his writing contra Noetum with the same formula), the Canons of Hippolytus and the Apostolic Constitutions. Cf. v. d. Goltz, Gebet, p. 135.

[220] Because of the connection with the preceding, probably also II Tim. 4:18; certainly II Pet. 3:18; Mart. Polyc. 21; 22.3; Acta Pauli et Thecl. 42. Cf. Passio Perpetuae et Felic. 1.4 (21.11); perhaps I Pet. 4:11; Heb. 13:21, and I Clem. 50.7 (see note 219). On the hymns of the Apocalypse, see below; εὐλογητός of Christ first in Mart. Polyc. 14.1.

[221] K L cop Chrys. Theodoret.

ᾄδοντες τῷ Χριστῷ, and that in Eph. 5:19 it is already expressed as ᾄδοντες καὶ ψάλλοντες τῷ κυρίῳ. Such a hymn is found in I Tim. 3:16. The Revelation of John with its hymns to the Lamb considerably advances the development. The apocalyptist cannot conceive of the conditions in heaven as anything but a service of worship[222] in which hymns are sung to God *and "the Lamb."* [223] In this he probably is aware of the novelty of the hymns to the Lamb in the church's usage: καὶ ᾄδουσιν ᾠδὴν καινήν (5:9; cf. 14:3; 15:4). Similarly, it is said in the Martyrdom of Polycarp that the blessed martyr who is abiding in heaven δοξάζει τὸν θεὸν καὶ πατέρα παντοκράτορα καὶ εὐλογεῖ τὸν κύριον ἡμῶν 'I. Χρ. (19:1; cf. the following verse).[224] The worship on earth with its characteristic features is transferred to heaven. Ignatius says to the Ephesians[225] that in the unanimity of the community and their loving harmony 'Ιησοῦς Χριστὸς ᾄδεται, by which he is probably thinking first of all of the Christians' worship.[226] Here, quite unconsciously, a significant and consequential event takes place. The word with which Pliny characterizes the Christians in his letter to Trajan, *carmenque Christo quasi deo dicere secum invicem,*[227] offers us the best insight into its import. In a later age, when people sought proofs of the deity of Jesus in ancient times, they appealed to the psalms and hymns, sung from the very beginning by believing brethren, which praise Christ, the Logos of God, by calling him God (θεολογοῦντες).[228] Here in fact Christ already takes his place at the side of God. And it is characteristic that it occurs in the singing of the community.[229] Singing is something

---

[222] Cf. the reminiscences of the liturgy: the song of the Seraphim in 4:8, the repeated ἄξιος (liturgy: ἄξιον καὶ δίκαιον).

[223] Hymns to the Lamb in 5:9, 12, (13); (7:10); (11:15-16); 15:3-4; 19:6-8 (marriage of the Lamb), (hymns to God alone, 11:17-18; 19:1-2, 5).

[224] Cf. E. v. d. Goltz, *Das Gebet in der ältesten Christenheit,* p. 136.

[225] Ign. Eph. 4.1, then of course the formula ἐν ἑνότητι ᾄδετε ἐν φωνῇ μιᾷ διὰ 'Ιησοῦ Χριστοῦ τῷ πατρί (4:2); cf. Rom. 2.2 and the δοξάζειν 'I. Χρ. in Eph. 2.2 and Philad. 10.1.

[226] Cf. further Clement, Paid. III, 101.2: αἰνοῦντες εὐχάριστον αἶνον τῷ μόνῳ πατρὶ καὶ υἱῷ . . . σὺν καὶ τῷ ἁγίῳ πνεύματι. Later passages in Schermann, *Der liturgische Papyrus von Der-Balyzeh,* 1910 (TU XXXVI, 1), p. 24.1. Cf. v. d. Goltz, *Das Gebet in der ältesten Christenheit,* p. 137; A. Jacoby, *Ein neues Evangelienfragment* (1900).

[227] Pliny suggests antiphonal choral singing. Cf. H. Lietzmann in *Gesch. Studien für Hauck* (1916), pp. 34-38. An illustration of this is provided by the portrayal of the celestial worship (see above) in Rev. 5:1. Cf. further Od. Sol. 10.7, if Gressmann's conjecture (ZNW XI [1910], 311) is correct: "They confessed me with psalms" (instead of "in the heights").

[228] Eus. CH V, 28.5.

[229] Cf. v. d. Goltz, *Das Gebet . . .* , p. 139.

different from the hard, fixed formula of doctrine and even from prayer. Enthusiasm and the rapture of inspiration are expressed most easily in it.

IV. *The Sacrificial Death and Its Significance.* This Kyrios, who occupies such a central position in the cultus of the community, is surrounded and enmeshed by a great mystery. He is the one who died for his community, who offered his life as a sacrifice for them. This view, for which the way was evidently prepared, perhaps already in the Palestinian primitive community but in any case in the pre-Pauline Gentile Christian church and which Paul set in the center of the Christian thought-world, was understood everywhere. Nothing could be more impressive than the picture of the suffering and dying Jesus.[230] And in the Gentile Christian milieu people were just as much in agreement in particular on the ideas of sacrifice and atonement as in Judaism. The sentence in Heb. 9:22: καὶ χωρὶς αἵματεκχυσίας οὐ γίνεται ἄφεσις holds true for the religious feeling of the whole world of that time.

It is especially to be noted that the idea of sacrifice also penetrated the words of the last Supper and therewith into the eucharist in general, where of course it did not originally belong. Associated with the "this is my body" is the "(given, broken) for you," and with the "this is the covenant in my blood" is the "shed (for the remission of sins) for many"; even Paul, who has so strongly grasped the basic idea of the eucharist, the κοινωνία, here, as it appears, stands under the impact of the tradition.[231] Thus from the outset the motif of sacrifice and atonement sounds in the sacred action of the eucharist. The Lord who is present in body and blood (spiritually–corporeally), who enters into κοινωνία with the Christians, is the same Lord who was given for us in the sacrificial death. The present body is still at the same time the body which was broken in death, and the present blood is the blood which was shed on the cross (cf. John 19:34). Thus the idea

---

[230] Cf. I Clem. 16:2: τὸ σκῆπτρον τῆς μεγαλωσύνης τοῦ θεοῦ ὁ κύριος ᾽Ιησοῦς Χριστὸς οὐκ ἦχθεν ἐν κόμπῳ ἀλαζωνείας οὐδὲ ὑπερηφανίας . . . ἀλλὰ ταπεινοφρονῶν, and then as evidence the entire context of Isa. 53:1-12 is quoted, as well as Ps. 22:7-9.

[231] To be sure, only in the first half of the saying. Here he has, going beyond the text of the Synoptics, the ὑπὲρ ὑμῶν. On the other hand he is not acquainted with the addition τὸ ἐκχυνόμενον [εἰς ἄφεσιν ἁμαρτιῶν] ὑπὲρ πολλῶν. The words τοῦτο τὸ ποτήριον ἡ καινὴ διαθήκη ἐστὶν ἐν τῷ ἐμῷ αἵματι are only a paraphrase of τὸ αἷμά μου τῆς διαθήκης. Paul and the Synoptics go back to a common text in which that addition was still lacking! "τὸ αἷμα τῆς διαθήκης" however has nothing to do with the idea of atonement; the thought contained therein has been correctly interpreted by Paul with the κοινωνία τοῦ αἵματος. Heb. 10:29 fully confirms this: The phrase τὸ αἷμα τῆς διαθήκης κοινὸν ἡγησάμενος *refers directly* to the element of the eucharist.

of sacrifice, even though at first only as a subordinate idea, attains its place in the eucharist. This is more important than all the literary affirmations even of a Paul; in every solemn eucharistic service of worship it was in the inmost thoughts of the early Christians.

In order rightly to evaluate the ideas of sacrifice, blood, and atonement in ancient Christianity, we will after all have to proceed from the fact that all these are more expressions of inspired discourse than of specific thinking, more hymn and liturgy than theology.

Some begin to speak of Christ in solemn and exalted language as the Lamb of God. The Apocalypse shows plainly and powerfully how this language stems from hymn and liturgy. The hymns which it hands down are hymns to the Lamb.[232] The mysterious enigmatic language—the Lamb that is slain,[233] the bride of the Lamb[234]—is borrowed from hymns. The confessional saying which is put in the mouth of the Baptist also has a hymnlike sound: "Behold the Lamb of God, who takes away the sins of the world" (1:29, 36). And perhaps the solemn tones in which I Peter speaks of the precious blood of Christ, the innocent and spotless Lamb, come from a baptismal homily (*vide infra*).

Equally solemnly, mysteriously, people speak of the blood of Christ. Already Paul begins with: "We are justified through his blood" (Rom. 5:9). One will note in particular the paradox that "the blood cleanses." This again emerges most strongly in the metaphorical language of the Apocalypse: "They have washed their garments and made them white in the blood of the Lamb!" (7:14). The sprinkling with the blood of Christ is the mark of the new people of God.[235] "The blood of Jesus Christ cleanses us from all sins" (I John 1:7). Through the blood of Christ those who were far off have come nigh to God (Eph. 2:13).[236] I Clement uses the blood formula especially frequently and admonishes: "Let us gaze steadfastly (ἀτενίζωμεν) at the blood of Christ and recognize how precious it is to God his Father" (7:4). At the same time the blood of Christ is experienced as a power present in the sacrament, and thus the mysterious aspect of the view is heightened. Spirit, water, and blood are the living, present powers of Chris-

---

[232] See above, p. 304, ᾠδὴ τοῦ ἀρνίου! It does not matter to me whether these expressions are in part later insertions. Here the later element is more instructive than the earlier.

[233] Rev. 5:6, 9; 13:8.

[234] 19:7; 21:2, 9.

[235] I Pet. 1:1; cf. Heb. 12:24. Barn. 5.1.

[236] Eph. 1:7. Col. 1:14 (mss.). Rev. 1:5. I Clem. 12.7; (21.6;) 49.6. Cf. Acts 20:28.

tianity (I John 5:6-8). In the Ignatian epistles the blood (and flesh) of Christ is in the first place the power present in the sacrament (*vide infra*, Chap. VIII). The stoutest paradox, "blood of God," will be treated below.

Similarly the cross is the great mystery of the community. Paul begins with this manner of meditation in the great affirmations of I Cor. "I intend to glory only in the cross of our Lord Jesus Christ, by which the world is crucified to me and I to the world" (Gal. 6:14). In the Colossian Epistle (1:20) the two mysteries are bound together (διὰ τοῦ αἵματος τοῦ σταυροῦ αὐτοῦ). Originally people paid less attention to the shape of the cross. Cross and stake[237] (wood, ξύλον) are identical concepts. Barnabas cites the apocryphal prophecy: ὅταν ξύλον κλιθῇ καὶ ἀναστῇ, καὶ ὅταν ἐξ ξύλου αἷμα στάξῃ (12.1).[238] Then, however, people became aware of the mysterious shape of the cross. The same Barnabas interprets the 318 servants of Abraham as IH and the sign of the cross, T (9.8). Moses, who prays with outstretched arms for Israel's victory against Amalek, represents the sign of the cross (12.2). In the Odes of Solomon the outstretching of the hands as a symbol of the cross is a note repeatedly sounded: "The stretching out of my hands is his sign and my outstretching is the upright wood." [239]

The mysterious proclamation of the Christianity of the cross for this reason found special echoes and strong resonance because for a long time in wide circles people were used to regarding the cross (in the actual meaning of the word) as a mysterious, magically powerful, life-giving sign.[240] Here then, probably under the multiple appropriation of syncretistic motifs, Christian imagination grew abundantly and prolifically. Very early the fantasy of the ascension of the cross emerges.[241] This ascension of the cross is already mentioned in the spurious Gospel of Peter.[242] To this was joined the later widespread[243] fantasy that on his return Jesus would appear hanging upon the cross (of light). The σημεῖον ἐκπετάσεως [244] ἐν οὐρανῷ

[237] Cf. the relating of Deut. 21:23 to the cross in Gal. 3:13, Acts 5:30 and 10:39.

[238] The second half of the saying: IV Ezra 5:5. Cf. also the symbol of the serpent on the "stake" according to Num. 21:8 ff. Barn. 12.5-6 and even John 3:14.

[239] Od. Sal. 27; cf. 42.1 (21.1; 35.8; 37.1). The passages (particularly 42.1) are in part obscure.

[240] Cf. e.g. the Egyptian hooked cross (symbol of lordship and of life), the regular badge of all the deities. Further, the divine image of the Alexandrian aeon described by Epiphanius in Haer. 51.22 bears five crosses; this however is in no way Christian-Gnostic. A cross sign on the Host in the mysteries of Mithras in the famous account of the sacred meal of Mithras (e.g., in Wendland, *Hellenistisch-römische Kultur*, 2nd ed., Plate XIII, 4). The little writing by Schremmer, *Labarum und Steinaxt*, 1911, sheds light here on a broad area.

[241] Sibyll. VI, 26-27.

[242] X, 39 ff.; it is explicitly expressed in Sibyll. VI, 26-27.

[243] Cf. Bousset, *Antichrist*, pp. 154 ff.

[244] To be translated "sign of the extension," i.e., of the arms. Cf. the passages in the

in the Didache (XVI, 6) can hardly be understood other than under this presupposition. Indeed perhaps the σημεῖον τοῦ υἱοῦ τοῦ ἀνθρώπου in Matt. 24:30 receives its explanation from this. Thus was developed an entire theology of the cross[245] or mystagogy, examples of which are found in Ignatius' Eph. 9, in Polycarp's Phil. 7.1, in Barnabas' chap. 8.5 and chap. 11, in Justin's Apol. I, 55 (cf. chap. 60), and in particular in the many mysterious statements and cross prayers of the apocryphal acts of the apostles.[246] These last-named witnesses are perhaps of specifically Gnostic origin. Yet, as it appears, at first only isolated notes of this mythology penetrated into the language of worship of genuine Christianity.

It is the language of the mysteries which is developed in the expressions about the Lamb of God, the blood of Christ and the cross, and infant Christianity found in the surrounding world understanding for and resonance with this mystery language. Under this perspective we also have to understand in essence all the expressions about the death of Christ which are more obviously developed along conceptual lines. In all this there is no real theology present; rather, they are thankful confessions of a believing community to the Kyrios who has done so much for his own. Thus the images by which people seek to portray the significance of his death are constantly being changed, and the most diverse images stand peaceably side by side. The death of Christ is redemption, ransom (it is almost never said exactly who then actually receives the ransom money),[247] it signifies atonement and forgiveness,[248] it is purification, initiation and sanctification,[249] it washes away sins,[250] brings forgiveness of sins, is the sacrifice for sins.[251]

---

Odes of Solomon mentioned above. In Barn. 12.4 the ἐξεπέτασα τὰς χεῖράς μου from Isa. 65:4 is referred to the sign of the cross. Thus the conjectured reading ἐπεκτάσεως is not even necessary.

[245] Cf. Celsus' scorn (Orig. VI, 36) for this cross mysticism.

[246] Act. Joh. 97-101; Mart. Petri, chaps. 8-9; Act. Andr. (Bonnet II, 1, p. 54), chap. 14; Act. Thom., chap. 121. In this context I must refrain from a discussion of this theology of the cross and hope to be able to give it in another place. Cf. ZNW XIV (1913), 273-85. The sign of the cross at baptism: Act. Petri 5, pars. 50 and 51; Act. Pauli et Thecl. 25, par. 253; Act. Joh. 15, par. 215; Act. Thom. 27-28, pars. 142-45. Cf. Dölger, Sphragis, 1911.

[247] ἀπολύτρωσις, ἀπολυτροῦν, λύτρον, λύτρωσις, λυτροῦν, λύειν, in Mark 10:45; Col. 1:14; Eph. 1:7; Heb. 9:12; I Pet. 1:18; I Tim. 2:6 (ἀντίλυτρον); Tit. 2:14; I Clem. 12.7 (7.4); Rev. 1:5; Barn. 14.5.

[248] ἱλασμός, ἱλάσκεσθαι in Heb. 2:17; I John 2:2; 4:10.

[249] καθαρίζειν, καθαρισμός in Heb. 1:3; 9:14 (9:22); I John 1:7, 9; Tit. 2:14. ῥαντισμός, ῥαντίζειν in I Pet. 1:2; Heb. 12:24; Barn. 5.1. ἁγιάζειν in Heb. 10:10; 13:12; Eph. 5:25; Barn. 5.1.

[250] Rev. 7:14 (1:5 mss.).

[251] Matt. 26:28; Heb. 9:26; I John 3:5 (αἴρειν τὰς ἁμαρτίας); Heb. 9:28; I Pet. 2:24 (ἀνενεγκεῖν ἁμαρτίας). Sacrifice: Heb. 10:12 (μίαν ὑπὲρ ἁμαρτιῶν προσήνεγκεν θυσίαν); 7:27; (9:12); Eph. 5:2 (προσφορά, θυσία); Barn. 7.3, 5; cf. Acts 8:32.

It has broken the power of death [252] and the power of him who had command of death; by means of blood, suffering, and death, Christ has earned the community as a possession,[253] has led us back to God,[254] has bestowed upon us the great grace of μετάνοια.[255] But the one great idea always sounds through: death, blood, and cross are the powers which support the present life of Christians, maintain it and govern it.[256] The Christians are κλάδοι τοῦ σταυροῦ.[257] Woe to the Docetic false teachers who deny the reality of the cross: καὶ ὃς ἂν μὴ ὁμολογῇ τὸ μαρτύριον τοῦ σταυροῦ ἐκ τοῦ διαβόλου ἐστίν.[258]

Here the Christians all sensed their most original possession. As generally widespread as was the idea of the necessity of atonement through a blood sacrifice, and as understandable to that age as the application of this idea to the death of Christ was, this news, that a being of godlike kind and glory had appeared, τὸ σκῆπτρον τῆς μεγαλωσύνης τοῦ θεοῦ, here below on earth, and had taken upon himself suffering and death for his own, was something unheard of, new. The idea of the typical significance of the death and resurrection of a god, and the principle that the pious (the initiated) re-experience the suffering, death, and resurrection of the deity in the cultic assembly was current and widespread (vide supra, pp. 188 ff.). But the surrounding world had nothing of similar weight and strength to set over against the preaching of the Kyrios who suffers and dies for us, of the πάθος θεοῦ and αἷμα θεοῦ for us.

At the same time this preaching was intimately connected with cultus and praxis. For now, young Christianity proclaimed that the one great sacrifice is offered once for all time and no further bloody sacrifice is needed. All the old sacrificial worship in Judaism as well as in paganism sinks into nothingness. The former is a σκιὰ τῶν μελλόντων, and the latter

---

[252] Heb. 2:14; II Tim. 1:10; Barn. 5.6; 14.5. In the idea of liberation from death (and particularly from the fear of death in Heb. 2:15), motifs of the piety of the mystery religion echo. On the idea of the destruction of the dominion of the old powers, see below, Chap. IX; cf. Mart. Apollon. 36: διὰ τοῦ παθεῖν ἔπαυσεν τὰς ἀρχὰς τῶν ἁμαρτιῶν.

[253] Acts 20:28; Tit. 2:14.

[254] I Pet. 3:18; Heb. 7:25; Ign. Trall. 11.2 (ἐν τῷ πάθει αὐτοῦ προσκαλεῖται ἡμᾶς).

[255] I Clem. 7.4; cf. 21.6.

[256] Cf., e.g., I Clem. 2.1; 21.16; Ign. Smyrn. 6.1; 7.7; 12.2; Polyc. 1.2 (Ign. Eph. 1.1; Trall. 2.1; Philad. Proem; Barn. 7.2).

[257] Trall. 11.2 [cf. L. v. Sybel, ZNW XX (1921), 93. Krüger].

[258] Pol. Phil. 7.1.

is the work of demons. The omnipotent and merciful Father is once for all reconciled, and now the new worship of God in spirit and in truth begins.

V. *Kyrios Cult and Ruler Cult.* In the third chapter I have demonstrated how the Kyrios cult of Hellenistic primitive Christianity is rooted in the Hellenistic milieu and finds its closest parallels in the Hellenistic-Roman emperor cult. These contacts remained lively and influential and led to a further heightening of the Kyrios cult, partly because the Christians, in energetic opposition, most vigorously elevated the claim of their Kyrios to sole lordship, but partly simply because elements of religious language were directly taken over, particularly from the emperor cult.

First of all it is the title Soter-Savior which comes into view here and demands a more precise examination. As is known, we see this title only gradually make its way into the New Testament literature. It is highly noteworthy that Paul (in his authentic epistles) uses it only one single time (Phil. 3:20), and indeed there in an expression so specifically primitive-Christian-eschatological that nothing obliges us to go beyond the assumption of the influence of the eschatological language of the Old Testament, in which Yahweh appears as the *Goël.* But later on the use is increased. In the Pastoral Epistles the title appears connected with certain other expressions which will engage our attention later (II Tim. 1:10; Tit. 1:4; 2:13; 3:5).[259] Besides, there is a circle of perhaps rather closely related authors and writings. The Antiochian (?) "Luke" knows the title (Luke 2:11; Acts 5:31 ἀρχηγὸς καὶ σωτήρ; 13:23)[260]; likewise Ignatius of Antioch (Eph. 1.1; Magn. Proem; Philad. 9.2; Smyrn. 7.1); in addition to these, the Gospel of Peter (IV, 13), the earliest traces of which we find once again among Syrian Docetists in the vicinity of Antioch,[261] Polycarp (Proem), and the Martyrdom of Polycarp (19.2). In the Johannine literary circle we encounter the distinctive σωτὴρ τοῦ κόσμου (4:42; I John 4:14). The designation is especially frequent in II Peter (1:1, 11; 2:10; 3:2, 18). As the title κατ' ἐξοχήν, Σωτήρ is first demonstrable in Gnostic circles. We have already referred above to the tradition of Irenaeus, that the Valentinians assigned the title of Kyrios to Achamoth while calling Jesus σωτήρ. And

---

[259] Alongside this, of course, σωτήρ is here used even more often of God.

[260] Cf. further II Clem. 20.5: τὸν σωτῆρα καὶ ἀρχηγὸν τῆς ἀφθαρσίας.

[261] Testimony of Serapion of Antioch, Eus. CH VI, 12.3-4.

this report harmonizes most exactly with the state of things in the epistle of Ptolemaeus to Flora,[262] as well as in Heracleon's Commentary on John.[263] And in the Excerpta ex Theodoto, in the alternation of κύριος and σωτήρ one has in hand a means of distinguishing the genuinely Gnostic fragments from other pieces and from the hand of the editor. And it is highly noteworthy that here in Gnosticism at first the absolute ὁ Σωτήρ[264] (the savior) emerges, without a genitive and without a second title. The language usage of the Valentinians who made their compromises with the church, however, also lets us infer something of the language usage at least of certain circles in the Great Church. Thus around the middle of the second century people begin extensively to characterize Jesus as the "Savior."

To answer the question as to the origin[265] of this title which only so gradually made its way, the ruler cultus, in fact, suggests itself first of all. The fact that the designation Soter is most intimately connected with this cultus is shown by the names of Ptolemy Soter and Ptolemy Euergetes, which apparently already contain a religious meaning. The Soter concept then was especially connected with the veneration of the Roman emperors. These were indeed the saving powers who had brought order, peace, repose, and prosperity into the world, in place of sheer hopeless chaos and unspeakable confusion. Relieved of war, the earth lay at their feet. Yet even here it was not merely unprincipled Byzantinism when people celebrated them in rapturous tones as the benefactors of the whole human race, as the saviors of the world. An inscription[266] from Ephesus calls Caesar the manifest God who stems from Ares and Aphrodite, κοινοῦ τοῦ ἀνθρωπίνου βίου σωτῆρα.[267] In quite special and rapturous manner this Soter veneration is applied to the emperor Augustus. I recall only the famous calendar inscrip-

---

[262] Cf. Harnack, *Mission and Expansion of Christianity*, I, 103, n. 2.

[263] Dölger, ' Ι χθύς (RQ, Supplem. XVII), p. 409 (where a full listing of the passages that come into consideration).

[264] Dölger correctly calls attention to this, ' Ι χθύς, pp. 408 ff. Dölger also refers to the ὁ σωτήρ in the new Oxyrhynchus Fragment (cf. ZNW IX (1908), 2, 3, 7, 18).

[265] On the following cf. P. Wendland, "Soter," in ZNW V, 1904, pp. 335 ff. Lietzmann, *Der Weltheiland*, 1909; Deissmann, *Light from the Ancient East*, pp. 363 f.; Dölger, ' Ι χθύς, pp. 406-22 (with new and valuable material). Diels, AAB, 1916, No. 7, p. 66, n. 1: ὑμνεῖν καὶ τὸν σωτῆρα τὸν ἡμέτερον (Philodemus of Epicurus); cf. Crönert, Rh. Mus., LVI, 1901, p. 625.

[266] Documentation for the following in Wendland, *Soter*, pp. 342 ff. [Cf. E. Lohmeyer, *Christuskult und Kaiserkult*, 1919.]

[267] Dittenberger, *Syllog.*, 2nd ed., p. 347. The Athenians also call Caesar their σωτήρ and εὐεργέτης; Dittenberger, 2nd ed., p. 346. Cf. Wendland, *Hellenistisch-römische Kultur*, 2nd ed., p. 408.

tion of the communities in Asia Minor: "Providence has filled this man with power in such a way that it sent him to us and to the coming generations as savior." [268] Testimonies for the later Roman emperors continue.[269]

Of course one should not focus all too one-sidedly on the parallels in the Roman emperor cult. Wobbermin[270] for his part has connected the emergence of the title of Soter with the renascence of the mystery cults. In this he relies on the evidence which Anrich[271] in particular has produced from the Orphic hymns. Wendland in due time rejected this conjecture. The new flourishing of the mystery cults, he argues, comes only in the romanticism of the second century of the Christian era, and none of the testimonies adduced belongs to an earlier time (p. 353). It is the achievement of Dölger to have brought forward the proof that the gods of the mysteries also in the earlier times held the title σωτήρ. An inscription from the time of Ptolemy IV, which was found in the vicinity of Alexandria, runs: ὑπὲρ βασιλέως Πτολεμαίου καὶ βασιλίσσης Ἀρσινόης θεῶν φιλοπατόρων Σαράπιδι καὶ Ἴσιδι Σωτῆρσιν.[272] I add a second inscription, knowledge of which likewise I owe to Dölger,[273] and which to be sure is not distinctive for the title Σωτήρ, but is extraordinarily distinctive for the related Εὐεργέτης. It comes from the time of Ptolemy III and reads: Σαράπιδι καὶ Ἴσιδι καὶ Νείλῳ καὶ Βασιλεῖ Πτολεμαίῳ καὶ Βασιλίσσῃ Βερενίκῃ Θεοῖς Εὐεργέταις. For here apparently Serapis and Isis also appear alongside the royal pair as beneficent gods. The later Orphic hymns, in which the title σωτήρ plays so decisive a role, will likewise be of Egyptian origin. Still Dölger is right in warning against deriving the title one-sidedly from the mystery cults and when he points to the title's wide distribution in Greek worship in general (p. 240). And especially in this connection still another deity comes into view who does not belong to the narrower circle of the mystery gods and who yet must be called a savior deity in a real

[268] W. Otto, "Augustus Soter," *Hermes*, XLV (1910), 448-60. I single out the inscription on the island of Philae (12/13 B.C., Otto, p. 449): Αὐτοκράτορι Καίσαρι. Σεβαστῷ Σωτῆρι καὶ Εὐεργέτῃ. One should note the important double title.

[269] Examples of the Soter cult in Egypt under Nero, Hadrian, and Caracalla, in Otto, "Augustus Soter," p. 454.

[270] *Religionsgeschichtliche Studien* (1896), pp. 105-13.

[271] *Das antike Mysterienwesen* (1894), pp. 47 ff.

[272] *Bulletin de la Société archéologique d'Alexandrie*, N. Sér. II, 2 (1908), p. 170. (Dölger, Ἰχθύς, p. 420, 2). Cf. now also Preisigke, No. 597 (according to Preisigke, from the years 216-205 B.C.).

[273] *Bulletin* (see preceding footnote), N. Sér. II, 1 (1907), p. 99 (Dölger, p. 389). Cf. also Preisigke, No. 585. Also C. I. Gr. 4930*b* (Philae from the first century B.C.): τὴν μεγίστην θεὰν κυρίαν σώτειραν Ἴσιν. Preisigke, No. 169 (Abydos, Ptolemaic era): Σαράπιδι Ὀσείριδι μεγίστῳ σωτῆρι. 596: Διΐ μεγάλῳ Σωτῆρι Σ[αράπιδι].

sense. This is the ἰατρὸς–σωτήρ Asclepius. "On the altars of the savior-god stood the word σωτήρ in bold letters." [274] And again, there is also to be connected with this the fact that Christ gradually begins to be identified as the ἰατρός of men.[275] The physician and the Soter are closely related concepts.

Thus we encounter in the area of Hellenistic piety a widely branched Soter faith. In the veneration of the saving deities in the mystery cult, in the veneration of the physician-savior Asclepius, in the cult of the Roman Caesars it finds its most vigorous expression. There are various motifs and basic attitudes of different levels which are connected with it. When people called the Roman rulers saviors, they celebrated them as restorers of civil order, as bringers of golden peace; from the Soter Asclepius one hoped for the healing of bodily illness and for aid in various needs of the external life; the σωτηρία which one sought from the gods of the mysteries was ultimately related to the beyond, to ἀθανασία, and to a favorable destiny in the life beyond.

But now there is the further fact that the Christian Soter faith could have one of its roots in the Old Testament eschatological ideas about Yahweh the redeemer (*Goël*) and liberator of the people of Israel. Of course, against this conjecture it may be objected that the very gradual and slow penetration of the Soter title rather points to a gradually increasing influence of Hellenistic piety and its language. On the other hand, the title is found—particularly in the Pastoral Epistles—more frequently precisely in especially eschatological contexts which point back to the Old Testament.

Thus one will be able to decide with some assurance upon a borrowing from the Hellenistic milieu only when still other reasons of a substantial and linguistic nature for the title Soter are produced. Now in fact in most of the passages coming into consideration, such convincing impetus is given, and it is highly noteworthy that these in part refer us again to the ruler

---

[274] Dölger, p. 419.

[275] Earliest passage, Ign. Eph. 7.2: εἷς ἰατρός ἐστιν σαρκικός τε καὶ πνευματικός. For the equation of ἰατρός and σωτήρ Dölger has rightly referred to Clem. Alex. Paid. I, 12.100 (p. 418). The designation of Christ as the physician is frequent in the apocryphal acts of the apostles (Act. Joh. 22, 108; Act. Phil. 41, 118; Act. Thom. 10, 37, 143, 156): J. Ott, *Katholik*, IV, Ser. V (1910), pp. 454-58. For the strata in which these legends were read, such an attitude of opposition to the ἰατρός-Asclepius cult is especially understandable. Celsus places the cult of the Soter Asclepius directly in opposition to the savior cult of the Christians (Origen, contra Celsum III, 3). On the whole, cf. Harnack: "The Gospel of the Saviour and of Salvation" in *Mission and Expansion of Christianity*, I, 101-24.

cult as the closest parallel to the Christian Soter cult. When, for example, in the Johannine writings (John 4:42; I John 4:14) the ceremonious σωτήρ τοῦ κόσμου appears, this is a title which in particular is explained, both as to content and as to form, in terms of the Caesar cult.[276] For the use of Soter in the Pastoral Epistles, the question is decided by the expressions which are closely connected with this title, such as ἐπιφάνεια, ἐπιφαίνειν (*vide infra*, p. 315). Furthermore, it is significant that in some passages precisely this title occurs in close connection with the designation of Jesus as θεός (Tit. 2:13; II Pet. 1:1).[277] We have already pointed out that in Acts the title σωτήρ stands together with the other ἀρχηγός (5:31; cf. II Clem. 20.5), which then recurs in Heb. 2:10 (τὸν ἀρχηγὸν τῆς σωτηρίας) and 12:2 (τὸν τῆς πίστεως ἀρχηγὸν καὶ τελειωτήν). Wendland is right in surmising that here we have the belief in the beneficent savior deity who destroys the old evil kingdom of chaotic disorder and has become the κτίστης (ἀρχηγός) of a new kingdom[278] (cf. Heb. 2:14). Thus one must raise the further question whether the Lucan form of the Christian message: "To you is born this day a savior," with the following: "Peace on earth," does not acquire new illumination in this context. The judgment will be justified that thus "the concept σωτήρ, in which Jewish and Greek views flowed together, became one of the forms in which the impression of the significance of Jesus which towers above the human sphere was made vivid also to the pagans, into which the content of Christian soteriology was poured." [279] That the title of savior was not simply appropriated but was filled with new content in Christianity hardly requires proof. A fragment of the Odes of Solomon (41.12) probably best illustrates the attitude which was joined with the belief in the savior in the Christian community:

The Savior who makes alive and does not cast away our souls,
The Man who was humbled and was exalted through his righteousness,
The Son of the Most High appeared in the perfection of his Father, . . .
The Anointed one is in truth one . . .
Who makes the souls alive forever through the truth of his name.[280]

[276] Cf., e.g., the inscription of Ephesus to Caesar, and the calendar inscription of the communities in Asia Minor to Augustus. Lietzmann, *Weltheiland*. Deissmann, *Light from the Ancient East*, p. 364.

[277] Cf. further Act. Petr., chap. 4: (Simon) *deus tu Romanorum salvator*. chap. 27: (Christus) *deus invisibilis et salvator*. Θεὸς σωτήρ referring to God in Jude 25; I Tim. 1:1; 2:3; 4:10; Tit. 1:3; 2:10; 3:4. On the μέγας θεὸς καὶ σωτήρ in Tit. 2:13, cf. Wobbermin, p. 111.1; Wendland, *Soter*, p. 349.2.

[278] Wendland, *Soter*, p. 350 (cf. 350.3, the reference to the Hellenistic parallels).

[279] Wendland, *Soter*, p. 350.

[280] Following the translation of Ungnad-Staerk.

In connection with this it may further be pointed out that even the word εὐαγγέλιον, which some for a long time have treasured as a wholly peculiar possession of Christian language, now has been proved to be pre-Christian, and exactly in the area of the cult of the Caesars. In the calendar inscription of the communities in Asia Minor, already mentioned so often, is found the sentence: ἦρξεν δὲ τῷ κόσμῳ τῶν δι᾽ αὐτοῦ εὐαγγελίων ἡ γενέθλιος τοῦ θεοῦ (of Augustus).[281] There is thus at least a great probability that in the summing up of its message in the splendid word εὐαγγέλιον, the infant religion was making use of an already-minted coin.[282] We will return once more to the Pastoral Epistles and turn our attention to the striking passages in which the ἐπιφάνεια or ἐπιφαίνειν of the Soter is discussed. The idea of the god who has become manifest dominates the ruler cult. The ruler is the god who has appeared on earth, the tangible and visible god, the living earthly copy of his heavenly prototype: εἰκὼν ζῶσα τοῦ Διός, as it is put in the Rosetta inscription. In the paean which the Athenians sang to Demetrios Poliorketes, the ἐναργὴς ἐπιφάνεια of the deity in him is praised. People do not see and grasp the other gods, but he is alive and present: "Give us peace, for you are the Lord." [283] The same view is already contained in the adjectives Antiochus *Epiphanes* and Ptolemy *Epiphanes* (Rosetta inscription). On the inscription of Ephesus, Caesar is celebrated as ἐπιφανὴς θεός. Ovid hymns Augustus: *ut mihi di faveant, quibus est manifestior ipse* (ex ponto I, 63).[284] Here we clearly grasp the connections.[285] It is this language that grips us in the Pastoral Epistles with its peculiarly powerful note: "God . . . has saved us . . . according to his grace, which was given to us in Christ Jesus before all ages, but now is made manifest through the *epiphany* of our savior Jesus Christ, who *has destroyed death and has brought life and immortality to light"* [286] (II Tim. 1:8 ff.). "The *saving* (σωτήριος) *grace* of God has appeared to all men"

[281] A second example in Deissmann, *Light from the Ancient East*, p. 366. No weight is to be placed upon the fact that the concept παρουσία is likewise demonstrable in the cult of the Caesars (presence of the emperor in the province, Deissmann, pp. 368 ff.). The Christian concept παρουσία can be fully explained in terms of the Jewish eschatological language.

[282] The word does not belong to Jesus' language, but to the older gospel tradition (see above, p. 79, n. 18).

[283] Athenaios VI, p. 253.

[284] Deissmann, p. 373; Ramsay, "The Manifest God," *Expository Times*, X, 208.

[285] Wendland, *Soter*, p. 349.

[286] The destruction of death and the giving of life are clear echoes from Hellenistic mystery religions. Still clearer is that in Heb. 2:14 (Barn. 14.5). Yet see also above, p. 314, n. 278.

(Tit. 2:11); then, of course, eschatologically: "We await the blessed hope and *epiphany*[287] of the glory of our *great God and savior* Jesus Christ" (Tit. 2:13). "But when the goodness and love (φιλανθρωπία) of *God our Savior* appeared (here to be sure it is God, not Christ, that is meant), . . . he saved us through the washing of regeneration" (Tit. 3:4). "I adjure you before God and Christ Jesus, the future judge of the living and the dead, and his *epiphany* and his kingdom." [288] Sounds of Jewish eschatology and others from the Hellenistic religion of the savior of the world (which by the way can appear in eschatological garb) here join in a peculiar harmony, and in giant's proportions, far beyond all human scales, there is raised the figure of the world savior Jesus Christ, the God become manifest. It is no accident that, next to Easter, the oldest festival of Christianity is that of the "Epiphany." The word in John's Gospel at the close of the narrative of the wedding at Cana likewise rests on this basis: "He revealed his glory and his disciples believed on him."

We possess still another writing in the New Testament in which the Christ cult is sensed to be in a conflicting relation to the Caesar cult. This is of course the Apocalypse of John. The beast which here emerges from the sea at the magical command of the devil (12:18), which together with the devil is worshiped by the whole world, is the Roman imperium, which demands worship from its subjects. The apocalyptist sees in the Roman state religion with its cultus of the living emperor the incarnation of Satan; in the struggle of the Christians against this cultus he sees the last great decisive battle, the time of dire peril before the end. Here are required "patience and faithfulness of the saints" (13:10). Over against the beast appears the Lamb, surrounded by the 144,000, the few in the world who do not worship the beast (14:1). Besides God, only this lamb deserves honor and worship. All the heavenly choirs of the supra-terrestrial powers confess him. "Worthy is the Lamb that was slain, to receive power and wealth and wisdom and strength and honor and glory and praise" (5:12; 7:12). His followers on earth bear his name on their foreheads (14:1), as the followers of the beast bear his name and sign (13:16). And now begins the struggle: "Here the endurance of the saints is needed. Blessed are those who die in the *Lord* from now on!" (14:13). But the outcome of the battle is sure. The apocalyptist already sees (19:11 ff.) the heavens opened and

---

[287] The thought in I Tim. 6:14 is also eschatological.

[288] II Tim. 4:1; cf. 4:8; II Clem. 12.1 (ἐπιφάνεια referring to God); 17.4 (referring to Christ).

the victor, in blood-stained garments and surrounded by his hosts clad in white, ride forth seated on a white horse. He is called *King of kings and Lord of lords*. And the beast is seized, and the false prophet (the priesthood of the emperor cult?) with him, and the beast and his followers, who worshiped his image and bore his sign, will all be cast alive into the lake of hell. Here the Roman imperium and the Caesar cult—here the new Kyrios and his community; *this* is the theme of the Revelation.

VI. *The Deity of Christ*. Thus the deification of Jesus develops gradually and with an inner necessity out of the veneration of the Kyrios in earliest Christianity. The Kyrios becomes the θεὸς 'Ιησοῦς Χριστός. It cannot escape the attentive observer how all the lines which have been previously drawn point to this end. In a certain sense the line from the dogma of Jesus' office as judge of the world, which had already emerged in the primitive community, leads to the assumption of the full deity of Christ. The preacher of the so-called Second Epistle of Clement plainly draws this consequence when he begins at the very first: "We must think of Christ as of God, as the judge of the living and the dead." On the other hand, the parallelism with the ruler cultus goes further. It is no accident that with the title of savior, the name of God for Christ also appears, and that it is now said: ὁ μέγας θεὸς καὶ σωτὴρ ἡμῶν 'Ιησοῦ Χριστοῦ and ἐπεφάνη γὰρ ἡ χάρις τοῦ θεοῦ σωτήριος.[289] In an environment in which the *Dominus ac Deus* gradually began to be the official style for every Roman emperor,[290] Christianity could not withhold from its hero this highest title of honor. We are no longer surprised when the Gospel of John puts in the mouth of Thomas the word of confession, "My Lord and my God" (20:28). And perhaps we should accordingly translate the great confession of faith (17:3) of the high-priestly prayer[291]: "Herein is eternal life, that they know thee, the only true God, and Jesus Christ whom thou hast sent (as the only true God)." Thus the author or the final redactor of I John will certainly already have understood this sentence, when he closes the epistle: "And he has given us the mind that we might know the true one; and we

---

[289] Tit. 2:13; 2:11; see above, pp. 315-16.

[290] See above, pp. 139-40.

[291] The alternation of persons (in 17:1*b*-3 the third person, then the first person) perhaps indicates that in 17:1-3 an earlier piece (stemming from the liturgy?) has been reworked.

are in the true one, in his Son Jesus Christ. This is the *true God* and eternal life." [292]

But the main motif which presses to the front here is the practical-cultic one. Once the Lord Jesus has attained such a position in the cultus of the Christians as has been demonstrated above, then he must also be God. This is a general and popular impression. People sing hymns in worship only to (one) God. The judgment of Pliny about *carmen quasi Deo dicere*[293] simply reflects the naïve impression of the times. The glorious and holy name whose power one invokes in baptism, about which people assemble in the eucharist, without which no prayer in worship and no doxology is possible, to which prayer is offered even in the widest circles, which people confess, for which some fight, suffer, and die—this must be the name of God, regardless of all the mountainous difficulties and paradoxes in which one thereby involves himself. A bit of monotheistic feeling is also hidden in it; we are to worship and reverence God alone. This religious feeling, of primordial power and free of all reflections, breaks through again and again in the history of christological dogma. It is no accident that the most radical denier of the deity of Christ, Paul of Samosata, removes from the church the "new" hymns to Christ.[294] The most dangerous weapon which Athanasius used in the battle against Arius was this, that he labeled the cultic veneration of a subordinate deity—for thus Jesus appeared in the doctrine of Arius—as paganism.[295] "The worship of Christ, which has been handed down from the beginning and which even our opponents do not dispute, already settles the question: God alone is to be worshiped; it is pagan to reverence creatures." If we go back into the third century, we

---

[292] I am doubtful whether the reading of the Prologue μονογενὴς θεός (B ℵ) is the original one. The alteration from θεός into υἱός is more difficult to imagine for a later period than the reverse. It is possible, however, that here the simple μονογενής is original, and both υἱός and θεός are additions. But even the variation, which must be very old, is significant for the history of Christology. Other such variations: the famous adulteration in I Tim. 3:16, θεὸς ἐφανερώθη ἐν σαρκί (to be sure only in the revised text, yet already presupposed by Hippolytus, contra Noet., chap. 17, and perhaps even by Ignatius, Eph. 19.3); above all, Gal. 2:20: ἐν πίστει τοῦ θεοῦ καὶ Χριστοῦ (B D G).

[293] With the following, cf. what was said above about primitive Christian hymnody.

[294] Eusebius, CH VII, 30.10: ψαλμοὺς δὲ τοὺς μὲν εἰς τὸν κύριον ἡμῶν Ἰησοῦν Χριστὸν παύσας ὡς δὴ νεωτέρους καὶ νεωτέρων ἀνδρῶν συγγράμματα.

[295] Harnack, *Dogmengeschichte*, 4th ed., II, 209. Athanasius, Orat. contra Arian. III, 16: διατί οὖν οἱ Ἀρειανοὶ τοιαῦτα λογιζόμενοι καὶ νοοῦντες οὐ συναριθμοῦσιν ἑαυτοὺς μετὰ τῶν Ἑλλήνων; καὶ γὰρ κἀκεῖνοι ὥσπερ καὶ οὗτοι τῇ κτίσει λατρεύουσι παρὰ τὸν κτίσαντα τὰ πάντα θεόν. . . . εἰ δὲ οἱ μὲν Ἕλληνες ἑνὶ ἀγενήτῳ καὶ πολλοῖς γενητοῖς λατρεύουσιν, οὗτοι δὲ ἑνὶ ἀγενήτῳ καὶ ἑνὶ γενητῷ, οὐδ' οὕτω διαφέρουσιν Ἑλλήνων.

meet the author of the Little Labyrinth who, among the witnesses to the deity of Christ, in addition to Justin, Miltiades, Tatian, Clement, Irenaeus, and Melito, above all lists the psalms and hymns which have been sung by believing brethren from the first (*vide supra*, p. 304).[296]

Accordingly, in the *eucharistic liturgy* of the Didache—to be sure, in a piece which could have been inserted only later—we no longer find "Hosanna to the Son of David," in spite of the fact that this formula was hallowed by the Old Testament usage and by the gospel narrative, but: "Hosanna to the *God* of David" (10.5). Its total attitude corresponds to the above-cited beginning of the homily in II Clement. It is true that nowhere here is Christ exactly called God, but the persons of God and Christ are so intermingled that a line of demarcation can no longer be recognized.[297] A saying of the Lord is introduced with λέγει ὁ θεός (13.4) or is cited as a sacred word of God (2.4); or a κύριος saying from the Old Testament is cited as an utterance of Jesus (3.5). Christ is described as the Lord who has called and redeemed us (5.1; 8.2; 9.5). The author speaks of a ποιεῖν τὸ θέλημα τοῦ Χριστοῦ (6.7). Corresponding to the beginning, in 17.4 ff. the judgment which Jesus will render is pictured. In this connection, his epiphany, his glory and his kingdom, his redemption and his mercy are spoken of (16.2), and the saying in Isa. 66:18 is referred to his appearing (17.4). "Above all, in the entire first section of the sermon (down to 9.5), the religious relationship is treated for the most part as though it consisted essentially of a relationship between the believers and Christ." [298] And again, on the other hand, everything that is said of Christ is also said of God: "We must think of Jesus Christ as of God." In the *worship praxis*—II Clement is just a sermon—all boundaries between Christ and God disappear. Such observations could easily be multiplied; I refer in passing especially to large parts of the Epistle of Barnabas (*vide supra*, pp. 290-91).[299]

In view of this one must actually be amazed at how negligible is the

---

[296] Eusebius, CH V, 28.4-5: ψαλμοὶ δὲ ὅσοι καὶ ᾠδαὶ ἀδελφῶν ἀπ' ἀρχῆς ὑπὸ πιστῶν γραφεῖσαι τὸν λόγον τοῦ θεοῦ τὸν Χριστὸν ὑμνοῦσιν θεολογοῦντες. Note here and in the preceding the expression θεολογεῖν. Justin is already familiar with κυριολογεῖν and θεολογεῖν as terms (see below). It is not impossible that in this connection there already stands the later nickname for John, ὁ θεολόγος, which Papias perhaps already knows (cf. the famous fragment from Philip Sidetes).

[297] In the following I am in agreement with Harnack's presentation, *Dogmengeschichte*, 4th ed., I, 207.

[298] Harnack, *Dogmengeschichte*, p. 208.

[299] Cf. particularly Barn. 6-7, 14, 16-17, 12.7: δόξα Ἰησοῦ, ὅτι ἐν αὐτῷ πάντα καὶ εἰς αὐτόν.

testimony in the immediately post-apostolic literature for the introduction of the full title of God for Jesus. Here the religious language of Paul and John had a powerful aftereffect. Through them the designation "Son of God" had become canonical, and this tradition—perhaps also a certain instinctive influence of the strong Old Testament and monotheistic feeling which was certainly present in Paul—overshadowed and conditioned the usage of the community. Still this feeling has its own set of conditions. Even if the history of the Son-of-God concept can be treated only at the close of this entire section, it must be already pointed out that in the title "Son of God" the community's faith simply heard the proclamation of the full deity of Christ of the earliest times.[300] Already in the death sentence which, according to the gospel account, the high priest pronounces over Jesus, there pulses this basic Christian feeling: Anyone who claims to be God's Son (without being such) blasphemes God, for he makes himself equal to God: either blasphemer of God or God (Son of God). This is quite openly expressed in the Gospel of John. The Jews—here, naturally, not the Jews of Jesus' lifetime, but the synagogue disputing with the "church" about the deity—accuse Jesus: "You, who are a man, make yourself to be *God*." To this Jesus responds with the reference to Ps. 82:6, "ye are gods," and from this derives the right—to call himself "Son of God" (10:33-36). The προσεκύνησεν αὐτῷ (9:38) follows the confession of the man born blind to Jesus, the Son of Man (mss., Son of God).[301] In the great proclamation of the *Son of God* at the beginning of the Hebrews, the Old Testament saying (LXX Deut. 32:43), καὶ προσκυνησάτωσαν αὐτῷ πάντες ἄγγελοι θεοῦ is connected with the returning Jesus, the πρωτότοκος of God.[302] In the Martyrdom of Polycarp it is said forthrightly τοῦτον μὲν γὰρ υἱὸν ὄντα τοῦ θεοῦ προσκυνοῦμεν (17:2), and indeed this

---

[300] Dölger, Ἰχθύς, RQ, Supplem. 17, p. 397, refers to Justin, Apol. I, 22, for evidence of how long the more indefinite expression "Son of God" was preserved and maintained in the moral sense: υἱὸς δὲ θεοῦ ὁ Ἰησοῦς λεγόμενος . . . εἰ καὶ κοινῶς μόνον ἄνθρωπος διὰ σοφίαν ἄξιος υἱὸς θεοῦ λέγεσθαι. (Here, by the way, cf. also the saying of the Jews in Celsus (Origen I, 57): εἰ τοῦτο λέγεις, ὅτι πᾶς ἄνθρωπος κατὰ θείαν πρόνοιαν γεγονὼς υἱός ἐστι θεοῦ, τί ἂν σὺ ἄλλου διαφέροις.) But here Justin is speaking in the explicitly apologetic attempt to make rational and plausible the irrational element in the Christian faith. A special case exists for the title παῖς θεοῦ, to which Dölger also has recourse (see above, p. 96, n. 67). Od. Sol. 36.3 (although I was a man, I am called the light, the Son of God) deals with the deification of the initiate in the actual sense of the word.

[301] In this connection I refer once more to how the προσκυνεῖν of Jesus penetrates into the latest stratum of the gospel tradition. In Mark only once, in 5:6 (the demoniac of Gadara); in Matthew 11 times! Cf. esp. 28:9, 17. Luke 24:52, worship of the resurrected One, in Luke only here.

[302] One should note what difficulties this passage caused Origen (περὶ εὐχῆς 15.3)!

προσκυνεῖν is expressly distinguished from the veneration of the martyrs.[303] In the basic Pseudo-Clementine writing,[304] this popular-catholic view is opposed under the guise of Simon. Here it is said: ὁ κύριος ἡμῶν . . . οὔτε ἑαυτὸν θεὸν εἶναι ἀνηγόρευσεν, υἱὸν δὲ θεοῦ τοῦ τὰ πάντα διακοσμήσαντος. Simon Magus' counter-question, however, has a characteristic sound: οὐ δοκεῖ σοι τὸν ἀπὸ θεοῦ θεὸν εἶναι?. Above all, the testimony of Celsus is important here; in numerous passages he regards the titles θεός and υἱὸς (παῖς) θεοῦ (here mostly=υἱὸς θεοῦ) as identical.[305] In the testimony of outsiders and spectators from a distance, the main lines of development of an intellectual movement often emerge more clearly.

Thus the concepts of God and Son move quite close together for the community and its understanding. The υἱὸς προσκυνητός is God himself, if it is correct that one is to worship God with his whole heart, and God alone.

The first literary document in which the half-instinctive, half-traditional reluctance to speak without embarrassment of the deity of Christ is abandoned, not merely occasionally but throughout and fundamentally, is the body of *Ignatian epistles*. How this fits together with the peculiarly defined Christianity of Ignatius will be further explained later on in context. Here only the fact is to be stressed that in the opening salutation of the Ephesian epistle and of the Roman epistle (twice), and in the closing expression of his epistle to Polycarp, Ignatius speaks altogether naturally of "our God Jesus Christ." He exhorts the Trallians not to separate themselves from "the God Jesus Christ" and the bishop and the apostles (7.1). He calls the deacons servants of the "God Christ" (Smyrn. 10.1).[306] He speaks of our God Jesus Christ, who is in the Father (Rom. 3.3), of the ἐν σαρκὶ γενόμενος (another reading ἐν ἀνθρώπῳ) θεός (Eph. 7.2, a

---

[303] Cf. Martyr. Carpos 5: Χριστιανός εἰμι, Χριστὸν τὸν υἱὸν τοῦ θεοῦ σέβομαι.

[304] Homil. XVI, 15. It is proved by the parallels in Rec. II, 49 and particularly III, 2-12 that something of this sort must have stood in the basic document (cf. XVI, 15-18). The Recognitions oppose in longer statements the use of the designations αὐτογένητος (and αὐτοπάτωρ) for God, which the Homilies (XVI, 16) use without embarrassment. The statements of the Homilies are also reworked.

[305] Origen, c. Cels. II, 30 (θεὸς καὶ θεοῦ υἱος); IV, 2 (Christians and Jews: οἱ μὲν καταβεβηκέναι λέγουσιν, οἱ δὲ καταβήσεσθαι εἰς τὴν γῆν τινα θεὸν ἢ θεοῦ υἱόν); V, 2 (θεὸς μὲν . . . καὶ θεοῦ παῖς οὐδεὶς οὔτε κατῆλθεν οὔτε κατέλθοι). Cf. precisely the same formula in the epistle of Abgar (Eus. CH I, 13.6), "That *you either are God* himself and have come down from heaven . . . *or that you are God's Son.*"

[306] θεὸς χριστός overwhelmingly attested in the mss. Cf. the addition on Smyrn. 6.1, τὸ αἷμα Χριστοῦ ὅτι (?) θεοῦ ἐστιν in one textual witness (Timoth.).

stylized confessional formula), of the θεὸς ἀνθρωπίνως φανερούμενος.[307] He praises Jesus Christ, the God τὸν οὕτως ὑμᾶς σοφίσαντα (Smyrn. 1.1). He no longer shies away from the violent paradox of the αἷμα θεοῦ (Eph. 1.1)[308] and the πάθος θεοῦ (Rom. 6.3); indeed, he already appears to take pleasure in it.[309] He begins the solemn confession in Eph. 18.2 with "Our God Jesus Christ."

But all this now may not be regarded as an isolated and singular phenomenon. Instead it must be judged that here for the first time in the literature something rises to a higher level which had existed for a long time in massive faith.

Above all, there is Justin's testimony,[310] which we here draw into the discussion in anticipation. Of course, characteristically, only the Dialogue and not the Apology offers the material. This fact has its own good reasons. Justin, who in the Apology so strongly emphasizes the reasonableness of Christianity, naturally hesitates to speak openly here of the ultimate and highest mystery of Christianity. But in the Dialogue he shows how firmly and strongly he stands on the basis of the unbroken faith of the community.[311]

Here the confession of the deity of Christ is found again and again. And first of all, every emphasis should be placed upon the fact that the deity

[307] One may compare the entire sentence (Eph. 19.3): παλαιὰ βασιλεία διεφθείρετο θεοῦ ἀνθρωπίνως φανερουμένου εἰς καινότητα ἀϊδίου ζωῆς—reminiscence of the ceremonial hieratic style from the cultus of the beneficent savior-God, see above, p. 314.

[308] Cf. the Christian interpolator of the Testament of the Twelve Patriarchs, Levi 4: ἐπὶ τῷ πάθει τοῦ ὑψίστου.

[309] Harnack is inclined to make a strict distinction between ὁ θεὸς ἡμῶν and the absolute ὁ θεός (Dogmengeschichte, I, p. 208, note; 209.2) and regards the absolute ὁ θεός (Trall. 7.1; Smyrn. 6.1; 10.1) as critically dubious. It is to be conceded to Harnack at the outset that the whole process of the deification of Christ takes its point of departure in the cultus and practice (Jesus Christ "our" God) and from that beginning point doctrinally and dogmatically makes its way. But the main thing is precisely this cultic development. It has much more significance than doctrine and dogma. Whether Christ is called θεός or ὁ θεός, ὁ θεὸς ἡμῶν or, absolutely, ὁ θεός—all this is relatively irrelevant in comparison with the most momentous of all the processes, that the deification is shaped out of the cultus.

[310] No weight should be placed upon the textually uncertain θεὸς Ἰησοῦς Χριστός in Polyc. Phil. 12.2. The alleged reference of τὰ παθήματα αὐτοῦ to God (I Clem. 2.1) is explained by the correct reading ἐφοδίοις τοῦ Χριστοῦ (lat. syr. cop.; θεοῦ only A). On the false reading in Acts 20:28, see above, p. 289, n. 145.

[311] To this corresponds the other observation that Justin gives expression to his Logos theology quite significantly in the Apology, and hardly touches it in the Dialogue. He developed and determined the two writings for different circles. He hardly intended to develop the Christian faith in them in stages. The atmosphere is different in the two cases. If we had from the other apologists writings like the Dialogue with Trypho, they too would be presented to us in a much closer approximation to the church's faith.

of Jesus signifies for Justin something thoroughly practical and does not at all emerge as theological speculation. For Justin deity and worship belong together.[312]

In Dial. 38, Justin has himself accused by his adversary that he proposes πολλὰ βλάσφημα, namely the Christ who was preexistent, appeared as man, was crucified, ascended to heaven, and will return. But last of all there follows the main thing: καὶ προσκυνητὸν εἶναι. In chap. 63 Justin summarizes the result of his proof with respect to this accusation: ὅτι γοῦν καὶ προσκυνητός ἐστι καὶ θεὸς καὶ Χριστός . . . οἱ λόγοι οὗτοι διαρρήδην σημαίνουσι. But Trypho answers: He will leave this Lord and Christ and God to the Gentiles who, following his name, are called Χριστιανοί. ἡμεῖς δὲ τοῦ θεοῦ τοῦ καὶ αὐτὸν τοῦτον ποιήσαντος λατρευταὶ ὄντες, οὐ δεόμεθα τῆς ὁμολογίας αὐτοῦ οὐδὲ τῆς προσ-κυνήσεως. In Dial. 68 (293 B) Justin again asserts: μήτι ἄλλον τινὰ προσκυνητὸν καὶ κύριον καὶ θεὸν λεγόμενον ἐν ταῖς γραφαῖς νοεῖτε εἶναι πλὴν τοῦ τοῦτο ποιήσαντος τὸ πᾶν καὶ τοῦ Χριστοῦ. Then again in 294 C: (γραφὰς) αἳ διαρρήδην τὸν Χριστὸν καὶ παθητὸν καὶ προσ-κυνητὸν καὶ θεὸν ἀποδεικνύουσιν. In the lengthy enumeration of titles of honor in Dial. 126 we read: υἱὸς ἀνθρώπου . . . παιδίον . . . Χριστὸς καὶ θεὸς προσκυνητός . . . λίθος, σοφία.[313] Or—Justin can also express this in another way—the important thing is that one offer to Christ the same τιμή as to the Father: "Anyone who, filled with a God-fearing mind, loves God with all his heart and all his strength, will worship no other God. And (yet) he will worship (as God) that emissary (ἄγγελος), since God wills it" (Dial. 93, 323 A).[314] And the practical attitude of Justin is shown by the

---

[312] It is also characteristic that Justin, where he associates God the Father, the Son, the host of angels, and the Spirit in that curious manner (Apol. I, 6), first speaks quite generally of a ὁμολογεῖν. This refers to the angels (Justin intends to prove that the Christians, theoretically considered, are not atheists). Not till we come to the Spirit do we find the expression πνεῦμά τε τὸ προφητικὸν σεβόμεθα καὶ προσκυνοῦμεν. In this connection he is not concerned with the προσκύνησις. Hence the obscuring of the situation.

[313] Cf. further the Didascalia (ch. 25, Achelis-Flemming, p. 122): "We have established and determined that you should worship God the Father Almighty and Jesus his Son, Christ, and the Holy Spirit" (cf. ch. 3, p. 9). In the Acts of Pionius 9.8, Asclepiades answers the question, τίνα σέβῃ; τὸν Χριστὸν Ἰησοῦν. And to the further question, οὗτος οὖν ἄλλος ἐστίν (than the previously confessed θεὸς παντοκράτωρ) there comes the answer: οὐχί, ἀλλ' ὁ αὐτὸς ὃν καὶ οὗτοι εἰρήκασι (otherwise in 16.4).

[314] From this perspective we can understand what John means when he says that all should honor the Son as they honor the Father, and when he adds, threateningly, "Whoever does not honor the Son also does not honor the Father" (5:22-23; cf. 8:49). It is a matter of the veneration of the Son in worship, the kernel of the dispute between synagogue and church (see above, p. 215).

fact that for him the two predicates κύριος and θεός so closely coincide. This is shown by almost all the passages already mentioned, but especially the important statement in Dial. 56, 277 C, where in reference to Ps. 110 and Ps. 45 Justin speaks of a θεολογεῖν[315] and κυριολογεῖν of the Holy Spirit or of the Scripture in connection with Christ.[316] And as the concepts κύριος and θεός coincide for him, so also do the designations θεός and υἱὸς θεοῦ. He accuses the Jews: ἐξηρνεῖσθε αὐτὸν εἶναι θεόν, τοῦ μόνου καὶ ἀγεννήτου θεοῦ υἱόν (126, 355 C). His own confession runs: οὔτε οὖν 'Αβραὰμ οὔτε 'Ισαὰκ οὔτε 'Ιακὼβ . . . εἶδε τὸν πατέρα καὶ ἄρρητον κύριον τῶν πάντων . . . ἀλλ' ἐκεῖνον τὸν κατὰ βουλὴν τὴν ἐκείνου καὶ θεὸν ὄντα, υἱὸν αὐτοῦ, καὶ ἄγγελον (Dial. 127, 357 B). Still more interesting is a second passage in which the title "Christ" is set over against the title υἱὸς θεοῦ on one side and θεός on the other side. "It is no less true that this one is the *Christ* of God because I am not able to show that from the beginning he was the Son of the Creator of the world, that he is God and as a man was born of a virgin" (Dial. 48, 267 C).[317] Justin also naturally finds this ἕτερος θεός—οὐχ ὀνόματι μόνον . . . ἀλλὰ καὶ ἀριθμῷ (chap. 128)—everywhere in the Old Testament.[318] Thus passages in which the Old Testament itself appears to speak of a second κύριος and particularly of a second θεός became especially important. So Justin also likes to dwell upon the much-used forty-fifth Psalm, or upon Ps. 47:6, ἀνέβη ὁ θεὸς ἐν ἀλαλαγμῷ, κύριος ἐν φωνῇ σάλπιγγος (Dial. 37).[319] Now one may not assume that Justin and his time have derived the θεὸς προσκυνητός from the Old Testament. Such important developments do not take place by way of scribal study. People rather read back into the Old Testament the already firmly established belief in the ἕτερος θεός (cf. Apol. I, 63, p. 96 C).

With all this, there actually are no better witnesses than Justin for the community's faith in connection with Christ as the new God. When this man whom people are inclined to abuse as a rationalist, who so strongly

---

[315] See above, p. 304.

[316] Cf. further Dial. 34, 251 D: βασιλεὺς καὶ ἱερεὺς καὶ θεὸς καὶ κύριος καὶ ἄγγελος καὶ ἄνθρωπος καὶ ἀρχιστρατηγὸς καὶ λίθος καὶ παιδίον, 36, 254 D.

[317] Cf. further Dial. 61, 284 B: υἱός, σοφία, ἄγγελος, θεός, κύριος λόγος (!); cf. 284 C, chap. 116, 343 B. It is said of Joshua: ἅτε οὐ Χριστὸς ὁ (!) θεὸς ὢν οὐδὲ υἱὸς θεοῦ, 113, 340 C. Naturally Justin is also acquainted with the paradox θεὸς καὶ ἄνθρωπος; for example, chaps. 71, 297 B, 34, 251 D.

[318] Justin affords whole series of such passages: Dial. 34, 36, 38-39, 63, etc. Cf. esp. also the long statements in Dial. 56 on Gen. 18-19, in Dial. 62 on Gen. 1:27, etc.

[319] With Dial. 38 and 63, cf. Heb. 1:8. Apparently the author of Hebrews already referred the purportedly addressed ὁ θεός σου to Christ.

emphasizes in his apologetic statements the absolute reasonableness of Christianity, whose theology actually went in an utterly different direction; when this man does not tire of proclaiming again and again the colossal paradox of a ἕτερος θεός προσκυνητός, there stands just behind him the community's tradition to which he submits, or better, the community's cultus and worship praxis to which he clings with all his heart and in spite of all his emphasis upon the Logos. His proclamation of the δεύτερος θεός springs from piety, not from speculation. His *speculation* has sought here again to moderate and to retreat. But this can be discussed only further on.

We associate with Justin a second witness to the Christian community's faith. As a witness for the deity of Christ, the Little Labyrinth lists in the last place, after Irenaeus, Melito of Asia Minor, θεόν καὶ ἄνθρωπον καταγγέλλοντα τὸν Χριστόν (Eus. CH V, 28.5). What we possess from him in fragments indeed justifies the judgment that he was hardly a theologian, a man of thought. He is first of all the transmitter of the massive faith of the community. So then we find in him also, as in Ignatius, the paradox ὁ θεὸς πέπονθεν ὑπὸ δεξιᾶς Ἰσραηλιτίδος.[320] This fragment preserved for us by Anastasius Sinaita from Melito's writing εἰς τὸ πάθος is found again in an extended Syriac fragment,[321] whose genuineness for this reason should not be disputed (as little as that of the other Syriac fragments closely connected with it). But precisely these fragments are characteristic. What we have here is really no theology; these are declamations of a preacher who revels in the incomprehensibilities of the Christian community's belief. The fragments are so typical that I cannot refrain from setting forth here some passages from the Latin translation by Otto, which appear to me to be a good representation of their style. Thus in the first fragment (Fr. 13) we read:

> quidnam est hoc novum mysterium?
> judex judicatur et quietus est;
> invisibilis videtur neque erubescit;
> incomprehensibilis prehenditur neque indignatur;
> incommensurabilis mensuratur neque repugnat;
> impassibilis patitur neque ulciscitur,
> immortalis moritur neque respondet verbum,
> coelestis sepelitur et <id> fert.

[320] Otto, *Corpus Apologet.* IX, 416, Fragment 7.
[321] Otto, IX, 419-23.

Or in the second fragment (Fr. 15):

> qui agnus visus est, pastor mansit;
> qui servus reputatus est, dignitatem filii non denegavit;
> a Maria portatus et patre suo indutus;
> terram calcans et coleum impleus;
> puer apparens et aeternitatem naturae suae non fallens;
> corpus induens et simplicitatem naturae suae divinae non coarctans;
> cibo in quantum *homo* erat, indigens,
> et non desineus mundum alere, in quantum *deus* erat.

And at the close of the third fragment, after the presentation of a long christological, confession-like kerygma (Fr. 15), it is said:

> auriga Cherubim,
> princeps exercitus angelorum,
> *Deus ex deo,* filius ex patre
> Jesus Christus, rex in saecula.

This is just hieratically formulated language,[322] a hymn, authentic or imitation community liturgy. Here we actually have the soil in which there grew the paradoxes of the Χριστὸς προσκυνητὸς θεός, the God who has suffered and died, the God-man, the θεὸς ἐκ θεοῦ. Cool reflective consideration and speculation somehow inspired by the spirit of Hellenistic theology did not stand sponsor for them. They have thrived in the hot atmosphere of an enthusiastic faith which lives fully in common worship, in hymn and song. A man who lived essentially on this atmosphere is also to be credited with having taught: "For since he was God and perfect man in one person (ὁ αὐτός), he proved both his natures (οὐσία)"; the deity through his miracles in the three-year activity after the baptism, the humanity in the thirty years before the baptism, during which, on account of his fleshly imperfection, he concealed the miracles of his deity, καίπερ θεὸς ἀληθὴς προαιώνιος ὑπάρχων.[323] In particular, when behind all this one perceives no

---

[322] Note the stylizing in the fifth fragment, the ever-repeated οὗτος ὅς, then nothing but beginnings with σύ. On the evaluation of the style, cf. Norden, *Agnostos Theos,* pp. 177 ff.

[323] Otto, IX, 415, Fragm. 6. On the fragment, cf. Harnack, *Chronologie,* p. 518: The genuineness is not to be disputed on external grounds; Harnack has reservations about the contents, but then has reservations about his own reservations. Loofs, *Dogmengeschichte,* 4th ed., p. 151, is convinced, probably correctly, of the genuineness of the fragment. The second, Syriac fragment cited above also speaks of the *simplicitas naturae divinae.* The same paradoxical ideas here and there.

theology, one is amazed at how the style of thought of a naïve faith, which is determined by the cultus and the liturgy and which is not deterred by any impossibilities, anticipates the development of centuries.

But now from here a light falls back upon a series of confession-like statements of Ignatius. When we find him writing (Eph. 7):

εἷς ἰατρός ἐστιν σαρκικός τε καὶ πνευματικός,

γεννητὸς καὶ ἀγέννητος,

ἐν σαρκὶ γενόμενος θεός,

ἐν θανάτῳ ζωὴ ἀληθινή,

καὶ ἐκ Μαρίας καὶ ἐκ θεοῦ

πρῶτον παθητὸς καὶ τότε ἀπαθής

Ἰησοῦς Χριστὸς ὁ κύριος ἡμῶν . . .

or (to Polyc. 3): τὸν ὑπὲρ καιρὸν προσδόκα τὸν ἄχρονον,

τὸν ἀόρατον τὸν δι' ἡμᾶς ὁρατόν,

τὸν ἀψηλάφητον,

τὸν ἀπαθῆ τὸν δι' ἡμᾶς παθητόν,[324]

τὸν κατὰ πάντα τρόπον δι' ἡμᾶς ὑπομείναντα . . .

who would fail to recognize there the same hieratic style and the close connection of the whole as to content and form? What is basic and in common to Ignatius and Melito is not "Asia Minor theology," is indeed no theology at all; it is the language of the Christ hymn and of the community's faith. Thus from there also must stem the presbyter's saying cited by Irenaeus (IV, 4.2), which we find again in Melito almost word for word: ipsum immensum patrem in filio mensuratum esse,[325] mensura enim patris filius, quoniam et capit eum.

This sort of hymnological community theology, the distinctive mark of which is a reveling in contradiction, finally had to lead to a complete deification, i.e., to the supplanting of God the Father or the denial of any difference between Father and Son. What is stirring here is the naïve Modalism which the Logos theologians later met as their most suspicious and intolerant opponent. Christ is *the* God who has become visible and tangible, in him

---

[324] Cf. further Melito (Otto, p. 419): invisibilem visum esse [et incomprehensibilem prehensum esse] et impassibilem passum esse et immortalem mortuum esse et coelestem sepultum esse. Numerous examples of this style are found in the apocryphal acts of the apostles; cf., e.g., the Preaching of Peter at the Agape, chap. 20 of the Acta Petri, and above all, the Acta Thomae.

[325] The Christ—Adam fantasies and speculations which are found in the work of Melito are to be treated below (Chap. X) in context. The descent into Hades also appears to have played a role precisely in the liturgy of the early church. Melito may get it from there (see above, pp. 62-63).

God's eternal and infinite nature has inclined itself to earth. But this is in no wise to be modernized. Behind this sentence there does not stand some sort of representation of the ethically religious personal image of Jesus of Nazareth—one must not at all think in these terms—but the God who is reverenced in the community's worship! Justin appears to know some Christians who indeed call Christ the Logos[326] but who regard him as a Dynamis inseparable and indistinguishable from the Father; just as the sunlight is related to the sun, so also is the relation between God-Father and Son: δύναμιν αὐτοῦ προπηδᾶν ποιεῖ καί, ὅταν βούληται, πάλιν ἀναστέλλει εἰς ἑαυτόν. What Justin appears to oppose here could be this naïve, already somewhat theologically colored Modalism,[327] which he would consequently make it possible for us to pursue directly into an early period. Over against it he sets his προσκυνητὸς θεός, ἕτερος ἀριθμῷ οὐ γνώμῃ (Dial. 128).

Finally, we have one last witness for the popular faith of the masses of the Christian communities in the second Christian century. This is the group of the apocryphal acts of the apostles. In their actual intellectual foundation they are probably not gnostically heretical, though a Gnostic veneer in many of them (Acts of John, Acts of Thomas) is certainly not to be overlooked. They perhaps reflect the popular belief of the catholic church since the second half of the second century. It is true that we cannot employ them directly as testimonies to the post-apostolic (pre-Justinian) age. But with its sources, our literature reaches back into still earlier times; and the broad undercurrent of the faith of the masses usually changes its direction little. It may already have looked around A.D. 100 as it looked in the second half of the second century.

And here Christ has simply become the God.[328] He is the new God, the new manifestation of the new God,[329] the living God[330]; he alone is the

---

[326]Cf. the characteristic explanation originating in Hellenistic allegory: λόγον καλοῦσιν ἐπειδὴ καὶ τὰς παρὰ τοῦ πατρὸς ὁμιλίας φέρει τοῖς ἀνθρώποις (358 AB). Thus this Dynamis is also the angel which appeared temporarily to the patriarchs and is also called ἀνήρ or ἄνθρωπος, because the Father appears to men, changing himself into such forms as he chooses (see below, Chap. IX).

[327] It must be conceded that Justin also could have had in view some Jewish opponents, possibly Alexandrian Logos speculations.

[328] As indeed also, even though here less frequently, in the acts of Paul, which occupy a special position in comparison with the rest of the corpus of the apocryphal acts. Cf. Acta Pauli et Thecl., chap. 29: My *God*, thou *Son* of the Most High; 42: My *God* and God of this house . . . Jesus Christ, *God's Son*. Mart. of Paul, chap. 4: We fight for a king . . . who is from heaven, for the *living God* who . . . comes as judge (cf. the following).

[329] Acta Thom., chap. 123.

[330] Acta Petri, chap. 2.

God of truth,[331] indeed he himself the Father of truth,[332] Father of the heights,[333] true and only God,[334] the hidden mystery, God from God,[335] the deity who for our sakes appeared in a human image,[336] thou who dwellest in the heights and now art found in the depths,[337] the great one who came down to slavery,[338] our God Jesus Christ.[339] To him the prayers are usually addressed,[340] especially the sacramental prayers: "O God Jesus Christ, in thy name I have just spoken, and he has been signed with thy holy sign," it says in the baptismal prayer in the Acts of Peter (chap. 5); and in another: "Lord God merciful Father, redeemer Christ." [341] Naïve Modalism cannot be more strongly expressed, and here it is expressed in the unreflective language of prayer.

And finally, the testimony of the pagan observer Celsus may be produced here by way of conclusion. In his criticism of Christianity, as already noted, he drew the lines somewhat crudely. But with his interpretation of the Christ faith of the Christians he is right in the end with respect to the average belief of the community. To him Christ is in fact the God who is addressed in prayer by the first Christians[342]; he returns to this again and again. We have already pointed out above that for him θεός and θεοῦ υἱός (παῖς) in the mouth of the Christians mean the same thing.[343] For the Christians indeed pray to this Son of God and devote to him specifically divine reverence: ὁ ὑπὸ Χριστιανῶν προσκυνούμενος καὶ θαυμαζόμενος [344] θεός (I, 51, p. 102.16). τὸν δὲ καὶ αὐτῶν ὡς ἀληθῶς εἰδώλων ἀθλιώτερον καὶ μηδὲ εἴδωλον ἔτι, ἀλλ᾽ ὄντως νεκρὸν σέβοντες καὶ πατέρα ὅμοιον αὐτῷ ζητοῦντες[345] (VII, 36). How can a God suffer fear, be betrayed,

---

[331] Acta Thom., chap. 25.

[332] Acta Thom., chap. 26.

[333] Acta Thom., chap. 143.

[334] Acta Joh., chap. 43.

[335] Acta Thom., chap. 47.

[336] Acta Thom., chap. 80.

[337] Acta Thom., chap. 37.

[338] Acta Joh., chap. 77.

[339] Acta Joh., chap. 107.

[340] Acta Petr., chap. 18: "Let us bow our knees to Jesus." Of course almost the same level of the Christ cultus has already been reached in Paul, Phil. 2:9 ff.

[341] Acta Thom., chap. 97.

[342] That Origen is not wholly in agreement with this view of Celsus is self-explanatory; cf. contra Celsum II, 9; III, 41, 62.

[343] See the passages above on p. 321, n. 305; in addition perhaps II, 9, III, 41, et passim.

[344] The θαυμάζειν here has somewhat the same meaning as in Rev. 13:3 and 17:8 (worshiping "admiration" of the beast, "devout amazement"); cf. John 5:20.

[345] Cf. II, 8 (of the Jews), ἐπεὶ μὴ πεπιστεύκασιν ὡς εἰς θεὸν Ἰησοῦν. Cf. II, 49, διότι τοῦτον οὐ νομίζομεν θεόν.

deserted by his own, arrested and condemned? Why, if he was God, did he not seek out better disciples? How can a God recline at the table with men? How can he suffer pain? His wondrous works testify to the false gods, not to God; that a God should sojourn among men is utterly incredible—all this Celsus ironically and scornfully hurls at the Christians or has these charges raised by the Jews in dialogue.[346]

Thus the proofs come together from all sides. And in conclusion it may once more be pointed out: The belief of early Christianity in the deity of Christ arises altogether out of the veneration of the κύριος in worship. Over against this, one may not refer to the fact that indeed the religious language in the milieu surrounding Christianity was very generous with the title "God." [347] The comparison does not fit. When the Christians spoke of their God Jesus Christ, they did not give him this predicate in the manner of an exaggerated praise in rhetorical figurative language. For them there stood behind this title a very strong and tangible reality, the everyday Christian worship, at the center of which stood the προσκυνούμενος θεός and κύριος Ἰησοῦς Χριστός. When Justin speaks of the ἕτερος θεός (προσκυνητός), who is distinguished from God not γνώμῃ but indeed ἀριθμῷ, he is fully aware that he and the faith which he represents give to Christ therewith an exceptional and unique position. As actual parallels, there come into consideration only those instances in the ancient world in which the *cultus* is bound up with the predicate of deity.[348] Such instances are in fact present.

---

[346] II, 8, 20, 21, 23, 38, 49, 74. Cf. III, 41, 62; IV, 5; VII, 53.

[347] Harnack (p. 209) points for evidence to Tertullian, Apol. 10, 11. One can also refer to the statements in the Pseudo-Clementines (Rec. II, 42; Hom. XVI, 14; XVIII, 4) about the way in which the Old Testament speaks of God and gods (statements which are made here in the perspective of defending the monarchy of God). Particularly distinctive here is the seventeenth Homily of Aphrahat (TU III, 3, 4, pp. 279-89), which Dölger, Ἰχθύς, p. 400, brings into this connection. In order to refute the Jewish charge that the Christians call a son of man God, Aphrahat points to a whole series of Old Testament passages in which men are called gods, and he even justifies the *proskynesis* of Jesus with the reference to the custom of the adoration of rulers. But all this is still spoken in an apologetic fashion and does not conform to the actual attitude of the church's faith. In Hermas, Vis. I, 1.7, where Hermas says to his lady: οὐ πάντοτέ σε ὡς θεὰν ἡγησάμην, this most unusual expression perhaps points to a Hellenistic source. The Epistle to Diognetus, whose testimony (X, 6) is regularly cited in this connection, is a unique product of a most highly disputed date: cf. Acta Joh., chap. 27 (Bonnet, II, 1.166.3-4).

[348] On the following, cf. the significant statements of Harnack, p. 138, n. 1. Under the point of view discussed above, however, all the witnesses in which the wise man (later the pious man, or the mystagogue) is spoken of as the θεῖος ἄνθρωπος and simply as a θεός do not belong here. Neither does, at least not directly, the fact that the ideal of deification penetrates Christian piety out of Hellenistic piety (Hippolytus, Ref. X, 34: γέγονας θεός; see above, Chap. IV, and also below, Chap. X). The expressed ideal of deification in Christianity is more recent than the Kyrios cult and worship of the God

The cult of the rulers has already been discussed adequately. In addition we must consider the cultic reverence which philosophical schools bestow upon their heads and founders. The Gnostic sects were frequently accused of veneration of their school leaders as divine. Irenaeus found cultic veneration of the picture of Christ and also of the pictures of the Greek philosophers among the Carpocratians (I, 25.6). Clement (Strom. III, 2.5)[349] knows of a cult in Cephallenia in honor of Carpocrates' son Epiphanes. The Simonians worshiped Simon and Helena as their κύριος and their κυρία (*vide supra*, pp. 144-45). Hellenes, Christians, heretics are charged with a predilection for such veneration and deification of men.[350] But in this connection it may once more be pointed out that in the Martyrdom of Polycarp (17.3), in response to the accusation of the worship of martyrs as divine, a sharp boundary line is drawn: τοῦτον μὲν γὰρ υἱὸν ὄντα τοῦ θεοῦ προσκυνοῦμεν, τοὺς δὲ μάρτυρας ὡς μαθητὰς καὶ μιμητὰς τοῦ κυρίου ἀγαπῶμεν ἀξίως ἕνεκα εὐνοίας ἀνυπερβλήτου.

One could continue in this enumeration,[351] and yet, with all this, one does not dilute the tremendous significance of the religio-historical fact that earliest Christianity accepted the Kyrios cult into the center of its religion, and that the belief in the deity of Jesus grew out of the Kyrios cult. One only makes the process historically comprehensible; all these observations only prove ever anew that with the development of the Kyrios cult, Christianity paid tribute to its time and its milieu, that it is affected by Hellenistic piety to its very center. Observations do not indicate that the parallel phenomena in Christianity are something relatively accidental and peripheral. On the contrary, Christianity indeed developed the Kyrios cult in its entire unique weight and force; for it, the κύριος became the *one* beside whom there is no other, the ἕτερος θεὸς προσκυνητός, that One to whom alone his position of honor alongside God appertains. Within that (formally)

---

Christ. How its acceptance into Christian piety was again in part rationalized by the Christ dogma will be discussed further below (Chap. X).

[349] Yet here there is probably an underlying simple confusion of Epiphanes with a moon deity (θεὸς Ἐπιφανής).

[350] Cf. Lucian, Peregrinus Proteus, chap. 11 (veneration of Peregrinus by the Christians); Caecilius in Minucius Felix, Octavius 9.4 (veneration of the priests among the Christians); the anti-Montanist in Eusebius, CH VI, 8.6 (veneration of the prophets among the Montanists). More in Harnack, *Dogmengeschichte*, 4th ed., I, 139.

[351] A real and most interesting parallel is found in Manichaeism. As we now know, Mani in the cult of his community became the worshiped Lord and God. F. W. K. Müller, *Ein Doppelblatt aus einem manichäischen Hymnenbuch* (1913), pp. 20 ff. Line 259: Thee will I bless, Nazd Mar Mani. Line 269: O God invulnerable Mari Mani; line 307: God Mari Mani; lines 375, 379: illuminating God Mari Mani. Cf. lines 233 and 263; also Flügel, *Mani*, p. 96.

given basic pattern, it developed its force of originality; here the impulse and impetus which had come from the person of Jesus of Nazareth continued to have a powerful influence; here also, in this stressing of the εἷς κύριος, the Old Testament monotheism of fundamental import—of course in such a way that there emerged all the sharper the paradox and the riddle of the δεύτερος θεός which was to torment all future generations.

VII. *Theological Reflection.* All this, the Kyrios cult in the whole broad abundance of its occurrences and the veneration of the God Jesus Christ all the way to an almost complete identification with God the Father, took place almost without theological or conceptual reflection. It was not made and shaped, it came to be and grew. This also accounts for the great unity and uniformity in the development. Hence also the possibility of portraying it all on one surface. In vain we look, so far as we can survey—even Gnosticism, insofar as it is affected by Christianity, hardly differs at this point—in vain we look around for an opposition to this development. Nowhere do we find any sort of polemic which is directed against the Christ *cult,* and which thus attacks at its roots the development here present. If we would become aware of how tremendous a development Christianity went through, we must first of all observe the polemic against *Judaism* as it found its classical expression in the Fourth Gospel or in Justin's Dialogue with Trypho.[352] The latter most clearly shows how foreign Old Testament monotheism was to the deification of the Son, the cultic veneration of the same, and the entire proclamation of the ἕτερος θεὸς προσκυνητός, and with what inward aversion it encountered all this. But within genuine Christianity we detect nothing of restraining and countering forces; this shows with what inner necessity the development took place. Perhaps the situation would be different if Palestinian Jewish Christianity had not lost, with the destruction of Jerusalem, apparently all influence upon the further development and had not become a sect in the country east of the Jordan. Perhaps we would still be able to show that this Jewish Christianity was not dragged into the general stream of development if our reports in the church fathers were not so utterly scanty. Apart from one isolated expression in Justin,[353] the

---

[352] Cf. the statements of Harnack in TU XXXIX, 1 (1913), 47 ff.: *Judentum und Judenchristentum in Justins Dialog mit Thryphon.* Here Harnack has proposed a topic whose fuller statement would be very instructive. Cf. particularly pp. 73 ff.

[353] The "τινές" who according to Justin (Dial. 48, 267 D) indeed acknowledge that Jesus is the Christ but say that he is ἄνθρωπον ἐξ ἀνθρώπων γινόμενον are Jewish Christians. For here we should read ἐκ τοῦ ὑμετέρου γένους. Cf. the collation of the

reports about the opposing position of the Jewish Christians on Christology first emerge in Irenaeus and here are of the most scanty and general nature. And even the later notices of the church fathers do not take us far beyond the paltry sketch of Irenaeus, if we except the reports of gnosticizing Jewish Christianity. So we find here in fact a polemical attitude toward the decisive affirmations into which the church's Christology *developed*. From the time of Irenaeus the assertion that the Ebionites deny the miraculous birth belongs to the fixed stock-in-trade of the polemic against the heretics. In the Clementine Homilies is found an interesting polemic against the dogma of the deity of Christ and an attempt to draw a distinction between the concepts "Son of God" and "God" (Hom. XVI, 15-16. *Vide supra*, p. 320). But all this does not concern the beginnings and the foundation of the Christian movement. And the question whether and to what extent authentic (or even gnostically influenced) Jewish Christianity was set on the basis of the Kyrios cult of the Hellenistic communities must, because of the lack of all more exact sources, remain unanswered.[354]

Within the Great Church, however, we have here a uniformity and continuity of development unequaled. The theological differences, which some have thought they found here and which are in fact present, are of an extraordinarily limited importance. Whether some thought more "adoptianistically" in their Christology and others proposed a more "pneumatic" Christology is, even if this distinction can be at all strictly employed, of very little import, since for both tendencies Jesus was the Kyrios reverenced in the cultus. Whether one considered the present position of dignity of the Kyrios (Theos) to rest upon his primordial preexistent nature, or whether one assumed that a man (by means of the implantation of a supernatural nature) had been elevated to divine dignity, for the praxis and the cultus it finally came to one and the same thing. Both conceptions alike lay within the range of conceptual possibilities for the Hellenistic world in which Chris-

---

Paris ms. in Harnack, *Judentum und Judenchristentum* . . . , pp. 93 ff. "Yet Justin did not make this point a decisive point of controversy" (Harnack, *Dogmengeschichte*, I, 4th ed., 320, n. 1; see in general the statements in I, 4th ed., 310 ff.).

[354] One should note that the boundaries here are fluid. Jewish Christianity must have had healings in the name of Jesus and a baptism in the name of Jesus (?), from the earliest period onward. But from this to the introduction of the Kyrios cultus into the very center of piety is still a long way. In the Jewish-Christian–Gnostic basic writing of the Pseudo-Clementines the proper title for the Christ is the true prophet, not the κύριος, although here naturally the usual terminology has penetrated the sources preserved for us in many passages. In the Gospel of the Hebrews the designation ὁ κύριος has penetrated several passages (not, however, in the fragments of the Ebionite gospel in Epiphanius, but here the material available for observation is very limited).

tianity moved. We shall have to consider later how it happened that the former view prevailed over the latter all along the line. But all that does not immediately belong to the essence and the core of the development.

1. Nevertheless at this point we must give a brief survey of the christological reflections which in this period accompany and surround the actual and momentous practical foundation of Christian piety. Such reflections will move, from the outset, along two lines; first, the question will be raised as to how the greatness of the Kyrios who is worshiped in the cultus is related to the one God and Father. It is characteristic of the post-apostolic age that actual reflection on *this* point still had hardly begun to stir. People simply let the two magnitudes stand peaceably side by side; along the lines of Pauline-Johannine ideas people almost everywhere comprehended the two under the figure of the Father and the Son.[355] Consequently, on the one hand they placed Christ as the Son quite close to God in his nature and his dignity, and yet sought again to differentiate between them as Father and Son. Of course we have already seen, on the other hand, how already in the post-apostolic period the concepts "God" and "Son of God" again run together. Here again for the broad masses the fine distinctions and delimitations disappeared. Confessions of a naïve Modalism, such as that the Son is the Father become visible, that the infinite and intangible Father has become finite and tangible in the Son (*vide supra*, p. 327), will have met with approval far and wide. Alongside this, the more simple and naïve belief, as it shows forth in part in the apocryphal legends of the apostles, and above all among the Gnostics, Marcion and others: the belief in the new God Christ, whereby the belief in God the Father is then utterly supplanted and absorbed, must now already have blazed its trail. But all this still lies peacefully side by side; actual reflection, with its demoralizing and divisive effect, has hardly begun yet.[356]

[355] After all, the title υἱὸς θεοῦ did not exercise absolute domination. It is significant that in Acts it occurs only once (9:21), in the summary of the preaching of Paul. Moreover, it is lacking in James, I Peter, II Peter, Jude, in Revelation (exception in 2:18), in I (!) and II Clement (I Clem. 36.4 is a quotation from Hebrews). In Ignatius the title again recedes in the face of the designation as "God."

[356] But the Logos theologians collided with the instinctive antipathy of this "naïve modalism" which then later, in the battle with the Logos theology, was structured into a thought-out theological Modalism, if one may speak at all of a theology in connection with these resolute representatives of the community's faith. Especially distinctive here is Tertullian's testimony in adv. Prax. 3: simplices quique, ne dixerim inprudentes et idiotae, *quae major pars semper credentium est*, . . . non intelligentes unicum quidem [*sc.*, deum] sed cum sua οἰκονομία esse credendum, *expavescunt ad* οἰκονομίαν. . . . itaque duos et tres iam jactitant a nobis praedicari, se vero unius dei cultores praesumunt . . . monarchiam, inquiunt, tenemus. The boast of monotheism is already reflected and theological. Monotheism

2. The second question has occupied minds and thoughts even more. In what relation does the divine essence, which people reverence as present in the Kyrios Jesus, stand to the earthly phenomenon of Jesus of Nazareth?

For post-apostolic Christianity, in particular the more sharply it began to divorce itself from the Gnostic movement, one thing was already fixed with dogmatic certainty: that the divine nature of Christ had appeared upon earth, not as an apparition (as an angel or a phantasm), but in tangible and human reality.

People expressed this, as well as they could, with the formula that Christ had appeared in the flesh. The Johannine writings began with this formulation. They said that "the Word became flesh."[357] And every true Christian must confess that Christ has come in the flesh.[358] Ignatius vigorously takes up this line of attack against Docetism. Two of his letters, to the Trallians and to the Smyrnaeans, are altogether essentially aimed at these false teachings. But this polemic also permeates his other letters. The two characteristic confessions, Trall. 9 and Smyrn. 1, acquired their distinctive stamp from this struggle. And just as Ignatius here likes to use the formula ἀληθῶς ἐγεννήθη, ἐσταυρώθη, ἀπέθανεν,[359] so also in other passages we encounter the characteristic emphasis upon the σάρξ of Jesus. In the confession of the Ephesian letter (7) we read εἷς ἰατρὸς σαρκικός τε καὶ πνεματικός, ἐν σαρκὶ γενόμενος θεός. One is to confess Jesus as the σαρκοφόρος (Smyrn. 5.2). He likes to speak of a ἕνωσις σαρκικὴ καὶ πνευματικὴ of the Christians with their Lord (Magn. 13). *Polycarp* united the confession of the Johannine epistles with a confession of the μαρτύριον σταυροῦ (reality of the suffering on the cross; Phil. 7.1).[360] The author of the Epistle of Barnabas repeatedly emphasizes the appearing of Jesus in the flesh.[361] Of course when he expresses the opinion that Christ had to appear in the flesh in order to veil his deity, which would otherwise have been unendurable for men,

---

was not the original impelling interest, but the belief in the new God. Very characteristic in this sense is Noetus (in Hippolytus, contra Noetum 1-2): τί οὖν κακὸν ποιῶ δοξάζων Χριστόν (δοξάζω almost=ἀποθεοῦν). . . . Χριστὸς ἦν θεὸς καὶ ἔπασχεν δι' ἡμᾶς αὐτὸς ὢν πατήρ.

[357] John 1:14. It is also anti-docetic when in the passion narrative John emphasizes that Jesus himself (not Simon of Cyrene) bore his cross (19:17; against the well-known Gnostic speculations about the crucifixion of Simon).

[358] I John 4:2-3; II John 7.

[359] Cf. πάθος ἀληθινόν in Ephesians, Proemium.

[360] In this connection (denial of a bodily resurrection) he speaks of a μεθοδεύειν τὰ λόγια τοῦ κυρίου πρὸς τὰς ἰδίας ἐπιθυμίας.

[361] 5.1, 6; 6.7, 9; 7.5; 12.10 (the body σκεῦος τοῦ πνεύματος in 7.3).

this again borders on Docetism (5.10).[362] The homilist of II Clement briefly sums up the confession: ὁ Χριστὸς ὢν μὲν τὸ πρῶτον πνεῦμα ἐγένετο σάρξ (9.5).[363] The author or an editor of the Shepherd of Hermas[364] proposes a quite unique Christology. In an artificial explanation of the parable of the faithful servant and his son he refers the son, who is named (inserted) in the parable alongside the servant, to the Holy Spirit, and the servant to the σάρξ, the bodily flesh which the Spirit wore. Thus here is presupposed something of a Christology such as is proposed in II Clement. The point of the explanation is the close connection of Jesus' σάρξ with his pneumatic nature. The σάρξ is to be co-inheritor of his glory after the resurrection; thus also the flesh of the Christians is to have a share in the resurrection, and therefore they are to preserve it pure and undefiled (cf. II Clem. 14.5).

With this strong emphasis upon the flesh of Christ one is gradually removed ever further and further from the view of Paul. According to him Christ has appeared, it is true, ἐν ὁμοιώματι σαρκὸς ἁμαρτίας (so far as I can see, no one took over the expression from Paul). But what took place here was, according to Paul, at the same time an unnatural connection, from which death has freed Christ himself and, following him, us also (vide supra, pp. 180-81). But now the σάρξ becomes in a wholly different way an integrating component part of the being of Jesus Christ, and the union of flesh and spirit becomes a great mystery, important for the present Christian faith. Related to this is the fact that people now not only begin to speak of the κοινωνία τοῦ σώματος in the Supper, but also stress the taking of the σάρξ of Christ. The Gospel of John has led the way here also (6:53 ff.).[365] Ignatius follows and in numerous passages emphasizes the eating of the σάρξ of Jesus in the eucharist. The connections become especially clear here in the polemic against the Docetists in Ignatius' letter to the Smyrnaeans 7.1: εὐχαριστίας καὶ προσευχῆς ἀπέχονται διὰ τὸ μὴ ὁμολογεῖν τὴν εὐχαριστίαν σάρκα εἶναι τοῦ σωτῆρος ἡμῶν Ἰ. Χρ. The

---

[362] Further traces of a naïve Docetism in Harnack, Dogmengeschichte, 4th ed., I, 215, n. 2.

[363] In I Tim. 3:16 the confession (cf. also I Pet. 3:18) is oriented in the other direction: ὃς ἐφανερώθη ἐν σαρκί, ἐδικαιώθη ἐν πνεύματι. The comparison is instructive. It shows how the accent was gradually shifted from the post-existence to the pre-existence. A similar view of the relation of the spirit and the flesh in Christ in the Acts of Paul (correspondence with the Corinthians, 3.14), here connected with the dogma of the miraculous birth.

[364] I have in mind here only the extremely artificial interpretation in Sim. V, 6.4-7.1 (cf. also 7.1b-4), for whose character as an appended supplement most recently J. v. Walter has taken a position (ZNW XIV (1913), 133 ff.).

[365] Here belongs also John 19:34, in comparison with I John 5:6-8.

stress upon the fleshly resurrection of Jesus as well as of the believers is also related to this.[366] In all these views people were moving ever further and further from the bold spiritualism of Paul.

3. But if the true and real bodily human actuality of Jesus was well established, how then were people to conceive of the union of the higher divine element and the lower sarkical element (of the one whom Paul had called the υἱὸς θεοῦ κατὰ σάρκα and κατὰ πνεῦμα)? Here we meet the opposites which we are accustomed to summarize with the terms "adoptionist and pneumatic Christology." We have already pointed out how little, practically considered, of an essential significance accrued to these theological differences. It must still be added that the contrasts here are not at all so clear and so palpable as they appear at first glance. One will still, for example, certainly count Paul as a representative of a pneumatic Christology, and yet he speaks in the programmatic passage Phil. 2 of a ὑπερυψοῦν which God has bestowed on Christ, speaks of the installation of a Son of God in power (Rom. 1:3), and thus finally knows again of a υἱοθεσία of Christ which takes place with the exaltation. Thus for him the pretemporal Jesus (whom he conceives of quite indefinitely ἐν μορφῇ θεοῦ after the analogy of an angelic being [?]) certainly does not have the same position of dignity and power as does the post-existent one. So conversely, even where one talks of the resurrection of Jesus as his installation as Son of God or of the birth of the Son of God at the baptism, the assumption of a preexistent nature of Jesus is not flatly ruled out. Here conceptions which are for us apparently altogether different have, as it appears, existed peacefully side by side.

If one wishes to speak of pneumatic Christology everywhere where the idea of preexistence is held to, one will be permitted to judge that the first view held and maintained unqualified dominance from the beginning onward. Indeed, it could hardly have been possible otherwise. For if it is true that the christological dogma of the primitive community was already summed up in the title "Son of Man," and that here people simply took over with the title the Jewish messianology related to it, then the idea of preexistence would be given from the earliest time, and on this point the Johannine-Pauline theology would be proposing no innovation at all. Thus,

---

[366] John 20:20 and 20:24-29, Luke 24:39-43 lie on the same line as Ignat. Smyrn. 3 (7.1), only that in the latter passage everything is doubly and triply underscored. Cf. also the just discussed editing of Hermas, Sim. V. Emphasis on the sarkic resurrection: I Clem. 23-28. II Clem. 8.4-5; 9.1; 14.5. Barn. 5.6.

then, the myth of a heavenly spiritual being, who sinks into this world of humiliation and is raised again out of it powerful, living, and mighty, has been dominant in Christianity from the outset.

Over against this one may speak only of "adoptionist" side currents and undercurrents. When Luke has Peter conclude his first speech with the thought that God has *made* this Jesus both Lord [367] and Christ (Acts 2:36), we will do well to remember that Paul also speaks of a ὁρισθεὶς υἱὸς θεοῦ ἐν δυνάμει. If Luke and the author of Hebrews connect the word in Ps. 2:7 to the resurrection act and thus interpret this act as the adoption of Jesus to be Son of God (Acts 13:33; Heb. 1:5), we will not for this reason be able to deny a pneumatic Christology at least for the Letter to the Hebrews (but also hardly for Luke); the ideas still lie unexplained beside each other.

In this connection we may place the great weight upon the early Christian baptismal account and upon the significant role which this account played in the tradition of earliest Christianity. I have already suggested (p. 82) that the baptismal account of our oldest gospel tradition, as it is found in Mark, is already legendary through and through, and in its setting in opposition of the Christian baptism with the Spirit and the Johannine baptism with water, as well as in its artificial proof from prophecy for the figure of the forerunner, is affected by a dogmatic tendency. Here the question must be raised whether this dogmatic tendency does not extend further and deeper. What then did the evangelist (or the tradition which he followed) intend to say thereby, when he placed this baptismal account at the beginning of his Gospel? Surely he did not intend to enlighten us as to the emergence and development of the messianic consciousness and an inward process in the spiritual life of Jesus, as modern interpreters are always trying to read into this utterly naïve dogmatic account. The evangelist or his predecessor rather intended here to answer for himself and his readers the question of how the divine element which according to him was effective in Jesus not only after the resurrection but already during Jesus' lifetime was related to the human phenomenon of Jesus of Nazareth. He stands on the ground of the Pauline ὁ δὲ κύριος τὸ πνεῦμά ἐστιν. For Paul this sentence is essentially and almost solely oriented to the reality of the exalted Lord, and alongside this the abstract idea of preexistence (which moreover is in no way excluded even for Mark) entered into his theology. But the evangelist explicitly draws into that Pauline equation the total earthly

---

[367] The expression "κύριον" καὶ Χριστόν proves that here "Luke" is setting forth his theology, *not* that of the primitive community.

activity of Jesus and poses the dogmatic theory of the complete union of the Spirit with Jesus at the beginning of the gospel narrative. Still more clearly than in the Marcan account this view is brought to expression through a series of tradition variations on the baptismal tradition. I recall the voice at the baptism which is preserved for us in a branch of Luke's tradition,[368] with the clear identification of the baptismal event as an adoption: "Thou art my Son, this day have I begotten thee." Particularly distinctive here is the account of the Gospel of the Hebrews: *descendit fons omnis spiritus sancti et requievit super eum et dixit illi: Fili mi in omnibus prophetis expectabam te, ut venires et requiescerem in te. Tu es enim requies mea, tu es filius meus, primogenitus, qui regnas in sempiternum.*[369]

Finally, it is significant that the so-called Ebionite Gospel, which in other respects, according to the reports of the church fathers, must have relied heavily upon Matthew's Gospel, began, according to the explicit statement of Epiphanius (Haer. 30. 13-14), with the pericope about the Baptist and baptism, and dwelt especially in detail upon the narrative of the baptism of Jesus.

With these traditions we are again standing on Jewish-Christian soil, yet it can be demonstrated that the interpretation of the baptism as an event of fundamental significance for the person of Jesus remained alive for a long time. Especially characteristic in this connection are Justin's arguments with Trypho in Dial. 87-88. To the Jew's objection that the assumption that the Christos is θεὸς προϋπάρχων σαρκοποιηθείς is not compatible with the conception of his being filled with the Spirit, Justin answers: νουνεχέστατα μὲν καὶ συνετώτατα ἠρώτησας (314 C). Thus he recognizes here a serious problem, which apparently also concerns the Christian circles, and now he endeavors in lengthier discussions to solve this perplexity. According to him, the descending (resting) of the divine spiritual powers upon Jesus signifies the fact that with him the prophetic powers of the Old Testament have ceased to be active. The event of the baptism and the voice at the

---

[368] D., vet. lat., Justin; cf. the Ebionite gospel in Epiphanius, Haer. 30.13. That this tradition is secondary is probably already proved by the fact that the saying from the Psalms is still connected in the earlier tradition with the resurrection of Jesus (see above, p. 338).

[369] Jerome in Isa. comment. IV (on 11:2). Whether the so-called Gospel of the Hebrews was already familiar with the birth story I do not venture to decide. Here everything has been thrown into uncertainty by the most recent investigations of Schmidtke, *Judenchristliche Evangelien*, 1911, and H. Waitz, "Das Evangelium der 12 Apostel," ZNW XIII (1912), 338-48, and XIV (1913), 38-64, and 117-32. Still it appears to me very likely that the Fragments 1 and 2 in Preuschen, *Antilegomena*, p. 4, do not belong to the Gospel of the Hebrews.

baptism do not mean that Jesus has become the Messiah, but that he has come to be known as such: τότε γένεσιν αὐτοῦ γίνεσθαι τοῖς ἀνθρώποῖς, ἐξ ὅτου ἡ γνῶσις αὐτοῦ μέλλει γίνεσθαι (316 D).[370] The view of the significance of the baptismal event which is here opposed by Justin and therefore is presupposed may also be documented elsewhere. In a whole series of later witnesses the baptism appears as the moment of the rebirth of Jesus himself.[371] Further related to this is the fact that in the earliest formulated christological Kerygma accessible to us[372] the allusion to the baptism of Jesus appears as a fixed component part, only later then to disappear. We have already referred above (pp. 276-77) to the theologoumenon, which is demonstrable in Gnostic as well as in ecclesiastical circles, that the miracle-working activity of Jesus began only with the baptism and on the basis of the baptism. It is Gnosticism, however, which affords us the strongest testimony for the part which the baptism of Jesus played in the early Christian reflection upon the person of Jesus. It has already been proved how widespread the use of the theologoumenon of the descent of a higher being (the Christ) upon Jesus at his baptism was in the Gnostic circles, and how the Gnostics made use of this idea, in order to bring their wholly mythological figure of the redeemer together with Jesus of Nazareth and thus to effect their compromise with ecclesiastical Christology (*vide supra*, p. 276). This, however, presupposes that when the Gnostics' theory of the baptism was created, the corresponding view of a fundamental significance of the baptism was widely recognized in ecclesiastical circles.

When now moreover, in connection with this, the day of Jesus' baptism was observed as a high festival in Gnostic circles (*vide supra*, p. 276) with a Pannychian celebration,[373] and when on the other hand particularly in the churches of the Orient until well into the fourth century and even beyond, the baptismal day, the Feast of the Epiphany (January 6) served as the actual festival of the birth of Jesus, it may be concluded that even in the second century the Gnostics were not alone in their celebration of the baptismal festival, but that we have here an ancient cultic tradition which

[370] Also in Clement, Ecl. proph. 7, there is an attempt to remove the assumption of a significance in the baptism of Jesus for his own person: καὶ διὰ τοῦτο ὁ σωτὴρ ἐβαπτίσατο μὴ χρῄζων αὐτός, ἵνα τοῖς ἀναγεννωμένοις τὸ πᾶν ὕδωρ ἁγιάσῃ (cf. Euchologion of Serapion 19; Funk, *Didascalia et Const. apost.*, II, 180). The same idea incidentally is already present in Ignatius. Eph. 18.2: ὃς ἐγεννήθη καὶ ἐβαπτίσθη, ἵνα τῷ πάθει τὸ ὕδωρ καθαρίσῃ.

[371] Cf. Heitmüller, *Im Namen Jesu*, p. 279.1.

[372] Ignatius, Eph. 18.2. Smyrn. 1.1.

[373] Clement, Strom. I, 21.146: ἑορτάζουσι προδιανυκτερεύοντες ἐν ἀναγνώσεσι.

extends beyond the Gnostic circles. The early Christian cultus testifies to the significance which belonged to the baptism of Jesus in the earliest interpretation: For the early Christians in wide circles baptism and Epiphany were identical.

But it must once more be emphasized that all this remained an undercurrent within the church's Christology. The "pneumatic" Christology continued to have absolute predominance; the differences and difficulties present here were not at all widely felt. In this period there is not one single trace to be found of a detailed and thought-out "adoptionist" Christology.[374]

The actual Adoptianists, who appear at the beginning of the third century, were isolated "theologians" who knew how to gain a certain following for a short time, but whose rational doubts, resting upon a study of the Scriptures and the work of comparing sources, had to be shattered, powerless against the inexorable course of development of things. This holds true for the Alogoi[375] as well as for the Roman Adoptianists. When the latter

---

[374] It is worthy of note that Harnack, who places such a strong accent upon this Christology, still must concede that it is contained in full form in only one work, namely the Shepherd of Hermas. But the statements of the Shepherd are hardly usable for a history of the Christology. In the supplement in Sim. V, 6.4–7.1, already treated above (p. 336), there is no adoptionist Christology at all, but an explicitly pneumatic one (the σάρξ of Jesus is the δοῦλος of his πνεῦμα). Then in the entire *explication of the parable* the distinction between δοῦλος and υἱός is no longer found at all, apart from the sentence in V, 5.2 which is hardly tenable even on text-critical grounds (preserved only in L¹): ὁ δὲ υἱὸς τὸ πνεῦμα ἅγιόν ἐστιν. Elsewhere the δοῦλος of the parable is simply applied to the υἱός. Consequently even in the original parable the Son of God can have had no place. Perhaps even the entire episode of the friends and counselors of God (alongside the mention of the Son and Heir) in V, 2.6-8, 11b has been inserted by the same hand which added the strained interpretation in V, 6.4–7.1. The insertion of the interpretation of the "friends" to mean the angels in the first half of the exposition of the parable then would have prompted the doublet, that the angels sometimes appear as χάρακες, and then again as φίλοι (V, 5.3; cf. Grosse-Brauckmann, *De compos. Past. Hermae*, Dissertation, Göttingen, 1910, pp. 48 ff.). Originally there were only two active persons in the parable, God and the servant, and it is not until the second exposition in V, 4-5 that the servant is interpreted to mean Jesus (the Son). To all this an editor has added the artificial reflections about the relationship of Jesus' πνεῦμα and σάρξ. The "Adoptionism" of Hermas however hangs on the one textually uncertain gloss: ὁ δὲ υἱὸς τὸ πνεῦμα ἅγιόν ἐστιν. Of course this sentence is also repeated in Sim. IX, 1.1. But this verse represents an artificial thread by which Sim. IX (a doublet of Vis. III) is subsequently connected with the whole. Outside of Similitude V the term υἱός is found only in Vis. II, 2.8, Sim. VIII, 3.2 (a gloss!) and 11.1, and (*passim*) Sim. IX.

[375] On them, cf. Epiph. 51.18, τῶν νομιζόντων ἀπὸ Μαρίας καὶ δεῦρο Χριστὸν αὐτὸν καλεῖσθαι [καὶ υἱὸν θεοῦ?] καὶ εἶναι μὲν πρότερον ψιλὸν ἄνθρωπον, κατὰ προκοπὴν δὲ εἰληφέναι τὴν τοῦ υἱοῦ τοῦ θεοῦ προσηγορίαν. I place these theological Adoptianists in this connection, in spite of the fact that they acknowledged the miraculous birth. For in their patterns of thought they are still essentially oriented to the event of the baptism and its dogmatic interpretation. Harnack, *Dogmengeschichte*, 4th ed., I, 709-10.

(according to Eusebius CH V, 28.3) appealed, to support their view, to the tradition which was said to have been altered only since the time of Victor, this judgment only proves that theological tendencies always find ways and means of showing that tradition is to be found on their side. All this has hardly any significance for the broad course of the development. In other respects, so far as we can see, none of those theologians laid the axe to the root and demanded an actual revision of the cultic veneration of Christ. They all limited themselves, even on irrational phenomena, most of all the complete deification[376] of Christ, to opposing a development whose roots lay much deeper and which thus were not at all touched by the opposition.

That view of the significance of the baptism of Christ as the hour of birth of the Son of God, from the beginning on, continued to be, strictly speaking, an alien element in the development. Even John does not know what to do with Jesus' baptism, and so he reshapes it into a revelation to John the Baptist about the One who was from the beginning onward the only begotten Son of God. Justin is somewhat embarrassed by this remnant of an earlier speculation. But it appears to have disappeared or to have been thrust altogether into the background only when the Gnostics enlarged it into the myth of the Christ who descended upon Jesus at the baptism.[377]

4. So now there emerges a new interpretation of the coming-into-the-flesh of the Son of God which is in a better position to be joined with the supernaturally, metaphysically structured Christology which had been dominant from the first. The concept "Son of God" acquires a natural, crudely drawn interpretation which suggests itself to the simple mind, in particular on the basis of Hellenistic mythology. The dogma of the miraculous birth emerges. It is of relatively quite late origin. Neither the earliest evangelist,

---

[376] At this point also characteristic variations are exhibited: Hippolytus, Ref. VII, 35.2, p. 222.11 W. θεὸν δὲ οὐδέποτε τοῦτον γεγονέναι αὐτὸν θέλουσιν ἐπὶ τῇ καθόδῳ τοῦ πνεύματος, ἕτεροι δὲ μετὰ τὴν ἐκ νεκρῶν ἀνάστασιν.

[377] Could not the legend of the transfiguration also, like the account of the baptism, originally have come out of such a dogmatic tendency? It has long been recognized that it is certainly a doublet of the latter. Perhaps we would then have here the *first* (and earlier) attempt at a dating back into the earthly life of Jesus of his exaltation to the rank of Son of God. In any case this legend played a role in Christian imagination. Cf. the statements in II Pet. 1:12 ff., Exc. ex Theod., chaps. 4–5 (cf. here the interpretation of the scene as a fulfillment of Mark 9:1). Acta Petri, chap. 20, Acta Joh., chap. 90. A parallel to the transfiguration scene (but transposed to the period after Jesus' earthly life) is found in Pistis Sophia, chaps. 5 ff., and here the transfiguration indeed means deification.

Mark, nor Paul,[378] nor the Fourth Gospel [379] knew it. The genealogies of Jesus in our first two Gospels stand in irreconcilable contradiction to it. The only witnesses in the New Testament are Matthew and Luke with their birth legends.[380] And in the Lucan narrative the dogma depends on two verses (1:34-35), in the elimination of which the context of the presentation would be freed of a crude disruption. Only with Ignatius do the testimonies begin to flow more abundantly. Ignatius already is familiar with a christological kerygma in which the birth from a virgin had a fixed place. Now it is said: ὁ γὰρ θεὸς ἡμῶν 'Ι. ὁ Χρ. ἐκυοφορήθη ὑπὸ Μαρίας κατ' οἰκονομίαν θεοῦ ἐκ σπέρματος μὲν Δαβὶδ [381] πνεύματος δε ἁγίου (Eph. 18.2).[382] Still more characteristic for the understanding of the dogma is the "καὶ ἐκ Μαρίας καὶ ἐκ θεοῦ" (Eph. 7.2). Now the term υἱὸς ἀνθρώπου (alongside υἱὸς θεοῦ) also acquires a new meaning, wholly alien to its origin, when it is said: τῷ κατὰ σάρκα ἐκ γένους Δαβίδ, τῷ υἱῷ ἀνθρώπου καὶ υἱῷ θεοῦ.[383] To this emergence of the dogma of the miraculous birth only in the last decades of the first century corresponds the fact that of the earlier Gnostics,[384] actually only the Valentinian schools and their immediate predecessors, the so-called Barbelo-Gnostics, accepted this view and, as well as could be done with their basic views, related this to the doctrine that the miraculously prepared body of the redeemer had passed through the womb of Mary as through a pipe.[385] Finally, it requires no further proof that for

[378] Rom. 1:3-4; Gal. 4:4.

[379] John 1:13 is decisive (the copyist who corrected the ὃς ἐγεννήθη already saw this), but 7:26 ff. is also significant.

[380] It requires no proof that in both, the legend of the miraculous birth is in contradiction with the genealogies. Von Soden has recently accepted into the text even the wording of the syr. sin. in Matt. 1:16, which allows the contradiction to emerge clearly: 'Ιωσὴφ δέ, ᾧ ἐμνηστεύθη παρθένος Μαριάμ, ἐγέννησεν 'Ιησοῦν τὸν λεγόμενον Χριστόν.

[381] It is noteworthy that at first the emphasis of the ἐκ σπέρματος Δαβίδ is held along with the virgin birth; cf. Eph. 20.2, Trall. 9, Smyrn. 1.1.

[382] Cf. Eph. 19.1, Trall. 9, Smyrn. 1.1 (υἱὸν θεοῦ κατὰ θέλημα καὶ δύναμιν θεοῦ γεγεννημένον.

[383] Cf. Eph. 20.2, et passim. Barn. 12.10 (without reference to the miraculous birth), οὐχὶ υἱὸς ἀνθρώπου ἀλλὰ υἱὸς τοῦ θεοῦ. Cf. Tertullian, adv. Marc. III, 11; IV, 10.

[384] Even the (Alogoi and the) Roman Adoptianists, who accept the dogma of the miraculous birth, continue to put all the stress upon the baptism of Jesus; see above, pp. 341-42.

[385] Perhaps it is for this reason that in the Roman baptismal symbol the ἐκ . . . Μαρίας παρθένου is fixed, while earlier, still in Justin (Hahn, Bibliothek der Symbole, 3rd ed., § 3), the διά is also common: (cf. Harnack, Chronologie, I, 531). Cf. Acta Petri, chap. 7: deus filium suum . . . per virginem protulit. (Correspondence of Paul with the Corinthians, 3.14: "God sent the Holy Spirit into Mary in Galilee . . . and she conceived in her body the Holy Spirit.")

Justin[386] and the confessional formula which he presupposed, the virgin birth belonged to the permanent assets.[387]

It is clear that this dogma is not to be understood as some sort of necessary consequence of the doctrine of preexistence, or of the metaphysical, Pauline-Johannine Christology. The motives prompting its admission can hardly be determined more exactly. Popular fantasy probably has functioned here in dependence on the concept of the Son of God. Perhaps the so surprisingly rapid spread of this dogma to wide circles was helped by the consideration that with it the separation of Christ and Jesus by the Gnostic baptismal myth would best be avoided. The doctrine of the virgin birth is set forth as a parallel formation to the doctrine of the baptism, in that here again the Pneuma (of God) is regarded as the effectual factor (Matt. 1:20; Luke 1:35). Just as according to the doctrine of Jesus' baptism the Pneuma descends upon him and begets the Son of God, so now the virgin Mary[388] conceives by the Holy Spirit. In all this, Paul's ὁ δὲ κύριος τὸ πνεῦμά ἐστιν is still at work. In other respects, as we have said, the dogma represents a popular coarsening of the idea of the supra-terrestrial Son of God, a coarsening which becomes clearest when we think of the Ignatian καὶ ἐκ Μαρίας καὶ ἐκ θεοῦ and the new contrast "Son of Man–Son of God." For this reason also one will not be able to avoid the conclusion that influences of the surrounding Hellenistic milieu were exerted upon this folk theology of the infant Christianity. Matters are so clear that it serves no purpose to cite other parallels and to introduce all the legends of miraculously born sons of God. This has already been done long ago and does not need to be repeated.[389]

But in this context we may at least refer to one religio-historical parallel,

[386] Harnack in Hahn, *Bibliothek der Symbole*, 3rd ed., § 3.

[387] We might further refer to the curious apocryphal quotations which appear (alongside Isa. 7:13) in Acta Petri, chap. 24. "In the last times a boy is born of the Holy Spirit; his mother does not know a man, and no one claims to be his father." "She has given birth and has not given birth." "We have neither heard her (?) voice (Ascensio Jesaiae XI, 13), nor has a midwife come in." The following quotation is already completely Gnostic.

[388] Cf. above the πνεῦμα-σάρξ speculations in II Clem. and in the Shepherd of Hermas. Cf. Tertullian, adv. Marc. III, 16, *spiritus creatoris, qui est Christus*. Later, in the apologists, the Logos appears in the place of the Pneuma. Justin, Apol. I, 33; Tatian, Or. 7. See below, Chap. IX.

[389] Cf. the compilation in Petersen, *Die wunderbare Geburt des Heilandes*, RV I, 17, 1909. Up to the present we have no evidence in the tradition for the assumption that the acceptance of the miraculous birth was mediated by the Jewish messianology. The reference to long-past Old Testament reminiscences of such a myth does not suffice. Naturally it comes out to one and the same thing for the evaluation, regardless of whether the appropriation came about directly or by way of a myth that was accepted in Judaism.

which comes into question for the tradition of Jesus' baptism as well as for the borrowing of the legend of the miraculous birth. The ancient baptismal festival of Christianity on January 6 (10) has already been discussed often. But now it can be shown that the festival of the epiphany of Dionysos was celebrated on January 6. Pliny relates, with an appeal for confirmation to the Roman consul Mucianus, that on January 5 every year a fountain in the temple of the Father Liber on the island of Andros[390] flowed with water that tasted like wine (Hist. Nat. II, 106.11). The report of Pausanias (VI, 26.1) confirms this: "The inhabitants of Andros also say that every year at the *feast of Dionysos* wine flows for them spontaneously from the holy place." When Pliny in another place (XXXI, 13) says that on Andros on each of "seven certain days of this god" wine flows from the fountain of the Father Liber, we may surmise with great probability that here *one* hebdomadal festival of the god, beginning on January 5, is meant. It is likely moreover that the festival began with a nighttime ceremony, that is, on the evening of January 5. This appears first to be attested by the parallel cult tradition of Elis, which again is preserved for us by Pausanias (VI, 26.1; cf. Athenaios I, 61, p. 34 A). According to him the inhabitants of Elis venerate the god Dionysos most of all, and "also say that the god visits them at the festival of Thyien." At this festival of the epiphany of the god, the date of which unfortunately is not given, at the beginning three pots were placed in a shrine empty, and then the doors to the shrine were sealed. On the next day, then, the pots were found filled with wine. Thus the festival of the epiphany of Dionysos appears to begin with the miracle which takes place in the night.[391]

Associated with this is further the observation that in fact in later syncretistic tradition we encounter the festival of the miraculous birth (epiphany) of a God on January 6, which began with a vigil (on the night of January 5/6). Epiphanius has preserved the interesting account for us in Haer. 51.22. On this date in Alexandria in the Koreion, a great temple of

---

[390] We have similar traditions from the island of Teos. Diod. Sic. III, 66: Τήιοι μὲν τεκμήριον φέρουσι τῆς παρ' αὐτοῖς γενέσεως τοῦ θεοῦ τὸ μέχρι τοῦ νῦν τεταγμένοις χρόνοις ἐν τῇ πόλει πηγὴν αὐτομάτως ἐκ τῆς γῆς οἴνου ῥεῖν εὐωδίᾳ διαφερόντως. Cf. the material in Nilsson, *Griechische Feste*, pp. 291-93; de Jong, *Das antike Mysterienwesen*, pp. 168 ff.; on the whole matter, cf. also Arnold Meyer, *Entstehung und Entwicklung des Weihnachtsfestes* (1913), 2nd ed.; above all, also Usener, *Weihnachtsfest* (1911), 2nd ed., and Cumont, "Le Natalis Invicti," Extr. des Comptes rendues des séances de l'Acad. des Inscr. et Belles Lettres (1911), 292 ff.

[391] The parallels to the miracle at the wedding in Cana, which here present themselves, are discussed above, pp. 102-3.

Kore, a *pannychian* ceremony took place, accompanied by song and the playing of flutes; and on the next morning after the cock crowing, people carried an image of the god, ornamented with golden crosses and simply enthroned on a litter, in a solemn procession seven times around the temple with the cry: "*Today at this hour Kore* (i.e., the virgin) *has given birth to the Aeon.*" The parallel cult tradition of the Arabian capital Petra (and of Elusa in the vicinity of Gaza), which Epiphanius relates in the same context, shows us who this anonymous God-Aeon is. There, on the same day, they celebrated the birthday of the similarly virgin-born god Dusares, whose name is said to mean μονογενής (!) τοῦ Δεσπότου,[392] as whose virgin mother an Arabian goddess with a variously reported name[393] is identified. But now Dusares is that god who generally is identified with the Greek Dionysos![394] Consequently now we should have established the festival, which began with a Pannychis, of the epiphany (the miraculous birth) of the god Dionysos-Dusares on January 5/6. Of course in reference to this we must remember that the Eleusinian, Orphic cult tradition actually knows no myth of a (virgin) birth or rebirth of Dionysos. (For the myth of Dionysos' birth from Semele, who nowhere appears as a goddess, can hardly come into question here.) Nevertheless we can at least show, in later tradition also, this feature within the milieu in question. In the so-called Naassene Preaching we encounter a peculiar (probably secondary) Eleusinian cult tradition: according to it, at the nighttime ceremony in Eleusis, the hierophant[395] is said to have cried out at the light of the torches (ὑπὸ πολλῷ πυρί): ἱερὸν ἔτεκε πότνια κοῦρον Βριμὼ Βριμόν [τουτέστι ἰσχυρὰ ἰσχυρόν]. This is an exact parallel to the cultic ceremony in the Koreion in

---

[392] Cf. the combination connected with this name in Cheyne, *Bible Problems* (1904), p. 74.

[393] Epiphanius, Χααμοῦ; in the parallel tradition of Cosmas of Jerusalem, to be discussed below, Χαμαρᾶ—a scholion on the Cosmas text, χαβαρα. John of Damascus, de haeresibus I, 111 (Migne, PSG XCIV, 764) speaks of an Ἀφροδίτη, ἣν δὴ Χαβὰρ (Χαβὲρ) τῇ ἑαυτῶν ἐπωνόμασαν γλώσσῃ, ὅπερ σημαίνει μεγάλη. (Khabir, in fact,= great). I cannot see, in view of the widely variant tradition present here, how Clemen (*Christentum und Mysterienreligion*, p. 63) intends actually to prove his assertion that the note in Epiphanius stems only from a linguistic misunderstanding. Clemen appears to depend here primarily upon Wellhausen's statements about Epiphanius' Haer. 51.22 in *Skizzen und Vorarbeiten*, III, 46. Yet cf. *contra* W. Robertson Smith, *The Religion of the Semites*, p. 56.

[394] To be compared on the god Aeon, whom the Alexandrians worship in the Koreion, is Suidas (s. v. Heraiskos, I 872, ed. Bernhard): τὸ ἄρρητον ἄγαλμα τοῦ αἰῶνος . . . ὃ Ἀλεξανδρεῖς ἐτίμησαν Ὄσιριν ὄντα καὶ Ἄδωνιν ὁμοῦ. *Osiris* however is again *Dionysos.*

[395] Hippolytus, Ref. V, 8.40, p. 96.18 W.

Alexandria and in Petra-Elusa.[396] Here it may have appended Oriental motifs to the Greek cult tradition. One further tradition, which likewise fits into this context in a surprising manner, points to this. Cosmas of Jerusalem, in his συναγωγὴ καὶ ἐξήγησις ὧν ἐμνήσθη ἱστοριῶν ὁ θεῖος Γρηγόριος, has handed on to us the following unusually important notice[397]: ταύτην ἦγον ἐκπάλαι δὲ τὴν ἡμέραν ἑορτὴν Ἕλληνες, καθ᾽ ἣν ἐτελοῦντο κατὰ τὸ μεσονύκτιον ἐν ἀδύτοις τισὶν ὑπεισερχόμενοι, ὅθεν ἐξιόντες ἔκραζον: ἡ Παρθένος ἔτεκεν, αὔξει φῶς. Unfortunately it cannot be determined exactly which ἡμέρα the author has in mind.[398] At this late time it may have been the birth celebration of Christ on December 25 that he was thinking about. But at the same time, for his account he refers in unmistakable fashion to the passage in Epiphanius which we discussed above: ταύτην . . . τὴν ἑορτὴν καὶ Σαρρακηνοὺς ἄγειν τῇ παρ᾽ αὐτῶν σεβομένῃ Ἀφροδίτῃ, ἣν δὲ Χαμαρᾶ . . . προσαγορεύουσι. But since on the other hand the cultic saying appears in Cosmas with a distinctive alteration (αὔξει φῶς), it is perhaps to be assumed that for Cosmas two cultic traditions have intermingled, both of which deal with the miraculous birth of a god and which involve different dates. The αὔξει φῶς[399] appears to refer to the miraculous birth of a sun-god. This perspective may also suggest the conjecture that the idea of the miraculous birth could have been related to the cultic ceremonies of Dionysos-Dusares only in a later period in the Orient.

But be that as it may, the suspicion can no longer be avoided that the

[396] The feature may only have been transferred erroneously to the old cultic ceremony of Eleusis. This cultic tradition then is again present in Gnostic-Christian editing, when it is said later in the Naassene Preaching with reference to Isa. 7:14 that the virgin had borne μακάριον Αἰῶνα Αἰώνων (V, 8.45, p. 97.17 W).

[397] Migne, PSG XXXVIII, 342 ff. I owe this and the following notices to Cumont's essay, "Le Natalis Invicti" (see above, p. 345, n. 390).

[398] Immediately before this there is a reference to that curious legend which is preserved in context in the Ἐξήγησις τῶν ἐν Περσίδι πραχθέντων (Bratke, Ein Religionsgespräch am Hof der Sassaniden, Leipzig, 1899). One may note that here at the close, after the account of the miraculous conception of the fountain (Pege) and the overthrow of the images of the gods, Dionysos appears without the usual following of Satyrs and proclaims to the old gods their overthrow. Might there be here also the parallel Dionysos–Christ? Here also it is a matter of a holy Pannychis. Unfortunately nothing is yielded by the context about the αὔτη ἡ ἡμέρα.

[399] Cumont points to the αὔξει φῶς in the calendar of the astrologer Antiochus (Boll, Griech. Kalender, SAH, 1910, p. 16). There on December 25 it is noted: Ἡλίου γενέθλιον, αὔξει φῶς. With this, one should compare further the cultic saying related to it: χαῖρε νύμφιε, χαῖρε νέον φῶς which Firmicus Maternus (de errore prof. relig., 19.1) has handed down. Dieterich, Mithras-Liturgie, p. 214, connects it with Dionysos (on this, cf. Wobbermin, Religionsgeschichtliche Studien, pp. 16 ff.). Thus here also the figure of Dionysos moves into the picture. Incidentally, Clement of Alexandria also appears to be familiar with the cultic expression, χαῖρε φῶς (Protr. XI, 114; see above, p. 234, n. 91).

celebration of the ancient Christian festival of the Epiphany on January 6 arose from an adaptation from the cultus of Dionysos. The probability significantly increases when we hear from the lively portrayal of the Aquitanian pilgrim (Aetheria)[400] that the later Christian festival of the Epiphany (and that as birth festival, not as baptismal festival) began already with a preliminary ceremony on the eve of January 6. People went from Jerusalem to Bethlehem, in order there to observe the nocturnal ceremonies, especially the midnight mass in the cave of the nativity,[401] and then returned to Jerusalem in solemn procession. Here we have the characteristic celebration of the Pannychis on January 5/6! And the cultic tradition from Jerusalem is so especially important because that cult adaptation must have had its origin in Palestine, Syria, and Egypt (cf. the parallels in Alexandria, Petra, and Elusa).

But the feast of the Epiphany in Christianity has a very old tradition of its own. We find it, as has been said, already among the Basilidians,[402] thus in the first half of the second century. That means we would approach the time of the emergence of the legend and of the dogma of the miraculous birth. Of course, against this combination one can object that January 6 first served as the baptismal day of Jesus and not as the day of the miraculous birth (*vide* p. 276). But the later ecclesiastical tradition did celebrate the birth of the Lord on January 6. What was taken over from the cult of Dionysos was first the Epiphany on January 6, which people connected with the baptism as the time of Jesus' birth. Then it was a second step when people appropriated out of the same cultic milieu the idea of the birth from a virgin.[403]

The worship of the god Dionysos can be demonstrated all around Palestine. We have already spoken of the veneration of Dionysos-Dusares in Petra and Elusa. His cult can be documented in Caesarea, Damascus, Scythopolis, and the Hauran region. The founding of Scythopolis[404] was combined with

---

[400] On this, see Usener, *Weihnachtsfest*, 2nd ed., pp. 208 ff.

[401] Cf. Jerome, epist. (58.3, 5, p. 532.7 H) ad Paulinum, on the Tammuz cult in the cave of Bethlehem: *et in specu, ubi quondam Christus parvulus vagiit, Veneris amasius plangebatur.*

[402] The difference in dates (the 10th and 14th of Tybi) which we encounter in the Gnostic tradition may well have developed because the ceremony of the Dionysos festival was a hebdomadal one.

[403] [On the whole matter, cf. K. Holl, *Der Ursprung des Epiphanienfestes*, SAB, 1917, pp. 402-48. Also O. Weinreich, *Archiv für Religionswissenschaft*, XIX (1918), 174-90, and F. Boll, *ibid.*, pp. 190-91. Bultmann.]

[404] Pliny, hist. nat. V, 18, 74.

the legend of Dionysos, as were the beginnings of Damascus and Raphia.[405] Dionysos frequently appears on the coins of Phoenician cities (Sidon, Berytus, Tyre, Orthosia, etc.).[406] The belief that the Jews worshiped Dionysos appears to have had a certain circulation.[407] Thus the cult of Dionysos will also have been in the first place a rival of Palestinian-Syrian primitive Christianity. The apologist Justin himself calls attention to the devil's imitations of Christian faith's motifs in the cult of Dionysos.[408] The symbol of Dionysos is the sacred vine, and the figurative language connected with this symbol (cf. Didache 9-10. John 15)[409] perhaps is related to the Dionysian cult. In any case, the legend of the wedding in Cana, as has already been brought out, is an adaptation of a Dionysian cultic legend to Jesus.

In view of all this, the possibility should be considered[410] whether it was not precisely the legend of the virgin birth of Dionysos-Dusares, of the νέον φῶς, which gave the first suggestion for the formation of the dogma of the miraculous birth.[411]

---

[405] Cf. the material in Schürer, *Gesch. des jüdischen Volkes*, 4th ed., for Caesarea (II, 35), Damascus (II, 37, 56), Scythopolis (II, 38, 56), Hauran (II, 44), and Raphia (II, 55).

[406] Cf. Baudissin, *Adonis und Esmun*, pp. 231-41.

[407] Cf. Plutarch, Symposium, V, 6 (Theme: τίς ὁ παρὰ 'Ιουδαίοις θεός). The view is rejected by Tacitus as folly; hist. V, 5. Lydus, de mensibus IV, 53 (likewise a treatment περὶ τοῦ παρ' Ἑβραίων τιμωμένου θεοῦ; all the answers presuppose the identification of Osiris and Dionysos). In the verses of Cornelius Labeo (probably from the first century A.D.) found in Macrobius, Saturnal. I, 18, 19, "Jao" is identified with Hades, Zeus, Helios, and Jakchos (to be read thus instead of Jao). (Jao, God of the Jews, according to Lydus, de mensibus IV, 51). Cf. Papyrus Parthey, AAB, 1866, p. 128, l. 300.

[408] Apol. I, 54; Dialogue 69.

[409] Weinel, *Neutestamentliche Theologie*, 2nd ed., p. 541.

[410] Robertson Smith (*Religion of the Semites*, p. 56, n. 3) sees in the virgin-mother-goddess found in Epiphanius' Haer. 51.22 the Arabian Allât, and in the divine son Dusares the deity of the morning star. He appeals there to Herodotus I, 131 and III, 8, and particularly to Jerome, who in the Life of Hilarion, chap. 25, mentions the temple of a Venus in Elusa, who was worshiped there "ob Luciferum," and in his commentary on Amos 5 (Migne, PSL XXV, 1055) directly asserts that among the Arabians the *morning star* was referred to as a male deity. I add the explicit testimony of John of Damascus, haer. I, 111 (Migne, PSG XCIV, 764): οὗτοι (the Arabians) προσκυνήσαντες τῷ ἑωσφόρῳ ἄστρῳ καὶ τῇ 'Αφροδίτῃ, ἣν δὴ Χαβὲρ (Χαβὲρ) τῇ ἑαυτῶν ἐπωνόμασαν γλώσσῃ, ὅπερ σημαίνει μεγάλη (see above, p. 346, n. 393). (Detailed evidence as to the male character of the morning star [Azizos] in the milieu under consideration also to be found in Dussaud, *Rev. Archéolog.*, 1903, pp. 128-33. I mention all this in order to point out that the expression in Rev. 22:16, ἐγώ εἰμι . . . ὁ ἀστὴρ ὁ λαμπρὸς ὁ πρωϊνός perhaps becomes understandable in these terms (cf. the enigmatic δώσω αὐτῷ τὸν ἀστέρα τὸν πρωϊνόν in 2:28.)

[411] Nothing can be concluded or inferred for the miraculous birth from the other birth legends in Matthew and Luke, for these were earlier than it.

# 8

## THE STRUCTURING OF CHRISTIANITY ON THE BASIS OF THE CHRIST CULT AND ITS VARIOUS TYPES

I. *Introduction*. In this section it will be our object to show what the Christ cult meant for the total development of the Christian life and of the basic Christian convictions. To pose the question means at the same time to confront characteristic differences in the forms and types which the Christianity of the post-apostolic era assumed. There are instances in the post-apostolic era in which the Christian religion is presented altogether as the cultus of the new God, and again there are others in which the cultic element, as over against the generally religious and moral, so definitely moves into the background that it requires some effort to demonstrate it at all.

In general, of course, one will have to conclude that the cultus dominated early Christian life in a way into which we can project ourselves only in a remote fashion. Worship and assemblies for worship were a part of the everyday life of the Christians. From Paul's portrayal in I Cor. 11, one gains the impression that the Christians came together daily for the common meal of the κυριακὸν δεῖπνον. This will have remained so later also, as Sunday, the κυριακὴ ἡμέρα, gradually acquired its predominant place in the cultus and the Sunday worship of the community was formally developed, as the earliest witnesses such as the Didache (14), Justin (I, 67) and Pliny's report to Trajan (*stato die*) show us. The Didache gives the prescriptions for the worship meals in particular along with the regulation of the Sunday worship (9–10). Wherever we look, we find the admonition

350

that the Christians are to come together as frequently as possible,[1] even in a time in which the regulated Sunday assemblies had been long established. Origen still vigorously exhorts the believers to come to worship daily *ad puteos scripturarum*, and he does not admit the excuse that one comes to church on feast days! [2]

Thus, insofar as possible, the Christian communities gathered every day, at least a large part of their members. And by and large their assemblies were more than simple meetings, they were communal ceremonial meals which bound the participants, socially and religiously, with one another most intimately and closely. As a rule they gathered in the evening (κυριακὸν δεῖπνον). During the day the Christians, mostly belonging to the poorer classes, were at their work in the dispersion in harsh slavery to the "world." From hard labor,[3] out of loneliness, the individuals then came to the κοινωνία, to the Christian fellowship. There something new and marvelous came to life in them, the spirit of the fellowship seized them and raised the individuals to a level above themselves. When Paul repeatedly emphasized that the Christians are a body, in their relationship with the exalted Lord as well as in the fellowship among themselves, he sounded a basic attitude of the early Christian era. In the meetings for worship people in fact felt themselves to be the "Soma," a unitary structure of unprecedented inward cohesiveness. The spirit blazed forth, prophets appeared and talked in visionary, mysteriously ecstatic fashion about the dread mysteries of the future and about the blessed joys of the heavenly kingdom,[4] or they disclosed hidden events in the life of the community

---

[1] Cf. Heb. 10:25, and on it, the passages cited by Windisch HNT, IV, 3). Did. 16.2: πυκνῶς συναχθήσεθε ζητοῦντες τὰ ἀνήκοντα ταῖς ψυχαῖς ἡμῶν. Also the parallel in Barn. 4.10: μὴ καθ᾽ ἑαυτοὺς ἐνδύνοντες μονάζετε . . . ἀλλ᾽ ἐπὶ τὸ αὐτὸ συνερχόμενοι συνζητεῖτε περὶ τοῦ κοινῆ συμφέροντος. Perhaps both passages come from the common (Jewish?) basic writing which is also used in the first chapters of the Didache. Hennecke, *Neutest. Apokr.*, p. 185; II Clem. 17.3: πυκνότερον προσερχόμενοι πειρώμεθα προκόπτειν ἐν ταῖς ἐντολαῖς τοῦ κυρίου. Ignatius, Eph. 13. Cf. Magn. 4; Eph. 20.2; Trall. 12.2; Polyc. 4.2; I Clem. 29.1; Pseudo-Clem. Diamartyr. Jac. 9. Cf. the reproach expressed in Hermas, Sim. IX, 26.3: μὴ κολλώμενοι τοῖς δούλοις τοῦ θεοῦ, ἀλλὰ μονάζοντες ἀπολλύουσι τὰς ἑαυτῶν ψυχάς; Didasc., chaps. 9, 13; Clement to James 17.

[2] Homil. in Genes. X, 2 (Migne, PSG XII, 215 ff.), cf. Schermann, *Ägyptische Abendmahlsliturgie* (1912), pp. 34 ff. In the ecclesiastical decrees of the Pseudo-Clementine Homilies (from the time of Callistus) it is said in III, 69: πρὸ δὲ πάντων . . . συνεχέστερον συνέρχεσθε εἴθε καθ᾽ ὥραν, ἐπεί γε ἐν ταῖς νομισμέναις τῆς συνόδου ἡμέραις. In Mart. Apollon. 9 we hear of a daily prayer for the ruler κατὰ πρόσταγμα δικαίας ἐντολῆς, which apparently is connected with the daily worship of the Christians.

[3] One rightly connects the ἀλλήλους ἐκδέχεσθε in I Cor. 11:33 with the poorer brethren who come from work.

[4] Cf. already II Cor. 2:6 ff., and above all Ign. Trall. 5.

and in the individual souls.[5] People speaking in tongues babbled in unintelligible sounds of highest rapture and inspiration. Miraculous powers were aroused, sick people were healed and demons expelled.[6] Prayers were uttered by the entire congregation together and aloud [7] in the name of the Lord Jesus; in hymns and antiphons in honor "of God and the Lamb," enthusiasm burned high. All that the Christians had of new religious and moral conviction they owed to the teaching and the admonition in these worship services. In the solemn act of the eucharist one experienced the presence of the Lord, the "Maranatha," the κοινωνία τοῦ αἵματος καὶ τοῦ σώματος Χριστοῦ. With pride and joy they led the Christians who had just been admitted through baptism to this great and wonderful mystery. Moral discipline was bound up most of all with the celebration of the eucharist. No unworthy person, especially no one who had a quarrel with his brother, might come to the table of the Lord.[8] Thus the confession of sins and the forgiveness of sins were connected with Christian worship, although from the outset other tendencies (the view of baptism as the sacrament which cleansed from sin, the conviction as to the unforgivable character of gross sins) worked against their occupying a central position.[9] Indeed the whole perspective of the primitive Christian communities grows out of worship. The ἐπίσκοποι and διάκονοι were first of all cultic officials of the community; they supplanted the enthusiasts and pneumatics, the free prophets and teachers in the leadership of worship; and in the leadership of worship they found the center of their activity. And finally: the entire social structure of the Christian community life is determined and governed by worship. As the Christian worship services gradually

[5] I Cor. 14:24-25 (2:15). Esp. characteristic is Ign. Philad. 7.

[6] In I Cor. 12:9 (cf. 12:28, 30), Paul apparently counts the healings and ἐνεργήματα δυνάμεων among the phenomena of the life of worship. In I Cor. 5:4 the assembled community is supposed to perform the marvel of the παραδοῦναι τῷ σατανᾷ. The σημεῖα τοῦ ἀποστόλου of which he boasts apparently have reference to the (worship-) life of the community (II Cor. 12:12; Rom. 15:19). See further examples in the statements below concerning Ignatius. The connection of exorcism with baptism is best explained if the exorcisms belonged from the very first to the ingredients of the life of worship.

[7] Justin, Apol. I, 65.1: κοινὰς εὐχὰς ποιησόμενοι . . . εὐτόνως (cf. the συντόνως in the summons to the long (deacon's) prayer in Apost. Const. VIII, 10); I, 67.5: ἔπειτα ἀνιστάμεθα κοινῇ πάντες καὶ εὐχὰς πέμπομεν.

[8] Didache 10.6, εἴ τις ἅγιός ἐστιν ἐρχέσθω, εἴ τις οὐκ ἐστὶ μετανοείτω; cf. particularly 14. Ignat. Trall. 8.2 continues immediately after a clear reference to the Supper (σάρξ and αἷμα Ἰησοῦ): μηδεὶς ὑμῶν κατὰ τοῦ πλησίον (τι) ἐχέτω. Cf. the admonitions of the deacon in all the great liturgies immediately before the Anaphora, e.g. in Apost. Const. VIII, 12.

[9] Strong emphasis on the ἐξομολόγησις in Didache 14; cf. the detailed exomologesis in the congregational prayer in I Clem. 59. See below, p. 356.

ceased to be communal meals, and the Agape was completely separated from the eucharistic celebration, the character of social service continued to be maintained for the worship in the broadest measure. It appeared under the category of θυσία[10]; probably in place of contributions to the common meals there appeared the freewill offering of gifts, the New Testament sacrifice corresponding to the Old Testament cult. The bishop receives the gifts[11] and regulates their distribution to the widows, the poor, and the sick, the prisoners, and even the strangers; for φιλοξενία is the bond which embraces and holds together the common organism of the individual congregations, the church. Alongside this the Agapae maintain the character of an explicitly caritative institution,[12] and over them as well the bishop's authority is extended. The chief characteristic of the heretics is that they absent themselves from the common assemblies, and again, a doctrinal view is above all felt to be divisive if it divides in worship.[13] Thus worship stands altogether in the center of the religious life of the new religious community; the lines run out from it in all directions, and everything is conditioned and determined from here. The cultus is the heart of the total sociological body, from which the circulation of blood throughout this body is regulated, and the one Kyrios Jesus Christos, much more than thought, dogma, and idea, an ever anew tangible, living reality, with all his powers holds sway over the worship.

II. *The Christianity of Ignatius.* We have a classic witness for this development of the Christian religion as a predominant cultic piety or, to put it more exactly, as a cultus which is determined by the Kyrios and Theos Jesus Christ. This is none other than Bishop Ignatius of Antioch. And we

---

[10] Didache 14; cf. above all the decisive statements of Irenaeus about the New Testament oblations in IV, 17.5-6; 18.2-4.

[11] In Justin I, 67 this procedure clearly appears as the final act of the eucharistic celebration. There also the instructions about the administration of gifts by the bishop. Cf. also Acta Pauli et Thecl., chap. 25; Act. Thom., chap. 29 and 50; and Ignatius. See p. —. Cf. H. Achelis, *Das Christentum in den ersten drei Jahrhunderten*, II, 79.

[12] Cf. above all the instructive and best portrayal of the Agapae in the so-called Egyptian Church Order (chaps. 17[47]-22[52], Funk, *Didasc. et const. apost.* II, 112). Also Tertullian, Apol. 39. The (widows') Agape in Acta Petri, chap. 20 ff., is also instructive. E. Schwartz ingeniously translates the fragment of the Gospel of the Hebrews which reads *"numquam laeti sitis, nisi cum fratrem vestrum videritis in caritate"* to read: "You should not celebrate a feast except when you see your brethren in the Agape." ZNW VII (1906), 1.

[13] Cf. Smyrn. 6.2 and 7.1 and further documentation below in the statements about Ignatius. The earliest divisions among the Christians are prompted by the question of the εἰδωλόθυτα φαγεῖν; cf. Irenaeus IV, 18.5, ἡμῶν δὲ σύμφωνος ἡ γνώμη (doctrine!) τῇ εὐχαριστίᾳ καὶ ἡ εὐχαριστία βεβαιοῖ τὴν γνώμην.

may regard him as a fully qualified witness. For even if his epistles in many respects—thus in the question of the monarchical episcopate—show a surprisingly rapid development of Christianity, still we actually have no weighty reasons for doubting the authenticity of the seven writings which are preserved under his name. And one will probably have to hold to the customary dating of the epistles[14] within the reign of Trajan (Eus. CH III, 34 ff.). For Ignatius, in fact, Christianity at its center is set forth as an organic cultic fellowship in which the Christos is the determinative factor. "Hence it is fitting for you to agree with the judgment of the bishop. . . . For in your unanimity and harmonious love *Jesus Christ is sung* (ᾄδεται).[15] And become all of you a choir, that you, harmonizing in unanimity in the special key of God in unity, with one voice praise the Father through Jesus Christ, so that he may hear you and recognize you in your well-doing as members of his Son. It is indeed profitable to you to be in blameless unity, so that thereby you may always have a part with God." (Eph. 4.21.) Again and again Ignatius expresses this conviction, that the incorporation of the believers into the ecclesiastical organism which is summed up in the bishop represents their fellowship with God and Christ. The believers are to be in inseparable union with the God Jesus Christ and the bishop and the decrees of the apostles (Trall. 7). "For those belong to God and Jesus Christ who are with the bishop, and as many repent and come to the unity of the church as belong to God, so that they may live according to Jesus Christ" (Philad. 3). "Where the bishop appears, there the congregation is to be, just as where Jesus Christ appears, there is the catholic church" (Smyrn. 8.2). "Cleave to the bishop, and then God will cleave to you" (ad Polyc. 6.1).[16]

The unity of outlook however means, above all, unity in worship and cultic association. "There is to be one prayer, one supplication, one mind (νοῦς), one hope in love and blameless joy, which is Jesus Christ (ὅ ἐστιν Ἰησοῦς Χριστός). . . . You all should hasten (as) to one temple of God, to one altar, to the one Jesus Christ, who has proceeded from the Father,

[14] Harnack, *Chronologie*, I, 406, after consideration of all the arguments: "The epistles of Ignatius and the epistle of Polycarp are genuine, and they were composed in the last years of Trajan (110–117) or perhaps a few years later (117–125)."

[15] Similarly the admonition δοξάζειν Ἰησοῦν Χριστόν runs parallel to the exhortation to single-minded submission to the bishop: Eph. 2.2; cf. Rom. 2.2: ἵνα ἐν ἀγάπῃ χορὸς γενόμενοι ᾄσητε τῷ πατρὶ ἐν Ἰησοῦ Χριστῷ; 4.2, λιτανεύσατε τὸν Χριστόν.

[16] Cf. also Eph. 5.1: ὑμᾶς μακαρίζω τοὺς ἐγκεκραμένους αὐτῷ ὡς ἡ ἐκκλησία Ἰησοῦ Χριστοῦ καὶ ὡς Ἰησοῦς Χριστὸς τῷ πατρί, ἵνα πάντα ἐν ἑνότητι σύμφωνα ᾖ. Philad. 2.1, ὅπου δὲ ὁ ποιμήν ἐστιν, ἐκεῖ ὡς πρόβατα ἀκολουθεῖτε.

and is in one and returns to one" (Magn. 7). The Christian community is represented in his eyes as a sacred worship procession: "You are all traveling companions, bearers of God, bearers of the temple, bearers of Christ, bearers of holiness, in every way adorned with the decrees of Jesus Christ" (Eph. 9.2). This unity and this association are best represented in the πυκνότερον συνέρχεσθαι εἰς εὐχαριστίαν θεοῦ καὶ εἰς δόξαν (Eph. 13). This unity in worship of the Christians has a marvelous power. "The powers of Satan are destroyed and his mischief is nullified by the concord of your faith" (Eph. 13).[17] False Christians are those who do something without the bishop, i.e., perform the actions pertaining to worship. "Such people have no good conscience, because they do not hold their assemblies exactly according to the commandment" (Magn. 4).

And this unity and unanimity in worship comes into question above all in the common observance of the special sacramental actions. This is already defined in the oft-repeated admonition[18] that one is to "do" nothing without the bishop (and the presbyters). The prophetic saying which Ignatius wishes to have suddenly thrust into the company of the Philadelphians begins: χωρὶς τοῦ ἐπισκόπου μηδὲν ποιεῖτε (Philad. 7.2). It is the ideal of good Christians to be ἐντὸς τοῦ θυσιαστηρίου. "One who is within the altar is pure; i.e., anyone who does anything without bishop and presbyter and deacon is stained in his conscience" (Trall. 7.2). In the Ephesian epistle it is said still more clearly: "If one is not within the altar, he lacks the *bread of God*" (Eph. 5.2). "You are to obey the bishop . . . and break *one bread*, which is the medicine of immortality" (Eph. 20.2). Or: (one eucharist) "one flesh of our Lord Jesus Christ, one cup for unity with his blood, *one altar*" (Philad. 4.1). *Only* that eucharist is to be regarded as valid (βεβαία) which takes place under the bishop (Smyrn. 8.1). Without the bishop one is not to baptize nor to observe the Agape (Smyrn. 8.2).[19] The polemic against the false teachers which recurs in almost all the letters also belongs wholly within this context. Their separation is pernicious above all because they disturb the harmony of the cultus. This

[17] Cf. Eph. 5.2: εἰ γὰρ ἑνὸς καὶ δευτέρου προσευχὴ τοιαύτην ἰσχὺν ἔχει, πόσῳ μᾶλλον ἥ τε τοῦ ἐπισκόπου καὶ πάσης τῆς ἐκκλησίας.

[18] Magn. 4; 7.1; Trall. 2.2; 7.1; Smyrn. 8.1; 9.1, ὁ λάθρα ἐπισκόπου τι ποιῶν τῷ διαβόλῳ λατρεύει.

[19] Note that it is said of the deacons: they are not ministers of "food and drink, but ministers of the church" (Trall. 2.3). That does not mean that the deacons did not in the first place have to administer food and drink, but that in this outward ministry they administer the spiritual goods of the church.

is the worst thing about the false doctrine of the Docetists: "They absent themselves *from the eucharist and from prayers* because they do not confess that the eucharist is the flesh of our savior Jesus Christ" (Smyrn. 7.1). "They care nothing about the 'Agape,'[20] nothing about widows and orphans, nothing about the oppressed, the prisoners or the liberated ones, nothing about the hungry and thirsty" (6.2).

In general, Christ is near to his community in the sacrament.[21] The powers overflow from the *Unio mystica* in the eucharist into the totality of the community life. The bread which the Christians break is the medicine of immortality; it signifies: ζῆν ἐν Ἰησοῦ Χριστῷ διὰ παντός (Eph. 20).

When Ignatius (Trall. 8) admonishes: "Renew yourselves (ἀνακτίσασθε ἑαυτούς)[22] in faith, the flesh of the Lord, and in love, the blood of the Lord," one may not on the basis of this passage arrive at a spiritualizing view of the sacrament. Here the lively sense is expressed that all spiritual gifts of grace for the believers flow from the common cultus of the sacrament. The "Agape" of the Christians creates brotherly love. The blood of Christ, with which the Christians are united in the sacrament, is a presently effective power. Thus it is to be explained when at the beginning of the Ephesian letter it is said of the Christians: ἀναζωπυρήσαντες ἐν αἵματι θεοῦ τὸ συγγενικὸν ἔργον τελείως ἀπηρτίσατε.[23]

Everywhere the same picture comes to our view. Christianity is Christ cultus, a Christian community is a cultic society which is focused upon the person of Christ. The bishops and deacons are the cultic officials, without whom this new religious structure is no longer conceivable. In the common cultus are focused all the powers of the new religion, and from here they overflow into everyday life. Here the Christians experience their union with

---

[20] Note here also the connection of worship with social concern (see above, p. 353).

[21] Over against that, the pure doctrine guaranteed by the episcopate is only rarely stressed, as in Magn. 6.2, ἑνώθητε τῷ ἐπισκόπῳ . . . εἰς τύπον καὶ διδαχὴν ἀφθαρσίας. The polemic against the false teachers of course plays its part in all the letters. But the main point remains, as brought out above, that of the practical union in the cultus. The words διδαχή, διδασκαλία, διδάσκειν are found in only a few places in the Ignatian letters (see the index in Zahn's edition).

[22] In Rom. 7.3 Ignatius expresses the wish to participate in the heavenly sacrament. (τὸ αἷμα αὐτοῦ), ὅ ἐστιν ἀγάπη ἄφθαρτος=heavenly Agape.

[23] Cf. ἡδρασμένους ἐν ἀγάπῃ ἐν τῷ αἵματι Χριστοῦ, Smyrn. 1.1. ἣν ἀσπάζομαι ἐν αἵματι Ἰησοῦ Χριστοῦ, Philad. Proem. ἐὰν μὴ πιστεύσωσιν εἰς τὸ αἷμα Χριστοῦ, Smyrn. 6.1. (ἀσπάζομαι) ἐν ὀνόματι Ἰησοῦ Χριστοῦ καὶ τῇ σαρκὶ αὐτοῦ καὶ τῷ αἵματι, πάθει δὲ καὶ ἀναστάσει, Smyrn. 12.2. In Ign. Polyc. 6.2, βάπτισμα, πίστις, ἀγάπη, ὑπομονή are named as defensive weapons of the Christian life. Here a comparison with the prototype of this passage in Eph. 6:12 ff. is instructive.

the flesh and blood of Christ, and the fruits of this union are faith and love. "All now, having received God's attitude (ὁμοήθειαν θεοῦ λαβόντες), should respect one another (ἐντρέπεσθε), and no one is to regard his neighbor according to the flesh, but in Jesus Christ you should love one another" (Magn. 6.2). At the heart of the entire new life and action, however, stands the Kyrios Christos. The Christians are κεκτημένοι ἀδιάκριτον πνεῦμα, ὅς ἐστιν Ἰησοῦς Χριστός (Magn. 15).[24] And in this connection a quite special significance accrues to the fact that in ever repeated expressions Ignatius already speaks of the God [25] Jesus Christ. *Christ is the new God of the new cultic society.*

The sharp and evident distance from Pauline-Johannine piety may be brought out once more. Paul's great spiritual conceptions have here almost totally disappeared or are greatly reduced. Christ is no longer first of all the bearer of a new personal, moral-religious life, but the foundation of the cultus and of the whole sacramental-worship structure, and only in the second place of the new life, insofar as the latter takes its point of departure from the former. The proud self-consciousness, the intense individualism of the pneumatic, the characteristic of Pauline piety, to be sure has not completely disappeared. It is preserved in part in the ecstatic martyr's delight of the bishop. But on the whole here, in place of pneumatic subjectivism there appears the objective entity of the community organized in cultus around the bishop. And corresponding to this is the fact that while in Paul the sacramental element is indeed already present, but is held down by the ethically personal element, the piety of Ignatius appears simply sacramentally, mysteriously determined. In Ignatius the corollary of the new God Christ is the organism of the community organized in cultus around the bishop.

III. *The Christianity of Certain Epistles.* The question may be posed, however, whether Ignatius is actually to be regarded as a type for the history of the faith in Christ in the post-apostolic era, or whether we have to do here only with an isolated phenomenon. Now of course it is to be conceded that in many things the bishop of Antioch represents a development of Christianity that is, in comparison with the general state of things, ad-

---

[24] Cf. Eph. 3.2, Ἰησοῦς Χριστὸς τὸ ἀδιάκριτον ἡμῶν ζῆν. 5.1, τοὺς ἐνκεκραμένους αὐτῷ (sc., τῷ ἐπισκόπῳ) ὡς ἡ ἐκκλησία Ἰησοῦ Χριστοῦ καὶ ὡς Χριστὸς τῷ Πατρί. 11.1, ἐν Ἰησοῦ Χριστῷ εὑρεθῆναι εἰς τὸ ἀληθινὸν ζῆν. 15.3, πάντα οὖν ποιῶμεν ὡς αὐτοῦ ἐν ἡμῖν κατοικοῦντος, ἵνα ὦμεν αὐτοῦ ναοί.

[25] See the evidence in the larger context above, pp. 321-22.

vanced. The monarchical episcopate and its central position, the strong emphasis upon the deity of Christ, the basic sacramental feature of piety are manifestations which show that Ignatius was running ahead of the development of his time. We shall not go astray in the judgment that in the Ignatian epistles the more rapid development of Christianity in the East (Syria and Asia Minor) is reflected.

But alongside Ignatius appear other manifestations which show how strongly the worship contexts and the attitudes of cultic piety determine and dominate the whole of the Christian religion and the position of the Kyrios Christos in this totality.

In the first place here stands the so-called Epistle to the Hebrews, perhaps an old anonymous homily which has only been artificially reshaped into an epistle. Indeed, one can actually summarize the statements of this homily in a motto: Ἰησοῦς ὁ ἀρχιερεὺς τῆς ὁμολογίας ἡμῶν. Already at the end of chap. 2, after a long proem of speculative character, which is essentially intended to prove the superiority of the υἱός (ἀρχιερεύς) to the angelic world, there stands the motto of *the merciful and faithful high priest;* chap. 3 then takes up the theme of the high priest "of our confession." But the comparison with the leader of the old confession prompts the speaker to take a longer warning backward look at the ancient people and their unbelief (3:7–4:13). Immediately after the excursus is ended, the theme is sounded again: "Now since we have a great *high priest* who has passed through the heavens, let us hold fast to the confession" (4:14). Now begins (5:1 ff.) the Christ–Melchizedek parallel. Once again the theme is interrupted—περὶ οὗ πολὺς ἡμῖν ὁ λόγος καὶ δυσερμήνευτος (5:11)—and the author (speaker) ponders the question whether the readers are ready for the mysteries ,which he intends to communicate to them. They really are not. Yet it is time at last to leave the rudiments[26] and to turn to perfection (τελειότης),[27] i.e. to the communication of the higher mysteries. And this is (6:20) the doctrine of Jesus: κατὰ τὴν τάξιν Μελχισεδὲκ ἀρχιερεὺς γενόμενος εἰς τὸν αἰῶνα. Now begins the heart of the epistle, the doctrinal discussion of this high priest. His mysterious,

[26] One should note that even ὁ τῆς ἀρχῆς τοῦ Χριστοῦ λόγος is essentially referring to questions of the cultus: "Repentance from dead works and faith in God (i.e., in this context, turning away from pagan worship and turning to the Christian community), teaching concerning baptisms (!) and the laying-on of hands (!)"; then "resurrection of the dead and eternal judgment"; the new cultic community guarantees certainty as to one's fate in the world beyond.

[27] On τέλειος and τελειότης, see above, p. 260, n. 58.

supra-terrestrial ancestry (ἀπάτωρ, ἀμήτωρ), his superiority to the ancestral lord of the old covenant and to the Old Testament priesthood, his confirmation by a divine oath, his eternal lordship, his sinlessness, his higher ministry in the heavenly holy place, which corresponds to the fact that he is the mediator of a higher covenant, his entrance into the heavenly holy place through the offering of a sacrifice accomplished once for all, not of the blood of animals but of his own blood—all this is now stated in a broader and more powerful presentation (7:1–10:18). But most of all there is one thing in this that is noteworthy. The presentation concerns the *present* high priest, who now holds sway from heaven as the mediator of the new covenant. The great once-performed sacrifice, in which this high priest offered himself, appears under the perspective of a precondition of his present position of dignity and honor. In this connection the death has, as in Paul, simply a connection with the past: θανάτου γινομένου εἰς ἀπολύτρωσιν τῶν ἐπὶ τῇ πρώτῃ διαθήκῃ παραβάσεων (9:15). Now the gateway of the second, higher covenant with its promises of an eternal inheritance is opened, and over this second covenant the high priest holds sway eternally after the manner of Melchizedek and continually guarantees for his own people entry into the heavenly sanctuary.

Only now do we understand the full import of the thought with which the speaker continues (10:19 ff.): "Since we now have such boldness to enter into the (heavenly) sanctuary . . . and (such) a high priest, . . . let us hold fast the confession of our hope without wavering . . ." and "let us not forsake *the assembling* of ourselves, as some are wont to do." With fearful gravity he points out, as earlier in 6:4 ff., that such a falling-away[28] from the fellowship means an unforgivable sin. One treads under foot the Son of God whom one has confessed and whom one now denies; one sins against the Spirit of grace who abundantly pours out his gifts, particularly in the worship experience of the Christians (10:29). And as in 6:4 ff. he has stressed the unpardonable sin with respect to baptism (τοὺς ἅπαξ φωτισθέντας), of which one becomes guilty through apostasy, here he says in an unmistakable allusion to the Supper, that in such an apostasy one profanes the blood of the covenant. The Christians are to recall the bravery of earlier days and not cravenly forsake their cause. Remembering the heroes of faith of earlier days, they are to rally around their hero:

---

[28] The ἐκουσίως ἁμαρτάνειν μετὰ τὸ λαβεῖν τὴν ἐπίγνωσιν τῆς ἀληθείας in 10:26 consists of the deliberate apostasy from the religious community, just as does the παραπεσεῖν in 6:6.

ἀφορῶντες εἰς τὸν τῆς πίστεως ἀρχηγὸν καὶ τελειωτὴν Ἰησοῦν, who
has gone before them in courageous endurance of suffering (12:2). They
are to be aware that they belong to the *ecclesia triumphans,* to the heavenly
Jerusalem with its myriads of angels, with its solemn assembly and congregation of the firstborn whose names are written in heaven, the spirits of
the perfected righteous, and to the mediator of the new covenant, Jesus
(12:22 ff.). They are to remember—again and again the cultic connections
are stressed—that they have a θυσιαστήριον,[29] from which "those who
serve in the tabernacle" have not the right to eat (13:10). As the sin
offering in ancient Israel was offered outside the camp, so has Jesus died
outside the gates (13:11 ff.): τοίνυν ἐξερχώμεθα πρὸς αὐτὸν ἔξω τῆς
παρεμβολῆς (13:13). They are to offer their sacrifice of praise through
Jesus Christ, by confessing his name (13:15-16). Jesus Christ is the same
yesterday, today, and forever.

One must imagine this entire context in order to comprehend how
strongly dominant is the cultic viewpoint here. Christianity also emerges
quite clearly as the new cultic society with its assemblies for worship, its
θυσιαστήριον and its sacred actions (sacraments). But over this cultus the
ἀρχιερεὺς τῆς ὁμολογίας, Jesus, holds sway. It is not yet, as in Ignatius,
God whom this cultus concerns, it is the μεσίτης, the ἀρχηγὸς τῆς
πίστεως[30] and the effective example of the pious; the humanity of this
high priest, who in all points (only with the exception of sin) has become
like us so that he could sympathize with us, who in his days on earth had
given adequate proof of this humanity, is a favorite thought of the
author.[31] But this Jesus is still the supra-terrestrial Son of God, far
superior in glory to all the angels and super-worldly beings, the ἀρχιερεύς
who from his sanctuary which he has entered victorious, from heaven, rules
and governs. Here the cult's mediator himself becomes the object of be-

[29] Note also the stressing of the distance separating the Old Testament sacrifice from
the New Testament one. The former were only presented ἐπὶ βρώμασιν καὶ πόμασιν
καὶ διαφόροις βαπτισμοῖς, the latter purifies the conscience from dead works to the
service of the living God, 9:10, 14; cf. the οὐ βρώμασιν (βεβαιοῦσθαι) in 13:9. The
διδαχὴ βαπτισμῶν (6:2) also has reference to the difference between the Jewish washings
and the Christian baptism.
[30] 8:6; 9:15; 12:24; 12:2 (ἀρχηγός); on the religio-historical connections of this latter
expression, see above, p. 314. Characteristic also is the sentence in 2:11, ὅ τε γὰρ
ἁγιάζων καὶ οἱ ἁγιαζόμενοι ἐξ ἑνὸς πάντες, δι' ἣν αἰτίαν οὐκ ἐπαισχύνεται ἀδελφοὺς
αὐτοὺς καλεῖν. In the mysteries the initiating priest (mystagogue) and the one initiated
again belong together as brothers. In the mystery religions also people experience liberation
from the fear of death as did the Christians in Heb. 2:15.
[31] 2:10 ff.; 2:18; 4:15-16; 5:7-8.

lieving veneration; the two modes of regarding him can no longer be separated. The passage in the Psalms: διὰ τοῦτο ἔχρισέ σε ὁ θεός, ὁ θεός σου ἐλαίῳ ἀγαλλιάσεως will have been understood already by the author in the sense in which people later understood it: "Therefore, O God, your God has anointed you." Likewise he will have connected with Jesus[32] the beginning: ὁ θρόνος σου ὁ θεός (1:8-9).

I Clement shows a quite different picture. With its piety it stands in connections which are to be discussed later. There is very little said in it of cultus and sacrament; here Christianity appears essentially as a refined belief in God and a purified new morality. But here and there is shown a different basic attitude, and indeed always at those points where definite and tangible cultic connections are present. It is the merit of Drews to have drawn attention to the fact that in chap. 34 [33] there are clear echoes of the Lord's Supper liturgy. The author is probably alluding to the "Holy, Holy, Holy" in the liturgy of the Supper when, after the quotations from Dan. 7:10 and Isa. 6:3, he continues: καὶ ἡμεῖς οὖν ἐν ὁμονοίᾳ ἐπὶ τὸ αὐτὸ συναχθέντες τῇ συνειδήσει ὡς ἐξ ἑνὸς στόματος βοήσωμεν πρὸς αὐτὸν εἰς τὸ μετόχους γενέσθαι τῶν μεγάλων καὶ ἐνδόξων ἐπαγγελιῶν αὐτῶν (34.7).[34]

It is no accident when now, almost immediately in this connection (chap. 36), Christ is celebrated in a more exuberant manner than we are otherwise accustomed to in this author. He is called the ἀρχιερεὺς τῶν προσφορῶν ἡμῶν, the προστάτης καὶ βοηθὸς τῆς ἀσθενείας. Thus Christ here is not the high priest who has brought his sacrifice in the past, but the one who holds sway over the present cultus of the community, its patron. Then it is said further:

διὰ τούτου ἀτενίζομεν εἰς τὰ ὕψη τῶν οὐρανῶν,
διὰ τούτου ἐνοπτριζόμεθα τὴν ἄμωμον καὶ ὑπερτάτην ὄψιν αὐτοῦ,
διὰ τούτου ἠνεώχθησαν ἡμῶν οἱ ὀφθαλμοὶ τῆς καρδίας,
διὰ τούτου ἡ ἀσύνετος καὶ ἐσκοτωμένη διάνοια ἡμῶν ἀναθάλλει εἰς
    τὸ θαυμαστὸν αὐτοῦ φῶς,
διὰ τούτου ἠθέλησεν ὁ δεσπότης τῆς ἀθανάτου γνώσεως ἡμᾶς γεύσασθαι.

We probably do not err when we here suspect sounds of, or at least echoes from, the liturgy of the Supper. Everything becomes more vivid

---

[32] Immediately preceding this goes πρὸς δὲ τὸν υἱόν (sc. λέγει).

[33] Drews, *Studien zur Geschichte des Gottesdienstes*, No. 2–3, 1906, p. 13.

[34] Perhaps the saying in I Cor. 2:9 which is frequently quoted in the later liturgy of the Supper is also already a reminiscence of the liturgy.

when we relate the experiences which are gloried in here to the inspiration and enthusiasm of Christian worship. The expression, "Through him the Master willed that we should taste imperishable knowledge," reminds us directly of the eucharistic prayers of the Didache.[35] It has long since been shown how the author uses the cultic language of the Old Testament in his discussion of partisan disputes (40 ff.). God, *Christ,* the apostles, the bishops and the deacons form for him a great, holy, and indestructible unity: woe to him who disturbs it through insubordination. The apostles are οἱ ἐν Χριστῷ πιστευθέντες (43.1). The ones installed in office by them are λειτουργήσαντες ἀμέμπτως τῷ ποιμνίῳ τοῦ Χριστοῦ (44.3). Again, at the conclusion of the long prayer in which Clement reproduces a good part of the Roman community prayer, we read: σοὶ ἐξομολογούμεθα διὰ τοῦ ἀρχιερέως καὶ προστάτου τῶν ψυχῶν ἡμῶν Ἰησοῦ Χριστοῦ (61.3; cf. 62.4).[36]

If we go back somewhat further from Ignatius, Hebrews, and I Clement, and approach very near to the Pauline era, a comparison of Ephesians with Colossians shows how quickly and strongly even here the cultic connections of the Christian religion and therewith the estimation of Jesus as the cultic head of his community moves into the center of consideration.

In Colossians as well as in Ephesians, in the long hymnic section the idea is stressed from the very beginning that Christ is the head of his church. But while in Colossians this thought is overshadowed by the further one, that the whole divine pleroma dwelt in Christ, in order to reconcile the world, the hymn in Ephesians climaxes in the sentence: καὶ αὐτὸν ἔδωκεν κεφαλὴν ὑπὲρ πάντα τῇ ἐκκλησίᾳ (1:22-23). And the ἐκκλησία, not the celestial world of aeons, is viewed as the pleroma of the Christos. While the continuation of the Colossian epistle is dominated by the simple idea of redemption and by the opposition to the gnosticizing assumption of mediatorial powers, the author of the Ephesian epistle, although he frequently works with the tools of the Colossian epistle, writes above the entire following section (2:1–3:21) the theme: "The Church and Its Head." He cele-

---

[35] It is worthy of note that there follows immediately, in 36.2 ff., an explicit reminiscence from the Epistle to the Hebrews.

[36] Cf. further Ignatius, Philad. 9.1: Christ (in contrast to the priests of the old covenant) ὁ ἀρχιερεὺς ὁ πεπιστευμένος τὰ ἅγια τῶν ἁγίων (a door for Abraham, Isaac, and Jacob, and the prophets). Cf. the prayer of Polycarp (likewise with strong echoes of the liturgy) in Martyr. Polyc. 14.3, αἰώνιος καὶ ἐπουράνιος ἀρχιερεύς. I Pet. 5:4: ἀρχιποιμήν. Finally, Polyc. Phil. 12.2, ὁ αἰώνιος ἀρχιερεὺς θεός (Latin, dei filius) Ἰησοῦς Χριστός

brates its wonderful organism which unites in itself the two previously separated halves of humanity. Christ's death on the cross, which according to the Colossian letter blots out the law's sentence of guilt that stands between God and man, here takes on the ultimate aim of tearing down the dividing wall between Jew and Gentile (2:14). Thus is erected before the mind of the author the proud new structure, on the foundation of the apostles and prophets, and built upon Jesus Christ the cornerstone (2:20). The mystery of God hidden before all ages, the manifold wisdom of God—here in the church they have become manifest (3:10). The angels look on in wonder; but in Christ all the threads of this mysterious divine economy run together! And again at the close of this section, after he had for the moment sounded a more subjective-sounding note—κατοικῆσαι τὸν Χριστὸν ἐν ταῖς καρδίαις ὑμῶν— the author turns his gaze to the great new total structure; his readers are to behold τί τὸ πλάτος καὶ μῆκος καὶ ὕψος καὶ βάθος (3:19). A characteristic doxology[37] concludes the whole: αὐτῷ ἡ δόξα ἐν τῇ ἐκκλησίᾳ καὶ ἐν Χριστῷ Ἰησοῦ εἰς πάσας τὰς γενεὰς τοῦ αἰῶνος τῶν αἰώνων.

Once again the author begins with a consideration of this marvelous work of Christ: ἓν σῶμα καὶ ἓν πνεῦμα . . . εἷς κύριος, μία πίστις, ἐν βάπτισμα[38] (4:5). He connects the gifts which the one who has ascended to heaven has bestowed on men (following Ps. 68:19) with the guides and leaders of the new organism, the apostles and prophets, evangelists, shepherds and teachers (4:8-11). Thus the image, borrowed from the Colossian letter (2:19), of the new body with its marvelous structure, whose head is Christ, is wrought out with an entirely different sculpture (4:13-16). The paraenetic statements that follow are of a general ethical attitude and are closely related to those of Colossians. Ecclesiastical viewpoints are struck only here and there.[39] But once again the whole, here in direct dependence on Colossians, is crowned with an ideal portrayal of the structure of Christian worship (5:18-20).[40] The "house rules" (5:22–6:9) are constructed in dependence upon the Colossian epistle, but the statements about married people once more give the author opportunity in a distinctive manner to return to his favorite theme, the great mystery: Christ and church! [41]

[37] On its further influence, see above, p. 303, n. 219.

[38] In Col. 2:15 only ἐκλήθητε ἐν ἑνὶ σώματι.

[39] Cf. 4:29 (ἀγαθὸς λόγος πρὸς οἰκοδομήν). 5:12 (the characteristic ἐλέγχειν).

[40] On the ᾄδοντες καὶ ψάλλοντες τῷ κυρίῳ (instead of θεῷ), see above, pp. 303-4.

[41] On the old myth which is applied here to Christ and the church ("the mystery is great; I refer to Christ and the church," Eph. 5:32), see above, p. 268. Cf. further Ignat.

When at the close he finally portrays the armor of the Christians, it is essentially the objective powers that hold sway over the whole of the church: "the" truth, righteousness, the gospel, the faith (i.e., in this context the confessionally formulated faith), the salvation (τὸ σωτήριον); and the Spirit is objectified into the ῥῆμα θεοῦ (6:17), the wonder-working, mysterious word [42] (cf. 5:26 τὸ λουτρὸν ἐν ῥήματι).[43]

Finally, we turn to the writings of this period which are specifically concerned with constitution and questions of ecclesiastical order. The testimony of the Pastoral Epistles is especially important for the changed situation, insofar as the compiler of these epistles has the apostle Paul speak and outline an ideal picture of Christian community life. Yet how different is that which this "Paul" has to say on the whole to the Christian community, compared with the preaching of the genuine Paul. Apart from II Timothy, the notes of personal Christianity are scanty and sporadic and almost everywhere bear the stamp of painstaking imitation and of jargon. Polemics against the heretics who disrupt the unity of the church and its life of worship,[44] instructions about the office of the bishops and deacons,[45] about the remuneration of the καλῶς προεστῶτες πρεσβύτεροι,[46] the institution of the widows,[47] the activity of the bishop in the leadership of worship[48] (ἀνάγνωσις, παράκλησις, διδασκαλία), prayer in public worship,[49] the treatment of sinners in the church[50] and of heretics,[51] laying-on of hands and ordination[52]—these are the themes in which the statements of the epistles are fairly well exhausted. It is also characteristic that, apart from the paraenetic concluding expressions of the epistles, in which Christ appears

Eph. 17 (5.1); II Clem. 14; the enigmatic reference in Did. 11.11 (ποιῶν εἰς μυστήριον κοσμικὸν τῆς ἐκκλησίας); the marriage of the lamb with the bride, Rev. 19:7; 21:2, 9; 22:17.

[42] Cf. II Tim. 3:16.

[43] A comparison between Colossians and Ephesians under the perspective of the theme of the ἐκκλησία proves beyond any doubt that the two epistles come from different authors. The Ephesian epistle lies in a completely different sphere of thought from that of the Colossian epistle.

[44] I Tim. 1:3-11, 19, 20; 4:1-5; 6:3-10; II Tim. 1:15-18; 2:17-19 (25); 3:1-9, 13; 4:3-4; Titus 1:10-16.

[45] I Tim. 3:1-13; Titus 1:5-9; 2:1 ff.

[46] I Tim. 5:3-18.

[47] I Tim. 5:3-16.

[48] I Tim. 4:6-7, 11-16; 5:1-2; II Tim. 3:14-16 (ἐλεγμός, ἐπανόρθωσις, παιδεία); 4:1-2 (κήρυξον τὸν λόγον, ἐπίστηθι, ἔλεγξον, ἐπιτίμησον, παρακάλεσον).

[49] I Tim. 2:1-15; 4:4-5; Titus 3:15.

[50] I Tim. 5:20-21, 24-25.

[51] I Tim. 1:4; 4:7; 6:20; II Tim. 2:14, 16, 22 ff.; 3:5; Titus 1:13; 3:9-10.

[52] I Tim. 5:22 (cf. I Tim. 1:18; 4:14; 6:12; II Tim. 1:6-7; one should note in the last-named passage the connection of the πνεῦμα with the spirit of office!).

as judge and savior and his miraculous and glorious epiphany is extolled,[53] and except for the repeated praise of the "beneficent" grace of God that has already appeared in him,[54] the mention of the person of Christ occurs in a series of expressions which have an already confessionally formulated character.[55] Here the statements of I Timothy are most striking. The center of the church, the στῦλος καὶ ἑδραίωμα τῆς ἀληθείας, is the great mystery of piety: Χριστὸς ὃς ἐφανερώθη ἐν σαρκί, ἐδικαιώθη ἐν πνεύματι.

In all this it is characteristic of the Pastoral Epistles that the sacramental element plays such a limited role in them. The sacrament that is *frequently* mentioned in them is that of ordination. With the constantly repeated portrayals of the official activity of the bishop (or of the president), baptism and eucharist are never mentioned. This is in harmony with the fact that all the stress falls, as is known, upon the teaching activity of the bishop: The bishop is to be διδακτικός, and ὑγιαίνουσα διδασκαλία is "the" ideal of the author. The false doctrine of the heretics is attacked, not schism. In this sober and rational attitude the Pastoral Epistles appear almost a unique phenomenon. Related to this also is the fact that the Christ mysticism, the Pauline ἐν Χριστῷ, is almost completely lacking in the Epistles.[56] In all this they are separated also from the Ignatian epistles by a great distance.

Quite different is the character of the Didache in this respect. Here the sacramental cultus stands in the center. Baptism, eucharist (Agape), eucharistic worship occupy the broadest setting in the discussions. Associated with these are the prohibition to participate in sacrifices to idols (6), the control of fasting, and the regulation of prescribed prayer (three times daily). In connection with the prescriptions concerning Sunday worship, there follows the regulation about the election of bishops and deacons (14–15). The prescriptions about wandering teachers, apostles, and prophets stand in the midst of these as a remnant left over from an earlier age, and the precautionary rules which are found to be valuable in those instances are distinctive. In the sacrament of the eucharist the community experiences the presence of

---

[53] I Tim. 6:14; II Tim. 4:1, 18; Titus 2:13.

[54] II Tim. 1:10-11; Titus 2:11; 3:4-5; (I Tim. 1:12-16).

[55] I Tim. 3:14-16; 6:13 (Christ the example in the making of the ὁμολογία!); II Tim. 2:8.

[56] I Tim. 1:14 (πίστεως καὶ ἀγάπης τῆς ἐν Χριστῷ Ἰησοῦ) is an imitation of the Pauline style. The same is true of II Tim. 1:9, 2:1 (χάρις ἐν), 1:13 (πίστις καὶ ἀγάπη ἐν), 2:10 (σωτηρία ἐν); cf. I Tim. 3:15; II Tim. 3:15 (πίστις ἐν); II Tim. 1:1; 3:12 (ζωὴ ἐν).

its Lord (10.6). The ethical instructions in 1.1–6.2 lead up to this entire structure of the cultus. But in characteristic fashion it is a *Jewish* ethical catechism which here has been accepted, expanded with some sayings of the Lord.[57]

Some further observations may be added here in conclusion. We have already referred more explicitly (pp. 316-17) to the fact that the major theme of the Apocalypse is the contrast between the worship of the Lamb and the cultus and self-deification of the Roman empire. Recently the thesis has been proposed that I Peter, in its first and larger half (1:3–4:11), contains a baptismal homily; in my judgment it deserves serious consideration.[58] The Shepherd of Hermas works for the most part with appropriated material, which it probably owes throughout to the synagogue. But it is well known and generally conceded that Hermas' peculiar and personal interest attaches to the proclamation of the possibility of a second repentance after baptism. In any case, we nowhere find such a vivid picture of what baptism meant for the first Christian community as here (*vide supra*, pp. 296-97). Finally, it is generally acknowledged that the so-called II Clement is the earliest Christian sermon which we can with certainty claim as such (19.1). At its beginning (chap. 2), there stands an exultant statement about how *the church* has surpassed the synagogue: "But now we believers have become more numerous than those who think that they have God." At the climax, however, there appears a mysterious statement about the conjugal relationship between Christ and the church (chap. 14). The Christian life finally stands under the ideal that one should preserve baptism, the seal, pure and undefiled (6.9; 8.5).[59]

What was to be proved is, in my judgment, proved. When in the Ignatian epistles Christianity appears as a new mystery cult whose center is the new God Jesus Christ, we have here no singular phenomenon. It is only that

---

[57] See the following section and below, p. 371.

[58] R. Perdelwitz, *Die Mysterienreligionen und das Problem des I. Petrusbriefes*, pp. 5-28. It is unfortunate for the thesis that the reference to rebirth through baptism does not clearly emerge in 1:3 (cf. the δι' ἀναστάσεως 'Ιησοῦ Χριστοῦ; or should this expression be closely joined with ζῶσαν?). In any case it is hardly to be denied that the statements in 1:3–4:11, regarded as addressed to Christians who have just been baptized, acquire a good internal interconnection.

[59] One should note further how the interest of the apocryphal acts of the apostles is quite significantly directed to the communication and detailed portrayal of sacramental acts of worship and the prayers connected therewith. Acta Petri 5 (baptism); 19 ff. (*agape* and *agape* preaching); Acta Joh. 94-96 (mystical worship); 109-10 (eucharist); Acta Thom. 6, 26-27, 49-50, 120-21, 131-33, 152-57. Also the many prayers about the mystery of the cross belong here: Mart. Petri, chaps. 8–10; Acta Joh., chaps. 97–101; Acta Andr. Bonnet II, 1, 54.18–55.19.

here a development has arrived at its ultimate goal with especial vigor and clarity, a goal toward which Christianity everywhere in its broad masses was pressing.

IV. *The Christianity of I Clement.* Another observation must be placed beside this; without it, what has been said previously would give a one-sided picture of the development of Christianity. Though actually present everywhere in praxis, the cultic sacramental element and its closely related placing of Jesus as Kyrios did not everywhere find expression in the same conscious manner. On the foundation described in Chapter VII, a much simpler, more rational, and, let us say it once, healthier religious life could be developed. Above, we have set forward the figure of Ignatius as the most concrete representative of the development of Christianity into mysterious piety; another single figure may appear over against him: the Roman Clement: Rome against Antioch, Orient against Occident.

The Christianity of Clement—as secondary witnesses of this type we can set forth James, Barnabas, the Shepherd of Hermas, as well as II Clement and others—may be characterized in a word as Diaspora-Judaism liberated to a complete universalism.

It is *liberated*, universalized Diaspora-Judaism. Universalism became a matter of course for the infant religion throughout the whole wide world.[60] The Christians or the Ἐκκλησία of the believers are the new people of God.[61] Through his appearing in the flesh, through his suffering and death Christ has prepared and acquired this new people for his own possession.[62] They are the new miraculous work of God, the great new fellowship in which God unites Jews, Greeks (and Barbarians): ἵνα τοὺς δύο κτίσῃ ἐν αὐτῷ εἰς ἕνα καινὸν ἄνθρωπον ποιῶν εἰρήνην καὶ ἀποκαταλλάξῃ τοὺς ἀμφοτέρους ἐν ἑνὶ σώματι (Eph. 2:15-16). The Christians are the third race,[63] neither Jews nor Greeks, but a new race formed out of both. The

---

[60] On the following, cf. Harnack, *Mission and Expansion of Christianity*, I, 240 ff.

[61] I Pet. 2:9. γένος ἐκλεκτόν, βασίλειον ἱεράτευμα, ἔθνος ἅγιον, λαὸς εἰς περιποίησιν; cf., e.g., Justin, Dial. 119.

[62] Acts 20:28; Titus 2:14; Barn. 3:6, ὁ λαὸς ὃν ἡτοίμασεν ἐν τῷ ἠγαπημένῳ αὐτοῦ. 5.7, (Χριστὸς) ἑαυτῷ τὸν λαὸν τὸν καινὸν ἑτοιμάζων. 7.5, ὑπὲρ ἁμαρτιῶν μέλλων τοῦ λαοῦ τοῦ καινοῦ προσφέρειν τὴν σάρκα. 14.5.

[63] Kerygma Petri in Clem. Strom. VI, 5.41, ὑμεῖς δὲ οἱ καινῶς αὐτὸν τρίτῳ γένει σεβόμενοι Χριστιανοί. Cf. the matter in the Epistle to Diognetus 5. Aristides, Apol. 2, 16: "And verily, this is a new people, and there is something divine [lit.: a divine admixture] in the midst of them" [ANF trans., IX, 278]. Orac. Sib. I, 383-84, βλαστὸς νέος ἀνθήσειεν ἐξ ἐθνῶν.

angels themselves have suspected nothing of this πολυποίκιλος σοφία of God (Eph. 3:10) which is revealed to them in the church; in astonishment they crane their necks in order to behold from heaven this marvelous establishment.[64] And as the Christians are the new people, so also they are the ancient people, chosen from the beginning. The thought that God's electing counsel governs the believers from all eternity[65] is expressed in the imaginative language of the time, in that the church is grasped as a pre-existent entity. The church, like our Lord Jesus, is pneumatic,[66] and became visible at the end of time in order to save us. Hermas beholds the church as an old woman, "because she was first created before all things." [67]

This new people of God simply takes its place in all the rights of the alleged ancient people of God. The claims of this Christianity are stretched far beyond the form in which Paul had defined the relationship of the new community of God to the old one. In place of the apostle's conception that the Gentiles are grafted into the ancient, holy stem that belongs to God, there appears the assertion of the dispossession of the old race, or more precisely, the principle that Judaism had never been the people of God. This standpoint is already maintained with special severity in the Fourth Gospel; the Jews do not follow the Father, they are children of the devil, they do not belong to the flock of Jesus.[68] And this opinion is so generally in vogue that the author of the epistle of Barnabas counts it as a gross sin when certain people declare: "Your covenant is also our covenant," and in the face of such admonishes that we may surrender nothing of that which we possess (4.6, 9).

Thus to the Christian church, which also gradually becomes aware of

[64] Cf. I Pet. 1:12, εἰς ἃ ἐπιθυμοῦσιν ἄγγελοι παρακύψαι.

[65] In I Clem. 29.1-2, Deut. 32:8-9 is simply applied to the election of the new people of God.

[66] ἦν γὰρ πνευματική, II Clem. 14.3. In this context πνευματικός means almost the same as preexistent (from heaven).

[67] Vis. II, 4.1. Cf. Vis. I, 3.4, (θεὸς) τῇ ἰδίᾳ σοφίᾳ καὶ προνοίᾳ κτίσας τὴν ἁγίαν ἐκκλησίαν. I, 1.6 (the whole world is created for the sake of the church).

[68] John 6:37 ff., 44 ff.; 8:44; 10:26. Cf., by way of example, the sharp contrasting of Ἰουδαϊσμός and Χριστιανισμός in Ign. Magn. 9-10; the way in which the book of Revelation even takes over the name "Jew" for the Christians in 2:9 and 3:9; the appropriation of the title "people of the twelve tribes of the Diaspora" in the proem of James and of I Peter; Justin's discussion with Jewish Christianity in Dial. 47-48; the designation of the Jews simply as sinners in Barn. 12.10, and so on. The major theme of the so-called Fifth Book of Ezra, which probably comes from the second century, is that of the replacement of the old people of God by the new: "I shall turn to other peoples and give my name to them, in order that they may keep my statutes" (I, 24).

being superior to the synagogue in numbers and significance (II Clem. 2.2), belongs all that previously had been the property of the latter.[69] To it belongs Abraham (and the patriarchs); Paul had already laid claim to him as the ancestral lord of faith. To it belongs the covenant, to it also the law. Moses had received from God the covenant and the law of the two tables, but the people of Israel were not worthy of these. Therefore Moses broke the tablets: αὐτὸς δὲ κύριος ἡμῖν ἔδωκεν εἰς λαὸν κληρονομίας δι' ἡμᾶς ὑπομείνας.[70] That Christ κατὰ σάρκα stems from the seed of David gradually disappears (in spite of Paul) from the christological confession of early Christianity, although Ignatius is still acquainted with the sentence (vide supra, p. 300, n. 209). To the Christian community belongs the true cultus, worship in spirit and in truth, the true high priest of the higher, better covenant, the θυσιαστήριον, to share in which the adherents of the synagogue have no right.[71]

Christianity is Diaspora-Judaism become universal, *freed of its limitations*, but it is also *Diaspora-Judaism* in spite of the removal of its limitations. It continues the development which had already successfully begun in Diaspora-Judaism, in the same direction. It developed into the religion of monotheism, of belief in the almighty Creator God, of the spiritual morality free from all particular obligatory character and from all ritual essence, of belief in responsibility and retribution after death, of confidence in the sin-forgiving divine mercy, of worship in spirit and in truth.

1. The most significant characteristic is the simple belief in the one almighty Creator God. The Shepherd of Hermas places this commandment, whose formulation he perhaps borrowed from Judaism, even to the very wording, ahead of all other commandments: πρῶτον πάντων πίστευσον, ὅτι εἷς ἐστιν ὁ θεός, ὁ τὰ πάντα κτίσας καὶ καταρτίσας καὶ ποιήσας ἐκ τοῦ μὴ ὄντος εἰς τὸ εἶναι τὰ πάντα καὶ πάντα χωρῶν, μόνος δὲ ἀχώρητος ὤν.[72]

---

[69] We possess a characteristic passage which shows us how Judaism on its own part was offended at this. In Schemoth Rabba Par. 6, 47 (trans. by Wünsche, p. 324) it is told that Moses had intended to write down the Mishna also. "But God foresaw that the Gentiles would translate the Torah and say, 'We are Israel, God's sons.'" The unwritten Torah would remain the only advantage of Israel (Bousset, *Religion des Judentums*, 2nd ed., p. 180).

[70] Barn. 14.4. Cf. 4.6.

[71] Cf. the views of Hebrews, esp. 13:8-15.

[72] Cf. the almost verbatim repetition in the Kerygma Petri, Clem. Strom. VI, 5.39. The newly discovered liturgical papyrus of Dêr Balyzeh proves that this confession was also taken up into the liturgy (Schermann, TU XXXVI 1, p. 12). Perhaps it even originally comes from there.

When we read I Clement, we are surprised to see that here Christianity is hardly anything other than this belief in the one almighty Creator God, who rules over the world in his omnipotence and guides it with his fatherly care. In solemn, choice language, which now and then rises to the level of a majestic hymn and which clearly shows the influence of Stoic popular philosophy which probably had been filtered through Judaism, Clement celebrates this Creator God [73]: ἀτενίσωμεν εἰς τὸν πατέρα καὶ κτίστην τοῦ σύμπαντος κόσμου! His figure still towers above and completely overshadows the figure of Jesus[74]; it is distinctive here how the Pauline "the Father of our Lord Jesus Christ" [75] was completely suppressed by the connection of the name "Father" to the creation. In general one can observe throughout that in one part of the post-apostolic literature the simple designations of God (θεός, πατήρ), which we encounter in the classical witnesses of primitive Christianity, retreat into the background in favor of a fuller and richer language, the tone of which is familiar to us from the later Jewish literature and the Jewish liturgy of prayers.[76]

[73] Cf. particularly chap. 20, and also the beginning of the long prayer in 59.3-4. On the stressing of the idea of creation, cf. Acts 17:24, 26; Hermas, Vis. I, 1; Mand. XII, 4.2; II Clem. 15.2; Didache 10.3 (a eucharistic prayer!). I Tim. 6:13, θεὸς ὁ ζωογονῶν τὰ πάντα (cf. I Clem. 59.3). Acta Pionii, chap. 8; Mart. Just. 2.5.

[74] See above, p. 294, n. 179, the proof of the exclusive connection of the ἅγιον καὶ ἔνδοξον ὄνομα with God.

[75] πατήρ in referring to Christ only in I Clem. 7.4. In 23.1, ὁ οἰκτίρμων κατὰ πάντα καὶ εὐεργετικὸς πατήρ with reference to the election of the new people of God. In 29.1, ἐπιεικὴς καὶ εὔσπλαγχνος πατήρ in an eschatological context. 19.2, πατὴρ καὶ κτίστης τοῦ σύμπαντος κόσμου. 62.2, πατὴρ καὶ θεὸς καὶ κτίστης. In 46.6 and 58.2 the trinitarian formula runs θεός—Χριστός—πνεῦμα. Cf. δημιουργὸς καὶ πατὴρ τῶν αἰώνων ὁ πανάγιος in 35.3. ὁ (μέγας) δημιουργὸς τῶν ἀπάντων, 20.11; 26.1; 33.2; 59.2; (38.3; 7.3). παντὸς πνεύματος κτίστης, 59.3.

[76] Cf., e.g., the borrowing of the δεσπότης which was common in Judaism (as distinguished from κύριος); see above, p. 287; further, θεὸς παντοκράτωρ in Revelation (passim; elsewhere in the New Testament only in II Cor. 6:18, in a quotation from the Old Testament); I Clem. Proem, 2.3; 32.4 (60.4); 62.2; Did. 10.3; Mart. Polyc. 14.1; 19.2; Hermas, Vis. III, 3.5; Sim. V, 7.4; Mart. Apollon. 46; Mart. Pion. 8; Acta Perpetuae 21.11 (omnipotens)—further, the characteristic and genuinely Jewish (parables of Enoch!) κύριος (θεός, δεσπότης) τῶν πνευμάτων in I Clem. 64.1 (59.3, εὐεργέτης πνευμάτων καὶ θεὸς πάσης σαρκός), Heb. 12:9; cf. Rev. 22:6, also θεὸς τῶν (ἀγγέλων καὶ) δυνάμεων in Hermas, Vis. I, 3.4; Mart. Polyc. 14.1; ὕψιστος in I Clem. 45.7; 59.3, Luke passim; Acts 7:48; 16:17; Heb. 7:1; Ignat. Rom. Proem; πανεπόπτης in I Clem. 55.6, 64.1; Polyc. Phil. 7.2; ἅγιος πανάγιος in I Clem. 30.1, 35.3, (58.1), 59.3 (τὸν μόνον ὕψιστον ἐν ὑψίστοις ἅγιον ἐν ἁγίοις ἀναπαυόμενον). Did. 10.2; θεὸς ζῶν (II Cor. 3:3, 6:16, I Thess. 1:9); I Tim. 3:15, 4:10, 6:17, Heb. 3:12, 9:14, 10:31, 12:22; I Pet. 1:23; Rev. 4:9-10, 7:2, 10:6, 15:7; Hermas, Vis. II, 3.2, III, 7.2; ζωογονῶν (τὰ πάντα) in I Tim. 6:13, τὸ ἀρχέγονον πάσης κτίσεως ὄνομα in I Clem. 59.3; θεὸς μόνος in I Clem. 59.4 (59.3); II Clem. 20.5; Jude 4, 25; Rom. 16:27; I Tim. 1:17; ὄνομα ἀληθινὸν καὶ μόνον in I Clem. 43.6; cf. John 17:3 (I John 5:20); βασιλεὺς (μέγας) in Hermas, Vis. III,

2. But further, this Christianity perfects the tendency of the Jewish Diaspora with its demand for a genuine morality that is free from all particularism and all ritual. It is true that Judaism was not able of itself to strike off the last fetters and confining conditions, but it had in essence loosened them. Now the last barriers fall. At the same time, Christianity can simply appropriate the rich treasure of a spiritual, lofty ethic, from the Old Testament which it had adopted as a holy book as well as from the later Jewish literature. The author of I Clement lives altogether in the ethic of the Old Testament. For him the Holy Scripture has become the great picture book of morality which he opens up before his readers in almost all ethical exhortations. But not only the Old Testament is made fruitful in this respect; the later Jewish literature also is exploited. The Christian religion kept in its bosom the Jewish (now so-called apocryphal, pseudepigraphical) literature, while the synagogue renounced it, and this is to a great extent *ethical* literature. I refer only to the speeches of Sirach, the book of Tobit, the Wisdom of Solomon, II and IV Maccabees, and most of all the early Christian re-editing of the Testament of the Patriarchs. In the Didache, the ethical closing sections of the Epistle of Barnabas, and the so-called Apostolic Constitutions, a Jewish catechism ("the Two Ways") has been incorporated. The suspicion can hardly be avoided that the author of the Shepherd of Hermas, especially in the Mandates, but also in the Visions and the Similitudes, in preponderant measure has simply reproduced Jewish material and has expanded it only a little with his own material.[77] One will have to conclude the same of the author of the Epistle of James. Even in the reinterpretation of the Old Testament ceremonial law into moral prescriptions, of which the Epistle of Barnabas may serve as the chief and classic document, the literature of Diaspora-Judaism has led the way for Christianity (cf. above all the letter of Aristeas and the abundant statements of Philo in this direction). So now Christianity appears in the comprehensive and classical formulation as "the new law" which yet is actually the old one.[78] This old law, in its proper exposition and stripped of its external and

---

9.8; I Tim. 1:17 (βασιλεὺς τῶν αἰώνων); Rev. 15:3; ἀόρατος θεός in I Tim. 1:17; Heb. 11:27; II Clem. 20.5; μακάριος θεός in I Tim. 1:17. Ceremonial heaping up of epithets, e.g., in I Tim. 1:17, 6:15-16; Rom. 16:25-27 (probably not genuine); I Clem. 59; II Clem. 20.5.

[77] Here we can only indicate that this Jewish ethic of Hermas again is profoundly affected by the Hellenistic (Stoic) popular ethic.

[78] I John 2:7, οὐκ ἐντολὴν καινήν . . . ἡ ἐντολὴ ἡ παλαιά ἐστιν, ὁ λόγος ὃν ἠκούσατε (it is the old commandment, the [Old Testament] word, which you hear [have heard]).

ceremonial nature, which however is actually only an apparent understanding and a misunderstanding and which rests upon a false interpretation of the wording; yet again the new law, the royal commandment of love, the perfect law of liberty.[79]

3. This ethical basic attitude is supported by the belief in imminent retribution and by the fear of the approaching judgment.[80] In the first Mandate of Hermas it is said: πίστευσον οὖν αὐτῷ καὶ φοβήθητι αὐτόν, φοβηθεὶς δὲ ἐγκράτευσον . . . ζήσῃ τῷ θεῷ, ἐὰν φυλάξῃς τὴν ἐντολὴν ταύτην. Just as the author of IV Ezra in a striking confession-like passage of his book connects the idea of God the creator of the world with that of the judge of the world (5.56–6.6), so now for the writer of I Clement, creation and resurrection appear in an immediate connection as beginning point and end point of the mighty acts of God, to whom for this reason one owes fear and obedience (20-28). God is[81] the creator and the judge.[82] Thus Jewish eschatology empties into Christian eschatology, and with the eschatology, the Jewish materialist doctrine of the resurrection of the flesh, in spite of Paul,[83] and the whole of fantastic Jewish apocalyptic. Here on this soil the literatures merge into each other completely, so that the boundary between what is Jewish and what is Christian is often very difficult to draw. This is attested by the Apocalypse which goes under the name of John, by so many other early Christian apocalypses, and once again by the fact that almost the entire body of apocalyptic-pseudepigraphical literature is preserved for us only through the medium of Christian tradition (and partial reworking). The earliest church order, the Didache, closes with a little apocalypse which, perhaps like the ethical catechism at the beginning, is of Jewish origin. Only in the one point that in looking at the end, triumphant hope is more stoutly placed beside trembling anxiety and fear—a classical example of this

[79] Cf. James 1:25; 2:8 (2:10-12; 4:11); see the further evidence below in the section on Christ the lawgiver. Barn. 2.6, ὁ καινὸς νόμος ἄνευ ζυγοῦ ἀνάγκης. In connection with the perfect law the thought often is more of the commandments of asceticism than of love. Worthy of note here and there is the connection with the dogma of the Stoa of the natural world- and moral law: Tatian, Oration 28: διὰ τοῦτο καὶ τῆς παρ' ὑμῖν κατέγνων νομοθεσίας· μίαν μὲν γὰρ ἔχρην εἶναι καὶ κοινὴν ἁπάντων τὴν πολιτείαν. Harnack, Dogmengeschichte, 4th ed., I, 191. Cf. also Mission and Expansion of Christianity, I, 208.4.

[80] Cf. Barn. 1.6, δικαιοσύνη κρίσεως ἀρχὴ καὶ τέλος. II Clem. 12.1.

[81] Cf. also in Heb. 11:2, 6, the two motifs combined.

[82] The fact that relatively few witnesses to the judgeship of God are to be found is due to the fact that for the most part the office of judge of the world appears transferred to Christ. Yet cf. I Pet. 1:17; James 4:12; 5:4; 5:8-9 (?); Rev. 1:8; 4:8; 11:17-18; 19:2; 20:11 ff.; I John 4:17; II Pet. 3:12, τὴν παρουσίαν τῆς τοῦ θεοῦ ἡμέρας.

[83] See above, p. 174.

is I Peter[84]—does the spirit of the new religion distinguish itself from the old.

4. In fact, this Christianity could acquire from the synagogue even the central idea of the present forgiveness of sins. For it is by no means true that this idea had disappeared from the piety of late Judaism.[85] The belief that God, the strict judge, yet at the same time is the compassionate God who forgives the pious their sins is not altogether alien to this late Jewish piety. The petition for the forgiveness of sins characterizes Jewish prayer literature to a great extent. Indeed, one might almost conclude that the stronger emphasis upon the forgiveness of sins was preserved in Christianity precisely where strong connections between Christianity and the Jewish Diaspora piety are present (thus in the literary circle which we are treating). Still, in general, the idea of the forgiveness of sins in the present recedes in early Christianity. The fact that the new religion appears to be dominated by the idea of the great sacrifice which was offered on the cross should not confuse us. For this belief continues essentially to be directed toward the broad concepts. As a rule what is involved is the redemption and reconciliation of humanity, the one great sacrifice which was offered for the (past) sins of humanity, the victory over the accursed powers of the past, the shattering of the dominion of death and the devil, the acquisition of a peculiar people. The idea of the individual and of present sin of the individual life recedes sharply into the background. The psychological connection between Christ's suffering death and the assurance of forgiveness of current sins for the individual soul is not very frequently presented. Moreover, it is well known how strongly dominant from Paul onward is the conviction that in essence the forgiveness of sins comes at the beginning of the Christian life, that the Christian actually no longer sins, and that the task of the Christian consists in keeping himself pure and undefiled until God's great judgment day. We have already brought out the fact that in the author of the Gospel of John we seek in vain for the expression "forgiveness of sins," and that the only passage in which we find it concerns the institution of the (outward) forgiveness by the apostles. In I John (3:6) there emerges with vigor the proud and strong (though somewhat naïve and robust) consciousness that the Christian no longer sins: "Everyone who abides in him does not sin; everyone who sins has not seen or

---

[84] Cf. Barn. 1.4, πίστις, ἀγάπη, ἐλπίς. In 1.6 it is even said that the hope of life is the beginning and end of our faith (righteousness, love).

[85] Bousset, *Religion des Judentums*, 2nd ed., pp. 446 ff.

known him" (3:6).[86] Ignatius[87] also hardly knows the idea of "sin and forgiveness." That proud (Pauline-Johannine) basic attitude is then stiffened and hardened into the familiar dogmatic view that in baptism, previous sins, which were placed in the Old Testament category of sins of ignorance,[88] are forgiven, and that it is necessary to preserve the seal of baptism pure and unspotted. The Epistle to the Hebrews sharply stresses the unforgivability[89] of certain gross offenses after baptism, in particular that of apostasy. The chief concern of the Shepherd of Hermas, the preaching of a second repentance after baptism, rests altogether on this basic attitude.[90] "If we do not preserve baptism pure and undefiled, how *then* shall we enter with confidence into the kingdom of God?" In these words the preacher of the homily which is II Clement fittingly summarizes this basic attitude.[91]

It is of course to be conceded that the various views and attitudes here pass over into one another. The concept of sins which are committed in ignorance is not a clearly bounded concept and is capable of a very vigorous extension. Thus the belief in the forgiveness of sins can be held even where the ideal of the preservation in purity of the seal of baptismal grace dominates the Christian life. It cannot be denied, however, that the pneumatic enthusiasm of Paul, the churchly view (based thereupon) of the necessity of purity of the Christian life, the ever increasing emphasis upon sacramental grace, all served in general to muffle and suppress the gospel of the forgiveness of sins.

The plain, simple, and obvious way in which the author of I Clement

[86] The statements in I John 1:7–2:2, in my judgment coming from another hand, do not agree in all points with this, unless people connected the confession of sin and conversion with the baptismal act. But this is impossible because of 2:1.

[87] *One time* he has the formal expression that Christ has suffered for our sins, in Smyrn. 7.1 (cf. Polyc. Phil. 7.2). The οὐ παρὰ τοῦτο δεδικαίωμαι in Rom. 5.1 (Philad. 8.2) which is reminiscent of Paul has somewhat the meaning of τετελείωμαι. Ignatius explains the concept of μετανοεῖν by means of ἔρχεσθαι ἐπὶ τὴν ἑνότητα τῆς ἐκκλησίας (Philad. 3.2) or μετανοεῖν εἰς ἑνότητα θεοῦ καὶ συνέδριον τοῦ ἐπισκόπου (8.1); cf. Smyrn. 4.1, 5.3; everywhere Ignatius has in view the ecclesiastical penance of the heretics; even in Smyrn. 9.1 the εἰς θεὸν μετανοεῖν stands immediately before the demand that they do nothing without the bishop (once in Eph. 10.1 the formula with reference to non-Christians).

[88] I Pet. 1:14; Eph. 4:18; Acts 3:17, 17:30; Heb. 5:2 (9:7); I Clem. 2.3; Acta Thom. 58; Kerygma Petri (Clem. Strom. VI, 6, 48.6); Aristides, Apol. 17.

[89] Heb. 6:4 ff.; 10:26 ff. (here the Epistle speaks quite generally of ἑκουσίως ἁμαρτάνειν—apparently in contrast to the sins κατ' ἄγνοιαν); 12:16-17.

[90] Cf. Vis. I, 3.2; II, 2.4-5; II, 3.1; III, 5.5; Mand. IV, 1.7–3.7; Sim. VIII, 6.1-3; Sim. IX (*passim*). Over against this second repentance, then, the sins which are committed before this second repentance are set under the perspective of the ἀγνοήματα in Sim. V, 7.3.

[91] II Clem. 6.9; cf. 8.4-5. Cf. Acta Joh., chap. 107; Acta Thom. chap. 58.

speaks of the present forgiveness of sins[92] and of the prayer for the forgiveness of sins oddly arises out of this entire milieu. It is of utmost importance that in the concluding prayer handed down by him, the petition for the forgiveness of sins plays such a central role (60.1-2):

ἐλεῆμον καὶ οἰκτίρμον,
ἄφες ἡμῖν τὰς ἀνομίας ἡμῶν
καὶ τὰς ἀδικίας καὶ τὰ παραπτώματα καὶ πλημμελείας.
μὴ λογίσῃς πᾶσαν ἁμαρτίαν δούλων σου καὶ παιδισκῶν,
ἀλλὰ καθαριεῖς ἡμᾶς τὸν καθαρισμὸν τῆς σῆς ἀληθείας
καὶ κατεύθυνον τὰ διαβήματα ἡμῶν.
ἐν ὁσιότητι καρδίας πορεύεσθαι.

The petition for the forgiveness of sins is perhaps nowhere in primitive Christianity more purely and more clearly expressed, and this is all the more significant because we have every reason to assume that here it is not a private man speaking, but that we have before us in the main the every Sunday prayer of the Roman congregation. But at the same time here again the connections with Old Testament Jewish religion are opened up. For in all probability the prayer of Clement ultimately stems from the synagogue's worship. We may suspect the same worship connections[93] when we read in the Didache (14.1) the decree that Christians are to celebrate the eucharist every Sunday: προ[σ]εξομολογησάμενοι τὰ παραπτώματα ὑμῶν, ὅπως καθαρὰ ἡ θυσία ὑμῶν ᾖ. In other respects also Clement does not stand alone. The author of the Epistle of Barnabas very nicely sums up the preaching of the twelve apostles: "who have proclaimed to us the glad message of the forgiveness of sins and the purifying of the heart" (8.3). "Luke," in his Gospel as well as in the book of Acts, energetically stresses the blessing of the forgiveness of sins as the specifically Christian blessing of salvation. Yet it cannot be precisely determined whether in all this he is not thinking essentially of the once-for-all forgiveness in baptism.[94] Certain parts of I John, which however, as already pointed out, do not harmonize with the characteristic basic outlook of the Epistle, provide a

[92] I Clem. 2.3; 9.1 (34.7); 48.1; 50.5; 51.1; 56.1; 20.11 (τοὺς προσπεφευγότας τοῖς οἰκτιρμοῖς αὐτοῦ διὰ τοῦ κυρίου ἡμῶν Ἰησοῦ Χριστοῦ).

[93] Cf. Did. 4.14, ἐν ἐκκλησίᾳ ἐξομολογήσῃ τὰ παραπτώματά σου καὶ οὐ προσελεύσῃ ἐπὶ προσευχήν σου ἐν συνειδήσει πονηρᾷ. Perhaps the admonition was already in the Jewish writing that lies behind the Two Ways, only without the important ἐν ἐκκλησίᾳ. (Reconstruction in Harnack, Die Apostellehre und die jüdischen beiden Wege, p. 57). It is very characteristic that one seeks almost in vain in the later liturgies of the Christian church for this exomologesis.

[94] Luke (1:77); 24:47; Acts 2:38; 5:31; 10:43; 13:38; 26:18.

simply classical formulation of the attitude of the assurance of the forgiveness of sins.[95] We find a splendid echo of the Gospel in Polycarp (ad Phil. 6.2 [96]): πάντες ὀφειλέται ἐσμὲν ἁμαρτίας. εἰ οὖν δεόμεθα τοῦ κυρίου, ἵνα ἡμῖν ἀφῇ, ὀφείλομεν καὶ ἡμεῖς ἀφιέναι.[97] But to be sure, the generally dominant attitude no longer presents this view. We will have the right to assert this feature as a characteristic of that variety of Christianity which in closest relationship with Jewish-Old Testament piety—yet also with Jesus' words, especially the Lord's Prayer—is presented as belief in the Creator God, in judgment and retribution, as conduct in keeping with God's commandments and as the hope of eternity.[98]

5. Finally, it is extremely important to note that even with its cultus and its worship praxis, this Christianity is rooted, at least with one of its main roots, in the worship of the synagogue. Of course we should openly concede that one entire side of Christian worship cannot be comprehended from the perspective of Judaism. To this side belongs the whole Kyrios cultus; the development as sacraments of the sacred actions (the washing of baptism and the eucharistic meal) which in part had been borrowed from Judaism; perhaps the early, more copious hymnological development of worship; the creation of a confession; and, with all that and most of all, the barring of the outside world from the climax of worship and the reserving of that moment for the initiated,[99] as well as the gradually prevailing view of the cultus as a holy mystery. However, these are of course precisely those things which more and more come to occupy a central place in the new religion. The bishop, as he appears to us in the Ignatian epistles as the bearer of the Christian cultus, has hardly anything to do with the Jewish rabbi and *darshan*.

And yet the church owes a good part of her worship forms to the synagogue. From thence come the three important factors of worship: Scripture

[95] I John 1:7–2:2; 5:16-17; cf. I Clem. 56.1.
[96] Cf. 7.2 (here also the influence of the Lord's Prayer).
[97] II Clem. 18.2, καὶ γὰρ αὐτὸς πανθαμαρτωλός is preaching jargon.
[98] Cf. the summaries, e.g. in Titus 2:12-13: ἵνα ἀρνησάμενοι τὴν ἀσέβειαν καὶ τὰς κοσμικὰς ἐπιθυμίας σωφρόνως καὶ δικαίως καὶ εὐσεβῶς ζήσωμεν προσδεχόμενοι τὴν μακαρίαν ἐλπίδα. Mart. Apollon. 37: θεὸν σέβειν μόνον ἀθάνατον, ψυχὴν ἀθάνατον πιστεύειν, δίκην μετὰ θάνατον πεπεῖσθαι, γέρας πόνων ἀρετῆς μετὰ τὴν ἀνάστασιν ἐλπίζειν. This simple and plain Christianity is especially well summed up in the Acts of Peter and Paul, chap. 58 (Lipsius-Bonnet I, 201-2) and in other passages (cf. Lipsius, *Apokr. Apostelgesch.*, II, 1 (1887), 551 ff.).
[99] The beginnings are already evident in Did. 9.5; Justin, in his portrayal of the Christian worship, already certainly presupposes that in the actual eucharistic worship only the believers are present. He is already familiar with the solemn service of worship in which the newly baptized person after baptism is admitted to the mystery of the eucharist.

reading, preaching, and prayer, thus all that one usually classifies as worship in the word of God as over against worship in the sacrament. Christianity simply borrowed from Judaism the sacred book which was read in the synagogue, and the New Testament canon also developed in such a way that people gradually began in cultic use to place new lectionaries alongside the holy Scripture κατ' ἐξοχήν. The Jewish prayer liturgy influenced the Christian liturgy in more prominent and richer measure than people up until recently suspected. The eucharistic prayers of the Didache, the great congregational prayer which Clement handed down, are proofs of this.[100] Christian preaching, although from the beginning more independent of the letter of Scripture, learned to move more freely, and placed the edifying and theoretical (pure doctrine) elements alongside the purely practical, pedagogical element, yet has its origin in the Jewish Midrash. Indeed, the church even owes to the synagogue the custom of the weekly gathering for worship, which of course appears only gradually to have been developed out of a much more abundant life of worship, so that the assembly on Sunday began only with the passing of time to overshadow the daily assemblies of the Christians. From that source also comes a part of the church's calendar (Pasch and Pentecost, the weekly fast days—of course not the festival of Epiphany and the much later festival of Christmas). And, if in conclusion we may go a bit further, the Christian exorcists and miracle-workers only replaced the Jewish ones.[101]

## V. *The Significance of the Person of Jesus for This Type of Christianity.*

One must form a picture of the totality of this kind of Christianity with

[100] Cf. von der Goltz, *Das Gebet in der ältesten Christenheit*, pp. 192 ff., 207 ff. A thoroughgoing investigation is needed of the later connections of the Jewish and Christian liturgies. Notably the song of the seraphim with its Trisagion (soon after the "Bor'chu" and before the recitation of the Shema) still has its fixed place in the Jewish liturgy of the present day (S. R. Hirsch, *Israels Gebete* (1895), p. 110), as in the Christian liturgy before the anaphora. The beginning of the prayer אמת ויציב (shortly before the recitation of the Sh'mone-Esre; Hirsch, p. 122) has been compared, probably correctly, with the ἄξιον καὶ δίκαιον of the Christian liturgy. Above all, I call attention to the long prayer of supplication on the Sabbath after the reading of the Torah (for teachers, the whole community, the founders of synagogues, for the wine for Habdala and Kiddush, for bread and alms for the poor, for kings and rulers, finally for the martyrs) with its various parallels to the Christian prayer liturgy (Hirsch, p. 350). Memorial prayer for "every spirit and every soul" in the Mussaph prayer for the New Year (Hirsch, p. 642).

[101] For most of the details, cf. the good and concise summary in Loeschke, *Jüdisches und Heidnisches im christlichen Kult*, Bonn, 1910. But Loeschke goes too far when he asserts (p. 15): "The Christian cult has its roots in Judaism" and therewith concedes an influence by pagan cultic practices only in details. The Christian cultus, like Christianity itself, is a syncretistic structure and is rooted in two settings.

its rational, easily surveyed and comprehensible individuality, its simplicity and powerful vitality, in order to comprehend how alongside the Kyrios cult a very much simpler and more rational evaluation of the person of Jesus Christ took on life and could be maintained.

Once again it is a simple, bare formula in which the significance of the person of Jesus is presented in this milieu. *He is the new lawgiver and, as the lawgiver, also the future judge.* We need only leaf through I Clement to meet everywhere with expressions to that effect. Christianity consists in our fulfilling the commandments and instructions of the Lord. The portrayal of the earlier ideal state of the Corinthian community *begins* with the words: τοὺς λόγους αὐτοῦ[102] ἐπιμελῶς ἐνεστερισμένοι ἦτε τοῖς σπλάγχνοις, and ends: τὰ προστάγματα καὶ τὰ δικαιώματα τοῦ κυρίου ἐπὶ τὰ πλάτη τῆς καρδίας ὑμῶν ἐγέγραπτο (chap. 2).[103] The community of Christ is πολιτεύεσθαι κατὰ τὸ καθῆκον τῷ Χριστῷ (3.4); they are to perform their service in the army ἐν τοῖς ἀμώμοις προστάγμασιν αὐτοῦ (37.1). The hymn to love, which imitates that in I Cor., begins: ὁ ἔχων ἀγάπην ἐν Χριστῷ ποιησάτω τὰ τοῦ Χριστοῦ παραγγέλματα[104] (49.1).

In the Johannine writings, particularly in the Epistles, in spite of all the mysticism, this point of view occupies the central position; Christianity is but keeping his commandments. And it is distinctive that in II John which, in my judgment, stands with III John at the beginning of the Johannine literature, the commandment appears still as ἐντολὴ τοῦ πατρός; that then in the First Epistle the point of view changes (in essence still God's commandment[105] but now also Jesus' commandment[106]), and then finally, in the farewell discourses of the Gospel we read "my commandments." [107]

The author of the Epistle of Barnabas speaks, in the introduction to the Epistle, of the τρία δόγματα τοῦ κυρίου (hope, righteousness, love: 1.6), and then there occurs the great slogan ὁ καινὸς νόμος τοῦ κυρίου ἡμῶν

---

[102] *Sc.* Χριστοῦ; thus (and not θεοῦ) in the preceding sentence (with lat syr copt *contra* A).

[103] On the other hand, cf. ἐν τοῖς νόμοις τοῦ θεοῦ πορεύεσθε in 1.3; immediately preceding the sentence quoted above we read πάντα τὰ ἐν τῷ φόβῳ αὐτοῦ (i.e., of God) τελεῖτε. Similarly in 3.4 (see above), ἐν τοῖς νομίμοις τῶν προσταγμάτων αὐτοῦ (i.e., θεοῦ) πορεύεσθαι; cf. 58.2.

[104] Cf. 13.3. The author probably is also thinking of Jesus' commandments when he warns in 7.2: ἔλθωμεν ἐπὶ τὸν εὐκλεῆ καὶ σεμνὸν τῆς παραδόσεως ἡμῶν κανόνα.

[105] I John 3:22, 23, 24 (?); 4:21; 5:2-3.

[106] I John 2:3-4, 7; (3:24?); cf. 2:5, λόγον τηρεῖν.

[107] John 13:34-35; 14:15, 21; 15:10, 12.

Ἰησοῦ Χριστοῦ (2.6).[108] The Shepherd of Hermas refers the food provisions, with which God compensates his servant and which the servant then shares with his fellow servants, to the commandments which he has given to his people through his Son (Sim. V, 5.3). The homilist in II Clem. speaks sometimes of the commandments of God [109] and at other times of those of the Lord Christ.

Even Ignatius also once speaks of the ἐντολαὶ Ἰησοῦ Χριστοῦ (Eph. 9.2), of the Christians ἡνωμένοις πάσῃ ἐντολῇ αὐτοῦ (Rom., Proem),[110] and still more characteristically of the δόγματα τοῦ κυρίου καὶ τῶν ἀποστόλων (Magn. 13.1).[111]

Thus Christ is the καινὸς νομοθέτης (Justin, Dial. 18, p. 236 A). Indeed, he is in his person the new law itself. The author of Hermas used a Jewish source in which the law of God was presented under the image of a tree casting its shadow over the world. He adds this interpretation: ὁ δὲ νόμος οὗτος υἱὸς θεοῦ ἐστι κηρυχθεὶς εἰς τὰ πέρατα τῆς γῆς (Sim. VIII, 3.2). In Justin, Christ is called ὁ καινὸς νόμος, ἡ καινὴ διαθήκη[112]; in the Petrine Kerygma, probably in direct dependence on the basic concepts of the Stoic world view, νόμος καὶ λόγος.[113]

This principle can be expressed still more simply: Christ himself is the great example of virtuous conduct! The author of I John in particular strikes this note: "One who claims to abide in him ought also to behave as he himself behaved." [114] I Clement concludes its great declaration about ταπεινοφροσύνη thus: ὁρᾶτε ἄνδρες ἀγαπητοί, τίς ὁ ὑπογραμμὸς ὁ δεδομένος ὑμῖν.[115] Polycarp begins his comprehensive ethical exhortation:

[108] Cf. 2.1, δικαιώματα κυρίου; in 4.11, on the other hand, ἐντολαί, δικαιώματα of God, and similarly in 16.9. Cf. Justin, Dial. 34, p. 251 C (καινὸς νόμος καὶ καινὴ διαθήκη); cf. 93, p. 321 A.

[109] II Clem. 3.4 (cf. 4); note here the equation of ὁμολογία and keeping the commandments: 3.4; 4.3. On the other hand, according to the context the commandments and instructions of the "Lord" are to be referred to Jesus in 8.4; 17. (1,) 3, 6; cf. 6.7.

[110] When in Magn. 2 the presbytery is called νόμος Ἰησοῦ Χριστοῦ, we find ourselves already in the train of thought peculiar to Ignatius (cf. Trall. 13.1).

[111] Cf. Trall. 7.1 (3.3), διατάγματα τῶν ἀποστόλων, and esp. II Pet. 3:2, τῆς τῶν ἀποστόλων ὑμῶν ἐντολῆς τοῦ κυρίου καὶ σωτῆρος. ἐντολὴ κυρίου also in Polyc. Phil. 4.1 (yet the ἀξίως τῆς ἐντολῆς αὐτοῦ . . . περιπατεῖν in 5.1 is to be referred to God). Mart. Apollon. 5: τὰς σεμνοπρεπεῖς καὶ λαμπρὰς ἐντολὰς μεμαθήκαμεν ἀπὸ τοῦ λόγου τοῦ θεοῦ (26, κατὰ τὰς θείας ζῆν ἐντολάς). 36: ὁ σωτὴρ ἡμῶν Ἰησοῦς Χριστὸς . . . φιλανθρώπως ἐδίδαξεν ἡμᾶς, τίς ὁ τῶν ὅλων θεὸς καὶ τί τέλος ἀρετῆς ἐπὶ σεμνὴν πολιτείαν ἁρμόζον.

[112] Dial. 11, p. 228 E.

[113] Clem. Strom. I, 29, 182; II, 15, 68; Ecl. proph. 58 (see below, Chap. IX).

[114] I John 2:6, 3:3 (ἁγνίζει ἑαυτὸν καθὼς ἐκεῖνος ἁγνός ἐστιν); 4:17; John 13:15.

[115] 16.17; cf. 33.8 (the ἔργα ἀγαθά of the κύριος as ὑπογραμμός).

"Follow the example of the Lord. . . . Forestall one another in the gentleness of the Lord" (10.1). Along this same line, then, lies the oft-repeated proclamation by Justin[116] of Jesus as the διδάσκαλος.[117]

Here enters the fact that it was the words of the Lord that first gained a position on a level with the sacred writings of the Old Testament. They are the most highly preferred documents of the new giving of the law. The author of I Clement admonishes his readers: μάλιστα μεμνημένοι τῶν λόγων τοῦ κυρίου Ἰησοῦ, οὓς ἐλάλησεν διδάσκων ἐπιείκειαν καὶ μακροθυμίαν (13.1). And after he quotes some words of Jesus, he admonishes: ταύτῃ τῇ ἐντολῇ καὶ τοῖς παραγγέλμασιν τούτοις στηρίξωμεν ἑαυτοὺς εἰς τὸ πορεύεσθαι ὑπηκόους ὄντας τοῖς ἁγιοπρεπέσιν λόγοις αὐτοῦ.[118] The homily of II Clement subsists altogether on words of Jesus,[119] the Didache introduces the appropriated Jewish document of the Two Ways with a mosaic of logia of Jesus. In his Apology Justin seeks to make the nature and character of Christianity understandable in a series of Jesus' utterances (Apol. I, 15 ff.). The procedure in Athenagoras 11 is not different. The author of the Epistle of Barnabas, even though he does not directly cite any words of Jesus, still brings to his history reminiscences in abundant measure. Even for the Gnostics the κύριος is an authority, though for the most part they must interpret his words allegorically, and his story stimulates their fantasy in rich measure. It is a fully comprehensible process, how in the Christians' worship the Lord's words and thereby the Gospels that contain them gradually appear alongside the Old Testament as sacred texts for reading—and thus the kernel of the New Testament canon emerges.[120]

One can hardly overestimate the importance of these facts. It signifies something tremendous for Christianity that a large part of Christendom frequently drew its spiritual nourishment (apart from the Old Testament)

[116] Cf. Act. Justin. 2.5: σωτηρίας κῆρυξ καὶ διδάσκαλος καλῶν μαθημάτων.

[117] More mysteriously, in certain connections Jesus is thought of as the originator of the new race of Christians. Justin, Dial. 123, p. 353 B, ἀπὸ τοῦ γεννήσαντος ἡμᾶς εἰς θεὸν Χριστοῦ.

[118] I Clem. 13; cf. 46.

[119] Cf. the introductory formula ὁ κύριος λέγει in 4.5, 5.3, 6.1, 9.11, 12.2 (+ἐν τῷ εὐαγγελίῳ, 8.5); 13.3 even ὁ θεὸς λέγει; cf. Polycarp 2.2-3, μνημονεύοντες δὲ ὧν εἶπεν ὁ κύριος διδάσκων (quotations follow), 7.2 (the Lord's Prayer); cf. 6.2.

[120] The placing side by side of the authority of the Lord's words and of the Scripture is clearest already in John 2:22 (cf. 18:9, 32). The ἀπομνημονεύματα τῶν ἀποστόλων as sacred books for reading alongside the "prophets" in Justin, Apol. I, 67.3. Cf. II Pet. 3:2; Polyc. 7.2 (see above), Hegesippus in Eusebius CH IV, 22.3 (ὡς ὁ νόμος κηρύσσει καὶ οἱ προφῆται καὶ ὁ κύριος).

not from the epistles of Paul but from the words of Jesus. That this was possible at all, in spite of the fact that the Pauline preaching of the πνεῦμα–κύριος and of the present power of his death and resurrection had completely overshadowed the life picture of Jesus of Nazareth, and in spite of the fact that for the piety of the masses Jesus was first of all the Lord who is present in the cultus and the sacrament, is a fact that is astonishing in the highest degree. To be sure, the gospel of Jesus of Nazareth becomes effectual here only in abbreviation. The words of Jesus were essentially considered under a one-sidedly ethical viewpoint, as the new commandments and the new law; his person and the picture of his life were first of all set in the perspective of the example of virtuous conduct. Of the center of his being, of his religious individuality, some little bits only became incidentally relevant; the fact that here a new, unique, and powerful impulse was given did not actually achieve conscious acknowledgment.[121] And yet, even in this abridgment, the figure of Jesus which here again became alive was a power that contributed to the health of the young religion's life.

We must add one further aspect to this picture. Corresponding to the evaluation of Jesus as the new lawgiver, there is on the other side obviously the strong emphasis on his office as world judge. We have already shown how since the very beginning of the development Christ appeared in the place of God, and his figure begins to overshadow that of the Father (*vide supra,* p. 47). The Gospel of John, recalling the old Jewish dogma, proclaims that the Father has given the judgment to the Son because he is the Son of Man,[122] the author of Acts speaks of the ὡρισμένος ὑπὸ τοῦ θεοῦ κριτὴς ζώντων καὶ νεκρῶν (10:42; cf. 17:31), and the author of the Pastoral Epistles speaks of the God and Christ Jesus who is to judge the living and the dead.[123] Similar formulas occur in Barnabas (the Son of God, although he is the Lord and has someday to judge the living and the dead),[124] and in Polycarp (ὃς ἔρχεται κριτὴς ζώντων καὶ νεκρῶν)[125]; and the early Christian sermon begins: "We are to think of Jesus Christ as of God, as of the judge of the living and the dead" (II Clem. 1.1).[126]

---

[121] Yet cf. what is said above (pp. 374-76) about the proclamation of the forgiveness of sins.

[122] John 5:27; cf. I John 2:28 (*contra* 4:17).

[123] II Tim. 4:1; cf. 4:8, 18; Titus 2:13.

[124] 7.2; cf. 5.7, 4.12, 15.4.

[125] Phil. 2:2.

[126] Cf. the context in II Clem. 17.1-7.

The "whence he shall come to judge the quick and the dead" belongs to the earliest common basic convictions of Christianity. This is matched by the fact that out of the βασιλεία τοῦ θεοῦ of our Gospels, there emerges on such an extensive scale a βασιλεία Χριστοῦ.[127]

With all this, one part of the eschatological attitude of primitive Christianity still is propagated. Christianity continues to be, to a degree, the expectation of "our Lord Jesus Christ," who is to come from heaven as savior and judge, and the good and honorable conduct in view of the imminent end of things and of the rewards and punishments which this Lord will mete out. The eschatology retains this personal note which distinguishes it from Jewish eschatology. With the Messiah whom one expects, one already knows one part of the otherwise unknown future. This attitude probably often remained the dominant one, particularly among the broad, non-literary masses. These people listened to the notes of the Apocalypse of John and similar writings, they were enchanted with the pictures of the blood-spattered conqueror on a white horse, or of the bridegroom who fetches his bride. These people prayed with fervor, ἀμὴν ἔρχου κύριε Ἰησοῦ. But even a Christian belonging to the upper classes, peaceable, substantially interested in the questions of the present Christian life in worship and order, such as the author of the Pastoral Epistles, speaks of the expectation of the blessed hope and of the epiphany of our great God and Savior (Titus 2:13; cf. II Tim. 4:1), and admonishes to keep the commandment pure and undefiled until the epiphany of our Lord Jesus Christ (I Tim. 6:14). For him it is not so imminently near; the blessed and only ruler (God) will cause it to come to view at the appropriate time; and yet his gaze is, still always directed toward this hope. With exultant joy I Peter speaks of the "future revelation of Jesus Christ," "whom not having seen you love, in whom now, though you do not see him, you believe, rejoicing with unutterable and glorious joy, receiving as the end of faith the salvation of your souls" (1:7-8).[128]

We must, however, affirm in conclusion that this Christianity which, except for the apocalyptic attitude which progressively fades with every passing decade, was so simple and rational, this piety of the liberated Diaspora-Judaism for which Jesus is lawgiver, teacher, and judge, is not actually found anywhere in its pure form, and to a certain extent represents

---

[127] Cf. Matt. 13:41; 16:28; 20:21; (Luke 22:29-30); I Cor. 15:24; Col. 1:13; II Tim. 4:1, 18; Eph. 5:5; II Pet. 1:11; I Clem. 50.3 (contra 42.3); II Clem. 17.5.

[128] Cf. further Heb. 9:28 (11:1); II Clem. 5.5; 17.1-7; Barn. 15; Did. 16; etc.

an abstraction. It arises on the basis of a community praxis and a life of worship for which the Kyrios cult and the sacrament become more and more the driving and determining factors. At first, with respect to this altogether unique "more" which the new religion actually has over and above the religion of Diaspora-Judaism, this piety miscarries with the spoken word and does not give this "more" an adequate expression and a fitting formula. But that element is present and it continues to flow beneath the surface. It daily imperceptibly affects and shapes the common life of Christians. And it must with certainty overcome all rational resistance and gradually come to the surface. The process appears to have occurred more rapidly in the East than in the West; the Ignatian epistles almost startle us with the quickness with which Christianity here has been developed into a mystery religion whose cult-hero is the κύριος Χριστός. The development in the West took place much more slowly, since the West was never so absorbed in the mystery system as was the East. The Epistle of Clement, which was written not much earlier, appears over against the Ignatian epistles at a characteristic distance. But the line in which the Christianity of Ignatius lies will be the one determining the development. A keener ear already detects in I Clement the sounds of the new cultically determined religion. Christianity will not exist as a religion of unrestricted monotheism, of liberated and purified morality, of the forgiveness of sins and of hope, but as a cultic fellowship, in the center of which the sacrament stands. Christ will not be the lawgiver and teacher, to whom God has handed over the judgment, but the God to whom people pray. The cultus will overwhelmingly dominate the whole life of the young religion, constitution and pure doctrine will enlist wholly in its service, the social life (and therewith the morals) and even the financial economy will be determined from that perspective, its leaders will first of all be cult officials. The basic eschatological outlook will gradually be cooled off and will evaporate, but in its place the certainty of the presence of the Lord in the cultus and most of all in the sacrament will determine the piety of the new religion. In the life of worship the simple and rational elements of Jewish worship will be suppressed; not the sermon but the eucharist will provide the middle point, around which the worship is gradually formed into an immense and complicated structure. A cultic-sacramentally determined God- and Christ-mysticism will move in as the distinctive feature of the new religion, in which the two figures of faith, God and Christ, merge into one another and become blurred, although on the other hand, dogmatic thought will be carefully exerted in centuries-long efforts again to introduce in the right way a distinction between them.

At first, of course, in the Christianity of the Apologists, that rational basic outlook experienced its thoroughgoing formation into a unified total outlook. With the following chapter we turn to this phenomenon.

# 9
## THE APOLOGISTS

The overall intellectual tendency of the apologists may be conceived as a continuation of that rational and simple Christianity which is set forth above all in I Clement. In fact, it is fundamentally, even more than is I Clement, the extension and the removal in principle of the restraints upon the Jewish piety of the Diaspora. The whole body of apologetic literature is a continuation of the argument with polytheism which the Jewish Diaspora had begun in polemic and apologetic.[1]

In this section, however, we do not need to begin with a general portrayal of the basic character of apologetic Christianity and to draw into this the Christology. The interpretation of Christ peculiar to the apologists is so central to their total way of looking at things and so clearly characterizes this outlook that in this section we can begin at once with the main theme itself. The Christology of the apologists is summed up in the phrase: Christ, the Logos of God.

I. *The Logos Theology.* The concept of the Logos, which is set by the apologists in the central and dominant position, already has a prehistory in the pre-apologetic period. So far as we can see, it was the author of the Fourth Gospel who first introduced it into Christian usage. And the way

---

[1] On these connections, cf. Geffcken, *Zwei griechische Apologeten* (1907), pp. IX-XLIII.

in which he does it suggests at the outset the idea that he is taking up and repeating a term which was coined in the non-Christian, Hellenistic milieu. The word appears, then, to have played the role of a shibboleth, as it were, in the Johannine circles. The first "Epistle" of John is opened, in the form in which it is handed down to us, with the catchword λόγος τῆς ζωῆς. And the Apocalypse of John, which likewise must once have passed through the tradition of Johannine circles (even though in no way developed out of them), acquires the Johannine seal in 19:13: καὶ κέκληται τὸ ὄνομα αὐτοῦ ὁ λόγος τοῦ θεοῦ.[2] Bishop Ignatius is familiar with the term and speaks of the λόγος ἀπὸ σιγῆς προελθών, an expression which is of peculiar worth for the question as to the content of the concept.[3] Moreover, it is of great significance that the Kerygma Petri, which one can regard as a forerunner of the apologetic literature, according to the thrice-given testimony of Clement of Alexandria[4] calls the Kyrios (Jesus) Logos and Nomos, and offers this expression about God[5]: ὃς τὰ πάντα ἐποίησεν λόγῳ δυνάμεως αὐτοῦ (τῆς γνωστικῆς γραφῆς) τουτέστι τοῦ υἱοῦ.[6] Justin (Dial. 128) is already familiar with earlier, yet probably Christian, expositors of the Old Testament (particularly of Exod. 3:6), whose opinion he disputes. These already had a Logos theology: καὶ λόγον καλοῦσιν, ἐπειδὴ καὶ τὰς παρὰ τοῦ πατρὸς ὁμιλίας φέρει τοῖς ἀνθρώποις (p. 358 D). To be sure they understood this Logos—and it was just this point with which Justin was not in agreement—as a power inseparable from God, related to him as the sunlight is related to the sun: οὕτως ὁ πατὴρ ὅταν βούληται, λέγουσι, δύναμιν αὐτοῦ προπηδᾶν ποιεῖ καί, ὅταν βούληται, πάλιν ἀναστέλλει εἰς ἑαυτόν. Over against this, then, Justin emphatically represents his view, that the Logos is distinguished from the Father ἀριθμῷ.

Further, a look at the Gnostic speculations can help us in determining the age of the Logos doctrine, for on the whole the figure of the Logos re-

[2] Cf. also Acta Joh. 8: ὁ λόγος καὶ υἱὸς τοῦ θεοῦ τοῦ ζῶντος, ὅς ἐστιν Ἰησοῦς Χριστός. 94, 96 (δόξα σοι λόγε). 98 (ποτὲ μὲν λόγος καλεῖται, ποτὲ δὲ νοῦς; cf. Act. Petri 20), 101, 109.

[3] Magn. 8.2 (cf. Rom. 2.1, λόγος γενήσομαι θεοῦ); Smyrn. Proem (λόγος alongside πνεῦμα); also Eph. 3.1: Ἰησοῦς Χριστὸς τοῦ πατρὸς ἡ γνώμη (17.2).

[4] Strom. I, 29.182; II, 15.68; Ecl. proph. 58.

[5] Strom. VI, 5.39. Cf. further the application of the ἐν ἀρχῇ in Gen. 1:1 to the πρωτόγονος υἱός. Strom. VI, 7.58.

[6] The important identification of the Logos with the Son must belong to the Kerygma (cf. Stählin's edition, II, 451.12). τῆς γνωστικῆς γραφῆς is an incomprehensible addition; the conjecture τῇ γνωστικῇ γραφῇ (according to Gnostic interpretation of Scripture?) does not render it much more comprehensible.

mained foreign to the Gnostic systems.[7] But we do find this figure as the Syzygos of Zoë in the Ogdoad of the usual Valentinian (Ptolemaic) system. In the customary tradition these two occupy the third place (next after Pater and Aletheia) in the ogdoadic system. But this tradition is not uniform. According to other sources they exchange places with a pair of aeons otherwise occupying fourth place, Anthropos and Ecclesia. The suspicion cannot entirely be avoided that the pair Logos-Zoë first gained acceptance into the Gnostic speculation under specifically New Testament (Johannine) influence. In the earlier Gnostic speculation the Primal Man (ἄνθρωπος) stands immediately alongside the (unknown) Father.[8] Perhaps the specifically Valentinian figure of Sigē also sprang from the contrast with the Logos (cf. Ignatius' "λόγος ἀπὸ σιγῆς προελθών"), as then the Valentinian Bythos similarly is only a doubling of the (unknown) Father. Of course the master of the school, Valentinus himself, had been acquainted with the figure of the Logos. He is said to have seen in a vision a child who was announced to him as the Logos (Hipp. Ref. VI, 42). Moreover, the *Excerpta ex Theodoto* and Heracleon both know the figure.[9] The Gnostic Marcus, in a curious fashion which will further interest us later on, identifies the Logos with the archangel Gabriel.[10] Thus the entire Valentinian school, which of course also treasured its belonging to the Christian church, is acquainted with the Logos speculation. Outside this school, apart from some fragmentary notices,[11] we find the

[7] Cf. moreover the hymn to the Word, the Logos, which comes from the early period of Gnosticism, in Od. Sol. 12: "The Most High gave it (the Word) to his Aeons. And the Aeons spoke with one another through it" (cf. 16.8-9). 41.14-15: "The son of the Most High has appeared in the perfection of his Father, and a light has gone forth from the Logos which was always within him" (λόγος ἐνδιάθετος!).

[8] Cf. the speculations of the Gnostics which of course are already distorted, in Iren. I, 30. 1-2, the system of the Naassenes in Hippolytus, Ref. V, 7 (Father, Mother, and Anthropos), the Hermetic tractate Poimandres, in which the Logos also is an inserted figure.

[9] In some fragments of the Excerpta ex Theodoto, the Logos plays a more active role than elsewhere in the Valentinian system. He appears to be identical with the Christos or Soter; cf. 2.1; 21.2; 25.1. In the Valentinian (Italian) system in Hippolytus, Ref. VI, 35, p. 165.8 W, the Spirit which descends upon Jesus at the baptism is called ὁ Λόγος ὁ τῆς μητρὸς ἄνωθεν τῆς Σοφίας. On Heracleon, cf. Hilgenfeld, *Ketzergeschichte*, pp. 499, 501.

[10] Irenaeus I, 15.3. Following Luke 1:35, he then further identifies the Holy Spirit with Zoë, the δύναμις θεοῦ with the Anthropos, and the Ecclesia with Mary, and thus construes an incorporation of the holy tetrad in Jesus.

[11] Cf. e.g. the term υἱὸς λόγος ὄφις among the Peratae in Hippolytus, Ref. V, 17, p. 114.18 W, and the Sethians, *ibid.*, V, 19, p. 120.16 W: ὁ ἄνωθεν τοῦ φωτὸς τέλειος Λόγος. If in III, 11.1 Irenaeus has correctly reported and has not gotten something confused, Cerinthus also knew the Logos as the Son of Monogenes.

figure of the Logos only in the late and complicated system of Barbelo-Gnosticism which is found in the Coptic Apocryphon of John and in the excerpt in Irenaeus I, 29. Here are the four male aeons which emanate from the primal Father and Barbelo: Christ (Monogenes), Nous, Thelema, and Logos. "For Christ created all things through the Logos." [12]

Accordingly[13] the Logos idea gradually entered into Christianity after the turn of the century (i.e., *ca.* 100). It was not, however, a creation of Christianity itself, but entered from without.

The religio-historical position and the character of this concept may easily be established in general. Here we have to do with a speculation which belongs to hypostasis theology. It must clearly be stated with utter definiteness that such concepts belong to philosophy as little as they belong to naïve popular belief. These concepts that move back and forth between person and quality are to be attributed to the theological or theosophical speculation which mediates between concrete and abstract, between popular belief and rational reflection. They are religio-historically of great importance. They first of all occur everywhere the monotheistic idea struggles free from the older polytheism, and where the monotheistic tendency volatilizes originally concrete figures of deities into abstract figures which are half person and half qualities of God.[14] The classic and at the same time perhaps the earliest example is found in the speculation of the Persian Gathas concerning the Ameshas-Spentas, in which, e.g., the old shepherd-god Vohumano becomes the εὔνοια of God (Ahura-Mazda), and the earth-goddess Spent-Armaiti becomes σοφία.[15] Moreover, the reinterpretations, later to be discussed, of Greek (and foreign) gods in Stoic allegory and in the popular theosophical speculation dependent on the Stoa, which flourished particularly on Egyptian soil, are an especially good example of such hypostasis theology. Later Judaism adopted an abundance of such

---

[12] C. Schmidt in *Philotesia Kleinert,* 1907, p. 324.

[13] Cf. some later extra-apologetic testimonies in Acta Thom. 26 (σφραγὶς τοῦ λόγου), 80 (λόγε σοφέ, ὁ ἐπουράνιος λόγος τοῦ πατρός); the unusual speculations in Mart. Petri. 9 on the λόγος τετάμενος, λόγος꞊ἦχος. Mart. Petri a Lino 14 (Bonnet 17.26), Christus . . . *qui est constitutus nobis sermo unus et solus.* In the literarily reworked martyr acts of Apollonius and Pionius, whose speeches have the character of apologetic discourses, naturally the figure of the Logos is also found: Apollon. 5.35 (here curiously in the mouth of the procurator; see below); Pionius IV, 24, VIII, 3.

[14] Naturally it is not to be denied that often the reverse process is also demonstrable: personification of an abstract attribute of the deity.

[15] Cf. the Greek interpretations of the name; Plutarch, de Iside et Osir. 47.

speculations, partly in the attempt to cling to naïve popular conceptions—both native and alien immigrant ones—insofar as they could be related to pure monotheism, partly in order to find in this middle term a means of satisfying the ever intensifying demand for a transcendent, purely spiritual interpretation of God.[16] Thus were figures like the Spirit, the Wisdom, the Shekinah, and the Word (Memra) of God created. The Alexandrian Philo, whose speculations especially belong in this context, is by no means a singular phenomenon in the development of the Jewish spirit.

Within the thought-world of early Christianity, the hypostasis theology in clearly defined form and in a dominant role occurs first, strictly speaking, in the Logos idea. The speculations about the Spirit were of a more incidental nature. In Paul they grew out of the popular view of the Spirit. The apologists retained these speculations concerning the Spirit, which soon became common Christian property, alongside their Logos doctrine as appropriated property. But they know little or nothing to do with it. Where they refer to the Spirit, they clearly do so in a simple taking-over of formulas which were earlier coined in the community's faith.[17] Where we encounter detailed speculations, they are often marked by hopeless confusion.[18] Then again, often Logos and Pneuma are simply identified.[19] But above all, for the apologists, and especially for Justin, the Spirit is still always τὸ προφητικὸν πνεῦμα, τὸ ἅγιον προφητικὸν πνεῦμα.[20] Furthermore, the Spirit was for them a living entity insofar as he stood behind the Old Testament canon and distinctly spoke to them in every Christian worship service in which the Scripture was read.

Actual Christian speculation begins with the Logos idea. Indeed, this at first appears of itself to introduce an objection to the above-discussed principle that such formations of concepts do not belong to philosophical re-

---

[16] Cf. my *Religion des Judentums*, 2nd ed., pp. 394-409.

[17] Cf. Harnack, *Dogmengeschichte*, 4th ed., I, 532; Loofs, *Dogmengeschichte*, 4th ed., pp. 125-26. Justin, Apol. I, 5-6, Athenagoras 10, Tatian 12-13.

[18] Theophilus, To Autolycus II, 10 ff. Theophilus identifies the Spirit with Wisdom (cf. the explicit mention of the "triad" God, Logos, Wisdom, II, 15, 94 D). This further heightens the confusion.

[19] Cf. the curious opinion of Justin that Jesus was conceived by the Logos (=πνεῦμα and δύναμις, Luke 1). Apol. I, 33.6; 32.9; 46.5. Identification of Logos and Pneuma also in Irenaeus; cf. Loofs, p. 141, notes 1 and 2. Valentinians in Hippolytus, Ref. VI, 35, p. 164.24 W.

[20] Justin, Apol. I, 6.2 (πνεῦμά τε τὸ προφητικὸν σεβόμεθα); 13.3; 32.2; 35.3; 39.1; 40.1; 44.1; 51.1; 53.4; 59.1. Even in the baptismal formula in I, 61.13 the prophetic Spirit is the subject. Dial. 7, etc. Athenagoras 10, p. 11.16 Schw.: τὸ ἐνεργοῦν τοῖς ἐκφωνοῦσιν προφητικῶς ἅγιον πνεῦμα. Theophilus, To Autolycus I, 14. Cf. also Celsus in Origen, III, 1, VII, 45.

flection and are not to be explained from that perspective. For at first glance the Logos appears altogether to stem from Stoic philosophy. The Stoa is dominated by this idea of the world-governing divine reason. For it the Logos is the bond which embraces all things, which holds together and supports individual things,[21] the might which again (as λόγος τομεύς) bestows upon each thing its individuality, its definiteness, and its place, the power which separates and again unites, which shapes the world into a cosmos, on the one hand a spiritual principle, providence and Heimarmene, on the other hand the natural element which pervades all things (πνεῦμα πυρῶδες),[22] finally, as ὀρθὸς λόγος, the moral law which also determines the human spirit and points out to it its ways. In inspired words Cleanthes already celebrates Zeus as the divine Logos who governs the world, as the world-determining Nomos.

But it never occurred to actual Stoic philosophers to affirm the Logos as a second figure beside the deity or even to set the Logos, as a power mediating the creation, between God and the world. *According to the Stoics' monistic world view, God, world, and Logos in essence always coincide.*

Accordingly, when we first encounter in Philo—to be sure, within the environment of numerous other hypostatized divine powers—such a figure of the Logos separated from the highest deity, who in a peculiar way occupies a mediating role between God and the world, this phenomenon confronts us with a problem not easily solved. One cannot be satisfied with conceiving of Philo as a new variety of a platonizing Stoicism, but must see that here a μετάβασις εἰς ἄλλο γένος has occurred, that here we have left the actual soil of Greek philosophy.[23]

On the other hand, it cannot be overlooked that in his individual concrete statements Philo again and again refers to the contemporary Hellenic-idealistic philosophy, in particular the platonizing Stoicism of a Poseidonius. We shall therefore have to pose the question of the subsidiary influences which lie between Philo and his models and which have been made so vividly noticeable.

[21] When Theophilus (To Autolycus I, 5, p. 72 C) writes οὕτως ἡ πᾶσα κτίσις περιέχεται ὑπὸ πνεύματος θεοῦ, the Pneuma here stands somewhat in the place of the Logos.
[22] τὸ δι᾽ ὅλου κεχωρηκὸς πνεῦμα, Theophilus, To Autolycus II, 4, p. 82 B.
[23] It is in particular the merit of Emil Bréhier clearly to have recognized and expressed this in his splendid work, *Les idées philosophiques et religieuses de Philon d'Alexandrie* (1908). Cf. the section on the Logos, pp. 83-111. Also Norden, in his *Agnostos Theos* (pp. 85-87), readily and correctly emphasizes the non-Hellenic, Oriental (but not purely Old Testament-Jewish) character of Philo's speculations.

What distinguishes the Philonic Logos idea is not a special nuance of philosophical doctrinal opinion; it is apparently first of all the inescapable mythological character of his speculation. Philo's Logos is through and through a mythological figure.

We can also still determine what concrete figures of gods stand behind these more or less mythological speculations and constructions. It is first of all the Greek god Hermes, and together with him, his Egyptian double, Thoth. Already in a relatively early time the Stoic spiritualizing and etymologizing allegorical method had discovered all sorts of ideas in the figure of this god, ideas which in the soil of the truly philosophical Stoa remained a mere juggling act with concepts, but then when transplanted to a different soil, came to be taken seriously and took on a religious meaning. The best and most detailed testimony for this occurs in the Ἑλληνικὴ θεολογία of Cornutus (in the first half of the first Christian century), in which one detects in considerable measure a residue from statements of Chrysippus.[24]

Here[25] Hermes is called the *Logos* whom the gods have sent from heaven to men because they have made him alone, above all being, λογικός. He is therefore the leader whom they have placed in association with men. He is the herald of the gods (κῆρυξ), because he communicates to men what comes from the gods, because he brings to the hearing through the voice what is signified according to the Logos (τὰ κατὰ τὸν λόγον σημαινόμενα). He is messenger (ἄγγελος), since we recognize the will of the gods out of the insights (ἐννοιῶν) given to us according to the Logos. His name is connected with the fact that the Logos is our defense (ἔρυμα) and our fortress (ὀχύρωμα) (p. 20.22). The goddess Hygieia is associated with him, for the Logos is present, not for doing evil and injury, but for healing (σώζειν).[26] He is the leader of the graces. His father is Zeus, his mother Maia, for the Logos is the offspring of vision (θεωρία) and meditation (ζήτησις).[27]

[24] Bréhier, *Les idées* . . . , p. 109.

[25] Cf. 16, pp. 20-21.

[26] This is remarkably reminiscent of passages in the Gospel of John, where it is emphasized that Jesus has come not to judge but to save. John 3:17, *et al.*

[27] In chap. 3, Zeus is interpreted to mean the ψυχή which holds the κόσμος together, and thus this has to do with (astronomical) θεωρία. Maia is interpreted as ζήτησις. There is much speculation about the birth of Hermes from Zeus and Maia. Important also is the passage in Lydus, de mensibus IV, 76, p. 129. 9 Wünsch: νοῦν μὲν εἶναι τὸν Δία, Μαῖαν δὲ τὴν φρόνησιν, παῖδα δὲ ἐξ ἀμφοῖν Ἑρμῆν λόγιον. Immediately before this

Thus again and again Hermes is the Logos, and in fact here the Logos in the double meaning of the inner perception and the word which expresses the thought comes into view. The perspective alternates between the two interpretations. But the interpretation of Hermes as the herald and the messenger of the gods is especially significant. Already here there appears the view of the Logos as the word of revelation which mediates the intercourse between gods and men.

We can definitely trace such allegorical views back into the first century B.C. (and on Greek soil beyond that point) by means of a comparison with Varro's statements about Mercury which Augustine (de civitate Dei VII, 14) has preserved.[28] Here the allegory even more clearly arises from the meaning of Logos-Word. Mercury is *sermo,* and like Hermes is related to ἑρμηνεία.[29] Hence Hermes as the Word establishes commerce among men, his wings indicate the swift word, he is called *nuntius,* because through the word the thought is made known. But Varro appears to have connected Hermes not only to the word of men with one another, but also to the revealing word of God. Augustine continues: *Mercurius, si sermonis etiam deorum potestatem gerit, ipsi quoque regi deorum dominatur, si secundum eius arbitrium Jupiter loquitur aut loquendi ab illo accepit facultatem; quod utique absurdum est.*[30]

This interpretation of Hermes as the (revelatory) Word (of the deity) then was later established and became widely known. Plutarch[31] interprets Hermes, who exhibits the true lineage of Horos as contrasted with the accusations of Typhon, by saying that Hermes ὁ λόγος μαρτυρῶν is καὶ δεικνύων. At another place he brings Hermes together with the graces,[32] ὡς μάλιστα τοῦ λόγου τὸ κεχαρισμένον καὶ προσφιλὲς ἀπαιτοῦντος.

---

(p. 128.11), Lydus notes a view of Akylinos (it is well known that Porphyry mentions a Gnostic Ἀκυλῖνος: vit. Plot. 16): ἡ Μαῖα ἀντὶ τῆς εἰς τοὔμφανὲς προόδου ἐστί, κυρίως μὲν τοῦ λόγου τοῦ διὰ πάντων πεφυκότος διατακτικοῦ τῶν ὄντων· διὸ δὴ καὶ Ἑρμοῦ μητέρα φασί (cf. Reitzenstein, *Poimandres,* pp. 43, 44.1). To be compared also is Macrobius, Somn. Scip. I, 14, "*Hic* (the most high God) *superabundanti majestatis fecunditate de se mentem creavit.*"

[28] Cf. Reitzenstein, *Zwei religionsgeschichtliche Fragen,* p. 81. I am indebted to Reitzenstein also for the material for the following in several respects.

[29] Plato (Cratylus 23, p. 407 E) already easily proposes the interpretation: ἔοικε περὶ λόγον τι εἶναι ὁ Ἑρμῆς καὶ τὸ ἑρμηνέα εἶναι καὶ τὸ ἄγγελον καὶ τὸ κλοπικόν τε. . . . περὶ λόγου δύναμίν ἐστιν πᾶσα αὕτη ἡ πραγματεία. In the following, Pan-Logos the son or brother of Hermes.

[30] Cf. Reitzenstein, *Zwei religionsgeschichtliche Fragen,* p. 81.1.

[31] De Is. et Osir. 54, p. 375 B.

[32] περὶ τοῦ ἀκούειν, 13, p. 44 E; cf. the above-quoted (p. 391) statements of Cornutus 16 and 20.15.

But of special importance here is the testimony of Justin,[33] who is still conscious of these religio-historical connections to a certain degree. For the Logos speculations of the Christians, he appeals to the Greek speculations about Hermes. And the Greeks on their part call Hermes the λόγον ἑρμηνευτικὸν καὶ πάντων διδάσκαλος or the λόγον τὸν παρὰ θεοῦ ἀγγελτικόν, just as Christ is Logos and "teacher" for the Christians.[34]

Here already, with the interpretation of Hermes as the revelatory word of the gods, the speculation about Hermes begins to take a religious turn, through which it is gradually removed far from its origin in philosophical fancy and etymological play and becomes religiously influential and significant.

This turn of affairs shows up still more clearly when now the significance of Hermes as the revelatory word is expanded in a curious fashion to that of the world-creating word of the deity. That this expansion took place is plain to see. In Philo, the Logos is first of all the power through which God frames the world. But the same turn in the speculation also occurs on the basis of purely Hellenistic (not affected by Judaism or Christianity) speculation. Thus in the Naassene doctrine, which probably was originally pagan, it is said:[35] Hermes is the Logos, (ὃς) ἑρμηνεὺς ὢν καὶ δημιουργὸς τῶν γεγονότων ὁμοῦ καὶ γινομένων καὶ ἐσομένων. And Porphyry likewise knows it [36]: τοῦ δὲ λόγου τῶν πάντων ποιητικοῦ τε καὶ ἑρμηνευτικοῦ ὁ Ἑρμῆς παραστατικός.[37]

[33] Apol. I, 21.2, 22.2. To be compared here also is the fact that in the Orphic Hymns (XXVIII), Hermas is characterized as Διὸς ἄγγελε (V, 1), λόγου θνητοῖσιν προφήτα (V, 4), and then as γλώσσης δεινὸν ὅπλον (V, 10). Cf. further Pseudo-Clem. Rec. X, 41: *Mercuriam verbum esse tradunt, per quod sensui doctrina confertur.*

[34] When Justin speaks (Dial. 128, p. 358 A) of opponents who speak of the "Logos," ἐπειδὴ καὶ τὰς παρὰ τοῦ πατρὸς ὁμιλίας φέρει τοῖς ἀνθρώποις, this is immediately reminiscent of the Hermetic speculations. Finally, to this category also belongs Acts 14:12. Paul is venerated alongside Zeus as mighty in word, as Hermes (the revealing messenger of the gods).

[35] Hippolytus, Ref. V, 7.29, p. 85.19 W. Cf. further Plutarch, de Is. et Osir. 62, the application of the Horos (with the legs grown together, which Isis alone can separate) to the Logos: ὅτι καθ᾽ ἑαυτὸν ὁ τοῦ θεοῦ νοῦς καὶ λόγος ἐν τῷ ἀοράτῳ καὶ ἀφανεῖ βεβηκὼς εἰς γένεσιν ὑπὸ κινήσεως προῆλθεν.

[36] Eusebius, Praep. Evang. III, 11, p. 114 C.

[37] These passages also have in common the fact that they interpret the distinguishing mark of Hermes, τὸ (ἐντεταμένον) αἰδοῖον as a symbol of his creative power. Porphyry, vit. Plot. 16: ὁ δὲ ἐντεταμένος Ἑρμῆς δηλοῖ τὴν εὐτονίαν, δείκνυσι δὲ καὶ τὸν σπερματικὸν λόγον τὸν διήκοντα διὰ πάντων. Similarly the Naassene teaching (cf. Hippolytus, Ref. V, 7). More material in Reitzenstein, p. 96; cf. also above all Cornutus 16. Here one does not see altogether clearly whether an allegorical interpretation of the figure of Hermes was the first occasion of interpreting the god as the world-creating Word, or whether conversely, after this interpretation had once emerged, the αἰδοῖον was equated

How might Hermes have come to this significance of the world creator or of the world-creating word? It is fair to suspect that behind this turning point there is the combination of the Greek divine figure with that of the Egyptian Thoth. This combination took place early. The cultic center of Thoth is called Hermopolis in the Greek tradition. The first certain documentation of this identification is brought to us by Hecataeus, from whom Diodorus I, 15-16 has preserved for us the detailed Egyptian-Greek myth of Hermes. Plutarch or his sources (Apion?) in *de Iside et Osiride* presupposed this equation as taken for granted. In the lists of the gods handed down in Cicero *nat. deor.* III, 56, two Egyptian figures of Hermes are specified as the fourth and fifth Hermes.[38]

Thoth is the moon-god, then the ancient Egyptian god of writing,[39] the inventor of the symbols of writing, of language, the bearer of all culture and all knowledge. As the lord of writing and of the word, he is also the great and powerful god of magic. He stands—and this facilitated his identification with Hermes—in the closest connection with the realm of the dead, is the lord patron of the dead, and plays a special role in the judgment of the dead. His sacred bird is the ibis, and thus the ibis becomes the symbol for "heart." For the heart is the seat of the understanding and of the will which is guided by the understanding. Thus in Horapollon I, 36, in a passage in which the identification of Hermes with Thoth occurs, it is said: καρδίαν βουλόμενοι γράφειν ἶβιν ζωογραφοῦσιν. τὸ γὰρ ζῷον Ἑρμῇ ᾠκείωται πάσης καρδίας[40] καὶ λογισμοῦ δεσπότῃ. In the cosmogony of the Leiden Papyrus W,[41] Hermes appears as the Nous (ἢ φρένες) καρδίαν ἔχων. And this Egyptian Hermes-Thoth now, in a peculiar manner, is subordinated to[42] or amalgamated with a higher god, usually (the sun-god) Ra, and thus appears in a peculiar way as the heart of Ra, the word of Ra, or even, as in the temple inscription of Dendera[43] from the time of the emperor Nero, as "heart of Ra, tongue of Tum, throat of the god whose name is hidden."[44] Thus, as a subordinate god of a

---

with the λόγος σπερματικός. The latter is the more likely. Cf. moreover the expression, τεταμένος λόγος in Mart. Petr. 9 (Bonnet I, 96.7).

[38] More detailed material in Reitzenstein, pp. 87-92.

[39] Cf. Erman, *Die ägypt. Religion* (1905), pp. 11 and 104.

[40] In this milieu, καρδία and λόγος have the same significance.

[41] Dieterich, *Abraxas*, p. 8.9.

[42] Cf. Reitzenstein, pp. 72-73.

[43] Brugsch, *Religion der Ägypter*, pp. 50 ff.

[44] This unique way of overcoming original polytheism in favor of a monotheism or a pantheistic monism could be regarded as an earlier and naïve-popular form of the

higher god, Thoth is then also creator of the world. On the inscription of the temple of Dendera it is said: "Revelation of the god of light, Ra, existent from the very first, Thoth, who rests upon the truth; whatever springs from his heart happens at once, and whatever he has spoken, that is eternally."

With this figure of Thoth, that of Hermes, in many respects related, is merged. But when the Greek spirit came over these strange materialistic speculations about a god who is heart and tongue (word) of another, then this conception had to be spiritualized into the conception which was already familiar to that spirit from Stoic philosophy. So now Hermes-Thoth becomes the inner thought as well as the revelatory word of the most high god, but in both senses the Logos.

In a remarkable way a statement of Aelian (probably following Apion) combines these conceptions of Egyptian provenance with the later Stoic doctrine of the λόγος ἐνδιάθετος and προφορικός. Accordingly the sacred bird of Hermes-Thoth is the ibis, ἐπεὶ ἔοικε τὸ εἶδος τῇ φύσει τοῦ λόγου. The black feathers of the bird correspond τῷ τε σιγωμένῳ καὶ ἔνδον ἐπιστρεφομένῳ λόγῳ, and on the other hand the white ones τῷ προφερομένῳ τε καὶ ἀκουομένῳ ἤδη καὶ ὑπηρέτῃ τοῦ ἔνδον καὶ ἀγγέλῳ ὡς ἂν εἴποις.[45]

Thus we may assume that in consequence of the identification of Hermes with Thoth, the conception of the world-creating word is also transferred to him.[46]

However, in order to understand this transition, we must here bring in for explanation a still broader conception which particularly stems from the cultus. In this entire development the conception of the significance

---

hypostasis theology. The subordinate gods become members of the most high God. That peculiar speculation is already present in an eighth-century inscription in the British Museum which Breasted has deciphered (*Zeitschrift für ägyptische Sprache* [1901], pp. 39 ff.). Here Ptah first appears as heart and tongue of the most high God; then in the following this position is assigned to Horos (heart) and Thoth (tongue), who appear with Ptah once again in mystical union. Reitzenstein, *Poimandres*, pp. 59, 62 ff.

[45] Aelian, Hist. An. X, 29. Reitzenstein, p. 72. Among the Christian apologists, Theophilus (To Autolycus II, 10, p. 88 B) expressly took over the conception of the λόγος ἐνδιάθετος.

[46] In the Strassburg Cosmogony published by Reitzenstein (*Zwei religionsgeschichtliche Fragen*, p. 56) Hermes, here thought of as the father of the Logos (Pan?), emerged as the creator of the world. In the cosmogony of the Papyrus Leiden W, Hermes (Νοῦς Φρένες) is characterized thus: καὶ ἐκλήθη Ἑρμῆς, δι᾽ οὗ τὰ πάντα μεθερμηνεύεται. ἔστιν δὲ ἐπὶ τῶν φρενῶν, δι᾽ οὗ οἰκονομήθη τὸ πᾶν (cf. Dieterich, *Abraxas*, p. 8). In the cosmogony of the Κόρη Κόσμου (Stobaeus, Ecl. I, 928 ff.) he plays a prominent role alongside the most high God. Also the first Tractate of the Hermetic Corpus (Poimandres) belongs here in part (see below).

and power of the *cultic word* must also have been influential from the out-set.[47] The secret religions of that time had their sacred Logos which was communicated to the initiate in a ceremonial manner at his initiation. But this Logos has a quite special, consecrating, life-preserving and life-creating power. Primitive conceptions of the magical power and significance of the word, which were still alive and which, though standing one level lower and developing in a belief in magic, yet were related in various manners with the belief of the mystery religions, also had their effect here. This conception of the power of the "word" was heightened to the same degree that in the gradual spiritualizing of the mysteries the really barbaric cultic practices and sacramental initiations declined. Therewith the word became everything,[48] the sacred text handed down from father to son,[49] from the mystagogues to the initiate, the reciting, hearing, or reading of which alone was already regarded as effectual. Thus the sacred word of revelation be-comes a divine, personified potency, whose effectiveness is thought of some-times purely in terms of magic and sorcery, other times more mystically. We have already (pp. 228-30) presented evidence to show how the view of the Fourth Gospel concerning the wonder-working Logos stands in this con-text. Here it may be especially pointed out how precisely this writing offers us a splendid example of how easily the secrecy-filled mysterious word could be personified. In John 12:48 he appears as judge of unbelieving men.

If, however, the word as a cultic-magical entity thus becomes a power effective in itself and endowed with energies, then it was to become of special significance that this concept of the revelational word could be combined with a half-concrete, half-idealized divine figure. And again, it now becomes all the more clear from this perspective how the ideas of the revealing word of the deity and the all-powerful word of creation could be connected. It is the same magical power of the word which is shown in the cultus and is effective in the emergence of the worlds. In the latter case, as in the former, the same personified power of God is effective. Ac-cording to the Egyptian conception, Thoth is the god of all magic; he has revealed the cultus with its secrets, with his all-powerful word he creates the world.

[47] It is the merit of Bréhier, *Philon*, pp. 101 ff., that he has called attention to this connection in the clarification of the Philonic concept of the Logos.

[48] On this development, cf. Reitzenstein, *Hellenistische Mysterienreligionen*, p. 24 [2nd ed., p. 24] (91 [102], 155 [179]); esp. also his statements about the expressions λογικὴ λατρεία, λογικὴ θυσία.

[49] Dieterich, *Abraxas*, pp. 162-63, *Mithras-Liturgie*, pp. 52, 146 ff.; Norden, *Agnostos Theos*, p. 290.

We have been able to follow step by step how that which began with allegoristic etymological play could finally acquire a serious religious and cultic significance. Or it is more correct to say: two different worlds, independent of each other, meet here. Stoic allegorical method and perverted etymological cunning meet a world of seriously minded religious speculations. And this latter now takes the former into its service, takes those conceptions at face value, gives to them real religious content, while on its own part, through the absorption of philosophical theorems this world undergoes an ever-increasing spiritualizing and a turning away from the original popular realism.

Two great and, for the religio-historical development, extraordinarily important phenomena stand even before the apologists on the basis of this unusual mixture of Hellenistic philosophy and Oriental mystical speculation. These are first the Hermetic literature and second the Jewish "philosopher" Philo.

The discussion of the Hermetic literature here can only be brief, first-because Reitzenstein in his so meritorious studies (*Zwei religionsgeschichtliche Fragen, Poimandres, Hellenistische Mysterienreligionen*) has already treated it in a manner which is completely adequate for our purposes. Another reason is that in this literary circle the *figure* of the Logos plays no prominent role. The *matter* to be sure is present here also. Hermes-Thoth, who here appears in a special way as the older God alongside "Tat," is spiritualized in these writings into the Nous. But the Nous has also become a quite specific supernatural figure, the revealer of hidden divine secrets, the teacher and the friend, the guide and the shepherd of the human soul, the supernatural redeeming power, who frees the soul from its lower world and bestows upon it the divine vision and eternal life, the judge and punisher of the wicked and insolent, a religious figure about whom the faith of pious communities is gathered. If the *Logos* idea here recedes, it is because we have here a mysticism heightened through piety which places the divine vision above revelation in the Word and intentionally devalues the latter.[50] Only a later editing appears to have brought into the cosmogony of the funda-

[50] It is the merit of Zielinski to have called attention to this connection in his essay on the Corpus Hermeticum (*Archiv für Religionswissenschaft,* VIII and IX). Cf. in I, 30 along with the praise of σιωπή the expression ἡ τοῦ λόγου ἐκφορά (this is the correct reading, following Zielinski, instead of ἐκφορά) γεννήματα ἀγαθῶν. IV, 3 (distinction in worth of Logos and Nous). IX, 10, ὁ γὰρ λόγος οὐ (instead of μου with Zielinski) φθάνει μεχρὶ τῆς ἀληθείας. XV, 16, καὶ ὁ λόγος, οὐκ ἔρως, ἔστιν ὁ πλανώμενος καὶ πλανῶν. Moreover, a similar opinion is to be found in Philo. Again and again Philo separates the Logos from the Nous in man and places the Logos one level below the

mental first Hermetic tractate the figure of the Logos, which now appears in an uncertain position alongside the Nous.

For the Philonic Logos doctrine the evidence of its connection with the Hellenic-Egyptian mythology and of the currency of the Logos in the pagan mystery religion is produced in a decisive and convincing fashion. Here I can content myself with referring to the most important points. Behind the figure of the Philonic Logos there stands, in all probability, the god Hermes.

It is Bréhier's merit[51] to have pointed to a number of noteworthy points of contact between Philo's Logos speculations and the allegorizing of Cornutus. In Philo also the Logos is the ἄγγελος[52] whom the Deity sends to the human soul,[53] he is the κῆρυξ who proclaims peace after the war,[54] he is the "psychopomp" who guides the soul of man (ascetics).[55] As Hermes is related to Hygieia, thus also Philo speaks of the ὑγιὴς λόγος.[56] As Hermes is the leader of the graces, so God is said to send down upon the Logos his virgin graces.[57] And even those plays on words with the name of Hermes found in Cornutus (=ἔρυμα ὀχύρωμα) recur when Philo asserts: ὡς γὰρ τῶν ἄλλων ἕκαστον ζῴων ἡ φύσις οἰκείοις ἕρκεσιν ὠχύρωσε, . . . καὶ ἀνθρώπῳ μέγιστον ἔρυμα καὶ φρουρὰν ἀκαθαίρετον λόγον δέδωκεν.[58]

The mythological element in Philo's conception comes out especially strongly when he proffers the opinion that the Logos, as the image of which he regards the Old Testament high priest (οὐκ ἄνθρωπον ἀλλὰ θεῖον λόγον), comes from a pair of divine parents: διότι οἶμαι γονέων ἀφθάρτων καὶ καθαρωτάτων ἔλαχεν, πατρὸς μὲν θεοῦ, ὃς καὶ τῶν συμπάντων ἐστὶ πατήρ, μητρὸς δὲ σοφίας, δι' ἧς τὰ ὅλα ἦλθεν εἰς γένεσιν.[59] We recall the

---

Nous. His highest goal is also the holy silence. Hence the communion of the soul with the Logos is only a preliminary to its communion with God which, if it is possible at all, takes place in the holy stillness of complete absorption. The documentation is to be found in Bréhier, pp. 101 ff. To this category also belongs the stressing of silence in Ignatius, Eph. 6, 19, Magn. 8: λόγος ἀπὸ σιγῆς προελθών; the figure of Sige among the Valentinians. Cf. Mart. Petri 10 (Bonnet, 96.17).

[51] *Philon*, p. 107.

[52] De Cherub. 35-36.

[53] De Somn. I, 69, 103.

[54] Quaest. in Exod. II, 118: *ut quippe colligaret et commisceret . . . universorum partes et contrarietates . . . ad concordiam, unionem osculumque pacis cogens conduceret.*

[55] De sacr. Ab. et Ca. 8.

[56] Leg. Alleg. III, 150 (τὸν ὑγιῆ καὶ ἡγεμόνα λόγον).

[57] De post. Ca. 32, ὄντος τοῦ πλουτοδότου θεοῦ τὰς παρθένους καὶ ἀθανάτους Χάριτας αὐτοῦ. Cf. the passage in Plutarch, περὶ ἀκούειν 13 (see above, p. 392, n. 32).

[58] De Somn. I, 103.

[59] De fuga et invent. 109. Cf. therewith Theophilus, To Autolycus II, 10: ἔχων οὖν ὁ θεὸς τὸν ἑαυτοῦ λόγον ἐνδιάθετον ἐν τοῖς ἰδίοις σπλάγχνοις ἐγέννησεν αὐτὸν μετὰ τῆς ἑαυτοῦ σοφίας ἐξερευξάμενος πρὸ τῶν ὅλων.

analogous speculations in Cornutus and Lydus (Aquilinus), and also Macrobius (*vide supra*, p. 391, n. 27) on Hermes as the son of Zeus and Maia. In fact, still other examples for Philo out of Egyptian mythology could come into consideration here. In particular, the allegorical fantasies which Plutarch offers in *de Is. et Os.* 53-54 appear to be closely related. According to this account, Isis is τὸ τῆς φύσεως θῆλυ καὶ δεκτικὸν ἁπάσης γενέσεως (cf. matter as ὑποδοχή and εἶδος πανδεχές in the speculation of Plato)[60]; Osiris is the Logos; the rending of his body is the entering of the Logos into matter; the son of the two, Horos, is this world of the senses which, however, is only an impure copy of the κόσμος νοητός. Therefore the latter is accused by Typhon, the principle of evil (of evil matter), of inauthenticity, and is defended and vindicated by the Logos Thoth. In this context, of course, the son of the celestial parents is not the Logos but the Cosmos.[61] The two, however, do belong very closely together. Indeed, Philo himself also expresses the idea that ἐπιστήμη (Wisdom) has conceived the world by God the Father: ἡ δὲ παραδεξαμένη τὰ τοῦ θεοῦ σπέρματα τελεσφόροις ὠδῖσι τὸν μόνον καὶ ἀγαπητὸν αἰσθητὸν υἱὸν ἀπεκύησε, τόνδε τὸν κόσμον.[62] And in another place he speaks of the world as the younger, the Logos as the elder, son of God.[63]

Thus the Philonic statements about the Logos appear to be immediately affected by Hermetic speculations and Egyptian mythology and from this perspective they find, in part, their explanation.

II. *Appropriation of the Logos Idea.* The Logos theology is multicolored tapestry in which both warp and woof are made up of quite variegated threads. A great many hands had a part in the weaving of it: Greek-Stoic philosophy and allegorical interpretation of myths, but also living piety and Oriental mysticism, veneration of Hermes and Egyptian religion. Out of the Logos a very complicated entity has developed: He is no longer the world-dominating reason, identical on the one side with God and on the other side with the world; he has become the δεύτερος θεός, the Word which mediates between men and Deity, the bearer of all the mysterious revelation of God, the world-creating power, the mediator between God and the world.

---

[60] Timaeus 18, p. 51 A.

[61] In the first Hermetic tractate (Poimandres), § 8 says that the world has emerged ἐκ Βουλῆς θεοῦ ἥτις λαβοῦσα τὸν Λόγον καὶ ἰδοῦσα τὸν καλὸν κόσμον ἐμιμήσατο.

[62] De ebr. 30.

[63] Quod deus sit immutabilis 31. Reitzenstein, *Poimandres*, p. 41, and Bréhier, p. 110, suspect that the prototype of this speculation is the Egyptian myth of the elder and younger Horos.

Christianity then took over this complex concept just as it was, adding nothing at all of its own to the concept, but taking only the one further step: It applied it in its richness and its great diversity to the person of Jesus Christ. The Christians laid their hands on this structure of thought of Hellenistic origin and announced: *all this is our property*. What Greek philosophy and Oriental mystery, belief in Hermes and worship of Thoth had dimly intimated has here become truth; the power which joins and unites God and humanity has appeared in Jesus of Nazareth! Thus did the author of the Fourth Gospel put it. It is no new theory of the Logos that he proclaims; he refers to a conception which is well known to all the world. He says only the one tremendous new thing: "The Word became flesh and we beheld his glory." And in similar fashion the author of the Kerygma Petri evidently connected the υἱὸς τοῦ θεοῦ with the Logos idea (*vide supra*, p. 385). Justin's statements about Hermes (*vide supra*, p. 393)[64] show that people were not yet fully aware of the connections of this concept with Hellenistic speculations. In confrontation with the Christians, Celsus concedes, or has his Jews acknowledge, that the Logos is indeed the Son of God.[65] The Acts of Apollonius (35) have the examining magistrate say: ἴσμεν καὶ ἡμεῖς, ὅτι ὁ λόγος τοῦ θεοῦ γενήτωρ καὶ ψυχῆς καὶ σώματός ἐστιν τῶν δικαίων, ὁ λογώσας καὶ διδάξας ὡς φίλον ἐστὶν τῷ θεῷ.

Not that the apologists first were interested in cosmological questions and solved the problem of the relationship between the transcendent God and the material world through the assumption of a mediatorial and world-creating nature of the Logos, only then to transfer this Logos idea to Jesus Christ. Against this interpretation there stands the one observation that they practically never gave a definition of the Logos idea and a precise and explicit exposition of the Logos doctrine.[66] No, they simply took over those elements of Logos speculations which they found already present in their environment. For this reason it is also a relatively unfruitful effort to seek to establish the peculiarities in the Logos doctrine of an individual apologist: strictly speaking, none of them possessed his own Logos doctrine.

But they took over the concept in order, through it, in apologetic battle with an environment which was more and more inclined to philosophical

---

[64] Cf. according to Clement, Strom. VI, 15.132: Ἑρμῇ, ὃν δὴ λόγον εἶναί φασι διὰ τὴν ἑρμηνείαν, καθιεροῦσι τῆς ῥοίας τὸν καρπόν. πολυκευδὴς γὰρ ὁ λόγος.

[65] Origen, contra Celsum II, 31. Celsus also is familiar with the principle that the κόσμος is the Son of God; *ibid.*, VI, 47.

[66] Tatian 5 and Theophilus II, 10 ff. may serve as possible exceptions. But how confused are the statements of the latter especially!

monotheism, to defend and justify the fact that the Christians rendered divine honors to the Jesus of Nazareth who had appeared and had been crucified here below on earth. The apologists stand altogether on the basis of the community's faith and the community's cultus as regards this veneration of Jesus, and they too acknowledge it.[67] Even if only Justin—and he essentially in the Dialogue with Trypho—clearly expresses it, for all of them Jesus is the δεύτερος θεός (vide supra, pp. 323 ff.). And in the face of this state of things, they required a justification, even for their own consciences. For what they had to proclaim to the Hellenic world was just this, that polytheism is pernicious folly and monotheism is the only proper religion. Then was not the divine honor rendered to the crucified Jesus polytheism of the worst and most obvious kind? They thought to avoid the charge when they proclaimed that for Christians Jesus is the Logos of God. The Christians do not worship a man but the incarnate Logos, who belongs altogether to the very essence of deity. This worship is no folly but precisely a sign of the loftiest reason: ὅσα οὖν παρὰ πᾶσιν καλῶς εἴρηται, ἡμῶν τῶν Χριστιανῶν ἐστι· τὸν γὰρ ἀπὸ ἀγεννήτου καὶ ἀρρήτου θεοῦ λόγον μετὰ τὸν θεὸν προσκυνοῦμεν (Justin, Apol. II, 13.4).

Against this, one must not object that the apologists in their speculations stop with the idea of the pre-temporal Logos and do not further trouble themselves with the incarnation of the Logos and with the manner of the union with Jesus of Nazareth. This is true enough of some of the later apologists; but Justin, who indeed essentially inaugurates the whole tendency, must be excepted from this defense at the start, as must also Tertullian, the most powerful of them all, and even in Athenagoras the close connection between the Logos speculation and the worship of Jesus is plainly present. But even before Justin, John and the author of the Kerygma Petri appear as witnesses for the fact that the interest in the Logos depends first of all on the appreciation of the person of Jesus which is achieved thereby. Naturally then later on, after people had once accepted the Logos idea and had placed it in the apologetic arsenal, the cosmological and speculative interest clung to this concept and occasionally became so strong that it completely displaced the original,[68] and that it might appear that the apologists were

[67] Cf. Justin, Apol. I, 6 and the point on this passage noted above, p. 323, n. 312; similarly Athenagoras 10.

[68] Thus e.g. in Tatian we miss any statements about the Logos that appeared in Jesus. But at one point (21, p. 23.5 Schw.) in his work it does emerge where the real apologetic interest lay: οὐ γὰρ μωραίνομεν, ἄνδρες Ἕλληνες, οὐδὲ λήρους ἀπαγγέλλομεν, θεὸν ἐν ἀνθρώπου μορφῇ γεγονέναι καταγγέλλοντες. Then of course Tatian immediately passes

interested above all in pure concepts of the relation of God and the world. But all this is still only appearance. Christianity accepted the Logos idea, in order particularly to make understandable to the educated world, in a philosophical-appearing formula, the veneration of Christ and the Christ cult.[69]

This procedure also must not be viewed as if now all at once by means of the adoption of the Logos formula the fall of early church thought into speculation and metaphysics occurs at the same time and as if thus for the first time the way is trod which would lead from the understanding of God in his historical revelation more and more into the maze of speculation and of metaphysically oriented dogma. Speculation and myth accompanied Christianity from the outset; the fantasy of the heavenly Son of Man or Man was already a speculative myth which almost wholly diverged from the person of the earthly Jesus of Nazareth. Speculative-metaphysical is the concept of the Son of God also in Paul and John; altogether a speculative myth is Paul's conception of the pneumatic being who descended into this world from the celestial heights in order to redeem us, through death and resurrection, from this world. The Logos idea is distinguished from all

---

over from the defensive to the offensive and empties his vessel of ridicule on the unworthy conceptions of God in Hellenism. People were gradually growing sure of themselves in the main point of the justification of the δεύτερος θεός and did not continually repeat the one great conception.

[69] In the above I have attempted to set forth to what extent I am not convinced by Harnack's derivation (*Dogmengeschichte*, 4th ed., I, 334-35) of the appropriation of the Logos idea among the apologists from general cosmological interests and those theological ones oriented to the idea of revelation. On the other hand, I agree with his judgment on page 699: "That they (the apologists) viewed Christ as the personal manifestation of the Logos is only a proof of the fact that they wished to say the highest possible things about him, *to justify the rendering of worship to him* and to demonstrate the absolute and unique contents of the Christian religion." Only the last phrase appears to me to be formulated in too modern a fashion and to misplace, by ascribing too much to deliberate intent, an effect which simply resulted. Loofs, *Dogmengeschichte*, 4th ed., p. 120, is unquestionably correct when he emphasizes the apologetic intention, "with the aid of the Logos concept which was understood by the culture of the time, to make comprehensible the Christian estimate of Jesus." It is hardly correct to recognize, as Loofs does, the cosmological motif even in addition to this. Further, the effort to preserve the otherworldliness of God over against the accounts in the Old Testament, by ascribing now all the all-too-human features reported there to the Logos, was not the primary determinative motive. This motive is, rather, quite uniform and quite transparent. After people had once accepted the Logos concept and the idea of a δεύτερος θεός, then of course they also utilized this idea in the interpretation of the Old Testament after the pattern of Philonic and kindred speculations. Cf. esp. the comprehensive judgment of Justin, Dial. 127; Theophilus II, 22. Tertullian made special use of this device in his discussion with Marcion in order to preserve for Christianity the *ut ita dixerim philosophorum deum* in the invisible Father and to ascribe everything in the Old Testament that was too human to the Logos; adv. Marc. II, 27.

these patterns of thought in that it was somewhat less mythical, somewhat more purely intellectual and philosophical, although the myth, as we have already seen and shall see still more precisely, had its full share even in this pattern of thought. The Logos theology was a renewed attempt to render the belief in Christ comprehensible in a changed milieu. It does not represent a break in the development. If one insists upon wishing to point to the place where the development of the gospel of Jesus suffered the break, one finds it in the very beginnings, in the emergence of the Christ cult.

III. *Import of the Logos Idea.* The Logos theology occupies a truly central position in the interpretation of Christianity by the apologists. Their total outlook is determined by it. And the tones which are struck by them and which now come distinctly to our ear are completely new and unprecedented ones. For this is what they proclaim in triumph: The Christian faith is the absolutely reasonable, the perfect religious truth, the perfect practical truth; Christianity is the universally valid, that which has always been true and will always hold, only that now for the first time it has come to light, wholly plain and clear, for human knowledge; it is that at which human nature, which in its essence is so truly rational, has aimed from the very beginning; it is that to which the human soul, when it correctly recognizes its own nature, must say yes and Amen.

Thus, in triumphant awareness that he speaks in the name of reason, Justin[70] addresses himself to the rulers. People call them pious ones and philosophers and guardians of justice; now it will be shown whether they are indeed all these (I, 2.2). It is not in accord with true *reason* (λόγος ἀληθής) to persecute innocent people because of an idle and evil rumor (I, 3). In such actions irrational passion (ἄλογος ὁρμή, πάθος) is shown. The worship of idols and the cult of sacrifice are irrational things (I, 9, 12). Every reasonable person (σωφρονῶν) must agree with the Christians' worship (I, 13.2). Their veneration of Christ is reasonable (μετὰ λόγου). Most of all, the ethical instructions of Jesus are reasonable.[71] Justin's presentation of this ethic of Jesus (I, 15) begins with statements about σωφροσύνη.[72] The heretics (Marcionites) offer no proof for their doctrines, for they are ἀλόγως συνηρπασμένοι (I, 58.2). Justin now intends to set the

---

[70] Cf. also Athenagoras 7.

[71] Cf. Athenagoras 11, 35.

[72] The exposition of the ethic in Jesus' discourses is generally designed properly to bring out the "philosophical" ideal of life of the Christians.

doctrines of the Christians before the rulers quite openly and without concealment: ὑμέτερον δέ, ὡς αἱρεῖ λόγος, ἀκούοντας ἀγαθοὺς εὑρίσκεσθαι κριτάς (I, 3.4).

Justin is convinced of this: In his struggle he has on his side the illustrious example of all Hellenic wisdom of life, Socrates. He, the εὐτονώτερος of all philosophers, persuaded by the Logos, once upon a time sought to deliver men from the service of the demons and attempted to lead them to the knowledge of the unknown God. For this the demons killed him as an atheist, through the men who reveled in their wickedness. Now the Christians carry on the same struggle with the same results (I, 5.4; II, 10.8). And not only in Socrates has the Logos held sway. It was from the very beginning a common possession of the human race: τὸ ἔμφυτον παντὶ γένει ἀνθρώπων σπέρμα τοῦ λόγου (II, 8.1).[73] The whole human race participated in the firstborn Christ, who is indeed the Logos. Hence all who have ever lived with the Logos, Socrates and Heraclitus and the men of God in the Old Testament, were Christians (I, 46). Plato and the Stoa, the poets and the historians proclaimed the same thing as did Christ, though indeed not in every respect, but in part: ἕκαστος γάρ τις ἀπὸ μέρους τοῦ σπερματικοῦ θείου λόγου τὸ συγγενὲς ὁρῶν καλῶς ἐφθέγξατο (II, 13.3). The Stoics, for example, were especially strong in ethics (II, 8.1), others in another connection. But whatever good the philosophers and lawgivers thought and proclaimed was elaborated by them κατὰ λόγου μέρος δι' εὑρέσεως καὶ θεωρίας (II, 10.2). Hence the proud confession: Whatever good has been said among all men is the property of us Christians! (II, 13.4).

Even if the other apologists do not all in this manner stress[74] and underscore the traces of the Logos who holds sway in human culture, the note which is struck here is distinctly echoed in all of them, even more strongly in the Latin than in the Greek-speaking apologists.[75] At the end of the series stands Tertullian. Nowhere did that conviction of the universality

---

[73] Cf. II, 13.5, διὰ τῆς ἐνούσας ἐμφύτου τοῦ λόγου σπορᾶς ἀμυδρῶς ἐδύναντο ὁρᾶν τὰ ὄντα.

[74] Even Athenagoras no longer sets forth the doctrine of the λόγος σπερματικός. Tatian and Theophilus cannot do enough in one-sided attacks on Hellenic philosophy. However, even though in an obscure way, still there recurs the concession that the philosophers frequently proclaim the same thing as do the Christians. And people move consciously as well as unconsciously along their ways of thought. Even Theophilus must reluctantly concede the moments of truth in the heathen philosophy and dwells upon them in all sorts of conjectures (see below), I, 14; II, 8, 12, 37-38.

[75] Cf. Harnack, pp. 520-21. Harnack however rightly emphasizes that the distinction seen as a whole is a relative one.

and reasonableness of Christian truth find a more gripping expression than in his *"Testimonium animae."* He addresses the human soul [76] in itself, not the one educated or miseducated in the schools and philosophical lecture halls, but the soul of the simple, the ignorant, the uneducated, as it comes from the alley, the street corners, and the workshops: "I desire to elicit from thee what thou bringest into men, what thou hast learned either from thyself or from thy author, whoever he may be. For as far as I know, thou art no Christian. For a man becomes a Christian, he is not born one! Nevertheless one now demands of thee a testimony" (chap. 1). "These testimonies of the soul are as true as simple, as simple as commonplace (*vulgaria*), as commonplace as universal, *as universal as natural, as natural as divine"* (chap. 5). "Without doubt the soul existed before writing, and speech before books, the thought before the pen, and man himself before the philosopher and the poet" (chap. 5). "And so then believe your own testimonies, and on the basis of our commentaries (commentarii=ἀπομνημο-νεύματα) believe also the divine testimonies; but on the basis of the free choice of the soul itself believe Nature just as firmly." . . . "Again, in order to acquire belief in Nature and in God, only believe the soul. Thus it will come about that you also believe yourself" (*ut et naturae et deo credas, crede animae*). "Every soul loudly proclaims in its own right those things which we (Christians) are not even allowed to whisper!" (chap. 6.)

This is the general world view which grew up on the basis of that Logos theology. And with holy wrath Tertullian defends this world view against the irrationalism of Marcion, against the Gnostic proclamation of the alien God who appeared in an alien world in order to bring to it an alien and unprecedentedly new good, and of the "unnaturalness" of that which Christ has brought. Over against these he intends to exhibit principles concerning the goodness of God. This goodness must be natural and original: *Omnia enim in deo naturalia et ingenita esse debebunt, ut sint aeterna* (I, 22). But it must also be rational: *Nego rationalem bonitatem dei Marcionis jam hoc primo, quod in salutem processerit hominis alieni* (I, 23). It must happen according to age-old sacred order: *Nulla res sine ordine rationalis potest vindicari.* Everywhere we encounter this demand for the rational, the universally valid, the orderly.

Yet all this is only one side of the coin, the reverse of which must now

---

[76] Similarly Minucius Felix, Octavius 16.5 (cf. 1.4), explains the Christian truth as that planted by nature in every man. In his dialogue with philosophical skepticism he works with the tools of the Stoic popular philosophy. Harnack, pp. 520-21.

be examined. In the very moment in which the apologists make the claim that they proclaim to the world the Logos, the absolutely rational, they surprise this world with the very strongest conceivable and most irrational paradox. This paradox does not lie in the assertion of the Logos as the δεύτερος θεός beside the Deity. To be sure even this idea, as we have shown, had not grown in rational, philosophical soil. But in the age and the environment of the apologists this mythological twisting of a philosophical idea apparently had lost the astounding and unusual aspect. The myth has extensively penetrated into philosophy, in particular in the levels of halfway education in which the apologists function. But the unprecedented thing, the thing which itself is in contradiction with the apologists' own premises of the general reasonableness of Christianity, is that they now asserted that the Logos has appeared bodily and totally in the *one man* Jesus of Nazareth. The writer of the Fourth Gospel had already flung this paradox into the world with unprecedented force: καὶ λόγος σάρξ ἐγένετο. The author of the Kerygma Petri follows when he calls the Son of God λόγος καὶ νόμος in the special sense. Justin provided a theoretical underpinning for this view. For him Christ is just the μορφωθεὶς λόγος, the Logos in bodily form (I, 5, 56 A).[77] In contrast thereto, through the use of a Stoic motif for the power which was also in the pagan philosophers and pious men, he coined the term (ἔμφυτον παντὶ γένει ἀνθρώπων) σπέρμα τοῦ λόγου or σπερματικὸς λόγος (σπερματικοῦ λόγου μέρος). In contrast to them the Christians have τὴν τοῦ παντὸς λόγου, ὅ ἐστι Χριστοῦ, γνῶσιν καὶ θεωρίαν.[78] For this reason the former have never recognized the full truth. Socrates was never able to persuade anyone to go to death for the truth which he knew (II, 10.8). Plato's doctrines agree with those of Christ, but only in part. The same can be said of the Stoics and of the poets and historians. They have recognized the truth only in part, ἀπὸ μέρους τοῦ σπερματικοῦ θείου λόγου, one thus, another differently (τὸ συγγενὲς ὁρῶν). Hence so many contradictions are also found in their teachings (II, 13.3; cf. II, 10.3). All of them have gained only an unclear comprehension of reality by means of the seed of the Logos implanted within them (by Nature). For there is a difference between the seed and the imitation on the one hand, and that on which that partnership and the imitation rests on the other (II, 13.6). Therefore Justin speaks only of a human

[77] Cf. II, 10.1: διὰ τὸ λογικὸν τὸ ὅλον τὸν φανέντα δι᾽ ἡμᾶς Χριστὸν γεγονέναι καὶ σῶμα καὶ λόγον καὶ ψυχήν.
[78] II, 8.3.

philosophy and strongly emphasizes the absolute superiority of Christianity: πάσης μὲν φιλοσοφίας ἀνθρωπείου ὑπερτέρα (II, 15.3). Christianity is δύναμις τοῦ ἀρρήτου πατρὸς καὶ οὐχὶ ἀνθρωπείου λόγου κατασκευή (II, 10.8). In the introduction to the Dialogue, Justin still more strongly bade farewell to all high esteem for Hellenic philosophy and wisdom. Here he associates himself with the skepticism that doubts all philosophical conclusions—a procedure not new then and to be repeated often in the future. The Hellenic philosophers have indeed posed questions, but they have given no answers. They have bogged down in sheer uncertainty and contradictions; an absolutely new and different route must be taken if one wants to arrive at the goal of knowledge. For the Deity is known by men only to the extent that he gives himself to be known by them.[79]

In all this some very important and basic problems are touched, which are most profoundly to influence the intellectual history of Christianity. For example, here there emerges for the first time a thought-out theory of supernatural revelation. The Logos who has appeared in Christ is something *toto genere* different from the λόγος σπερματικός which is effective in the human race. It is not merely an accidental empirical state of affairs that the perceptions of the philosophers are only partially correct, imperfect, and in contradiction with one another. There is here an inner, higher necessity; men require the authority of revelation. In related fashion Athenagoras develops this theory in his Apology. All the philosophers and poets have spoken of ultimate divine matters only in conjectural fashion (στοχαστικῶς). Touched by the divine breath,[80] they have each been set on the search after God from within their own soul and have not been able to find him (οὐ παρὰ θεοῦ περὶ θεοῦ ἀξιώσαντες μαθεῖν). For this reason they have set forth such varied and contradictory teachings. We Christians,

---

[79] The attacks upon pagan philosophy become much sharper in the successors of Justin, esp. in Tatian and Theophilus. And in spite of his own rational stance, Tertullian appears, as does Minucius Felix, as a grim opponent of that philosophy. Cf. the passages in Harnack, pp. 515 ff., 518, 522. Associated with this is the charge borrowed from Jewish polemics that the Greek philosophers have stolen their wisdom from the philosophy of the barbarians. Even in Justin, I, 44.9, 59.1; esp. in Tatian (see his proof from antiquity, 31 ff.); Theophilus I, 14; II, 12, 37; Minucius Felix 34. Harnack (p. 511) correctly brings out the fact that at least in Justin this view does not stand on the level of his doctrine of the λόγος σπερματικός and represents an alien element that has been adopted into his thought. The forms of criticism stand in closest proximity in Clement of Alexandria, so that one could be tempted on the basis of these contradictions to distinguish separate sources that have been used.

[80] Athenagoras 7, p. 8.10 Schw.: κινηθέντες κατὰ συμπαθείαν τῆς παρὰ τοῦ θεοῦ πνοῆς. The distinction between πνοή and πνεῦμα indicated here is already found in Philo, Leg. Alleg. I, 42.

however, he goes on, have as witnesses for our truth the prophets who, moved by the divine spirit, have spoken of God. How unreasonable it would be to abandon belief in the Spirit who moved the prophets as his instruments, and to believe human opinions (δόξαις)! [81] And after Athenagoras defends the belief in the one God in fuller detail, he turns once more to the idea of revelation. "If we now were satisfied with such ideas, then one could rightly regard our proclamation as human. But since the voices of the prophets attest our thoughts. . . ." (chap. 9.)

As to contents, on both sides the same truths are involved [82]: the one supra-terrestrial God; his Son, the Logos, and the creation of the world through him; providence, moral freedom, and responsibility; retribution after death, and directions for a perfect moral life. [83] Only here and there it is emphasized that a Christian truth is not found among the heathen philosophers. In particular the belief in the bodily resurrection as a specific of the Christian religion plays a role in this connection. But for the whole of the consideration this hardly matters. Only in form is there a great difference. There we have human thoughts and conjectures, and here we have supernatural divine truth assured by authority. It cannot be surprising that in these statements the prophets and the prophetic spirit for the most part appear as the authority for revelation. [84] For on the one hand and in the first place, apologetic reasons seem to have been present here. By means of this placing of the special Christian revelation in a revelation history of age-old and venerable antiquity one escaped the accusations of the arbitrary and arrogant self-esteem of a new and young religion. On the other hand— and this is shown again here quite plainly—Christianity is still just a liberated Diaspora-Judaism. The tangible external authority for the Christians, upon which their worship and indeed their whole spiritual frame of mind was

[81] Cf. also the contrast between the truth and the δόξαι παλαιῶν in Justin, Apol. I, 2.1.

[82] Cf. the enumeration of truths common to Christianity and philosophy in Justin, Apol. I, 20. Athenagoras 5–7 (even the philosophers have had in part a true knowledge of God and have opposed the false demons. Christianity is not something unprecedentedly new, and for this reason also is not to be opposed). Cf. Theophilus, II, 8.

[83] Note the curious comment in Pseudo-(?) Justin, resurr. 10, 595 B: "If the savior . . . had brought only the knowledge of the life of the *soul*, what would he have brought that was new in comparison with Pythagoras, Plato and the throng of their followers?"

[84] See above (p. 389, n. 20) the passages on the προφητικὸν πνεῦμα. Tatian also knows nothing of a distinction between the revelation through the prophets and that through Christ. Cf. chap. 29, p. 30.4 Schw.; chap. 12, p. 13.13; chap. 13, p. 15.1; chap. 20, p. 22.30; Harnack, p. 517.2. Cf. Minucius Felix, Octav. 34. Theophilus, I, 14 (further passages in Harnack, p. 518.3).

based, is in the first place always the Old Testament. It still is not long since that the ἀπομνημονεύματα τοῦ κυρίου had begun to be placed beside the Old Testament. Thus the prophetic revelation offers a fixed point of contact for the thought-world of the apologists. Indeed even Justin, who most strongly emphasized the concentration of revelation in the Logos-Christos, again requires the authority of the prophets or the Old Testament for proof of his thesis that the full and complete Logos has appeared in Jesus, the Son of God. For him the authority of his Logos Christos depends upon the external condition that the predictions of the prophets who were filled with God's spirit referred to the one Jesus Christ and have been fulfilled in the figure of this one.

But whether now the revelation faith of the apologists may be oriented more to the prophecy of the Old Testament or to the Logos which has taken shape in Christ, it dominates their thoughts and gives their rationalism a supernatural crowning element. According to their opinion there is a peculiar state of affairs with reference to the truth of the proclamation of the Christian faith. Its proclaimers set forth the truths which are contained in the faith without any sort of proof: οὐ γὰρ μετὰ ἀποδείξεως πεποίηνται . . . τοὺς λόγους, ἅτε ἀνωτέρω πάσης ἀποδείξεως ὄντες ἀξιόπιστοι μάρτυρες τῆς ἀληθείας. They proclaim the truth authoritatively, and they provide the proof of their authority by means of their fulfilled prophecies and the miracles which they perform.[85] The divine truth, according to the author of the pseudo-Justinian (?) writing De resurrectione, is elevated above demonstration: ὁ μὲν τῆς ἀληθείας λόγος ἐστὶν ἐλεύθερός τε καὶ αὐτεξούσιος, ὑπὸ μηδεμίαν βάσανον ἐλέγχου θέλων πίπτειν μηδὲ τὴν παρὰ τοῖς ἀκούουσι δι' ἀποδείξεως ἐξέτασιν ὑπομένειν (chap. 1). On this, the belief that the truth requires no proof, rests the plain and comprehensible simplicity of their presentation, the artlessness of their discourse.[86] Hence it comes about that the Christian faith wins its adherents among the plain and simple, the uneducated and the old women, and that these with their wisdom put the philosophers to shame. Socrates persuaded none of his followers to die for his conviction. But the Christian faith has the experience

---

[85] Justin, Dial. 7, p. 224 D, 225 A.; cf. Tatian, 12, p. 14.8 Schw.: τὰ τῆς ἡμετέρας παιδείας ἐστὶν ἀνωτέρω τῆς κοσμικῆς καταλήψεως.

[86] Cf. the characteristic statements of Tatian, 29, p. 30.7 Schw.: καί μοι πεισθῆναι ταύταις (the γραφαὶ βαρβαρικαί) διά τε τῶν λέξεων τὸ ἄτυφον καὶ τῶν εἰπόντων τὸ ἀνεπιτήδευτον καὶ τῆς τοῦ παντὸς ποιήσεως τὸ εὐκατάληπτον καὶ τῶν μελλόντων τὸ προγνωστικὸν καὶ τῶν παραγγελμάτων τὸ ἐξαίσιον καὶ τῶν ὅλων τὸ μοναρχικόν.

that not only "philosophers and philologists, but craftsmen and uneducated people" learn to scorn the fear of death.[87]

Finally, the reasoning which the apologists offer for these theses of theirs is distinctive. They give a unanimous answer to the question why then the divine revelation through the prophets or the Logos was necessary, why the Logos had to appear in Christ, and human thought and will had not been able to lead to the goal. It is the domination by the demons which renders the human understanding incapable and makes the revelation and illumination from above a necessity. I have already shown in the course of this investigation how the view of the redemption of the human race through Jesus and his cross was affected by a myth, which worked its way into Christianity from the very beginning, of the battle of the redeemer-hero with the demons of the depths. In the idea of the descent into Hades (*vide supra*, pp. 60 ff.), which is also present in the apologists, and already in some pointedly mythical statements of the apostle Paul about the death of Christ (*vide supra*, pp. 179-81),[88] the influences of this myth are quite evident. In the apologists this mythical way of considering the work of Christ has become the almost completely dominant one. They return again and again to this theory. In conjunction with the well-known Jewish fantasies, particularly of the Book of Enoch, they develop a detailed theory as to the source and origin of the demons.[89] These demons, the descendants of the fallen angels, are the forces at work in paganism. They are worshiped by the pagans as gods.[90] They stand back of the sacrificial and image worship of the heathen; the miraculous powers which the images exhibit are their work.[91] They are the authors of the persecution of Christians,[92] they are the creators of all the slanders[93] which are directed against the Christians; it is their doing that people threaten with death the readers of the wholesome prophecies of the Sibyl and of Hystaspes.[94] On the basis of Old Testament prophecies, which they nevertheless have not rightly understood, they have caused the

[87] Justin, Apol. II, 10.8; cf. Athenag. 11; Tatian, 32, 33.

[88] I Cor. 2:6, 8; 15:24 ff.; Col. 1:18-20; 2:15; Heb. 2:14; I Pet. 3:22; Eph. 1:21-22; 4:8; I Tim. 3:16; Rev. 12:10-11; John 12:31; 14:30; 16:11; cf. Justin, Apol. I, 45.1; I, 63.10.

[89] Justin, Apol. I, 5, II, 5. Athenagoras 25 (29). Tatian, 7 ff.; above all the Pseudo-Clementines, Hom. VIII, 12 ff.; Rec. IV, 26-27.

[90] Justin, Apol. I, 5.2, 9.1.

[91] Justin, Apol. I, 9.1. Athenagoras, 23. Pseudo-Clem., Hom. IX, 7 ff., 16-17, Rec. IV, 14 ff., 20-21.

[92] Justin, Apol. I, 12.5.

[93] Justin, Apol. I, 10.6.

[94] Justin, I, 44.12.

imitation of Christian truths and the Christian sacraments in pagan belief and cultus.[95] They are also the originators of Christian heresy.[96] From them stem the bad laws of mankind.[97]

Thus the demons are the misfortune of men. Because of them the appearance of the Logos upon earth has become necessary. Christ has appeared on earth in order to break their power: Ἰησοῦς δὲ καὶ ἄνθρωπος καὶ σωτὴρ γέγονε κατὰ τὴν τοῦ θεοῦ καὶ πατρὸς βουλὴν ἀποκυηθείς . . . ἐπὶ καταλύσει τῶν δαιμόνων.[98] The apologists prove the truth of this view in a noteworthy fashion by means of the constantly repeated reference to the fact that even now the demons, when they are exorcized in the name of Jesus Christ, flee and leave the men who are possessed by them.[99]

This teaching of the apologists is significant in several respects. For one thing, it again shows the close relationship between dogmatic theory and cultus. It is the opposition to the polytheistic cultus of paganism which is expressed in this appropriation and the strong emphasis of ancient mythological elements. To the apologists the demons were first of all not a theory but a living reality which is revealed in their corrupting dominion over minds, and which they daily saw before their eyes with amazement and terror. Over against the demons, the highest thing they could say of the Christos-Logos was that he had come to destroy the dominion of the demons and to enlighten the human race with the true knowledge of God. And in the exorcisms, which must have played a major role in their days, they saw the practical demonstration of the power and lordship of the Lord Christ. Everywhere the living cultic reality stands close beside the theory.

However, it is of importance to observe how external is this proof of the necessity of a supernatural intervention in human history and of an

---

[95] Justin, I, 54 ff., I, 62; Dial. 69, 78.

[96] Justin, I, 26.1.

[97] Tatian, 15, p. 17.4 Schw.

[98] Justin, II, 6.5, cf. Dial. 41, p. 260 A: καὶ τὰς ἀρχὰς καὶ τὰς ἐξουσίας καταλελυκέναι (sc., θεόν) τελείαν κατάλυσιν διὰ τοῦ παθητοῦ γενομένου κατὰ τὴν βουλὴν αὐτοῦ. Clem. Alex., Protr. 1.3.2: καταλύσων τὴν δουλείαν τὴν πικρὰν τῶν τυραννούντων δαιμόνων; cf. XI, 111.1.

[99] Harnack, Dogmengeschichte, 4th ed., I, 545.3. Justin, Apol. II, 6.6., 8.4. Dial. (11) 30, p. 247 C; 35, p. 254 B; 39, p. 258 C; 76, p. 302 A; 85, p. 311 B; 111, p. 338 B; 121, p. 350 B. Tatian 16, p. 18.4 Schw. Tertullian, Apol. 23, 27, 32, 37. Origen, contra Celsum I, 6 (cf. 24), 67, III, 36; cf. IV, 92. Act. Pion. 13. According to Dial. 85, p. 311 B, the formula of exorcism ran thus: κατὰ γὰρ τοῦ ὀνόματος τοῦ υἱοῦ τοῦ θεοῦ τοῦ πρωτοτόκου πάσης κτίσεως καὶ διὰ παρθένου γεννηθέντος καὶ παθητοῦ γεναμένου ἀνθρώπου καὶ σταυρωθέντος ἐπὶ Ποντίου Πιλάτου . . . καὶ ἀποθανόντος καὶ ἀναστάντος ἐκ νεκρῶν καὶ ἀναβάντος εἰς τὸν οὐρανόν. On the connections between formula of exorcism and baptismal symbol (the Apostolicum), cf. Heitmüller, Im Namen Jesu, pp. 334 ff.

enlightenment of human knowledge through revelation. Only the dominion of the demons has deluded men and made them unfit; nowhere is anything said of a fundamental corruption of the very nature of the human race. Such an assumption would even have been in contradiction with basic apologetic ideas. For according to their basic outlook God has given man freedom and reason as original equipment. Therewith he has made him the free master of his fate and responsible for it. His initial emergence does not lie within man's power, but after this it does lie within the scope of his free decision, by virtue of the λογικαὶ δυνάμεις given by God, to pursue that which is pleasing in God's sight and to attain incorruptibility (ἀφθαρ-σία).[100] Life and death are in his hands; God has made man neither mortal nor immortal, but by keeping the commandments he can attain ἀθανασία, through disobedience he can incur death. For either of the two possibilities it is not God but men who bear the responsibility.[101] If they miss the goal they are ἀναπολόγητοι, because God has created them θεωρητικοί and λογικοί.[102] The apologists are bitter opponents of any doctrine of fate; for them the belief in divine justice and the idea of retribution depend upon the idea of freedom.[103]

The dominion of the demons does not alter anything in this respect. Afterward as beforehand, there remain for man even under this dominion both the freedom and the moral obligation to escape from the irrational dominion of the demons.[104] Theophilus one time voices the conjecture that if the philosophers had grasped some truths about the oneness of God and the judgment, this therefore means that for a while they had been freed from the dominion of the demons (II, 8.87 C). Tatian indeed offers the opinion, in the propositions (Orat. 12–15) which are singular within his milieu,[105] that the human soul is not by nature immortal but could achieve this freedom only through the connection with the divine spirit, but has lost that connection through the dominion of the demons. But Tatian himself teaches that the precondition of the return of the spirit to man is the

---

[100] Justin, Apol. I, 10.4.

[101] Theophilus, To Autolycus II, 27, p. 103 C, D.

[102] Justin I, 28.3.

[103] Justin I, 43, II, 7. Dial. 88, p. 316 A; 141. Athenagoras 24. In the Pseudo-Clementine Rec. IX and X there is heaped up a whole arsenal of weapons for fighting the doctrine of Heimarmene.

[104] Cf. Harnack, pp. 536-37, 538.4.

[105] Tatian's statements lie on the way to the one-sided Gnostic religion of redemption, but they stop halfway. Still more Gnostic are the broad statements of Arnobius, adv. nat. II, which move in the same directions in a lively discussion with platonizing (Hermetic) speculations about the divinity of the soul.

proper exercise of human freedom, and thus he remains within the apologetic framework. And it is still an apologetic pattern of thought when he says that Christ frees us from slavery to many lords and tyrants, but yet has given us no blessings which we had not already received; he rather has given us such as we indeed had received but, in consequence of error, had not been able to retain.[106]

IV. *Concluding Estimate.* It is an overall outlook full of contradictions which confronts us in the apologists. Christianity is the absolutely rational; but this rational has come into the world through a supernatural revelation. Christianity is the universally valid, which always was and always will be, the Logos; but this Logos has entered into the world at one particular point and has been concentrated in a historical figure. In Christ the Logos has acquired bodily form, but the Spirit has spoken in a long succession of prophetic men, and it is difficult to say what the λόγος μορφωθείς has brought that is new in comparison with the revelation of the prophets. Christianity is utterly different from all human philosophy, and yet again, seen in respect to the contents, they are almost identical. In Hellenic philosophy the λόγος σπερματικός was active, but basically this philosophy stopped with merely empty and contradictory human opinions; indeed, it perhaps owes its best parts to wisdom stolen from the prophets. Through the rule of the demons men have become so greatly weakened in their knowledge that they require the supernatural revelation, but they have not lost their freedom, and thus they did not actually require that supernatural intervention.

How are we to evaluate this bundle of contradictory views? Where are errors and where is the correct element?

The error does *not* lie in the basic affirmation of the apologists of the reasonableness and universality of Christian truth. People have taken this principle quite amiss; some believe that on the basis of this they have discovered in the apologists a defect as to religion, and explain the apologists' world view as intellectualistic, and the apologists themselves as essentially moved by a cosmological and moral interest. And yet one may not so completely deny a religious character to these men. It is of course true that they are lacking all notes of religious mysticism, and there is missing an inwardness of religious experience, but nevertheless, in the midst of a con-

---

[106] Chap. 29, p. 30.14 Schw.: δίδωσι δὲ ἡμῖν οὐχ ὅπερ μὴ ἐλάβομεν, ἀλλ' ὅπερ λαβόντες ὑπὸ τῆς πλάνης ἔχειν ἐκωλύθημεν.

tradictory world they fought for the purity of the belief in God and risked their lives for it. Their passionateness is displayed in the opposition of Hellenic-Roman polytheism; before their souls there stands in utter majesty the glory of the one God, the creator, ruler and judge of the world, the compassionate Father, who gave to men their freedom and responsibility. Moreover, there can hardly be a stronger religious estimate of the person of Jesus than when these Christians proclaimed Christ as the incarnate divine reason, the λόγος μορφωθείς. Therein they stand fundamentally and wholly on the basis of the faith of the Christian community.

What is proper in the amazed consternation with which people regard the apologists is this: They stand in sharp contrast to that form of Christianity for which Paul and John prepared the way and which the Gnostics coined and perfected. If religion is summed up in the one-sided idea of redemption through a power alien to man and coming from above, if it is indeed true that the best and highest that man possesses stands in contradiction to his natural essence, if Christianity is exhaustively represented in the Pauline-Gnostic redemption belief, then to be sure the apologists possessed very little of religion. But measured by this standard, a decisive deficiency is shown also in the gospel of Jesus. It is of course much too simple to provide an explicit and clear answer to the questions raised here. That in the gospel of Jesus, as also in the tradition of his community, those notes of the single-minded redemption mysticism are still altogether lacking should be clear—unless one confuses that idea of redemption with the simple proclamation of a God who forgives sins. When Jesus points the minds of men to the highest goal, the reflection that thereby he thrusts into human nature something foreign, something that is contrary to his essence, is utterly remote from his mind.[107]

Thus in the simple obviousness with which religion (and Christianity as its embodiment) is understood as something ultimately native to the human soul, we have to see a certain return from the virtuosity of Pauline-Gnostic piety to the plainness and simplicity of the gospel. Indeed, even if we now have to concede, as will become clear shortly, that the apologists pushed the pendulum too far, that they made out of the reasonableness of Christianity almost a bare obviousness, and out of the universality a com-

---

[107] The great μετανοεῖτε of Jesus' preaching does not argue to the contrary. For Jesus, it is a matter of the return of the sons who are in a foreign land to the paternal home to which they belong, the self-recollection of man of the nature which is originally his, implanted by the Creator God.

monplace (*simplex et vulgare!* Tertullian), we recognize here, over against the Pauline-Gnostic one-sidedness, a justified and refreshing counter-stroke to the other side. *How rich and vigorous was the life of early Christianity to conceal within itself such opposites!*

Of course, the rationalism of the apologists is one-sided and distorted, and with this one-sidedness all sorts of contradictions and complications were introduced into their world of thought. The apologists did not succeed in rightly distinguishing between religion and philosophy. It is not so very important to establish whether this or that apologist called himself a philosopher or talked of a Christian philosophy. What is important, however, is to recognize that here they were lacking any proper standards for making the distinction. That religion is something original on its own basis: the relation of the human soul to God—this *tu nos fecisti ad te, ac cor nostrum inquietum est, donec requiescat in te*—and again, that all religious utterances about God and human nature have to take their departure from this point, all this they did not recognize. To them religion was a bundle of truths accessible to human knowledge, a sensible world view. And they stood on the foundation of a popular philosophy which was credited with having arrived at these ultimate truths by way of evidence that was in accordance with understanding. For the later idealistic Platonic-Stoic philosophy, which nourished the apologists in all their ideas, the *theologia physica* is indeed the highest theology; i.e., theology is the crown of natural science, and the natural-scientific consideration of the world reaches its climax in belief in God. But religious and ethical truths are demonstrable, as are other objects of science also, and philosophy an ἐπιστήμη θείων καὶ ἀνθρωπίνων πραγμάτων. The apologists now mix this intellectual world view with the Christian religion. Thus, whether they really intended it or not, for them the Christian religion becomes philosophy, and the Logos Christos not the creative author of the new life in God, but the διδάσκαλος, who proclaims religious and ethical truths.

Here lay the seed and kernel of all sorts of difficulties. For now ancient idealist philosophy and intellectually adulterated Christianity became rivals in the same territory. And now began that strange game in which what one hand gave the other took away. One had to acknowledge that, as to content, Christian proclamation brings the same as Hellenic philosophy— of course not the individual philosopher, but pious (i.e., idealist) philosophy on the whole—had already approximately done in its proclamation. And yet again, one had to hold to the claim that Christianity was something completely different from Hellenic philosophy. Thus one had to reduce the achievements of philosophy to the vanishing point, had to unite with skepticism and with the help of this dangerous ally, which nevertheless was gladly claimed by all "revelational" theology, prove that the philosophers had done nothing more than pose questions, and answer these questions with empty and contradictory conjectures. Yet one could not have an easy conscience in this, for with this judgment one renounces a world by which one lives. And that skeptical attitude ill accorded with the bold rationalism with which people beheld in Christ the incarnate Logos. And so the apologists had to make some concessions after all in some corner of this Hellenic philosophy, even though not all were honest enough to apply at least in part to the culture of the Hellenic poets, thinkers, and lawgivers the attractive interpretation, which corresponds so well to the basic apologetic outlook, of the λόγος σπερματικός.

They escaped to the idea and the assumption of a supernatural revelation in the prophetic men of God which somehow climaxed in the Logos Christos. But this assumption did not actually harmonize with the foundations of the apologetic thought-world. It is not comprehensible why thoughts which are accessible to human knowledge yet are revealed supernaturally; why there should be needed a supernatural access to a world of thought which is thoroughly rational and which coincides as to contents with the basic ideas of the popular Greek philosophy, according to the apologists' own admission. The skepticism with which they argue the idea of the necessity of revelation is, however, only an assumed mask, and another face peers out from behind it. At the moment when they boldly assert that the Christian faith stands above all demonstration (a correct principle, but suited only for further confusion if it is not based on a proper understanding of faith)—they cheerfully proceed to offer proof of it. Or conversely, after they have presented proof to the best of their ability, say, of the singleness of God, they conclude the exposition with the thought that Christian truth does not rest upon such proofs but on prophetic revelation. Rationalism and authoritative faith are there quite superficially glued together. For the appealing thought that Christ is the Logos, they find a proof (the mistake is that one even seeks a proof and does not appeal to the testimony of the human soul) in the external authority of the prophets, which rests upon the external basis of fulfilled predictions. But, as we saw, the establishing of the necessity of revelation with the theory of the demons' dominion over the human race is utterly superficial. For because the freedom of men is not affected by this rule of the demons, we have to do here only with an empirical competence, in terms of which any metaphysical conclusions as to the necessity of revelation are actually impossible. But the fact that the apologists cling to the idea of human freedom and responsibility demonstrates once again where their most profound interests and impulses lay. Here also they are shown not so much as moralists, but rather as determined opponents of all the Pauline-Gnostic religion of redemption.

Thus the problem of faith and knowledge, at that point where it first emerges in Christian history, is found immediately in a hopeless confusion. A Clement of Alexandria, in association with Aristotle, expressed clever ideas about the necessity of faith. He argues that all human knowledge ultimately rests upon the ultimate unprovable principles (axioms), which one just has to accept in faith and confidence (Strom. II, 2-6). At first glance a new world of thought appears to be opened up here. But if one looks closer, one discovers that Clement understands by the basic presuppositions which one must accept by faith the traditional phrases of the community's faith which rests upon external authority. He did not possess the means of going further on the way and searching in the human soul for the ultimate basic axioms of all religion or of Christianity. The problem of "faith and knowledge" [108] remained for this period an insoluble one, because people did not know how to say what faith is and where are the limits of knowledge-type perception and of rational demonstration. And therewith a proper evaluation of the person of Jesus, beyond his interpretation as the philosophical teacher and the model of virtue, remained unattainable. For what the apologists supply concerning forgiveness of sins and redemption through Christ's sacrificial death are only adopted ideas without vital and convincing power.

There remains *one* contradiction in the total outlook of the apologists which needs a closer scrutiny, namely the contradiction between the rationalism of their Logos view in general and their proclamation of the incarnate concentration of the Logos in Jesus Christ. In the preceding we were able to conclude that all those antirationalist sentences which we discovered in the apologists stemmed more from emergency needs and

---

[108] Here Philo has already delved much deeper; he suspected that faith, in terms of its whole structure and its nature, is different from human philosophical knowledge (see above, p. 201). But he did not carry this to its conclusion, because he was too much of a mystical ecstatic.

from the difficulties traceable to their own inadequate clarity; but this contradiction goes much deeper. Immediately behind this irrationalism stands the community's faith. We must not forget that the apologists are men who stand with both feet on the ground of the community dogma and the community cultus. And the content, center, and circumference of this community faith was the conviction of Christ's deity. In his Dialogue, Justin confesses in ever repeated expressions this dogma of Christ as the δεύτερος θεός. And in the Christian cultus, on the basis of which they stand, this Christ was an object of pious veneration. The whole doctrine of the apologists of the λόγος μορφωθεὶς ἐν Χριστῷ is indeed, as we saw, set forth only in order to justify, with the means of apparently philosophical reflection, this Christian belief in the δεύτερος θεός and in particular his veneration in the cultus, in the face of the monotheistic demands of the educated upon the new religion. Thus people said: Christ is the Logos of God, who forms an indissoluble unity with God and yet again is distinguished from him. This was of course a myth, yet it was clothed in philosophical garb, and the irrationalism of the dogma was at least somewhat tempered, but it remains doubtful whether dogma and community faith will submit to this moderating or weakening.

Here however we see quite clearly that it is not correct to say that the apologists emptied and hollowed out the Christian community's faith and in its place put a rational religious philosophy. They consistently maintained and defended the community's faith in its central concern, i.e., at the point of the deity of Christ and the cultically sacramental reverence paid to him. The details do not matter. The doctrine of justification and the Pauline concept of faith, belief in the Spirit as the new supernatural life force of the Christians, one-sided dualistic theories of redemption, indeed even a strictly followed theory of satisfaction or sacrifice—all these do not belong to the common property of the Christian faith. Indeed it may be said on behalf of the apologists that in them, most clearly in their leader Justin, the simple ethical content of the gospel has shone forth anew, even though through a mirror dimmed by Stoic thought. We must not forget that Justin developed a description of the nature of Christianity in the speeches of Jesus.[109]

But the fact that the apologists were bound to the Christian community's faith and to the dogma of the deity of Christ also means that their

---

[109] Apol. I, 14 ff.; cf. Athenagoras 11. Aristides 15.

great basic conviction of the reasonableness and universality of the Christian religion found an absolute hindrance to its free development. Even its proclamation was at the very center burdened with a contradiction and an irrationalism which has nothing to do with the depths of authentic religion, the dogma of the δεύτερος θεός. Thus that daring idea was at first only a vanishing ripple in the current of the development, and it had a continuing effect only in greatly attenuated form and a changed direction. The apologists would have had to be much freer spirits with respect to the tradition and much more profound thinkers for it to have been otherwise. The time was not ripe for the interpretation of religion or of Christianity as an eternal and universally valid necessity of the human soul; perhaps it will never be altogether ripe.

# 10
## IRENAEUS

The Christianity of the second century is immensely rich in possibilities for development. Of course for the piety of the community and the conviction of the masses, the new religion was more and more definitely summed up in the cultus of the κύριος Jesus Christ. And in worship and sacrament this cultus dominates the life of the Christians in its entire breadth. Thus the content of the young religion is formed more and more as the proclamation of the new God.

But on this foundation the most diverse configurations are possible. On the one side stands the Pauline-Johannine interpretation, continued in Gnosticism, of Christianity as the religion of redemption in an absolute and blunt sense, the conviction that with the gospel the absolutely alien, the unheard-of, has come into the world, and with it the tendency toward the mythologizing of the person of Jesus of Nazareth. On the other side stands a basically quite rational view: Christianity is unshackled Diaspora-Judaism; all the emphasis falls on what is unhistorical in it, on the eternal and universally valid, what always was; indeed Christianity itself is the absolutely reasonable; the Son of God is the Logos who has appeared in bodily form, and everything historical comes into consideration actually only as evidential material (in the proof from prophecy) for the eternal truth of Christianity.

How may the development further turn out? Which of the two views that in their side-by-side existence prove the immense wealth, the many-sidedness, and the formative power of the new religion will be victorious? Or will neither of them gain the victory? A consideration of the Christianity or of the Christ faith of Irenaeus gives us the answer to these questions.[1] Irenaeus is actually *the* theologian in the second half of the second Christian century who presents the future formation of things in a way in which no other beside him or immediately after him does. None is like him in wealth and diversity of the motifs taken up and further spun out, or in the power of unified and complete summary. One can actually call him the Schleiermacher of the second century. With the presentation of his piety and theology we can break off our study, because we actually gain the impression that here we stand before a provisional conclusion in the development.

It is hardly necessary to stress that Irenaeus is altogether the theologian of the dominant community piety. For him the deity of Christ [2] in the full sense of the word is the beginning point of all his thought; for him the concepts "Son of God" and "God" coincide completely. And just as decisively he protests against the Gnostic dissolution of the human figure of Jesus into a myth. Just as certainly as Jesus is the *filius dei*, he is the *filius hominis*[3]: *Jesus Christus vere homo vere deus* (IV, 6.7).[4] "Τὰ Εἰρηναίου τε καὶ Μελίτωνος καὶ τῶν λοιπῶν τίς ἀγνοεῖ βιβλία θεὸν καὶ ἄνθρωπον καταγγέλλοντα τὸν Χριστόν." [5]

Irenaeus already stands beyond the age of the apologists in that for him the proclamation of the second God, the other God, causes no more difficulties. For him this proclamation has passed over into flesh and blood. He is thoroughly familiar with the basic concept of the apologists, the "Logos." Again and again the great key expression "Verbum dei" sounds

---

[1] I cite Irenaeus' *Adversus Haereses* following the usual numbers (not according to Harvey); the ἐπίδειξις according to the translation of S. Weber, *Bibliothek der Kirchenväter*, Kempten, 1912.

[2] Connection between deity and worship in the cultus, IV, 5.2 (in dependence upon the LXX, Bel and the Dragon, v. 25: *dominum deum meum adorabo, quoniam hic est deus vivus*): *qui igitur a prophetis adorabatur deus vivus, hic est vivorum deus et verbum eius. . . . ipse igitur Christus cum patre vivorum est deus.*

[3] It is worthy of note how this title (ὁ υἱὸς τοῦ ἀνθρώπου) even in Irenaeus appears totally alienated from its original sense and by means of its being connected with the humanity and the contrasting interpretation of *filius dei* receives a new content. III, 16.3, 7; 17.1 (end); 19.1, 3; 22.1; IV, 33.2, 11; V, 21.1. See above, p. 343.

[4] V, 1.1: *verbum potens et homo verus*. V, 17.3: *quoniam homo et quoniam deus*.

[5] Author of the "Little Labyrinth" in Eusebius, CH V, 28.5.

forth from his expositions. But he no longer employs this basic concept in order to make understandable to himself and others the nature of the second God and the strange doubling of the cultic object in the worship of Christianity. For him the Logos has already become one of the many traditional elements which Christianity carried along with itself in the constantly widening stream of the tradition. He characteristically uses the idea of the Logos in another place for the removal of a difficulty. Over against the Gnostics' preaching of the Agnostos Theos and their appeal to the saying of Jesus that no one knows the Father except the Son, he can, since he thoroughly accepts the idea of the exclusive revelation in the Son, point to the fact that the Son is the preexistent Logos and all revelation has always proceeded from him (IV, 6-7).

On the other hand, Irenaeus' proclamation of Jesus' deity or of his true godhood and true manhood is by no means a simple acceptance of the tradition, a simple bowing before the facts of the Kyrios cultus[6] and the language of the community's liturgy, although naturally there are numerous echoes of the community's liturgy to be discovered in him, precisely in his Christology.[7]

Irenaeus can instead dispense with the Logos theology of the apologists because he himself possessed an inward argument for the appearance of the incarnate God. His entire thought revolved around this proof of *Cur deus homo*. He really wishes to know why the redeemer has descended to earth. He sets himself against the possibility that the pagan philosophers had already known the truth. "And if they actually knew it, then the descent of the Savior into this world is superfluous: *Ad quid enim descendebat?*" (II, 14.7.)

I. *God Must Become Man, in Order That Men May Become Gods.* This question, *"ad quid enim descendebat,"* Irenaeus answered conclusively and clearly, interpreting matters from within. And this answer which, once it had been expressed, became centrally dominant in Christian piety, runs

---

[6] Note the characteristic juxtaposition of *dominus* and *deus: neque igitur dominus, neque spiritus sanctus, neque apostoli eum, qui non esset deus, definitive et absolute deum nominassent aliquando, nisi esset vere deus; neque dominum appellassent aliquem ex sua persona, nisi qui dominatur omnium: deum patrem et filium eius, qui dominium accepit a patre suo.* III, 6.1; III, 9.1; III, 10.1.

[7] Cf. for example III, 16.6: *invisibilis visibilis factus est et incomprehensibilis factus comprehensibilis et impassibilis passibilis et verbum homo.* Cf. III, 11.5; also the statements about the death of Christ in II, 20.3. See above, pp. 325 ff.

thus: Christ, God, had to become man so that men could become Gods or humanity could be united to God.

Irenaeus speaks actually without embarrassment of the point that we men are to become Gods. He takes up Ps. 82 [8] with special pleasure: "God stood in the assembly of the gods, in their midst he judges the gods." Then he speaks of the Father and the Son and of those who have received the *adoption, that is, of the church*. This, namely, is the assembly of God, which God, i.e. the Son, himself has instituted through himself. Concerning it, again we read: "God, the Lord of gods (according to Irenaeus=Jesus Christ) has spoken and has called to the earth" (Ps. 50:1). . . . But who are the gods? Those to whom he has said, "you are gods and sons of the Most High," namely those who have received the grace of sonship (III, 6.1).[9] Against the hasty questions as to why God did not make man perfect at once, Irenaeus objects: *Nos enim imputamus ei, quoniam non ab initio dii facti sumus, sed primo quidem homines, tunc demum dii*[10] (then again follows the quotation from Ps. 82:6-7), (IV, 38.4).

In another passage Irenaeus addresses himself, and in fact with an appeal to the same psalm, to those who explain Jesus as a mere man: πρὸς τοὺς μὴ δεξαμένους τὴν δωρεὰν τῆς υἱοθεσίας ἀλλ' ἀτιμάζοντας τὴν σάρκωσιν τῆς καθαρᾶς γεννήσεως τοῦ λόγου τοῦ θεοῦ καὶ ἀποστεροῦντας τὸν ἄνθρωπον τῆς εἰς θεὸν ἀνόδου καὶ ἀχαριστοῦντας τῷ ὑπὲρ αὐτῶν σαρκωθέντι λόγῳ τοῦ θεοῦ (III, 19.1).

When one observes how in all these passages deification (ἡ εἰς θεὸν ἀνόδου) and sonship to God (υἱοθεσία, adoptio) are for Irenaeus synonymous concepts,[11] then the closing sentence with which he concludes these expositions of fundamental importance increases in significance quite noticeably: "For the Logos became man and the Son of God became the Son of Man for this purpose, ἵνα ὁ ἄνθρωπος τὸν Λόγον χωρήσας καὶ τὴν

---

[8] On this point Irenaeus already has a predecessor in Justin. The latter in Dial. 124, p. 353 D also exegetes Ps. 82 in a quite similar fashion: τὸ πνεῦμα τὸ ἅγιον ὀνειδίζει τοὺς ἀνθρώπους τοὺς καὶ θεῷ ὁμοίως ἀπαθεῖς καὶ ἀθανάτους, ἐὰν φυλάξωσι τὰ προστάγματα αὐτοῦ, γεγενημένους, καὶ οὕτως ἀποδέδεικται, ὅτι θεοὶ κατηξίωνται γενέσθαι καὶ υἱοὶ ὑψίστου πάντες δύνασθαι γενέσθαι κατηξίωνται. Incidentally the interesting statement in John 10:33 ff. already runs along the same line, only that the saying from the Psalm is used here in the defense of the deification of Jesus. Cf. II Pet. 1:4, θείας κοινωνοὶ φύσεως.

[9] IV, 1.1: *neminem alterum deum et dominum a spiritu praedicatum, nisi eum, qui dominatur omnium deus cum verbo suo, et eos qui adoptionis spiritum accipiunt.*

[10] IV, 39.2; *oportet enim te primo quidem ordinem hominis custodire, tunc deinde participari gloriae dei.*

[11] Just as for Irenaeus the Son of God is God, so also are the sons of God gods.

υἱοθεσίαν λαβών, υἱὸς γένηται θεοῦ." This means that the God-like Logos has become man so that man could become God's son, absorbing in himself the fullness of the deity (the Logos): ἢ πῶς ἄνθρωπος χωρήσει εἰς θεὸν εἰ μὴ ὁ θεὸς ἐχωρήθη εἰς ἄνθρωπον? (IV, 33.4.)[12]

Also in Irenaeus, there clearly shows through the conviction which is fundamental to all this, that likeness to God or deification lies first of all in the sharing of eternal life, the special blessing in which deity enjoys an advantage over man.[13] In the passage cited above, Irenaeus continues: "For we could receive imperishability and immortality in no other way except that we were united with imperishability and immortality. But how could we be *united* with imperishability and immortality if imperishability and immortality had not first become what we also are?"[14]

But with Irenaeus the idea goes much further. For him it depends on the whole marvelous mystical unity in which God's nature and that of man are joined, as an example in the Son of God, *vere deus et vere homo,* and in imitation of the example in the members of the church.

Irenaeus stands in reverence in the presence of this miracle of the redeemer: *Filius dei hominis filius factus est, ut per eum adoptionem percipiamus, portante homine et capiente et complectente filium dei.* ἥνωσεν οὖν τὸν ἄνθρωπον τῷ θεῷ. . . . ἔδει γὰρ τὸν μεσίτην θεοῦ τε καὶ ἀνθρώπων διὰ τῆς ἰδίας πρὸς ἑκατέρους οἰκειότητος εἰς φιλίαν καὶ ὁμόνοιαν τοὺς ἀμφοτέρους συναγαγεῖν καὶ θεῷ μὲν παραστῆσαι τὸν ἄνθρωπον, ἀνθρώποις δὲ γνωρίσαι τὸν θεόν. "For how could we participate in the adoption of sons unless we had shared through his Son in that fellowship with himself, if the Word, having been made flesh, had not mediated that fellowship to us?"[15] (III, 18.6-7.) Irenaeus never wearies of extolling

---

[12] With the χωρεῖν, cf. Poimandres 32: εἰς ζωὴν καὶ φῶς χωρῶ (thus speaks the mystic who experiences his deification).

[13] See above, pp. 227-28. Cf. also the sharp formulation of Theophilus, To Autolycus II, 27: εἰ γὰρ ἀθάνατον αὐτὸν ἀπ' ἀρχῆς πεποιήκει, θεὸν αὐτὸν πεποιήκει, ἵνα μισθὸν κομίσηται παρ' αὐτοῦ τὴν ἀθανασίαν καὶ γένηται θεός.

[14] III, 19.1. Cf. also the beginning of the chapter. Ps. 82:6, "You are sons of the Most High and gods, you will die like men," is readily interpreted by Irenaeus to mean the men who on account of their unbelief do not accept the gift of eternal life from the Son of God. Cf. III, 18.7: εἰ μὴ συνηνώθη ὁ ἄνθρωπος τῷ θεῷ, οὐκ ἂν ἐδυνήθη μετασχεῖν τῆς ἀφθαρσίας. Cf. IV, 14.1.

[15] (Domino) effundente spiritum patris in adunitionem et communionem dei et hominis, ad homines quidem deponente deum per spiritum, ad deum autem rursus imponente hominem per suam incarnationem et firme et vere in adventu suo donante nobis incorruptelam per communionem quae est ad eum (deum), V, 1.1. (filius hic est enim, qui in communionem et unitatem dei hominem inducit, IV, 13.1. Jesus Christus, qui novissimis temporibus homo in hominibus factus est, ut finem conjungeret principio . . . per quem com-

this wonder of all wonders over and over, in constantly repeated expressions. Again and again he proclaims the marvelous υἱοθεσία (adoptio) which makes men gods; the ἕνωσις and κοινωνία of deity and humanity: the weak human nature which begins to bear and to grasp the fullness of deity; God and humanity united into one!

For him the entire gospel of the appearance of the Son of God upon earth is concentrated in this mystery. Before this all-encompassing thought all else completely recedes into the background. Indeed it can hardly be otherwise than that Irenaeus, who is so much at home in the epistolary literature of Paul, should speak also of the cross of Christ and seek to stress the significance of the death on the cross. But here he makes it all in all only a mechanical repetition of the notes sounded in the New Testament, or a heaping up of liturgical declamations.[16] We find almost nowhere an original discussion and exposition of the meaning of the suffering on the cross, only that again and again, in opposition to Gnostic-Docetic speculations, Irenaeus emphasizes the reality of Christ's suffering on the cross. He only knows to give a fixed though subordinate place within his recapitulation theory, to be discussed below, to the train of thought taken over from the apologists, that the crucifixion signifies a conquest of the devil and triumph over the evil spirits, as well as the contrast borrowed from Paul of Christ's obedience and Adam's disobedience. One must read in context the passages in which Irenaeus expresses himself about the crucifixion in order to recognize how everywhere and from all sides he returns to his main thought of the union of divine and human nature, and all special theology of the cross is completely overshadowed by this thought.[17] For him the cross of Christ is the culmination and highest

---

*mixtio et communio dei et hominis secundum placitum patris facta est,* IV, 20.4. *prophetas vero praestruebat in terra, assuescens hominem portare eius spiritum et communionem habere cum deo, ipse quidem nullius indigens, his vero, qui indigent eius, suam praebens communionem,* IV, 14.2. ἕνωσις τοῦ Λόγου τοῦ θεοῦ πρὸς τὸ πλάσμα αὐτοῦ, IV, 33.11. *Nunc autem partem aliquam a spiritu eius sumimus ad perfectionem et praeparationem incorruptelae, paulatim assuescentes capere et portare deum,* V, 8.1. *Ex virgine generationem sustinuit ipse per se hominem adunans deo,* III, 4.2. *Homo verbum dei factum est, semetipsum homini et hominem sibimet ipsi assimilans,* V, 16.2. *quoniam homo et quoniam deus: ut quomodo homo compassus est nobis, tamquam deus misereatur nobis et remittat nobis debita nostra, quae factori nostro debemus deo,* V, 17.3. *fides hominum aucta est, additamentum accipiens, filium dei, ut et homo fieret particeps dei,* IV, 28.2.

[16] II, 20.3, *Dominus . . . per passionem mortem destruxit et solvit errorem, corruptionemque exterminavit et ignorantiam destruxit; vitam autem manifestavit et ostendit, veritatem et incorruptionem donavit.*

[17] Cf. esp. V, 1.1; Epideixis 31. Also III, 16.9; III, 18.1-7.

concentration of Christ's manifestation on earth; therefore everything that is true of this manifestation in general is also potentially true of the cross,[18] but nothing special beyond this. From Paul's special cross mysticism (dying and rising with Christ) Irenaeus took over at the most the outward words, but not the substance; we shall see later why this was true. What concerns Irenaeus above all else is the arrangement of the natures, the positive salvific benefit of ἕνωσις and κοινωνία θεοῦ, and again in the first place of the ἀφθαρσία and ἀθανασία, of this being promoted into a higher divine existence. Sin, guilt, forgiveness of sin and guilt, all retreat into the background for him, as they do in the Johannine writings.

II. *Deification by Means of the Vision of God.* Nevertheless, in Irenaeus one may not speak of a natural redemption theology or of a redemption mysticism essentially concentrated in cult and sacrament. His mysticism remained predominantly a spiritual-personal one. Consciously or unconsciously, Irenaeus walked the paths of Johannine mysticism. With him also the union of the human nature with the divine comes about through the miraculous vision of God: ὥσπερ οἱ βλέποντες τὸ φῶς ἐντός εἰσι τοῦ φωτὸς καὶ τῆς αὐτοῦ λαμπρότητος μετέχουσιν, οὕτως οἱ βλέποντες τὸν θεὸν ἐντός εἰσι τοῦ θεοῦ μετέχοντες αὐτοῦ τῆς λαμπρότητος (IV, 20.5). And the object of this vision of God is the God-Logos who has appeared upon earth. Indeed this mystical piety of deification through the vision of God, which we had to construe in the Johannine literature out of individual fragments, appears before us here in the most vivid and detailed testimonies.

Irenaeus presented this great theme in detail particularly in the twentieth chapter of his fourth book. Nowhere do we gain a more intimate look into his personal piety than here. One cannot know God in his greatness— *impossibile est enim mensurari patrem*—but indeed with respect to his love: with this enigmatic sentence he begins his expositions.[19] But the love of God is Jesus Christ who has appeared upon earth.

No one was able to open the book of the Father and to behold him except the slain Lamb. But now the Word has become flesh, *ut viderent omnia suum regem, et ut in carne domini nostri occurrat paterna lux, et a carne eius rutila veniat in nos, et sic homo deveniat in incorruptelam. circumdatus*

---

[18] Cf. the above quoted passage, II, 20.3.

[19] Cf. III, 24.2: *Quoniam propter dilectionem suam et immensam benignitatem in agnitionem venit hominibus (in agnitionem autem non secundum magnitudinem, nec secundum substantiam, nemo enim mensus est eum nec palpavit).*

*paterno lumine* (IV, 20.2). καὶ διὰ τοῦτο ὁ ἀχώρητος καὶ ἀκατάληπτος καὶ ἀόρατος ὁρώμενον ἑαυτὸν καὶ καταλαμβανόμενον καὶ χωρούμενον τοῖς πιστοῖς παρέσχεν, ἵνα ζωοποιήσῃ τοὺς χωροῦντας καὶ βλέποντας αὐτὸν διὰ πίστεως[20] (IV, 20.5). "Thus men are to behold God, so that they may live, having become immortal through that vision, and attaining even unto God" (20.6). "And thus the Word became the dispenser of paternal grace for the blessing of men . . . and disclosed God to men, but also presented men to God. . . . For the glory (δόξα) of God is a living man, but the life of man is the vision of God" (20.7). All this is concisely and briefly summarized in the Epideixis: "He united man with God and again established fellowship and harmony between God and man, while we would not have been in a position otherwise to gain a legitimate share in immortality if he had not come to us. For if immortality had remained *invisible* and *unknown*, then it would not have brought us salvation. So *it became visible, that thereby we might gain a share in every respect in the gift of immortality*" (31).[21]

This mystical vision of God is likewise γνῶσις: ἡ δὲ ὕπαρξις τῆς ζωῆς ἐκ τῆς τοῦ θεοῦ περιγίνεται μετοχῆς. μετοχὴ δὲ θεοῦ ἐστιν τὸ γινώσκειν θεὸν καὶ ἀπολαύειν τῆς χρηστότητος αὐτοῦ[22] (IV, 20.5). But both, or all three, the vision of God, faith, Gnosis, are kindled at the picture of the incarnate Logos who has appeared upon earth. Here at this point humanity has been able to see and grasp that which has become visible of the invisible and immeasurable Father. This image of Jesus, however, is not a fact of a remote and closed past. The person of Jesus as it is presented in the Gospels is present for Irenaeus. This fourfold gospel which contains the sacred picture of Jesus is for him almost a cosmological necessity, as necessary as the four winds and the four corners of the world (III, 11.8). In this basic outlook Irenaeus' statements are in line with the Fourth Gospel, and Paul's neglect of the earthly Jesus is utterly alien to him.

For him this earthly Jesus is the divine proclaimer of the secrets of the

[20] Here again, as in the Gospel of John, the concept πίστις incorporates that of vision.

[21] Conceived more eschatologically, but in the same conceptual sphere: θεὸς γὰρ ὁ μέλλων ὁρᾶσθαι· ὅρασις δὲ θεοῦ περιποιητικὴ ἀφθαρσίας, ἀφθαρσία δὲ ἐγγὺς εἶναι ποιεῖ θεοῦ, in IV, 38.3. Cf. IV, 26.1: Et praenuntians, quoniam in tantum homo diligens deum proficiet, ut etiam videat deum et audiat sermonem eius, et ex auditu loquelae eius in tantum glorificari, ut reliqui non possint intendere in faciem gloriae eius.

[22] Cf. IV, 36.7, τὴν γνῶσιν τοῦ υἱοῦ τοῦ θεοῦ, ἥτις ἦν ἀφθαρσία. The concept πίστις in V, 28.1 also fits into this connection: οἱ μὲν προστρέχουσι τῷ φωτί, καὶ διὰ τῆς πίστεως ἑνοῦσιν ἑαυτοὺς τῷ θεῷ. Clement, Strom. III, 5.42, ἐξομοιοῦσθαι τῷ κυρίῳ ἢ γνῶσιν ἔχειν θεοῦ.

celestial world. He is the great mystagogue who initiates us into the divine secrets. The Johannine saying, "No man has seen God; the only begotten Son who is in the bosom of the Father has proclaimed him to us," is repeatedly used by Irenaeus as a *Leitmotiv*, as one can observe in the use of the word ἐξηγεῖσθαι (enarrare). In the great mystical chapter he says: *enarrat ergo ab initio filius patris, quippe qui ab initio est cum patre.*[23]

Thus also frequently Irenaeus' reference to the *magister* Jesus is to be understood. The *magister* is just the mystagogue. It is a context full of mystical piety: *non enim aliter nos discere poteramus, quae sunt dei, nisi magister noster verbum existens homo factus fuisset.*[24] It is true that the mysticism developed by Irenaeus can easily turn into a certain rationalism; the Gnosis which rests upon the vision of God can assume an intellectual character; the character of the mystagogue who initiates into the heavenly secrets can merge into that of the teacher. But in general one will do well to interpret Irenaeus from the mystical side.[25]

III. *The Deification Ideal of Irenaeus and the Community Piety.* The total outlook of Irenaeus signifies a quite fundamental deepening of the community piety, from which he proceeds and in which he is rooted with all his expositions. In that world of the common Christian faith, the deity of Christ, or better, his position as θεὸς προσκυνητός in the cultus was an undoubted fact which people accepted without reflection. Christianity was actually focused in the cultus of the new God. But to the question *Cur deus homo* Irenaeus gives an answer of previously unachieved clarity: πῶς ἄνθρω-

---

[23] IV, 20.7. Note how in the context there is a reference to the *visiones propheticas et divisiones charismatum*, and then follows the formula: *hominibus quidem ostendens deum, deo autem exhibens hominem.*

[24] Cf. the continuation: *neque enim alius poterat e n a r r a r e nobis quae sunt patris nisi proprium ipsius verbum . . . neque rursus nos aliter discere poteramus, nisi magistrum nostrum v i d e n t e-s et per auditum nostrum vocem eius percipientes, ut imitatores quidem operum, factores autem sermonum eius facti, c o m m u n i o n e m habeamus cum ipso,* V, 1.1. The passage in IV, 34.1 should be compared with this: *(cum) perceperunt eam, quae est ab eo, libertatem et p a r t i c i p a n t v i s i o n e m eius et audierunt sermones eius et fruiti sunt muneribus ab eo, non jam requiretur quid novi[us] attulit . . . semetipsum enim attulit.* IV, 5.1: *sed quoniam impossibile erat sine deo discere deum, per verbum suum docet homines scire deum.* IV, 6.3: *quum sit inenarrabilis (pater) ipse enarrat eum nobis, agnitio enim patris est filii manifestatio.* Cf. also IV, 28.1 with its strongly mystical-sacramental statements about the significance of Jesus' appearing upon earth.

[25] Of all the documentation which Harnack (p. 592, n. 3) brings forward for the Teacher Jesus in Irenaeus, most significant is the repeated indication that Jesus has brought *libertas* to men. But even this is in part a reminiscence of the Fourth Gospel. See below for fuller treatment.

πος χωρήσει εἰς θεόν, εἰ μὴ ὁ θεὸς ἐχωρήθη εἰς ἄνθρωπον. If the *matter* actually had already been in existence since Paul, still the *form* is new and almost unprecedented. No one had previously set the proclamation of the deification of man in the central position with such certainty as did Irenaeus. And by precisely this means his ideas achieve this unprecedented force and decisiveness.

With all that, however, the great riddle of the Christian cultus, the second God, is saturated and thereby spiritualized. As paradoxical as it sounds, one could say, the Christ cult is set on a rational basis, it ceases to be pure cultic mystery, pure worship praxis. And as irrational as Irenaeus' thought-world is, still it is a coherent, conceivable system. The deity of Christ must necessarily lose something of the purely miraculous, the irrational, when we hear that the ultimate goal of all Christians is that they shall one day become gods. The union of deity and humanity in Christ ceases to be the unique, incomprehensible; it becomes the symbol of that which is to occur everywhere in the fellowship in every individual Christian.

Thus, thought triumphs in Irenaeus; he is a theologian, not a preacher of mysteries as was Ignatius. In his statements the sacrament plays a relatively limited role. Only in a few passages of his great work against heresies does he speak more explicitly of it, and in every case it really is only chance that leads him to this theme.[26] In the summary presentation of the Epideixis he hardly touches the topic at all. Nevertheless one must not underestimate the significance of the cultus and the sacramental in Irenaeus. These things were for him already self-evident, like the air which one breathes. And essentially in the worship service, where one read and explained the Gospels, and where one felt in the sacrament the κοινωνία with the body and blood of the Logos, he experienced deification through the living and visible-tangible reality of the incarnate *verbum dei*. Once he also portrays the communion which the Logos, who has become tangible on earth in lowliness, establishes between God and man, in words that certainly stem from the cultus of the sacrament: καὶ διὰ τοῦτο ὡς νηπίοις ὁ ἄρτος ὁ τέλειος τοῦ πατρὸς γάλα ἡμῖν ἑαυτὸν παρέσχεν, ὅπερ ἦν ἡ κατ' ἄνθρωπον αὐτοῦ παρουσία, ἵνα ὡς ἀπὸ μασθοῦ τῆς σαρκὸς αὐτοῦ τραφέντες καὶ διὰ τῆς

---

[26] In the two chief passages in which Irenaeus discusses the sacrament of the eucharist, he is led to do this in the one case by the discussion of the Old Testament sacrificial cultus (IV, 17-18), and in the other case by the defense of the resurrection of the flesh (V, 2; cf. IV, 18.5).

τοιαύτης γαλακτουργίας ἐθισθέντες τρώγειν καὶ πίνειν τὸν λόγον τοῦ θεου, τὸν τῆς ἀθανασίας ἄρτον, ὅπερ ἐστὶ τὸ πνεῦμα τοῦ πατρός, ἐν ἡμῖν αὐτοῖς κατασχεῖν δυνηθῶμεν (VI, 38.1). And where he actually speaks of the eucharist, the main thought which he presents is the immediate κοινωνία with the Lord's body and blood, a κοινωνία which extends into the sarkic side of man's nature.[27]

Thus Irenaeus lives in the actuality of a cultus which creates the great κοινωνία between deity and humanity. But for him this cultus is no mere pure actuality, but is permeated and spiritualized by the idea.

Finally, it is significant in the history of religions that Irenaeus, with the clear enunciation of the ideal of deification, gave assistance to an essential bit of Hellenistic piety toward ultimate victory in Christianity. In the section on the Johannine form of piety we have already brought out how the idea that one could become like God through the vision of God and that one could acquire eternal life through the vision is rooted in the soil of this piety. Here, where deification is set forth as the ultimate goal of man, these relationships emerge even more perceptibly and clearly. When Irenaeus says so flatly that we are to change from being men to being gods, the connections with a piety rooted in polytheistic soil are no longer to be denied.

It is perfectly clear that this ideal of deification stems from Hellenistic piety. Of course it has not been long since eminent scholars explained with great decisiveness that the conception in the poem of Pseudo-Phocylides (V. 104), "ὀπίσω δὲ θεοὶ τελέθονται," is not Greek.[28] Now we read on one of the gold tablets from the graves of the Orphic-Pythagorean brotherhoods in lower Italy:

ὄλβιε καὶ μακαριστέ, θεὸς δ' ἔσῃ ἀντὶ βροτοῖο
ἔριφος ἐς γαλ' ἔπετον.[29]

---

[27] IV, 18.5: τὴν σάρκα . . . τὴν ἀπὸ τοῦ σώματος τοῦ κυρίου καὶ τοῦ αἵματος αὐτου τρεφομένην. V, 2.2: τὸ ἀπὸ τῆς κτίσεως ποτήριον αἷμα ἴδιον ὡμολόγησεν, ἐξ οὗ τὸ ἡμέτερον δεύει αἷμα, καὶ τὸν ἀπὸ τῆς κτίσεως ἄρτον ἴδιον σῶμα διεβεβαιώσατο, ἀφ' οὗ τὰ ἡμέτερα αὔξει σώματα. V, 2.3: (σάρξ) ἥτις καὶ ἐκ τοῦ ποτηρίου αὐτοῦ, ὅ ἐστι τὸ αἷμα αὐτοῦ, τρέφεται καὶ ἐκ τοῦ ἄρτου, ὅ ἐστι τὸ σῶμα αὐτοῦ, αὔξεται. Cf. the mystical statements about baptism in III, 17.2.

[28] Bernays, "Über d. Phok. Gedicht," *Ges. Schriften*, I, 205. For this reason Harnack in turn explained this expression as Christian by adducing a number of parallels (which originate in Hellenistic piety) in TLZ, 1885, col. 160. Dieterich, *Nekyia*, p. 88.2.

[29] Dieterich, de hymnis orphicis 31, *Kleine Schriften*, p. 92. An almost literal parallel to this in Kaibel I, Gr. Si. 642. Dieterich, *Nekyia*, p. 85.2. Cf. therewith Diels, "Ein orphischer Totenpass" (*Philotesia Kleinert,* 1907), pp. 44-45.

The conclusion of the Pythagorean χρυσᾶ ἔπη runs (V. 71)

ἔσσεαι ἀθάνατος θεὸς ἄμβροτος οὐκέτι θνητός.[30]

In later times deification is the ultimate aim of the cultus in the mystery religions and in all sorts of religious piety. The Hermetic writings offer abundant documentation. τοῦτο ἔστιν τὸ ἀγαθὸν τέλος τοῖς γνῶσιν ἐσχηκόσι· θεωθῆναι, so it is put in Poimandres I, 26, and in the concluding prayer of the λόγος τέλειος (Asclepius): ἐν σώμασιν ἡμᾶς ὄντας ἀπεθέωσας τῇ σεαυτοῦ θέᾳ. In the Hermetic tractate κλεῖς the ascent of man into the world of the demons and of the double choir of gods, of πλανώμενοι and ἀπλανεῖς, is described: καὶ αὕτη ψυχῆς ἡ τελειοτάτη δόξα (X, 7).[31] In the consecration of prophets it is ἐθεώθημεν τῇ γενέσει (XIII, 10) or: θεὸς πέφυκας καὶ τοῦ ἑνὸς παῖς (XIII, 14).

When at the end of the so-called Mithras Liturgy the initiate breaks out into the words: "Lord, reborn I expire, and since I am exalted, I die," [32] the underlying conception, that the man dies and the god is born, is obvious. The members of the cultic society, when the initiate who was initiated in the taurobolium climbed out of the pit, spattered with blood, greeted him as god: *omnes salutant atque adorant eminus.*[33] In the Isis mysteries, the initiate who has experienced the highest rites is robed in sacred garments and adorned with a divine halo, and a blazing torch is put in his hand. "So I was adorned like the sun and was set up like a statue, when the curtains were suddenly drawn back and the people hung on the sight of me." [34] Finally, we should recall the allusion to the rites of the Attis mysteries which is found in the account of the entrance into the cave of Hierapolis, by Damascius: ἐδόκουν ὄναρ ὁ Ἄττης γενέσθαι καί μοι ἐπιτελεῖσθαι παρὰ τῆς Μητρὸς τῶν θεῶν τὴν τῶν Ἱλαρίων καλομένην ἑορτήν.[35]

Wherever we look—the examples could easily be multiplied—the striving for deification everywhere dominates the Hellenistic mystery piety. The characteristic thing is that here all boundaries between divine and human

[30] Dieterich, *Nekyia*, p. 88.2. Cf. already Empedocles (V. 355, Stein):
χαίρετ᾽, ἐγὼ δ᾽ ὕμμιν θεὸς ἄμβροτος οὐκέτι θνητός
πωλεῦμαι μετὰ πᾶσι τετιμημένος.
It must be assumed as likely that these views which were widespread in Orphic-Pythagorean circles were also developed in these circles into mysteries in which the deification of the initiate was already experienced in this world.
[31] Cf. X, 6, δυνατὸν γὰρ τὴν ψυχὴν ἀποθεωθῆναι ἐν σώματι ἀνθρώπου κειμένην.
[32] Dieterich, *Mithras-Liturgie*, pp. 14-15.
[33] Prudentius, Peristephan. X, 1048. Hepding, *Attis*, p. 66.
[34] Apuleius, Metamorphoses XI, 24.
[35] Damascius, vita Isidori in Photius, cod. 242, p. 345a, ed. Becker.

fade away in an utterly astonishing fashion. It is a widely held belief of that age that through picture magic[36] one could invoke the divine element into the statues and thus could make gods; this is then again set parallel to the divine rites in which the initiate takes into himself the divine element. Thus we now read in the Hermetic tractate Asclepius (Ps.-Apul.) 23: *homo fictor est deorum . . . et non solum inluminatur*[37] (in the mystery rites) *verum etiam inluminat, nec solum ad deum proficit*[38] *verum etiam conformat deos.* It is an oppressive, overheated hothouse atmosphere of piety into which the Christianity of the second century got itself. One must marvel that it still remained comparatively so healthy. But a broad wave of this Hellenistic mystery piety struck the young religion. Christian piety was more and more filled with this striving for deification, with the longing for the higher, heavenly manner of being. The substance had already long been in existence, and now the express word is joined to it: deification through the vision of God which occurs in the incarnate Logos of God, and the incarnation of the *Logos* essential for the aim of the deification of the human race! So far as we can see, Irenaeus is the first one decisively to put these ideas in the center of his interpretation of Christianity and thus to give to the young religion the form in which it would permanently be understood within this milieu.[39]

IV. *The Christology That Arises on the Basis of the Idea of Deification.* The Christology of Irenaeus now is determined throughout by this basic outlook. If the Logos of God who has appeared on earth is to produce the ἕνωσις and κοινωνία between God and Man, it must be both: true God and true man, *vere homo vere deus.*

This is true first of all of the true manhood of Jesus. This is not only maintained, over against Docetism, on the basis of the authority of tradition and custom, but to a certain extent is comprehended in its intrinsic merit.

---

[36] On picture magic, de Jong, *Das antike Mysterienwesen* (1909), pp. 88 ff., 101 ff., and cf. above, pp. 165-66 and 223, n. 46.

[37] Here *illuminare* takes on exactly the meaning of ἀποθεοῦσθαι.

[38] On *proficere*, cf. Iren. IV, 26.1: *In tantum homo diligens deum proficiet, ut etiam videat deum* (then follows the reference to the heavenly glorification=δόξα). IV, 20.7: *ut semper haberet ad quod proficeret.* IV, 38.3: τοῦ δὲ ἀνθρώπου ἠρέμα προκόπτοντος καὶ πρὸς τέλειον ἀνερχομένου τουτέστι πλησίον τοῦ ἀγεννήτου γενομένου.

[39] How strongly the statements of Irenaeus have prevailed here, or how much these ideas were in the air, is shown by the parallels from Tertullian and Hippolytus given in Harnack, p. 613.3. Cf. further Clem. Strom. VII, 14.84; 16.101.4 (ἐν σαρκὶ περιπολῶν θεός) *et passim.* Tertullian, adv. Marc. II, 25. Hippolytus, Ref. X, 34. Mart. Carp. 7 (ἀφομοιοῦνται τῇ δόξῃ θεοῦ καί εἰσιν μετ᾽ αὐτοῦ ἀθάνατοι).

How strong this high evaluation of Jesus' humanity is in Irenaeus will emerge with full clarity only from a comparison with Paul, which will be undertaken later. But already here it is clear: for Irenaeus' faith the humanity of Jesus is an intrinsically valuable good. For him the reality of the idea of redemption depends on the fact that Christ really and truly was man. To him the humanity is not something that is temporarily put on and then laid aside again; it has eternal worth. For the final goal which hovers before Irenaeus' eyes is indeed the miraculous unity of divine and human. Hence Christ assumed and bore full humanity, not merely, as it could appear now and then in his utterances, fleshliness: "For if he did not assume from man the substance of the flesh and did not become man or son of man, and if he did not become what we were, then by his suffering and dying he accomplished nothing great. But everyone will acknowledge that we consist of a body which is taken from earth and a soul which receives the spirit from God. Thus the Word of God has come to be . . . and for this reason he is confessed as Son of Man" (III, 22.1). In this fashion again and again the *filius hominis* appears for him of equal worth and with equal stress alongside the *filius dei*. *Filius dei hominis filius factus, ut per eum adoptionem percipiamus, portante homine et capiente et complectente filium dei* (III, 16.3).[40] *Hic igitur filius dei, dominus noster, existens verbum dei, quoniam ex Maria,*[41] *quae ex hominibus habebat genus . . . , habuit secundum hominem generationem, factus est filius hominis* (III, 19.3).

Irenaeus did not reflect upon the way in which the human nature has been united with the divine. He is glad to rely on the Johannine formula, "the Word became flesh."[42] But it is distinctive for his fuller emphasis on

---

[40] III, 16.7: *Verbum dei incarnatum . . . in quo filium hominis fieri oportebat filium dei* (a peculiar formulation, one that hardly ever recurs elsewhere). III, 17.1: *unde et (spiritus) in filium dei, filium hominis factum descendit.* III, 19.1: εἰς τοῦτο γὰρ ὁ Λόγος ἄνθρωπος et qui filius dei est, filius hominis factus est.

[41] It is worthy of note that for Irenaeus the *full humanity* of Jesus depends on the actual birth from the virgin. IV, 33.2: *et quare se filium hominis confitebatur, si non eam, quae ex homine est, generationem sustinuisset?* Hence also the repeated strong polemic against the Valentinian opponents who, connecting the dogma of the miraculous birth with Docetism, asserted "μηδὲν εἰληφέναι ἐκ τῆς παρθένου" (III, 22.1; V, 1.2). The way in which Irenaeus, without here sensing the difficulties, connects the idea of Jesus' humanity with the idea of Jesus' miraculous *birth* makes it likely again that this dogma had already emerged in opposition to Docetism and the dogma of the descent of the Christ upon Jesus. The full humanity of the divine one who has appeared upon earth was intended to be maintained by the acceptance of the (miraculous) birth.

[42] Cf. for example V, 18.3: *(Verbum dei) propter hoc in sua [in]visibiliter venit et caro factum est.* IV, 33.11.

the humanity of Jesus that he prefers the formulas *verbum homo*[43] *factus est* and *filius dei filius hominis factus est.*[44] *"Mundi enim factor vere verbum dei est; hic autem est dominus noster, qui in novissimis temporibus homo factus est"* (V, 18.3).

Irenaeus usually contented himself with this formula, "the Word of God has become man." Yet he could not altogether fail to reflect upon this miraculous union between God and man. The formulas, "Christ assumed flesh," and "he appeared ἐν ὁμοιώματι σαρκὸς ἁμαρτίας," and even the formula "the Word became flesh" or "came in the flesh" did not afford the same occasion for this reflection. However strongly one could emphasize with them the reality and tangibility of the human appearance—the flesh, the external, sensual manner of appearance, could still, seen as a whole, appear as the "accidents," as the robe which the Logos puts on, only to take it off again. The case is different now with the stressing of the full and genuine humanity. One could now pose the question as to what in the total phenomenon of the *vere deus vere homo* belongs to the "Son of Man" and what to the "Son of God." In particular, one could attempt to soften the all-too-paradoxical aspect of the assertion that the full Deity had descended to earth in the appearance of Jesus of Nazareth, and to alleviate the difficulties resulting therefrom, by more strongly stressing the share of the humanity in the total being. Justin had already been busily engaged with an ancient difficulty as to what the bestowal of the Spirit at baptism signified for the eternal Son of God and how the birth from the Spirit harmonized with the idea of the miraculous birth. Irenaeus now attempts to solve this difficulty by assuming that the Spirit descended only on the *man* Jesus.[45] But his statements in III, 19.3 go much further: ὥσπερ γὰρ ἦν ἄνθρωπος ἵνα πειρασθῇ, οὕτως καὶ Λόγος ἵνα δοξασθῇ· ἡσυχάζοντος μὲν τοῦ Λόγου ἐν τῷ πειράζεσθαι <καὶ ἀτιμάζεσθαι> καὶ σταυροῦσθαι καὶ ἀποθνήσκειν, συγγινομένου δὲ τῷ ἀνθρώπῳ ἐν τῷ νικᾶν καὶ ὑπομένειν καὶ χρηστεύεσθαι

---

[43] III, 18.6: *verbum dei patris filius hominis factus.* V, 1.1: *nisi magister noster verbum existens homo factus fuisset. . . . Verbum potens et homo verus.* III, 19.1, Λόγος ἄνθρωπος.

[44] Cf. above, p. 421, n. 3. III, 16.3, 7; III, 17.1; III, 19.1, 3; III, 22.1; IV, 33.11: *Verbum caro erit et filius dei filius hominis;* cf. IV, 33.4: *filius dei factus est homo.* III, 16.6.

[45] III, 9.3. *Nam secundum id quod verbum dei homo erat ex radice Jessae et filius Abrahae, secundum hoc requiescebat spiritus dei super eum . . . secundum autem quod deus erat, non secundum gloriam judicabat* (i.e., οὐ κατὰ δόξαν ἔκρινεν; cf. John 7:24, μὴ κρίνετε κατ' ὄψιν). Cf. III, 17.1: *unde et in filium dei filium hominis factum descendit, cum ipso assuescens habitare in genere humano.*

καὶ ἀνίστασθαι καὶ ἀναλαμβάνεσθαι. With these statements Irenaeus already stands in the middle of the speculations concerning the two natures in Christ which would later dominate Christian theology, and again on the other side moves into a certain dubious proximity to the Gnostic fantasies about the Jesus *patibilis* and the impassible Christ. Still on the whole he stopped with the simple stressing of the great mystery of the God-man.

On the second question, as to how the relationship of the God-Logos to the God-Father is to be thought of, Irenaeus made his judgment altogether on the basis of his total outlook regarding the benefits of salvation, deification through the vision of God. The actual opinion which best corresponds to the basic outlook of Irenaeus may be summed up in the words: The Word who has appeared upon earth is God himself become visible and tangible, the *deus manifestus*. Again and again Irenaeus expresses this thought in pointed formulation: καὶ διὰ τοῦτο ὁ ἀχώρητος καὶ ἀκατάληπτος καὶ ἀόρατος (namely God) ὁρώμενον ἑαυτὸν καὶ καταλαμβανόμενον καὶ χωρούμενον τοῖς πιστοῖς παρέσχεν, ἵνα ζωοποιήσῃ τοὺς χωροῦντας καὶ βλέποντας αὐτὸν διὰ πίστεως (IV, 20.5).[46] *et hominem ergo in semetipsum recapitulans est, invisibilis visibilis factus et incomprehensibilis factus comprehensibilis et impassibilis passibilis et verbum homo* (III, 16.6). It is perhaps most precisely summed up in the phrase: *invisibile filii pater, visibile autem patris filius* (IV, 6.6) or in that saying of an earlier authority which Irenaeus approvingly cites: *et bene qui dixit ipsum immensum patrem in filio mensuratum: mensura enim patris filius, quoniam et capit eum* (IV, 4.2). Thus Christ is the God who has become visible and tangible—we recall the ἐπιφανὴς θεός, the *deus manifestus*, as we encountered him in the region of Hellenistic piety, particularly in the ruler cult and in the festivals of the epiphany of God (*vide supra*, pp. 315-16). The same basic attitude is exhibited here as was there. The interest of Irenaeus' piety in Christology is actually exhausted in this sentence: "For if immortality had remained invisible and unknown, then it would not have brought us salvation. So it became visible, that thereby we might gain a share in every respect in the gift of immortality" (Epideixis 31). In reference to this position one can in fact speak of a practical Modalism of Irenaeus. To faith and piety, the

[46] Cf. further IV, 6.5: *Omnibus igitur revelavit se pater, omnibus verbum suum visibile faciens. 6.6: et per ipsum verbum visibilem et palpabilem factum pater ostendebatur.* IV, 20.7: *hominibus quidem ostendens deum, deo exhibens hominem . . . et invisibilitatem patris custodiens . . . visibilem autem rursus hominibus per multas dispositiones ostendens deum.*

Father and the Word who has appeared on earth coincide. All that faith can comprehend of God is given it in Jesus Christ, the God who has become visible and tangible, and faith has no ambition to comprehend still more.[47]

Irenaeus' *reflection*, of course, goes beyond this. In his thought-world the significance of the *verbum dei* is not exhausted in the incarnation, in the Word's role of the God who emerges from invisibility into visibility. We have already pointed out above (pp. 421-22) that Irenaeus, against the Gnostics' insistence on Matt. 11:27, refers to the continuing revelation of the Father in the Son since the Creation, indeed from all eternity (IV, 6). In the second major division of the Epideixis, he gives us a whole anthology of passages from the Old Testament in which the δεύτερος θεός appears alongside God. Here Irenaeus is walking altogether in the paths of the apologists' speculations about the pre-temporal Logos of God who is at work in the history of salvation, only here, in keeping with his basic stance and tendency, he combines the persons of the Father and the Son most closely. He is no longer familiar with the doctrine that God has only created the world through the Logos and the necessary middle position, connected with that doctrine, of the Logos between God and the world, as the entire rational side of the Logos theology in general is hardly of interest to him any longer. In his works one time God appears as the Creator of the world, and another time it is the Logos. He even ventures the expression: *"fabricator, qui fecit ea (mundum) per semetipsum, hoc est per verbum et per sapientiam suam"* (II, 30.9). Again following apologetic suggestions, in that he thus almost eliminates the idea of their own personal hypostases, he likes to interpret the Son and the Spirit as the two hands with which God makes the world.[48] He did not make an apologetic use of the thought that the Logos already held sway in the salvation history of the Old Testament in order to transfer to the Logos expressions that appear unworthy of almighty God. Instead, even in connection with this salvation history the unity is emphasized: *quum sit unus et idem deus, pater et verbum eius semper assistens humano generi* (IV, 28.2). And most of all, it is characteristic how he transfers his basic thought, that the Father has become

---

[47] Here and there Irenaeus of course speaks of the vision of God in the world beyond, by which the vision in the Son is overshadowed: *visus quidem tunc* (in the Old Testament) *per spiritum prophetiae, visus autem et per filium adoptive, videbitur autem in regno caelorum paternaliter,* IV, 20.5. Cf. IV, 38.3; V, 36.2. On this idea of the gradual ascent, which Irenaeus perhaps took over from the elders, see below.

[48] IV Praefatio 3, 20.1; V, 1.3, 6.1, 28.4; cf. III, 21.10; IV, 7.4. Cf. Pseudo-Clem. Hom. XI, 22, τὸ πνεῦμα ὥσπερ χεὶρ αὐτοῦ τὰ πάντα δημιουργεῖ (=Rec. VI, 7).

visible in the Son, to the relationship of the pre-temporal Logos to God, so
that for him the Logos is in the first place the *revealer* of the hidden God:
"The Son, who is with the Father from eternity, always and even from the
very beginning reveals the Father to the angels and archangels and mights
and powers and all whom God wills to share in the revelation." [49] Also
with reference to the Son who is active in the Old Testament it is said:
"Through the Son, who is in the Father and has the Father in himself, the
God who is is revealed, in that the Father testifies for the Son and the Son
proclaims the Father" (III, 6.2). Thus Irenaeus strove here to assert the
essential unity and togetherness of the Father and the Son.[50] But even all
these speculations—this is actually the distinctive thing—only occasionally
appear. His main interest remains the principle that the Father and the
Son are identical for the eye of faith, that the entire fullness of the invisible God has become bodily visible in the Son.

V. *The Theory of Recapitulation.* The actual conceptual interest of Irenaeus
is concentrated at another point. Irenaeus theologically reflected quite
thoroughly upon the great cardinal principle of his piety, of the uniting of
the divine and human natures which is brought about through Jesus Christ.
He poses the fundamental question of how this great marvel, the κοινωνία
of deity and humanity, is possible and how the human nature which is
taken into this unity was constituted. He answers this question with his
*recapitulation theory.*[51]

The whole doctrine of *recapitulatio* in Irenaeus is thoroughly anti-Gnostic
in orientation. He answers the question as to why man could be united to
God with the triumphant reference to the unity of the Redeemer-God and
the Creator-God. The first man, quite apart from that which has come from

---

[49] II, 30.9, cf. III, 16.6, IV, 6.7, IV, 7.1-3.—Thus the basic Gnostic idea of the Agnostos
Theos here comes into its own in a limited way.

[50] There are also some passages of a decidedly subordinationist character; Harnack, p.
585.1.

[51] Iren. IV, 6.2 has the words which apparently still belong to the preceding quotation
from Justin (from the Syntagma against Marcion): *Sed quoniam ab uno deo . . . unigenitus
filius venit ad nos, suum plasma in semetipsum recapitulans, firma est mea ad eum fides et
immobilis erga patrem dilectio.* If these words actually came from Justin, then the latter
had already prefigured the theory of recapitulation. But it appears to me likely that only
the sentence handed down by Eusebius, CH IV, 18.9, actually comes from Justin and that
after this quotation Irenaeus again resumes his own statements with the sentence quoted
above. Justin's placing in parallel the virgin Mary and Eve, Dial. 100, p. 327 C, does not
presuppose the presence of a developed theory of recapitulation. Incidentally, a kind of
theory of recapitulation is found in the Christian Sibylline oracles, VIII, 269-70.

him historically, or more precisely the *substantia antiqua* of man (man in himself) has come forth from the will of God pure and destined for the loftiest goals. He is the *plasma* of the living God himself. He is created by the two hands to which God said at the beginning of the world, "Let us make man" (*vide supra*, p. 436, n. 48). To this first (earthly) man, Irenaeus connects without hesitation the characterization of Gen. 1:26-27 [52]: From the beginning man possesses the εἰκών and ὁμοίωσις θεοῦ. He was originally intended for immortality.[53] He has indeed fallen and has lost the εἰκών and ὁμοίωσις. But his revolt against God was not primarily his fault. It is charged to the enemy, the tempter, upon whom for this reason God has placed the whole curse, while he showed mercy to Adam.[54] But above all, this victory of the devil has occurred contrary to justice and nature: *quoniam injuste dominabatur nobis apostasia, et cum natura essemus dei omnipotentis, alienavit nos contra naturam* (V, 1.1). So this tragic and fateful occurrence demands a corrective. The bond between God and man is not finally broken. *Non enim effugit aliquando Adam manus Dei, ad quas pater loquens dicit: faciamus hominem ad imaginem et similitudinem nostram* (V, 1.3). Hence for Irenaeus it is a lie and godless heresy when a person like Tatian disputes the ultimate salvation of the first Adam (III, 23.8). It would be a defeat for God if the man who is created after God's image and likeness should finally be lost. The salvation of Adam results from an inner necessity (III, 23.2). If God punished him with death, this was grace and mercy, for therewith he placed a barrier between Adam and the transgression which otherwise would have been perpetuated in him (III, 23.6). But God reserved to himself the final deliverance of Adam from the dominion of death. It could not at all be said with justice that death is swallowed up in victory "if that man over whom death first gained dominion had not been set free" (III, 23.7). But again Adam in fact is only a prototype and symbol; what is true of him is true with him and in him of the whole of humanity and of all its members singly.

Thus the redeeming work of Jesus is defined as ἀνακεφαλαίωσις, *recapitulatio*. Redemption is nothing but the reestablishment of the original nature of man. This original and pure nature of the first man (man in himself) has been assumed by the Redeemer in his incarnation and united with himself: *Verbum patris et spiritus dei adunitus antiquae substantiae*

---

[52] III, 23.2.

[53] Epideixis I, 15.

[54] IV, 40.3, τὸν ἀμελῶς μὲν ἀλλὰ κακῶς παραδεξάμενον τὴν παρακοὴν ἐλέησεν.

*plasmationis Adae viventem et perfectum effecit hominem, capientem per-fectum patrem, ut quemadmodum in animali omnes mortui sumus, sic in spiritali omnes vivificemur* (V, 1.3).

"And hence the Lord confesses himself to be the Son of Man, in that he comprises within himself that original man (*principalem hominem*) from whom the form of woman came" (V, 21.1).[55] He could do this because in fact the pure and unadulterated substance of human nature was his own creation,[56] and had come forth from his own hands. In this assumption of human nature the beginning appears bound up with the end, the work of redemption with the original work of creation, in a marvelous manner: *Jesus Christus, qui novissimis temporibus homo in hominibus factus est, ut finem conjungeret principio* (IV, 20.4).

Through this uniting of the divine and human natures, the restoration of human nature to its original purity and uncorrupted state occurs, or more precisely, what men have lost through Adam, that they regain in Christ: *ut quod perdideramus in Adam:* i.e. *secundum imaginem et similitudinem esse dei, hoc in Christo Jesu reciperemus* (III, 18.1). *Necesse ergo fuit dominum . . . recapitulationem facientem. . . . illum ipsum hominem salvare, qui factus fuerat secundum imaginem et similitudinem eius* (III, 23.1).

It is actually true that the outset reappears in the outcome. The golden age of Paradise has again dawned, the first man again walks upon earth as he came forth from God's hand. The line is rounded into a circle, and at the end, which is also the point of beginning, stands Jesus Christ, *vere homo et vere deus,* who sums up in himself this entire long development intended by God [57]—*longam hominum expositionem in se ipso recapitulavit*

[55] The corresponding Greek saying in V, 1.2: τὴν ἀρχαίαν πλάσιν τοῦ 'Αδὰμ εἰς ἑαυτὸν ἀνεκεφαλαιώσατο.. IV, 38.1: καὶ ὁ κύριος ἡμῶν ἐπ' ἐσχάτων τῶν καιρῶν ἀνακε-φαλαιωσάμενος εἰς αὐτὸν πάντα ἦλθεν πρὸς ἡμᾶς.

[56] This is stressed again and again. III, 16.6: *unitus et consparsus suo plasmati secundum placitum patris et caro factus.* III, 18.1: *Verbum . . . unitum suo plasmati passi-bilem hominem factum.* III, 19.3: *quaerentem ovem quae perierat, quod quidem erat pro-prium ipsius plasma.* III, 22.1: *suum plasma in semetipsum recapitulans.* III, 23.1: *tantae dispositionis recapitulationem facientem et suum plasma requirentem.* IV, 6.2: *suum plasma in semetipsum recapitulans.* IV, 33.4: *filius dei factus est homo antiquam plasma-tionem in semetipsum suscipiens.* 33.11: ἕνωσις τοῦ Λόγου τοῦ θεοῦ πρὸς τὸ πλάσμα αὐτοῦ.

[57] Naturally we can speak of development only *cum grano salis.* It is actually the "development" of a closed circulating system which feeds back into itself. In this sense Irenaeus speaks of ἀνακεφαλαιοῦν (summarize, sum up), which the Latin, in that he properly stresses the one side of the event, reproduces with *recapitulare.* Irenaeus is think-ing of this "development" when he so often in this connection speaks of *dispositio* (οἰκονομία) and *expositio* (see the next note).

(III, 18.1)—a development over which again he held sway and watched through all the ages from the beginning: *veniens per universam dispositionem et omnia in semetipsum recapitulans.*[58]

The beginnings reappear at the end. This is skillfully carried through by Irenaeus down to details. As in the beginning Adam, through the will and the wisdom of God, came from the *virgin earth* (!),[59] so also the Word of God, recapitulating Adam, in fitting fashion took his beginning from the virgin Mary. As through a disobedient virgin man was caused to fall, did fall, and died, so through a virgin who hearkened to God's Word man, again vivified with life, received life: *quod alligavit virgo Eva per incredulitatem, hoc virgo Maria solvit per fidem.*[60] And as there was a tree in Paradise at which Adam's disobedience was displayed, so now at the tree which is the cross the obedience of the New Testament has been displayed.[61] And again as at the beginning a mighty contest with the devil is involved; then Adam was overcome by him and unjustly robbed of his nature. But now the devil should be conquered by the new man. And for this reason our Lord took the same body as was in Adam, so that therewith he might fight for the fathers and through Adam might overcome the one who had smitten us through Adam.[62] And in order that the devil might be overcome, that miraculous blending of deity and humanity was necessary: Ἥνωσεν οὖν τὸν ἄνθρωπον τῷ θεῷ, εἰ γὰρ μὴ ἄνθρωπος ἐνίκησεν τὸν ἀντίπαλον τοῦ ἀνθρώπου, οὐκ ἂν δικαίως ἐνικήθη ὁ ἐχθρός· πάλιν τε, εἰ μὴ ὁ θεὸς ἐδωρήσατο τὴν σωτηρίαν, οὐκ ἂν βεβαίως ἔσχομεν αὐτήν. Thus Irenaeus sees in the temptation experience of Jesus the recapitulating counterpart of Adam's temptation experience (V, 21). Altogether, he has inserted into this context of the recapitulation theory the view which he often repeated, that Jesus' life and particularly his death was a conquest of Satan.[63]

---

[58] III, 16.6; III, 23.1: *et tantae dispositionis recapitulationem faciens.* Cf. III, 22.3, IV, 28.2: *unus et idem deus, pater et verbum eius, semper adsistens humano generi variis quidem dispositionibus.* III, 17.4: τοῦ υἱοῦ τοῦ θεοῦ μονογενοῦς . . . σαρκωθέντος καὶ πᾶσαν τὴν κατὰ ἄνθρωπον οἰκονομίαν ἐκπληρώσαντος.

[59] Epideixis I, 32. Adv. haer. III, 21.10. Epideixis 31: "And for this reason our Lord assumed the same body as was in Adam." 33: "Thus also he did not become a new creation, but preserved the creaturely relationship with those who were of Adam's race."

[60] Epideixis 33. Adv. haer. III, 22.4. Cf. III, 21.7.

[61] V, 16.3. Epideixis 34. Even the day of Christ's death is, according to Irenaeus' calculation, a recapitulation of the day of Adam's death.

[62] Epideixis 31. Cf. adv. haer. III, 18.6. Irenaeus also takes up in III, 20.2 the Pauline idea of the condemnation of sin in the flesh (Rom. 8:3).

[63] III, 18.6; 23.1; V, 21.1, 3; 22.1; cf. particularly also V, 1.1: *verbum potens et homo verus sanguine suo rationabiliter redimens nos, redemptionem semetipsum dedit pro his,*

It is an interesting mythical view which everywhere appears here. It is the old song of the return of the primeval times, of the return of the golden age or of Paradise, which is sung here. Authentically mythical also is the way in which in Irenaeus' interpretation, all history becomes a drama which is performed between the devil and man. The devil overcame the first man and led him into captivity. For this he is now conquered and bound by the second man. Is Irenaeus perhaps actually stimulated in his fantasies here by the myth of the Primal Man, by that speculation about a divine redeemer figure, the first creation of God, which appears in the world in various figures, as these for example are found in the pseudo-Clementine literary circle? [64] Much could point to this: the favorable treatment, indeed even the glorification of the first Adam which is found so frequently in Irenaeus; the passion with which he opposes the teaching that Adam is condemned; the interpretation of the devil as the great adversary of Adam.[65] When he asserts of the Ebionites (V, 1.3): *perseverantes autem in eo, qui victus est Adam et projectus est de paradiso,* the expression suggests the question whether he could not have known something of the Adam speculation of Gnostic Jewish Christianity. Methodius[66] later proposes precisely the speculation that the Son of God assumed in himself, not human nature, but the first Adam himself. But of course the statements of Irenaeus are sharply distinguished from that Adam (Primal Man) myth. For him, Christ is not the returning Adam, not even Adam as he came forth pure from God's hands before the fall. He has restored the nature of man *because he was more than man,* the *verbum dei* who was united with the original substance of man. Still, perhaps it is sufficient to conclude that in Irenaeus at this point we have only expanded and strongly redirected motifs of Pauline theology.

---

*qui in captivitatem ducti sunt.* In what follows it is explained how he himself acted therein with right and uprightness. The myth of the outwitting of the devil is still remote, but an actual legal process between the God-man and the devil is already suggested. Further, the descent into Hades, which Irenaeus often stresses, belongs in this connection (IV, 6.7 also probably has reference in part to this: as *vere homo et vere deus* Christ received his testimony: *ab apostaticis spiritibus et daemoniis et ab inimico et novissime ab ipsa morte).*

[64] For the religio-historical connections, cf. Bousset, *Hauptprobleme,* pp. 160 ff.

[65] On the devil as the opponent of the true prophets and of the first men in the doctrine of the Clementines, cf. Bousset, *Hauptprobleme,* pp. 136 ff. On the antagonism between Adam and the devil in Jewish literature (particularly in the Slavonic Book of Enoch), cf. *ibid.,* p. 174.

[66] Convivium III, 4 ff., Harnack, *Dogmengeschichte* I, 785 ff.

VI. *Irenaeus' Tendency Toward the Idea of Evolution.* But a more important observation obtrudes itself here. Irenaeus apparently places such value upon the unity of creation and redemption that here and there he is almost inclined to assume a straight line of development from the first to the second man and to interpret the incarnate Logos of God at the end of this line as the crown and goal of the human race.

It is worthy of note, first of all, that Irenaeus is in a position not only to excuse the fall of Adam (*vide supra,* p. 438) but also to set it under a teleological point of view. So the fall almost appears not only as something permitted by God, but directly willed, as something requisite for the development of man. "As God once permitted Jonah to be swallowed by the sea monster, not that he might utterly perish, but that, cast up by the monster, he might the more submit to God and the more praise him, so also in the beginning God let man be swallowed up by the great monster, not that he should thereby completely perish, but because he prepared the discovery of salvation, which then took place through the word in the sign of Jonah" (III, 20.1). *Haec ergo fuit magnanimitas dei, ut per omnia pertransiens homo et mortis* (instead of *morum*) *agnitionem percipiens, dehinc veniens ad resurrectionem, quae est a mortuis, et experimento discens unde liberatus est, semper gratus existat domino, munus incorruptelae consecutus ab eo, ut plus diligeret eum* (III, 20.2). For we treasure all goods all the more when we have come to know their opposite (cf. IV, 37.7). Through the fall Adam acquired knowledge of good and evil. *Magnanimitatem igitur praestante deo cognovit homo et bonum obedientiae et malum inobedientiae, uti oculus mentis utrorumque accipiens experimentum, electionem meliorum cum judicio faciat et numquam segnis neque negligens praecepta fiat dei* (IV, 39.1).[67] In general Irenaeus, in his unique and remarkable way, prefers the idea of evolution. He answers in detail the question[68] of why God could not have created man perfect, by reference to the fact that as a created being man is an evolving being and could not possess perfection from the very beginning. God would have been able to give him this perfection, but it would have been worth nothing to him, for

---

[67] Cf. the following: *quaemadmodum enim lingua per gustum accipit experimentum dulcis et amari . . . sic et mens per utrorumque experimentum disciplinam boni accipiens firmior ad conservationem eius efficitur obediens deo, inobedientiam quidem primum respuens per poenitentiam, quoniam amarum et malum est.*

[68] Cf. the entire chap. IV, 38.

it is to be attained in freedom.[69] We are not gods at the very beginning, but first men and then gods. *Opertuerat autem primo naturam*[70] *apparere, post deinde vinci et absorbi mortale ab immortalitate et corruptibile ab incorruptibilitate et fieri hominem secundum imaginem et similitudinem dei, agnitione accepta boni et mali* (IV, 38.4).

Irenaeus also proclaims the idea of evolution otherwise in varied ways. Apparently he was prompted in the conception of this idea by the Gnostics and the contest with them. That something happens in the salvation history of God, that an *advance* is presented, was apparently a favorite idea of those who for this reason perhaps will have more often described themselves as the "advanced ones." Irenaeus disputes this slogan: *si autem hoc est proficere*[71] (προκόπτειν) *alterum adinvenire patrem—et sic semper putans proficere talis sensus numquam in uno stabit deus* (IV, 9.3). And in just this connection he now develops his fine and lofty ideas about the relation of the two Testaments and about the advance in the moral revelation of God from the patriarchs to Moses to Jesus.[72] Therein again general expressions of fitting terseness about the necessity of evolution occur: *et hoc deus ab homine differt, quoniam deus quidem facit, homo autem fit; et quidem qui facit, semper idem est; quod autem fit, et initium et medietatem et adjectionem et augmentum accipere debet . . . quemadmodum enim deus semper idem est; sic et homo in deo inventus semper proficiet ad deum* (IV, 11.2). In fact, Irenaeus even introduces the idea of development into eschatology. From this perspective he interprets the necessity and the meaning of the earthly interregnum and of the conquest of the antichrist. In the interim men are to grow through the vision of the Lord and gradually become accustomed to the glory of God and finally attain fellowship with the angels and unity with spiritual being.[73] The idea of chiliasm evolutionistically interpreted and transfigured! Thus then the whole of salvation can also appear to Irenaeus as a gradual revelation and a graded ascent from the Holy Spirit to the Son to the Father: διὰ ταύτης . . . τῆς τάξεως καὶ τῶν τοιούτων ῥυθμῶν καὶ τῆς τοιαύτης ἀγωγῆς ὁ γεννητὸς καὶ πεπλασ-

---

[69] Immediately preceding this, in IV, 37, goes the detailed treatment of human freedom.

[70] That is, the lower, unredeemed human nature. This of course sounds different from the same Irenaeus when he says that the devil unjustly rules over man *quum natura essemus domini omnipotentis* (see above, p. 438).

[71] Cf. the προκόπτειν in II Tim. 2:16; 3:9, 13, and the προάγειν in II John 9.

[72] Cf. the entire section IV, 9-16.

[73] *Cum sanctis angelis conversationem et communionem et unitatem spiritalium* (=κοινωνίαν καὶ ἕνωσιν τῶν πνευματικῶν) *in regno capient.* V, 35.1; cf. V, 32.1.

μένος ἄνθρωπος κατ' εἰκόνα καὶ ὁμοίωσιν τοῦ ἀγεννήτου γίνεται θεοῦ τοῦ μὲν πατρὸς εὐδοκοῦντος καὶ κελεύοντος, τοῦ δὲ υἱοῦ πράσσοντος καὶ δημιουργοῦντος, τοῦ δὲ πνεύματος τρέφοντος καὶ αὔξοντος, τοῦ δὲ ἀνθρώπου ἠρέμα προκόπτοντος καὶ πρὸς τέλειον ἀνερχομένου, τουτέστι πλησίον τοῦ ἀγεννήτου γινομένου (IV, 38.3).[74]

But all this stands under the sign of human freedom. Here Irenaeus is completely determined by rational-apologetic concerns. The idea of freedom belongs so completely to the permanent assets of all the idealistic philosophy of that time that the denial of it simply appeared as godlessness and libertinism. Moreover, here lay the contrast with Gnosticism which was well known to and repeatedly emphasized by all the representatives of the genuine church. At this point in Irenaeus also there enters all the theodicy and all the response to the question as to the necessity of sin and imperfection. From the very beginning onward God has made man free, in possession of his powers and his soul: *vetus lex libertatis hominis*. One must read the entire section (IV, 37) in the work of Irenaeus which begins with this saying, in order to recognize what a dominant role the idea of freedom has in his theology. Irenaeus does not even think of expressing the idea that man's freedom was lost through the fall. Afterward as well as beforehand the principle holds true: Man can decide upon disobedience toward God (IV, 37.4).

Not only with respect to works, however, but even with regard to faith God has preserved man's freedom and self-determination (IV, 37.5). Where Irenaeus speaks of Christ's having brought freedom to men, he does not mean this in the actual and strict sense of the word, but only in a relative sense.[75] It is man's freedom which, in the salvation history of God's grace and goodness, is led and guided to the goal.

Some, of course, have wished to see a complete contrast between these two patterns of thought—I will sum them up in the key words: *redemption* through *recapitulation* which takes place in the God-man, and *evolution*— as though two disparate basic outlooks lay before us here. The tension between the two sets of ideas should be acknowledged, and yet it must not be overestimated.

In Irenaeus the two circles of ideas nevertheless form a unity. The most

---

[74] The idea of the ascent from the Spirit to the Son to the Father is still clearer in IV, 20.5 and V, 36.2 (here with appeal to the presbyters). Epideixis I, 7.

[75] Freedom from the (outward) captivity in the power of the devil, from the Jewish legal prescriptions and so on, III, 23.2; IV, 34.1.

extreme aspects and consequences have been eliminated from both. As much as he likes the idea of evolution and from that perspective considers matters and brings them into the picture, he never clearly draws the consequent implication[76] that Jesus is simply the crown of human development which began with Adam, the *perfectus homo* in whom the Logos of God has been fully revealed. For him Jesus continues to be the *divine Logos* which has assumed human nature; in fact, even the Adam who came forth pure from God's hand is only a poor likeness of the pattern of the incarnate Logos (V, 16).

It is the grace that comes from above that speaks the last word in the entire development; at the decisive point a full supernaturalism is maintained.

And on the other hand, this supernaturalism still is nowhere overdrawn in such a way that the incarnate Logos and the higher human nature represented in him appears in radical opposition to the lower and natural kind of man. What Christ assumed remains this human nature which came forth from the hand of God itself, only divested of all the accidents of historical sinful development. And even by the fall human nature is not actually essentially altered. Though it forfeited the εἰκών and ὁμοίωσις of God, still it retained the determination some day to attain it. Indeed, it actually never rightly possessed this likeness, for one can possess nothing that one has not freely attained. And again, the (lower) *natura* of Adam which has been manifested through his fall can be regarded as the beginning point for the development which leads man upward to the likeness of God. *Non enim effugit aliquando Adam manus dei, ad quas pater loquens dicit, faciamus hominem ad imaginem et similitudinem nostram* (V, 1.3). A re-formation and alteration of nature has never occurred; man never completely lost his freedom. And yet again, the whole of salvation history is by no means an unequivocal development from below upward, it is likewise a working of God from above downward and from without inward. *Secundum autem dilectionem et virtutem vincet*[77] *factae naturae substantiam* (IV, 38.4).

Thus Irenaeus has already set up that complicated system of *natura* and *gratia*, that interweaving of evolution and supernaturalism which then should so extensively attain dominance in the history of the church. All this

---

[76] Harnack, p. 604.
[77] Here also what is spoken of is a conquering, not an annihilation.

is actually summed up in the word ἀνακεφαλαίωσις. To a certain degree the concept of ἀνακεφαλαίωσις embraces that of development, a summation of the *longa expositio,* of the manifold *dispositiones dei.* However, it is a development, not in the sense of a straight line, but in such a way that the end comes back to the beginning, or more precisely, in such a way that the end point lies one step higher than the beginning point. One must not finally separate the two patterns of thought of Irenaeus from one another; the characteristic thing is precisely their interweaving and their shading off into one another.

VII. *Irenaeus and Paul.* Now we have in hand all the threads and can move on to the comparison which here obtrudes itself immediately and which once more is brightly to illumine the whole: *Irenaeus and Paul.* The comparison immediately obtrudes itself! Irenaeus is that theologian who for us at least for the first time breaks the church's long and painful silence about Paul. While down to this point, apart from some exceptions, we encounter the *apostolos* essentially as the authority and the teacher of the Gnostic circles, in Irenaeus Paul now appears, not, it is true, as the only authority besides the Lord, but still as fully valid authority to whom Irenaeus refers again and again. Indeed if, as we saw, the theology of Irenaeus finds its foundation in the theory of recapitulation, it appears at first glance quite actually to have been Pauline ideas and motifs which provided the basis of his total theological outlook, only that here incidental remarks of Paul have grown into a system. If the Pauline-rabbinic Adam-Christ theology so thoroughly became the foundation of the ordinary Christian dogmatics, we owe this to Irenaeus.

And yet the harmony between Paul and Irenaeus is in essence only a semblance.[78] One can even say: Irenaeus ecclesiastically accepted Paul and made him into a recognized theologian at a price, the price being that in a grandiose manner he distorted the genuine Pauline ideas and divested them of their essential nature.

The contrasts between Irenaeus and Paul are obvious. According to Irenaeus, the first man, as he came forth from God's hand, is a lofty godlike being which possesses the εἰκών and ὁμοίωσις of God; according to Paul the first man is essentially a less worthy being which is "only" ψυχή

---

[78] In characteristic fashion Irenaeus, even where he intends to sum up the apostle's preaching to the Gentiles, attaches to this his own basic views; IV, 24.1.

ζῶσα, and for this reason belongs to this lower world. When Irenaeus describes the nature of the original man, he proceeds altogether from Gen.
1:26, while Paul takes his point of departure from the second chapter of
the Creation narrative, calls *Christ* the εἰκὼν τοῦ θεοῦ, and would never
have been able to use this expression of Adam. Paul nowhere expresses the
teaching that Adam suffered an essential loss through the fall; it is in fact
ruled out by the statements in I Corinthians. What Paul teaches is merely
this, that the fate of death has ruled in the human race since Adam. But
one must not read further speculations about an original loftier nature of
Adam even into Rom. 5:12 ff. Accordingly, for Paul Christ's appearance
in no wise signifies an ἀνακεφαλαίωσις or *recapitulatio*, a return of the
end to the beginning. For Paul, Christ is not, even as ἄνθρωπος πνευματικός, the restoration of the Adamic nature before the fall, but
he is "as man" of an essentially higher kind than the first man. Irenaeus
thinks in the context of evolutionary thought; and in spite of the strong
supernatural touch which this contains, one can still say in his sense that the
God-Logos who appeared on earth and united with human nature is the
consummation and transfiguration of the nature of man established in the
creation. Paul sees only the sharp antithetical contrasts: For him Christ is
*not the consummation and transfiguration, but the death of the old Adam,*
of the old sensual nature of man (not merely of the evil tendency of the
will in this nature). According to Irenaeus' view, there remains even to
fallen man, in spite of his loss of God's image and likeness, his freedom,
and God, in his mysterious wisdom, leads free man to completion. But
Paul loudly proclaims the absolute lack of freedom and the inability of
the old fleshly man who, like his ancestor, is only psychical, and expects
*everything* from the supernatural spirit of God which as an absolute
miracle is inserted into the human being. For Irenaeus, in spite of all the
supernaturalism, creation and redemption form a great inner unity. It is the
same God and the same Word which create man and place in him the
disposition to the Highest and then in redemption lead to this preestablished
goal. For Paul, however, the spheres of creation and redemption are
separated from each other[79]; he strongly feels the contrasting distinction
between the two. To be sure, he did not draw the implications for his belief's

---

[79] The contrasts which Harnack (p. 569) formulates for the relationship between
Irenaeus and Gnosticism can be transferred for the most part to the relationship between
Irenaeus and Paul.

view of God and the creation; he stopped with the radical contrast of the first and the second man without further reflecting upon how the essentially less worthy nature of the first man could be explained. But, unnoticed, that basic attitude of Paul also colored his world view. Thus then the apostle ventures the bold principle of the θεὸς τοῦ αἰῶνος τούτου. Irenaeus, however, complains that the heretics appeal to this saying, and is able to adopt it only in a violent distortion (*vide supra*, p. 255). It is simply a fundamental difference in basic attitude, between the supernaturalist optimism of the church father and the radical pessimism of the apostle.

From here a number of further consequences emerge. Both Irenaeus and Paul appear to stress in the same way the reality of the redeemer's appearance here upon earth. And yet there is again a fundamental difference between the two. For Irenaeus, even though he once speaks from the standpoint of the redeemer's deity of humiliation and self-emptying, the human nature which the redeemer assumed is something lofty and glorious: the *natura* which came forth from God's own hands, the εἰκών and ὁμοίωσις τοῦ θεοῦ. For Paul, the σάρξ of Christ, the reality of which he does not deny, is at most slightly limited by means of expressions such as ἐν ὁμοιώματι σαρκὸς ἁμαρτίας, μορφὴν δούλου λαβών, ἐν ὁμοιώματι ἀνθρώπων γενόμενος καὶ σχήματι εὑρεθεὶς ὡς ἄνθρωπος, yet only something lower, a burden which he patiently bears, still something which is ultimately externally attached to him. For Irenaeus, the uniting of deity and humanity in Jesus is the greatest miracle, before which he stands in awe, marveling; something abidingly valuable, existing to all eternity. For Paul the σάρξ of Christ is something temporarily assumed, a burden[80] from which he is finally freed by death. For Irenaeus, in this uniting of deity and complete humanity, including body and soul, Christ is an effectual symbol and the ultimate goal of all believers; for Paul, the dead and risen Christ is an effectual symbol for the liberation of the Christian from all that is base, sarkic as well as psychic, and for his elevation into the higher pneumatic world.

The differences between the two are sharpest in eschatology. Irenaeus energetically asserts the resurrection of the flesh as a fundamental principle of the Christian religion. In him it is this as no accident and externally incidental thing. His theory of recapitulation, his doctrine of the union of

---

[80] Paul would not have been able to speak of a sinlessness of the *flesh* of Christ (Irenaeus V, 14.3).

deity with complete and full humanity makes this implication inescapably necessary. The work of redemption appears to him in the battle with Gnosticism as incomplete; indeed the very heart of it appears to him to be removed if one dares to deny the resurrection of the flesh. For fleshly sensual matter also belongs to the *natura* of man created by God, and it is just this which the redeemer manifest in the flesh bore and united with deity. And in the holy sacrament of the eucharist Christ nourishes our flesh and blood with his own. "Our doctrine (of the resurrection) harmonizes with the eucharist, and the eucharist again confirms our doctrine" (IV, 18.5). πῶς δεκτικὴν μὴ εἶναι λέγουσιν τὴν σάρκα τῆς δωρεᾶς τοῦ θεοῦ, ἥτις ἐστὶ ζωὴ αἰώνιος, τὴν ἀπὸ τοῦ σώματος καὶ αἵματος τοῦ κυρίου τρεφομένην καὶ μέλος αὐτοῦ ὑπάρχουσαν (V, 2.3). At this point Irenaeus touches upon the expression of Paul in I Cor. 15:50: "Flesh and blood cannot inherit the kingdom of God." He must angrily concede: "In their madness all the heretics quote this passage against us, in order to show that the handiwork of God (!) cannot be saved" (V, 9.1). And now he devotes a large section to the discussion with this saying, for all the following expositions (V, 9-14) hinge on this. One must read the entire section in order to recognize how violently the ideas of Paul are twisted and distorted here. Indeed it cannot be denied that Paul himself, in his assumption of and emphasis upon a new body, already to some extent takes the path of a compromise theology, and that the relation between old and new body does not come to complete clarity in him. It is also to be conceded to Irenaeus that he knows skillfully to utilize the realistic side of Paul's hope of the resurrection. But when he comes back again and again to the interpretation that the flesh of God "cannot without the spirit" inherit the kingdom of God,[81] meaning that the flesh must be taken up by the Spirit of God [82]; when he reinterprets flesh and blood to mean the fleshly actions which deliver man to sin[83]; when he interprets the putting off of the old man to mean only the renunciation of the old way of life[84]; and when, following all this, he teaches that the entire man with flesh and blood is renewed by God [85]—then one sees at first glance that all this is completely un-Pauline, and how Paul would never have been able to

[81] V, 9.3; V, 12.3.
[82] V, 9.4.
[83] V, 14.4.
[84] V, 12.4.
[85] V, 12.6.

say that in the sacrament our flesh is nourished from the body and blood of the Lord.

The difference is simply a fundamental one. At the very end he treats the πνεῦμα-σάρξ doctrine which is dominant in Paul. Here too, of course, first of all is revealed the noteworthy fact that Irenaeus simply takes over Paul's language and terminology. He describes the scope of human nature in an apparently Pauline way[86]: *nos autem quoniam corpus sumus de terra acceptum, et anima accipiens a deo spiritum, omnis quicunque confitebitur* (III, 22.1). *Perfectus autem homo, commixtio et adunatio est animae assumentis spiritum patris et admixta ei carni, quae est plasmata secundum imaginem dei* (V, 6.2).[87] Directly Pauline—actually not at all fitting into Irenaeus' system, but borrowed from Paul's circle of thought—is the clause[88] ἵνα ὡς ἐν τῷ Ἀδὰμ πάντες ἀποθνήσκομεν ὅτι ψυχικοί, ἐν τῷ Χριστῷ ζήσομεν ὅτι πνευματικοί (V, 12.3). But all this is nothing more than borrowed words. We see Irenaeus, when he moves in Paul's tracks, also immediately jump the track again. Paul would not have been able to say of the σάρξ: *quae est plasmata secundum imaginem dei.* And after the last-quoted, strongly paulinizing sentence there follows Irenaeus' emendation: ἀποθέμενοι οὐ τὸ πλάσμα τοῦ θεοῦ (*sc.* the fleshly-psychic nature) ἀλλὰ τὰς ἐπιθυμίας τῆς σαρκός, λαβόντες τὸ πνεῦμα ἅγιον.

The basic concepts are simply totally different. For Irenaeus in those sentences quoted above the πνεῦμα is the supernatural *"additamentum"* of the human soul, through which soul and flesh are elevated into the divine sphere. Irenaeus no longer has even the most remote suspicion of the spirit of the Pauline doctrine of redemption with its sharp contrasts, of the import of a saying like ψυχικὸς δὲ ἄνθρωπος οὐ δέχεται τὰ τοῦ πνεύματος τοῦ θεοῦ, of what Paul means by the lusting of the flesh against the spirit. Irenaeus inaugurated the ecclesiastical understanding of Paul, he is the first representative of that exegetically tempered Paulinism which since then has been so widely dominant. Irenaeus has perhaps been the largest contributor to Paul's remaining "the" theologian of the church,

---

[86] The observation cannot be made against this that Irenaeus at one time, on the occasion of disputing the migration of souls, speaks of the πνεῦμα as an inalienable possession of the individual man.

[87] III, 22.3: *praeformante deo primum animalem hominem, videlicet ut a spiritali salvaretur.*

[88] Harnack (p. 595.2) rightly judges "It is Gnostic when Irenaeus at one point says, . . . [quoting the sentence]. But Paul also was close to this idea." I would judge that the idea is Pauline even to the very wording. But Paulinism and Gnosticism coincide here.

but only by means of a forcible abbreviation has he made Paulinism tolerable for the church.[89]

But what Irenaeus eliminated from the theology and the thought-world of Paul consisted of all the points of beginning which ultimately led to Gnosticism, the implications of which the Gnostics drew: that radical and one-sidedly sharp idea of redemption which ultimately endangers and disparages the idea of creation; that pessimistic basic outlook which introduces into all human nature a disharmony of unprecedented sharpness and which in essence takes away the unitariness of humankind and leads to its tearing asunder into the two classes of pneumatics and psychics; that excessively strong feeling of the completely new and unprecedented in the Christian redemption which at last not only disparages everything old but also threatens to eliminate the eternal and universally valid in the relationship of God to the human soul; that otherworldly longing which would experience the highest outside the whole world, which embraces the purely human life of the soul; in the spiritualized attitude of the pneumatic revelation, of vision and ecstasy; in a word, that pneumatic enthusiasm which was indeed in a position to explode and annihilate an old world but yet could not build a new world-embracing fellowship.

Since all this was eliminated from Paulinism, there remained the ecclesiastically usable Paulinism. The volcano burned out, and its flaming masses of lava became the fertile soil of a new world.

It was a masterpiece that the church fathers achieved here! Paul, the greatest genius whom the Christian primitive period produced, is wrested from the Gnostics, and thereby at the same time the fatal blow is struck at the Gnostic movement. What had been dangerous to the church about this movement was the connection of Gnosticism with Paulinism. Marcion, who presents this connection in its purest form, also became the more dangerous rival of the church. Now, after it proved this connection to be illegitimate, the church had nothing more to fear from that side. Irenaeus and Tertullian, Clement and Hippolytus are the men of the future.

At the same time, the thought-world of the apologists was to a certain degree vindicated and adopted. In every point in which Irenaeus dissents from Paul and Gnosticism, he obviously stands on the basis of the apologists.

[89] A fine example of the reinterpretation of central Pauline ideas in IV, 12.4 (how could Christ be the end of the law if he were not also its beginning?). Cf. with this how Clement of Alexandria interprets the ἐθανατώθητε τῷ νόμῳ in Strom. III, 12.84 (also in III, 18.106, "ζῷ δὲ οὐκέτι ἐγὼ" ὡς ἔζων κατὰ τὰς ἐπιθυμίας).

Yet again their rationalism is here far surpassed and excelled. The time for its internal conquest of course had not yet come, but it is surpassed by means of the introduction of a firm supernaturalism into the total outlook of the religion. The unity of creation and redemption is strenuously maintained: still for Irenaeus redemption has an *augmentum* and *additamentum* beyond creation, something which simply cannot be conceived from the latter alone, however much it appears to be based thereupon. Redemption becomes a real, great, divine miracle. The apologists, especially Justin, also had suggested something of this when they spoke of the Logos as having himself appeared in the fullness of his being in Jesus. But quite differently, Irenaeus knows how to speak of this in a much more massive and more commonly understandable way, and to answer the Marcionites' question: *quid (novi) igitur dominus attulit veniens,* thus: *quoniam omnem novitatem attulit, semetipsum afferens.* "But after the king came and the subjects were filled with the promised joy, and received the freedom which comes from him, and took part in his 'vision' and heard his word and received gifts from him—then one will no longer ask what new thing the king has brought. He has in fact brought himself, and has given to men the promised benefits into which the angels long to look" (IV, 34.1).

This stronger supernaturalism and the clearer grasp of the significance of redemption, however, is again apparently an effect of Pauline influence and of the dispute with Gnosticism. It is the residuum of the much sharper radical and dualistic pessimism of the Pauline Gnostic thought-world. On the other hand, it appears here tempered by a basically optimistic, brighter way of looking at things which places the whole under the perspective of evolution. With these conceptions, after all, Irenaeus has run far ahead of his time. Neither Tertullian nor Hippolytus, who even more walked the paths of the apologetic *Aufklärung,* nor Clement, who sought to overcome Stoicism with Platonic supernaturalism, equaled Irenaeus in exemplary significance. The future belongs to the simple and complete redemption supernaturalism of Irenaeus, in which *gratia* and *natura* are united in such a remarkable harmony and are so skillfully attuned one to the other.

And if one once more recalls that Irenaeus, with all that he contributed, knew how to place himself entirely on the basis of the community's dominant faith and simply and skillfully to establish and deepen this faith in such a way that his doctrine could simply pass for an exposition of it; that alongside this he proposed an interpretation of religion and its ultimate aim which in the surrounding milieu could be recognized as their own by all those of a more profound mind (deification by means of the vision of God)—then we can in some measure evaluate the role which he played for the Christ faith of the second century. The question *Cur deus homo?* is definitively answered for this period: The Logos of God had to become man in order to create the great and miraculous unity between God and human nature. Thus the deification of the person of Jesus in the cultus acquired, for the style of thinking of the then-current age, its intrinsic reason and justification.

Of course the development cannot and will not stop with this ecclesiastical mediational theology of Irenaeus, this *Sic et Non* of a christological supernaturalism, but it found here, and indeed for a long time, a temporary resting place.

# Index of Biblical Passages

Numbers in italic indicate references to footnotes.

## I. Old Testament

## II. New Testament

# Index of Other Literature Cited

Superior numbers refer to footnotes on pages indicated.

Barnabas—*cont'd*
12.5-6:307 [228]
12.7:319 [299]
12.9:291 [156]
12.10:35, 291 [156], 335 [361], 343 [383], 368 [68]
12.11:291 [156]
14:319 [299]
14.3:291 [155, 156]
14.4-5:291 [155]
14.4:369 [70]
14.5:308 [247], 309 [252], 315 [286], 367 [62]
14.7:291 [156]
15:382 [128]
15.4:291 [157], 381 [124]
15.5:291 [155]
15.9:60
16–17:319 [299]
16.2:291 [157]
16.6:291 [155, 156]
16.7-8:295 [184]
16.8:290 [155], 295 [184]
16.9:379 [108]
19.7:285

Canones Apostolorum 50:299 [203]
Carpos, Martyrdom of
5:321 [303]
7:432 [39]
Cicero
somnium Scipionis I.14:392 [27]
de nat. deorum III.56:394
I Clement
Proem: 370 [76]
1.1:294 [179]
1.3:378 [103]
2:378
2.1:309 [256], 322 [310]
2.2:284
2.3:370 [76], 374 [88], 375 [92]
3.4:378, 378 [103]
7.2:378 [104]
7.3:370 [75]
7.4:306, 308 [247], 309 [255], 370 [75]
9.1:375 [92]
12.7:306 [236], 308 [247]
13:380 [118]
13.1:380
13.3:378 [104]
16.2:305 [230]
16.17:379 [115]
19.2:370 [75]
20–28:372
20:370 [73]
20.11 ff.:303 [219]
20.11:370 [75], 375 [92]
21.6:306 [236], 309 [255]
21.16:309 [256]
23–28:337 [366]
23.1:370 [75]
24.1:287-88
25.2:214 [18]
26.1:370 [75]
29.1-2:368 [65]
29.1:351 [1], 370 [75]
30.1:370 [76]

I Clement—*cont'd*
32.4:303 [219], 370 [76]
33.2:370 [75]
33.8:379 [115]
34:361
34.7:361, 375 [92]
35.3:370 [75, 76]
36:361
36.2 ff.:362 [35]
36.2:293 [177], 294 [179]
36.4:334 [355]
37.1:378
38.3:266 [74], 370 [75]
38.4:303 [219]
40 ff.:362
42.3:284, 382 [127]
43.1:362
43.6:287 [139], 294 [179], 303 [219], 370 [76]
44.3:362
45.7:294 [179], 303 [219], 370 [76]
46:286 [137], 380 [118]
46.6:284, 298 [197], 370 [75]
47.3:284
47.7:294 [179]
48.1:288 [140], 375 [92]
49.1:378
49.6:288, 306 [236]
50.3:382 [127]
50.5:375 [92]
50.7:303 [219, 220]
51.1:375 [92]
53.5:287 [139]
55.6:370 [76]
56.1:375 [92], 376 [95]
58.1:294 [179], 370 [76]
58.2:284, 298 [197], 303 [219], 370 [75], 378 [103]
59 ff.:302
59:352 [9], 371 [76]
59.2:96, 294 [179], 370 [75]
59.3:96, 294 [179], 370 [73, 75, 76]
59.4:96, 370 [73, 76]
60.1-2:375
60.1:287
60.4:294 [179], 370 [76]
61.1, 2:287
61.3:303 [219], 362
62.2:370 [75, 76]
62.4:362
64:303 [219]
64.1:294 [179], 370 [76]
65.2:303 [219]

II Clement
1.1:381
1.2:266 [74]
2:366
2.2:369
2.4:319
3.4:379 [109]
3.5:319
4.3:379 [109]
4.5:380 [119]
5.1:319
5.3:380 [119]
5.5:382 [128]

Excerpta ex Theodoto—*cont'd*
57:262 [62]
58-59:273
58:260 [57], 273 [91, 92], 279 [125]
59:273 [91], 279 [125]
60-61:273 [90]
60:279 [125, 127]
61.6:277 [120]
64:262 [63], 269 [82]
76.3:298
78:265 [74]
80:297
80.3:298
81, 82, 83:297 [196]
86:297 [194]
IV Ezra: 47 [45], 177
5.56-6.6:372
5.5:307 [238]
6.32 [4]
7.28 ff.:56
7.28-29:93 [54]
13.3, 12:45
13.32, 37, 52:92
14.9:92
V Ezra 1.24:368 [68]

Firmicus Maternus
de errore prof. relig. II.4-5:224 [45]
9:192 [104]
XIX.1:224 [48],
234 [91], 347 [399]
XXII.1:192
XXV:62 [90]

Ginza, Right
Tractate 1 and 2:45 [39]
6 and 8:270 [84]

Heraiskos
I.872:346 [394]
873:189 [93]
Hermas, Shepherd
Vis.   I.1:370 [73]
1.3:286 [136]
1.6:368 [67]
1.7:330 [347]
2.4:286 [136]
3.2:374 [90]
3.4:368 [67], 370 [76]
II. 1.1:286 [136]
2.4-5:374 [90]
2.8:291 [158], 341 [374]
3.1:374 [90]
3.2:370 [76]
4.1:368 [67]
III: 291 [158], 341 [374]
1.9; 2.1:292 [166]
3.5:294 [178], 370 [76]
5.2:292 [166]
5.5:374 [90]
7.2:370 [76]
8.9:286 [136]
9.8:370 [76]
11.2; 13.2:286 [136]
Mand.   I:369, 372
III.1, 2, 4:286 [136]

Hermas, Shepherd—*cont'd*
IV.1.7-3.7:374 [90]
2.1-3.7:291 [158]
V.1.3:286 [136]
IX.11:286 [136]
X:286 [136]
XI:162, 283, 286
XII.2:286 [136]
4.2:370 [73]
Sim.   V:291 [158], 341 [378]
2.6-8; 11b:341 [378]
4-5:341 [378]
5.2:286, 341 [374]
5.3:341 [374], 379
6.4-7.1 (7.1b-4):336 [364],
337 [366], 341 [374]
6.5-7:286
7.1-2:286
7.3:374 [90]
7.4:286, 370 [76]
VIII:291 [158]
1.1:292 [165]
3.2:341 [378], 379
6.1-3:374 [90]
6.2-3:297 [190]
6.4:292 [170]
10.3:292 [162]
11.1:341 [378]
IX:286 [136], 291 [158], 294 [178],
341 [374], 374 [90]
1.1-2:286
1.1:341 [374]
12.4:292 [163]
12.8:292 [163], 297 [190]
13.2-3:292 [162], 297 [190]
13.2:286 [136]
13.5:286 [136]
13.7:286 [136], 292 [163]
14.3:286 [136], 292 [165]
14.5:294
15.6:286 [136]
16.1:286 [136]
16.3:292 [162], 296
16.5:61-62
16.7:292 [164]
17.4:286 [136], 292 [165]
18.4:286 [136]
24.2:286 [136]
24.4; 25.2:286
26.3:351 [1]
28.2:292 [166]
28.5-6:292 [166]
28.5:292 [162], 295 [183], 297 [190]
Hermetic Literature
Asclepius, Logos teleios
(Ps.=Apuleius)   7:186 [79, 82]
8:145 [100]
9:186 [79]
18:186 [79]
22:145 [100], 186 [79]
23:145 [100], 166,
302 [215], 432
26:145 [100]
29:145 [100], 203
38:302 [215]
41:224, 227 [67], 228,

# Index of Persons and Subjects

Superior numbers refer to footnotes on pages indicated.

482

Drews, 20, 361 [33]
δύναμις=Christ, 328 [326]; δ. Χριστοῦ,
162; δ. θεοπτική, 186 [82]; δ. θεοῦ=
Anthropos, 387 [10]; δ. μεγάλη,
109 [104]; δ. ὑψιστοῦ=demiurge,
279 [127]; δ. in Carpocrates, 277 [112]
Droysen, 14
dualism: in Paul, 172 ff., 178, 182, 199;
Paul and John, 243-44; Gnosticism,
245-46, 263-64, 280; anthropological
d. in Paul and in Gnosticism, 263-64.
Dusares, 142, 144 (Kyrios); 214, 346
(Monogenes); 346-47 (identical with
Dionysos; cultic legend of Petra and
Elusa); 349 [410] (morning star, son
of Allât)

earth, virgin, 440
Easter, Christian observance of, and cult
of Attis, 58 [76]
Easter Sunday, 58 [76], 59
'ebedh Yahweh, 92, 96
Ebionite gospel, 55, 277 [112], 333 [354], 339
Ebionites, 54 ff.; 97 (use of παῖς θεοῦ);
333, 441
Ecclesia, aeon, 387
"ecclesiastics," 200, 208
ecstasy, ecstatic piety, 161 ff., 169, 174-75
(Paul); 131 (Philo); 165
ecstatics (Paul), 174
Edem, aeon, 262
Eerdmans, 43 [29]
Egypt: occurrence of the Kyrios title,
140-41, 142-43; ruler cult, 140,
312 [269]; liturgy, 302 [214]; source of
Orphic hymns, 312. See Alexandria,
Aeon, Hermes, Horos, ibis, Isis, Min
(Pan), Ptah, Ptolemies, Ra, Serapis,
Thoth, Tum
Egyptian cross, 307 [240]
εἴδωλον, 165
εἰκών (θεοῦ)=Christ, 166 [31], 206, 447
(Paul); man (Iren.), 438, 445, 446
εἰκὼν ζῶσα, 166 [31], 206, 315
εἶναι: ἐν κυρίῳ, 130, 154-60, 168-69;
ἐν Χριστῷ, 154-60, 166, 168-69,
170 ff., 286; ἐν πνεύματι, 160; ἐν
θεῷ, 171-72
ἐκκλησία, 136;=body of the Kyrios, 179;
Pleroma of Christ, 362; the believers
=people of God, 367
Eleusinian mysteries (and the Naassene
Preaching), 346
ἐλευθερία (John), 231
Elis, cult of Dionysos (miracle of the
wine), 103, 345
El-Kargeh, inscription, 141
Elkesaites, 55-56, 298 [198]
Elohim, aeon in Justin's Gnosticism, 262
Elusa, cult of Dusares, 346-47, 349 [410]
Elxai, 55
emasculation (cult of Attis), 165, 190,
193
ἡμέρα: κυριακή, 60, 124 [22], 134, 140, 350;
ἡ τοῦ ἡλίου, 59

Empedocles (deification), 431 [30]
ἐναργής (ἐπιφάνεια), 139, 166 [31], 206,
315
Enoch, Ethiopic book of, 148 [105] (doctrine of angels); 410 (doctrine of demons); similitudes, 32, 44-45 (Son
of Man); 46 (preexistence, judgeship); 47 [45] (gathering of the dispersed)
Enoch, Slavonic book of, 104 [90], 264 [72],
441 [65]
Enos-Uthra, 45 [39], 75, 197 [113]
enthusiasm, pneumatic, 161-62, 221, 283
ἕνωσις τοῦ θεοῦ, 425-26
Ephesians, epistle to, 362-64; relation to
the Colossian epistle, 364 [43]
Ephesus, inscription, 311, 314 [76], 315
epiclesis, 302
Epictetus, 212 [4]
Epicureans, 260 [58]
Epicurus, 311 [265]
ἐπικαλεῖσθαι τὸ ὄνομα κυρίου, 130 ff.,
149, 153
ἐπιφαίνειν, ἐπιφάνεια, 139, 166 [31], 206,
314 ff.
Epiphanes, son of Carpocrates, 331
epiphany, of Dionysos, 103, 345 ff.; of the
new God, 103; of the Son of God
(John), 217; of Jesus (Basilides),
276; (Pastoral Epistles), 315-16; of
the Soter, 314
ἐπιφανής, 315, 435
Epiphanius, 61 [86] (descent into Hades);
261 [60]
Epiphany, festival of, 103 [87], 276, 316,
340, 348
episcopate, monarchical (Ignatius), 353 ff.
ἐπιστήμη: in the Stoics and Philo, 201;
ὀπτική (Philo), 226; mother of the
Logos, 399
epopteia, 222 ff.; 227 [68] (Paul); 230 [78]
(gospel of John); 234 [91], 236
ἐρχόμενος, ὁ, 34, 44, 110
ἔργα in the gospel of John, 217
Erman, 192 [105], 394 [89]
ἑρμηνεία (=Hermes), 392
ἔρυμα (=Hermes), 391, 398
eschatology: Jewish, 47, 198 (Paul), 213,
236-37 (John), 313, 315 [281], 316,
372; primitive Christian, 7, 47, 51-52,
133, 151-52, 198, 213, 236-37, 381-
82; Paul, 176, 178, 198, 210, 255;
gospel of John, 213-14, 222-23, 237;
Irenaeus, 443, 448-49 (Paul); Persian,
59, 197 [113]; Samaritan, 56
Esmun, 188
ἔσω (ἐντὸς) ἄνθρωπος, 175-76
Ἑστώς, designation for God, 109 [104], 202
ethics, influence of Judaism, 372; basic
lines of Christian ethics, 373 ff.;
Jesus' ethics in Justin, 403
Ethiopia (sealing), 296 [186]
εὐαγγέλιον, 79 [18], 315
Eucharist, 301-2, 351 ff.; in the Pauline
communities, 131; (anamnesis), 137-

γνῶσις—cont'd

John, 231; in Irenaeus, 427-28; ξένη γνῶσις (Marcionites), 250, 251

Gnosticism and magic, 266 [77]

Gnosticism, Jewish Christian, 55-56; (Odes of Solomon), 63-64; fantasies about the redeemer, 65-66; descent into Hades, 67; Jesus=original Adam, 275

Gnostics: in Irenaeus, I 30: 234 [91], 261 [60], 268 [80], 271-72, 274 [97], 276-77, 278 [122], 387 [8]; in Epiphanius 26: 260 [55], 266 [75], 269 [83], 274 [96], 278 [123]; of Plotinus, 246, 248-49; words and history of Jesus, 380

γνωστικοὶ τέλειοι, 260 [58]

God who raised Christ, 150

God the Father, belief in (Paul), 150-51, 209-10

God, the new, 251, 328

God, the suffering and dying, and his cult, 57, 188 ff.

God-man, in Irenaeus, 422-23, 432-33

God-mysticism: in Paul, 170-71; Hermetic literature, 171 [46]; Johannine literature, 171-72, 221 ff., 237 ff.

god-savior, 251

Goltz, E. v. d., 303 [219], 304 [224, 226, 229], 377 [100]

gospel, apocryphal, of the Gnostics, 274 [96]

gospel, fourfold, 220, 427

gospel, the pneumatic, 220

gospels, synoptic, 33, 67 [103], 69-118, 79, 91, 127, 150 [115], 200, 212 [5]

graces: and Hermes, 392; and the Logos, in Philo, 398

gratia and natura (Irenaeus), 445-46

Gressmann, 45 [36], 56 [66], 63 [95], 64 [96], 188 [89], 222 [41, 42], 298 [198], 304 [227]

Grosse-Brauckmann, 341 [374]

guilt: idea in Paul, 194; in Irenaeus, 426

Gunkel, 7, 14, 20, 63 [95], 64 [96], 82 [21], 161 [11, 12]

Haase, 270 [84]

Habdala, 377 [100]

Hades, descent into, 60-68, 270 [84], 410, 441 [63]

Hades, preaching of wisdom, 62 [89], 64

Hadrian, 312 [269]

Haggada, 54

hands, the two, of God, 436, 438

Harnack, A. v., 12, 13, 34 [7], 54 [62], 62 [91], 63 [95], 90 [46], 138 [60], 145 [99], 250 [24], 255 [42], 283 [132], 286 [137], 290 [154], 300 [208, 210, 211], 310 [262], 313 [275], 318 [295], 319 [297, 298], 322 [309], 326 [323], 330 [347, 348], 331 [350], 332 [352], 333 [353], 336 [362], 341 [374, 375], 343 [385], 344 [386], 354 [14], 367 [60], 372 [79], 375 [93], 389 [17], 402 [69], 404 [75], 405 [76], 407 [79], 408 [84], 411 [99], 412 [104], 428 [25], 430 [28], 432 [39], 437 [50], 441 [66], 445 [76], 447 [79], 450 [88]

Hauran, cult of Dionysos, 348. See Auranitis

Haussleiter, 301 [211]

healing, ancient miracles of, 100-101

healing, by Jesus, 99, 107;=working of the Spirit, 161

healings, in the name of Jesus, 133-34, 294

heart, Egyptian representation, 394-95 (see Ibis)

hebdomad, 247

Hebrews, epistle to, 358-61; 204 (concept of faith); 289 (κύριος); 160, 300, 358 (confession); 374 (forgiveness of sins). See ἀρχηγός; see Index of Bibl. Passages

Hebrews, gospel of, 53 (Son of Man); 124-25, 333 [354] (κύριος); 82, 279 [127], 339 (account of baptism); 353 [12] (Agape)

Hecataeus, 394

Hecate Kyria, 142

Hegesippus, 47 (Son of Man); 53, 109 [104] (confession of James); 380 [120] (authority of the Lord's words)

Heimarmene, 194, 258, 390; in Paul, 257; in Gnosticism, 247-48; in the Apologists, 412. See fate

Heinze, 189 [94]

Heitmüller, W., 7, 14, 86 [32], 119 [1], 120 [3], 121 [4], 122 [6], 123 [13], 131 [42, 45], 154 [1], 157 [5], 296 [186], 297 [196], 298 [199], 340 [371], 411 [99]

Helena Kyria, 145-46, 331

Helios Kyrios, 141, 144 [95], 349 [407]

hell, descent into, 270

Hepding, 58 [76], 165 [24, 27], 188 [89], 190 [98], 212 [4], 431 [33]

Heracleon, 250, 273 [94]; 145 [99], 310 (Soter); 187 (dualism); 260 [56, 57], 262 [62], 263 [69] (anthropology); 269 [83] (sacrament of the bridal chamber); 296 [186] (branding); 387 (Logos)

Heracles Sandan, 188

Heraclitus in Justin, 404

heresy, the work of demons, 411

heretics: exclusion from worship, 353, 355-56, 364; in the Pastoral Epistles, 365

Hermas, Shepherd of: Jewish sources, Jewish material, 371, 379; on the Spirit, 285-86, 286 [136], 344 [388]; κύριος and θεός, 291 [158]; name of Jesus, 292; adoptionism, 341 [374]; second repentance, 366, 374; Christ the new law, 379; commandments of Christ, 379. See Index of Other Lit. Cited

Hermes, 142, 165

Hermes=Logos, 391 ff.; (creator of the world), 393-94, 395 [46]; =Nous, 146, 166 [34], 394; =Anthropos (awakener of souls), 265 [73]

Hermes, prayer to, 87-88, 165

Hermes=Thoth, 142, 394

Hermetic Literature, literary circle: 18; its age, 185 [76]; Kyrios, 146-47; supranatural psychology, 185-86; Gnosis, 87-88, 186; Anthropos myth, 191-92,

Marcosians—cont'd
the bridal chamber); 297 [196] (baptism); 298 [198] (baptismal formula)
Marcus Aurelius, 171 [46]
Marcus, Gnostic, Logos=Gabriel, 387
Marduk, 188 [89]
Mari, 126-27, 331 [351]
Mark, gospel of, 70-83, 339 (Messiah-dogma); 70, 78 [16], 98-99, 106 (character of its composition), 107; 338-39 (tendency of the baptismal narrative). See Index of Bibl. Passages
Marnas (Kyrios), 144
marriage, Paul's attitude toward, 256
marriage of the Soter and the Mother, 268-69; of the Soter and Sophia, 271-72; marriage of the Lamb, 304 [223]. See bridal chamber, γάμος, ἱερός
martyrdom, significance of, 115; martyrdom and Pneuma, 283
martyrs. See Apollonius, Carpos, Justin, Paul, Peter, Pionius, Polycarp
martyrs, cult of, 331
Mary (Valentinians), 272, 279; (Pistis Sophia), 274 [95]; =Ecclesia (Marcus), 387 [10]; and Eve (Justin), 437 [51]; (Iren.), 440; formula διά and ἀπό (ἐκ) Μαρίας, 278 [123]
Mater deum (domina), 142 [77]
Matthew, gospel of, 89 ff. (Messiah-dogma); 123 (κύριος); 343 [380] (miraculous birth). See Index of Bibl. Passages
Mechilta on Exodus 20:23, 148
Melchizedek, 358-59
Melito of Sardis, 325 ff. (deity of Christ); 62, 327 [325] (descent into Hades); 277 (baptismal narrative)
Melkart of Tyre, 188
Memra, 389
Menander, 251 [26]
Mercury, sermo, 392
Merx, 56 [67]
Messiah ben Ephraim, 57
Messiah ben Joseph, 57
Messiah, idea of, in Jesus, 50 [55]
Messiah, the suffering and dying, 56, 71
Messianic secret, 95, 106 ff.
Messianology, Jewish, 31-32, 34, 56-57, 92-93, 110, 206-7, 213
μεταμορφοῦσθαι, 102, 159, 227 [68]
Μήτηρ, 145 [98], 146-47, 268-69
Methodius, Adam-theology, 441
Meyer, Arnold, 345 [390]
Midas, miracle of, 101 [78]
midrash and Christian preaching, 377
Min-Pan of Coptos (Kyrios), 143
Mind-reading (influence of the Spirit), 161
Minucius Felix, 331 [350], 405 [76], 407 [79], 408 [84]
miracles of Jesus, 98 ff.; only after the baptism, 276-77
Mishna, on pronouncing the name of God, 128 [33]; and oral tradition, 369 [69].

Mishna—cont'd
See Index of Other Lit. Cited
Mithras (Kyrios), 144 [95]
Mithras, cult of, stigmatizing, 296 [196]; sign of the cross on the Host, 307 [240]
Mithras liturgy, 144 [95], 187 [87], 192 [105], 261 [60], 431
Modalism, 327-28, 334, 435-36
Mohammed, 83
Monogenes, 214-15, 228, 318 [292]; 346 (name of Dusares); 388
μόνος, name for God, 370 [76]
monotheism, 369-70
Montanists, 162 [16], 263, 331 [350]
morning star, 349 [410]. See Dusares
mors voluntaria, 164 [22], 192 [105]
mother, among the Gnostics, 259, 264-65, 268-69, 280-81; Jesus and the "Mother," 273 [92]. See Mater
mother of the gods and Attis, 190. See Mater deum
Mucianus, consul, 345
Müller, F. W. K., 75 [12], 197 [113], 331 [351]
Müller, K., 228 [70], 298 [198]
Mussaph prayer, 377 [100]
Mygdonia (Acts of Thomas), 299 [201]
mystagogue, 168, 224, 266, 269 [83], 360 [30]; Jesus in John, 228; in Irenaeus, 428
mystery societies, 167-68
mystery initiation, 223-24; 230 [78] (ascent); 229-30, 395-96 (significance of the cultic utterance); deification, 222 ff., 430-31
mystery piety, 87-88, 164 ff., 223 ff., 308-9
mystic, initiate, 87, 167-68, 223-24, 269 [83]
mysticism. See Christ-mysticism, God-mysticism
mystics, aristocratic self-consciousness, 168
mythology: in Paul, 180-81; in Gnosticism, 186-87; redemption myths (myth and history) in the Gnostics, 267 ff.; in Irenaeus, 441

Naassenes (Naassene Preaching), 61 [84] (descent into Hades); 190 ff., 193, 267 [79] (the suffering and dying God); 234 [91] (φωστήρ τέλειος); 259 [54], 260 [57, 58], 262 (anthropology); 265 [73] (redemption); 274 (Primal Man); 346, 387 [8] (miraculous birth); 393 (Logos)
name, appeal to the name of Jesus, 130 ff., 292-93; in the gospel of John, 215; among the Valentinians, 277; the name in magic practice, 165; expulsion of demons in the name of Jesus, 411. See exorcism, prayer in the name, baptism in the name, ὄνομα
Name of God, 369-70
natural science and theology, 415
natures, two, in Christ, 435
Nazarenes, gospel of, 55; 97 (παῖς θεοῦ)
Neb=Kyrios, 142
Necys=Attis, 190
Neo-Platonism, 183, 189. See Iamblichus,

Poimandres—cont'd
  myth); 164, 166 [33, 34], 191, 192-93,
    194-95, 202, 235, 387 [8], 395 [46], 397,
    399 [61], 424 [12], 431. See Hermetic
    literature. See Index of Other Lit.
    Cited
Polycarp, letter to the Philippians: 362;
    Docetism, 216; use of κύριος, 290;
    forgiveness of sins, 376; words of
    Jesus, 380 [119]; Jesus as example, 379-
    80; Jesus judge of the world, 381.
    See Index of Other Lit. Cited
Polycarp, martyr, 140, 304
Polycarp, Martyrdom of, 214 [18], 292 [171];
    doxology, 304; veneration of martyrs,
    331. See Index of Other Lit. Cited
Polycarpos=Attis, 190
poor, care of, 353
Porphyry, 88, 392 [27]; on the Logos, 393
Poseidonius of Apamea, 184 [71], 225, 390
prayer, angels as mediators of (in Judaism),
    148
prayer to the Kyrios and in the name of
    the Kyrios, 131-32, 215, 302-3; prayer
    to God in the book of Acts, 288 [144];
prayer uttered together aloud, 352
prehistory of the life of Jesus, 82, 92.
    See life of Jesus; baptism, account of
preaching, Christian and Jewish, 377
predestination, 242 (in Paul and John);
    264
preexistence, idea of, 337
preexistence of the soul, 193
Preisigke, 143 [83, 85], 312 [272, 273]
Prepon, Marcionite, 250 [25], 275 [102]
Preuschen, 124 [21], 339 [369]
Priene, inscription, 251 [30], 311-12, 314 [276],
    315
priests, veneration of, among Christians,
    331 [350]
Primal Man, 54, 57, 178, 190, 194 ff.,
    267-68, 274 [96], 441. See Adam, An-
    thropos
προάγειν, προκόπτειν, 443
Prodicians, 250, 260 [56]
proficere, 432 [38], 443
prophecy, proof from, 109 ff.; in the
    Apologists, 408-9
prophet, the true, 333 [354]
prophets, authorities on the truth for the
    Apologists, 408-9, 416
prophets, cult of, among the Montanists,
    331 [350]
προσκυνεῖν, προσκύνησις, 135 [56], 320,
    330
προσφορά, 308 [251]
Prudentius, on the cult of Attis, 165 [24],
    296 [186], 431 [33]
Psalms, 109 ff. (messianic interpretation);
    304, 318 (Christian worship)
Pseudo-Clementines, 54-55, 195, 275, 441
    (doctrine of Adam); 234 [91] (light-
    theology); 274 [96], 321 (Simon
    Magus); 298 (baptismal formula);
    330 [347] (Gods in the Old Testa-

Pseudo-Clementines—cont'd
    ment); 333 [354] (the true prophet);
    393 [33] (Hermes-Logos); 410 [89] (de-
    mons); 412 [103] (against fate); 441 [65]
    (the devil and Adam). See Index of
    Other Lit. Cited
ψυχή, ψυχικός in Paul, 172, 174 (passim,
    esp. 187 [88]); in the Gnostics, 186,
    261 ff., 450; 282 (I Peter)
psychics: in Paul, 169, 174, 178, 199,
    263; in the Valentinians, 261-62, 272-
    73; Jesus the redeemer of the psy-
    chics, 273
Psychopomp, Hermes-Logos, 398
Ptah, 395 [44]
Ptolemaeus, Valentinian, Ptolemaeans,
    233 [90], 273 [91, 94]; epistle to Flora,
    145 [99], 260 [57], 310
Ptolemies, 138, 311-12; Ptolemy Al-
    exander, 142; Ptolemy Auletes,
    142 [80]; Ptolemy Soter, 311; Ptolemy
    III, Euergetes, 311, 312; Ptolemy IV,
    Philopator, 140 [64], 312; Ptolemy V,
    Epiphanes, 140, 315; Ptolemy XIII,
    140
πῦρ=God, 233
Pythagoras (in Justin), 408 [83]
Pythagorean brotherhoods, 430-31 (lower
    Italy)

Ra, 394-95
rabba, Schemoth, 369 [69]
rabbi, title, 36 [13], 123 [17], 126
race, the third, 367
Ramsay, 315 [284]
ῥαντίζειν, ῥαντισμός, 308 [249]
Raphia, cult of Dionysos, 349
rebirth, 194, 217-18, 238 [98], 340
recapitulare, recapitulatio, 437 ff.
recapitulation and evolution in Irenaeus,
    442 ff.
redeemer-hero, descent into Hades, 66;
    struggle with the demons, 268-69;
    remaining unrecognized, 66, 68 [104];
    and Gnosticism, 267; multiform,
    274 [96]
redeemer-myth and the figure of Jesus,
    192 ff.; 254 (Paul)
redeemer, various forms of, 274 [96], 275 [99]
redemption myth, 192-93, 254-55, 267 ff.,
    410
redemption, religion of (one-sided), 182-
    83, 186, 249, 266, 280, 412 [105]
redemption: in Paul, 180 ff., 193; Paul
    and John, 243-44; Gnosticism, 249,
    267 ff. (Gnosticism and Paul); Ire-
    naeus, 438-39, 444-45
Reich, 114 [120]
Reitzenstein, R., 45 [39], 47 [45], 54 [62], 57 [69],
    [70], 76-77, 87 [37], 88 [41], 90 [46], 100 [76],
    131 [40], 145 [100], 159 [8], 164 [22, 23],
    165, 167 [34, 35], 168 [39], 170 [42], 171 [46],
    174 [54], 185 [74, 75, 76], 187 [87, 88], 188,
    189 [94], 190 [96], 191 [102], 195, 196 [111],
    202 [126], 203 [127], 223 [47], 224 [50, 52],

Reitzenstein, R.—*cont'd*
227 [68], 228 [69, 70], 231 [83, 84], 234 [91], 235 [92], 238 [98], 240 [106], 247 [8], 252 [33], 259 [55], 261 [59, 60], 266 [74], 267 [77, 79], 274 [96], 392 [27, 28, 30], 393 [37], 394 [38], [42], 395 [44, 45, 46], 396 [48], 399 [63]

resurrection, 50, 103-6; r. of Jesus, 103-6; r. of the flesh, 256, 335 [360], 337, 372, 408; Paul, 104, 174, 179 ff., 256; John, 104 [91], 237 [96]; Gnostics, 256; Ignatius, 285, 336-37; Apologists, 409; Irenaeus, 449; predictive proof, 109 ff.

revelation (in Gnosticism), 252; and Spirit, 283-84; theory of revelation among the Apologists, 407 ff., 415-16; in Irenaeus, 422, 436-37, 443-44

Revelation. *See* John

Riggenbach, 299 [204]

Rohde, 188 [89]

Roma, Dea, 139

Romans, epistle to, 157-58, 159-60, 175, 256

Rome: community in, 120, 121 [4]; baptismal confession, 300; community prayer, 375

Roscher, 141 [74, 75], 142 [77], 143 [84]

Rosetta, inscription, 140, 142 [79], 166 [81], 315

*ruach* and *nephesh*, 187 [88]

rulers, cult of, 138 ff., 206, 207 [142], 251, 310 ff., 435

Sabaoth (demiurge), 274 [95]

Sabazios (Kyrios), 142

Sabbath, 78-79, 99

sacrifice, theory of: in the primitive community, 115-16; in Paul, 180; John (?), 231; in the post-apostolic era, 305 ff., 373; in Irenaeus, 425 ff.

sacrament, in Paul, 157-58; 179, 181, 194 (spiritualizing); in the gospel of John, 213, 218, 221, 230; in the Hermetic writings, 186, 203; in Gnosticism, 186, 253, 269 (*see* bridal chamber), 271; in Ignatius, 285, 307, 355-56; Ignatius and Paul, 357; in the Pastorals, 365; the Didache, 365-66; in Irenaeus, 429-30, 449; sacraments and the Spirit, 284. *See* consecration, bridal chamber, eucharist, γυμφών, baptism

sage, the Greek, 183; as leader, 168; rarity of the wise men, 201

salvation-history in Irenaeus, 445

Samaritans. *See* eschatology

Sanguis, day of mourning, 58, 192. *See* Attis

Saracens, festival of the virgin birth, 347

σαρκικοί: in Paul, 173-74; in the Gnostics, 261

σαρκοφόρος (Jesus), 335

σάρξ. *See* flesh

Satornilus, 259 [53], 263, 275

Saturnus (dominus), 144 [92]

savior of the world, 139, 243, 311, 316

skepticism and revelational theology, 405 [76], 406, 416-17

Sceva, sons of, 133-34

Schemoth. *See* rabba

Schermann, 63 [93], 96 [67], 299 [203], 302 [214], 304 [226], 351 [2], 369 [72]

Schlatter, 9, 146 [101]

Schmidt, C., 60 [82], 233 [90], 278 [122], 388 [12]

Schmidt, H., 66 [102], 270 [84]

Schmidt, K. L., 70 [2]

Schmidtke, 55, 56, 97 [69], 339 [369]

Schremmer, 307 [240]

Schürer, 144 [88], 349 [405]

Schwartz, Ed., 60 [80, 81], 63 [93], 97 [68], 105 [92, 94], 255 [42], 273 [89], 299 [203], 353 [12]

Schweitzer, A., 20

Scripture, reading of, 377

Scythopolis, cult of Dionysos, 348-49

sealing, general religious custom, 296. *See* σφραγίς, baptism

Sebaste, emperor's day, 141 [73]

Seleucids, 138

Seneca, 202 [125] (on the sages); 225 (astronomic piety)

Septuagint, Kyrios-title, 128, 145; influence on the Hermetic literature, 185 [76]; influence on Pauline terminology, 187 [88]. *See* Index of Bibl. Passages under Old Testament

Seraphim, song of: in the liturgy, 361; in the Jewish liturgy, 377 [100]

Serapion, Euchologion, 310 [261]

Serapis, 131 (cultic meal); 143, 146 (κύριος); 165 [25], 188; 312 (Soter)

Sermo=Hermes, 392

servant of God, 56, 111-12

Sethians, 233 [90], 259 [53, 55], 261 [59], 263 [70], 265 [73], 275 [103], 278 [121], 387 [11]

Shekinah, 90, 389

Sibyl, 410, 437 [51]

Sibyllina, Oracula, 61 [85] (descent into Hades); 367 [63], 437 [51]

Sidon, cult of Dionysos, 349

Sige, aeon, 387, 398 [50]

silence, holy, 397 [50]

Simon of Cyrene, 219 [33], 335 [357]

Simon Magus (Kyrios), 145, 331; 94, 109 [104], 259 [53], 274 [96], 314 [277], 321

Simonians, 145, 331

sinlessness of the redeemer and Docetism, 275

Sirach. *See* Jesus ben Sirach

σκότος, 232, 235, 259 [53]

Smith, 346 [393], 349 [410]

Smyrna, inscription, 143 [83]

social concern and cultus, 353, 356 [20]

Socrates in Justin, 404, 406, 409

Soknopaios (κύριος), 143 [85]

Solomon, Odes of, 63-64 (descent into Hades); 168 [39] (the religious leader); 233 [90], 234 [91] (light-theology); 64 [97], 270 (the "I" of the Odes); 270 [85] (journey to heaven and hell);

Talmud, Babylonian, the title Mar (Rabbi), 127 [29]. *See* Index of Other Lit. Cited

Talmud, Jerusalem, 53 [60] (Son of Man); 101 (miracles); 148 (cult of angels). *See* Index of Other Lit. Cited

Tammuz, 188, 348 [401]

Targum, Jerusalem, on Exod. 20:23 (cult of angels), 148. *See* Index of Other Lit. Cited

Tarsus, 119, 129

Tatian, 389 [17], Logos and Spirit; 399 ff. *passim;* 412, esp. anthropology; 438 on Adam. *See* Index of Other Lit. Cited

Taurobolium, 165 [24], 431

teacher, Jesus as, 380, 428

τέλειος (τέλειοι), -ον, 260 [57, 58]

τέλειος λόγος, 260 [58]

τελειότης, 260 [58], 358

Teos, island of, Dionysos cult, miracle of the wine, 103, 345 [390]

Tertullian, 404 ff., *passim,* 452; descent into Hades, 65 [98]; on Marcion, 251, 405; I Cor. 15, 256 [46]; the title God, 330 [347]; Agape, 353 [12]; Jesus' birth by the Holy Spirit, 344 [388]; Modalism, 334 [356]; Logos in the OT, 402 [69]; the testimony of the soul, 405; one-sided rationalism, 415. *See* Index of Other Lit. Cited

Testaments, the two (Irenaeus), 443

Testament of the Patriarchs, 124 [18], 232 [86], 322 [308], 371

tetrad, holy, 387 [10]

Thaddaeus, Acts of, descent into Hades, 63

θαυμάζειν (in the sense of cultic reverence), 329 [344]

Thelēma, aeon, 388

Themistios, 203 [128]

theodicy in Irenaeus, 444

Theodotion, Dan. 7:13, 44 [34]

θεοκρασία μυστική, 189

θεολογεῖν, 304, 319 [296], 324

*theologia physica,* 415

Theon, Christian, 297

Theophilus, apologist, 389 [18] (spirit and wisdom); (Pneuma=Logos), 390 [21, 22], 395 [45] (λόγος ἐνδιάθετος); 404 [74], 407 [79] (Hellenistic philosophy); 399 ff. *passim*

θεωρεῖν, 231

θεωρία, 391

θεός, 224; θεός and κύριος in Paul, 147 [103], 205; in Justin, 323-24; θεός and ὁ θεός, 322 [309]

θεὸς τοῦ αἰῶνος τούτου, 255, 448

third day, 56-60, 113

Thomas, Acts of, descent into Hades, 63; hymns, 253 [35], 327 [324]; sealing, 296 [189]; baptism, baptismal formula, 297 [195, 196], 298-99; eucharist, 301-2; Logos, 388 [13]. *See* Index of Other Lit. Cited

Thoth, 391, 394-95; =Logos, 399

Thoth of Pnubis (κύριος), 142 [81]

Thrace, Kyrios title, 141

threefold division of men by the Valentinians, 261

throat, Thoth the throat of the most high God, 394

θυσία (θυσίαι), 204 [130], 308 [251], 396 [48]; in the Eucharist, 353

θυσιαστήριον, 360, 369

Thyien, festival of, 345

Tiberius, 140, 250

Timaeus, creation myth, 264

τιμωρὸς δαίμων, 185-86

I Timothy, Spirit, 284; confession (hymn to Christ), 300

Tiridates, 144 [95]

Tischendorf, 62 [90]

Tobit, book of, 148, 371

tomb, the empty, 103-5

tongues, speaking in, 161, 162 [17]

Torah, appropriation by the "Gentiles," 369 [69]

Trachonitis, inscriptions, 144 [88]

tradition and Pneuma, 120

tradition of the community, 71-74

tradition of the gospels, oral, 69 [2]

transfiguration legends, 83 [23], 95, 106 [95], 342 [377]

triad: Father, Mother, Son, 207; God, Logos, Wisdom, 389 [18]

trial of Jesus before the high priest, 46, 71, 73; before Pilate, 71

triumphal entry, 34, 50 [55], 71-72, 110 [107], 114, 123

truth: in the gospel of John, 231; property of Thoth, 395

Tum, 394

Turfan, find, 196

Typhon, 189, 392, 399

Tyre, cult of Dionysos, 349

υἱοθεσία=deification, 423 ff.

*unio mystica,* 165 [29], 166, 191, 225, 248, 356

ὕψωμα, 258

ὑψωθῆναι, 53, 104 [91], 213 [7]

Urmarkus, 69 [2], 70

Usener, 207 [144], 276 [107], 279 [128], 299 [200], 345 [390], 348 [400]

Valentinians, Anatolian and Italian branches, 273 [94]; use of the Kyrios title, 145, 259 [54], 261 [60]; use of Monogenes, 214; light-theology, 234 [91]; canon, 255 [42]; idea of redemption, 265-66; world view formulas, 266 [74]; bridal chamber, 269 [82, 83]; redemption myth, 268-69; the redeemer and Jesus, 272-73; Christology, 277-78; miraculous birth, 279, 343, 433 [41]; title Soter, 145, 310-11; Logos, 387, 389 [19]

Valentinus, 168 [39]; early account of Irenaeus, I, II, 277 [120]; fragments, 253 [35]; dualism, 250; anthropology,